EDWARD ELINSKI

PROJECT MANAGEMENT FOR CONSTRUCTION

PROJECT MANAGEMENT FOR CONSTRUCTION

Fundamental Concepts for Owners, Engineers, Architects, and Builders

Chris Hendrickson
CARNEGIE MELLON UNIVERSITY

Tung Au
CARNEGIE MELLON UNIVERSITY

PRENTICE HALL, Englewood Cliffs, New Jersey 07632

Library of Congress Cataloging-in-Publication Data

Hendrickson, Chris.
  Project management for construction : fundamental concepts
for owners, engineers, architects, and builders / CHRIS HENDRICKSON,
TUNG AU.
    p.   cm.—(Civil engineering and engineering mechanics
  series)
  Bibliography: p.
  Includes index.
  ISBN 0-13-731266-0
    1. Construction industry—Management.   2. Industrial project
management.   I. Au, Tung, [date].   II. Title.   III. Series:
Prentice-Hall civil engineering and engineering mechanics series.
HD9715.A2H39   1989
624'.068–dc19

                                                    88-29055
                                                       CIP

CIVIL ENGINEERING AND ENGINEERING MECHANICS SERIES
William J. Hall, Editor

Editorial/production supervision: *Edith Riker*
Cover design: *Lundgren Graphics, Ltd.*
Manufacturing buyer: *Mary Noonan*
Cover photo: *The Manitowoc Company, Inc.*

 © 1989 by Prentice-Hall, Inc.
A Division of Simon & Schuster
Englewood Cliffs, New Jersey 07632

Printed in the United States of America

10 9 8 7 6 5 4 3 2 1

ISBN   0-13-731266-0

PRENTICE-HALL INTERNATIONAL (UK) LIMITED, *London*
PRENTICE-HALL OF AUSTRALIA PTY. LIMITED. *Sydney*
PRENTICE-HALL CANADA INC., *Toronto*
PRENTICE-HALL HISPANOAMERICANA. S.A., *Mexico*
PRENTICE-HALL OF INDIA PRIVATE LIMITED. *New Delhi*
PRENTICE-HALL OF JAPAN. INC.. *Tokyo*
SIMON & SCHUSTER ASIA PTE. LTD.. *Singapore*
EDITORA PRENTICE-HALL do BRASIL. LTDA.. *Rio de Janeiro*

DOONESBURY By Garry Trudeau. Copyright 1986 G.B. Trudeau. Reprinted with permission of Universal Press Syndicate. All rights reserved.

Contents

3   THE DESIGN AND CONSTRUCTION PROCESS   47

4   LABOR, MATERIAL, AND EQUIPMENT UTILIZATION   76

5   COST ESTIMATION   121

Preface

This book develops a specific viewpoint in discussing the participants, the processes, and the techniques of project management for construction. This viewpoint is that of owners who desire completion of projects in a timely, cost-effective fashion. Some profound implications for the objectives and methods of project management result from this perspective:

- The "life cycle" of costs and benefits from initial planning through operation of a facility are relevant to decision making. An owner is concerned with a project from the cradle to the grave. Construction costs represent only one portion of the overall life-cycle costs.

- Optimizing performance at one stage of the process may not be beneficial overall if additional costs or delays occur elsewhere. For example, saving money on the design process will be a false economy if the result is excess construction costs.

- Fragmentation of project management among different specialists may be necessary, but good communication and coordination among the participants is essential to accomplish the overall goals of the project.

- Productivity improvements are always of importance and value. As a result, introducing new materials and automated construction processes is always desirable as long as they are less expensive and are consistent with desired performance.

- Quality of work and performance are critically important to the success of a project since it is the owner who will have to live with the results.

In essence, adopting the viewpoint of the owner focuses attention on the cost effectiveness of facility construction rather than on competitive provision of services by the various participants.

While this book is devoted to a particular viewpoint with respect to project management for construction, it is not solely intended for owners and their direct representatives. By understanding the entire process, all participants can respond more effectively to the owner's needs in their own work, in marketing their services, and in commmunicating with other participants. In addition, the specific techniques and tools discussed in this book (such as economic evaluation, scheduling, management information systems, etc.) can be readily applied to any portion of the process.

As a result of the focus on the effective management of entire projects, a number of novel organizational approaches and techniques become of interest. First and foremost is the incentive to replace confrontation and adversarial relationships with a spirit of joint endeavor and accomplishment. For example, we discuss the appropriate means to evaluate risks and the appropriate participants to assume the unavoidable risks associated with constructed facilities. Scheduling, communication of data, and quality assurance have particular significance from the viewpoint of an owner, but not necessarily for individual participants. The use of computer-based technology and automation also provides opportunities for increased productivity in the process. Presenting such modern management options in a unified fashion is a major objective of this book.

The unified viewpoint of the entire process of project management in this book differs from virtually all other literature on the subject. Most textbooks in the area treat special problems, such as cost estimating, from the viewpoint of particular participants such as construction managers or contractors. This literature reflects the fragmentation of the construction process among different organizations and professionals. Even within a single profession such as civil engineering, there are quite distinct groups of specialists in planning, design, management, construction, and other subspecialties. Fragmentation of interest and attention also exists in nearly all educational programs. While specialty knowledge may be essential to accomplish particular tasks, participants in the process should also understand the context and role of their special tasks.

This book is intended primarily as a text for advanced undergraduates or beginning graduate students in engineering, construction, architecture, or facilities management. Examples and discussion are chosen to remind readers that project management is a challenging, dynamic, and exciting enterprise and not just a record of past practices. It should also be useful to professionals who wish an up-to-date reference on project management.

Chapters 1 to 3 present an overview of the construction management and design process which should be of interest to anyone engaged in project management for construction. One need not have detailed knowledge about individual tasks or techniques for this part. Individuals can read these chapters and understand the basic philosophy and principles without further elaboration.

Chapters 4 through 14 describe specific functions and techniques useful in the process of project management. This part presents techniques and requirements during project planning, including risk assessment, cost estimation, forecasting, and economic evaluation. It is during this planning and design phase in which major cost savings may be obtained during the eventual construction and operation phases. It also addresses programming and financing issues, such as contracting and bidding for services, financing, organizing communication, and ensuring effective use of information. It further discusses techniques for control of time, cost, and quality during the construction phase. Beginning courses in engineering economics (including cash flow analysis and discounting), use of computers, probability, and statistics would be useful. Furthermore, access to a personal computer with spreadsheet or equation-solving software would be helpful for readers attempting some of the problems in Chapters 4 to 14. Numerous software programs could be used for this purpose, including both spreadsheet and equation-solving programs. Problems in some chapters could also be done on any number of existing software packages for information management and project scheduling. However, the use of personal computers in this fashion is not required in following the text material. Each instructor may exercise discretion in omitting some of the material in these chapters if it is redundant with that offered in other classes or too advanced for students in his or her own class.

The last two chapters of this book discuss some future prospects for new technology in the construction field. We expect that these new technologies will have a substantial impact on productivity improvement in the next two decades even though they are not part of standard practice today. By including these chapters, we are challenging readers with the remarkable opportunities for innovation and improvement that exist in the field. These chapters may also be reserved for an advanced course.

It is our hope that students beginning their career in project management for construction will be prepared to adopt the integrated approach emphasized in this book. Furthermore, experienced professional in various fields may discover in this book some surprises that even they have not anticipated. High-level decision makers in owner organizations who are not directly involved in the project management process may find the basic philosophy and principles of interest, especially in Chapters 1 through 3, as owners must invariably pay for constructed facilities, for better or worse. It the book can fulfill even a small part of its promises to influence the future of project management for construction, our efforts will have been amply rewarded.

We wish to acknowledge our appreciation to Dr. William J. Hall for his encouragement and assistance in expediting the publication of this book. We are indebted to several colleagues at Carnegie Mellon University, Drs. Paul Christiano, Steven Fenves, Francis McMichael, and Daniel Rehak, who reviewed parts of the manuscript and offered valuable suggestions. We also wish to thank Debbie Scappatura and Shirley Knapp for their efforts in typing the manuscript. This book also reflects the contributions of numerous students and colleagues in industry who have challenged us with problems and shared their own ideas and experience over many years. We are grateful to all these individuals.

Some material in this book has been taken from several papers authored by us and published by the American Society of Civil Engineers. Materials taken from other sources are acknowledged in footnotes, tables, or figures. We gratefully acknowledge the permissions given to us by these individuals, publishers, and organizations.

Finally, a series of photographs depicting various stages of construction of the PPG building in Pittsburgh, Pennsylvania is inserted in sequence between chapters. We wish to thank PPG Industries for its cooperation in providing these photographs.

PROJECT MANAGEMENT FOR CONSTRUCTION

1

The
Owners' Perspective

1.1 INTRODUCTION

Like the five blind men encountering different parts of an elephant, each of the numerous participants in the process of planning, designing, financing, constructing, and operating physical facilities has a different perspective on project management for construction. Specialized knowledge can be very beneficial, particularly in large and complicated projects, since experts in various specialties can provide valuable services. However, it is advantageous to understand how the different parts of the process fit together. Waste, excessive cost, and delays can result from poor coordination and communication among specialists. It is particularly in the interest of owners to ensure that such problems do not occur. And it behooves all participants in the process to heed the interests of owners because, in the end, it is the owners who provide the resources and call the shots.

By adopting the viewpoint of the owners, we can focus our attention on the complete process of *project management* for constructed facilities rather than the historical roles of various specialists such as planners, architects, engineering designers, constructors, fabricators, material suppliers, financial analysts, and others. To be sure, each specialty has made important advances in developing new techniques and tools for efficient implementation of construction projects. However, it is through the understanding of the entire process of project management that these specialists can respond more effectively to the owner's desires for their services, in marketing their specialties, and in improving the productivity and quality of their work.

The introduction of innovative and more effective project management for construction is not an academic exercise. As reported by the "Construction Industry Cost Effectiveness Project" of the Business Roundtable:[1]

> By common consensus and every available measure, the United States no longer gets its money's worth in construction, the nation's largest industry . . . The creeping erosion of construction efficiency and productivity is bad news for the entire U.S. economy. Construction is a particularly seminal industry. The price of every factory, office building, hotel or power plant that is built affects the price that must be charged for the goods or services produced in it or by it. And that effect generally persists for decades . . . Too much of the industry remains tethered to the past, partly by inertia and partly by historic divisions.

Improvement of project management not only can aid the construction industry, but may also be the engine for the national and world economy. However, if we are to make meaningful improvements, we must first understand the construction industry, its operating environment, and the institutional constraints affecting its activities as well as the nature of project management.

[1] The Business Roundtable, *More Construction for the Money*, Summary Report of the Construction Industry Cost Effectiveness Project, January 1983, p. 11.

1.2 THE PROJECT LIFE CYCLE

The acquisition of a constructed facility usually represents a major capital investment, whether its owner happens to be an individual, a private corporation, or a public agency. Since the commitment of resources for such an investment is motivated by market demands or perceived needs, the facility is expected to satisfy certain objectives within the constraints specified by the owner and relevant regulations. With the exception of the speculative housing market, where the residential units may be sold as built by the real estate developer, most constructed facilities are custom made in consultation with the owners. A real estate developer may be regarded as the sponsor of building projects, as much as a government agency may be the sponsor of a public project and turns it over to another government unit upon its completion. From the viewpoint of project management, the terms "owner" and "sponsor" are synonymous because both have the ultimate authority to make all important decisions. Since an owner is essentially acquiring a facility on a promise in some form of agreement, it will be wise for any owner to have a clear understanding of the acquisition process to maintain firm control of the quality, timeliness, and cost of the completed facility.

From the perspective of an owner, the project life cycle for a constructed facility may be illustrated schematically in Figure 1-1. Essentially, a project is conceived to meet market demands or needs in a timely fashion. Various possibilities may be considered in the conceptual planning stage, and the technological and economic feasibility of each alternative will be assessed and compared to select the best possible project. The financing schemes for the proposed alternatives must also be examined, and the project will be programmed with respect to the timing for its completion and for available cash flows. After the scope of the project is clearly defined, detailed engineering design will provide the blueprint for construction, and the definitive cost estimate will serve as the baseline for cost control. In the procurement and construction stage, the delivery of materials and the erection of the project on site must be carefully planned and controlled. After the construction is completed, there is usually a brief period of start-up or shakedown of the constructed facility when it is first occupied. Finally, the management of the facility is turned over to the owner for full occupancy until the facility lives out its useful life and is designated for demolition or conversion.

Of course, the stages of development in Figure 1-1 may not be strictly sequential. Some of the stages require iteration, and others may be carried out in parallel or with overlapping time frames, depending on the nature, size, and urgency of the project. Furthermore, an owner may have in-house capacities to handle the work in every stage of the entire process, or it may seek professional advice and services for the work in all stages. Understandably, most owners choose to handle some of the work in-house and to contract outside professional services for other components of the work as needed. By examining the project life cycle from an owner's perspective, we can focus on the proper roles of various activities and participants in all stages regardless of the contractual arrangements for different types of work.

In the United States, for example, the U.S. Army Corps of Engineers has

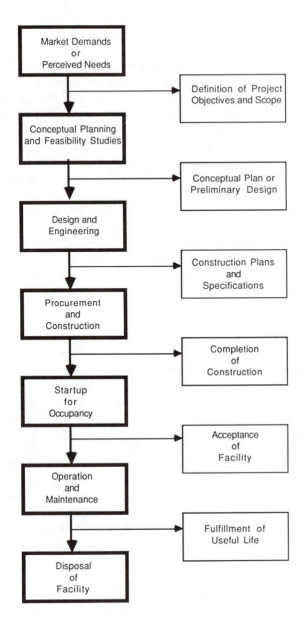

Figure 1-1 The Project Life Cycle of a Constructed Facility

in-house capabilities to deal with planning, budgeting, design, construction, and operation of waterway and flood control structures. Other public agencies, such as state transportation departments, are also deeply involved in all phases of a construction project. In the private sector, many large firms such as DuPont, Exxon, and IBM are adequately staffed to carry out most activities for plant expansion. All these owners, both public and private, use outside agents to a greater or lesser degree when it becomes more advantageous to do so.

The project life cycle may be viewed as a process through which a project is implemented from cradle to grave. This process is often very complex; however, it can be decomposed into several stages as indicated by the general outline in Figure 1-1. The solutions at various stages are then integrated to obtain the final outcome. Although each stage requires different expertise, it usually includes both technical and managerial activities in the *knowledge domain* of the specialist. The owner may choose to decompose the entire process into more or less stages based on the size and nature of the project and thus obtain the most efficient result in implementation. Very often, the owner retains direct control of work in the planning and programming stages, but increasingly, outside planners and financial experts are used as consultants because of the complexities of projects. Since operation and maintenance of a facility will go on long after the completion and acceptance of a project, it is usually treated as a separate problem except in the consideration of the life-cycle cost of a facility. All stages from conceptual planning and feasibility studies to the acceptance of a facility for occupancy may be broadly lumped together and referred to as the design/construct process, while the procurement and construction alone are traditionally regarded as the province of the construction industry.

Owners must recognize that there is no single best approach in organizing project management throughout a project's life cycle. All organizational approaches have advantages and disadvantages, depending on the knowledge of the owner in construction management as well as the type, size, and location of the project. It is important for the owner to be aware of the approach which is most appropriate and beneficial for a particular project. In making choices, owners should be concerned with the life-cycle costs of constructed facilities rather than simply the initial construction costs. Saving small amounts of money during construction may not be worthwhile if the result is much larger operating costs or not meeting the functional requirements for the new facility satisfactorily. Thus, owners must be very concerned with the quality of the finished product as well as the cost of construction itself. Since facility operation and maintenance is a part of the project life cycle, the owners' expectation to satisfy investment objectives during the project life cycle will require consideration of the cost of operation and maintenance. Therefore, the facility's operating management should also be considered as early as possible, just as the construction process should be kept in mind at the early stages of planning and programming.

1.3 MAJOR TYPES OF CONSTRUCTION

Since most owners are generally interested in acquiring only a specific type of constructed facility, they should be aware of the common industrial practices for the type of construction pertinent to them. Likewise, the *construction industry* is a conglomeration of quite diverse segments and products. Some owners may procure a constructed facility only once in a long while and tend to look for short-term advantages. However, many owners require periodic acquisition of new facilities and/or rehabilitation of existing facilities. It is to their advantage to keep the construction industry healthy and productive. Collectively, the owners have more power to influence the construction industry than they realize because, by their individual actions, they can provide incentives or disincentives for innovation, efficiency and quality in construction. It is to the interest of all parties that the owners take an active interest in the construction and exercise beneficial influence on the performance of the industry.

In planning for various types of construction, the methods of procuring professional services, awarding construction contracts, and financing the constructed facility can be quite different. For the purpose of discussion, the broad spectrum of constructed facilities may be classified into four major categories, each with its own characteristics.

Residential Housing Construction

Residential housing construction includes single-family houses, multifamily dwellings, and highrise apartments. (An illustration appears in Figure 1-2.) During the development and construction of such projects, the developers or sponsors who are familiar with the construction industry usually serve as surrogate owners and take charge, making necessary contractual agreements for design and construction and arranging the financing and sale of the completed structures. Residential housing designs are usually performed by architects and engineers, and the construction executed by builders who hire subcontractors for the structural, mechanical, electrical, and other specialty work. An exception to this pattern is for single-family houses which may be designed by the builders as well.

The residential housing market is heavily affected by general economic conditions, tax laws, and the monetary and fiscal policies of the government. Often, a slight increase in total demand will cause a substantial investment in construction, since many housing projects can be started at different locations by different individuals and developers at the same time. Because of the relative ease of entry, at

Figure 1-2   Residential Housing Construction (courtesy of Caterpillar, Inc.)

least at the lower end of the market, many new builders are attracted to the residential housing construction. Hence, this market is highly competitive, with potentially high risks as well as high rewards.

Institutional and Commercial Building Construction

Institutional and commercial building construction encompasses a great variety of project types and sizes, such as schools and universities, medical clinics and hospitals, recreational facilities and sports stadiums, retail chain stores and large shopping centers, warehouses and light manufacturing plants, and skyscrapers for offices and hotels. (An illustration appears in Figure 1-3.) The owners of such buildings may or may not be familiar with construction industry practices, but they usually are able to select competent professional consultants and arrange the financing of the constructed facilities themselves. Specialty architects and engineers are often engaged for designing a specific type of building, while the builders or general contractors undertaking such projects may also be specialized in only that type of building.

Because of the higher costs and greater sophistication of institutional and commercial buildings in comparison with residential housing, this market segment

Figure 1-3 Construction of the PPG Building in Pittsburgh, Pennsylvania (courtesy of PPG Industries, Inc.)

is shared by fewer competitors. Since the construction of some of these buildings is a long process which once started will take some time to proceed until completion, the demand is less sensitive to general economic conditions than that for speculative housing. Consequently, the owners may confront an *oligopoly* of general contractors who compete in the same market. In an oligopoly situation, only a limited number of competitors exist, and a firm's price for services may be based in part on its competitive strategies in the local market.

Specialized Industrial Construction

Specialized industrial construction usually involves very-large-scale projects with a high degree of technological complexity, such as oil refineries, steel mills, chemical processing plants, and coal-fired or nuclear power plants. (An illustration appears in Figure 1-4.) The owners usually are deeply involved in the development of a project and prefer to work with designer-builders such that the total time for the completion of the project can be shortened. They also want to pick a team of designers and builders with whom the owner has developed good working relations over the years.

Although the initiation of such projects is also affected by the state of the economy, long-range demand forecasting is the most important factor since such

Figure 1-4 Construction of a Benzene Plant in Lima, Ohio (courtesy of Manitowoc Company, Inc.)

projects are capital intensive and require considerable amount of planning and construction time. Governmental regulation such as the rulings of the Environmental Protection Agency and the Nuclear Regulatory Commission in the United States can also profoundly influence decisions on these projects.

Infrastructure and Heavy Construction

Infrastructure and heavy construction includes projects such as highways, mass transit systems, tunnels, bridges, pipelines, drainage systems, and sewage treatment plants. (An illustration appears in Figure 1-5.) Most of these projects are publicly owned and therefore financed either through bonds or taxes. This category of construction is characterized by a high degree of mechanization, which has gradually replaced some labor-intensive operations.

Figure 1-5 Construction of the Dame Point Bridge in Jacksonville, Florida (courtesy of Mary Lou Maher)

The engineers and builders engaged in infrastructure construction are usually highly specialized since each segment of the market requires different types of skills. However, demands for different segments of infrastructure and heavy construction may shift with saturation in some segments. For example, as the available highway construction projects are declining, some heavy construction contractors quickly move their work force and equipment into the field of mining where jobs are available.

1.4 SELECTION OF PROFESSIONAL SERVICES

When an owner decides to seek professional services for the design and construction of a facility, he is confronted with a broad variety of choices. The type of services selected depends to a large degree on the type of construction and the experience of the owner in dealing with various professionals in the previous projects undertaken by the firm. Generally, several common types of professional services may be engaged either separately or in some combination by the owners.

Financial Planning Consultants

At the early stage of strategic planning for a capital project, an owner often seeks the services of financial planning consultants such as certified public accounting (CPA) firms to evaluate the economic and financial feasibility of the constructed facility, particularly with respect to various provisions of federal, state, and local tax laws which may affect the investment decision. Investment banks may also be consulted on various options for financing the facility to analyze their long-term effects on the financial health of the owner organization.

Architectural and Engineering Firms

Traditionally, the owner engages an architectural and engineering (A/E) firm or consortium as technical consultant in developing a preliminary design. After the engineering design and financing arrangements for the project are completed, the owner will enter into a construction contract with a general contractor either through competitive bidding or negotiation. The general contractor will act as a constructor and/or a coordinator of a large number of subcontractors who perform various specialties for the completion of the project. The A/E firm completes the design and may also provide on-site quality inspection during construction. Thus, the A/E firm acts as the prime professional on behalf of the owner and supervises the construction to ensure satisfactory results. This practice is most common in building construction.

In the past two decades, this traditional approach has become less popular for a number of reasons, particularly for large-scale projects. The A/E firms, which are engaged by the owner as the prime professionals for design and inspection, have become more isolated from the construction process. This has occurred because of pressures to reduce fees to A/E firms, the threat of litigation regarding construction defects, and lack of knowledge of new construction techniques on the part of architect and engineering professionals. Instead of preparing a construction plan along with the design, many A/E firms are no longer responsible for the details of construction nor do they provide periodic field inspection in many cases. As a matter of fact, such firms will place a prominent disclaimer of responsibilities on any shop drawings they may check, and they will often regard their representatives in the field as observers instead of inspectors. Thus, the A/E firm and the general contractor on a project often become antagonists who are looking after their own competing interests. As a result, even the constructibility of some engineering designs may become an issue of contention. To carry this protective attitude to the extreme, the specifications prepared by an A/E firm for the general contractor often protects the interest of the A/E firm at the expense of the interests of the owner and the contractor.

To reduce the cost of construction, some owners introduce *value engineering*, which seeks to reduce the cost of construction by soliciting a second design that might cost less than the original design produced by the A/E firm. In practice, the second design is submitted by the contractor after receiving a construction contract at a stipulated sum, and the saving in cost resulting from the redesign is shared by the contractor and the owner. The contractor is able to absorb the cost of redesign from the profit in construction or to reduce the construction cost as a result of the redesign. If the owner had been willing to pay a higher fee to the A/E firm or to direct the design process better, the A/E firm might have produced an improved design which would have cost less in the first place. Regardless of the merit of value engineering, this practice has undermined the role of the A/E firm as the prime professional acting on behalf of the owner to supervise the contractor.

Design/Construct Firms

A common trend in industrial construction, particularly for large projects, is to engage the services of a design/construct firm. By integrating design and construction management in a single organization, many of the conflicts between designers and constructors might be avoided. In particular, designs will be closely scrutinized for their constructibility. However, an owner engaging a design/construct firm must ensure that the quality of the constructed facility is not sacrificed by the desire to reduce the time or the cost for completing the project. Also, it is difficult to make use of competitive bidding in this type of design/construct process. As a result, owners must be relatively sophisticated in negotiating realistic and cost-effective construction contracts.

One of the most obvious advantages of the integrated design/construct process is the use of *phased construction* for a large project. In this process, the project is divided up into several phases, each of which can be designed and constructed in a staggered manner. After the completion of the design of the first phase, construction can begin without waiting for the completion of the design of the second phase, and so on. If proper coordination is exercised, the total project duration can be greatly reduced. Another advantage is to exploit the possibility of using the *turnkey* approach, whereby an owner can delegate all responsibility to the design/construct firm which will deliver to the owner a completed facility that meets the performance specifications at the specified price.

Professional Construction Managers

In recent years, a new breed of construction managers (CM) offers professional services from the inception to the completion of a construction project. These construction managers mostly come from the ranks of A/E firms or general contractors who may or may not retain dual roles in the service of the owners. In any case, the owner can rely on the service of a single prime professional to manage the entire process of a construction project. However, like the A/E firms of several decades ago, construction managers are appreciated by some owners but not by others. Before long, some owners find that the construction managers too may try to protect their own interest instead of that of the owners when the stakes are high.

It should be obvious to all involved in the construction process that the party which is required to take higher risk demands larger rewards. If an owner wants to engage an A/E firm on the basis of low fees instead of established qualifications, it often gets what it deserves or if the owner wants the general contractor to bear the cost of uncertainties in construction such as foundation conditions, the contract price will be higher even if competitive bidding is used in reaching a contractual agreement. Without mutual respect and trust, an owner cannot expect that construction managers can produce better results than other professionals. Hence, an owner must understand its own responsibility and the risk it wishes to assign to itself and to other participants in the process.

Operation and Maintenance Managers

Although many owners keep a permanent staff for the operation and maintenance of constructed facilities, others may prefer to contract such tasks to professional managers. Understandably, it is common to find in-house staff for operation and maintenance in specialized industrial plants and infrastructure facilities, and the use of outside managers under contracts for the operation and maintenance of rental properties such as apartments and office buildings. However, there are exceptions to these common practices. For example, maintenance of public roadways can be contracted to private firms. In any case, managers can provide a spectrum of operation and maintenance services for a specified time period in accordance to the terms of contractual agreements. Thus, the owners can be spared the provision of in-house expertise to operate and maintain the facilities.

Facilities Management

As a logical extension for obtaining the best services throughout the project life cycle of a constructed facility, some owners and developers are receptive to adding strategic planning at the beginning and facility maintenance as a follow-up to reduce space-related costs in their real estate holdings. Consequently, some architectural/engineering firms and construction management firms with computer-based expertise, together with interior design firms, are offering such front-end and follow-up services in addition to the more traditional services in design and construction. This spectrum of services is described in *Engineering News-Record (now ENR)* as follows:[2]

> Facilities management is the discipline of planning, designing, constructing and managing space—in every type of structure from office buildings to process plants. It involves developing corporate facilities policy, long-range forecasts, real estate, space inventories, projects (through design, construction and renovation), building operation and maintenance plans and furniture and equipment inventories.

A common denominator of all firms entering into these new services is that they all have strong computer capabilities and heavy computer investments. In addition to the use of computers for aiding design and monitoring construction, the service

[2] "Hot New Market Lures A-E Players to Cutting Edges," *Engineering News-Record*, April 4, 1985, pp. 30–37.

includes the compilation of a computer record of building plans that can be turned over at the end of construction to the facilities management group of the owner. A computer database of facilities information makes it possible for planners in the owner's organization to obtain overview information for long-range space forecasts, while the line managers can use as-built information such as lease/tenant records, utility costs, et cetera, for day-to-day operations.

1.5 CONSTRUCTION CONTRACTORS

Builders who supervise the execution of construction projects are traditionally referred to as *contractors*, or more appropriately called *constructors*. The *general contractor* coordinates various tasks for a project while the *specialty contractors* such as mechanical or electrical contractors perform the work in their specialties. Material and equipment suppliers often act as *installation contractors*; they play a significant role in a construction project since the conditions of delivery of materials and equipment affect the quality, cost, and timely completion of the project. It is essential to understand the operation of these contractors to deal with them effectively.

General Contractors

The function of a general contractor is to coordinate all tasks in a construction project. Unless the owner performs this function or engages a professional construction manager to do so, a good general contractor who has worked with a team of superintendents, specialty contractors, or subcontractors together for a number of projects in the past can be most effective in inspiring loyalty and cooperation. The general contractor is also knowledgeable about the labor force employed in construction. The labor force may or may not be unionized, depending on the size and location of the projects. In some projects, no member of the work force belongs to a labor union; in other cases, both union and nonunion craftsmen work together in what is called an open shop, or all craftsmen must be affiliated with labor unions in a closed shop. Since labor unions provide hiring halls staffed with skilled journeyman who have gone through apprentice programs for the projects as well as serving as collective bargain units, an experienced general contractor will make good use of the benefits and avoid the pitfalls in dealing with organized labor.

Specialty Contractors

Specialty contractors include mechanical, electrical, foundation, excavation, and demolition contractors among others. They usually serve as subcontractors to the general contractor of a project. In some cases, legal statutes may require an owner to deal with various specialty contractors directly. In the state of New York, for example, specialty contractors, such as mechanical and electrical contractors, are not subjected to the supervision of the general contractor of a construction project and must be given separate prime contracts on public works. With the exception of such special cases, an owner will hold the general contractor responsible for negotiating and fulfilling the contractual agreements with the subcontractors.

Material and Equipment Suppliers

Major material suppliers include specialty contractors in structural steel fabrication and erection, sheet metal, ready-mixed concrete delivery, reinforcing steel bar detailers, roofing, glazing, et cetera. Major equipment suppliers for industrial construction include manufacturers of generators, boilers, and piping and other equipment. Many suppliers handle on-site installation to ensure that the requirements and contractual specifications are met. As more and larger structural units are prefabricated off site, the distinction between specialty contractors and material suppliers becomes even less obvious.

1.6 FINANCING OF CONSTRUCTED FACILITIES

A major construction project requires an enormous amount of capital that is often supplied by lenders who want to be assured that the project will offer a fair return on the investment. The direct costs associated with a major construction project may be broadly classified into two categories: (1) the construction expenses paid to the general contractor for erecting the facility on site and (2) the expenses for land acquisition, legal fees, architect/engineer fees, construction management fees, interest on construction loans, and the opportunity cost of carrying empty space in the facility until it is fully occupied. The direct construction costs in the first category represent approximately 60 to 80 percent of the total costs in most construction projects. Since the costs of construction are ultimately borne by the owner, careful financial planning for the facility must be made prior to construction.

Construction Financing

Construction loans to contractors are usually provided by banks or savings and loan associations for construction financing. Upon the completion of the facility, construction loans will be terminated and the postconstruction facility financing will be arranged by the owner.

Construction loans provided for different types of construction vary. In the case of residential housing, construction loans and long-term mortgages can be obtained from savings and loans associations or commercial banks. For institutional and commercial buildings, construction loans are usually obtained from commercial banks. Since the value of specialized industrial buildings as collateral for loans is limited, construction loans in this domain are rare, and construction financing can be done from the pool of general corporate funds. For infrastructure construction owned by government, the property cannot be used as security for a private loan, but there are many possible ways to finance the construction, such as general appropriation from taxation or special bonds issued for the project.

Traditionally, banks serve as construction lenders in a three-party agreement among the contractor, the owner, and the bank. The stipulated loan will be paid to the contractor on an agreed schedule upon the verification of completion of various portions of the project. Generally, a payment request together with a standard progress report will be submitted each month by the contractor to the owner, which in turn submits a draw request to the bank. Provided that the work to date has been performed satisfactorily, the disbursement is made on that basis during the construction period. Under such circumstances, the bank has been primarily concerned with the completion of the facility on time and within the budget. The economic life of the facility after its completion is not a concern because of the transfer of risk to the owner or an institutional lender.

Facility Financing

Many private corporations maintain a pool of general funds resulting from retained earnings and long-term borrowing on the strength of corporate assets, which can be used for facility financing. Similarly, for public agencies, the long-term funding may be obtained from the commitment of general tax revenues from the federal, state, and/or local governments. Both private corporations and public agencies may issue special bonds for the constructed facilities which may obtain lower interest rates than other forms of borrowing. Short-term borrowing may also be used for bridging the gaps in long-term financing. Some corporate bonds are convertible to stocks under circumstances specified in the bond agreement. For public facilities, the assessment of user fees to repay the bond funds merits consideration for certain types of facilities such as toll roads and sewage treatment plants.[3] The use of mortgages is primarily confined to rental properties such as apartments and office buildings.

Because of the sudden surge of interest rates in the late 1970s, many financial institutions offer, in addition to the traditional fixed rate long-term mortgage commitments, other arrangements such as a combination of debt and a percentage of ownership in exchange for a long-term mortgage or the use of adjustable rate mortgages. In some cases, the construction loan may be granted on an open-ended basis without a long-term financing commitment. For example, the plan might be issued for the construction period with an option to extend it for a period of up to three years in order to give the owner more time to seek alternative long-term financing on the completed facility. The bank will be drawn into situations involving financial risk if it chooses to be a lender without long-term guarantees.

1.7 LEGAL AND REGULATORY REQUIREMENTS

The owners of facilities naturally want legal protection for all the activities involved in the construction. It is equally obvious that they should seek competent legal advice. However, there are certain principles that should be recognized by owners in order to avoid unnecessary pitfalls.

[3] See C. Hendrickson, "Financing Civil Works with User Fees," *Civil Engineering*, Vol. 53, no. 2, February 1983, pp. 71–72.

Legal Responsibilities

Activities in construction often involve risks, both physical and financial. An owner generally tries to shift the risks to other parties to the degree possible when entering into contractual agreements with them. However, such action is not without cost or risk. For example, a contractor who is assigned the risks may either ask for a higher contract price to compensate for the higher risks or end up in nonperformance or bankruptcy as an act of desperation. Such consequences can be avoided if the owner is reasonable in risk allocation. When risks are allocated to different parties, the owner must understand the implications and spell them out clearly. Sometimes there are statutory limitations on the allocation of liabilities among various groups, such as prohibition against the allocation of negligence in design to the contractor. An owner must realize its superior power in bargaining and hence the responsibilities associated with this power in making contractual agreements.

Mitigation of Conflicts

It is important for the owner to use legal counselors as advisors to mitigate conflicts before they happen rather than to wield conflicts as weapons against other parties. There are enough problems in design and construction due to uncertainty rather than bad intentions. The owner should recognize the more enlightened approaches for mitigating conflicts, such as using owner-controlled *wrap-up* insurance which will provide protection for all parties involved in the construction process for unforeseen risks or using arbitration, mediation, and other extrajudicial solutions for disputes among various parties. However, these compromise solutions are not without pitfalls and should be adopted only on the merit of individual cases.

Government Regulation

To protect public safety and welfare, legislatures and various government agencies periodically issue regulations which influence the construction process, the operation of constructed facilities, and their ultimate disposal. For example, building codes promulgated by local authorities have provided guidelines for design and construction practices for a very long time. Since the 1970s, many federal regulations that are related directly or indirectly to construction have been established in the United States. Among them are safety standards for workers issued by the Occupational Health and Safety Administration, environmental standards on pollutants and toxic wastes issued by the Environmental Protection Agency, and design and operation procedures for nuclear power plants issued by the Nuclear Regulatory Commission. The proliferation of environmental protection laws in recent decades can be noted from Figure 1-6.

Owners must be aware of the impacts of these regulations on the costs and durations of various types of construction projects as well as possibilities of litigation due to various contentions. For example, owners acquiring sites for new construction may be strictly liable for any hazardous wastes already on the site or removed from the site under the U.S. Comprehensive Environmental Response Compensation and

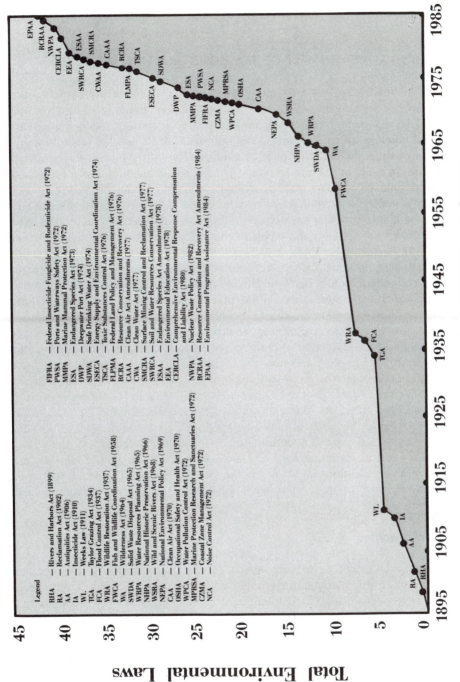

Figure 1-6 U.S. Laws on Environmental Protection, 1895–1985 (Copyright © 1985 Electric Power Research Institute. EPRI Report P-4391-SR *Electricity Outlook: The Foundation for EPRI R&D Planning*; reprinted with permission.)

Legend

RHA	— Rivers and Harbors Act (1899)	
RA	— Reclamation Act (1902)	
AA	— Antiquities Act (1906)	
IA	— Insecticide Act (1910)	
WL	— Weeks Law (1911)	
TGA	— Taylor Grazing Act (1934)	
FCA	— Flood Control Act (1937)	
WRA	— Wildlife Restoration Act (1937)	
FWCA	— Fish and Wildlife Coordination Act (1958)	
WA	— Wilderness Act (1964)	
SWDA	— Solid Waste Disposal Act (1965)	
WRPA	— Water Resources Planning Act (1965)	
NHPA	— National Historic Preservation Act (1966)	
WSRA	— Wild and Scenic Rivers Act (1968)	
NEPA	— National Environmental Policy Act (1969)	
CAA	— Clean Air Act (1970)	
OSHA	— Occupational Safety and Health Act (1970)	
WPCA	— Water Pollution Control Act (1972)	
MPRSA	— Marine Protection Research and Sanctuaries Act (1972)	
CZMA	— Coastal Zone Management Act (1972)	
NCA	— Noise Control Act (1972)	

FIFRA	— Federal Insecticide Fungicide and Rodenticide Act (1972)	
PWSA	— Ports and Waterways Safety Act (1972)	
MMPA	— Marine Mammal Protection Act (1972)	
ESA	— Endangered Species Act (1973)	
DWP	— Deepwater Port Act (1974)	
SDWA	— Safe Drinking Water Act (1974)	
ESECA	— Energy Supply and Environmental Coordination Act (1974)	
TSCA	— Toxic Substances Control Act (1976)	
FLPMA	— Federal Land Policy and Management Act (1976)	
RCRA	— Resource Conservation and Recovery Act (1976)	
CAAA	— Clean Air Act Amendments (1977)	
CWA	— Clean Water Act (1977)	
SMCRA	— Surface Mining Control and Reclamation Act (1977)	
SWRCA	— Soil and Water Resources Conservation Act (1977)	
ESAA	— Endangered Species Act Amendments (1978)	
EEA	— Environmental Education Act (1978)	
CERCLA	— Comprehensive Environmental Response Compensation and Liability Act (1980)	

NWPA	— Nuclear Waste Policy Act (1982)	
RCRAA	— Resource Conservation and Recovery Act Amendments (1984)	
EPAA	— Environmental Programs Assistance Act (1984)	

Liability (CERCL) Act of 1980. For large-scale projects involving new technologies, the construction costs often escalate with the uncertainty associated with such restrictions.

1.8 THE CHANGING ENVIRONMENT OF THE CONSTRUCTION INDUSTRY

The construction industry is a conglomeration of diverse fields and participants that have been loosely lumped together as a sector of the economy. The construction industry plays a central role in national welfare, including the development of residential housing, office buildings, and industrial plants and the restoration of the nation's infrastructure and other public facilities. The importance of the construction industry lies in the function of its products which provide the foundation for industrial production, and its impacts on the national economy cannot be measured by the value of its output or the number of persons employed in its activities alone.

To be more specific, construction refers to all types of activities usually associated with the erection and repair of immobile facilities. Contract construction consists of a large number of firms that perform construction work for others and is estimated to be approximately 85 percent of all construction activities. The remaining 15 percent of construction is performed by owners of the facilities and is referred to as *force-account* construction. Although the number of contractors in the United States exceeds 1 million, over 60 percent of all contractor construction is performed by the top 400 contractors. The value of new construction in the United States (expressed in constant dollars) and the value of construction as a percentage of the gross national products from 1955 to 1985 are shown in Figure 1-7. It can be seen that construction is a significant factor in the gross national product, although its importance has been declining in recent years.[4] Not to be ignored is the fact that as the nation's constructed facilities become older, the total expenditure on rehabilitation and maintenance may increase relative to the value of new construction.

Owners who pay close attention to the peculiar characteristics of the construction industry and its changing operating environment will be able to take advantage of the favorable conditions and to avoid the pitfalls. Several factors are particularly noteworthy because of their significant impacts on the quality, cost, and time of construction.

New Technologies

In recent years, technological innovation in design, materials, and construction methods have resulted in significant changes in construction costs. Computer aids have improved capabilities for generating quality designs as well as reducing the time required to produce alternative designs. New materials not only have enhanced the quality of construction but also have shortened the time for shop fabrication and

[4] The graph is derived from data in "Value of New Construction Put in Place, 1960–1983," *Statistical Abstract of the United States*, 1985 105th edition, U.S. Department of Commerce, Bureau of Census, 1985, pp. 722–723, as well as from information in other editions.

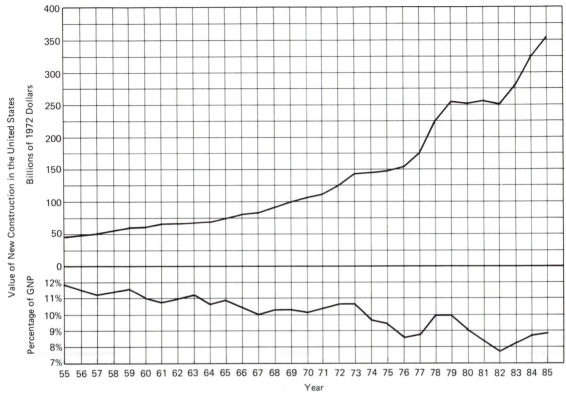

Figure 1-7   Value of New Construction in the United States, 1955-1985

field erection. Construction methods have gone through various stages of mechanization and automation, including the latest development of construction robotics.

The effects of new technologies on construction costs have been mixed because of the high development costs for new technologies. However, it is unmistakable that design professionals and construction contractors who have not adapted to changing technologies have been forced out of the mainstream of design and construction activities. Ultimately, construction quality and cost can be improved with the adoption of new technologies which are proved to be efficient from both the viewpoints of performance and economy.

Labor Productivity

The term *productivity* is generally defined as a ratio of the production output volume to the input volume of resources. Since both output and input can be quantified in a number of ways, there is no single measure of productivity that is universally applicable, particularly in the construction industry where the products are often unique, and there is no standard for specifying the levels for aggregation of data. However, since labor constitutes a large part of the cost of construction, labor productivity in terms of output volume (constant dollar value or functional units) per person-hour is a useful measure. Labor productivity measured in this way does not necessarily indicate the efficiency of labor alone but rather measures the combined effects of labor, equipment, and other factors contributing to the output.

While aggregate construction industry productivity is important as a measure of national economy, owners are more concerned about the labor productivity of basic units of work produced by various crafts on site. Thus, an owner can compare the labor performance at different geographic locations, under different working conditions, and for different types and sizes of projects.

Construction costs usually run parallel to material prices and labor wages. Actually, over the years, labor productivity has increased in some traditional types of construction and thus provides a leveling or compensating effect when hourly rates for labor increase faster than other costs in construction. However, labor productivity has been stagnant or even declined in unconventional or large-scale projects.

Public Scrutiny

Under the present litigious climate in the United States, the public is increasingly vocal in the scrutiny of construction project activities. Sometimes it may result in considerable difficulty in siting new facilities as well as additional expenses during the construction process itself. Owners must be prepared to manage such crises before they get out of control.

Figure 1-8 can serve to indicate public attitudes toward the siting of new facilities. It represents the cumulative percentage of individuals who would be willing to accept a new industrial facility at various distances from their homes. For example, over 50 percent of the people surveyed would accept a 10-story office building within 5 miles of their home, but only 25 percent would accept a large factory or coal-fired power plant at a similar distance. An even lower percentage would accept a hazardous waste disposal site or a nuclear power plant. Even at a distance of 100 miles, a significant fraction of the public would be unwilling to accept hazardous waste facilities or nuclear power plants.

This objection to new facilities is a widespread public attitude, representing considerable skepticism about the external benefits and costs which new facilities will impose. It is this public attitude which is likely to make public scrutiny and regulation a continuing concern for the construction industry.

International Competition

A final trend which deserves note is the increasing level of international competition in the construction industry. Owners are likely to find nontraditional firms bidding for construction work, particularly on large projects. Separate bids from numerous European, North American, and Asian construction firms are not unusual. In the United States, overseas firms are becoming increasingly visible and important. In this environment of heightened competition, good project management and improved productivity are more and more important.

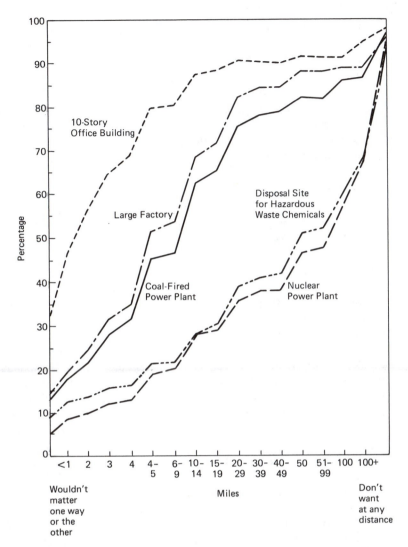

Figure 1-8 Public Acceptance Toward New Facilities (Reprinted from *Environmental Quality-1980*, the Eleventh Annual Report of the Council on Environmental Quality, U.S. Government Printing Office, Washington, DC, December 1980.)

A bidding competition for a major new offshore drilling platform illustrates the competitive environment in construction. As described in *The Wall Street Journal*,[5]

Through most of the postwar years, the nation's biggest builders of offshore oil platforms enjoyed an unusually cozy relationship with the Big Oil Companies they served. Their top officials developed personal friendships with oil executives, entertained them

[5] See Thomas Petzinger, Jr., "Upstart's Winning Bid for Offshore Platform Stuns Its Older Rivals," *The Wall Street Journal*, November 20, 1985, p.1, c.6.

at opulent hunting camps, and won contracts to build nearly every major offshore oil platform in the world. . . . But this summer, the good-old boy network fell apart. Shell [Oil Co.] awarded the main contract for [a new] platform—taller than Chicago's Sears Tower, four times heavier than the Brooklyn Bridge—to a tiny upstart.

The winning bidder arranged overseas fabrication of the rig, kept overhead costs low, and proposed a novel assembly procedure by which construction equipment was mounted on completed sections of the platform to speed the completion of the entire structure. The result was lower costs than those estimated and bid by traditional firms.

Of course, U.S. firms including A/E firms, contractors, and construction managers are also competing in foreign countries. Their success or failure in the international arena may also affect their capacities and vitality to provide services in the domestic U.S. market.

Contractor-Financed Projects

Increasingly, some owners look to contractors or joint ventures as a resource to design, to build, and to finance a constructed facility. For example, a utility company may seek a consortium consisting of a design/construct firm and a financial investment firm to assume total liability during construction and thereby eliminate the risks of cost escalation to ratepayers, stockholders, and the management. On the other hand, a local sanitation district may seek such a consortium to provide private ownership for a proposed new sewage treatment plant. In the former case, the owner may take over the completed facility and service the debt on construction through long-term financing arrangements; in the latter case, the private owner may operate the completed facility and recover its investment through user fees. The activities of joint ventures among design, construction, and investment firms are sometimes referred to as *financial engineering*.

This type of joint venture has become more important in the international construction market where aggressive contractors often win contracts by offering a more attractive financing package rather than superior technology. With a deepening shadow of international debts in recent years, many developing countries are not in a position to undertake any new project without contractor-backed financing. Thus, the contractors or joint ventures in overseas projects are forced into very risky positions if they intend to stay in the competition.

1.9 THE ROLE OF PROJECT MANAGERS

In the project life cycle, the most influential factors affecting the outcome of the project often reside at the early stages. At this point, decisions should be based on competent economic evaluation with due consideration for adequate financing, the prevalent social and regulatory environment, and technological considerations. Architects and engineers might specialize in planning, in construction field management, or in operation, but as project managers, they must have some familiarity with all such aspects to understand properly their role and be able to make competent decisions.

Since the 1970s, many large-scale projects have run into serious problems of management, such as cost overruns and long schedule delays. Actually, the management of *megaprojects* or *superprojects* is not a practice peculiar to our time. Witness the construction of transcontinental railroads in the Civil War era and the construction of the Panama Canal at the turn of this century. Although the megaprojects of this generation may appear in greater frequency and present a new set of challenge, the problems are organizational rather than technical. As noted by Hardy Cross,[6]

> It is customary to think of engineering as a part of a trilogy, pure science, applied science and engineering. It needs emphasis that this trilogy is only one of a triad of trilogies into which engineering fits. This first is pure science, applied science and engineering; the second is economic theory, finance and engineering; and the third is social relations, industrial relations and engineering. Many engineering problems are as closely allied to social problems as they are to pure science.

As engineers advance professionally, they often spend as much or more time on planning, management, and other economic or social problems as they do on the traditional engineering design and analysis problems which form the core of most educational programs. It is upon the ability of engineers to tackle all such problems that their performance will ultimately be judged.

The greatest stumbling block to effective management in construction is the inertia and historic divisions among planners, designers, and constructors. While technical competence in design and innovation remains the foundation of engineering practice, the social, economic and organizational factors that are pervasive in influencing the success and failure of construction projects must also be dealt with effectively by design and construction organizations. Of course, engineers are not expected to know every detail of management techniques, but they must be knowledgeable enough to anticipate the problems of management so that they can work harmoniously with professionals in related fields to overcome the inertia and historic divisions.

Paradoxically, engineers who are creative in engineering design are often innovative in planning and management since both types of activities involve problem solving. In fact, they can reinforce each other if both are included in the education process, provided that creativity and innovation instead of routine practice are emphasized. A project manager who is well educated in the *fundamental principles* of engineering design and management can usefully apply such principles once he or she has acquired basic understanding of a new *application area*. A project manager who has been trained by rote learning for a specific type of project may merely gain one year of experience repeated 20 times even if he or she has been in the field for 20 years. A broadly educated project manager can reasonably hope to become

---

[6] See H. Cross, *Engineers and Ivory Towers*, McGraw-Hill Book Company, Inc, New York, 1952.

a leader in the profession; a narrowly trained project manager is often relegated to the role of his or her first job level permanently.

The owners have much at stake in selecting a competent project manager and in providing her or him with the authority to assume responsibility at various stages of the project regardless of the types of contractual agreements for implementing the project. Of course, the project manager must also possess the leadership quality and the ability to handle effectively intricate interpersonal relationships within an organization. The ultimate test of the education and experience of a project manager for construction lies in her or his ability to apply fundamental principles to solving problems in the new and unfamiliar situations which have become the hallmarks of the changing environment in the construction industry.

1.10 REFERENCES

1-1. Au, T., and C. Hendrickson, "Education in Engineering Planning and Management," *Proceedings of the ASCE Conference on Civil Engineering Education,* Columbus, Ohio, 1985.

1-2. Barrie, D. S. (editor), *Directions in Managing Construction*, John Wiley and Sons, Inc., New York, 1981.

1-3. Bonny, J. B., and J. P. Frein, *Handbook of Construction Management and Organization*, 2nd ed., Van Nostrand Reinhold Co., New York, 1980.

1-4. Lange, J. E., and D. Q. Mills, *The Construction Industry*, Lexington Books, D.C. Heath and Co., Lexington, MA, 1979.

1-5. Walker, N., E. N. Walker, and T. K. Rohdenburg, *Legal Pitfalls in Architecture, Engineering and Building Construction*, 2nd ed., McGraw-Hill Book Company, New York, 1979.

1-6. *Building for Tommorow: Global Enterprise and the U.S. Construction Industry*, National Academy Press, Washington D.C., 1988.

2

Organizing
for
Project Management

2.1 WHAT IS PROJECT MANAGEMENT ?

The management of construction projects requires knowledge of modern management as well as an understanding of the design and construction process. Construction projects have a specific set of objectives and constraints such as a required time frame for completion. While the relevant technology, institutional arrangements or processes will differ, the management of such projects has much in common with the management of similar types of projects in other specialty or technology domains such as aerospace, pharmaceutical, and energy developments.

Generally, project management is distinguished from the general management of corporations by the mission-oriented nature of a project. A project organization will generally be terminated when the mission is accomplished. According to the Project Management Institute, the discipline of project management can be defined as follows:[7]

> Project management is the art of directing and coordinating human and material resources throughout the life of a project by using modern management techniques to achieve predetermined objectives of scope, cost, time, quality and participation satisfaction.

By contrast, the general management of business and industrial corporations assumes a broader outlook with greater continuity of operations. Nevertheless, there are sufficient similarities as well as differences between the two so that modern management techniques developed for general management may be adapted for project management.

The basic ingredients for a project management framework[8] may be represented schematically in Figure 2-1. A working knowledge of general management and familiarity with the special knowledge domain related to the project are indispensable. Supporting disciplines such as computer science and decision science may also play an important role. In fact, modern management practices and various special knowledge domains have absorbed various techniques or tools which were once identified only with the supporting disciplines. For example, computer-based information systems and decision support systems are now commonplace tools for general management. Similarly, many operations research techniques such as linear programming and network analysis are now widely used in many knowledge or application domains. Hence, the representation in Figure 2-1 reflects only the sources from which the project management framework evolves.

Specifically, project management in construction encompasses a set of objectives which may be accomplished by implementing a series of operations subject to resource constraints. There are potential conflicts between the stated objectives with regard to scope, cost, time, and quality and the constraints imposed on human mate-

---

[7] See R. M. Wideman, "The PMBOK Report—PMI Body of Knowledge Standard," *Project Management Journal*, Vol. 17, no.3, August 1986, pp.15–24.

[8] See L. C. Stuckenbruck, "Project Management Framework," *Project Management Journal*, Vol. 17, no. 3, August 1986, pp. 25–30.

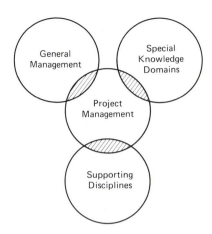

Figure 2-1 Basic Ingredients
in Project Management

rial and financial resources. These conflicts should be resolved at the onset of a project by making the necessary trade-offs or creating new alternatives. Subsequently, the functions of project management for construction generally include the following:

1. Specification of project objectives and plans including delineation of scope, budgeting, scheduling, setting performance requirements, and selecting project participants.
2. Maximization of efficient resource utilization through procurement of labor, materials, and equipment according to the prescribed schedule and plan.
3. Implementation of various operations through proper coordination and control of planning, design, estimating, contracting, and construction in the entire process.
4. Development of effective communications and mechanisms for resolving conflicts among the various participants.

2.2 TRENDS IN MODERN MANAGEMENT

In recent years, major developments in management reflect the acceptance to various degrees of the following elements: (1) the management process approach, (2) the management science and decision support approach, and (3) the behavioral science approach for human resource development. These three approaches complement each other in current practice and provide a useful groundwork for project management.

The management process approach emphasizes the systematic study of management by identifying management functions in an organization and then examining each in detail. There is general agreement regarding the functions of planning, organizing, and controlling. A major tenet is that by analyzing management along functional lines, a framework can be constructed into which all new management activities can be placed. Thus, the manager's job is regarded as coordinating a process of interrelated functions that are neither totally random nor rigidly predetermined but are dynamic as the process evolves. Another tenet is that management principles can be derived from an intellectual analysis of management functions. By dividing the manager's job into functional components, principles based upon each function can be extracted. Hence, management functions can be organized into a hierarchical structure designed to improve operational efficiency, such as the example of the organization for a manufacturing company shown in Figure 2-2. The basic management functions are performed by all managers, regardless of enterprise, activity, or hierarchical levels. Finally, the development of a management philosophy results in helping the manager to establish relationships between human and material resources. The outcome of following an established philosophy of operation helps the manager win the support of the subordinates in achieving organizational objectives.

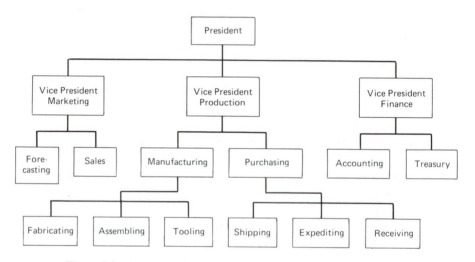

Figure 2-2 Illustrative Hierarchical Structure of Management Functions

The management science and decision support approach contributes to the development of a body of quantitative methods designed to aid managers in making complex decisions related to operations and production. In decision support systems, emphasis is placed on providing managers with relevant information. In management science, a great deal of attention is given to defining objectives and constraints and to constructing mathematical analysis models in solving complex problems of inventory, materials, and production control, among others. A topic of major interest in management science is the maximization of profit, or in the absence of a workable model for the operation of the entire system, the suboptimization of the operations of its components. The optimization or suboptimization is often achieved by the use of operations research techniques, such as linear programming, quadratic programming, graph theory, queueing theory, and Monte Carlo simulation. In addition to the increasing use of computers accompanied by the development of sophisticated mathematical models and information systems, management science and decision support systems have played an important role by looking more carefully at problem inputs and relationships and by promoting goal formulation and measurement of performance. Artificial intelligence has also begun to be applied to provide decision support systems for solving ill-structured problems in management.

The behavioral science approach for human resource development is important because management entails getting things done through the actions of people. An effective manager must understand the importance of human factors such as needs, drives, motivation, leadership, personality, behavior, and work groups. Within this context, some place more emphasis on interpersonal behavior which focuses on the individual and his or her motivations as a sociopsychological being; others emphasize more group behavior in recognition of the organized enterprise as a social organism, subject to all the attitudes, habits, pressures, and conflicts of the cultural environment of people. The major contributions made by the behavioral scientists to the field of management include (1) the formulation of concepts and explanations about individual and group behavior in the organization, (2) the empirical testing of these concepts methodically in many different experimental and field settings, and (3) the establishment of actual managerial policies and decisions for operation based on the conceptual and methodical frameworks.

2.3 STRATEGIC PLANNING AND PROJECT PROGRAMMING

The programming of capital projects is shaped by the strategic plan of an organization, which is influenced by market demands and resources constraints. The programming process associated with planning and feasibility studies sets the priorities and timing for initiating various projects to meet the overall objectives of the organizations. However, once this decision is made to initiate a project, market pressure may dictate early and timely completion of the facility.

Among various types of construction, the influence of market pressure on the timing of initiating a facility is most obvious in industrial construction.[9] Demand for an industrial product may be shortlived, and if a company does not hit the market first, there may not be demand for its product later. With intensive competition for national and international markets, the trend of industrial construction moves toward shorter project life cycles, particularly in technology-intensive industries.

To gain time, some owners are willing to forgo thorough planning and feasibility study so as to proceed on a project with inadequate definition of the project scope. Invariably, subsequent changes in project scope will increase construction costs; however, profits derived from earlier facility operation often justify the increase in construction costs. Generally, if the owner can derive reasonable profits from the operation of a completed facility, the project is considered a success even if construction costs far exceed the estimate based on an inadequate scope definition. This attitude may be attributed in large part to the uncertainties inherent in construction

[9] See, for example, J. T. O'Connor, and C. G. Vickory, *Control of Construction Project Scope*, a Report to the Construction Industry Institute, The University of Texas at Austin, December 1985.

projects. It is difficult to argue that profits might be even higher if construction costs could be reduced without increasing the project duration. However, some projects, notably some nuclear power plants, are clearly unsuccessful and abandoned before completion, and their demise must be attributed at least in part to inadequate planning and poor feasibility studies.

The owner or facility sponsor holds the key to influence the construction costs of a project because any decision made at the beginning stage of a project life cycle has far greater influence than those made at later stages, as shown schematically in Figure 2-3. Therefore, an owner should obtain the expertise of professionals to provide adequate planning and feasibility studies. Many owners do not maintain an in-house engineering and construction management capability, and they should consider the establishment of an ongoing relationship with outside consultants to respond quickly to requests. Even among those owners who maintain engineering and construction divisions, many treat these divisions as reimbursable, independent organizations. Such an arrangement should not discourage their legitimate use as false economies in reimbursable costs from such divisions can indeed be very costly to the overall organization.

Finally, the initiation and execution of capital projects places demands on the resources of the owner and the professionals and contractors to be engaged by the owner. For very large projects, it may bid up the price of engineering services as well as the costs of materials and equipment and the contract prices of all types. Consequently, such factors should be taken into consideration in determining the timing of a project.

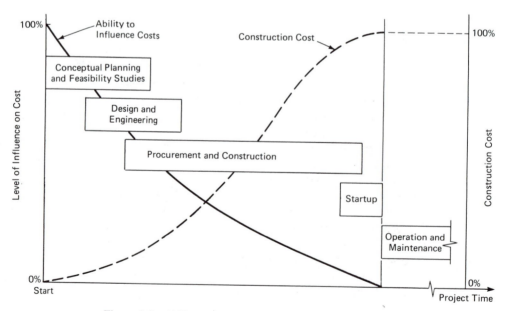

Figure 2-3 Ability to Influence Construction Cost over Time

Example 2-1: Setting Priorities for Projects

A department store planned to expand its operation by acquiring 20 acres of land in the southeast of a metropolitan area which consists of well-established suburbs for middle-income families. An architectural and engineering (A/E) firm was engaged to design a shopping center on the 20-acre plot with the department store as its flagship plus a large number of storefronts for tenants. One year later, the department store owner purchased 2,000 acres of farmland in the northwest outskirts of the same metropolitan area and designated 20 acres of this land for a shopping center. The A/E firm was again engaged to design a shopping center at this new location.

The A/E firm was kept completely in the dark while the assemblage of the 2,000 acres of land in the northwest quietly took place. When the plans and specifications for the southeast shopping center were completed, the owner informed the A/E firm that it would not proceed with the construction of the southeast shopping center for the time being. Instead, the owner urged the A/E firm to produce a new set of similar plans and specifications for the northwest shopping center as soon as possible, even at the sacrifice of cost-saving measures. When the plans and specifications for the northwest shopping center were ready, the owner immediately authorized its construction. However, it took another three years before the southeast shopping center was finally built.

The reason behind the change of plan was that the owner discovered the availability of the farmland in the northwest which could be developed into residential real estate properties for upper-middle-income families. The immediate construction of the northwest shopping center would make the land development parcels more attractive to home buyers. Thus, the owner was able to recoup enough cash flow in three years to construct the southeast shopping center in addition to financing the construction of the northeast shopping center, as well as the land development in its vicinity.

While the owner did not want the construction cost of the northwest shopping center to run wild, it apparently was satisfied with the cost estimate based on the detailed plans of the southeast shopping center. Thus, the owner had a general idea of what the construction cost of the northwest shopping center would be and did not wish to wait for a more refined cost estimate until the detailed plans for that center were ready. To the owner, the timeliness of completing the construction of the northwest shopping center was far more important than was reducing the construction cost in fulfilling its investment objectives.

Example 2-2: Resource Constraints for Megaprojects

A major problem with megaprojects is the severe strain placed on the environment, particularly on the resources in the immediate area of a construction project. "Mega" or "macro" projects involve construction of very large facilities such as the Alaska pipeline constructed in the 1970s or the Panama Canal constructed in the 1900s. The limitations in some or all of the basic elements required for the successful completion of a megaproject include

- Engineering design professionals to provide sufficient personnel to complete the design within a reasonable time limit.
- Construction supervisors with capacity and experience to direct large projects.
- The number of construction workers with proper skills to do the work.
- The market to supply materials in sufficient quantities and of required quality on time.

- The ability of the local infrastructure to support the large number of workers over an extended period of time, including housing, transportation, and other services.

To compound the problem, megaprojects are often constructed in remote environments away from major population centers and subject to severe climate conditions. Consequently, special features of each megaproject must be evaluated carefully.

2.4 EFFECTS OF PROJECT RISKS ON ORGANIZATION

The uncertainty in undertaking a construction project comes from many sources and often involves many participants in the project. Since each participant tries to minimize its own risk, the conflicts among various participants can be detrimental to the project. Only the owner has the power to moderate such conflicts as it alone holds the key to risk assignment through proper contractual relations with other participants. Failure to recognize this responsibility by the owner often leads to undesirable results. In recent years, the concept of "risk-sharing/risk-assignment" contracts has gained acceptance by the federal government.[10] Since this type of contract acknowledges the responsibilities of the owners, the contract prices are expected to be lower than those in which all risks are assigned to contractors.

In approaching the problem of uncertainty, it is important to recognize that incentives must be provided if any of the participants is expected to take a greater risk. The willingness of a participant to accept risks often reflects the professional competence of that participant as well as its propensity to risk. However, society's perception of the potential liabilities of the participant can affect the attitude of risk taking for all participants. When a claim is made against one of the participants, it is difficult for the public to know whether a fraud has been committed, or simply that an accident has occurred.

Risks in construction projects may be classified in a number of ways.[11] One form of classification is as follows:

1. Socioeconomic factors
   - Environmental protection
   - Public safety regulation
   - Economic instability
2. Organizational relationships
   - Contractual relations
   - Attitudes of participants
   - Communication

[10] See, for example, Federal Form 23-A and EPA's Appendix C-2 clauses.

[11] See E. D'Appolonia, "Coping with Uncertainty in Geotechnical Engineering and Constuction," *Special Proceedings of the 9th International Conference on Soil Mechanics and Foundation Engineering*, Tokyo, Japan, Vol. 4, 1979, pp. 1–18.

3. Technological problems
- Design assumptions
- Site conditions
- Construction procedures
- Construction occupational safety

The environmental protection movement has contributed to the uncertainty for construction because of the inability to know what will be required and how long it will take to obtain approval from the regulatory agencies. The requirements of continued reevaluation of problems and the lack of definitive criteria which are practical have also resulted in added costs. Public safety regulations have similar effects, which have been most noticeable in the energy field involving nuclear power plants and coal mining. The situation has created constantly shifting guidelines for engineers, constructors, and owners as projects move through the stages of planning to construction. These moving targets add a significant new dimension of uncertainty which can make it virtually impossible to schedule and complete work at budgeted cost. Economic conditions of the past decade have further reinforced the climate of uncertainty with high inflation and interest rates. The deregulation of financial institutions has also generated unanticipated problems related to the financing of construction.

Uncertainty stemming from regulatory agencies, environmental issues, and financial aspects of construction should be at least mitigated or ideally eliminated. Owners are keenly interested in achieving some form of breakthrough that will lower the costs of projects and mitigate or eliminate lengthy delays. Such breakthroughs are seldom planned. Generally, they happen when the right conditions exist, such as when innovation is permitted or when a basis for incentive or reward exists. However, there is a long way to go before a true partnership of all parties involved can be forged.

During periods of economic expansion, major capital expenditures are made by industries and bid up the cost of construction. To control costs, some owners attempt to use fixed price contracts so that the risks of unforeseen contingencies related to an overheated economy are passed on to contractors. However, contractors will raise their prices to compensate for the additional risks.

The risks related to organizational relationships may appear to be unnecessary but are quite real. Strained relationships may develop between various organizations involved in the design/construct process. When problems occur, discussions often center on responsibilities rather than project needs at a time when the focus should be on solving the problems. Cooperation and communication between the parties are discouraged for fear of the effects of impending litigation. This barrier to communication results from the ill-conceived notion that uncertainties resulting from technological problems can be eliminated by appropriate contract terms. The net result has been an increase in the costs of constructed facilities.

The risks related to technological problems are familiar to the design/construct professions which have some degree of control over this category. However, because of rapid advances in new technologies which present new problems to designers and constructors, technological risk has become greater in many instances. Certain design assumptions which have served the professions well in the past may become obsolete in dealing with new types of facilities which may have greater complexity or scale or both. Site conditions, particularly subsurface conditions which always present some degree of uncertainty, can create an even greater degree of uncertainty for facilities with heretofore unknown characteristics during operation. Because construction procedures may not have been fully anticipated, the design may have to be modified after construction has begun. An example of facilities which have encountered such uncertainty is the nuclear power plant, and many owners, designers, and contractors have suffered for undertaking such projects.

If each of the problems just cited can cause uncertainty, the combination of such problems is often regarded by all parties as being out of control and inherently risky. Thus, the issue of liability has taken on major proportions and has influenced the practices of engineers and constructors, who in turn have influenced the actions of the owners.

Many owners have begun to understand the problems of risks and are seeking to address some of these problems. For example, some owners are turning to those organizations that offer complete capabilities in planning, design, and construction and tend to avoid breaking the project into major components to be undertaken individually by specialty participants. Proper coordination throughout the project duration and good organizational communication can avoid delays and costs resulting from fragmentation of services, even though the components from various services are eventually integrated.

Attitudes of cooperation can be readily applied to the private sector, but only in special circumstances can they be applied to the public sector. The ability to deal with complex issues is often precluded in the competitive bidding which is usually required in the public sector. The situation becomes more difficult with the proliferation of regulatory requirements and resulting delays in design and construction while awaiting approvals from government officials who do not participate in the risks of the project.

2.5 ORGANIZATION OF PROJECT PARTICIPANTS

The top management of the owner sets the overall policy and selects the appropriate organization to take charge of a proposed project. Its policy will dictate how the project life cycle is divided among organizations and which professionals should be engaged. Decisions by the top management of the owner will also influence the organization to be adopted for project management. In general, there are many ways to decompose a project into stages. The most typical are

- Sequential processing, whereby the project is divided into separate stages and each stage is carried out successively in sequence.

- Parallel processing, whereby the project is divided into independent parts such that all stages are carried out simultaneously.
- Staggered processing, whereby the stages may be overlapping, such as the use of phased design/construct procedures for fast-track operation.

It should be pointed out that some decompositions may work out better than others, depending on the circumstances. In any case, the prevalence of decomposition makes the subsequent integration particularly important. The critical issues involved in organization for project management are

- How many organizations are involved?
- What are the relationships among the organizations?
- When are the various organizations brought into the project?

There are two basic approaches to organize for project implementation, even though many variations may exist as a result of different contractual relationships adopted by the owner and builder. These basic approaches are divided along the following lines:

1. **Separation of organizations.** Numerous organizations serve as consultants or contractors to the owner, with different organizations handling design and construction functions. Typical examples which involve different degrees of separation are
   - Traditional sequence of design and construction.
   - Professional construction management.
2. **Integration of organizations.** A single or joint venture consisting of a number of organizations with a single command undertakes both design and construction functions. Two extremes may be cited as examples:
   - Owner-builder operation in which all work will be handled in-house by force account.
   - Turnkey operation in which all work is contracted to a vendor which is responsible for delivering the completed project.

Since construction projects may be managed by a spectrum of participants in a variety of combinations, the organization for the management of such projects may vary from case to case. On one extreme, each project may be staffed by existing personnel in the functional divisions of the organization on an ad hoc basis as shown in Figure 2-4 until the project is completed. This arrangement is referred to as the matrix organization as each project manager must negotiate all resources for the project from the existing organizational framework. On the other hand, the organization may consist of a small central functional staff for the exclusive purpose of supporting various projects, each of which has its functional divisions as shown in Figure 2-5. This decentralized setup is referred to as the project-oriented

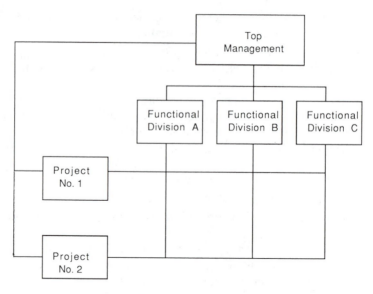

Figure 2-4 A Matrix Organization

organization as each project manager has autonomy in managing the project. There are many variations of management style between these two extremes, depending on the objectives of the organization and the nature of the construction project. For example, a large chemical company with in-house staff for planning, design, and construction of facilities for new product lines will naturally adopt the matrix organization. On the other hand, a construction company whose existence depends entirely on the management of certain types of construction projects may find the project-oriented organization particularly attractive. While organizations may differ, the same basic principles of management structure are applicable to most situations.

To illustrate various types of organizations for project management, we shall

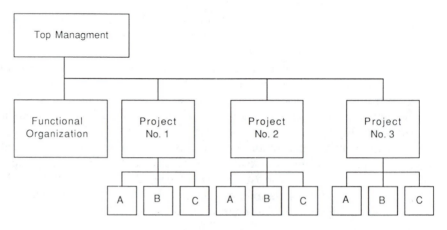

Figure 2-5 A Project-Oriented Organization

consider two examples, the first one representing an owner organization while the second one representing the organization of a construction management consultant under the direct supervision of the owner.

Example 2-3: Matrix Organization of an Engineering Division

The Engineering Division of an Electric Power and Light Company has functional departments as shown in Figure 2-6. When small-scale projects such as the addition of a transmission tower or a substation are authorized, a matrix organization is used to carry out such projects. For example, in the design of a transmission tower, the professional skill of a structural engineer is most important. Consequently, the leader of the project team will be selected from the Structural Engineering Department while the remaining team members are selected from all departments as dictated by the personnel requirements. On the other hand, in the design of a new substation, the professional skill of an electrical engineer is most important. Hence, the leader of the project team will be selected from the Electrical Engineering Department.

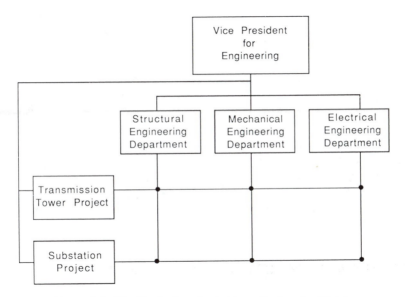

Figure 2-6   The Matrix Organization in an Engineering Division

Example 2-4: Example of Construction Management Consultant Organization

When the same Electric Power and Light Company in the previous example decided to build a new nuclear power plant, it engaged a construction management consultant to take charge of the design and construction completely. However, the company also assigned a project team to coordinate with the construction management consultant as shown in Figure 2-7.

Since the company eventually will operate the power plant upon its completion, it is highly important for its staff to monitor the design and construction of the plant. Such coordination allows the owner not only to assure the quality of construction but also to be familiar with the design to facilitate future operation and maintenance. Note

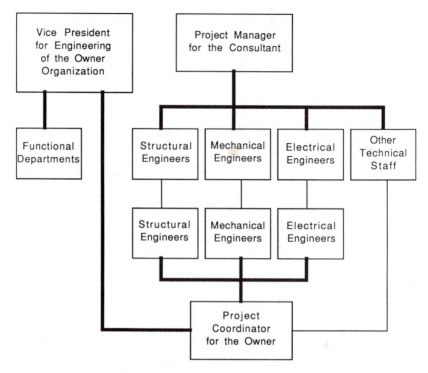

Figure 2-7   Coordination Between Owner and Consultant

the close direct relationships of various departments of the owner and the consultant. Since the project will last for many years before its completion, the staff members assigned to the project team are not expected to rejoin the Engineering Department but will probably be involved in the future operation of the new plant. Thus, the project team can act independently toward its designated mission.

2.6 TRADITIONAL DESIGNER/CONSTRUCTOR SEQUENCE

For ordinary projects of moderate size and complexity, the owner often employs a designer (an architectural/engineering firm) which prepares the detailed plans and specifications for the constructor (a general contractor). The designer also acts on behalf of the owner to oversee the project implementation during construction. The general contractor is responsible for the construction itself even though the work may actually be undertaken by a number of specialty subcontractors.

The owner usually negotiates the fee for service with the architectural/engineering firm. In addition to the responsibilities of designing the facility, the A/E firm also exercises to some degree supervision of the construction as stipulated by the owner. Traditionally, the A/E firm regards itself as design professionals representing the owner who should not communicate with potential contractors to avoid collusion or conflict of interest. Field inspectors working for an A/E firm usually follow through the implementation of a project after the design is completed and seldom have extensive input in the design itself. Because of the litigation climate in the last two decades, most A/E firms only provide observers rather than inspectors in the field. Even the shop drawings of fabrication or construction schemes submitted by the contractors for approval are reviewed with a disclaimer of responsibility by the A/E firms.

The owner may select a general constructor either through competitive bidding or through negotiation. Public agencies are required to use the competitive bidding mode, while private organizations may choose either mode of operation. In using competitive bidding, the owner is forced to use the designer/constructor sequence since detailed plans and specifications must be ready before inviting bidders to submit their bids. If the owner chooses to use a negotiated contract, it is free to use phased construction if it so desires.

The general contractor may choose to perform all or part of the construction work or act only as a manager by subcontracting all the construction to subcontractors. The general contractor may also select the subcontractors through competitive bidding or negotiated contracts. The general contractor may ask a number of subcontractors to quote prices for the subcontracts before submitting its bid to the owner. However, the subcontractors often cannot force the winning general contractor to use them on the project. This situation may lead to practices known as *bid shopping* and *bid peddling*. Bid shopping refers to the situation when the general contractor approaches subcontractors other than those whose quoted prices were used in the winning contract to seek lower-priced subcontracts. Bid peddling refers to the actions of subcontractors who offer lower-priced subcontracts to the winning general contractor to dislodge the subcontractors who originally quoted prices to the general contractor prior to its bid submittal. In both cases, the quality of construction may be sacrificed, and some state statutes forbid these practices for public projects.

Although the designer/constructor sequence is still widely used because of the public perception of fairness in competitive bidding, many private owners recognize the disadvantages of using this approach when the project is large and complex and when market pressures require a shorter project duration than that which can be accomplished by using this traditional method.

2.7 PROFESSIONAL CONSTRUCTION MANAGEMENT

Professional construction management refers to a project management team consisting of a professional construction manager and other participants who will carry out the tasks of project planning, design, and construction in an integrated manner. Contractual relationships among members of the team are intended to minimize adversarial relationships and contribute to greater response within the management group. A professional construction manager is a firm specialized in the practice of professional construction management, which includes

- Work with owner and the A/E firms from the beginning and make recommendations on design improvements, construction technology, schedules, and construction economy.
- Propose design and construction alternatives if appropriate and analyze the effects of the alternatives on the project cost and schedule.
- Monitor subsequent development of the project so that these targets are not exceeded without the knowledge of the owner.
- Coordinate procurement of material and equipment and the work of all construction contractors and monthly payments to contractors, changes, claims, and inspection for conforming design requirements.
- Perform other project-related services as required by owners.

Professional construction management is usually used when a project is very large or complex. The organizational features that are characteristics of megaprojects can be summarized as follows:[12]

- The overall organizational approach for the project will change as the project advances. The "functional" organization may change to a "matrix" which may change to a "project" organization (not necessarily in this order).
- Within the overall organization, there will probably be functional, project, and matrix suborganizations all at the same time. This feature greatly complicates the theory and the practice of management, yet is essential for overall cost effectiveness.
- Successful giant, complex organizations usually have a strong matrix-type suborganization at the level where basic cost- and schedule-control responsibility is assigned. This suborganization is referred to as a "cost center" or as a "project" and is headed by a project manager. The cost center matrix may have participants assigned from many different functional groups. In turn, these functional groups may have technical reporting responsibilities to several different and higher tiers in the organization. The key to a cost-effective effort is the development of this project suborganization into a single team under the leadership of a strong project manager.
- The extent to which decision making will be centralized or decentralized is crucial to the organization of the megaproject.

Consequently, it is important to recognize the changing nature of the organizational structure as a project is carried out in various stages.

Example 2-5: Managing of the Alaska Pipeline Project

The Alaska pipeline project was the largest, most expensive private construction project in the 1970s, which encompassed 800 miles, thousands of employees, and $10 billion.
    At the planning stage, the owner (a consortium) employed a construction man-

---

[12] These features and the following example are described in F. P. Moolin, Jr., and F. A. McCoy, "Managing the Alaska Pipeline Project," *Civil Engineering*, November 1981, pp. 51–54.

agement contractor (CMC) to direct the pipeline portion, but retained centralized decision making to assure single direction and to integrate the effort of the CMC with the pump stations and the terminals performed by another contractor. The CMC also centralized its decision making in directing over 400 subcontractors and thousands of vendors. Because there were 19 different construction camps and hundreds of different construction sites, this centralization caused delays in decision making.

At about the 15 percent point of physical completion, the owner decided to reorganize the decision-making process and change the role of the CMC. The new organization was a combination of owner and CMC personnel assigned within an integrated organization. The objective was to develop a single project team responsible for controlling all subcontractors. Instead of having nine tiers of organization from the general manager of the CMC to the subcontractors, the new organization had only four tiers from the senior project manager of the owner to subcontractors. Besides unified direction and coordination, this reduction in tiers of organization greatly improved communications and the ability to make and implement decisions. The new organization also allowed decentralization of decision making by treating five sections of the pipeline at different geographic locations as separate projects, with a section manager responsible for all functions of the section as a profit center.

At about the 98 percent point of physical completion, all remaining activities were to be consolidated to identify single bottom-line responsibility, to reduce duplication in management staff, and to unify coordination of remaining work. Thus, the project was first handled by separate organizations but later was run by an integrated organization with decentralized profit centers. Finally, the organization in effect became small and was ready to be phased out of operation.

2.8 OWNER-BUILDER OPERATION

In this approach an owner must have a steady flow of ongoing projects to maintain a large work force for in-house operation. However, the owner may choose to subcontract a substantial portion of the project to outside consultants and contractors for both design and construction, even though it retains centralized decision making to integrate all efforts in project implementation.

Example 2-6: U.S. Army Corps of Engineers Organization

The District Engineer's Office of the U. S. Army Corps of Engineers may be viewed as a typical example of an owner-builder approach as shown in Figure 2-8.

In the District Engineer's Office of the U. S. Corps of Engineers, there usually exist an Engineering Division and an Operations Division, and, in a large district, a Construction Division. Under each division, there are several branches. While the authorization of a project is usually initiated by the U. S. Congress, the planning and design functions are separated to facilitate operations. Since the authorization of the feasibility study of a project may precede the authorization of the design by many years, each stage can best be handled by a different branch in the Engineering Division. If construction is ultimately authorized, the work may be handled by the Construction Division or by outside contractors. The Operations Division handles the operation of locks and other facilities which require routine attention and maintenance.

When a project is authorized, a project manager is selected from the most appropriate branch to head the project, together with a group of staff drawn from

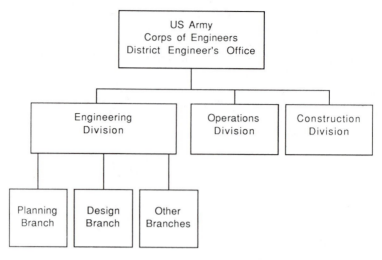

Figure 2-8 Organization of a District of Corps of Engineers

various branches to form the project team. When the project is completed, all members of the team including the project manager will return to their regular posts in various branches and divisions until the next project assignment. Thus, a matrix organization is used in managing each project.

2.9 TURNKEY OPERATION

Some owners wish to delegate all responsibilities of design and construction to outside consultants in a *turnkey* project arrangement. A contractor agrees to provide the completed facility on the basis of performance specifications set forth by the owner. The contractor may even assume the responsibility of operating the project if the owner so desires. For a turnkey operation to succeed, the owner must be able to provide a set of unambiguous performance specifications to the contractor and must have complete confidence in the capability of the contractor to carry out the mission.

This approach is the direct opposite of the owner-builder approach in which the owner wishes to retain the maximum amount of control for the design/construction process.

Example 2-7: An Example of a Turnkey Organization

A 150-Mw power plant was proposed in 1985 by the Texas-New Mexico Power Company of Fort Worth, Texas, which would make use of the turnkey operation.[13] Upon approval by the Texas Utility Commission, a consortium consisting of H. B. Zachry Co., Westinghouse Electric Co., and Combustion Engineering, Inc., would design, build, and finance the power plant for completion in 1990 for an estimated

[13] "Private Money Finances Texas Utility's Power Plant," *Engineering News Record*, July 25, 1985, p. 13.

construction cost of $200 million in 1990 dollars. The consortium would assume total liability during construction, including debt service costs, and thereby eliminate the risks of cost escalation to ratepayers, stockholders, and the utility company management.

2.10 LEADERSHIP AND MOTIVATION FOR THE PROJECT TEAM

The project manager, in the broadest sense of the term, is the most important person for the success or failure of a project. The project manager is responsible for planning, organizing, and controlling the project. In turn, the project manager receives authority from the management of the organization to mobilize the necessary resources to complete a project.

The project manager must be able to exert interpersonal influence to lead the project team. The project manager often gains the support of his or her team through a combination of the following:

- Formal authority resulting from an official capacity which is empowered to issue orders.
- Reward and/or penalty power resulting from his or her capacity to dispense directly or indirectly valued organization rewards or penalties.
- Expert power when the project manager is perceived as possessing special knowledge or expertise for the job.
- Attractive power because the project manager has a personality or other characteristics to convince others.

In a matrix organization, the members of the functional departments may be accustomed to a single reporting line in a hierarchical structure, but the project manager coordinates the activities of the team members drawn from functional departments. The functional structure within the matrix organization is responsible for priorities, coordination, administration, and final decisions pertaining to project implementation. Thus, there are potential conflicts between functional divisions and project teams. The project manager must be given the responsibility and authority to resolve various conflicts such that the established project policy and quality standards will not be jeopardized. When contending issues of a more fundamental nature are developed, they must be brought to the attention of a high level in the management and be resolved expeditiously.

In general, the project manager's authority must be clearly documented as well as defined, particularly in a matrix organization where the functional division managers often retain certain authority over the personnel temporarily assigned to a project. The following principles should be observed:

- The interface between the project manager and the functional division managers should be kept as simple as possible.
- The project manager must gain control over those elements of the project which may overlap with functional division managers.

- The project manager should encourage problem solving rather than role playing of team members drawn from various functional divisions.

2.11 INTERPERSONAL BEHAVIOR IN PROJECT ORGANIZATIONS

While a successful project manager must be a good leader, other members of the project team must also learn to work together, whether they are assembled from different divisions of the same organization or even from different organizations. Some problems of interaction may arise initially when the team members are unfamiliar with their own roles in the project team, particularly for a large and complex project. These problems must be resolved quickly to develop an effective, functioning team.

Many of the major issues in construction projects require effective interventions by individuals, groups, and organizations. The fundamental challenge is to enhance communication among individuals, groups, and organizations so that obstacles in the way of improving interpersonal relations may be removed. Some behavior science concepts are helpful in overcoming communication difficulties that block cooperation and coordination. In very large projects, professional behavior scientists may be necessary in diagnosing the problems and advising the personnel working on the project. The power of the organization should be used judiciously in resolving conflicts.

The major symptoms of interpersonal behavior problems can be detected by experienced observers, and they are often the sources of serious communication difficulties among participants in a project. For example, members of a project team may avoid each other and withdraw from active interactions about differences that need to be dealt with. They may attempt to criticize and blame other individuals or groups when things go wrong. They may resent suggestions for improvement and become defensive to minimize culpability rather than take the initiative to maximize achievements. All these actions are detrimental to the project organization.

While these symptoms can occur to individuals at any organization, they are compounded if the project team consists of individuals who are put together from different organizations. Invariably, different organizations have different cultures or modes of operation. Individuals from different groups may not have a common loyalty and may prefer to expand their energy in the directions most advantageous to themselves instead of the project team. Therefore, no one should take it for granted that a project team will work together harmoniously just because its members are placed physically together in one location. On the contrary, it must be assumed that good communication can be achieved only through the deliberate effort of the top management of each organization contributing to the joint venture.

2.12 PERCEPTIONS OF OWNERS AND CONTRACTORS

Although owners and contractors may have different perceptions on project management for construction, they have a common interest in creating an environment leading to successful projects in which performance quality, completion time and final costs are within prescribed limits and tolerances. It is interesting therefore to note the opinions of some leading contractors and owners who were interviewed in 1984.[14]

From the responses of six contractors, the key factors cited for successful projects are

- Well defined scope
- Extensive early planning
- Good leadership, management and first-line supervision
- Positive client relationship with client involvement
- Proper project team chemistry
- Quick response to changes
- Engineering managers concerned with the total project, not just the engineering elements

Conversely, the key factors cited for unsuccessful projects are

- Ill-defined scope
- Poor management
- Poor planning
- Breakdown in communication between engineering and construction
- Unrealistic scope, schedules and budgets
- Many changes at various stages of progress
- Lack of good project control

The responses of eight owners indicated that they did not always understand the concerns of the contractors although they generally agreed with some of the key factors for successful and unsuccessful projects cited by the contractors. The significant findings of the interviews with owners are summarized as follows:

- All owners have the same perception of their own role, but they differ significantly in assuming that role in practice.
- The owners also differ dramatically in the amount of early planning and in providing information in bid packages.
- There is a trend toward breaking a project into several smaller projects as the projects become larger and more complex.
- Most owners recognize the importance of schedule, but they adopt different requirements in controlling the schedule.
- All agree that people are the key to project success.

[14] See J. E. Diekmann and K. B. Thrush, *Project Control in Design Engineering*, A Report to the Construction Industry Institute, The University of Texas at Austin, May 1986.

From the results of these interviews, it is obvious that owners must be more aware and involved in the process to generate favorable conditions for successful projects. Design professionals and construction contractors must provide better communication with each other and with the owner in project implementation.

2.13 REFERENCES

2-1. Barrie, D. S., and B. C. Paulson, Jr., *Professional Construction Management,* 2nd ed; McGraw-Hill Book Company, New York, 1984.

2-2. Halpin, D. W., and R. W. Woodhead, *Construction Management*, John Wiley and Sons, Inc.,1980.

2-3. Hodgetts, R. M., *Management: Theory, Process and Practice*, W. B. Saunders Co., Philadelphia, 1979.

2-4. Kerzner, H., *Project Management: A Systems Approach to Planning, Scheduling and Controlling*, 2nd ed., Van Nostrand Reinhold Co., New York, 1984.

2-5. Levitt, R. E., R. D. Logcher, and N. H. Quaddumi, "Impact of Owner-Engineer Risk Sharing on Design Conservatism," *ASCE Journal of Professional Issues in Engineering*, Vol. 110, 1984, pp. 157–167.

2-6. Moolin, F. P., Jr., and F. A. McCoy, "Managing the Alaska Pipeline Project," *Civil Engineering*, November 1981, pp. 51–54.

2-7. Murray, L., E. Gallardo, S. Aggarwal, and R. Waywitka, "Marketing Construction Management Services," *ASCE Journal of Construction Division*, Vol. 107, 1981, pp. 665–677.

3

The Design
and
Construction Process

3.1 DESIGN AND CONSTRUCTION AS AN INTEGRATED SYSTEM

In the planning of facilities, it is important to recognize the close relationship between design and construction. These processes can best be viewed as an integrated system. Broadly speaking, design is a process of creating the description of a new facility, usually represented by detailed plans and specifications; construction planning is a process of identifying activities and resources required to make the design a physical reality. Hence, construction is the implementation of a design envisioned by architects and engineers. In both design and construction, numerous operational tasks must be performed with a variety of precedence and other relationships among the different tasks.

Several characteristics are unique to the planning of constructed facilities and should be kept in mind even at the very early stage of the project life cycle. These include the following:

- Nearly every facility is custom designed and constructed and often requires a long time to complete.
- Both the design and construction of a facility must satisfy the conditions peculiar to a specific site.
- Because each project is site specific, its execution is influenced by natural, social, and other locational conditions such as weather, labor supply, or local building codes.
- Since the service life of a facility is long, the anticipation of future requirements is inherently difficult.
- Because of technological complexity and market demands, changes of design plans during construction are not uncommon.

In an integrated system, the planning for both design and construction can proceed almost simultaneously, examining various alternatives which are desirable from both viewpoints and thus eliminating the necessity of extensive revisions under the guise of value engineering. Furthermore, the review of designs with regard to their constructibility can be carried out as the project progresses from planning to design. For example, if the sequence of assembly of a structure and the critical loadings on the partially assembled structure during construction are carefully considered as a part of the overall structural design, the impacts of the design on construction falsework and on assembly details can be anticipated. However, if the design professionals are expected to assume such responsibilities, they must be rewarded for sharing the risks as well as for undertaking these additional tasks. Similarly, when construction contractors are expected to take over the responsibilities of engineers, such as devising a very elaborate scheme to erect an unconventional structure, they too must be rewarded accordingly. As long as the owner does not assume the responsibility for resolving this risk-reward dilemma, the concept of a truly integrated system for design and construction cannot be realized.

It is interesting to note that European owners are generally more open to new technologies and to share risks with designers and contractors. In particular, they are more willing to accept responsibilities for the unforeseen subsurface conditions in geotechnical engineering. Consequently, the designers and contractors are also more willing to introduce new techniques to reduce the time and cost of construction. In European practice, owners typically present contractors with a conceptual design, and contractors prepare detailed designs, which are checked by the owner's engineers. Those detailed designs may be alternate designs, and specialty contractors may also prepare detailed alternate designs.

Example 3-1: Proposed Responsibility for Shop Drawings

The willingness to assume responsibilities does not come easily from any party in the current litigious climate of the construction industry in the United States. On the other hand, if owner, architect, engineer, contractor, and other groups that represent parts of the industry do not jointly fix the responsibilities of various tasks to appropriate parties, the standards of practice will eventually be set by court decisions. In an attempt to provide a guide to the entire spectrum of participants in a construction project, the American Society of Civil Engineers issued a preliminary edition of a *Manual of Professional Practice: Quality in the Constructed Project, 1988.* After an 18-month period for trial use and comment, a final version is expected to be published as recommended standards for industrywide adoption. It is hoped that this manual will help bring a turnaround of the fragmentation of activities in the design and construction process.

Shop drawings represent the assembly details for erecting a structure which should reflect the intent and rationale of the original structural design. They are prepared by the construction contractor and are reviewed by the design professional. However, since the responsibility for preparing shop drawings was traditionally assigned to construction contractors, design professionals took the view that the review process was advisory and assumed no responsibility for their accuracy. This justification was ruled unacceptable by a court in connection with the walkway failure at the Hyatt Hotel in Kansas City in 1985. In preparing the *ASCE Manual of Professional Practice: Quality in the Constructed Project, 1988,* the responsibilities for preparation of shop drawings proved to be the most difficult to develop.[15] The reason for this situation is not difficult to fathom since the responsibilities for the task are diffused, and all parties must agree to the new responsibilities assigned to each in the recommended risk-reward relations shown in Table 3-1.

Traditionally, the owner is not involved in the preparation and review of shop drawings, and perhaps is even unaware of any potential problems. In the recommended practice, the owner is required to take responsibility for providing adequate time and funding, including approval of scheduling, to allow the design professionals and construction contractors to perform satisfactorily.

Example 3-2: Model Metro Project in Milan, Italy [16]

Under Italian law, unforeseen subsurface conditions are the owner's responsibility, not the contractor's. This is a striking difference from U.S. construction practice where changed conditions clauses and claims and the adequacy of prebid site investigations are points of contention. In effect, the Italian law means that the owner assumes those

---

[15] See Vol. 1, p. 157 of this manual.

[16] See V. Fairweather, "Milan's Model Metro," *Civil Engineering*, December 1987, pp. 40–43.

TABLE 3–1 RECOMMENDED RESPONSIBILITY FOR SHOP DRAWINGS

Task	Responsible party		
	Owner	Design professional	Construction contractor
Provide adequate time and funding for shop drawing preparation and review	Prime		
Arrange for structural design	Prime		
Provide structural design		Prime	
Establish overall responsibility for connection design		Prime	
Accomplish connection design (by design professional)		Prime	
Alternately, provide loading requirements and other information necessary for shop drawing preparation		Prime	
Alternatively, accomplish some or all of connection design (by constructor with a licensed P.E.)			Prime
Specify shop drawing requirements and procedures	Review	Prime	
Approve proper scheduling	Prime	Assisting	Assisting
Provide shop drawings and submit the drawings on schedule			Prime
Make timely reviews and approvals		Prime	
Provide erection procedures, construction bracing, shoring, means, methods and techniques of construction, and construction safety			Prime

risks. But under the same law, a contractor may elect to assume the risks to lower the bid price and thereby beat the competition.

According to the technical director of Rodio, the Milan-based contractor which is heavily involved in the grouting job for tunneling in the Model Metro project in Milan, Italy, there are two typical contractual arrangements for specialized subcontractor firms such as theirs. One is to work on a unit-price basis with no responsibility for the design. The other is the "nominated subcontractor" or turnkey method: prequalified subcontractors offer their own designs and guarantee the price, quality, quantities, and, if they wish, the risks of unforeseen conditions.

At the beginning of the Milan metro project, the Rodio contract ratio was 50/50 unit price and turnkey. The firm convinced the metro owners that they would save money with the turnkey approach, and the ratio became 80 percent turnkey. What's more, in the work packages where Rodio worked with other grouting specialists, those subcontractors paid Rodio a fee to assume all risks for unforeseen conditions.

Under these circumstances, it was critical that the firm should know the subsurface conditions as precisely as possible, which was a major reason why the firm developed a computerized electronic-sensing program to predict stratigraphy and thus control grout mixes, pressures, and, most important, quantities.

3.2 INNOVATION AND TECHNOLOGICAL FEASIBILITY

The planning for a construction project begins with the generation of concepts for a facility which will meet market demands and owner needs. Innovative concepts in design are highly valued not for their own sake but for their contributions to reducing costs and to the improvement of aesthetics, comfort, or convenience as embodied in a well-designed facility. However, the constructor as well as the design professionals must have an appreciation and full understanding of the technological complexities often associated with innovative designs to provide a safe and sound facility. Since these concepts are often preliminary or tentative, screening studies are carried out to determine the overall technological viability and economic attractiveness without pursuing these concepts in great detail. Because of the ambiguity of the objectives and the uncertainty of external events, screening studies call for uninhibited innovation in creating new concepts and judicious judgment in selecting the appropriate ones for further consideration.

One of the most important aspects of design innovation is the necessity of communication in the design/construction partnership. In the case of bridge design, it can be illustrated by the following quotation from Lin and Gerwick concerning bridge construction:[17]

> The great pioneering steel bridges of the United States were built by an open or covert alliance between designers and constructors. The turnkey approach of designer-constructor has developed and built our chemical plants, refineries, steel plants, and nuclear power plants. It is time to ask, seriously, whether we may not have adopted a restrictive approach by divorcing engineering and construction in the field of bridge construction.
>
> If a contractor-engineer, by some stroke of genius, were to present to design engineers today a wonderful new scheme for long span prestressed concrete bridges that made them far cheaper, he would have to make these ideas available to all other constructors, even limiting or watering them down so as to "get a group of truly competitive bidders." The engineer would have to make sure that he found other contractors to bid against the ingenious innovator.
>
> If an engineer should, by a similar stroke of genius, hit on such a unique and brilliant scheme, he would have to worry, wondering if the low bidder would be one who had any concept of what he was trying to accomplish or was in any way qualified for high class technical work.

Innovative design concepts must be tested for technological feasibility. Three levels of technology are of special concern: technological requirements for operation or production, design resources, and construction technology. The first refers to the new technologies that may be introduced in a facility which is used for a certain type of production such as chemical processing or nuclear power generation. The second

[17] See T. Y. Lin and B. G. Gerwick, Jr., "Design of Long Span Concrete Bridges with Special References to Prestressing, Precasting, Structural Behavior and Economics," ACI Publication SP-23, First International Symposium, 1969, pp. 693–704.

refers to the design capabilities that are available to the designers, such as new computational methods or new materials. The third refers to new technologies which can be adopted to construct the facility, such as new equipment or new construction methods.

A new facility may involve complex new technology for operation in hostile environments such as severe climate or restricted accessibility. Large projects with unprecedented demands for resources such as labor supply, material, and infrastructure may also call for careful technological feasibility studies. Major elements in a feasibility study on production technology should include, but are not limited to, the following:

- Project type as characterized by the technology required, such as synthetic fuels, petrochemicals, nuclear power plants, and so on.
- Project size in dollars, design engineer's hours, construction labor-hours, and so on.
- Design, including sources of any special technology which require licensing agreements.
- Project location, which may pose problems in environmental protection, labor productivity, and special risks.

An example of innovative design for operation and production is the use of entropy concepts for the design of integrated chemical processes. Simple calculations can be used to indicate the minimum energy requirements and the least number of heat exchange units to achieve desired objectives. The result is a new incentive and criterion for designers to achieve more effective designs. Numerous applications of the new methodology have shown its efficacy in reducing both energy costs and construction expenditures.[18] This is a case in which innovative design is not a matter of trading off operating and capital costs, but better designs can simultaneously achieve improvements in both objectives.

The choice of construction technology and method involves both *strategic* and *tactical* decisions about appropriate technologies and the best sequencing of operations. For example, the extent to which prefabricated facility components will be used represents a *strategic* construction decision. In turn, prefabrication of components might be accomplished off-site in existing manufacturing facilities, or a temporary, on-site fabrication plant might be used. Another example of a strategic decision is whether to install mechanical equipment in place early in the construction process or at an intermediate stage. Strategic decisions of this sort should be integrated with the process of facility design in many cases. At the tactical level, detailed decisions about how to accomplish particular tasks are required, and such decisions can often be made in the field.

Construction planning should be a major concern in the development of facility designs, in the preparation of cost estimates, and in forming bids by contractors. Unfortunately, planning for the construction of a facility is often treated as an

---

[18] See B. Linnhoff, D. W. Townsend, D. Boland, G. F. Hewitt, B. E. A. Thomas, A. R. Guy, and R. H. Marsland, *User Guide on Process Integration for the Efficient Use of Energy,* Institution of Chemical Engineers, Rugby, Warks., England, 1982.

afterthought by design professionals. This contrasts with manufacturing practices in which the *assembly* of devices is a major concern in design. Design to ensure ease of assembly or construction should be a major concern of engineers and architects. As the Business Roundtable noted, "All too often chances to cut schedule time and costs are lost because construction operates as a production process separated by a chasm from financial planning, scheduling, and engineering or architectural design. Too many engineers, separated from field experience, are not up to date about how to build what they design, or how to design so structures and equipment can be erected most efficiently." [19]

Example 3-3: Innovative Use of Structural Frames for Buildings [20]

The structural design of skyscrapers offers an example of innovation in overcoming the barrier of high costs for tall buildings by making use of new design capabilities. A revolutionary concept in skyscraper design was introduced in the 1960s by Fazlur Khan, who argued that, for a building of a given height, there is an appropriate structural system which would produce the most efficient use of the material.

Before 1965, most skyscrapers were steel rigid frames. However, Fazlur Khan believed that it was uneconomical to construct all office buildings of rigid frames, and proposed an array of appropriate structural systems for steel buildings of specified heights as shown in Figure 3-1. By choosing an appropriate structural system, an

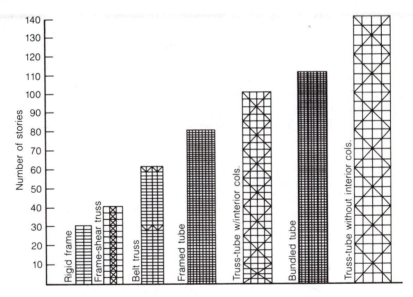

Figure 3-1 Proposed Structural Systems for Steel Buildings (Reprinted with permission from *Civil Engineering*, May 1983.)

[19] "More Construction for the Money," *Summary Report of the Construction Industry Cost Effectiveness Project*, The Business Roundtable, New York, 1983, p. 30.

[20] See "The Quiet Revolution in Skyscraper Design," *Civil Engineering*, May 1983, p. 54–59.

engineer can use structural materials more efficiently. For example, the 60-story Chase Manhattan Building in New York used about 60 pounds per square foot of steel in its rigid frame structure, while the 100-story John Hancock Center in Chicago used only 30 pounds per square foot for a trusted tube system. At the time the Chase Manhattan Building was constructed, no bracing was used to stiffen the core of a rigid-frame building because design engineers did not have the computing tools to do the complex mathematical analysis associated with core bracing.

3.3 INNOVATION AND ECONOMIC FEASIBILITY

Innovation is often regarded as the engine which can introduce construction economies and advance labor productivity. This is obviously true for certain types of innovations in industrial production technologies, design capabilities, and construction equipment and methods. However, there are also limitations due to the economic infeasibility of such innovations, particularly in the segments of the construction industry which are more fragmented and permit ease of entry, as in the construction of residential housing.

Market demand and firm size play an important role in this regard. If a builder is to construct a larger number of similar units of buildings, the cost per unit may be reduced. This relationship between the market demand and the total cost of production may be illustrated schematically as in Figure 3-2. An initial threshold or fixed cost F is incurred to allow any production. Beyond this threshold cost, total cost increases faster than the units of output but at a decreasing rate. At each point on this total cost curve, the average cost is represented by the slope of a line from the origin to the point on the curve. At a point H, the average cost per unit is at a minimum. Beyond H to the right, the total cost again increases faster than the units of output and at an increasing rate. When the rate of change of the average cost slope is decreasing or constant as between 0 and H on the curve,

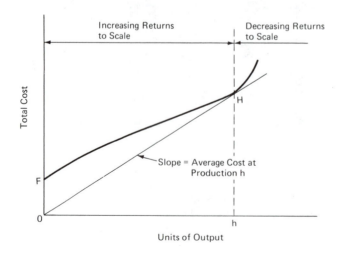

Figure 3-2 Market Demand and Total Cost Relationship

the range between 0 and *H* is said to be *increasing return to scale*; when the rate of change of the average cost slope is increasing as beyond *H* to the right, the region is said to be *decreasing return to scale*. Thus, if fewer than *h* units are constructed, the unit price will be higher than that of exactly *h* units. On the other hand, the unit price will increase again if more than *h* units are constructed.

Nowhere is the effect of market demand and total cost more evident than in residential housing.[21] The housing segment in the last few decades accepted many innovative technical improvements in building materials which were promoted by material suppliers. Since material suppliers provide products to a large number of homebuilders and others, they are in a better position to exploit production economies of scale and to support new product development. However, homebuilders themselves have not been as successful in making the most fundamental form of innovation which encompasses changes in the technological process of homebuilding by shifting the mixture of labor and material inputs, such as substituting large-scale off-site prefabrication for on-site assembly.

There are several major barriers to innovation in the technological process of homebuilding, including demand instability, industrial fragmentation, and building codes. Since market demand for new homes follows demographic trends and other socioeconomic conditions, the variation in home-building has been anything but regular. The profitability of the homebuilding industry has closely matched aggregate output levels. Since entry and exit from the industry are relatively easy, it is not uncommon during periods of slack demand to find builders leaving the market or suspending their operations until better times. The inconsistent levels of retained earnings over a period of years, even among the more established builders, are likely to discourage support for research and development efforts which are required to nurture innovation. Furthermore, because the homebuilding industry is fragmented with a vast majority of homebuilders active only in local regions, the typical homebuilder finds it excessively expensive to experiment with new designs. The potential costs of a failure or even a moderately successful innovation would outweigh the expected benefits of all but the most successful innovations. Variation in local building codes has also caused inefficiencies although repeated attempts have been made to standardize building codes.

In addition to the scale economies visible within a sector of the construction market, there are also possibilities for scale economies in individual facilities. For example, the relationship between the size of a building (expressed in square feet) and the input labor (expressed in labor-hours per square foot) varies for different types and sizes of buildings. As shown in Figure 3-3, these relationships for several types of buildings exhibit different characteristics.[22] The labor-hours per square foot decline as the size of the facility increases for houses, public housing, and public buildings. However, the labor-hours per square foot almost remains constant for all sizes of school buildings and increases as the size of a hospital facility increases.

---

[21] See J. Landis, "Why Homebuilders Don't Innovate," *Built Environment*, Vol. 8, no. 1, 1982, pp. 46–53.

[22] See P. J. Cassimates, *Economics of the Construction Industry*, National Industry Conference Board (SBE No. 111), 1969.

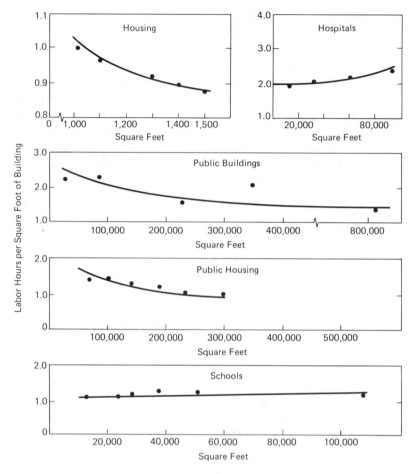

Figure 3-3 Illustrative Relationships between Building Size and Input Labor by Types of Building (Reprinted with permission from P. J. Cassimatis, *Economics of the Construction Industry*, The National Industry Conference Board, SEB No. 111, 1969, p. 53.)

Example 3-4: Use of New Materials [23]

In recent years, an almost entirely new set of materials is emerging for construction, largely from the aerospace and electronics industries. These materials were developed from new knowledge about the structure and properties of materials as well as new techniques for altering existing materials. Additives to traditional materials such as concrete and steel are particularly prominent. For example, it has been known for some time that polymers would increase concrete strength, water resistance, and ability to insulate when they are added to the cement. However, their use has been limited by their costs since they have had to replace as much as 10 percent of the cement to

[23] See F. Moavenzadeh, "Construction's High Technology Revolution," *Technology Review*, October 1985, 32–39.

be effective. However, Swedish researchers have helped reduce costs by using polymer microspheres 8 millionths of an inch across, which occupy less than 1 percent of the cement. Concretes made with these microspheres meet even the strict standards for offshore structures in the North Sea. Research on microadditives will probably produce useful concretes for repairing roads and bridges as well.

Example 3-5: Habitat [24]

Habitat was an experimental residential complex designed by Moshe Safdie and constructed in modules with an on-site factory for the 1967 Exposition in Montreal, Canada. The original proposal called for a self-contained community with 1,000 to 2,000 apartments, but was scaled down to a single 10-story complex with 158 units built on Cité du Havre, a landfill peninsula in Montreal's inner harbor. The project was budgeted for $11.5 million, and almost half of that was spent building the factories and acquiring special cranes. This start-up cost was absurdly high for a single 10-story apartment complex, but might have been justified in the original proposal for a whole community. As a result of the small scale, development costs amounted to $85,500 for an apartment at a time when average Montreal apartments were selling for $10,000 to $16,000. However, even if mass production was possible, steep increases in urban land costs and interest rates in recent years would have overshadowed the projected savings from production. Thus, an innovation which was hailed at one time as the solution for urban housing has not materialized due to a combination of economic factors.

3.4 DESIGN METHODOLOGY

While the conceptual design process may be formal or informal, it can be characterized by a series of actions: formulation, analysis, search, decision, specification, and modification. However, at the early stage in the development of a new project, these actions are highly interactive as illustrated in Figure 3-4.[25] Many iterations of redesign are expected to refine the functional requirements, design concepts and financial constraints, even though the analytic tools applied to the solution of the problem at this stage may be very crude.

The series of actions taken in the conceptual design process may be described as follows:

- Formulation refers to the definition or description of a design problem in broad terms through the synthesis of ideas describing alternative facilities.
- Analysis refines the problem definition or description by separating important from peripheral information and by pulling together the essential detail. Interpretation and prediction are usually required as part of the analysis.
- Search involves gathering a set of potential solutions for performing the specified functions and satisfying the user requirements.

[24] This example is based on a review of the project 20 years after its completion. See *The New York Times*, July 26, 1987, Sec. 8, p. 1.

[25] See R. W. Jensen and C. C. Tonies (editors), *Software Engineering*, Prentice Hall, Inc., Englewood Cliffs, NJ, 1979, p. 22.

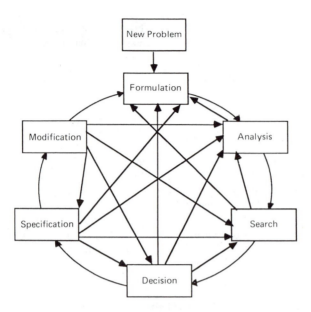

Figure 3-4 Conceptual Design Process (Adapted with permission from R. W. Jensen and C. C. Tonies, *Software Engineering*, Prentice Hall, Englewood Cliffs, NJ, 1979, p. 22.)

- Decision means that each of the potential solutions is evaluated and compared to the alternatives until the best solution is obtained.
- Specification is to describe the chosen solution in a form which contains enough detail for implementation.
- Modification refers to the change in the solution or redesign if the solution is found to be wanting or if new information is discovered in the process of design.

As the project moves from conceptual planning to detailed design, the design process becomes more formal. In general, the actions of formulation, analysis, search, decision, specification, and modification still hold, but they represent specific steps with less random interactions in detailed design. The design methodology thus formalized can be applied to a variety of design problems. For example, the analogy of the schematic diagrams of the structural design process and of the computer program development process is shown in Figure 3-5.[26]

The basic approach to design relies on decomposition and integration. Since design problems are large and complex, they have to be decomposed to yield subproblems that are small enough to solve. There are numerous alternative ways to decompose design problems, such as decomposition by functions of the facility, by spatial locations of its parts, or by links of various functions or parts. Solutions to subproblems must be integrated into an overall solution. The integration often creates conceptual conflicts which must be identified and corrected. A hierarchical structure with an appropriate number of levels may be used for the decomposition of a design problem to subproblems. For example, in the structural design of a

[26] See S. J. Fenves, "Computer Applications," in E. H. Gaylord and C. N. Gaylord, eds., *Structural Engineering Handbook*, McGraw-Hill Book Company, New York, 1979.

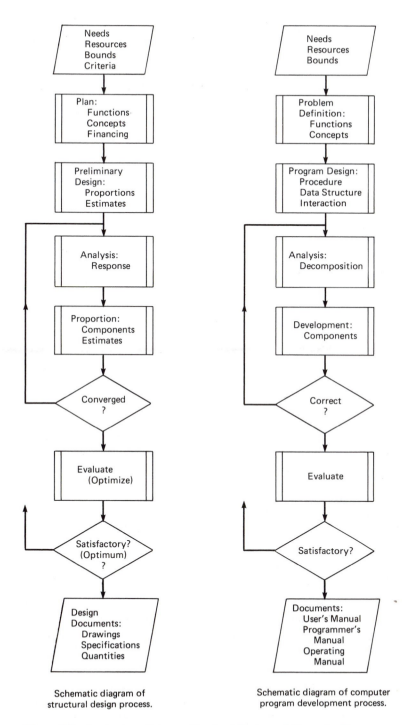

Schematic diagram of
structural design process.

Schematic diagram of computer
program development process.

Figure 3-5 An Analogy Between Structural Design and Computer Program
Development Processes (Reprinted with permission from E. H. Gaylord and
C. N. Gaylord, eds., *Structural Engineering Handbook*, 2nd Ed., McGraw-Hill
Book Company, New York, 1979.)

multistory building, the building may be decomposed into floors, and each floor may in turn be decomposed into separate areas. Thus, a hierarchy representing the levels of building, floor, and area is formed.

Different design styles may be used. The adoption of a particular style often depends on factors such as time pressure or available design tools, as well as the nature of the design problem. Examples of different styles are

- **Top-down design**. Begin with a behavior description of the facility and work toward descriptions of its components and their interconnections.
- **Bottom-up design**. Begin with a set of components, and see if they can be arranged to meet the behavior description of the facility.

The design of a new facility often begins with the search of the files for a design that comes as close as possible to the one needed. The design process is guided by accumulated experience and intuition in the form of heuristic rules to find acceptable solutions. As more experience is gained for this particular type of facility, it often becomes evident that parts of the design problem are amenable to rigorous definition and algorithmic solution. Even formal optimization methods may be applied to some parts of the problem.

3.5 FUNCTIONAL DESIGN

The objective of functional design for a proposed facility is to treat the facility as a complex system of interrelated spaces which are organized systematically according to the functions to be performed in these spaces to serve a collection of needs. The arrangement of physical spaces can be viewed as an iterative design process to find a suitable floor plan to facilitate the movement of people and goods associated with the operations intended.

A designer often relies on a heuristic approach, that is, applying selected rules or strategies serving to stimulate the investigation in search for a solution. The heuristic approach used in arranging spatial layouts for facilities is based generally on the following considerations:

1. Identification of the goals and constraints for specified tasks
2. Determination of the current state of each task in the iterative design process
3. Evaluation of the differences between the current state and the goals
4. Means of directing the efforts of search toward the goals on the basis of past experience

Hence, the procedure for seeking the goals can be recycled iteratively to make trade-offs and thus improve the solution of spatial layouts.

Consider, for example, an integrated functional design for a proposed hospital.[27] Since the responsibilities for satisfying various needs in a hospital are divided among different groups of personnel within the hospital administrative structure, a hierarchy of functions corresponding to different levels of responsibilities is proposed in the systematic organization of hospital functions. In this model, the functions of a hospital system are decomposed into a hierarchy of several levels:

1. **Hospital**—conglomerate of all hospital services resulting from top policy decisions.
2. **Division**—broadly related activities assigned to the same general area by administrative decisions.
3. **Department**—combination of services delivered by a service or treatment group.
4. **Suite**—specific style of common services or treatments performed in the same suite of rooms.
5. **Room**—all activities that can be carried out in the same internal environment surrounded by physical barriers.
6. **Zone**—several closely related activities that are undertaken by individuals.
7. **Object**—a single activity associated with an individual.

In the integrated functional design of hospitals, the connection between physical spaces and functions is most easily made at the lowest level of the hierarchy and then extended upward to the next higher level. For example, a bed is a physical object immediately related to the activity of a patient. A set of furniture consisting of a bed, a night table, and an armchair arranged comfortably in a zone indicates the sphere of private activities for a patient in a room with multiple occupancy. Thus, the spatial representation of a hospital can be organized in stages starting from the lowest level and moving to the top. In each step of the organization process, an element (space or function) under consideration can be related directly to the elements at the levels above it, to those at the levels below it, and to those within the same level.

Since the primary factor relating spaces is the movement of people and supplies, the objective of arranging spaces is the minimization of movement within the hospital. On the other hand, the internal environmental factors such as atmospheric conditions (pressure, temperature, relative humidity, odor, and particle pollution), sound, light, and fire protection produce constraining effects on the arrangement of spaces since certain spaces cannot be placed adjacent to other spaces because of different requirements in environmental conditions. The consideration of logistics is important at all levels of the hospital system. For example, the travel patterns between objects in a zone or those between zones in a room are frequently equally important for devising an effective design. On the other hand, the adjacency desir-

---

[27] See T. Au, E. W. Parti, and A. K. C. Wong, "Computer Applications for Health Care Facility Design," *Computers in Biology and Medicine*, Vol. 1, no. 4, 1971, pp. 299–316.

ability matrix based upon environmental conditions will not be important for organization of functional elements below the room level since a room is the lowest level that can provide a physical barrier to contain desirable environmental conditions. Hence, the organization of functions for a new hospital can be carried out through an interactive process, starting from the functional elements at the lowest level that is regarded as stable by the designer and moving step by step up to the top level of the hierarchy. Due to the strong correlation between functions and the physical spaces in which they are performed, the arrangement of physical spaces for accommodating the functions will also follow the same iterative process. Once a satisfactory spatial arrangement is achieved, the hospital design is completed by the selection of suitable building components which complement the spatial arrangement.

Example 3-6: Top-Down Design Style

In the functional design of a hospital, the designer may begin with a "reference model," that is, the spatial layouts of existing hospitals of similar size and service requirements. On the basis of past experience, spaces are allocated to various divisions as shown schematically in Figure 3-6. The space in each division is then divided further for various departments in the division, and all the way down the line of the hierarchy. In every step along the way, the pertinent information of the elements immediately below the level under consideration will be assessed in order to provide input for making necessary adjustments at the current level if necessary. The major drawback of the top-down design style is that the connection between physical spaces and functions at lower levels cannot be easily anticipated. Consequently, the new design is essentially based on the intuition and experience of the designer rather than an objective analysis of the functions and space needs of the facility. Its greatest attraction is its simplicity which keeps the time and cost of design relatively low.

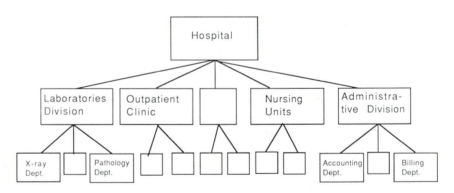

Figure 3-6 A Model for Top-Down Design of a Hospital

Example 3-7: Bottom-Up Design Style

A multipurpose examination suite in a hospital is used as an illustration of bottom-up design style. In Figure 3-7, the most basic elements (furniture) are first organized into zones which make up the room. Thus the size of the room is determined by spatial

The Design and Construction Process   Chap. 3

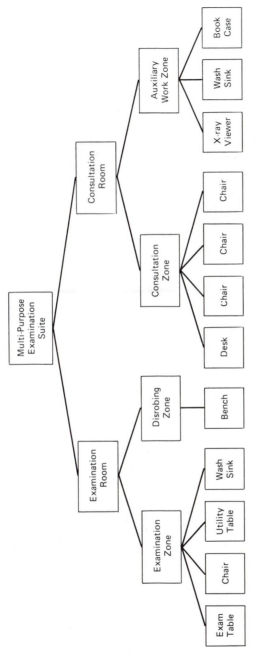

Figure 3-7 A Model for Bottom-Up Design of an Examination Suite

layout required to perform the desired services. Finally, the suite is defined by the rooms which are parts of the multipurpose examination suite.

3.6 PHYSICAL STRUCTURES

The structural design of complex engineering systems generally involves both synthesis and analysis. Synthesis is an inductive process; analysis is a deductive process. The activities in synthesis are often described as an art rather than a science and are regarded more akin to creativity than to knowledge. The conception of a new structural system is by and large a matter of subjective decision since there is no established procedure for generating innovative and highly successful alternatives. The initial selection of a workable system from numerous possible alternatives relies heavily on the judicious judgment of the designer. Once a structural system is selected, it must be subjected to vigorous analysis to ensure that it can sustain the demands in its environment. In addition, compatibility of the structural system with mechanical equipment and piping must be assured.

For traditional types of structures such as office buildings, there are standard systems derived from the past experience of many designers. However, in many situations, special systems must be developed to meet the specified requirements. The choice of materials for a structure depends not only on the suitability of materials and their influence on the form of the structure. For example, in the design of an airplane hangar, a steel skeleton frame may be selected because a similar frame in reinforced concrete will limit the span of the structure owing to its unfavorable ratio or resistance to weight. However, if a thin-shelled roof is adopted, reinforced concrete may prove to be more suitable than steel. Thus, the interplay of the structural forms and materials affects the selection of a structural system, which in turn may influence the method of construction including the use of falsework.

Example 3-8: Steel Frame Supporting a Turbo-Blower [28]

The design of a structural frame supporting a turbo-blower supplying pressurized air to a blast furnace in a steel mill can be used to illustrate the structural design process. As shown in Figure 3-8, the turbo-blower consists of a turbine and a blower linked to an air inlet stack. Since the vibration of the turbo-blower is a major concern to its operation, a preliminary investigation calls for a supporting frame which is separated from the structural frame of the building. An analysis of the vibration characteristics of the turbo-blower indicates that the lowest mode of vibration consists of independent vibration of the turbine shaft and the blower shaft, with higher modes for the coupled turbo-blower system when both shafts vibrate either in-phase or out-of-phase. Consequently, a steel frame with separate units for the blower side and the turbine side is selected. The columns of the steel frame are mounted on pile foundation, and all joints of the steel frame are welded to reduce the vibration levels.

Since the structural steel frame also supports a condenser, an air inlet and exhaust, and a steam inlet and exhaust in addition to the turbo-blower, a static analysis

[28] The authors are indebted to E. D'Appolonia for suggesting this example.

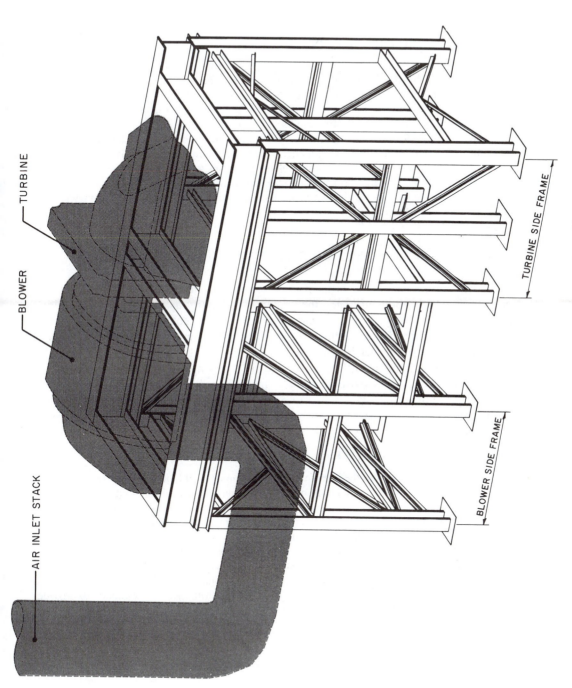

TURBINE

BLOWER

AIR INLET STACK

TURBINE SIDE FRAME

BLOWER SIDE FRAME

Figure 3-8 Steel Frame Supporting a Turbo-Blower

is made to size its members to support all applied loads. Then, a dynamic analysis is conducted to determine the vibration characteristics of the system incorporating the structural steel frame and the turbo-blower. When the limiting conditions for static loads and natural frequencies of vibration are met, the design is accepted as satisfactory.

Example 3-9: Multiple Hierarchy Descriptions of Projects

In the previous section, a hierarchy of functional spaces was suggested for describing a facility. This description is appropriate for functional design of spaces and processes within a building, but may be inadequate as a view of the facility's structural systems. A hierarchy suitable for this purpose might divide elements into *structural functions* such as slabs, walls, frames, footings, piles, or mats. Lower levels of the hierarchy would describe individual design elements. For example, frames would be made up of column, beam, and diagonal groups, which, in turn, are composed of individual structural elements. These individual structural elements comprise the limits on functional spaces such as rooms in a different hierarchical perspective. Designers typically will initiate a view appropriate for their own concerns, and these different hierarchical views must be synthesized to ensure consistency and adequacy of the overall design.

3.7 GEOTECHNICAL ENGINEERING INVESTIGATION

Since construction is site specific, it is very important to investigate the subsurface conditions which often influence the design of a facility as well as its foundation. The uncertainty in the design is particularly acute in geotechnical engineering so that the assignment of risks in this area should be a major concern. Since the degree of uncertainty in a project is perceived differently by different parties involved in a project, the assignment of unquantifiable risks arising from numerous unknowns to the owner, engineer, and contractor is inherently difficult. It is no wonder that courts or arbitrators are often asked to distribute equitably a risk to parties who do not perceive the same risks and do not want to assume a disproportionate share of such risks.

Example 3-10: Design of a Tie-Back Retaining Wall [29]

This example describes the use of a tie-back retaining wall built in the 1960s when such construction was uncommon and posed a considerable risk. The engineer designing it and the owner were aware of the risk because of potentially extreme financial losses from both remedial and litigation costs in the event that the retaining wall failed and permitted a failure of the slope. But the benefits were perceived as being worth the risk–benefits to the owner in terms of both lower cost and shorter schedule, and benefits to the engineer in terms of professional satisfaction in meeting the owner's needs and solving what appeared to be an insurmountable technical problem.

The tie-back retaining wall was designed to permit a cut in a hillside to provide additional space for the expansion of a steel-making facility. Figure 3-9 shows a cross

[29] See E. D'Appolonia, R. Alperstein, and D. J. D'Appolonia, "Behavior of Colluvial Slope," *ASCE Journal of Soil Mechanics and Foundations Division*, Vol. 93, no. SM4, 1967, pp. 447–473.

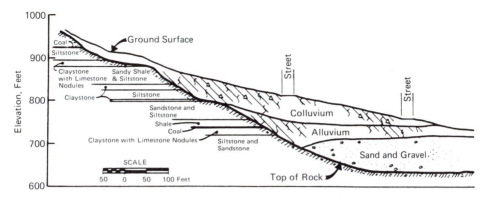

Figure 3-9 Typical Cross Section of Hillside Adjoining Site

section of the original hillside located in an urban area. Numerous residential dwellings were located on top of the hill which would have been prohibitively costly or perhaps impossible to remove to permit regrading of the hillside to push back the toe of the slope. The only realistic way of accomplishing the desired goal was to attempt to remove the toe of the existing slope and use a tie-back retaining wall to stabilize the slope as shown in Figure 3-10.

A commitment was made by both the owner and the engineer to accomplish what was a common goal. The engineer made a commitment to design and construct the wall in a manner which permitted a real-time evaluation of problems and the ability to

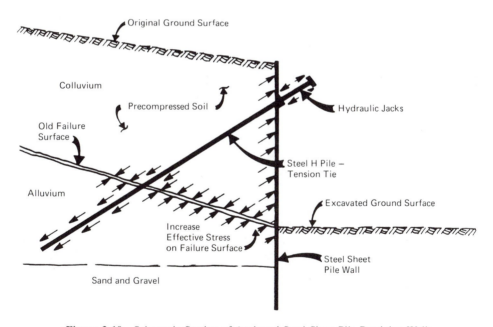

Figure 3-10 Schematic Section of Anchored Steel Sheet Pile Retaining Wall

take mitigating measures throughout the construction of the wall. The owner made a commitment to give the engineer both the professional latitude and resources required to perform his work. A design/construct contract was negotiated whereby the design could be modified as actual conditions were encountered during construction. But even with all the planning, investigation, and design efforts, there still remained a sizable risk of failure.

The wall was successfully built—not according to a predevised plan which went smoothly, and not without numerous problems to be resolved as unexpected ground-water and geological conditions were encountered. Estimated costs were exceeded as each unexpected condition was addressed. But there were no construction delays and their attendant costs as disputes over changed conditions and contract terms were reconciled. There were no costs for legal fees arising from litigation nor increased interest costs as construction stopped while disputes were litigated. The owner paid more than was estimated, but not more than was necessary and not as much as if he had to acquire the property at the top of the hill to regrade the slope. In addition, the owner was able to attain the desired facility expansion in far less time than by any other method.

As a result of the success of this experience and others, the use of tie-back retaining walls has become a routine practice.

3.8 CONSTRUCTION-SITE ENVIRONMENT

While the general information about the construction site is usually available at the planning stage of a project, it is important for the design professionals and construction manager as well as the contractor to visit the site. Each group will be benefited by firsthand knowledge acquired in the field.

For design professionals, an examination of the topography may focus their attention to the layout of a facility on the site for maximum use of space in compliance with various regulatory restrictions. In the case of industrial plants, the production or processing design and operation often dictate the site layout. A poor layout can cause construction problems such as inadequate space for staging, limited access for materials and personnel, and restrictions on the use of certain construction methods. Thus, design and construction inputs are important in the layout of a facility.

The construction manager and the contractor must visit the site to gain some insight in preparing or evaluating the bid package for the project. They can verify access roads and water and electrical and other service utilities in the immediate vicinity, with the view of finding suitable locations for erecting temporary facilities and the field office. They can also observe any interferences of existing facilities with construction and develop a plan for site security during construction.

In examining site conditions, particular attention must be paid to environmental factors such as drainage, groundwater, and the possibility of floods. Of particular concern is the possible presence of hazardous waste materials from previous uses. Cleaning up or controlling hazardous wastes can be extremely expensive.

Example 3-11: Groundwater Pollution from a Landfill [30]

The presence of waste deposits on a potential construction site can have substantial impacts on the surrounding area. Under existing environmental regulations in the United States, the responsibility for cleaning up or otherwise controlling wastes generally resides with the owner of a facility in conjunction with any outstanding insurance coverage.

A typical example of a waste problem is illustrated in Figure 3-11. In this figure, a small pushover burning dump was located in a depression on a slope. The landfill consisted of general refuse and was covered by a very sandy material. The inevitable infiltration of water from the surface or from the groundwater into the landfill will result in vertical or horizontal percolation of leachable ions and organic contamination. This leachate would be odorous and potentially hazardous in water. The pollutant would show up as seepage downhill, as pollution in surface streams, or as pollution entering the regional groundwater.

Before new construction could proceed, this landfill site would have to be controlled or removed. Typical control methods might involve

- Surface water control measures, such as contour grading or surface sealing.
- Passive groundwater control techniques such as underground barriers between the groundwater and the landfill.

---

[30] The material in this example is adapted from A. L. Tolman, A. P. Ballestero, W. W. Beck, and G. H. Emrich, *Guidance Manual for Minimizing Pollution from Waste Disposal Sites,* Report to the Municipal Environmental Research Laboratory, U.S. Environmental Protection Agency, EPA-600/2-78-142, August 1978.

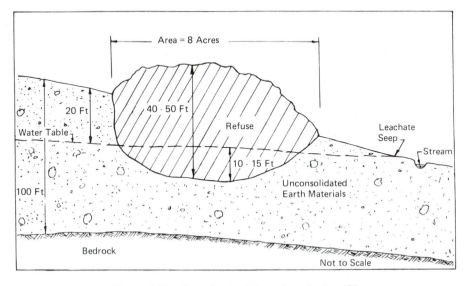

Figure 3-11 Cross-Section Illustration of a Landfill

- Plume management procedures such as pumping water from surrounding wells.
- Chemical immobilization techniques such as applying surface seals or chemical injections.
- Excavation and reburial of the landfill requiring the availability of an engineered and environmentally sound landfill.

The excavation and reburial of even a small landfill site can be very expensive. For example, the estimated reburial cost for a landfill like that shown in Figure 3-11 was in excess of $4 million in 1978.

3.9 VALUE ENGINEERING

Value engineering may be broadly defined as an organized approach in identifying unnecessary costs in design and construction and in soliciting or proposing alternative design or construction technology to reduce costs without sacrificing quality or performance requirements. It usually involves the steps of gathering pertinent information, searching for creative ideas, evaluating the promising alternatives, and proposing a more cost-effective alternative. This approach is usually applied at the beginning of the construction phase of the project life cycle.

The use of value engineering in the public sector of construction has been fostered by legislation and government regulation, but the approach has not been widely adopted in the private sector of construction. One explanation may lie in the difference in practice of engineering design services in the public and private sectors. In the public sector, the fee for design services is tightly monitored against the "market price" or may even be based on the lowest bid for service. Such a practice in setting professional fees encourages the design professionals to adopt known and tried designs and construction technologies without giving much thought to alternatives that are innovative but risky. Contractors are willing to examine such alternatives when offered incentives for sharing the savings by owners. In the private sector, the owner has the freedom to offer such incentives to design professionals as well as the contractors without being concerned about the appearance of favoritism in engaging professional services.

Another source of cost savings from value engineering is the ability of contractors to take advantage of proprietary or unusual techniques and knowledge specific to the contractor's firm. For example, a contractor may have much more experience with a particular method of tunneling that is not specified in the original design and, because of this experience, the alternative method may be less expensive. In advance of a bidding competition, a design professional does not know which contractor will undertake the construction of a facility. Once a particular contractor is chosen, then modifications to the construction technology or design may take advantage of peculiar advantages of the contractor's organization.

As a final source of savings in value engineering, the contractor may offer genuine new design or construction insights which have escaped the attention of the design professional even if the latter is not restrained by the fee structure from exploring more alternatives. If the expertise of the contractor can be utilized, of course, the best time to employ it is during the planning and design phase of the project life cycle. That is why professional construction management or integrated design/construction are often preferred by private owners.

3.10 CONSTRUCTION PLANNING

The development of a construction plan is very much analogous to the development of a good facility design. The planner must weigh the costs and reliability of different options while at the same time ensuring technical feasibility. Construction planning is more difficult in some ways since the building process is dynamic as the site and the physical facility change over time as construction proceeds. On the other hand, construction operations tend to be fairly standard from one project to another, whereas structural or foundation details might differ considerably from one facility to another.

Forming a good construction plan is an exceptionally challenging problem. There are numerous possible plans available for any given project. While past experience is a good guide to construction planning, each project is likely to have special problems or opportunities that may require considerable ingenuity and creativity to overcome or exploit. Unfortunately, it is quite difficult to provide direct guidance concerning general procedures or strategies to form good plans in all circumstances. There are some recommendations or issues that can be addressed to describe the *characteristics* of good plans, but this does not necessarily tell a planner how to discover a good plan. However, as in the design process, strategies of *decomposition* in which planning is divided into subproblems and *hierarchical planning* in which general activities are repeatably subdivided into more specific tasks can be readily adopted in many cases.

From the standpoint of *construction contractors* or the construction divisions of large firms, the planning process for construction projects consists of three stages that take place between the moment in which a planner starts the plan for the construction of a facility to the moment in which the evaluation of the final output of the construction process is finished.

The *estimate* stage involves the development of a cost and duration estimate for the construction of a facility as part of the proposal of a contractor to an owner. It is the stage in which assumptions of resource commitment to the necessary activities to build the facility are made by a planner. A careful and thorough analysis of different conditions imposed by the construction project design and by site characteristics are taken into consideration to determine the best estimate. The success of a contractor depends upon this estimate, not only to obtain a job but also to construct the facility with the highest profit. The planner has to look for the time-cost combination that will allow the contractor to be successful in his commitment. The result of a high estimate would be to lose the job, and the result of a low estimate could be to win the job, but to lose money in the construction process. When changes are done, they should improve the estimate, taking into account not only present effects, but also future outcomes of succeeding activities. It is very seldom the case in which the output of the construction process exactly echoes the estimate offered to the owner.

In the *monitoring and control stage* of the construction process, the construction manager has to keep constant track of both activities' durations and ongoing costs. It is misleading to think that if the construction of the facility is on schedule or ahead of schedule, the cost will also be on the estimate or below the estimate, especially if several changes are made. Constant evaluation is necessary until the construction of the facility is complete. When work is finished in the construction process, and information about it is provided to the planner, the third stage of the planning process can begin.

The *evaluation* stage is the one in which results of the construction process are matched against the estimate. A planner deals with this uncertainty during the estimate stage. Only when the outcome of the construction process is known is he or she able to evaluate the validity of the estimate. It is in this last stage of the planning process that he or she determines if the assumptions were correct. If they were not or if new constraints emerge, he or she should introduce corresponding adjustments in future planning.

3.11 INDUSTRIALIZED CONSTRUCTION AND PREFABRICATION

Another approach to construction innovation is to apply the principles and organizational solutions adopted for manufacturing. Industrialized construction and prefabrication would involve transferring a significant portion of construction operations from the construction site to more or less remote sites where individual components of buildings and structures are produced. Elements of facilities could be prefabricated off the erection site and assembled by cranes and other lifting machinery.

There are a wide variety and degrees of introducing greater industrialization to the construction process. Many components of constructed facilities have always been manufactured, such as air-conditioning units. Lumber, piping, and other individual components are manufactured to standard sizes. Even temporary items such as forms for concrete can be assembled off-site and transported for use. Reinforcing bars for concrete can also be precut and shaped to the desired configuration in a manufacturing plant or in an automated plant located proximate to a construction site.

A major problem in extending the use of prefabricated units is the lack of standardization for systems and building regulations.[31] While designers have long adopted standard sizes for individual components in designs, the adoption of standardized subassemblies is rarer. Without standardization, the achievement of a large market and scale economies of production in manufacturing may be impossible. An innovative and more thorough industrialization of the entire building process may be a primary source of construction cost savings in the future.

---

[31] For discussions of industrialized building, see R. Bender, *A Crack in the Rear View Mirror—A View of Industrialized Building,* Van Nostrand Reinhold Company, New York, 1983; or A. Warzawski, M. Avraham, and D. Carmel, "Utilization of Precast Concrete Element in Building," *ASCE Journal of Construction Engineering and Management,* Vol. 110, no. CO4, 1984, pp. 476–485.

Example 3-12: Planning of Prefabrication

When might prefabricated components be used in preference to components assembled on a construction site? A straightforward answer is to use prefabricated components whenever their cost, including transportation, is less than the cost of assembly on site. As an example, forms for concrete panels might be transported to a construction site with reinforcing bars already built in, necessary coatings applied to the forms, and even special features such as electrical conduit already installed in the form. In some cases, it might be less expensive to prefabricate and transport the entire concrete panel to a manufacturing site. In contrast, traditional construction practice would be to assemble all the different features of the panel on site. The relevant costs of these alternatives could be assessed during construction planning to determine the lowest-cost alternative.

In addition to the consideration of direct costs, a construction planner should also consider some other aspects of this technology choice. First, the planner must ensure that prefabricated components will satisfy the *relevant building codes* and *regulations*. Second, the *relative quality* of traditional versus prefabricated components as experienced in the final facility should be considered. Finally, the *availability of components* at the required time during the construction process should also be considered.

Example 3-13: Impacts of Building Codes [32]

Building codes originated as a part of the building regulatory process for the safety and general welfare of the public. The source of all authority to enact building codes is based on the police power of the state which may be delegated by the state legislature to local government units. Consequently, about 8,000 localities having their own building codes, either by following a national model code or developing a local code. The lack of uniformity of building codes may be attributed to a variety of reasons:

- Neighboring municipalities may adopt different national models as the basis for local regulation.
- Periodic revisions of national codes may not be adopted by local authorities before the lapse of several years.
- Municipalities may explicitly decline to adopt specific provisions of national model codes or may use their own variants of key provisions.
- Local authorities may differ in interpretation of the same language in national model codes.

The lack of uniformity in building codes has serious impact on design and construction as well as the regulatory process for buildings. Among the significant factors are

- Delay in the diffusion of new building innovations which may take a long time to find their ways to be incorporated in building codes.
- Discouragement to new production organizations, such as industrialized construction and prefabrication.
- Duplication of administrative cost of public agencies and compliance cost incurred by private firms.

[32] See C. G. Field and S. R. Rivkin, *The Building Code Burden*, Lexington Books, D. C. Heath and Co., Lexington, MA, 1975.

3.12 COMPUTER-AIDED ENGINEERING

In the past 20 years, the computer has become an essential tool in engineering, design, and accounting. The innovative designs of complicated facilities cited in the previous sections would be impossible without the aid of computer-based analysis tools. By using general-purpose analysis programs to test alternative designs of complex structures such as petrochemical plants, engineers are able to improve initial designs greatly. General-purpose accounting systems are also available and adopted in organizations to perform routine bookkeeping and financial accounting chores. These applications exploit the capability for computers to perform numerical calculations in a preprogrammed fashion rapidly, inexpensively and accurately.

Despite these advances, the computer is often used as only an incidental tool in the design, construction, and project management processes. However, new capabilities, systems, and application programs are rapidly being adopted. These are motivated in part by the remarkable improvement in computer hardware capability coupled with a extraordinary decline in cost. New concepts in computer design and in software are also contributing. For example, the introduction of personal computers using microcircuitry has encouraged the adoption of interactive programs because of the low cost and considerable capability of the computer hardware. Personal computers available for several thousand dollars in 1988 have essentially the same capability as expensive mainframe computer systems of 15 years earlier.

Computer graphics provide another pertinent example of a potentially revolutionary mechanism for design and communication. Graphical representations of both the physical and work activities on projects have been essential tools in the construction industry for decades. However, manual drafting of blueprints, plans, and other diagrams is laborious and expensive. Stand-alone, computer-aided drafting equipment has proved to be less expensive and fully capable of producing the requiring drawings. More significantly, the geometric information required for producing desired drawings might also be used as a database for computer-aided design and computer-integrated construction. Components of facilities can be represented as three-dimensional computer-based *solid models* for this purpose. Geometric information forms only one component of integrated design databases in which the computer can assure consistency, completeness, and compliance with relevant specifications and constraints. Several approaches to integrated computer-aided engineering environments of this type have already been attempted.[33]

Computers are also being applied more and more extensively to nonanalytical and nonnumerical tasks. For example, computer-based specification-writing assistants are used to assemble sets of standard specifications rapidly or to insert special clauses in the documentation of facility designs. As another example, computerized transfer of information provides a means to avoid laborious and error-prone transcription of project information. While most of the traditional applications and research in computer aids have emphasized numerical calculations, the use of com-

[33] See D. R. Rehak and L. A. Lopez, *Computer Aided Engineering Problems and Prospects*, Department of Civil Engineering, University of Illinois at Urbana-Champaign, 1981.

puters will rapidly shift toward the more prevalent and difficult problems of planning, communication, design, and management.

Knowledge-based systems represent a prominent example of new software approaches applicable to project management. These systems originally emerged from research in artificial intelligence in which human cognitive processes were modeled. In limited problem domains such as equipment configuration or process control, knowledge-based systems have been demonstrated to approach or surpass the performance of human experts. The programs are marked by a separation between the reasoning or "inference" engine program and the representation of domain-specific knowledge. As a result, system developers need not specify complete problem-solving strategies (or algorithms) for particular problems. This characteristic of knowledge-based systems makes them particularly useful in the ill-structured domains of design and project management. In Chapter 15 we consider knowledge-based systems in greater detail.

Computer program assistants will soon become ubiquitous in virtually all project management organizations. The challenge for managers is to use the new tools in an effective fashion. Computer-intensive work environments should be structured to aid and to amplify the capabilities of managers rather than to divert attention from real problems such as worker motivation.

3.13 REFERENCES

3-1. Au, T., and P. Christiano, *Structural Analysis*, Prentice Hall, Englewood Cliffs, NJ, 1987.

3-2. Building Research Advisory Board, *Exploratory Study on Responsibility, Liability and Accountability for Risks in Construction,* National Academy of Sciences, Washington, DC, 1978.

3-3. Drucker, P. F., *Innovation and Entrepreneurship: Practice and Principles*, Harper & Row, Publisher, Inc., New York, 1985.

3-4. Gaylord, E. H., and C. N. Gaylord (editors), *Structural Engineering Handbook*, 2nd ed., McGraw-Hill Book Company, New York, 1979.

3-5. Levitt, R. E., R. D. Logcher, and N. H. Quaddumi, "Impact of Owner-Engineer Risk Sharing on Design Conservatism," *ASCE Journal of Professional Issues in Engineering,* Vol. 110, 1984, pp. 157–167.

3-6. Simon, H. A., *The Science of the Artificial*, 2nd ed., MIT Press, Cambridge, MA, 1981.

3-7. Tatum, C. B., "Innovation on the Construction Project: A Process View," *Project Management Journal,* Vol. 18, no. 5, 1987, pp. 57–67.

4

Labor, Material, and Equipment Utilization

4.1 HISTORICAL PERSPECTIVE

Good project management in construction must vigorously pursue the efficient utilization of labor, material, and equipment. Improvement of labor productivity should be a major and continual concern of those who are responsible for cost control of constructed facilities. Material handling, which includes procurement, inventory, shop fabrication, and field servicing, requires special attention for cost reduction. The use of new equipment and innovative methods has made possible wholesale changes in construction technologies in recent decades. Organizations which do not recognize the impact of various innovations and have not adapted to changing environments have justifiably been forced out of the mainstream of construction activities.

Observing the trends in construction technology presents a very mixed and ambiguous picture. On the one hand, many of the techniques and materials used for construction are essentially unchanged since the introduction of mechanization in the early part of the twentieth century. For example, a history of the Panama Canal construction from 1904 to 1914 argues that:[34]

> [T]he work could not have done any faster or more efficiently in our day, despite all technological and mechanical advances in the time since, the reason being that no present system could possibly carry the spoil away any faster or more efficiently than the system employed. No motor trucks were used in the digging of the canal; everything ran on rails. And because of the mud and rain, no other method would have worked half so well.

In contrast to this view of one large project, one may also point to the continual change and improvements occurring in traditional materials and techniques. Bricklaying provides a good example of such changes:[35]

> Bricklaying . . . is said not to have changed in thousands of years; perhaps in the literal placing of brick on brick it has not. But masonry technology has changed a great deal. Motorized wheelbarrows and mortar mixers, sophisticated scaffolding systems, and forklift trucks now assist the bricklayer. New epoxy mortars give stronger adhesion between bricks. Mortar additives and cold-weather protection eliminate winter shutdowns.

Add to this list of existing innovations the possibility of robotic bricklaying; automated prototypes for masonry construction already exist. Technical change is certainly occurring in construction, although it may occur at a slower rate than in other sectors of the economy.

[34] D. McCullough, *The Path Between the Seas*, Simon & Schuster,Inc., New York, 1977, p. 531.

[35] S. Rosefielde and D. Q. Mills, "Is Construction Technologically Stagnant?" in J. E. Lange and D. Q. Mills, *The Construction Industry*, Lexington Books, D. C. Heath and Co., Lexington, MA, 1979, p. 83.

The U.S. construction industry often points to factors which cannot be controlled by the industry as a major explanatory factor in cost increases and lack of technical innovation. These include the imposition of restrictions for protection of the environment and historical districts, requirements for community participation in major construction projects, labor laws which allow union strikes to become a source of disruption, regulatory policies including building codes and zoning ordinances, and tax laws which inhibit construction abroad. However, the construction industry should bear a large share of blame for not realizing earlier that the technological edge held by the large U.S. construction firms has eroded in face of stiff foreign competition. Many past practices, which were tolerated when U.S. contractors had a technological lead, must now be changed in the face of stiff competition. Otherwise, the U.S. construction industry will continue to find itself in trouble.

With a strong technological base, there is no reason why the construction industry cannot catch up and reassert itself to meet competition wherever it may be. Individual design and/or construction firms must explore new ways to improve productivity for the future. Of course, operational planning for construction projects is still important, but such tactical planning has limitations and may soon reach the point of diminishing return because much that can be wrung out of the existing practices have already been tried. What is needed the most is strategic planning to usher in a revolution which can improve productivity by an order of magnitude or more. Strategic planning should look at opportunities and ask whether there are potential options along which new goals may be sought on the basis of existing resources. No one can be certain about the success of various development options for the design professions and the construction industry. However, with the availability of today's high technology, some options have good potential of success because of the social and economic necessity which will eventually push barriers aside. Ultimately, decisions for action, not plans, will dictate future outcomes.

4.2 LABOR PRODUCTIVITY

Productivity in construction is often broadly defined as output per labor hour. Since labor constitutes a large part of the construction cost and the quantity of labor-hours in performing a task in construction is more susceptible to the influence of management than are materials or capital, this productivity measure is often referred to as *labor productivity*. However, it is important to note that labor productivity is a measure of the overall effectiveness of an operating system in utilizing labor, equipment, and capital to convert labor efforts into useful output, and is not a measure of the capabilities of labor alone. For example, by investing in a piece of new equipment to perform certain tasks in construction, output may be increased for the same number of labor-hours, thus resulting in higher labor productivity.

Construction output may be expressed in terms of functional units or constant dollars. In the former case, labor productivity is associated with units of product per labor hour, such as cubic yards of concrete placed per hour or miles of highway paved per hour. In the latter case, labor productivity is identified with value of construction in constant dollars per labor hour.

Productivity at the Job Site

Contractors and owners are often concerned with the labor activity at job sites. For this purpose, it is convenient to express labor productivity as functional units per labor-hour for each type of construction task. However, even for such specific purposes, different levels of measure may be used. For example, cubic yards of concrete placed per hour is a lower level of measure than is miles of highway paved per hour. Lower-level measures are more useful for monitoring individual activities, while higher-level measures may be more convenient for developing industrywide standards of performance.

While each contractor or owner is free to use its own system to measure labor productivity at a site, it is a good practice to set up a system which can be used to track productivity trends over time and in varied locations. Considerable efforts are required to collect information regionally or nationally over a number of years to produce such results. The productivity indices compiled from statistical data should include parameters such as the performance of major crafts, effects of project size, type and location, and other major project influences.

To develop industrywide standards of performance, there must be a general agreement on the measures to be useful for compiling data. Then, the job-site productivity data collected by various contractors and owners can be correlated and analyzed to develop certain measures for each of the major segment of the construction industry. Thus, a contractor or owner can compare its performance with that of the industry average.

Productivity in the Construction Industry

Because of the diversity of the construction industry, a single index for the entire industry is neither meaningful nor reliable. Productivity indices may be developed for major segments of the construction industry nationwide if reliable statistical data can be obtained for separate industrial segments. For this general type of productivity measure, it is more convenient to express labor productivity as constant dollars per labor hours since dollar values are more easily aggregated from a large amount of data collected from different sources. The use of constant dollars allows meaningful approximations of the changes in construction output from one year to another when price deflators are applied to current dollars to obtain the corresponding values in constant dollars. However, since most construction price deflators are obtained from a combination of price indices for material and labor inputs, they reflect only the change of price levels and do not capture any savings arising from improved labor productivity. Such deflators tend to overstate increases in construction costs over a long period of time and consequently understate the physical volume or value of construction work in years subsequent to the base year for the indices.

4.3 FACTORS AFFECTING JOB-SITE PRODUCTIVITY

Job-site productivity is influenced by many factors which can be characterized either as project work conditions or as nonproductive activities. The project work conditions include, among other factors,

- Job size and complexity.
- Job-site accessibility.
- Labor availability.
- Equipment utilization.
- Contractual agreements.
- Local climate.
- Local cultural characteristics, particularly in foreign operations.

The nonproductive activities associated with a project may or may not be paid by the owner, but they nevertheless take up potential labor resources which can otherwise be directed to the project. The nonproductive activities include, among other factors,

- Indirect labor required to maintain the progress of the project.
- Rework for correcting unsatisfactory work.
- Temporary work stoppage due to inclement weather or material shortage.
- Time off for union activities.
- Absentee time, including late start and early quits.
- Nonworking holidays.
- Strikes.

Both categories of factors affect the productive labor available to a project as well as the on-site labor efficiency.

Project Work Conditions

Job-site labor productivity can be estimated either for each craft (carpenter, bricklayer, etc.) or each type of construction (residential housing, processing plant, etc.) under a specific set of work conditions. A *base labor productivity* may be defined for a set of work conditions specified by the owner or contractor who wishes to observe and measure the labor performance over a period of time under such conditions. A *labor productivity index* may then be defined as the ratio of the job-site labor productivity under a different set of work conditions to the base labor productivity and is a measure of the relative labor efficiency of a project under this new set of work conditions.

The effects of various factors related to work conditions on a new project can be estimated in advance, some more accurately than others. For example, for very large construction projects, the labor productivity index tends to decrease as the project size and/or complexity increase because of logistic problems and the "learning" that the work force must undergo before adjusting to the new environment. Job-site accessibility often may reduce the labor productivity index if the workers must perform their jobs in round-about ways, such as avoiding traffic in repaving the highway surface or maintaining the operation of a plant during renovation. Labor availability in the local market is another factor. Shortage of local labor will force the contractor to bring in nonlocal labor or schedule overtime work or both. In either case, the labor efficiency will be reduced in addition to incurring additional expenses. The degree of equipment utilization and mechanization of a construction project clearly will have direct bearing on job-site labor productivity. The contractual agreements play an important role in the utilization of union or nonunion labor, the use of subcontractors, and the degree of field supervision, all of which will impact job-site labor productivity. Since on-site construction essentially involves outdoor activities, the local climate will influence the efficiency of workers directly. In foreign operations, the cultural characteristics of the host country should be observed in assessing the labor efficiency.

Nonproductive Activities

The nonproductive activities associated with a project should also be examined to determine the *productive labor yield*, which is defined as the ratio of direct labor-hours devoted to the completion of a project to the potential labor-hours. The direct labor-hours are estimated on the basis of the best possible conditions at a job site by excluding all factors which may reduce the productive labor yield. For example, in the repaving of highway surface, the flaggers required to divert traffic represent indirect labor which does not contribute to the labor efficiency of the paving crew if the highway is closed to the traffic. Similarly, for large projects in remote areas, indirect labor may be used to provide housing and infrastructure for the workers hired to supply the direct labor for a project. The labor-hours spent on rework to correct unsatisfactory original work represent extra time taken away from potential labor-hours. The labor-hours related to such activities must be deducted from the potential labor-hours to obtain the actual productive labor yield.

Example 4-1: Effects of Job Size on Productivity

A contractor has established that under a set of "standard" work conditions for building construction, a job requiring 500,000 labor-hours is considered standard in determining the base labor productivity. All other factors being the same, the labor productivity index will increase to 1.1 or 110 percent for a job requiring only 400,000 labor-hours. Assuming that a linear relation exists for the range between jobs requiring 300,000 to 700,000 labor-hours as shown in Figure 4-1, determine the labor productivity index for a new job requiring 650,000 labor-hours under otherwise the same set of work conditions.

The labor productivity index I for the new job can be obtained by linear interpolation of the available data as follows:

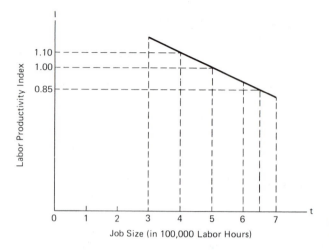

Figure 4-1 Illustrative Relationship Between Productivity Index and Job Size

Labor Productivity Index (y-axis)

Job Size (in 100,000 Labor Hours) (x-axis)

$$I = 1.0 + (1.1 - 1.0)\left(\frac{500,000 - 650,000}{500,000 - 400,000}\right) = 0.85$$

This implies that labor is 15 percent less productive on the large job than on the standard project.

Example 4-2: Productive Labor Yield [36]

In the construction of an off-shore oil drilling platform, the potential labor-hours were found to be $L = 7.5$ million hours. Of this total, the nonproductive activities expressed in thousand labor-hours were as follows:

- $A = 417$ for holidays and strikes
- $B = 1,415$ for absentees (i.e., vacation, sick time)
- $C = 1,141$ for temporary stoppage (i.e., weather, waiting, union activities)
- $D = 1,431$ for indirect labor (i.e., building temporary facilities, cleaning up the site, rework to correct errors)

Determine the productive labor yield after the foregoing factors are taken into consideration. The percentages of time allocated to various nonproductive activities, A, B, C and D are

$$\frac{A}{L} = \frac{417}{7,500} = 6\%; \quad \frac{B}{L} = \frac{1,415}{7,500} = 19\%$$

$$\frac{C}{L} = \frac{1,141}{7,500} = 15\%; \quad \frac{D}{L} = \frac{1,431}{7,500} = 19\%$$

[36] This example was adapted with permission from an unpublished paper "Managing Mega Projects" presented by G. R. Desnoyers at the Project Management Symposium sponsored by the Exxon Research and Engineering Company, Florham Park, NJ, November 12, 1980.

The total percentage of time X for all nonproductive activities is

$$X = \frac{A + B + C + D}{L} = 6\% + 19\% + 15\% + 19\% = 59\%$$

The productive labor yield, Y, when the given factors for A, B, C and D are considered, is as follows:

$$Y = \frac{L - A - B - C - D}{L} = 100\% - 6\% - 19\% - 15\% - 19\%$$
$$= 41\%$$

As a result, only 41 percent of the budgeted labor time was devoted directly to work on the facility.

Example 4-3: Utilization of On-Site Worker's Time

An example illustrating the effects of indirect labor requirements which limit productive labor by a typical craftsman on the job site was given by R. Tucker with the following percentages of time allocation:[37]

Productive time	40%
Unproductive time	
Administrative delays	20%
Inefficient work methods	20%
Labor jurisdictions and other work restrictions	15%
Personal time	5%

In this estimate, as much time is spent on productive work as on delays due to management and inefficiencies due to antiquated work methods.

4.4 LABOR RELATIONS IN CONSTRUCTION

The market demand in construction fluctuates greatly, often within short periods and with uneven distributions among geographical regions. Even when the volume of construction is relatively steady, some types of work may decline in importance while other types gain. Under an unstable economic environment, employers in the construction industry place great value on flexibility in hiring and laying off workers as their volumes of work wax and wane. On the other hand, construction workers sense their insecurity under such circumstances and attempt to limit the impacts of changing economic conditions through labor organizations.

There are many crafts in the construction labor forces, but most contractors hire from only a few of these crafts to satisfy their specialized needs. Because of the peculiar characteristics of employment conditions, employers and workers are placed in a more intimate relationship than in many other industries. Labor

[37] See R. L. Tucker, "Perfection of the Buggy Whip," *ASCE Journal of Construction Engineering and Management*, Vol. 111, no.2, 1988. pp.158–171.

and management arrangements in the construction industry include both union-ized and nonunionized operations which compete for future dominance. Most in-dustrial and utility construction is union. In the commercial building sector, nonunion contractors have made inroads, while in the housing sector, most con-tractors are nonunion. The heavy construction sector is primarily nonunion.

Unionized Construction

The craft unions work with construction contractors using unionized labor through various market institutions such as jurisdiction rules, apprenticeship programs, and the referral system. Craft unions with specific jurisdiction rules for different trades set uniform hourly wage rates for journeymen and offer formal apprenticeship train-ing to provide common and equivalent skill for each trade. Contractors, through the contractors' associations, enter into legally binding collective bargaining agreements with one or more of the craft unions in the construction trades. The system which binds both parties to a collective bargaining agreement is referred to as the "union shop." These agreements obligate a contractor to observe the work jurisdictions of various unions and to hire employees through a union operated referral system commonly known as the hiring hall.

The referral systems operated by union organizations are required to observe several conditions:

1. All qualified workers reported to the referral system must be made available to the contractor without discrimination on the basis of union membership or other relationship to the union. The "closed shop" which limits referral to union members only is now illegal.
2. The contractor reserves the right to hire or refuse to hire any worker referred by the union on the basis of his or her qualifications.
3. The referral plan must be posted in public, including any priorities of referrals or required qualifications.

While these principles must prevail, referral systems operated by labor organizations differ widely in the construction industry.

Contractors and craft unions must negotiate not only wage rates and working conditions, but also hiring and apprentice training practices. The purpose of trade jurisdiction is to encourage considerable investment in apprentice training on the part of the union so that the contractor will be protected by having only qualified workers perform the job even though such workers are not permanently attached to the contractor and thus may have no sense of security or loyalty. The referral system is often a rapid and dependable source of workers, particularly for a contractor who moves into a new geographical location or starts a new project which has high fluctuations in demand for labor. By and large, the referral system has functioned smoothly in providing qualified workers to contractors, even though some other aspects of union operations are not as well accepted by contractors.

Nonunionized Construction

In recent years, nonunion contractors have entered and prospered in an industry which has a long tradition of unionization. Nonunion operations in construction are referred to as "open shops." However, in the absence of collective bargaining agreements, many contractors operate under policies adopted by nonunion contractors' associations. This practice is referred to as the "merit shop," which follows substantially the same policies and procedures as collective bargaining although under the control of a nonunion contractors' association without union participation. Other contractors may choose to be totally "unorganized" by not following either union shop or merit shop practices.

The operations of the merit shop are national in scope, except for the local or state apprenticeship and training plans. The comprehensive plans of the contractors' association apply to all employees and crafts of a contractor regardless of their trades. Under such operations, workers have full rights to move through the nation among member contractors of the association. Thus, the nonunion segment of the industry is organized by contractors' associations into an integral part of the construction industry. However, since merit shop workers are employed directly by the construction firms, they have a greater loyalty to the firm and recognize that their own interest will be affected by the financial health of the firm.

Playing a significant role in the early growth and continued expansion of merit shop construction is the Associated Builders and Contractors Association. By 1987, it had a membership of nearly 20,000 contractors and a network of 75 chapters through the nation. Among the merit shop contractors are large construction firms such as Fluor Daniel, Blount International, and Brown & Root Construction. The advantages of merit shops as claimed by its advocates are

- The ability to manage their own work force.
- Flexibility in making timely management decisions.
- The emphasis on making maximum usage of local labor force.
- The emphasis on encouraging individual work advancement through continued development of skills.
- The shared interest that management and workers have in seeing an individual firm prosper.

By shouldering the training responsibility for producing skill workers, the merit shop contractors have deflected the most serious complaints of users and labor that used to be raised against the open shop. On the other hand, the use of mixed crews of skilled workers at a job site by merit shop contractors enables them to remove a major source of inefficiencies caused by the exclusive jurisdiction practiced in the union shop, namely, the idea that only members of a particular union should be permitted to perform any given task in construction. As a result, merit shop contractors are able to exert a beneficial influence on productivity and cost effectiveness of construction projects.

The unorganized form of open shop is found primarily in housing construction where a large percentage of workers are characterized as unskilled helpers. The skilled workers in various crafts are developed gradually through informal apprenticeships while serving as helpers. This form of open shop is not expected to expand beyond the type of construction projects in which highly specialized skills are not required.

4.5 PROBLEMS IN COLLECTIVE BARGAINING

In the organized building trades in North American construction, the primary unit is the international union, which is an association of local unions in the United States and Canada. Although only the international unions have the power to issue or remove charters and to organize or combine local unions, each local union has considerable degrees of autonomy in the conduct of its affairs, including the negotiation of collective bargaining agreements. The business agent of a local union is an elected official who is the most important person in handling the day-to-day operations on behalf of the union. The contractors' associations representing the employers vary widely in composition and structure, particularly in different geographical regions. In general, local contractors' associations are considerably less well organized than the union with which they deal, but they try to strengthen themselves through affiliation with state and national organizations. Typically, collective bargaining agreements in construction are negotiated between a local union in a single craft and the employers of that craft as represented by a contractors' association, but there are many exceptions to this pattern. For example, a contractor may remain outside the association and negotiate independently of the union, but it usually cannot obtain a better agreement than the association.

Because of the great variety of bargaining structures in which the union and contractors' organization may choose to stage negotiations, there are many problems arising from jurisdictional disputes and other causes. Given the traditional rivalries among various crafts and the ineffective organization of some of contractors' associations, coupled with the lack of adequate mechanisms for settling disputes, some possible solutions to these problems deserve serious attention.[38]

Regional Bargaining

Currently, the geographical area in a collective bargaining agreement does not necessarily coincide with the territory of the union and contractors' associations in the negotiations. There are overlapping of jurisdictions as well as territories, which may create successions of contract termination dates for different crafts. Most collective bargaining agreements are negotiated locally, but regional agreements with more comprehensive coverage embracing a number of states have been established. The role of national union negotiators and contractors' representatives in local

---

[38] For more detailed discussion, see D. Q. Mills, "Labor Relations and Collective Bargaining," Chapter 4, in J. E. Lang and D. Q. Mills, *The Construction Industry*.

collective bargaining is limited. The national agreement between international unions and a national contractor normally binds the contractors' association and its bargaining unit. Consequently, the most promising reform lies in the broadening of the geographic region of an agreement in a single trade without overlapping territories or jurisdictions.

Multicraft Bargaining

The treatment of interrelationships among various craft trades in construction presents one of the most complex issues in the collective bargaining process. Past experience on project agreements has dealt with such issues successfully in that collective bargaining agreements are signed by a group of craft trade unions and a contractor for the duration of a project. Project agreements may reference other agreements on particular points, such as wage rates and fringe benefits, but may set their own working conditions and procedures for settling disputes including a commitment of no strike and no lockout. This type of agreement may serve as a starting point for multicraft bargaining on a regional, nonproject basis.

Improvement of Bargaining Performance

Although both sides of the bargaining table are to some degree responsible for the success or failure of negotiation, contractors have often been responsible for the poor performance of collective bargaining in construction in recent years because local contractors' associations are generally less well organized and less professionally staffed than the unions with which they deal. Legislation providing for contractors' association accreditation as an exclusive bargaining agent has now been provided in several provinces in Canada. It provides a government board that could hold hearings and establish an appropriate bargaining unit by geographic region or sector of the industry, on a single-trade or multitrade basis.

4.6 MATERIALS MANAGEMENT

Materials management is an important element in project planning and control. Materials represent a major expense in construction, so minimizing *procurement* or *purchase* costs presents important opportunities for reducing costs. Poor materials management can also result in large and avoidable costs during construction. First, if materials are purchased early, capital may be tied up and interest charges incurred on the excess *inventory* of materials. Even worse, materials may deteriorate during storage or be stolen unless special care is taken. For example, electrical equipment often must be stored in waterproof locations. Second, delays and extra expenses may be incurred if materials required for particular activities are not available. Accordingly, ensuring a timely flow of material is an important concern of project managers.

Materials management is not just a concern during the monitoring stage in which construction is taking place. Decisions about material procurement may also be required during the initial planning and scheduling stages. For example, activities can be inserted in the project schedule to represent purchasing of major items such as elevators for buildings. The availability of materials may greatly influence the schedule in projects with a *fast track* or very tight time schedule: sufficient time for obtaining the necessary materials must be allowed. In some cases, more expensive suppliers or shippers may be employed to save time.

Materials management is also a problem at the organization level if central purchasing and inventory control is used for standard items. In this case, the various projects undertaken by the organization would present requests to the central purchasing group. In turn, this group would maintain inventories of standard items to reduce the delay in providing material or to obtain lower costs due to bulk purchasing. This organizational materials management problem is analogous to inventory control in any organization facing continuing demand for particular items.

Materials ordering problems lend themselves particularly well to computer-based systems to ensure the consistency and completeness of the purchasing process. In the manufacturing realm, the use of automated *materials requirements planning* systems is common. In these systems, the master production schedule, inventory records, and product component lists are merged to determine what items must be ordered, when they should be ordered, and how much of each item should be ordered in each time period. The heart of these calculations is simple arithmetic: the projected demand for each material item in each period is subtracted from the available inventory. When the inventory becomes too low, a new order is recommended. For items that are nonstandard or not kept in inventory, the calculation is even simpler, since no inventory must be considered. With a materials requirement system, much of the detailed record keeping is automated, and project managers are alerted to purchasing requirements.

Example 4-4: Examples of Benefits for Materials Management Systems [39]

From a study of 20 heavy-construction sites, the following benefits from the introduction of materials management systems were noted:

- In one project, a 6 percent reduction in craft labor costs occurred due to the improved availability of materials as needed on site. On other projects, an 8 percent savings due to reduced delay for materials was estimated.
- A comparison of two projects with and without a materials management system revealed a change in productivity from 1.92 person-hours per unit without a system to 1.14 person-hours per unit with a new system. Again, much of this difference can be attributed to the timely availability of materials.
- Warehouse costs were found to decrease 50 percent on one project with the introduction of improved inventory management, representing a savings of $92,000. Interest charges for inventory also declined, with one project reporting a cash flow savings of $35,000 from improved materials management.

[39] This example was adapted from G. Stukhart, and L. C. Bell, "Costs and Benefits of Materials Management Systems," *ASCE Journal of Construction Engineering and Management*, Vol. 113, no. 2, 1987, pp. 222–234.

Against these various benefits, the costs of acquiring and maintaining a materials management system has to be compared. However, management studies suggest that investment in such systems can be quite beneficial.

4.7 MATERIAL PROCUREMENT AND DELIVERY

The main sources of information for feedback and control of material procurement are requisitions, bids and quotations, purchase orders and subcontracts, shipping and receiving documents, and invoices. For projects involving the large-scale use of critical resources, the owner may initiate the procurement procedure even before the selection of a constructor to avoid shortages and delays. Under ordinary circumstances, the constructor will handle the procurement to shop for materials with the best price/performance characteristics specified by the designer. Some overlapping and rehandling in the procurement process is unavoidable, but it should be minimized to ensure timely delivery of the materials in good condition.

The materials for delivery to and from a construction site may be broadly classified as (1) bulk materials, (2) standard off-the-shelf materials, and (3) fabricated members or units. The process of delivery, including transportation, field storage, and installation, will be different for these classes of materials. The equipment needed to handle and haul these classes of materials will also be different.

Bulk materials refer to materials in their natural or semiprocessed state, such as earthwork to be excavated, wet concrete mix, and so on, which are usually encountered in large quantities in construction. Some bulk materials such as earthwork or gravels may be measured in bank (solid in situ) volume. Obviously, the quantities of materials for delivery may be substantially different when expressed in different measures of volume, depending on the characteristics of such materials.

Standard piping and valves are typical examples of standard off-the-shelf materials which are used extensively in the chemical processing industry. Since standard off-the-shelf materials can easily be stockpiled, the delivery process is relatively simple.

Fabricated members such as steel beams and columns for buildings are preprocessed in a shop to simplify the field erection procedures. Welded or bolted connections are attached partially to the members which are cut to precise dimensions for adequate fit. Similarly, steel tanks and pressure vessels are often partly or fully fabricated before shipping to the field. In general, if the work can be done in the shop where working conditions can better be controlled, it is advisable to do so, provided that the fabricated members or units can be shipped to the construction site in a satisfactory manner at a reasonable cost.

As a further step to simplify field assembly, an entire wall panel including plumbing and wiring or even an entire room may be prefabricated and shipped to the site. While the field labor is greatly reduced in such cases, "materials" for delivery are in fact manufactured products with value added by another type of labor. With modern means of transporting construction materials and fabricated units, the percentages of costs on direct labor and materials for a project may change if more prefabricated units are introduced in the construction process.

In the construction industry, materials used by a specific craft are generally handled by craftsmen, not by general labor. Thus, electricians handle electrical materials, pipefitters handle pipe materials, and so on. This multiple handling diverts scarce skilled craftsmen and contractor supervision into activities which do not contribute directly to construction. Since contractors are not normally in the freight business, they do not perform the tasks of freight delivery efficiently. All these factors tend to exacerbate the problems of freight delivery for very large projects.

Example 4-5: Freight Delivery for the Alaska Pipeline Project [40]

The freight delivery system for the Alaska pipeline project was set up to handle 600,000 tons of materials and supplies. This tonnage did not include the pipes which comprised another 500,000 tons and were shipped through a different routing system.

The complexity of this delivery system is illustrated in Figure 4-2. The rectangular boxes denote geographical locations. The points of origin represent plants and factories throughout the United States and elsewhere. Some of the materials went to a primary staging point in Seattle, and some went directly to Alaska. There were five ports of

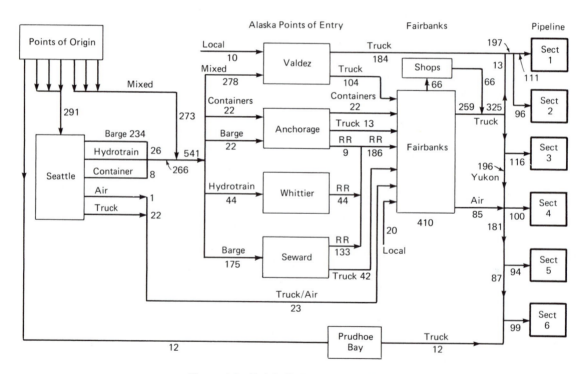

Figure 4-2 Freight Delivery to the Alaska Pipeline Project

[40] The information for this example was provided by Exxon Pipeline Company, Houston, TX, with permission from the Alyeska Pipeline Service Co., Anchorage, Alaska.

Labor, Material, and Equipment Utilization   Chap. 4

entry: Valdez, Anchorage, Whittier, Seward, and Prudhoe Bay. There was a secondary staging area in Fairbanks, and the pipeline itself was divided into six sections. Beyond the Yukon River, there was nothing available but a dirt road for hauling. The amounts of freight in thousands of tons shipped to and from various locations are indicated by the numbers near the network branches (with arrows showing the directions of material flows) and the modes of transportation are noted above the branches. In each of the locations, the contractor had supervision and construction labor to identify materials, unload from transport, determine where the material was going, repackage if required to split shipments, and then reload material on outgoing transport.

Example 4-6: Process Plant Equipment Procurement [41]

The procurement and delivery of bulk materials items such as piping, electrical and structural elements involves a series of activities if such items are not standard and/or in stock. The times required for various activities in the procurement of such items might be estimated to be as follows:

Activities	Duration (days)	Cumulative Duration
Requisition ready by designer	0	0
Owner approval	5	5
Inquiry issued to vendors	3	8
Vendor quotations received	15	23
Complete bid evaluation by designer	7	30
Owner approval	5	35
Place purchase order	5	40
Receive preliminary shop drawings	10	50
Receive final design drawings	10	60
Fabrication and delivery	60–200	120–260

As a result, this type of equipment procurement will typically require four to nine months. Slippage or contraction in this standard schedule is also possible, based on such factors as the extent to which a fabricator is busy.

4.8 INVENTORY CONTROL

Once goods are purchased, they represent an *inventory* used during the construction process. The general objective of inventory control is to minimize the total cost of keeping the inventory while making trade-offs among the major categories of costs: (1) purchase costs, (2) order cost, (3) holding costs, and (4) unavailable cost. These cost categories are interrelated since reducing cost in one category may increase cost in others. The costs in all categories generally are subject to considerable uncertainty.

---

[41] This example was adapted from A. E. Kerridge, "How to Develop a Project Schedule," in A. E. Kerridge and C. H. Vervalin eds., *Engineering and Construction Project Management*, Gulf Publishing Company, Houston, TX, 1986.

Purchase Costs

The *purchase cost* of an item is the unit purchase price from an external source including transportation and freight costs. For construction materials, it is common to receive discounts for bulk purchases, so the unit purchase cost declines as quantity increases. These reductions may reflect manufacturers' marketing policies, economies of scale in the material production, or scale economies in transportation. There are also advantages in having homogeneous materials. For example, a bulk order to ensure the same color or size of items such as bricks may be desirable. Accordingly, it is usually desirable to make a limited number of large purchases for materials. In some cases, organizations may consolidate small orders from a number of different projects to capture such bulk discounts; this is a basic saving to be derived from a central purchasing office.

The cost of materials is based on prices obtained through effective bargaining. Unit prices of materials depend on bargaining leverage, quantities, and delivery time. Organizations with potential for long-term purchase volume can command better bargaining leverage. While orders in large quantities may result in lower unit prices, they may also increase holding costs and thus cause problems in cash flow. Requirements of short delivery time can also adversely affect unit prices. Furthermore, design characteristics which include items of odd sizes or shapes should be avoided. Since such items normally are not available in the standard stockpile, purchasing them causes higher prices.

The transportation costs are affected by shipment sizes and other factors. Shipment by the full load of a carrier often reduces prices and assures quicker delivery, as the carrier can travel from the origin to the destination of the full load without having to stop for delivering part of the cargo at other stations. Avoiding transshipment is another consideration in reducing shipping cost. While the reduction in shipping costs is a major objective, the requirements of delicate handling of some items may favor a more expensive mode of transportation to avoid breakage and replacement costs.

Order Cost

The *order* cost reflects the administrative expense of issuing a purchase order to an outside supplier. Order costs include expenses of making requisitions, analyzing alternative vendors, writing purchase orders, receiving materials, inspecting materials, checking on orders, and maintaining records of the entire process. Order costs are usually only a small portion of total costs for material management in construction projects, although ordering may require substantial time.

Holding Costs

The *holding costs* or *carrying costs* are primarily the result of capital costs, handling, storage, obsolescence, shrinkage, and deterioration. Capital cost results from the opportunity cost or financial expense of capital tied up in inventory. Once payment for goods is made, borrowing costs are incurred or capital must be diverted from other productive uses. Consequently, a capital carrying cost is incurred equal to the value of the inventory during a period multiplied by the interest rate obtainable or paid during that period. Note that capital costs accumulate only when payment for materials actually occurs; many organizations attempt to delay payments as long as possible to minimize such costs. Handling and storage represent the movement and protection charges incurred for materials. Storage costs also include the disruption caused to other project activities by large inventories of materials that get in the way. Obsolescence is the risk that an item will lose value because of changes in specifications. Shrinkage is the decrease in inventory over time due to theft or loss. Deterioration reflects a change in material quality due to age or environmental degradation. Many of these *holding cost* components are difficult to predict in advance; a project manager knows only that there is some chance that specific categories of cost will occur. In addition to these major categories of cost, there may be ancillary costs of additional insurance, taxes (many states treat inventories as taxable property), or fire hazards. As a general rule, holding costs will typically represent 20 to 40 percent of the average inventory value over the course of a year; thus if the average material inventory on a project is $1 million over a year, the holding cost might be expected to be $200,000 to $400,000.

Unavailability Cost

The *unavailability cost* is incurred when a desired material is not available at the desired time. In manufacturing industries, this cost is often called the *stockout* or *depletion* cost. Shortages may delay work, thereby wasting labor resources or delaying the completion of the entire project. Again, it may be difficult to forecast in advance exactly when an item may be required or when a shipment will be received. While the project schedule gives one estimate, deviations from the schedule may occur during construction. Moreover, the cost associated with a shortage may also be difficult to assess; if the material used for one activity is not available, it may be possible to assign workers to other activities and, depending upon which activities are critical, the project may not be delayed.

4.9 TRADE-OFFS OF COSTS IN MATERIALS MANAGEMENT

To illustrate the type of trade-offs encountered in materials management, suppose that a particular item is to be ordered for a project. The amount of time required for processing the order and shipping the item is uncertain. Consequently, the project manager must decide how much lead time to provide in ordering the item. Ordering early and thereby providing a long lead time will increase the chance that the item is available when needed, but it increases the costs of inventory and the chance of spoilage on site.

Let T be the time for the delivery of a particular item, R be the time required for processing the order, and S be the shipping time. Then, the minimum amount of time for the delivery of the item is $T = R + S$. In general, both R and S are random variables; hence, T is also a random variable. For the sake of simplicity, we shall consider only the case of instant processing for an order, that is, $R = 0$. Then, the delivery time T equals the shipping time S.

Since T is a random variable, the chance that an item will be delivered on day t is represented by the probability $p(t)$. Then, the probability that the item will be delivered on or before t day is given by

$$P_r\{T \le t\} = \sum_{u=0}^{t} p(u) \tag{4.1}$$

If a and b are the lower and upper bounds of possible delivery dates, the expected delivery time is then given by:

$$E[T] = \sum_{t=a}^{b} t[p(t)] \tag{4.2}$$

The lead time L for ordering an item is the time period ahead of the delivery time and will depend on the trade-off between holding costs and unavailability costs. A project manager may want to avoid the unavailable cost by requiring delivery on the scheduled date of use or may be to lower the holding cost by adopting a more flexible lead time based on the expected delivery time. For example, the manager may make the trade-off by specifying the lead time to be D days more than the expected delivery time; that is,

$$L = E[T] + D \tag{4.3}$$

where D may vary from 0 to the number of additional days required to produce certain delivery on the desired date.

In a more realistic situation, the project manager would also contend with the uncertainty of exactly when the item might be required. Even if the item is *scheduled* for use on a particular date, the work progress might vary so that the desired date would differ. In many cases, greater than expected work progress may result in no savings because materials for future activities are unavailable.

Example 4-7: Lead Time for Ordering with no Processing Time

Table 4-1 summarizes the probability of different delivery times for an item. In this table, the first column lists the possible shipping times (ranging from 10 to 16 days), the second column lists the probability or chance that this shipping time will occur, and the third column summarizes the chance that the item arrives on or before a particular date. This table can be used to indicate the chance that the item will arrive on a desired date for different lead times. For example, if the order is placed 12 days in advance of the desired date (so the lead time is 12 days), then there is a 15 percent chance that the item will arrive exactly on the desired day and a 35 percent chance that the item will arrive on or before the desired date. Note that this implies that there is a $1 - 0.35 = 0.65$ or 65 percent chance that the item will not arrive by the desired date with a lead time of 12 days. Given the information in Table 4-1, when should the item order be placed?

Suppose that the scheduled date of use for the item is in 16 days. To be completely

TABLE 4–1 DELIVERY DATE ON ORDERS AND PROBABILITY
OF DELIVERY FOR AN EXAMPLE

Delivery date t	Probability of delivery on date t $p(t)$	Cumulative probability of delivery by day t $Pr\{T \leq t\}$
10	0.10	0.10
11	0.10	0.20
12	0.15	0.35
13	0.20	0.55
14	0.30	0.85
15	0.10	0.95
16	0.05	1.00

certain to have delivery by the desired day, the order should be placed 16 days in advance. However, the expected delivery date with a 16-day lead time would be:

$$E[T] = \sum_{t=10}^{16} t[p(t)]$$

$$= (10)(0.1) + (11)(0.1) + (12)(0.15) \\ + (13)(0.20) + (14)(0.30) + (15)(0.10)$$

$$= 13.0$$

Thus, the actual delivery date may be $16 - 13 = 3$ days early, and this early delivery might involve significant holding costs. A project manager might then decide to provide a lead time so that the *expected* delivery date was equal to the desired assembly date as long as the availability of the item was not critical. Alternatively, the project manager might negotiate a more certain delivery date from the supplier.

4.10 CONSTRUCTION EQUIPMENT

The selection of the appropriate type and size of construction equipment often affects the required amount of time and effort and thus the job-site productivity of a project. It is therefore important for site managers and construction planners to be familiar with the characteristics of the major types of equipment most commonly used in construction.[42]

Excavation and Loading

One family of construction machines used for excavation is broadly classified as a *crane-shovel* as indicated by the variety of machines in Figure 4-3. The crane-shovel consists of three major components:

[42] For further details on equipment characteristics, see, for example, S. W. Nunnally, *Construction Methods and Management*, 2nd ed., Prentice Hall, Englewood Cliffs, NJ, 1986.

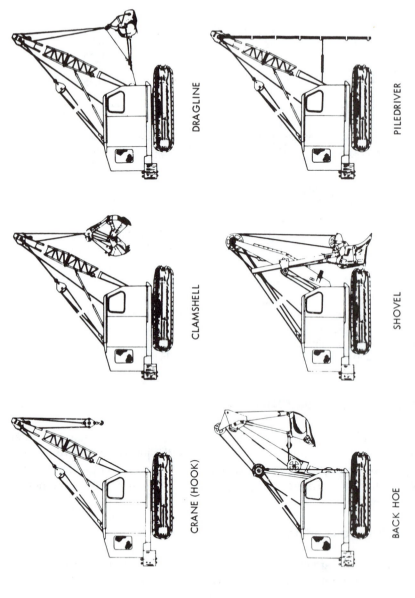

Figure 4-3 Typical Machines in the Crane-Shovel Family (Source: U.S. Department of Army.)

DRAGLINE

PILEDRIVER

CLAMSHELL

SHOVEL

CRANE (HOOK)

BACK HOE

1. A carrier or mounting which provides mobility and stability for the machine
2. A revolving deck or turntable which contains the power and control units
3. A front-end attachment which serves the special functions in an operation

The type of mounting for all machines in Figure 4-3 is referred to as *crawler mounting*, which is particularly suitable for crawling over relatively rugged surfaces at a job site. Other types of mounting include *truck mounting* and *wheel mounting*, which provide greater mobility between job sites, but require better surfaces for their operation. The revolving deck includes a cab to house the person operating the mounting and/or the revolving deck. The types of front-end attachments in Figure 4-3 might include a crane with hook, clam shell, dragline, backhoe, shovel, and piledriver.

A tractor consists of a crawler mounting and a nonrevolving cab. When an earth-moving blade is attached to the front end of a tractor, the assembly is called a bulldozer. When a bucket is attached to its front end, the assembly is known as a loader or bucket loader. There are different types of loaders designed to handle most efficiently materials of different weights and moisture contents.

Scrapers are multiple units of tractor-truck and blade-bucket assemblies with various combinations to facilitate the loading and hauling of earthwork. Major types of scrapers include single engine two-axle or three-axle scrapers, twin-engine all-wheel-drive scrapers, elevating scrapers, and push-pull scrapers. Each type has different characteristics of rolling resistance, maneuverability, stability, and speed in operation.

Compaction and Grading

The function of compaction equipment is to produce higher density in soil mechanically. The basic forces used in compaction are static weight, kneading, impact, and vibration. The degree of compaction that may be achieved depends on the properties of soil, its moisture content, the thickness of the soil layer for compaction, and the method of compaction. Some major types of compaction equipment are shown in Figure 4-4, which includes rollers with different operating characteristics.

The function of grading equipment is to bring the earthwork to the desired shape and elevation. Major types of grading equipment include motor graders and grade trimmers. The former is an all-purpose machine for grading and surface finishing; the latter is used for heavy construction because of its higher operating speed.

Drilling and Blasting

Rock excavation is an audacious task requiring special equipment and methods. The degree of difficulty depends on physical characteristics of the rock type to be excavated, such as grain size, planes of weakness, weathering, brittleness, and hardness. The task of rock excavation includes loosening, loading, hauling, and compacting. The loosening operation is specialized for rock excavation and is performed by drilling, blasting, or rippling.

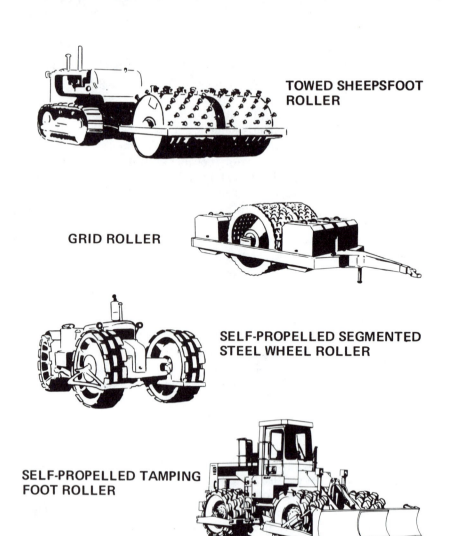

TOWED SHEEPSFOOT ROLLER

GRID ROLLER

SELF-PROPELLED SEGMENTED STEEL WHEEL ROLLER

SELF-PROPELLED TAMPING FOOT ROLLER

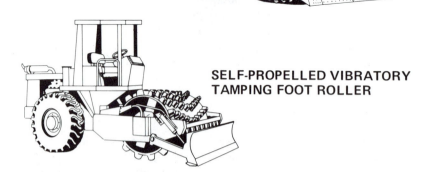

SELF-PROPELLED VIBRATORY TAMPING FOOT ROLLER

Figure 4-4 Some Major Types of Compaction Equipment (Reprinted with permission from Compaction Equipment, Caterpillar, Inc., 1979.)

Major types of drilling equipment are percussion drills, rotary drills, and rotary-percussion drills. A percussion drill penetrates and cuts rock by impact while it rotates without cutting on the upstroke. Common types of percussion drills include a jackhammer which is hand-held and others which are mounted on a fixed frame or on a wagon or crawl for mobility. A rotary drill cuts by turning a bit against the rock surface. A rotary-percussion drill combines the two cutting movements to provide a faster penetration in rock.

Blasting requires the use of explosives, the most common of which is dynamite. Generally, electric blasting caps are connected in a circuit with insulated wires. Power sources may be power lines or blasting machines designed for firing electric cap circuits. Also available are nonelectrical blasting systems which combine the precise timing and flexibility of electric blasting and the safety of nonelectrical detonation.

Tractor-mounted rippers are capable of penetrating and prying loose most rock types. The blade or ripper is connected to an adjustable shank which controls the angle at the tip of the blade as it is raised or lowered. Automated ripper control may be installed to control ripping depth and tip angle.

In rock tunneling, special tunnel machines equipped with multiple cutter heads and capable of excavating full diameter of the tunnel are now available. Their use has increasingly replaced the traditional methods of drilling and blasting.

Lifting and Erecting

Derricks are commonly used to lift equipment of materials in industrial or building construction. A derrick consists of a vertical mast and an inclined boom sprouting from the foot of the mast. The mast is held in position by guys or stifflegs connected to a base while a topping lift links the top of the mast and the top of the inclined boom. A hook in the road line hanging from the top of the inclined boom is used to lift loads. Guy derricks may easily be moved from one floor to the next in a building under construction while stiffleg derricks may be mounted on tracks for movement within a work area.

Tower cranes are used to lift loads to great heights and to facilitate the erection of steel building frames. Horizon boom-type tower cranes are most common in highrise building construction. Inclined boom-type tower cranes are also used for erecting steel structures.

Mixing and Paving

Basic types of equipment for paving include machines for dispensing concrete and bituminous materials for pavement surfaces. Concrete mixers may also be used to mix Portland cement, sand, gravel, and water in batches for other types of construction other than paving.

A truck mixer refers to a concrete mixer mounted on a truck which is capable of transporting ready-mixed concrete from a central batch plant to construction sites.

A paving mixer is a self-propelled concrete mixer equipped with a boom and a bucket to place concrete at any desired point within a roadway. It can be used as a stationary mixer or used to supply slipform pavers that are capable of spreading, consolidating, and finishing a concrete slab without the use of forms.

A bituminous distributor is a truck-mounted plant for generating liquid bituminous materials and applying them to road surfaces through a spray bar connected to the end of the truck. Bituminous materials include both asphalt and tar which have similar properties except that tar is not soluble in petroleum products. While asphalt is most frequently used for road surfacing, tar is used when the pavement is likely to be heavily exposed to petroleum spills.

Construction Tools and Other Equipment

Air compressors and pumps are widely used as the power sources for construction tools and equipment. Common pneumatic construction tools include drills, hammers, grinders, saws, wrenches, staple guns, sandblasting guns, and concrete vibrators. Pumps are used to supply water or to dewater at construction sites and to provide water jets for some types of construction.

Automation of Equipment

The introduction of new mechanized equipment in construction has had a profound effect on the cost and productivity of construction as well as the methods used for construction itself. An exciting example of innovation in this regard is the introduction of computer microprocessors on tools and equipment. As a result, the performance and activity of equipment can be continually monitored and adjusted for improvement. In many cases, automation of at least part of the construction process is possible and desirable. For example, wrenches that automatically monitor the elongation of bolts and the applied torque can be programmed to achieve the best bolt tightness. On grading projects, laser-controlled scrapers can produce desired cuts faster and more precisely than can wholly manual methods.[43] Possibilities for automation and robotics in construction are explored more fully in Chapter 16.

Example 4-8: Tunneling Equipment [44]

In the mid-1980s, some Japanese firms were successful in obtaining construction contracts for tunneling in the United States by using new equipment and methods. For example, the Japanese firm of Ohbayashi won the sewer contract in San Francisco because of its advanced tunneling technology. When a tunnel is dug through soft earth, as in San Francisco, it must be maintained at a few atmospheres of pressure to keep it from caving in. Workers must spend several hours in a pressure chamber

[43] See C. Paulson, "Automation and Robotics for Construction," *ASCE Journal of Construction Engineering and Management*, Vol. 111, no. CO-3, 1985, pp. 190–207.

[44] This example is adapted from F. Moavenzadeh, "Construction's High-Technology Revolution," *Technology Review*, October 1985, p.32.

before entering the tunnel and several more in decompression afterward. They can stay inside for only three or four hours, always at considerable risk from cave-ins and asphyxiation. Ohbayashi used the new Japanese "earth-pressure-balance" method, which eliminates these problems. Whirling blades advance slowly, cutting the tunnel. The loose earth temporarily remains behind to balance the pressure of the compact earth on all sides. Meanwhile, prefabricated concrete segments are inserted and joined with waterproof seals to line the tunnel. Then the loose earth is conveyed away. This new tunneling method enabled Ohbayashi to bid $5 million below the engineer's estimate for a San Francisco sewer. The firm completed the tunnel three months ahead of schedule. In effect, an innovation involving new technology and method led to considerable cost and time savings.

4.11 CHOICE OF EQUIPMENT AND STANDARD PRODUCTION RATES

Typically, construction equipment is used to perform essentially repetitive operations and can be broadly classified according to two basic functions: (1) operators such as cranes, graders, and so on that stay within the confines of the construction site and (2) haulers such as dump trucks, ready-mixed concrete trucks, and so on that transport materials to and from the site. In both cases, the cycle of a piece of equipment is a sequence of tasks which is repeated to produce a unit of output. For example, the sequence of tasks for a crane might be to fit and install a wall panel (or a package of eight wall panels) on the side of a building; similarly, the sequence of tasks of a ready-mixed concrete truck might be to load, haul, and unload 2 cubic yards (or one truck load) of fresh concrete.

To increase job-site productivity, it is beneficial to select equipment with proper characteristics and a size most suitable for the work conditions at a construction site. In excavation for building construction, for example, factors that could affect the selection of excavators include

1. **Size of the job.** Larger volumes of excavation will require larger excavators or smaller excavators in greater number.
2. **Activity time constraints.** Shortage of time for excavation may force contractors to increase the size or numbers of equipment for activities related to excavation.
3. **Availability of equipment.** Productivity of excavation activities will diminish if the equipment used to perform them is available but not the most adequate.
4. **Cost of transportation of equipment.** This cost depends on the size of the job, the distance of transportation, and the means of transportation.
5. **Type of excavation.** Principal types of excavation in building projects are cut and/or fill, excavation massive, and excavation for the elements of foundation. The most adequate equipment to perform one of these activities is not the most adequate to perform the others.
6. **Soil characteristics.** The type and condition of the soil is important when choosing the most adequate equipment since each piece of equipment has

different outputs for different soils. Moreover, one excavation pit could have different soils at different strata.

7. **Geometric characteristics of elements to be excavated.** Functional characteristics of different types of equipment makes such considerations necessary.

8. **Space constraints.** The performance of equipment is influenced by the spatial limitations for the movement of excavators.

9. **Characteristics of haul units.** The size of an excavator will depend on the haul units if there is a constraint on the size and/or number of these units.

10. **Location of dumping areas.** The distance between the construction site and dumping areas could be relevant not only for selecting the type and number of haulers, but also the type of excavators.

11. **Weather and temperature.** Rain, snow and severe temperature conditions affect the job-site productivity of labor and equipment.

Various types of machines for excavation can be compared for efficiency. For example, power shovels are generally found to be the most suitable for excavating from a level surface and for attacking an existing digging surface or one created by the power shovel; furthermore, they have the capability of placing the excavated material directly onto the haulers. Another alternative is to use bulldozers for excavation.

The choice of the type and size of haulers is based on the consideration that the number of haulers selected must be capable of disposing of the excavated materials expeditiously. Factors that affect this selection include

1. **Output of excavators.** The size and characteristics of the excavators selected will determine the output volume excavated per day.

2. **Distance to dump site.** Sometimes part of the excavated materials may be piled up in a corner at the job-site for use as backfill.

3. **Probable average speed.** The average speed of the haulers to and from the dumping site will determine the cycle time for each hauling trip.

4. **Volume of excavated materials.** The volume of excavated materials including the part to be piled up should be hauled away as soon as possible.

5. **Spatial and weight constraints.** The size and weight of the haulers must be feasible at the job site and over the route from the construction site to the dumping area.

Dump trucks are usually used as haulers for excavated materials as they can move freely with relatively high speeds on city streets as well as on highways.

The cycle capacity C of a piece of equipment is defined as the number of output units per cycle of operation under standard work conditions. The capacity is a function of the output units used in the measurement as well as the size of the equipment and the material to be processed. The cycle time T refers to units of time per cycle of operation. The standard production rate R of a piece of construction equipment is defined as the number of output units per unit time. Hence,

$$R = \frac{C}{T} \qquad (4.4)$$

or

$$T = \frac{C}{R} \qquad (4.5)$$

The daily standard production rate P_e of an excavator can be obtained by multiplying its standard production rate R_e by the number of operating hours H_e per day. Thus,

$$P_e = R_e H_e = \frac{C_e H_e}{T_e} \qquad (4.6)$$

where C_e and T_e are cycle capacity (in units of volume) and cycle time (in hours) of the excavator, respectively.

In determining the daily standard production rate of a hauler, it is necessary to determine first the cycle time from the distance D to a dump site and the average speed S of the hauler. Let T_t be the travel time for the round trip to the dump site, T_o be the loading time and T_d be the dumping time. Then the travel time for the round trip is given by

$$T_t = \frac{2D}{S} \qquad (4.7)$$

The loading time is related to the cycle time of the excavator T_e and the relative capacities C_h and C_e of the hauler and the excavator, respectively. In the optimum or standard case,

$$T_o = T_e \frac{C_h}{C_e} \qquad (4.8)$$

For a given dumping time T_d, the cycle time T_h of the hauler is given by

$$T_h = \frac{2D}{S} + T_e \frac{C_h}{C_e} + T_d \qquad (4.9)$$

The daily standard production rate P_h of a hauler can be obtained by multiplying its standard production rate R_h by the number of operating hours H_h per day. Hence,

$$P_h = R_h H_h = \frac{C_h H_h}{T_h} \qquad (4.10)$$

This expression assumes that haulers begin loading as soon as they return from the dump site.

The number of haulers required is also of interest. Let w denote the swell factor of the soil such that $w P_e$ denotes the daily volume of loose excavated materials resulting from the excavation volume P_e. Then the approximate number of haulers required to dispose of the excavated materials is given by

$$N_h = \frac{wP_e}{P_h} \qquad (4.11)$$

While the standard production rate of a piece of equipment is based on "standard" or ideal conditions, equipment productivities at job sites are influenced by actual work conditions and a variety of inefficiencies and work stoppages. As one example, various factor adjustments can be used to account in an approximate fashion for actual site conditions. If the conditions that lower the standard production rate are denoted by n factors $F_1, F_2, \ldots, F_n$, each of which is smaller than 1, then the actual equipment productivity R' at the job site can be related to the standard production rate R as follows:

$$R' \approx RF_1F_2 \ldots F_n \qquad (4.12)$$

On the other hand, the cycle time T' at the job site will be increased by these factors, reflecting actual work conditions. If only these factors are involved, T' is related to the standard cycle time T as

$$T' \approx \frac{T}{F_1F_2 \ldots F_n} \qquad (4.13)$$

Each of these various adjustment factors must be determined from experience or observation of job sites. For example, a bulk composition factor is derived for bulk excavation in building construction because the standard production rate for general bulk excavation is reduced when an excavator is used to create a ramp to reach the bottom of the bulk and to open up a space in the bulk to accommodate the hauler. In addition to the problem of estimating the various factors, $F_1, F_2, \ldots, F_n$, it may also be important to account for interactions among the factors and the exact influence of particular site characteristics.

Example 4-9: Daily Standard Production Rate of a Power Shovel[45]

A power shovel with a dipper of 1 cubic yard (yd^3) capacity has a standard operating cycle time of 30 seconds (sec). Find the daily standard production rate of the shovel.
For $C_e = 1$ yd^3, $T_e = 30$ sec, and $H_e = 8$ hr, the daily standard production rate is found from Eq. (4.6) as follows:

$$P_e = \frac{(1 \text{ yd}^3)(8 \text{ hr})(3,600 \text{ sec/hr})}{30 \text{ sec}} = 960 \text{ yd}^3$$

In practice, of course, this standard rate would be modified to reflect various production inefficiencies, as described in Example 4-11.

Example 4-10: Daily Standard Production Rate of a Dump Truck

A dump truck with a capacity of 6 yd^3 is used to dispose of excavated materials at a dump site 4 miles away. The average speed of the dump truck is 30 mph and the

---

[45] This and the following examples in this section have been adapted from E. Baracco-Miller and C. T. Hendrickson, *Planning for Construction*, Technical Report No. R-87-162, Department of Civil Engineering, Carnegie Mellon University, Pittsburgh, 1987.

dumping time is 30 sec. Find the daily standard production rate of the truck. If a fleet of dump trucks of this capacity is used to dispose of the excavated materials in Example 4-8 for 8 hrs per day, determine the number of trucks needed daily, assuming a swell factor of 1.1 for the soil.

The daily standard production rate of a dump truck can be obtained by using Eqs. (4.7) through (4.10):

$$T_t = \frac{(2)(4 \text{ mi})(3,600 \text{ sec/hr})}{(30 \text{ mi/hr})} = 960 \text{ sec}$$

$$T_o = (30 \text{ sec})\left(\frac{6 \text{ yd}^3}{1 \text{ yd}^3}\right) = 180 \text{ sec}$$

$$T_h = 960 + 180 + 30 = 1,170 \text{ sec}$$

Hence, the daily hauler productivity is:

$$P_h = \frac{(6 \text{ yd}^3)(8 \text{ hr})(3,600 \text{ sec/hr})}{(1,170 \text{ sec})} = 147.7 \text{ yd}^3$$

Finally, from Eq. (4.11), the number of trucks required is:

$$N_h = \frac{(1.1)(960 \text{ yd}^3)}{147.7 \text{ yd}^3} = 7.1$$

implying that 8 trucks should be used.

Example 4-11: Job Site Productivity of a Power Shovel

A power shovel with a dipper of 1 yd^3 (in Example 4-9) has a standard production rate of 960 yd^3 for an 8-hr day. Determine the job-site productivity and the actual cycle time of this shovel under the work conditions at the site that affects its productivity as shown:

Work Conditions at the Site	Factors
Bulk composition	0.954
Soil properties and water content	0.983
Equipment idle time for worker breaks	0.8
Management efficiency	0.7

Using Eq. (4.11), the job site productivity of the power shovel per day is given by

$$P_e' = (960 \text{ yd}^3)(0.954)(0.983)(0.8)(0.7) = 504 \text{ yd}^3$$

The actual cycle time can be determined as follows:

$$T_e' = \frac{(30 \text{ sec})}{(0.954)(0.983)(0.8)(0.7)} = 57 \text{ sec}$$

Noting Eq.(4.6), the actual cycle time can also be obtained from the relation $T_e' = \frac{C_e H_e}{P_e'}$. Thus,

$$T_e' = \frac{(1 \text{ yd}^3)(8 \text{ hr})(3,600 \text{ sec/hr})}{504 \text{ yd}^3} = 57 \text{ sec}$$

Example 4-12: Job-Site Productivity of a Dump Truck

A dump truck with a capacity of 6 yd^3 (in Example 4-10) is used to dispose of excavated materials. The distance from the dump site is 4 miles and the average speed of the dump truck is 30 mph. The job-site productivity of the power shovel per day (in Example 4-11) is 504 yd^3, which will be modified by a swell factor of 1.1. The only factors affecting the job-site productivity of the dump truck are 0.80 for equipment idle time and 0.70 for management efficiency. Determine the job-site productivity of the dump truck. If a fleet of such trucks is used to haul the excavated material, find the number of trucks needed daily.

The actual cycle time T'_h of the dump truck can be obtained by summing the actual times for traveling, loading, and dumping:

$$T'_t = \frac{T_t}{F_1 F_2} = \frac{(2)(4 \text{ mi})(3,600 \text{ sec/hr})}{(30 \text{ mi/hr})(0.8)(0.7)} = 1,714 \text{ sec}$$

$$T'_o = \frac{T'_e C_h}{F_1 F_2 C_e} = \left(\frac{57 \text{ sec}}{(0.8)(0.7)}\right)\left(\frac{6 \text{ yd}^3}{1 \text{ yd}^3}\right) = 342 \text{ sec}$$

$$T'_d = \frac{T_d}{F_1 F_2} = \frac{30 \text{ sec}}{(0.8)(0.7)} = 54 \text{ sec}$$

Hence, the actual cycle time is

$$T'_h = T'_t + T'_o + T'_d = 1,714 + 611 + 54 = 2,379 \text{ sec}$$

The job-site productivity P'_h of the dump truck per day is

$$P'_h = \frac{C_h H_h}{T'_h} = \frac{(6 \text{ yd}^3)(8 \text{ hr})(3,600 \text{ sec/hr})}{2,379 \text{ sec}} = 72.6 \text{ yd}^3$$

The number of trucks needed daily is

$$N'_h = \frac{w P'_e}{P'_h} = \frac{(1.1)(504 \text{ yd}^3)}{72.6 \text{ yd}^3} = 7.6$$

so 8 trucks are required.

4.12 CONSTRUCTION PROCESSES

The previous sections described the primary inputs of labor, material, and equipment to the construction process. At varying levels of detail, a project manager must ensure that these inputs are effectively coordinated to achieve an efficient construction process. This coordination involves both strategic decisions and tactical management in the field. For example, strategic decisions about appropriate technologies or site layout are often made during the process of construction planning. During the course of construction, foremen and site managers will make decisions about work to be undertaken at particular times of the day based upon the availability of the necessary resources of labor, materials, and equipment. Without coordination among these necessary inputs, the construction process will be inefficient or stop altogether.

Example 4-13: Steel Erection

Erection of structural steel for buildings, bridges, or other facilities is an example of a construction process requiring considerable coordination. Fabricated steel pieces must arrive on site in the correct order and quantity for the planned effort during a day. Crews of steelworkers must be available to fit pieces together, bolt joints, and perform any necessary welding. Cranes and crane operators may be required to lift fabricated components into place; other activities on a job site may also be competing for use of particular cranes. Welding equipment, wrenches, and other hand tools must be readily available. Finally, ancillary materials such as bolts of the correct size must be provided.

In coordinating a process such as steel erection, it is common to assign different tasks to specific crews. For example, one crew may place members in place and insert a few bolts in joints in a specific area. A following crew would be assigned to finish bolting, and a third crew might perform necessary welds or attachment of brackets for items such as curtain walls.

With the required coordination among these resources, it is easy to see how poor management or other problems can result in considerable inefficiency. For example, if a shipment of fabricated steel is improperly prepared, the crews and equipment on site may have to wait for new deliveries.

Example 4-14: Construction Process Simulation Models

Computer-based simulation of construction operations can be a useful although laborious tool in analyzing the efficiency of particular processes or technologies. These tools tend to be either oriented toward modeling resource processes or toward representation of spatial constraints and resource movements. Later chapters will describe simulation in more detail, but a small example of a construction operation model can be described here.[46] The process involved placing concrete within existing formwork for the columns of a new structure. A crane-and-bucket combination with a capacity of 1 yd^3 and a flexible "elephant trunk" was assumed for placement. Concrete was delivered in trucks with a capacity of 8 yd^3. Because of site constraints, only one truck could be moved into the delivery position at a time. Construction workers and electric immersion-type concrete vibrators were also assumed for the process.

The simulation model of this process is illustrated in Figure 4-5. Node 2 signals the availability of a concrete truck arriving from the batch plant. As with other circular nodes in Figure 4-5, the availability of a truck may result in a resource waiting or *queueing* for use. If a truck (node 2) and the crane (node 3) are both available, then the crane can load and hoist a bucket of concrete (node 4). As with other rectangular nodes in the model, this operation will require an appreciable period of time. On the completion of the load and hoist operations, the bucket (node 5) is available for concrete placement. Placement is accomplished by having a worker guide the bucket's elephant trunk between the concrete forms and having a second worker operate the bucket release lever. A third laborer operates a vibrator in the concrete while the bucket (node 8) moves back to receive a new load. Once the concrete placement is complete, the crew becomes available to place a new bucket load (node 7). After two buckets are placed, then the column is complete (node 9) and the equipment

---

[46] This model used the INSIGHT simulation language and was described in B. C. Paulson, W. T. Chan, and C. C. Koo, "Construction Operations Simulation by Microcomputer," *ASCE Journal of Construction Engineering and Management*, Vol. 113, no. 2, 1987, pp. 302–314.

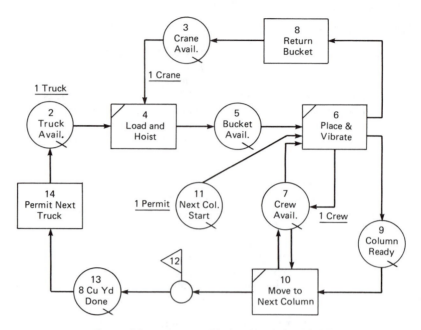

Figure 4-5 A Concrete-Placing Simulation Model

and crew can move to the next column (node 10). After the movement to the new column is complete, placement in the new column can begin (node 11). Finally, after a truck is emptied (nodes 12 and 13), the truck departs and a new truck can enter the delivery stall (node 14) if one is waiting.

Application of the simulation model consists of tracing through the time required for these various operations. Events are also simulated such as the arrival times of concrete trucks. If random elements are introduced, numerous simulations are required to estimate the actual productivity and resource requirements of the process. For example, one simulation of this process using four concrete trucks found that a truck was waiting 83 percent of the time with an average wait at the site of 14 mins. This type of simulation can be used to estimate the various productivity adjustment factors described in the previous section.

4.13 QUEUES AND RESOURCE BOTTLENECKS

A project manager needs to ensure that resources required for and/or shared by numerous activities are adequate. Problems in this area can be indicated in part by the existence of queues of resource demands during construction operations. A *queue* can be a *waiting line* for service. One can imagine a queue as an orderly line of customers waiting for a stationary server such as a ticket seller. However, the demands for service might not be so neatly arranged. For example, we can speak of the *queue* of welds on a building site waiting for inspection. In this case, demands do not come to the server, but a roving inspector travels among the waiting service points. Waiting for resources such as a particular piece of equipment or a particular individual is an endemic problem on construction sites. If workers spend appreciable portions of time waiting for particular tools, materials, or an inspector, costs increase and productivity declines. Ensuring adequate resources to serve expected demands is an important problem during construction planning and field management.

In general, there is a trade-off between waiting times and utilization of resources. Utilization is the proportion of time a particular resource is in productive use. Higher amounts of resource utilization will be beneficial as long as it does not impose undue costs on the entire operation. For example, a welding inspector might have 100 percent utilization, but workers throughout the job site might be wasting inordinate time waiting for inspections. Providing additional inspectors may be cost effective, even if they are not utilized at all times.

A few conceptual models of queueing systems may be helpful to construction planners in considering the level of adequate resources to provide. First, we shall consider the case of time-varying demands and a server with a constant service rate. This might be the situation for an elevator in which large demands for transportation occur during the morning or at a shift change. Second, we shall consider the situation of randomly arriving demands for service and constant service rates. Finally, we shall consider briefly the problems involving multiple serving stations.

Single Server with Deterministic Arrivals and Services

Suppose that the cumulative number of demands for service or "customers" at any time t is known and is equal to the value of the function $A(t)$. These "customers" might be crane loads, weld inspections, or any other defined group of items to be serviced. Suppose further that a single server is available to handle these demands, such as a single crane or a single inspector. For this model of queueing, we assume that the server can handle customers at some constant, maximum rate denoted as x "customers" per unit of time. This is a maximum rate since the server may be idle for periods of time if no customers are waiting. This system is *deterministic* in the sense that both the arrival function and the service process are assumed to have no random or unknown component.

A cumulative arrival function of customers, $A(t)$, is shown in Figure 4-6 in which the vertical axis represents the cumulative number of customers, while the horizontal axis represents the passage of time. The arrival of individual customers to the queue would actually represent a unit step in the arrival function $A(t)$, but these small steps are approximated by a continuous curve in the figure. The rate of arrivals for a unit time interval Δt from $t - 1$ to t is given by:

$$\Delta A_t = A(t) - A(t - 1) \qquad (4.14)$$

While an hour or a minute is a natural choice as a unit time interval, other time periods may also be used as long as the passage of time is expressed as multiples of such time periods. For instance, if half an hour is used as unit time interval for a process involving 10 hours, then the arrivals should be represented by 20 steps of a half-hour each. Hence, the unit time interval between $t - 1$ and

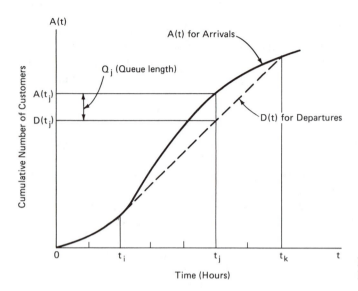

Figure 4-6 Cumulative Arrivals and Departures in a Deterministic Queue

Time (Hours)

t is $\Delta t = t - (t - 1) = 1$, and the slope of the cumulative arrival function in the interval is given by

$$A'(t) = \frac{A(t) - A(t - 1)}{\Delta t} = A(t) - A(t - 1) \qquad (4.15)$$

The cumulative number of customers served over time is represented by the cumulative departure function $D(t)$. While the maximum service rate is x per unit time, the actual service rate for a unit time interval Δt from $t-1$ to t is

$$\Delta D_t = D(t) - D(t - 1) \qquad (4.16)$$

The slope of the cumulative departure function is

$$D'(t) = \frac{D(t) - D(t - 1)}{\Delta t} = D(t) - D(t - 1) \qquad (4.17)$$

Any time that the rate of arrivals to the queue exceeds the maximum service rate, then a queue begins to form and the cumulative departures will occur at the maximum service rate. The cumulative departures from the queue will proceed at the maximum service rate of x "customers" per unit of time, so that the slope of $D(t)$ is x during this period. The cumulative departure function $D(t)$ can be readily constructed graphically by running a ruler with a slope of x along the cumulative arrival function $A(t)$. As soon as the function $A(t)$ climbs above the ruler, a queue begins to form. The maximum service rate will continue until the queue disappears, which is represented by the convergence of the cumulative arrival and departure functions $A(t)$ and $D(t)$.

With the cumulative arrivals and cumulative departure functions represented graphically, a variety of service indicators can be readily obtained as shown in Fig-

Labor, Material, and Equipment Utilization   Chap. 4

ure 4-6. Let $A'(t)$ and $D'(t)$ denote the derivatives of $A(t)$ and $D(t)$ with respect to t, respectively. For $0 \le t \le t_i$ in which $A'(t) \le x$, there is no queue. At $t = t_i$, when $A'(t) > D'(t)$, a queue is formed. Then $D'(t) = x$ in the interval $t_i \le t \le t_k$. As $A'(t)$ continues to increase with increasing t, the queue becomes longer since the service rate $D'(t) = x$ cannot catch up with the arrivals. However, when again $A'(t) \le D'(t)$ as t increases, the queue becomes shorter until it reaches 0 at $t = t_k$. At any given time t, the queue length is

$$Q(t) = A(t) - D(t) \tag{4.18}$$

For example, suppose a queue begins to form at time t_i and is dispersed by time t_k. The maximum number of customers waiting or queue length is represented by the maximum difference between the cumulative arrival and cumulative departure functions between t_i and t_k, that is, the maximum value of $Q(t)$. The total waiting time for service is indicated by the total area between the cumulative arrival and cumulative departure functions.

Generally, the arrival rates $\Delta A_t = 1, 2, \ldots, n$ periods of a process as well as the maximum service rate x are known. Then the cumulative arrival function and the cumulative departure function can be constructed systematically together with other pertinent quantities as follows:

1. Starting with the initial conditions $D(t - 1) = 0$ and $Q(t - 1) = 0$ at $t = 1$, find the actual service rate at $t = 1$:

$$\Delta D_1 = \text{minimum } \{x; A_1\} \tag{4.19}$$

2. Starting with $A(t - 1) = 0$ at $t = 1$, find the cumulative arrival function for $t = 2, 3, \ldots, n$ accordingly

$$A(t) = A(t - 1) + \Delta A_t \tag{4.20}$$

3. Compute the queue length for $t = 1, 2, \ldots, n$:

$$Q(t) = Q(t - 1) + \Delta A_t - \Delta D_t \tag{4.21}$$

4. Compute ΔD_t for $t = 2, 3, \ldots, n$ after $Q(t - 1)$ is found first for each t:

$$\Delta D_t = \text{minimum } \{x; Q(t - 1) + \Delta A_t\} \tag{4.22}$$

5. If $A'(t) > x$, find the cumulative departure function in the time period between t_i where a queue is formed and t_k where the queue dissipates:

$$D(t) = D(t - 1) + \Delta D_t \tag{4.23}$$

6. Compute the waiting time Δw for the arrivals which are waiting for service in interval Δt:

$$\Delta w = Q(t)(\Delta t) \tag{4.24}$$

7. Compute the total waiting time W over the time period between t_i and t_k:

$$W = \sum_{t=t_i}^{t_k} \Delta w \qquad (4.25)$$

8. Compute the average waiting time w for arrivals which are waiting for service in the process:

$$w = \frac{W^{\cdot}}{A(t_k) - A(t_i)} \qquad (4.26)$$

This simple, deterministic model has a number of implications for operations planning. First, an increase in the maximum service rate will result in reductions in waiting time and the maximum queue length. Such increases might be obtained by speeding up the service rate such as introducing shorter inspection procedures or installing faster cranes on a site. Second, altering the pattern of cumulative arrivals can result in changes in total waiting time and in the maximum queue length. In particular, if the maximum arrival rate never exceeds the maximum service rate, no queue will form, or if the arrival rate always exceeds the maximum service rate, the bottleneck cannot be dispersed. Both cases are shown in Figure 4-7.

A practical means to alter the arrival function and obtain these benefits is to inaugurate a reservation system for customers. Even without drawing a graph such as Figure 4-6, good operations planners should consider the effects of different operation or service rates on the flow of work. Clearly, service rates less than the expected arrival rate of work will result in resource bottlenecks on a job.

Single Server with Random Arrivals and Constant Service Rate

Suppose that arrivals of "customers" to a queue are not deterministic or known as in Figure 4-6. In particular, suppose that "customers" such as joints are completed

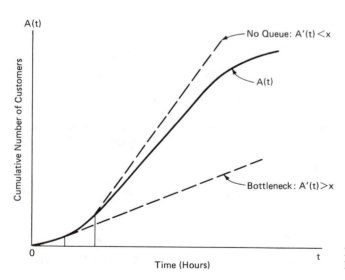

Figure 4-7   Cases of No Queue and Permanent Bottleneck

or crane loads arrive at random intervals. What are the implications for the smooth flow of work? Unfortunately, bottlenecks and queues may arise in this situation even if the maximum service rate is larger than the average or expected arrival rate of customers. This occurs because random arrivals will often bunch together, thereby temporarily exceeding the capacity of the system. While the average arrival rate may not change over time, temporary resource shortages can occur in this circumstance.

Let w be the average waiting time, a be the average arrival rate of customers, and x be the deterministic constant service rate (in customers per unit of time). Then, the expected average time for a customer in this situation is given by[47]

$$w = \frac{a}{2x^2(1 - a/x)}$$

If the average utilization rate of the service is defined as the ratio of the average arrival rate and the constant service rate, for example,

$$u = \frac{a}{x}$$

Then, Eq. (4.27) becomes

$$w = \frac{u}{2x(1 - u)} \qquad (4.29)$$

In this equation, the ratio u of arrival rate to service rate is very important: if the average arrival rate approaches the service rate, the waiting time can be very long. If $a \geq x$, then the queue expands indefinitely. Resource bottlenecks will occur with random arrivals unless a measure of extra service capacity is available to accommodate sudden bunches in the arrival stream. Figure 4-8 illustrates the waiting time resulting from different combinations of arrival rates and service times.

Multiple Servers

Both of the simple models of service performance just described are limited to single servers. In operations planning, it is commonly the case that numerous operators are available and numerous stages of operations exist. In these circumstances, a planner typically attempts to match the service rates occurring at different stages in the process. For example, construction of a highrise building involves a series of operations on each floor, including erection of structural elements, pouring or assembling a floor, construction of walls, installation of HVAC (heating, ventilating,

---

[47] In the literature of queueing theory, this formula represents an M/D/1 queue, meaning that the arrival process is Markovian or random, the service time is fixed, only one server exists, and the system is in "steady state," implying that the service time and average arrival rate are constant. Altering these assumptions would require changes in the waiting time formula; for example, if service times were also random, the waiting time formula would not have the 2 shown in the denominator of Eq. (4.27). For more details on queueing systems, see G. F. Newell, *Applications of Queueing Theory*, Chapman and Hall, London, 1982.

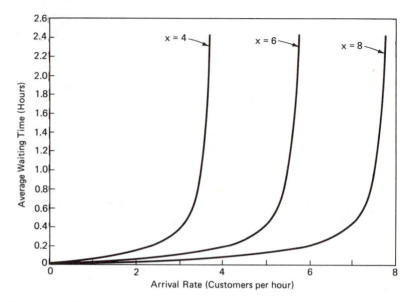

Figure 4-8 Waiting Times for Different Average Arrivals Rates and Service Times

and air conditioning) equipment, installation of plumbing and electric wiring, and so on. A smooth construction process would have each of these various activities occurring at different floors at the same time without large time gaps between activities on any particular floor. Thus, floors would be installed soon after erection of structural elements, walls would follow subsequently, and so on. From the standpoint of a queuing system, the planning problem is to ensure that the productivity or service rate per floor of these different activities are approximately equal, so that one crew is not continually waiting on the completion of a preceding activity or interfering with a following activity. In the realm of manufacturing systems, creating this balance among operations is called *assembly-line* balancing.

Example 4-15: Effect of a Crane Breakdown

Suppose that loads for a crane are arriving at a steady rate of 1 every 10 minutes. The crane has the capacity to handle one load every 5 minutes. Suppose further that the crane breaks down for 90 minutes. How many loads are delayed, what is the total delay, and how long will be required before the crane can catch up with the backlog of loads?

The cumulative arrival and service functions are graphed in Figure 4-9. Starting with the breakdown at time 0, 9 loads arrive during the 90-minute repair time.

From Figure 4-9, an additional 9 loads arrive before the entire queue is served. Algebraically, the required time for service, t, can be calculated by noting that the number of arrivals must equal the number of loads served. Thus,

$$A(t) = \frac{t}{10} \text{ for } t \geq 0$$

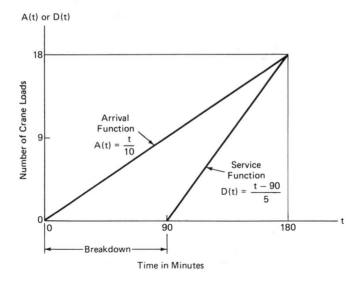

Figure 4-9 Arrivals and Services of Crane Loads with a Crane Breakdown

$$D_1(t) = 0 \text{ for } 0 \le t \le 90 \text{ min}$$

$$D_2(t) = \frac{t - 90}{5} \text{ for } t \ge 90 \text{ min}$$

A queue is formed at $t = 0$ because of the breakdown, but it dissipates at $A(t) = D_2(t)$. Let

$$\frac{t}{10} = \frac{t - 90}{5}$$

from which we obtain $t = 180$ min. Hence

$$A(180) = D_2(180) = 18 \text{ loads}$$

The total waiting time W can be calculated as the area between the cumulative arrival and service functions in Figure 4-9. Algebraically, this is conveniently calculated as the difference in the areas of two triangles:

$$W = \frac{(18)(180)}{2} - \frac{(18)(90)}{2} = 810 \text{ min}$$

so the average delay per load is $w = 810/18 = 45$ minutes

Example 4-16: Waiting Time with Random Arrivals

Suppose that material loads to be inspected arrive randomly but with an average of 5 arrivals per hour. Each load requires 10 minutes for an inspection, so an inspector can handle 6 loads per hour. Inspections must be completed before the material can be unloaded from a truck. The cost per hour of holding a material load in waiting is $30, representing the cost of a driver and a truck. In this example, the arrival rate, a, equals 5 arrivals per hour and the service rate, x, equals 6 material loads per hour. Then, the average waiting time of any material load for $u = 5/6$ is

$$\frac{5/6}{(2)(6) - (1 - 5/6)} = 0.4 \text{ hr}$$

At a resource cost of $30.00 per hour, this waiting would represent a cost of $(30)(0.4)(5) = \$60.00$ per hour on the project.

In contrast, if the possible service rate is $x = 10$ material loads per hour, then the expected waiting time of any material load for $u = 5/10 = 0.5$ is

$$\frac{0.5}{(2)(10)(1 - 0.5)} = 0.05 \text{ hr}$$

which has only a cost of $(30)\ (0.05)\ (5) = \$7.50$ per hour.

Example 4-17: Delay of Lift Loads on a Building Site

Suppose that a single crane is available on a building site and that each lift requires 3 minutes including the time for attaching loads. Suppose further that the cumulative arrivals of lift loads at different time periods are as follows:

6:00–7:00 A.M.	4 per hour	12:00–4:00 P.M.	8 per hour
7:00–8:00 A.M.	15 per hour	4:00–6:00 P.M.	4 per hour
8:00–11:00 A.M.	25 per hour	6:00 P.M.–6:00 A.M.	0 per hour
11:00–12:00 A.M.	5 per hour		

Using the foregoing information of arrival and service rates

1. Find the cumulative arrivals and cumulative number of loads served as a function of time, beginning with 6:00 A.M.
2. Estimate the maximum queue length of loads waiting for service. What time does the maximum queue occur?
3. Estimate the total waiting time for loads.
4. Graph the cumulative arrival and departure functions.

The maximum service rate $x = 60$ min/3 min per lift $= 20$ lifts per minute. The detailed computation can be carried out in the Table 4-2, and the graph of $A(t)$ and $D(t)$ is given in Figure 4-10.

4.14 REFERENCES

4-1. Bourdon, C. C., and R. W. Levitt, *Union and Open Shop Construction*, Lexington Books, D.C. Heath and Co., Lexington, MA, 1980.
4-2. *Caterpillar Performance Handbook*, 18th ed., Caterpillar, Inc., Peoria, IL, 1987.

TABLE 4–2 COMPUTATION OF QUEUE LENGTH AND WAITING TIME

Period	Arrival rate	Cumulative arrivals $A(t)$	Queue	Departure rate	Cumulative departures $D(t)$	Waiting time
5–7:00	4	4	0	4	4	0
7–8:00	15	19	0	15	19	0
8–9:00	25	44	5	20	39	5
9–10:00	25	69	10	20	59	10
10–11:00	25	94	15	20	79	15
11–12:00	5	99	0	20	99	0
12–1:00	8	107	0	8	107	0
1–2:00	8	115	0	8	115	0
2–3:00	8	123	0	8	123	0
3–4:00	8	131	0	8	131	0
4–5:00	4	135	0	4	135	0
5–6:00	4	139	0	4	139	9
6–7:00	0	139	0	0	139	0
7–8:00	0	139	0	0	139	0

Total waiting time = 30
Maximum queue = 15

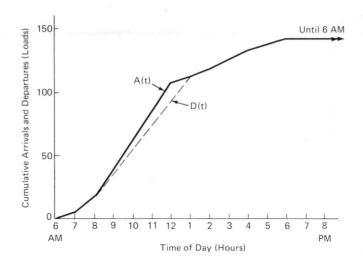

Figure 4-10 Delay of Lift Loads on a Building Site

4-3. Cordell, R. H., "Construction Productivity Management," *Cost Engineering*, Vol. 28, no. 2, February 1986, pp. 14–23.

4-4. Lange, J. E., and D. Q. Mills, *The Construction Industry*, Lexington Books, D.C. Heath and Co., Lexington, MA, 1979.

4-5. Nunnally, S. W., *Construction Methods and Management*, 2nd ed., Prentice Hall, Englewoood Cliffs, NJ, 1987.

4-6. Peurifoy, R. L., *Construction Planning, Equipment and Methods*, 2nd ed., McGraw-Hill Book Company, NY, 1970.

4-7. Tersine, R. J., *Principles of Inventory and Materials Management*, North Holland, NY, 1982.

4.15 PROBLEMS

P4-1. Using the relationship between the productivity index and job size in Example 4-1, determine the labor productivity for a new job requiring 350,000 labor-hours under otherwise the same set of work conditions.

P4-2. The potential labor-hours available for a large energy complex were found to be 5.4 million hours. The nonproductive activities in thousands of labor-hours were:

1. 360 for holidays and strikes
2. 1,152 for absentees
3. 785 for temporary stoppage
4. 1,084 for indirect labor

Determine the productive labor yield after the foregoing factors are taken into consideration.

P4-3. Labor productivity at job site is known to decrease with overtime work. Let x be the percentage of overtime over normal workweek. If x is expressed in decimals, the productivity index I as a function of the percentage of overtime is found to be

$$I = -0.8x^2 + 1 \qquad 0 \le x \le 0.5$$

Find the value of the index I for $x = 0, 0.1, 0.2, 0.3, 0.4,$ and 0.5, and plot the relationship in a graph.

P4-4. Labor productivity for a complex project is known to increase gradually in the first 500,000 labor-hours because of the learning effects. Let x be the number of 100,000 labor-hours. The labor productivity index I is found to be a function of x as follows:

$$I = \begin{cases} -0.016x^2 + 0.16x + 0.6 \text{ for } < x \le 5 \\ 1.0 \text{ for } x \ge 5 \end{cases}$$

Find the value of the index I for $x = 0, 1, 2, 3, 4,$ and 5 and plot the relationship in a graph.

P4-5. The probabilities for different delivery times of an item are given in the table. Find the expected delivery date of the item. Also find the lead time required to provide an expected delivery date one day less than the desired delivery date.

t	$p(t)$	$Pr\{T \le t\}$
12	0.05	0.05
13	0.10	0.15
14	0.25	0.40
15	0.35	0.75
16	0.15	0.90
17	0.10	1.00

P4-6. A power shovel with a dipper of 2 yd^3 capacity has a standard operating cycle time of 80 sec. The excavated material which has a swell factor of 1.05 will be disposed by a dump truck with an 8 yd^3 capacity at a dump site 6 miles away. The average speed of the dump truck is 30 mph and the dumping time is 40 sec. Find the daily standard production rates of the power shovel and the dump truck if both are operated 8 hr per day. Determine also the number of trucks needed daily to dispose of the excavated material.

P4-7. The power shovel in Problem P4-6 has a daily standard production rate of 720 yd^3. Determine the job site productivity and the actual cycle time of this shovel under the work conditions at the site that affect the productivity as shown:

Work conditions at site	Factors
Bulk composition	0.972
Soil properties and water content	0.960
Equipment idle time for breaks	0.750
Management inefficiency	0.750

P4-8. Based on the information given for Problems P4-6 and P4-7, find the job-site productivity of a dump truck, assuming that the only factors affecting work conditions are 0.85 for equipment idle time and 0.80 for management efficiency. Also find the number of dump trucks required.

P4-9. A power shovel with a dipper of 1.5 yd^3 capacity has a standard operating cycle time of 60 sec. The excavated material which has a swell factor of 1.08 will be disposed by a dump truck with a 7.5 yd^3 capacity at a dumpsite 5 miles away. The average speed of a dump truck is 25 mph and the dumping time is 75 sec. Both the power shovel and the dump truck are operated 8 hr per day.

  a. Find the daily standard production rate of the power shovel.
  b. Find the daily standard production rate of the dump truck and number of trucks required.
  c. If the work conditions at the site that affect the productivity of the shovel can be represented by four factors $F_1 = 0.940$, $F_2 = 0.952$, $F_3 = 0.850$, and $F_4 = 0.750$, determine the job-site productivity and the actual cycle time.
  d. If the work conditions at the site affect the productivity of the dump truck can be represented by three factors $F_1 = 0.952$, $F_2 = 0.700$ and $F_3 = 0.750$, determine the job-site productivity of the dump truck and the number of dump trucks required.

P4-10. Suppose that a single piece of equipment is available on a site for testing joints. Further, suppose that each joint has to be tested and certified before work can proceed. Joints are completed and ready for testing at random intervals during a shift. Each test requires an average of 10 minutes. What is the average utilization of the testing equipment and the average wait of a completed joint for testing if the number of joints completed is (a) five per hour or (b) three per hour.

P4-11. Suppose that the steel plates to be inspected are arriving steadily at a rate of one every 12 minutes. Each inspection requires 16 minutes, but two inspectors area available so the inspection service rate is one every 8 minutes. Suppose one inspector takes a break for 60 minutes. What is the resulting delay in the arriving pieces? What is the average delay among the pieces that have to wait?

P4-12. Suppose that three machines are available in a fabrication shop for testing welded joints of structural members so that the testing service rate of the three machines is one in every 20 minutes. However, one of the three machines is shut down for 90 minutes when the welded joints to be tested arrive at a rate of one in every 25 minutes. What is the total delay for the testing service of the arriving joints? What is the average delay? Sketch the cumulative arrivals and services versus time.

P4-13. Solve Example 4-17 if each lift requires 5 minutes instead of 3 minutes.

P4-14. Solve Example 4-17 if each lift requires 6 minutes instead of 3 minutes.

P-15. Suppose that up to 12 customers can be served per hour in an automated inspection process. What is the total waiting time and maximum queue with arrival rates for both cases (a) and (b):

	(a)	(b)
6–7:00 A.M.	0	0
7–8:00 A.M.	25	10
8–9:00 A.M.	25	10
9–10:00 A.M.	25	15
10–11:00 A.M.	25	15
11–12:00 A.M.	10	10
12–1:00 P.M.	8	15
1–2:00 P.M.	0	15
2–3:00 P.M.	0	10
3–4:00 P.M.	0	10
4–5:00 P.M.	0	10
After 5 P.M.	0	0
Total number of arrivals	118	120

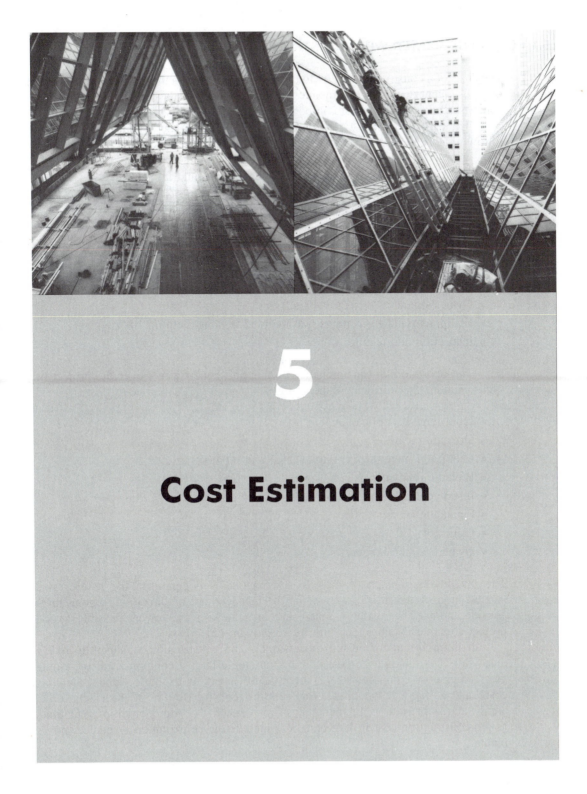

5

Cost Estimation

5.1 COSTS ASSOCIATED WITH CONSTRUCTED FACILITIES

The costs of a constructed facility to the owner include both the initial capital cost and the subsequent operation and maintenance costs. Each of these major cost categories consists of a number of cost components.

The capital cost for a construction project includes the expenses related to the following activities:

- Land acquisition, including assembly, holding, and improvement
- Planning and feasibility studies
- Architectural and engineering design
- Construction, including materials, equipment, and labor
- Field supervision of construction
- Construction financing
- Insurance and taxes during construction
- Owner's general office overhead
- Equipment and furnishings not included in construction
- Inspection and testing

The operation and maintenance cost in subsequent years over the project life cycle includes the following expenses:

- Land rent, if applicable
- Operating staff
- Labor and material for maintenance and repairs
- Periodic renovations
- Insurance and taxes
- Financing costs
- Utilities
- Owner's other expenses

The magnitude of each of these cost components depends on the nature, size, and location of the project as well as the management organization, among many considerations. The owner is interested in achieving the lowest possible overall project cost that is consistent with its investment objectives.

It is important for design professionals and construction managers to realize that while the construction cost may be the single largest component of the capital cost, other cost components are not insignificant. For example, land acquisition costs are a major expenditure for building construction in high-density urban areas, and construction financing costs can reach the same order of magnitude as the construction cost in large projects such as the construction of nuclear power plants.

From the owner's perspective, it is equally important to estimate the corresponding operation and maintenance cost of each alternative for a proposed facility to analyze the life-cycle costs. The large expenditures needed for facility maintenance, especially for publicly owned infrastructure, are reminders of the neglect in the past to consider fully the implications of operation and maintenance cost in the design stage.

In this chapter, we shall focus on the estimation of construction cost, with only occasional reference to other cost components. In Chapter 6, we shall deal with the economic evaluation of a constructed facility on the basis of both the capital cost and the operation and maintenance cost in the life-cycle of the facility. It is at this stage that trade-offs between operating and capital costs can be analyzed.

Example 5-1: Energy Project Resource Demands [48]

The resource demands for three types of major energy projects investigated during the energy crisis in the 1970s are shown in Table 5-1. These projects are (1) an oil shale project with a capacity of 50,000 barrels of oil product per day; (2) a coal gasification project that makes gas with a heating value of 320 billions of British thermal units per day, or equivalent to about 50,000 barrels of oil product per day; and (3) a tar sand project with a capacity of 150,000 barrels of oil product per day.

For each project, the cost in billions of dollars, the engineering personnel requirement for basic design in thousands of hours, the engineering personnel requirement for detailed engineering in millions of hours, the skilled labor requirement for construction in millions of hours, and the material requirement in billions of dollars are shown in Table 5-1. To build several projects of such an order of magnitude concurrently could drive up the costs and strain the availability of all resources required to complete the projects. Consequently, cost estimation often represents an exercise in professional judgment instead of merely compiling a bill of quantities and collecting cost data to reach a total estimate mechanically.

TABLE 5–1 RESOURCE REQUIREMENTS OF SOME MAJOR ENERGY PROJECTS

	Oil shale (50,000 barrels/day)	Coal gasification (320 billions BTU/day)	Tar sands (150,000 barrels/day)
Cost ($ billion)	2.5	4	8 to 10
Basic design (thousands of hours)	80	200	100
Detailed engineering (millions of hours)	3 to 4	4 to 5	6 to 8
Construction (millions of hours)	20	30	40
Materials ($ billion)	1	2	2.5

Source: Exxon Research and Engineering Company, Florham Park, NJ.

[48] This example was adapted with permission from a paper, "Forecasting Industry Resources," presented by A. R. Crosby at the Institution of Chemical Engineers in London, November 4, 1981.

5.2 APPROACHES TO COST ESTIMATION

Cost estimating is one of the most important steps in project management. A cost estimate establishes the baseline of the project cost at different stages of development of the project. A cost estimate at a given stage of project development represents a prediction provided by the cost engineer or estimator on the basis of available data. According to the American Association of Cost Engineers, cost engineering is defined as that area of engineering practice where engineering judgment and experience are utilized in the application of scientific principles and techniques to the problem of cost estimation, cost control, and profitability.

Virtually all cost estimation is performed according to one or some combination of the following basic approaches:

Production function.   In microeconomics, the relationship between the output of a process and the necessary resources is referred to as the production function. In construction, the production function may be expressed by the relationship between the volume of construction and a factor of production such as labor or capital. A production function relates the amount or volume of output to the various inputs of labor, material, and equipment. For example, the amount of output Q may be derived as a function of various input factors $x_1, x_2, \ldots, x_n$ by means of mathematical and/or statistical methods. Thus, for a specified level of output, we may attempt to find a set of values for the input factors so as to minimize the production cost. The relationship between the size of a building project (expressed in square feet) to the input labor (expressed in labor-hours per square foot) is an example of a production function for construction. Several such production functions are shown in Figure 3-3 of Chapter 3.

Empirical cost inference.   Empirical estimation of cost functions requires statistical techniques which relate the cost of constructing or operating a facility to a few important characteristics or attributes of the system. The role of statistical inference is to estimate the best parameter values or constants in an assumed cost function. Usually, this is accomplished by means of regression analysis techniques.

Unit costs for bill of quantities.   A unit cost is assigned to each of the facility components or tasks as represented by the bill of quantities. The total cost is the summation of the products of the quantities multiplied by the corresponding unit costs. The unit cost method is straightforward in principle but quite laborious in application. The initial step is to break down or disaggregate a process into a number of tasks. Collectively, these tasks must be completed for the construction of a facility. Once these tasks are defined and quantities representing these tasks are assessed, a unit cost is assigned to each and then the total cost is determined by summing the costs incurred in each task. The level of detail in decomposing into tasks will vary considerably from one estimate to another.

Allocation of joint costs.   Allocations of cost from existing accounts may be used to develop a cost function of an operation. The basic idea in this method is that each expenditure item can be assigned to particular characteristics of the operation. Ideally, the allocation of joint costs should be causally related to the category of basic costs in an allocation process. In many instances, however, a causal relationship between the allocation factor and the cost item cannot be identified or may not exist. For example, in construction projects, the accounts for basic costs may be classified according to (1) labor, (2) material, (3) construction equipment, (4) construction supervision, and (5) general office overhead. These basic costs may then be allocated proportionally to various tasks which are subdivisions of a project.

5.3 TYPES OF CONSTRUCTION COST ESTIMATES

Construction cost constitutes only a fraction, though a substantial fraction, of the total project cost. However, it is the part of the cost under the control of the construction project manager. The required levels of accuracy of construction cost estimates vary at different stages of project development, ranging from ballpark figures in the early stage to fairly reliable figures for budget control prior to construction. Since design decisions made at the beginning stage of a project life-cycle are more tentative than are those made at a later stage, the cost estimates made at the earlier stage are expected to be less accurate. Generally, the accuracy of a cost estimate will reflect the information available at the time of estimation.

Construction cost estimates may be viewed from different perspectives because of different institutional requirements. In spite of the many types of cost estimates used at different stages of a project, cost estimates can best be classified into three major categories according to their functions. A construction cost estimate serves one of the three basic functions: design, bid, and control. For establishing the financing of a project, either a design estimate or a bid estimate is used.

1. **Design Estimates.** For the owner or its designated design professionals, the types of cost estimates encountered run parallel with the planning and design as follows:
   - Screening estimates (or order of magnitude estimates)
   - Preliminary estimates (or conceptual estimates)
   - Detailed estimates (or definitive estimates)
   - Engineer's estimates based on plans and specifications.

   For each of these different estimates, the amount of design information available typically increases.

2. **Bid Estimates.** For the contractor, a bid estimate submitted to the owner either for competitive bidding or negotiation consists of direct construction cost including field supervision, plus a markup to cover general overhead and profits. The direct cost of construction for bid estimates is usually derived from a combination of the following approaches.
   - Subcontractor quotations
   - Quantity takeoffs
   - Construction procedures

3. Control Estimates. For monitoring the project during construction, a control estimate is derived from available information to establish

- Budget estimate for financing
- Budgeted cost after contracting but prior to construction
- Estimated cost to completion during the progress of construction

Design Estimates

In the planning and design stages of a project, various design estimates reflect the progress of the design. At the very early stage, the *screening estimate* or *order of magnitude estimate* is usually made before the facility is designed and must therefore rely on the cost data of similar facilities built in the past. A *preliminary estimate* or *conceptual estimate* is based on the conceptual design of the facility at the state when the basic technologies for the design are known. The *detailed estimate* or *definitive estimate* is made when the scope of work is clearly defined and the detailed design is in progress so that the essential features of the facility are identifiable. The *engineer's estimate* is based on the completed plans and specifications when they are ready for the owner to solicit bids from construction contractors. In preparing these estimates, the design professional will include expected amounts for contractors' overhead and profits.

The costs associated with a facility may be decomposed into a hierarchy of levels that are appropriate for the purpose of cost estimation. The level of detail in decomposing the facility into tasks depends on the type of cost estimate to be prepared. For conceptual estimates, for example, the level of detail in defining tasks is quite coarse; for detailed estimates, the level of detail can be quite fine.

As an example, consider the cost estimates for a proposed bridge across a river. A screening estimate is made for each of the potential alternatives, such as a tied arch bridge or a cantilever truss bridge. As the bridge type is selected, for example, the technology is chosen to be a tied arch bridge instead of some new bridge form, a preliminary estimate is made on the basis of the layout of the selected bridge form on the basis of the preliminary or conceptual design. When the detailed design has progressed to a point where the essential details are known, a detailed estimate is made on the basis of the well-defined scope of the project. When the detailed plans and specifications are completed, an engineer's estimate can be made on the basis of items and quantities of work.

Bid Estimates

The contractor's bid estimates often reflect the desire of the contractor to secure the job as well as the estimating tools at its disposal. Some contractors have well-established cost-estimating procedures while others do not. Since only the lowest bidder will be the winner of the contract in most bidding contests, any effort devoted to cost estimating is a loss to the contractor who is not a successful bidder. Consequently, the contractor may put in the least amount of possible effort for making a cost estimate if it believes that its chance of success is not high.

If a general contractor intends to use subcontractors in the construction of a facility, it may solicit price quotations for various tasks to be subcontracted to specialty subcontractors. Thus, the general contractor will shift the burden of cost estimating to subcontractors. If all or part of the construction is to be undertaken by the general contractor, a bid estimate may be prepared on the basis of the quantity takeoffs from the plans provided by the owner or on the basis of the construction procedures devised by the contractor for implementing the project. For example, the cost of a footing of a certain type and size may be found in commercial publications on cost data which can be used to facilitate cost estimates from quantity takeoffs. However, the contractor may want to assess the actual cost of construction by considering the actual construction procedures to be used and the associated costs if the project is deemed to be different from typical designs. Hence, items such as labor, material, and equipment needed to perform various tasks may be used as parameters for the cost estimates.

Control Estimates

Both the owner and the contractor must adopt some baseline for cost control during the construction. For the owner, a *budget estimate* must be adopted early enough for planning long-term financing of the facility. Consequently, the detailed estimate is often used as the budget estimate since it is sufficiently definitive to reflect the project scope and is available long before the engineer's estimate. As the work progresses, the budgeted cost must be revised periodically to reflect the estimated cost to completion. A revised estimated cost is necessary either because of change orders initiated by the owner or due to unexpected cost overruns or savings.

For the contractor, the bid estimate is usually regarded as the budget estimate, which will be used for control purposes as well as for planning construction financing. The budgeted cost should also be updated periodically to reflect the estimated cost to completion as well as to ensure adequate cash flows for the completion of the project.

Example 5-2: Screening Estimate of a Grouting Seal Beneath a Landfill [49]

> One of the methods of isolating a landfill from groundwater is to create a bowl-shaped bottom seal beneath the site as shown in Figure 5-1. The seal is constructed by pumping or pressure-injecting grout under the existing landfill. Holes are bored at regular intervals throughout the landfill for this purpose, and the grout tubes are extended from the surface to the bottom of the landfill. A layer of soil at a minimum of 5 ft thick is left between the grouted material and the landfill contents to allow for irregularities in the bottom of the landfill. The grout liner can be between 4 and 6 ft thick. A typical material would be Portland cement grout pumped under pressure through tubes to fill voids in the soil. This grout would then harden into a permanent, impermeable liner.

[49] This example is adapted from a cost estimate in A. L. Tolman, A. P. Ballestero, W. W. Beck, and G. H. Emrich, *Guidance Manual for Minimizing Pollution from Waste Disposal Sites,* Municipal Environmental Research Laboratory, U.S. Environmental Protection Agency, Cincinnati, Ohio, 1978.

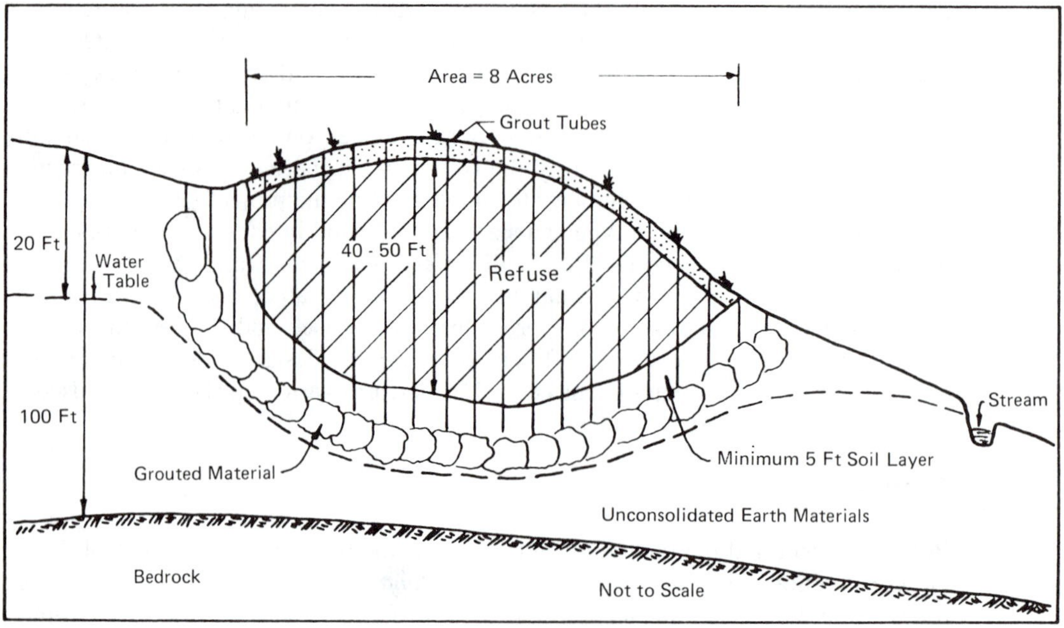
Area = 8 Acres
Grout Tubes
20 Ft
Water Table
40 - 50 Ft
Refuse
100 Ft
Stream
Grouted Material
Minimum 5 Ft Soil Layer
Unconsolidated Earth Materials
Bedrock
Not to Scale

Figure 5-1 Grout Bottom Seal Liner at a Landfill

The work items in this project include (1) drilling exploratory bore holes at 50 ft intervals for grout tubes and (2) pumping grout into the voids of a soil layer between 4 and 6 ft thick. The quantities for these two items are estimated on the basis of the landfill area:

$$8 \text{ acres} = (8)(43,560 \text{ ft}^2/\text{acre}) = 348,480 \text{ ft}^2$$

(As an approximation, use 360,000 ft^2 to account for the bowl shape.)

The number of bore holes in a 50-ft by 50-ft grid pattern covering 360,000 ft^2 is given by

$$\frac{360,000 \text{ ft}^2}{(50 \text{ ft})(50 \text{ ft})} = 144$$

The average depth of the bore holes is estimated to be 20 ft. Hence, the total amount of drilling is (144)(20) = 2,880 ft.

The volume of the soil layer for grouting is estimated to be:

For a 4 ft. layer, volume = (4 ft)(360,000 ft^2) = 1,440,000 ft^3
For a 6 ft. layer, volume = (6 ft)(360,000 ft^2) = 2,160,000 ft^3

It is estimated from soil tests that the voids in the soil layer are between 20 and 30 percent of the total volume. Thus, for a 4-ft soil layer;

Grouting in 20% voids = (20%)(1,440,000) = 288,000 ft^3
Grouting in 30% voids = (30%)(1,440,000) = 432,000 ft^3

and for a 6-ft soil layer:

$$\text{Grouting in 20\% voids} = (20\%)(2,160,000) = 432,000 \text{ ft}^3$$
$$\text{Grouting in 30\% voids} = (30\%)(2,160,000) = 648,000 \text{ ft}^3$$

The unit cost for drilling exploratory bore holes is estimated to be between \$3 and \$10 per foot (in 1978 dollars), including all expenses. Thus, the total cost of boring will be between $(2,880)(\$3) = \$8,640$ and $(2,880)(\$10) = \$28,800$. The unit cost of Portland cement grout pumped into place is between \$4 and \$10 per cubic foot including overhead and profit. In addition to the variation in the unit cost, the total cost of the bottom seal will depend upon the thickness of the soil layer grouted and the proportion of voids in the soil. That is,

For a 4-ft layer with 20% voids, grouting cost = \$1,152,000 to \$2,880,000
For a 4-ft layer with 30% voids, grouting cost = \$1,728,000 to \$4,320,000
For a 6-ft layer with 20% voids, grouting cost = \$1,728,000 to \$4,320,000
For a 6-ft layer with 30% voids, grouting cost = \$2,592,000 to \$6,480,000

The total cost of drilling bore holes is so small in comparison with the cost of grouting that the former can be omitted in the screening estimate. Furthermore, the range of unit cost varies greatly with soil characteristics, and the engineer must exercise judgment in narrowing the range of the total cost. Alternatively, additional soil tests can be used to estimate better the unit cost of pumping grout and the proportion of voids in the soil. Suppose that, in addition to ignoring the cost of bore holes, an average value of a 5 ft soil layer with 25 percent voids is used together with a unit cost of \$7 per ft^3 of Portland cement grouting. In this case, the total project cost is estimated to be

$$(5 \text{ ft})(360,000 \text{ ft}^2)(25\%)(\$7/\text{ft}^3) = \$3,150,000$$

An important point to note is that this screening estimate is based to a large degree on engineering judgment of the soil characteristics, and the range of the actual cost may vary from \$1,152,000 to \$6,480,000 even though the probabilities of having actual costs at the extremes are not very high.

Example 5-3: Example of Engineer's Estimate and Contractors' Bids [50]

The engineer's estimate for a project involving 14 miles of Interstate 70 roadway in Utah was \$20,950,859. Bids were submitted on March 10, 1987, for completing the project within 320 working days. The three low bidders were

1.	Ball, Ball & Brosame, Inc., Danville, CA	\$14,129,798
2.	National Projects, Inc., Phoenix, AR	\$15,381,789
3.	Kiewit Western Co., Murray, Utah	\$18,146,714

It was astounding that the winning bid was 32 percent below the engineer's estimate. Even the third lowest bidder was 13 percent below the engineer's estimate for this project. The disparity in pricing can be attributed either to the very conservative estimate of the engineer in the Utah Department of Transportation or to area contractors who are hungrier than usual to win jobs.

---

[50] See "Utah Interstate Forges On," *ENR*, July 2, 1987, p. 39.

The unit prices for different items of work submitted for this project by (1) Ball, Ball & Brosame, Inc., and (2) National Projects, Inc. are shown in Table 5-2. The similarity of their unit prices for some items and the disparity in others submitted by the two contractors can be noted.

TABLE 5–2 UNIT PRICES IN TWO CONTRACTORS' BIDS FOR ROADWAY CONSTRUCTION

Items	Unit	Quantity	Unit price 1	Unit price 2
Mobilization	ls	1	115,000	569,554
Removal, berm	lf	8,020	1.00	1.50
Finish subgrade	sy	1,207,500	0.50	0.30
Surface ditches	lf	525	2.00	1.00
Excavation structures	cy	7,000	3.00	5.00
Base course, untreated, ¾''	ton	362,200	4.50	5.00
Lean concrete, 4'' thick	sy	820,310	3.10	3.00
PCC, pavement, 10'' thick	sy	706,010	10.90	12.00
Concrete, ci AA(AE)	ls	1	200,000	190,000
Small structure	cy	50	500	475
Barrier, precast	lf	7,920	15.00	16.00
Flatwork, 4'' thick	sy	7,410	10.00	8.00
10'' thick	sy	4,241	20.00	27.00
Slope protection	sy	2,104	25.00	30.00
Metal, end section, 15''	ea	39	100	125
18''	ea	3	150	200
Post, right-of-way, modification	lf	4,700	3.00	2.50
Salvage and relay pipe	lf	1,680	5.00	12.00
Loose riprap	cy	32	40.00	30.00
Braced posts	ea	54	100	110
Delineators, type I	lb	1,330	12.00	12.00
type II	ea	140	15.00	12.00
Constructive signs fixed	sf	52,600	0.10	0.40
Barricades, type III	lf	29,500	0.20	0.20
Warning lights	day	6,300	0.10	0.50
Pavement marking, epoxy material,				
black	gal	475	90.00	100
Yellow	gal	740	90.00	80.00
White	gal	985	90.00	70.00
Plowable, one-way white	ea	342	50.00	20.00
Topsoil, contractor furnished	cy	260	10.00	6.00
Seedling, method A	acr	103	150	200
Excelsior blanket	sy	500	2.00	2.00
Corrugated, metal pipe, 18''	lf	580	20.00	18.00
Polyethylene pipe, 12''	lf	2,250	15.00	13.00
Catch basin grate and frame	ea	35	350	280
Equal opportunity training	hr	18,000	0.80	0.80
Granular backfill borrow	cy	274	10.00	16.00
Drill caisson, 2' × 6''	lf	722	100	80.00
Flagging	hr	20,000	8.25	12.50

TABLE 5–2 Continued

Items	Unit	Quantity	Unit price 1	Unit price 2
Prestressed concrete member				
type IV, 141′ × 4″	ea	7	12,000	16,000
132′ × 4″	ea	6	11,000	14,000
Reinforced steel	lb	6,300	0.60	0.50
Epoxy coated	lb	122,241	0.55	0.50
Structural steel	ls	1	5,000	1,600
Sign, covering	sf	16	10.00	4.00
type C-2 wood post	sf	98	15.00	17.00
24″	ea	3	100	400
30″	ea	2	100	160
48″	ea	11	200	300
Auxiliary	sf	61	15.00	12.00
Steel post, 48″ × 60″	ea	11	500	700
type 3, wood post	sf	669	15.00	19.00
24″	ea	23	100	125
30″	ea	1	100	150
36″	ea	12	150	180
42″ × 60″	ea	8	150	220
48″	ea	7	200	270
Auxiliary	sf	135	15.00	13.00
Steel post	sf	1,610	40.00	35.00
12″ × 36″	ea	28	100	150
Foundation, concrete	ea	60	300	650
Barricade, 48″ × 42″	ea	40	100	100
Wood post, road closed	lf	100	30.00	36.00

5.4 EFFECTS OF SCALE ON CONSTRUCTION COST

Screening cost estimates are often based on a single variable representing the capacity or some physical measure of the design such as floor area in buildings, length of highways, volume of storage bins, and production volumes of processing plants. Costs do not always vary linearly with respect to different facility sizes. Typically, scale economies or diseconomies exist. If the average cost per unit of capacity is declining, then scale economies exist. Conversely, scale diseconomies exist if average costs increase with greater size. Empirical data are sought to establish the economies of scale for various types of facility, if they exist, in order to take advantage of lower costs per unit of capacity.

Let x be a variable representing the facility capacity, and y be the resulting construction cost. Then, a linear cost relationship can be expressed in the form,

$$y = a + bx \qquad (5.1)$$

where a and b are positive constants to be determined on the basis of historical data. Note that in Eq.(5.1), a fixed cost of $y = a$ at $x = 0$ is implied as shown in Figure 5-2. In general, this relationship is applicable only in a certain range of

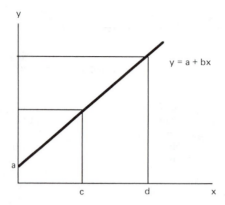

Figure 5-2 Linear Cost Relationship with Economies of Scale

the variable x, such as between $x = c$ and $x = d$. If the values of y corresponding to $x = c$ and $x = d$ are known, then the cost of a facility corresponding to any x within the specified range may be obtained by linear interpolation. For example, the construction cost of a school building can be estimated on the basis of a linear relationship between cost and floor area if the unit cost per square foot of floor area is known for school buildings within certain limits of size.

A nonlinear cost relationship between the facility capacity x and construction cost y can often be represented in the form,

$$y = ax^b \qquad (5.2)$$

where a and b are positive constants to be determined on the basis of historical data. For $0 < b < 1$, Eq.(5.2) represents the case of increasing returns to scale, and for $b > 1$, the relationship becomes the case of decreasing returns to scale, as shown in Figure 5-3. Taking the logarithm of both sides of this equation, a linear relationship can be obtained as follows:

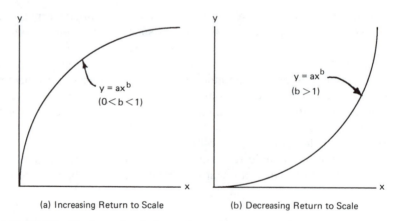

(a) Increasing Return to Scale

(b) Decreasing Return to Scale

Figure 5-3 Nonlinear Cost Relationship with Increasing or Decreasing Economies of Scale

$$\ln y = \ln a + b \ln x \tag{5.3}$$

Although no fixed cost is implied in Eq.(5.2), the equation is usually applicable only for a certain range of x. The same limitation applies to Eq. (5.3).

A nonlinear cost relationship often used in estimating the cost of a new industrial processing plant from the known cost of an existing facility of a different size is known as the *exponential rule*. Let y_n be the known cost of an existing facility with capacity Q_n and y be the estimated cost of the new facility which has a capacity Q. Then, from the empirical data, it can be assumed that:

$$y = y_n \left(\frac{Q}{Q_n} \right)^m \tag{5.4}$$

where m usually varies from 0.5 to 0.9, depending on a specific type of facility. A value of $m = 0.6$ is often used for chemical processing plants. The exponential rule can be reduced to a linear relationship if the logarithm of Eq. (5.4) is used:

$$\ln y = \ln y_n + m \ln \left(\frac{Q}{Q_n} \right) \tag{5.5}$$

or

$$\ln \left(\frac{y}{y_n} \right) = m \ln \left(\frac{Q}{Q_n} \right) \tag{5.6}$$

The exponential rule can be applied to estimate the total cost of a complete facility or the cost of some particular component of a facility.

Example 5-4: Determination of m for the Exponential Rule

The empirical cost data from a number of sewage treatment plants are plotted on a log-log scale for $\ln (Q/Q_n)$ and $\ln (y/y_n)$ and a linear relationship between these logarithmic ratios is shown in Figure 5-4. For $(Q/Q_n) = 1$ or $\ln (Q/Q_n) = 0$, $\ln (y/y_n) = 0$; and for $(Q/Q_n) = 2$ or $\ln (Q/Q_n) = 0.301$, $\ln (y/y_n) = 0.1765$. Since m is the slope of the line in the figure, it can be determined from the geometric relation as follows:

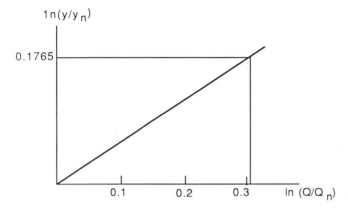

Figure 5-4 Log-Log Scale Graph of Exponential Rule Example

$$m = \frac{0.1765}{0.301} = 0.585$$

For $\ln (y/y_n) = 0.1765$, $y/y_n = 1.5$, while the corresponding value of Q/Q_n is 2. In words, for $m = 0.585$, the cost of a plant increases only 1.5 times when the capacity is doubled.

Example 5-5: Cost Exponents for Water and Wastewater Treatment Plants [51]

The magnitude of the cost exponent m in the exponential rule provides a simple measure of the economy of scale associated with building extra capacity for future growth and system reliability for the present in the design of treatment plants. When m is small, there is considerable incentive to provide extra capacity since scale economies exist as illustrated in Figure 5-3. When m is close to 1, the cost is directly proportional to the design capacity. The value of m tends to increase as the number of duplicate units in a system increases. The values of m for several types of treatment plants with different plant components derived from statistical correlation of actual construction costs are shown in Table 5-3.

TABLE 5–3 ESTIMATED VALUES OF COST EXPONENTS FOR WATER TREATMENT PLANTS

Treatment plant type	Exponent m	Capacity range (millions of gallons per day)
1. Water treatment	0.67	1–100
2. Waste treatment		
Primary with digestion (small)	0.55	0.1–10
Primary with digestion (large)	0.75	0.7–100
Trickling filter	0.60	0.1–20
Activated sludge	0.77	0.1–100
Stabilization ponds	0.57	0.1–100

Source: Data are collected from various sources by P. M. Berthouex. See the references in his article for the primary sources.

Example 5-6: Cost Data for the Exponential Rule

The exponential rule as represented by Equation (5.4) can be expressed in a different form as:

$$y = K Q^m$$

where

$$K = \frac{y_n}{(Q_n)^m}$$

If m and K are known for a given type of facility, then the cost y for a proposed new facility of specified capacity Q can be readily computed.

[51] This and the next example have been adapted from P. M. Berthouex, "Evaluating Economy of Scale," *Journal of the Water Pollution Control Federation*, Vol. 44, no. 11, November 1972, pp. 2111–2118.

TABLE 5–4 COST FACTORS OF PROCESSING UNITS FOR TREATMENT PLANTS

Processing unit	Unit of capacity	K Value (1968 $)	m Value
1. Liquid processing			
Oil separation	mgd	58,000	0.84
Hydroclone degritter	mgd	3,820	0.35
Primary sedimentation	ft²	399	0.60
Furial clarifier	ft²	700	0.57
Sludge aeration basin	mil. gal.	170,000	0.50
Tickling filter	ft²	21,000	0.71
Aerated lagoon basin	mil. gal.	46,000	0.67
Equalization	mil. gal.	72,000	0.52
Neutralization	mgd	60,000	0.70
2. Sludge handling			
Digestion	ft³	67,500	0.59
Vacuum filter	ft²	9,360	0.84
Centrifuge	lb dry solids/hr	318	0.81

Source: Data are collected from various sources by P. M. Berthouex. See the references in his article for the primary sources.

The estimated values of K and m for various water and sewage treatment plant components are shown in Table 5-4. The K values are based on 1968 dollars. The range of data from which the K and m values are derived in the primary sources should be observed in order to use them in making cost estimates.

As an example, take K = $399 and m = 0.60 for a primary sedimentation component in Table 5-4. For a proposed new plant with the primary sedimentation process having a capacity of 15,000 ft², the estimated cost (in 1968 dollars) is:

$$y = (\$399)(15,000)^{0.60} = \$128,000$$

5.5 UNIT COST METHOD OF ESTIMATION

If the design technology for a facility has been specified, the project can be decomposed into elements at various levels of detail for the purpose of cost estimation. The unit cost for each element in the bill of quantities must be assessed to compute the total construction cost. This concept is applicable to both design estimates and bid estimates, although different elements may be selected in the decomposition.

For design estimates, the unit cost method is commonly used when the project is decomposed into elements at various levels of a hierarchy as follows:

1. **Preliminary estimates**. The project is decomposed into major structural systems or production equipment items, for example, the entire floor of a building or a cooling system for a processing plant.
2. **Detailed estimates**. The project is decomposed into components of various major systems, that is, a single floor panel for a building or a heat exchanger for a cooling system.

3. **Engineer's estimates.** The project is decomposed into detailed items of various components as warranted by the available cost data. Examples of detailed items are slabs and beams in a floor panel or the piping and connections for a heat exchanger.

For bid estimates, the unit cost method can also be applied even though the contractor may choose to decompose the project into different levels in a hierarchy as follows:

1. **Subcontractor quotations**. The decomposition of a project into subcontractor items for quotation involves a minimum amount of work for the general contractor. However, the accuracy of the resulting estimate depends on the reliability of the subcontractors since the general contractor selects one among several contractor quotations submitted for each item of subcontracted work.
2. **Quantity takeoffs.** The decomposition of a project into items of quantities that are measured (or *taken off*) from the engineer's plan will result in a procedure similar to that adopted for a detailed estimate or an engineer's estimate by the design professional. The levels of detail may vary according to the desire of the general contractor and the availability of cost data.
3. **Construction procedures.** If the construction procedure of a proposed project is used as the basis of a cost estimate, the project may be decomposed into items such as labor, material, and equipment needed to perform various tasks in the projects.

Simple Unit Cost Formula

Suppose that a project is decomposed into n elements for cost estimation. Let Q_i be the quantity of the ith element and u_i be the corresponding unit cost. Then, the total cost of the project is given by

$$y = \sum_{i=1}^{n} u_i Q_i \qquad (5.7)$$

where n is the number of units. Based on characteristics of the construction site, the technology employed, or the management of the construction process, the estimated unit cost, u_i, for each element may be adjusted.

Factored Estimate Formula

A special application of the unit cost method is the "factored estimate" commonly used in process industries. Usually, an industrial process requires several major equipment components such as furnaces, towers, drums, and pumps in a chemical processing plant, plus ancillary items such as piping, valves, and electrical elements. The total cost of a project is dominated by the costs of purchasing and installing the major equipment components and their ancillary items. Let C_i be the purchase cost of a major equipment component i and f_i be a factor accounting for the cost of ancillary items needed for the installation of this equipment component i. Then, the total cost of a project is estimated by :

$$y = \sum_{i=1}^{n} C_i + \sum_{i=1}^{n} f_i C_i = \sum_{i=1}^{n} C_i(1 + f_i) \qquad (5.8)$$

where n is the number of major equipment components included in the project. The factored method is essentially based on the principle of computing the cost of ancillary items such as piping and valves as a fraction or a multiple of the costs of the major equipment items. The value of C_i may be obtained by applying the exponential rule so the use of Eq.(5.8) may involve a combination of cost estimation methods.

Formula Based on Labor, Material, and Equipment

Consider the simple case for which costs of labor, material, and equipment are assigned to all tasks. Suppose that a project is decomposed into n tasks. Let Q_i be the quantity of work for task i, M_i be the unit material cost of task i, E_i be the unit equipment rate for task i, L_i be the units of labor required per unit of Q_i, and W_i be the wage rate associated with L_i. In this case, the total cost y is :

$$y = \sum_{i=1}^{n} y_i = \sum_{i=1}^{n} Q_i(M_i + E_i + W_i L_i) \qquad (5.9)$$

Note that $W_i L_i$ yields the labor cost per unit of Q_i, or the labor unit cost of task i. Consequently, the units for all terms in Eq. (5.9) are consistent.

Example 5-7: Decomposition of a Building Foundation into Design and Construction Elements

The concept of decomposition is illustrated by the example of estimating the costs of a building foundation excluding excavation as shown in Table 5.5 in which the decomposed design elements are shown on horizontal lines and the decomposed contract elements are shown in vertical columns. For a design estimate, the decomposition of the project into footings, foundation walls, and elevator pit is preferred since

TABLE 5–5 ILLUSTRATIVE DECOMPOSITION OF BUILDING FOUNDATION COSTS

Design elements	Contract elements			Total cost
	Formwork	Rebars	Concrete	
Footings	$5,000	$10,000	$13,000	$28,000
Foundation walls	15,000	18,000	28,000	61,000
Elevator pit	9,000	15,000	16,000	40,000
Total cost	$29,000	$43,000	$57,000	$129,000

the designer can easily keep track of these design elements; however, for a bid estimate, the decomposition of the project into formwork, reinforcing bars, and concrete may be preferred, since the contractor can get quotations of such contract items more conveniently from specialty subcontractors.

Example 5-8: Cost Estimate Using Labor, Material and Equipment Rates

For the given quantities of work Q_i for the concrete foundation of a building and the labor, material, and equipment rates in Table 5-6, the cost estimate is computed on the basis of Eq. (5.9). The result is tabulated in the last column of the same table.

TABLE 5-6 ILLUSTRATIVE COST ESTIMATE USING LABOR, MATERIAL, AND EQUIPMENT RATES

Description	Quantity Q_i	Material unit cost M_i	Equipment unit cost E_i	Wage rate W_i	Labor input L_i	Labor unit cost W_iL_i	Direct cost Y_i
Formwork	12,000 ft^2	$0.4/ft^2	$0.8/ft^2	$15/hr	0.2 hr/ft^2	$ 3.0/ft^2	$50,400
Rebars	4,000 lb	0.2/lb	0.3/lb	15/hr	0.04 hr/lb	0.6/lb	4,440
Concrete	500 yd^3	5.0/yd^3	50/yd^3	15/hr	0.8 hr/yd^3	12.0/yd^3	33,500
Total							$88,300

5.6 METHODS FOR ALLOCATION OF JOINT COSTS

The principle of allocating joint costs to various elements in a project is often used in cost estimating. Because of the difficulty in establishing a causal relationship between each element and its associated cost, the joint costs are often prorated in proportion to the basic costs for various elements.

One common application is found in the allocation of field supervision cost among the basic costs of various elements based on labor, material, and equipment costs and the allocation of the general overhead cost to various elements according to the basic and field supervision cost. Suppose that a project is decomposed into n tasks. Let y be the total basic cost for the project and y_i be the total basic cost for task i. If F is the total field supervision cost and F_i is the proration of that cost to task i, then a typical proportional allocation is

$$F_i = F \frac{y_i}{y} \qquad (5.10)$$

Similarly, let z be the total direct field cost, which includes the total basic cost and the field supervision cost of the project, and z_i be the direct field cost for task i. If G is the general office overhead for proration to all tasks, and G_i is the share for task i, then

$$G_i = G \frac{z_i}{z} \qquad (5.11)$$

Finally, let w be the grand total cost of the project, which includes the direct field cost and the general office overhead cost charged to the project, and w_i be that attributable task i. Then,

$$z = F + y = F + \sum_{i=1}^{n} y_i \tag{5.12}$$

and

$$w = G + z = G + \sum_{i=1}^{n} z_i \tag{5.13}$$

Example 5-9: Prorated Costs for Field Supervision and Office Overhead

If the field supervision cost is $13,245 for the project in Table 5-6 (Example 5-8) with a total direct cost of $88,300, find the prorated field supervision costs for various elements of the project. Furthermore, if the general office overhead charged to the project is 4 percent of the direct field cost, which is the sum of basic costs and field supervision cost, find the prorated general office overhead costs for various elements of the project.

For the project, $y = \$88,300$ and $F = \$13,245$. Hence,

$$z = \$13,245 + \$88,300 = \$101,545$$

$$G = (0.04)(\$101,545) = \$4,062$$

$$w = \$101,545 + \$4,062 = \$105,607$$

The results of the proration of costs to various elements are shown in Table 5-7.

TABLE 5–7 PRORATION OF FIELD SUPERVISION AND OFFICE OVERHEAD COSTS

Description	Direct cost y_i	Allocated field supervision cost F_i	Total field cost z_i	Allocated overhead cost G_i	Total cost W_i
Formwork	$50,400	$ 7,560	$ 57,960	$2,319	$ 60,279
Rebars	4,400	660	5,060	202	5,262
Concrete	33,500	5,025	38,525	1,541	40,066
Total	$88,300	$13,245	$101,545	$4,062	$105,607

Example 5-10: A Standard Cost Report for Allocating Overhead

The reliance on labor expenses as a means of allocating overhead burdens in typical management accounting systems can be illustrated by the example of a particular product's standard cost sheet.[52] Table 5-8 is an actual product's standard cost sheet of a company following the procedure of using overhead burden rates assessed per direct labor hour. The material and labor costs for manufacturing a type of valve were estimated from engineering studies and from current material and labor prices. These amounts are summarized in columns 1 and 2 of Table 5-8. The overhead costs shown in column 3 were obtained by allocating the expenses of several departments to the various products manufactured in these departments in proportion to the labor

[52] See H. T. Johnson and R. S. Kaplan, *Relevance Lost: The Rise and Fall of Management Accounting,* Harvard Business School Press, Boston, 1987, p. 185.

TABLE 5–8 STANDARD COST REPORT FOR A TYPE OF VALVE

	(1) Material cost	(2) Labor cost	(3) Overhead cost	(4) Total cost
Purchased part	$1.1980			$1.1980
Operation				
Drill, face, tap (2)		$0.0438	$0.2404	0.2842
Degrease		0.0031	0.0337	0.0368
Remove burs		0.0577	0.3241	0.3818
Total cost, this item	1.1980	0.1046	0.5982	1.9008
Other subassemblies	0.3253	0.2994	1.8519	2.4766
Total cost, subassemblies	1.5233	0.4040	2.4501	4.3773
Assemble and test		0.1469	0.4987	0.6456
Pack without paper		0.0234	0.1349	0.1583
Total cost, this item	$1.5233	$0.5743	$3.0837	$5.1813
Cost component, %	29%	11%	60%	100%

Source: H. T. Johnson and R. S. Kaplan, *Relevance Lost: The Rise and Fall of Management Accounting*, Harvard Business School Press, Boston. Reprinted with permission.

cost. As shown in the last line of the table, the material cost represents 29 percent of the total cost, while labor costs are 11 percent of the total cost. The allocated overhead cost constitutes 60 percent of the total cost. Even though material costs exceed labor costs, only the labor costs are used in allocating overhead. Although this type of allocation method is common in industry, the arbitrary allocation of joint costs introduces unintended cross subsidies among products and may produce adverse consequences on sales and profits. For example, a particular type of part may incur few overhead expenses in practice, but this phenomenon would not be reflected in the standard cost report.

5.7 HISTORICAL COST DATA

Preparing cost estimates normally requires the use of historical data on construction costs. Historical cost data will be useful for cost estimation only if they are collected and organized in a way that is compatible with future applications. Organizations which are engaged in cost estimation continually should keep a file for their own use. The information must be updated with respect to changes that will inevitably occur. The format of cost data, such as unit costs for various items, should be organized according to the current standard of usage in the organization.

Construction cost data are published in various forms by a number of organizations. These publications are useful as references for comparison. Basically, the following types of information are available:

- Catalogs of vendors' data on important features and specifications relating to their products for which cost quotations are either published or can be obtained. A major source of vendors' information for building products is *Sweets' Catalog* published by McGraw-Hill Information Systems Company.

- Periodicals containing construction cost data and indices. One source of such information is *ENR*, the McGraw-Hill construction weekly, which contains extensive cost data including quarterly cost reports. *Cost Engineering*, a journal of the American Association of Cost Engineers, also publishes useful cost data periodically.
- Commercial cost-reference manuals for estimating guides. An example is the *Building Construction Cost Data* published annually by R. S. Means Company, Inc., which contains unit prices on building construction items. *Dodge Manual for Building Construction*, published by McGraw-Hill, provides similar information.
- Digests of actual project costs. The *Dodge Digest of Building Costs and Specifications* provides descriptions of design features and costs of actual projects by building type. Once a week, *ENR* publishes the bid prices of a project chosen from all types of construction projects.

Historical cost data must be used cautiously. Changes in relative prices may have substantial impacts on construction costs which have increased in relative price. Unfortunately, systematic changes over a long period of time for such factors are difficult to predict. Errors in analysis also serve to introduce uncertainty into cost estimates. It is difficult, of course, to foresee all the problems which may occur in construction and operation of facilities. There is some evidence that estimates of construction and operating costs have tended to understate the actual costs persistently. This is due to the effects of greater than anticipated increases in costs, changes in design during the construction process, or overoptimism.

Since the future prices of constructed facilities are influenced by many uncertain factors, it is important to recognize that this risk must be borne to some degree by all parties involved, that is, the owner, the design professionals, the construction contractors, and the financing institution. It is to the best interest of all parties that the risk-sharing scheme implicit in the design/construct process adopted by the owner is fully understood by all. When inflation adjustment provisions have very different risk implications to various parties, the price-level changes will also be treated differently for various situations.

Example 5-11: Cost Data from Commercial Publications

Cost data from commercial publications often provide useful information for cost estimating. An example of cost data for earthwork (bulk excavation with a backhoe) is shown in Figure 5-5, which is reproduced from *Building Construction Cost Data*, 1988, by R. S. Means Company, Inc. These excavation costs assume standard crews with the associated costs summarized in Figure 5-6. For example, operation of a 2-yd^3 capacity crawler-mounted hydraulic backhoe for bulk excavation would require standard crew B-12C, would have a standard daily output of $(130 \text{ yd}^3/\text{hr})(8 \text{ hr}) = 1,040 \text{ yd}^3$, and would require 0.015 labor-hours per cubic yard of excavation for a total of $(1,040 \text{ yd}^3)(0.015 \text{ hr/yd}^3) = 15.6$ labor-hours. Note that the labor-hours per cubic yard of excavation is based on a daily crew of 2 operators or 16 labor-hours. Thus,

022 200	Excav, Backfill, Compact	CREW	DAILY OUTPUT	MAN-HOURS	UNIT	MAT.	LABOR	EQUIP.	TOTAL	TOTAL INCL O&P	
234											**234**
3500	Blasting caps				Ea.	1.60			1.60	1.76	
3700	Explosives				Lb.	1.20			1.20	1.32	
3900	Blasting mats, rent, for first day				Ea.	37			37	41	
4000	Per added day					21			21	23	
4200	Preblast survey for 6 room house, individual lot, minimum	A-6	2.40	6.670			125		125	190	
4300	Maximum	"	1.35	11.850			225		225	335	
4500	City block within zone of influence, minimum	A-8	25,200	.001	S.F.		.02		.02	.03	
4600	Maximum	"	15,100	.002	"		.04		.04	.06	
238 0010	EXCAVATING, BULK BANK MEASURE Common earth piled										**238**
0020	For loading onto trucks, add								15%	15%	
0050	For mobilization and demobilization, see division 022-274 (16)										
0100	For hauling, see division 022-266										
0200	Backhoe, hydraulic, crawler mtd., 1 C.Y. cap. = 75 C.Y./hr.	B-12A	600	.027	C.Y.		.53	.84	1.37	1.71	
0250	1-½ C.Y. cap. = 100 C.Y./hr.	B-12B	800	.020			.40	.75	1.15	1.41	
0260	2 C.Y. cap. = 130 C.Y./hr. (17)	B-12C	1,040	.015			.31	.72	1.03	1.25	
0300	3 C.Y. cap. = 160 C.Y./hr.	B-12D	1,620	.010			.20	1.06	1.26	1.45	
0310	Wheel mounted, ½ C.Y. cap. = 30 C.Y./hr.	B-12E	240	.067			1.33	1.27	2.60	3.35	
0360	¾ C.Y. cap. = 45 C.Y./hr.	B-12F	360	.044			.89	.99	1.88	2.39	
0500	Clamshell, ½ C.Y. cap. = 20 C.Y./hr.	B-12G	160	.100			2	2.32	4.32	5.50	
0550	1 C.Y. cap. = 35 C.Y./hr.	B-12H	280	.057			1.14	1.55	2.69	3.38	
1000	Dragline, ¾ C.Y. cap. = 35 C.Y./hr.	B-12I	280	.057			1.14	1.33	2.47	3.15	
1050	1-½ C.Y. cap. = 65 C.Y./hr.	B-12P	520	.031			.61	1.16	1.77	2.18	
1200	Front end loader, track mtd., 1-½ C.Y. cap. = 70 C.Y./hr.	B-10N	560	.021			.42	.56	.98	1.24	
1250	2-½ C.Y. cap. = 95 C.Y./hr.	B-10O	760	.016			.31	.49	.80	1	
1300	3 C.Y. cap. = 130 C.Y./hr.	B-10P	1,040	.012			.23	.56	.79	.96	
1350	5 C.Y. cap. = 160 C.Y./hr.	B-10Q	1,620	.007			.15	.55	.70	.82	
1500	Wheel mounted, ¾ C.Y. cap. = 45 C.Y./hr.	B-10R	360	.033			.66	.55	1.21	1.57	
1550	1-½ C.Y. cap. = 80 C.Y./hr.	B-10S	640	.019			.37	.43	.80	1.02	
1600	2-¼ C.Y. cap. = 100 C.Y./hr.	B-10T	800	.015			.30	.48	.78	.96	
1650	5 C.Y. cap. = 185 C.Y./hr.	B-10U	1,480	.008			.16	.56	.72	.85	
1800	Hydraulic excavator, truck mtd., ½ C.Y. = 30 C.Y./hr.	B-12J	240	.067			1.33	2.28	3.61	4.47	
1850	48 inch bucket, 1 C.Y. = 45 C.Y./hr.	B-12K	360	.044			.89	1.87	2.76	3.36	
3700	Shovel, ½ C.Y. capacity = 55 C.Y./hr.	B-12L	440	.036			.73	.84	1.57	1.99	
3750	¾ C.Y. capacity = 85 C.Y./hr.	B-12M	680	.024			.47	.63	1.10	1.38	
3800	1 C.Y. capacity = 120 C.Y./hr.	B-12N	960	.017			.33	.51	.84	1.05	
3850	1-½ C.Y. capacity = 160 C.Y./hr.	B-12O	1,280	.013			.25	.54	.79	.96	
3900	3 C.Y. cap. = 250 C.Y./hr.	B-12T	2,000	.008			.16	.50	.66	.78	
4000	For soft soil or sand, deduct								15%	15%	
4100	For heavy soil or stiff clay, add								60%	60%	
4200	For wet excavation with clamshell or dragline, add								100%	100%	
4250	All other equipment, add								50%	50%	
4400	Clamshell in sheeting or cofferdam, minimum	B-12H	160	.100			2	2.71	4.71	5.90	
4450	Maximum	"	60	.267			5.30	7.25	12.55	15.80	
242 0010	EXCAVATING, BULK, DOZER Open site										**242**
2000	75 H.P., 50' haul, sand & gravel	B-10L	460	.026	C.Y.		.52	.48	1	1.29	
2200	150' haul, sand & gravel		230	.052			1.03	.96	1.99	2.58	
2400	300' haul, sand & gravel		120	.100			1.98	1.85	3.83	4.95	
3000	105 H.P., 50' haul, sand & gravel	B-10W	700	.017			.34	.50	.84	1.05	
3200	150' haul, sand & gravel		310	.039			.77	1.13	1.90	2.37	
3300	300' haul, sand & gravel		140	.086			1.70	2.49	4.19	5.25	
4000	200 H.P., 50' haul, sand & gravel	B-10B	1,400	.009			.17	.50	.67	.80	
4200	150' haul, sand & gravel		595	.020			.40	1.17	1.57	1.88	
4400	300' haul, sand & gravel		310	.039			.77	2.25	3.02	3.61	
5040	Clay	B-10M	1,025	.012			.23	.73	.96	1.15	
5400	300' haul, sand & gravel	"	470	.026			.51	1.60	2.11	2.51	
246 0010	EXCAVATION, BULK, SCRAPERS										**246**
0100	Elevating scraper 11 C.Y., sand & gravel 1500' haul	B-33F	690	.020	C.Y.		.41	1	1.41	1.70	

For expanded coverage of these items see *Means Site Work Cost Data 1988*

Figure 5-5 Cost Data For Earthwork–Bulk Excavating With Backhoe (Source: *Building Construction Cost Data, 1988,* p. 35. Reprinted with permission from R. S. Means Company, Inc., Kingston, MA.)

CREWS

Crew No.	Bare Costs		Incl. Subs O & P		Cost Per Man-hour	
Crew B-12B	Hr.	Daily	Hr.	Daily	Bare Costs	Incl. O&P
1 Equip. Oper. (crane)	$21.90	$175.20	$32.25	$258.00	$19.95	$29.37
1 Equip. Oper. Oiler	18.00	144.00	26.50	212.00		
1 Hyd. Excavator, 1.5 C.Y.		599.00		658.90	37.43	41.18
16 M.H., Daily Totals		$918.20		$1128.90	$57.38	$70.55
Crew B-12C	Hr.	Daily	Hr.	Daily	Bare Costs	Incl. O&P
1 Equip. Oper. (crane)	$21.90	$175.20	$32.25	$258.00	$19.95	$29.37
1 Equip. Oper. Oiler	18.00	144.00	26.50	212.00		
1 Hyd. Excavator, 2 C.Y.		751.00		826.10	46.93	51.63
16 M.H., Daily Totals		$1070.20		$1296.10	$66.88	$81.00
Crew B-12D	Hr.	Daily	Hr.	Daily	Bare Costs	Incl. O&P
1 Equip. Oper. (crane)	$21.90	$175.20	$32.25	$258.00	$19.95	$29.37
1 Equip. Oper. Oiler	18.00	144.00	26.50	212.00		
1 Hyd. Excavator, 3.5 C.Y.		1710.00		1881.00	106.87	117.56
16 M.H., Daily Totals		$2029.20		$2351.00	$126.82	$146.93
Crew B-12E	Hr.	Daily	Hr.	Daily	Bare Costs	Incl. O&P
1 Equip. Oper. (crane)	$21.90	$175.20	$32.25	$258.00	$19.95	$29.37
1 Equip. Oper. Oiler	18.00	144.00	26.50	212.00		
1 Hyd. Excavator, .5 C.Y.		304.40		334.85	19.02	20.92
16 M.H., Daily Totals		$623.60		$804.85	$38.97	$50.29
Crew B-12F	Hr.	Daily	Hr.	Daily	Bare Costs	Incl. O&P
1 Equip. Oper. (crane)	$21.90	$175.20	$32.25	$258.00	$19.95	$29.37
1 Equip. Oper. Oiler	18.00	144.00	26.50	212.00		
1 Hyd. Excavator, .75 C.Y.		354.60		390.05	22.16	24.37
16 M.H., Daily Totals		$673.80		$860.05	$42.11	$53.74
Crew B-12G	Hr.	Daily	Hr.	Daily	Bare Costs	Incl. O&P
1 Equip. Oper. (crane)	$21.90	$175.20	$32.25	$258.00	$19.95	$29.37
1 Equip. Oper. Oiler	18.00	144.00	26.50	212.00		
1 Power Shovel, .5 C.Y.		328.40		361.25		
1 Clamshell Bucket, .5 C.Y		42.60		46.85	23.18	25.50
16 M.H., Daily Totals		$690.20		$878.10	$43.13	$54.87

Figure 5-6 Cost Data For Crews Operating Construction Equipment (Source: *Building Construction Costs Data, 1988,* p. ix. Reprinted with permission from R. S. Means Company, Inc., Kingston, MA.

(16 labor-hrs) / (1,040 yd^3) = 0.0154 labor-hours / yd^3. The truncation of the number 0.0154 to 0.015 in Figure 5-5 leads to the approximation of 15.6 labor-hours. Costs exclusive of overhead and profit (i.e., "bare costs") as well as total costs including standard overhead and profit rates are shown in Figure 5-5. Thus, the total bare cost for a standard daily output of 1,040 yd^3 is (1,040 yd^3)($1.03 / yd^3) = $1,071. The

standard crew B-12C for this task consists of two equipment operators as shown in Figure 5-6. Using a daily total of 16 labor-hours, the daily bare cost is seen to be $1,070, which is essentially the same as the $1,071 obtained from Figure 5-5 except for the difference due to truncation of decimals in the process of computation. Note that costs would increase 15 percent if the excavated material must be loaded onto trucks (Figure 5-5).

5.8 COST INDICES

Since historical cost data are often used in making cost estimates, it is important to note the price-level changes over time. Trends in price changes can also serve as a basis for forecasting future costs. The input price indices of labor and/or material reflect the price-level changes of such input components of construction; the output price indices, where available, reflect the price-level changes of the completed facilities, thus to some degree also measuring the productivity of construction.

A price index is a weighted aggregate measure of constant quantities of goods and services selected for the package. The price index at a subsequent year represents a proportionate change in the same weighted aggregate measure because of changes in prices. Let I_t be the price index in year t and I_{t+1} be the price index in the following year $t + 1$. Then, the percentage change in price index for year $t + 1$ is:

$$j_{t+1} = \frac{I_{t+1} - I_t}{I_t}(100\%) \tag{5.14}$$

or

$$I_{t+1} = I_t(1 + j_{t+1}) \tag{5.15}$$

If the price index at the base year $t = 0$ is set at a value of 100, then the price indices $I_1, I_2, \ldots I_n$ for the subsequent years $t = 1, 2, \ldots n$ can be computed successively from changes in the total price charged for the package of goods measured in the index.

The best known indicators of general price changes are the GNP deflators compiled periodically by the U.S. Department of Commerce, and the consumer price index (CPI) compiled periodically by the U.S. Department of Labor. They are widely used as broad gauges of the changes in production costs and in consumer prices for essential goods and services. Special price indices related to construction are also collected by industry sources since some input factors for construction and the outputs from construction may disproportionately outpace or fall behind the general price indices. Examples of special price indices for construction input factors are the wholesale Building Material Price and Building Trades Union Wages, both compiled by the U.S. Department of Labor. In addition, the construction cost index and the building cost index are reported periodically in the *Engineering News–Record (ENR)*. Both *ENR* cost indices measure the effects of wage rate and material price trends, but they are not adjusted for productivity, efficiency, competitive conditions, or technology changes. Consequently, all these indices measure only the price changes of respective construction *input factors* as represented by constant quantities of material and/or labor. On the other hand, the price indices of various types of completed facilities reflect the price changes of construction output including all pertinent factors in the construction process. The building construction output indices compiled by Turner Construction Company and Handy-Whitman Utilities are compiled in the U.S. *Statistical Abstracts* published each year.

Figure 5-7 shows the gross national product (GNP) price deflator and the *ENR* building index from 1955 to 1985, using 1982 as the base year with an index of 100. Before 1976, the *ENR* building index rose more sharply than the GNP deflator except in 1973, whereas from 1976 to 1985, both indices practically coincide. The *ENR* building index is an input price index reflecting the cost of inputs to the building construction process such as wage rates and standard material costs. Figure 5-8

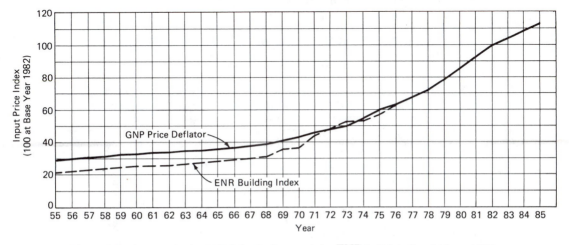

Figure 5-7 Changes in the GNP Price Deflator and the *ENR* Building Cost Indices, 1955–1985

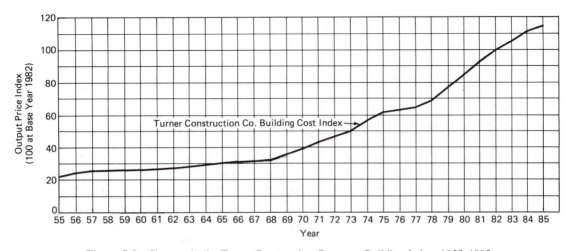

Figure 5-8 Changes in the Turner Construction Company Building Index, 1955–1985

shows the Turner Construction Company building cost index, also using 1982 as the base year for an index of 100. The Handy-Whitman Utilities building cost index and the GNP price deflator are almost identical to the Turner index, and therefore cannot be detected as separate curves if plotted in Figure 5-8. Both the Turner and the Handy-Whitman indices are referred to as output price indices because they represent the cost of completed buildings. Before 1982, the Turner index runs very close to the *ENR* building index, indicating no significant changes in productivity. However, from 1982 to 1985, the Turner index increases slightly faster than the *ENR* building index, suggesting a possible decline in productivity. In view of the fact that the productivity of manufacturing industries has improved significantly from 1955 to 1985, the performance of the construction industry has been viewed as being stagnant by comparison. A summary of these indices from 1970 to 1985 is also shown in Table 5-9 for illustration.

TABLE 5–9 SUMMARY OF INPUT AND OUTPUT PRICE INDICES, 1970–1985

Year	GNP deflator	ENR building cost index	Turner Construction Co. building cost index	Handy-Whitman utilities building cost index
1970	43	37	39	38
1971	45	43	44	41
1972	47	47	47	45
1973	50	51	49	49
1974	55	54	57	59
1975	60	58	61	66
1976	63	63	62	67
1977	67	67	64	70
1978	72	72	68	77
1979	79	79	76	86
1980	86	86	84	95
1981	94	94	93	100
1982	100	100	100	100
1983	104	104	105	103
1984	108	108	111	107
1985	112	112	115	110

Note: Index = 100 in base year of 1982.

Since construction costs vary in different regions of the United States and in all parts of the world, *locational indices* showing the construction cost at a specific location relative to the national trend are useful for cost estimation. *ENR* publishes periodically the indices of local construction costs at the major cities in different regions of the United States as percentages of local to national costs.

When the inflation rate is relatively small, that is, less than 10 percent, it is convenient to select a single price index to measure the inflationary conditions in construction and thus to deal only with a single set of price change rates in forecasting. Let j_t be the price change rate in year $t + 1$ over the price in year t. If the base year is denoted as year 0 ($t = 0$), then the price change rates at years 1, 2, ... t are $j_1, j_2, ... j_t$, respectively. Let A_t be the cost in year t expressed in base-year dollars and A'_t be the cost in year t expressed in then-current dollars. Then

$$A'_t = A_t(1 + j_1)(1 + j_2) \cdots (1 + j_{t-1})(1 + j_t) = A_t\left(\frac{I_t}{I_o}\right) \qquad (5.16)$$

Conversely

$$A_t = A'_t(1 + j_t)^{-1}(1 + j_{t-1})^{-1} \cdots (1 + j_2)^{-1}(1 + j_1)^{-1} = A'_t\left(\frac{I_o}{I_{t_\cdot}}\right) \qquad (5.17)$$

If the prices of certain key items affecting the estimates of future benefits and costs are expected to escalate faster than the general price levels, it may become necessary to consider the differential price changes over and above the general inflation rate. For example, during the period from 1973 through 1979, it was customary to assume that fuel costs would escalate faster than the general price levels. With hindsight in 1983, the assumption for estimating costs over many years would have been different. Because of the uncertainty in the future, the use of differential inflation rates for special items should be judicious.

Future forecasts of costs will be uncertain: the actual expenses may be much lower or much higher than those forecasted. This uncertainty arises from technological changes, changes in relative prices, inaccurate forecasts of underlying socioeconomic conditions, analytical errors, and other factors. For the purpose of forecasting, it is often sufficient to project the trend of future prices by using a constant rate j for price changes in each year over a period of t years, then

$$A'_t = A_t(1 + j)^t \qquad (5.18)$$

and

$$A_t = A'_t(1 + j)^{-t} \qquad (5.19)$$

Estimation of the future rate increase j is not at all straightforward. A simple expedient is to assume that future inflation will continue at the rate of the previous period:

$$j = j_{t-1} \qquad (5.20)$$

A longer-term perspective might use the average increase over a horizon of n past periods:

$$j = \sum_{i=1}^{n} \frac{j_{t-i}}{n} \qquad (5.21)$$

More sophisticated forecasting models to predict future cost increases include corrections for items such as economic cycles and technology changes.

Example 5-12: Changes in Highway and Building Costs

Table 5-10 shows the change of standard highway costs from 1940 to 1980, and Table 5-11 shows the change of residential building costs from 1970 to 1980. For these series, the quality of the finished product was held roughly equivalent. In each case, the rate of cost increase was substantially above the rate of inflation after 1970. Indeed, the real cost increase between 1970 and 1980 was in excess of 3 percent per year in both cases. However, these data also show some cause for optimism. For the case of the standard highway, real cost *decreases* took place in the period from 1940 to 1960. Unfortunately, comparable indices of outputs are not being compiled on a nationwide basis for other types of construction.

TABLE 5–10 COMPARISON OF STANDARD HIGHWAY COSTS, 1940–1980

Year	Standard highway cost (1972 = 100)	Price deflator (1972 = 100)	Standard highway Real cost (1972 = 100)	Percentage change per year
1940	26	29	90	
1950	48	54	89	−0.1%
1960	58	69	84	−0.6
1970	91	92	99	+1.8
1980	255	179	143	+4.4

Source: *Statistical Abstract of the United States*. GNP deflator is used for the price deflator index.

TABLE 5–11 COMPARISON OF RESIDENTIAL BUILDING COSTS, 1970–1980

Year	Standard residence cost (1972 = 100)	Price deflator (1972 = 100)	Standard residence real cost (1972 = 100)	Percentage change per year
1970	77	92	74	
1980	203	179	99	+3.4%

Source: *Statistical Abtract of the United States*. The GNP deflator is used for the price deflator index.

5.9 APPLICATIONS OF COST INDICES TO ESTIMATING

In the screening estimate of a new facility, a single parameter is often used to describe a cost function. For example, the cost of a power plant is a function of electricity generating capacity expressed in megawatts, or the cost of a sewage treatment plant as a function of waste flow expressed in million gallons per day.

The general conditions for the application of the single parameter cost function for screening estimates are

1. Exclude special local conditions in historical data.
2. Determine new facility cost on basis of specified size or capacity (using the methods described in Sections 5.3 to 5.6).

3. Adjust for inflation index.

4. Adjust for local index of construction costs.

5. Adjust for different regulatory constraints.

6. Adjust for local factors for the new facility.

Some of these adjustments may be done using compiled indices, whereas others may require field investigation and considerable professional judgment to reflect differences between a given project and standard projects performed in the past.

Example 5-13: Screening Estimate for a Refinery

The total construction cost of a refinery with a production capacity of 200,000 bbl/day in Gary, Indiana, completed in 1981 was $100 million. It is proposed that a similar refinery with a production capacity of 300,000 bbl/day be built in Los Angeles, for completion in 1983. For the additional information given here, make an order of magnitude estimate of the cost of the proposed plant.

1. In the total construction cost for the Gary, Indiana, plant, there was an item of $5 million for site preparation which is not typical for other plants.

2. The variation of sizes of the refineries can be approximated by the exponential rule, Eq. (5.4), with $m = 0.6$.

3. The inflation rate is expected to be 8 percent per year from 1979 to 1983.

4. The location index was 0.92 for Gary, Indiana, and 1.14 for Los Angeles in 1979. These indices are deemed to be appropriate for adjusting the costs between these two cities.

5. New air pollution equipment for the Los Angeles plant costs $7 million in 1983 dollars (not required in the Gary plant).

6. The contingency cost due to inclement weather delay will be reduced by the amount of 1 percent of total construction cost because of the favorable climate in Los Angeles (compared to Gary).

On the basis of the foregoing conditions, the estimate for the new project may be obtained as follows:

1. Typical cost excluding special item at Gary, Indiana is

$$\$100 \text{ million} - \$5 \text{ million} = \$95 \text{ million}$$

2. Adjustment for capacity based on the exponential law yields

$$(\$95)\left(\frac{300,000}{200,000}\right)^{0.6} = (95)(1.5)^{0.6} = \$121.2 \text{ million}$$

3. Adjustment for inflation leads to the cost in 1983 dollars as

$$(\$121.2)(1.08)^4 = \$164.6 \text{ million}$$

4. Adjustment for location index gives

$$(\$164.6)\left(\frac{1.14}{0.92}\right) = \$204.6 \text{ million}$$

5. Adjustment for new pollution equipment at the Los Angeles plant gives

$$\$204.6 + \$7 = \$211.6 \text{ million}$$

6. Reduction in contingency cost yields

$$(\$211.6)(1 - 0.01) = \$209.5 \text{ million}$$

Since there is no adjustment for other construction costs, the order of magnitude estimate for the new project is $209.5 million.

Example 5-14: Conceptual Estimate for a Chemical Processing Plant

In making a preliminary estimate of a chemical processing plant, several major types of equipment are the most significant parameters in affecting the installation cost. The cost of piping and other ancillary items for each type of equipment can often be expressed as a percentage of that type of equipment for a given capacity. The standard costs for the major equipment types for two plants with different daily production capacities in 1972 are as shown in Table 5-12. It has been established that the installation cost of all equipment for a plant with daily production capacity between 100,000 bbl and 400,000 bbl can best be estimated by using linear interpolation of the standard data.

TABLE 5–12 COST DATA FOR EQUIPMENT AND ANCILLARY ITEMS

Equipment type	Equipment cost ($1,000)		Cost of ancillary items as a percentage of equipment cost ($1,000)	
	100,000 bbl	400,000 bbl	100,000 bbl	400,000 bbl
Furnace	$3,000	$10,000	40%	30%
Tower	2,000	6,000	45	35
Drum	1,500	5,000	50	40
Pumps, etc.	1,000	4,000	60	50

A new chemical processing plant with a daily production capacity of 200,000 bbl was constructed in Memphis, Tennessee, in 1976. Determine the total preliminary cost estimate of the plant including the building and the equipment on the following basis:

1. The installation cost for equipment was based on linear interpolation from Table 5-12, and adjusted for inflation for the intervening four years using the *ENR* building cost index.
2. The location index for equipment installation is 0.95 for Memphis, Tennesee, in comparison with the standard cost.
3. An additional cost of $500,000 was required for the local conditions in Memphis, Tennessee.

The solution of this problem can be carried out according to the steps as outlined in the problem statement:

1. The costs of the equipment and ancillary items for a plant with a capacity of 200,000 bbl can be estimated in 1972 dollars by linear interpolation of the data in Table 5-12, and the results are shown in Table 5-13.

TABLE 5–13 RESULTS OF LINEAR INTERPOLATION FOR AN ESTIMATION EXAMPLE

Equipment type	Equipment cost (in $1,000)	Percentage for ancillary items
Furnace	$3,000 + (1/3)($10,000 − $3,000) = $5,333	40% − (1/3)(40% − 30%) = 37%
Tower	$2,000 + (1/3)($ 6,000 − $2,000) = $3,333	45% − (1/3)(45% − 35%) = 42%
Drum	$1,500 + (1/3)($ 5,000 − $1,500) = $2,667	50% − (1/3)(50% − 40%) = 47%
Pumps, etc.	$1,000 + (1/3)($ 4,000 − $1,000) = $2,000	60% − (1/3)(60% − 50%) = 57%

Hence, the total project cost in thousands of 1972 dollars is given by Eq.(5.8) as:

$$(\$5,333)(1.37) + (\$3,333)(1.42) + (\$2,667)(1.47) + (\$2,000)(1.57)$$

$$= \$2,307 + \$4,733 + \$3,920 + \$3,140 = \$19,100$$

2. The corresponding cost in thousands of 1976 dollars according to the *ENR* building cost index in Table 5-9 and using Eq. (5.16) is

$$(\$19,100)(63/47) = \$25,600$$

3. The total cost of the project after adjustment for location is

$$(0.95)(\$25,600,000) + \$500,000 \approx \$24,800,000$$

5.10 ESTIMATE BASED ON ENGINEER'S LIST OF QUANTITIES

The engineer's estimate is based on a list of items and the associated quantities from which the total construction cost is derived. This same list is also made available to the bidders if unit prices of the items on the list are also solicited from the bidders. Thus, the itemized costs submitted by the winning contractor may be used as the starting point for budget control.

In general, the progress payments to the contractor are based on the units of work completed and the corresponding unit prices of the work items on the list. Hence, the estimate based on the engineers' list of quanities for various work items essentially defines the level of detail to which subsequent measures of progress for the project will be made.

Example 5-15: Bid Estimate Based on Engineer's List of Quantities

Using the unit prices in the bid of contractor 1 for the quantitites specified by the engineer in Table 5-2 (Example 5-3), we can compute the total bid price of contractor 1 for the roadway project. The itemized costs for various work items as well as the total bid price are shown in Table 5-14.

TABLE 5–14   BID PRICE OF CONTRACTOR 1 IN A HIGHWAY PROJECT

Items	Unit	Quantity	Unit price	Item cost
Mobilization	ls	1	115,000	115,000.
Removal, berm	lf	8,020	1.00	8,020.
Finish subgrade	sy	1,207,500	0.50	603,750.
Surface ditches	lf	525	2.00	1,050.
Excavation structures	cy	7,000	3.00	21,000.
Base course, untreated, ¾''	ton	362,200	4.50	1,629,900.
Lean concrete, 4'' thick	sy	820,310	3.10	2,542,961.
PCC, pavement, 10'' thick	sy	706,010	10.90	7,695,509.
Concrete, ci AA(AE)	ls	1	200,000	200,000.
Small structure	cy	50	500	25,000.
Barrier, precast	lf	7,920	15.00	118,800.
Flatwork, 4'' thick	sy	7,410	10.00	74,100.
10'' thick	sy	4,241	20.00	84,820.
Slope protection	sy	2,104	25.00	52,600.
Metal, end section, 15''	ea	39	100	3,900.
18''	ea	3	150	450.
Post, right-of-way, modification	lf	4,700	3.00	14,100.
Salvage and relay pipe	lf	1,680	5.00	8,400.
Loose riprap	cy	32	40.00	1,280.
Braced posts	ea	54	100	5,400.
Delineators, type I	lb	1,330	12.00	15,960.
type II	ea	140	15.00	2,100.
Constructive signs fixed	sf	52,600	0.10	5,260.
Barricades, type III	lf	29,500	0.20	5,900.
Warning lights	day	6,300	0.10	630.
Pavement marking, epoxy material,				
black	gal	475	90.00	42,750.
Yellow	gal	740	90.00	66,600.
White	gal	985	90.00	88,650.
Plowable, one-way white	ea	342	50.00	17,100.
Topsoil, contractor furnished	cy	260	10.00	2,600.
Seedling, method A	acr	103	150	15,450.
Excelsior blanket	sy	500	2.00	1,000.
Corrugated, metal pipe, 18''	lf	580	20.00	11,600.
Polyethylene pipe, 12''	lf	2,250	15.00	33,750.
Catch basin grate and frame	ea	35	350	12,250.
Equal opportunity training	hr	18,000	0.80	14,400.
Granular backfill borrow	cy	274	10.00	2,740.
Drill caisson, 2' × 6''	lf	722	100	72,200.
Flagging	hr	20,000	8.25	165,000.
Prestressed concrete member				
type IV, 141' × 4''	ea	7	12,000	84,000.
132' × 4''	ea	6	11,000	66,000.
Reinforced steel	lb	6,300	0.60	3,780.
Epoxy coated	lb	122,241	0.55	67,232.55
Structural steel	ls	1	5,000	5,000.

TABLE 5–14 (Continued)

Items	Unit	Quantity	Unit price	Item cost
Sign, covering	sf	16	10.00	160.
type C-2, wood post	sf	98	15.00	1,470.00
24''	ea	3	100	300.
30''	ea	2	100	200.
48''	ea	11	200	2,200.
Auxiliary	sf	61	15.00	915.
Steel post, 48'' × 60''	ea	11	500	5,500.
type 3, wood post	sf	669	15.00	10,035.
24''	ea	23	100	2,300.
30''	ea	1	100	100.
36''	ea	12	150	1,800.
42'' × 60''	ea	8	150	1,200.
48''	ea	7	200	1,400.
Auxiliary	sf	135	15.00	2,025.
Steel post	sf	1,610	40.00	64,400.
12'' × 36''	ea	28	100	2,800.
Foundation, concrete	ea	60	300	18,000.
Barricade, 48'' × 42''	ea	40	100	4,000.
Wood post, road closed	lf	100	30.00	3,000.
Total				$14,129,797.55

5.11 ALLOCATION OF CONSTRUCTION COSTS OVER TIME

Since construction costs are incurred over the entire construction phase of a project, it is often necessary to determine the amounts to be spent in various periods to derive the cash flow profile, especially for large projects with long durations. Consequently, it is important to examine the percentage of work expected to be completed at various time periods to which the costs would be charged. More accurate estimates may be accomplished once the project is scheduled as described in Chapter 10, but some rough estimate of the cash flow may be required prior to this time.

Consider the basic problem in determining the percentage of work completed during construction. One common method of estimating percentage of completion is based on the amount of money spent relative to the total amount budgeted for the entire project. This method has the obvious drawback in assuming that the amount of money spent has been used efficiently for production. A more reliable method is based on the concept of *value of work completed*, which is defined as the product of the budgeted-labor-hours per unit of production and the actual number of production units completed and is expressed in budgeted labor-hours for the work completed. Then, the percentage of completion at any stage is the ratio of the value of work completed to date and the value of work to be completed for the entire project.

Regardless of the method of measurement, it is informative to understand the trend of work progress during construction for evaluation and control.

In general, the work on a construction project progresses gradually from the time of mobilization until it reaches a plateau; then the work slows down gradually and finally stops at the time of completion. The rate of work done during various time periods (expressed in the percentage of project cost per unit time) is shown schematically in Figure 5-9, in which 10 time periods have been assumed. The solid line A represents the case in which the rate of work is zero at time $t = 0$ and increases linearly to 12.5 percent of project cost at $t = 2$, while the rate begins to decrease from 12.5 percent at $t = 8$ to 0 percent at $t = 10$. The dotted line B represents the case of rapid mobilization by reaching 12.5 percent of project cost at $t = 1$ while beginning to decrease from 12.5 percent at $t = 7$ to 0 percent at $t = 10$. The dashed line C represents the case of slow mobilization by reaching 12.5 percent of project

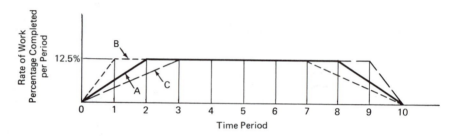

Figure 5-9   Rate of Work Progress Over Project Time

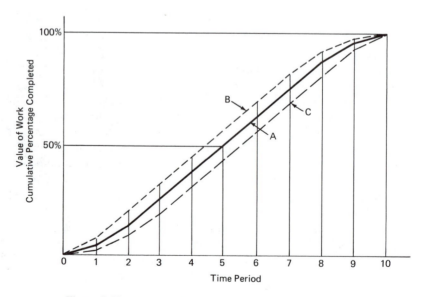

Figure 5-10   Value of Work Completed Over Project Time

cost at $t = 3$ while beginning to decrease from 12.5 percent at $t = 9$ to 0 percent at $t = 10$.

The value of work completed at a given time (expressed as a cumulative percentage of project cost) is shown schematically in Figure 5-10. In each case (A, B or C), the value of work completed can be represented by an "S-shaped" curve. The effects of rapid mobilization and slow mobilization are indicated by the positions of curves B and C relative to curve A, respectively.

While the curves shown in Figures 5-9 and 5-10 represent highly idealized cases, they do suggest the latitude for adjusting the schedules for various activities in a project. While the rate of work progress may be changed quite drastically within a single period, such as the change from rapid mobilization to a slow mobilization in periods 1, 2, and 3 in Figure 5-9, the effect on the value of work completed over time will diminish in significance as indicated by the cumulative percentages for later periods in Figure 5-10. Thus, adjustment of the scheduling of some activities may improve the utilization of labor, material, and equipment, and any delay caused by such adjustments for individual activities is not likely to cause problems for the eventual progress toward the completion of a project.

In addition to the speed of resource mobilization, another important consideration is the overall duration of a project and the amount of resources applied. Various strategies may be applied to shorten the overall duration of a project such as overlapping design and construction activities (as described in Chapter 2) or increasing the peak amounts of labor and equipment working on a site. However, spatial, managerial, and technical factors will typically place a minimum limit on the project duration or cause costs to escalate with shorter durations.

Example 5-16: Calculation of Value of Work Completed

From the area of work progress in Figure 5-9, the value of work completed at any point in Figure 5-10 can be derived by noting the area under the curve up to that point in Figure 5-9. The result for $t = 0$ through $t = 10$ is shown in Table 5-15 and is plotted in Figure 5-10.

TABLE 5–15 CALCULATION OF VALUE OF WORK COMPLETED

Time	Case A	Case B	Case C
0	0	0	0
1	3.1%	6.2%	2.1%
2	12.5	18.7	8.3
3	25.0	31.2	18.8
4	37.5	43.7	31.3
5	50.0	56.2	43.8
6	62.5	68.7	56.3
7	75.0	81.2	68.8
8	87.5	91.7	81.9
9	96.9	97.9	93.8
10	100.0	100.0	100.0

5.12 ESTIMATION OF OPERATING COSTS

To analyze the life-cycle costs of a proposed facility, it is necessary to estimate the operation and maintenance costs over time after the start-up of the facility. The stream of operating costs over the life of the facility depends upon subsequent maintenance policies and facility use. In particular, the magnitude of routine maintenance costs will be reduced if the facility undergoes periodic repairs and rehabilitation at periodic intervals.

Since the trade-off between the capital cost and the operating cost is an essential part of the economic evaluation of a facility, the operating cost is viewed not as a separate entity, but as a part of the larger parcel of life-cycle cost at the planning and design stage. The techniques of estimating life-cycle costs are similar to those used for estimating capital costs, including empirical cost functions and the unit cost method of estimating the labor, material, and equipment costs. However, it is the interaction of the operating and capital costs which deserve special attention.

As suggested earlier in the discussion of the exponential rule for estimating, the value of the cost exponent may influence the decision whether extra capacity should be built to accommodate future growth. Similarly, the economy of scale may also influence the decision on rehabilitation at a given time. As the rehabilitation work becomes extensive, it becomes a capital project with all the implications of its own life-cycle. Hence, the cost estimation of a rehabilitation project may also involve capital and operating costs.

While deferring the discussion of the economic evaluation of constructed facilities to Chapter 6, it is sufficient to point out that the stream of operating costs over time represents a series of costs at different time periods which have different values with respect to the present. Consequently, the cost data at different time periods must be converted to a common baseline if meaningful comparison is desired.

Example 5-17: Maintenance Cost on a Roadway [53]

Maintenance costs for constructed roadways tend to increase with both age and use of the facility. As an example, the following empirical model was estimated for maintenance expenditures on sections of the Ohio Turnpike,

$$C = 596 + 0.0019V + 21.7A$$

where C is the annual cost of routine maintenance per lane-mile (in 1967 dollars), V is the volume of traffic on the roadway (measured in equivalent standard axle loads, ESAL, so that a heavy truck is represented as equivalent to many automobiles), and A is the age of the pavement in years since the last resurfacing. According to this model, routine maintenance costs will increase each year as the pavement service deteriorates. In addition, maintenance costs increase with additional pavement stress due to increased traffic or to heavier axle loads, as reflected in the variable V.

---

[53] This example is adapted from S. McNeil, and C. Hendrickson, "A Statistical Model of Pavement Maintenance Expenditure," *Transportation Research Record*, no. 846, 1982, pp. 71–76.

For example, for $V = 500,300$ ESAL and $A = 5$ years, the annual cost of routine maintenance per lane-mile is estimated to be:

$$C = 596 + (0.0019)(500,300) + (21.7)(5)$$

$$= \$596 + \$950.5 + \$108.5$$

$$= \$1,655(\text{in 1967 dollars})$$

Example 5-18: Time Stream of Costs over the Life of a Roadway [54]

The time stream of costs over the life of a roadway depends upon the intervals at which rehabilitation is carried out. If the rehabilitation strategy and the traffic are known, the time stream of costs can be estimated.

Using a life-cycle model that predicts the economic life of highway pavement on the basis of the effects of traffic and other factors, an optimal schedule for rehabilitation can be developed. For example, a time stream of costs and resurfacing projects for one pavement section is shown in Figure 5-11. As described in the previous example, the routine maintenance costs increase as the pavement ages, but decline after each new resurfacing. As the pavement continues to age, resurfacing becomes more frequent until the roadway is completely reconstructed at the end of 35 years.

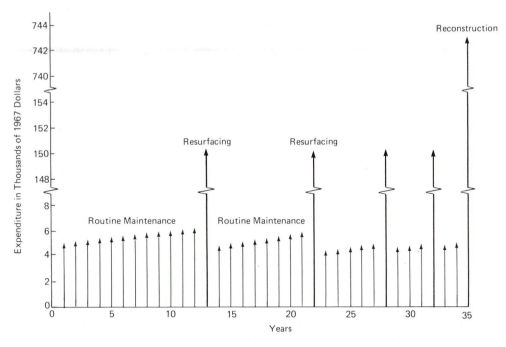

Figure 5-11   Time Stream of Costs over the Life of a Highway Pavement

[54] This example is adapted from S. McNeil, *Three Statistical Models of Road Management Based on Turnpike Data*, M.S. thesis, Carnegie-Mellon University, Pittsburgh, 1981.

5.13 REFERENCES

5-1. Ahuja, H. N. and W. J. Campbell, *Estimating: From Concept to Completion*, Prentice Hall, Inc., Englewood Cliffs, NJ, 1987.

5-2. Clark, F. D., and A. B. Lorenzoni, *Applied Cost Engineering*, Marcel Dekker, Inc., New York, 1978.

5-3. Clark, J. E., *Structural Concrete Cost Estimating*, McGraw-Hill Book Company, Inc., New York, 1983.

5-4. Diekmann, J. R., "Probabilistic Estimating: Mathematics and Applications," *ASCE Journal of Construction Engineering and Management*, Vol. 109, 1983, pp. 297-308.

5-5. Humphreys, K. K. (ed.), *Project and Cost Engineers' Handbook* (sponsored by American Association of Cost Engineers), 2nd ed., Marcel Dekker, Inc., New York, 1984.

5-6. Maevis, A. C., "Construction Cost Control by the Owners," *ASCE Journal of the Construction Division*, Vol. 106, 1980, pp. 435–446.

5-7. Wohl, M., and C. Hendrickson, *Transportation Investment and Pricing Principles*, John Wiley and Sons Inc., New York, 1984.

5.14 PROBLEMS

P5-1. Suppose that the grouting method described in Example 5-2 is used to provide a grouting seal beneath another landfill of 12 acres.(Use an approximation of 540,000 square feet to account for the bowl shape.) The grout line is expected to be between 4.5 and 5.5 ft thickness. The voids in the soil layer are between 25 and 35 percent. Using the same unit cost data (in 1978 dollars), find the range of costs in a screening estimate for the grouting project.

P5-2. To avoid submerging part of U.S. Route 40 south and east of Salt Lake City due to the construction of the Jardinal Dam and Reservoir, 22 miles of highway were relocated to the west around the site of the future reservoir. Three separate contracts were let, including one covering 10 miles of the work which had an engineer's estimate of $34,095,545. The bids were submitted on July 21, 1987, and the completion date of the project under the contract was August 15, 1989. (See *ENR*, October 8, 1987, p. 34.) The three lowest bids were

1. W. W. Clyde & Co., Springville, Utah	$21,384,919
2. Sletten Construction Company, Great Falls, Montana	$26,701,018
3. Gilbert Western Corporation, Salt Lake City, Utah	$30,896,203

Find the percentage of each of these bidders below the engineer's cost estimate.

P5-3. In making a screening estimate of an industrial plant for the production of batteries, an empirical formula based on data of a similar building completed before 1987 was proposed,

$$C = (16,000)(Q + 50,000)^{1/2}$$

where Q is the daily production capacity of batteries and C is the cost of the building in 1987 dollars. If a similar plant is planned for a daily production capacity of 200,000 batteries, find the screening estimate of the building in 1987 dollars.

P5-4. For the cost factor $K = \$46,000$ (in 1968 dollars) and $m = 0.67$ for an aerated lagoon basin of a water treatment plant in Table 5-4 (Example 5-6), find the estimated cost of a proposed new plant with a similar treatment process having a capacity of 480 million gallons (in 1968 dollars). If another new plant was estimated to cost $160,000 by using the same exponential rule, what would be the proposed capacity of that plant?

P5-5. Using the cost data in Figure 5-5 (Example 5-11), find the total cost including overhead and profit (O and P) of excavating 90,000 yd^3 of bulk material using a backhoe of 1.5 yd^3 capacity for a detailed estimate. Verify the total cost per daily output obtained from Figure 5-5 in comparison with the total cost of crew B-12B per day including O and P in Figure 5-6.

P5-6. The basic costs (labor, material, and equipment) for various elements of a construction project are given as follows:

Excavation	$240,000
Subgrade	$100,000
Base course	$420,000
Concrete pavement	$640,000
Total	$1,400,000

Assuming that field supervision cost is 10 percent of the basic cost, and the general office overhead is 5 percent of the direct costs (sum of the basic costs and field supervision cost), find the prorated field supervision costs, general office overhead costs, and total costs for the various elements of the project.

P5-7. In making a preliminary estimate of a chemical processing plant, several major types of equipment are the most significant components in affecting the installation cost. The cost of piping and other ancillary items for each type of equipment can often be expressed as a percentage of that type of equipment for a given capacity. The standard costs for the major equipment types for two plants with different daily production capacities are as shown in Table P5-7. It has been established that the installation cost of all equipment for a plant with daily production capacity between 150,000 bbl and 600,000 bbl can best be estimated by using linear interpolation of the standard data. A new chemical processing plant with a daily production capacity of 400,000 bbl is being planned. Assuming that all other factors remain the same, estimate the cost of the new plant.

TABLE P5-7

Equipment Type	Equipment cost ($1,000)		Factor for ancillary items	
	150,000 bbl	600,000 bbl	150,000 bbl	600,000 bbl
Furnace	$3,000	$10,000	0.32	0.24
Tower	2,000	6,000	0.42	0.36
Drum	1,500	5,000	0.42	0.32
Pumps, etc.	1,000	4,000	0.54	0.42

P5-8. The total construction cost of a refinery with a production capacity of 100,000 bbl/day in Caracas, Venezuela, completed in 1977 was $40 million. It was proposed that a similar refinery with a production capacity of $160,000 bbl/day be built in New Orleans for completion in 1980. For the additional information given, make a screening estimate of the cost of the proposed plant.

1. In the total construction cost for the Caracas, Venezuela, plant, there was an item of $2 million for site preparation and travel which is not typical for similar plants.
2. The variation of sizes of the refineries can be approximated by the exponential law with $m = 0.6$.
3. The inflation rate in U.S. dollars was approximately 9 percent per year from 1977 to 1980.
4. An adjustment factor of 1.40 was suggested for the project to account for the increase of labor cost from Caracas, Venezuela, to New Orleans.
5. New air pollution equipment for the New Orleans plant cost $4 million in 1980 dollars (not required for the Caracas plant).
6. The site condition at New Orleans required special piling foundation which cost $2 million in 1980 dollars.

P5-9. The total cost of a sewage treatment plant with a capacity of 50 million gallons per day completed in 1981 for a new town in Colorado was $4.5 million. It was proposed that a similar treatment plant with a capacity of 80 million gallons per day be built in another town in New Jersey for completion in 1985. For the additional information given now, make a screening estimate of the cost of the proposed plant.

1. In the total construction cost in Colorado, an item of $300,000 for site preparation is not typical for similar plants.
2. The variation of sizes for this type of treatment plant can be approximated by the exponential law with $m = 0.5$.
3. The inflation rate was approximately 5 percent per year from 1981 to 1985.
4. The locational indices of Colorado and New Jersey areas are 0.95 and 1.10, respectively, against the national average of 1.00.
5. The installation of special equipment to satisfy the new environmental standard cost an extra $200,000 in 1985 dollars for the New Jersey plant.
6. The site condition in New Jersey required special foundation which cost $500,000 in 1985 dollars.

P5-10. Using the *ENR* building cost index, estimate the 1985 cost of the grouting seal on a landfill described in Example 5-2, including the most likely estimate and the range of possible cost.

P5-11. Using the unit prices in the bid of contractor 2 for the quantitites specified by the engineer in Table 5-2 (Example 5-3), compute the total bid price of contractor 2 for the roadway project including the expenditure on each item of work.

P5-12. The rate of work progress in percentage of completion per period of a construction project is shown in Figure P5-12 in which 13 time periods have been assumed. The cases A, B, and C represent the normal mobilization time, rapid mobilization, and slow mobilization for the project, respectively. Calculate the value of work completed in cumulative percentage for periods 1 through 13 for each of the cases A, B, and C. Also plot the value of work completed versus time for these cases.

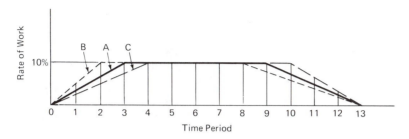

Figure P5-12

P5-13. The rate of work progress as a percentage of completion per period of a construction project is shown in Figure P5-13 in which 10 time periods have been assumed. The cases A, B, and C represent the normal mobilization time, rapid mobilization, and slow mobilization for the project, respectively. Calculate the value of work completed in cumulative percentage for periods 1 through 10 for each of the cases A, B, and C. Also plot the volume of work completed versus time for these cases.

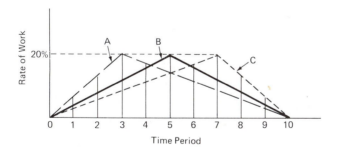

Figure P5-13

P5-14. Suppose that the empirical model for estimating annual cost of routine maintenance in Example 5-17 is applicable to sections of the Pennsylvania Turnpike in 1985 if the *ENR* building cost index is 30 in 1967, which can be applied to inflate the 1967 dollars for estimating the cost in 1985. Estimate the annual cost of maintenance per lane-mile of the turnpike for which the traffic volume on the roadway is 750,000 ESAL and the age of the pavement is 4 years in 1985.

P5-15. The initial construction cost for an electric power line is known to be a function of the cross-sectional area A (in square centimeters) and the length L (in kilometers).

Let C_1 be the unit cost of construction (in dollars per cubic centimeters). Then, the initial construction cost P (in dollars) is given by

$$P = C_1 AL(10^5)$$

The annual operating cost of the power line is assumed to be measured by the power loss. The power loss S (in kilowatt-hours) is known to be

$$S = \frac{J^2 R}{10^3} \left[\frac{L(10^5)}{A} \right] = \frac{J^2 RL}{A}(10^2)$$

where J is the electric current in amperes, and R is the resistivity in ohm-centimeters. Let C_2 be the unit operating cost (in dollars per kilowatt-hour). Then, the annual operating cost U (in dollars) is given by

$$U = C_2 \frac{J^2 RL}{A}(10^2)$$

Suppose that the power line is expected to last n years and the life-cycle cost T of the power line is equal to

$$T = P + UK$$

where K is a discount factor depending on the useful life-cycle n and the discount rate i (to be explained in Chapter 6). In designing the power line, all quantities are assumed to be known except A, which is to be determined. If the owner wants to minimize the life-cycle cost, find the best cross-sectional area A in terms of the known quantities.

6

Economic Evaluation
of
Facility Investments

6.1 PROJECT LIFE CYCLE AND ECONOMIC FEASIBILITY

Facility investment decisions represent major commitments of corporate resources and have serious consequences on the profitability and financial stability of a corporation. In the public sector, such decisions also affect the viability of facility investment programs and the credibility of the agency in charge of the programs. It is important to evaluate facilities rationally with regard to both the economic feasibility of individual projects and the relative net benefits of alternative and mutually exclusive projects.

This chapter will present an overview of the decision process for economic evaluation of facilities with regard to the project life cycle. The cycle begins with the initial conception of the project and continues though planning, design, procurement, construction, start-up, operation, and maintenance. It ends with the disposal of a facility when it is no longer productive or useful. Four major aspects of economic evaluation will be examined:

1. The basic concepts of facility investment evaluation, including time preference for consumption, opportunity cost, minimum attractive rate of return, cash flows over the planning horizon, and profit measures.
2. Methods of economic evaluation, including the net present value method, the equivalent uniform annual value method, the benefit-cost ratio method, and the internal rate of return method.
3. Factors affecting cash flows, including depreciation and tax effects, price-level changes, and treatment of risk and uncertainty.
4. Effects of different methods of financing on the selection of projects, including types of financing and risk, public policies on regulation and subsidies, the effects of project financial planning, and the interaction between operational and financial planning.

It is important to distinguish between the economic evaluation of alternative physical facilities and the evaluation of alternative financing plans for a project. The former refers to the evaluation of the cash flow representing the benefits and costs associated with the acquisition and operation of the facility, and this cash flow over the planning horizon is referred to as the *economic cash flow* or the *operating cash flow*. The latter refers to the evaluation of the cash flow representing the incomes and expenditures as a result of adopting a specific financing plan for funding the project, and this cash flow over the planning horizon is referred to as the *financial cash flow*. In general, economic evaluation and financial evaluation are carried out by different groups in an organization since economic evaluation is related to design, construction, operations, and maintenance of the facility while financial evaluations require knowledge of financial assets such as equities, bonds, notes, and mortgages. The separation of economic evaluation and financial evaluation does not necessarily mean one should ignore the interaction of different designs and financing requirements over time which *may* influence the relative desirability of specific design/financing combinations. All such combinations can be duly considered. In practice, however, the division of labor among two groups of specialists generally leads to sequential decisions without adequate communication for analyzing the interaction of various design/financing combinations because of the timing of separate analyses.

As long as the significance of the interaction of design/financing combinations is understood, it is convenient first to consider the economic evaluation and financial evaluation separately, and then combine the results of both evaluations to reach a final conclusion. Since the methods of analyzing economic cash flows are equally applicable to the analysis of financial cash flows, the *techniques* for evaluating financing plans and the combined effects of economic and financial cash flows for project selection are also included in this chapter. Consequently, this chapter is devoted primarily to the economic evaluation of alternative physical facilities while the effects of a variety of financing mechanisms will be treated in the next chapter.

6.2 BASIC CONCEPTS OF ECONOMIC EVALUATION

A systematic approach for economic evaluation of facilities consists of the following major steps:

1. Generate a set of projects or purchases for investment consideration.
2. Establish the planning horizon for economic analysis.
3. Estimate the cash flow profile for each project.
4. Specify the minimum attractive rate of return (MARR).
5. Establish the criterion for accepting or rejecting a proposal, or for selecting the best among a group of mutually exclusive proposals, on the basis of the objective of the investment.
6. Perform sensitivity or uncertainty analysis.
7. Accept or reject a proposal on the basis of the established criterion.

It is important to emphasize that many assumptions and policies, some implicit and some explicit, are introduced in economic evaluation by the decision maker. The decision-making process will be influenced by the subjective judgment of the management as much as by the result of systematic analysis.

The period of time to which the management of a firm or agency wishes to look ahead is referred to as the *planning horizon*. Since the future is uncertain, the period of time selected is limited by the ability to forecast with some degree of accuracy. For capital investment, the selection of the planning horizon is often influenced by the useful life of facilities, since the disposal of usable assets, once acquired, generally involves suffering financial losses.

In economic evaluations, project alternatives are represented by their cash flow profiles over the n years or periods in the planning horizon. Thus, the interest periods are normally assumed to be in years $t = 0, 1, 2, \ldots, n$ with $t = 0$ representing the present time. Let $B_{t,x}$ be the annual benefit at the end of year t for an investment project x, where $x = 1, 2, \ldots$ refer to projects no. 1, no. 2, and so on, respectively. Let $C_{t,x}$ be the annual cost at the end of year t for the same investment project x.

The net annual cash flow is defined as the annual benefit in excess of the annual cost and is denoted by $A_{t,x}$ at the end of year t for an investment project x. Then, for $t = 0, 1, \ldots, n$,

$$A_{t,x} = B_{t,x} - C_{t,x} \qquad (6.1)$$

where $A_{t,x}$ is positive, negative or zero depends on the values of $B_{t,x}$ and $C_{t,x}$, both of which are defined as positive quantities.

Once the management has committed funds to a specific project, it must forgo other investment opportunities which might have been undertaken by using the same funds. The *opportunity cost* reflects the return that can be earned from the best alternative investment opportunity forgone. The forgone opportunities may include not only capital projects but also financial investments or other socially desirable programs. Management should invest in a proposed project only if it will yield a return at least equal to the minimum attractive rate of return (MARR) from forgone opportunities as envisioned by the organization.

In general, the MARR specified by the top management in a private firm reflects the *opportunity cost of capital* of the firm, the market interest rates for lending and borrowing, and the risks associated with investment opportunities. For public projects, the MARR is specified by a government agency, such as the Office of Management and Budget or the Congress of the United States. The public MARR thus specified reflects social and economic welfare considerations and is referred to as the *social rate of discount*.

Regardless of how the MARR is determined by an organization, the MARR specified for the economic evaluation of investment proposals is critically important in determining whether any investment proposal is worthwhile from the standpoint of the organization. Since the MARR of an organization often cannot be determined accurately, it is advisable to use several values of the MARR to assess the sensitivity of the potential of the project to variations of the MARR value.

6.3 COSTS AND BENEFITS OF A CONSTRUCTED FACILITY

The basic principle in assessing the economic costs and benefits of new facility investments is to find the aggregate of individual changes in the welfare of all parties affected by the proposed projects. The changes in welfare are generally measured in monetary terms, but there are exceptions, since some effects cannot be measured directly by cash receipts and disbursements. Examples include the value of human lives saved through safety improvements or the cost of environmental degradation. The difficulties in estimating future costs and benefits lie not only in uncertainties and reliability of measurement, but also on the social costs and benefits generated as side effects. Furthermore, proceeds and expenditures related to financial transactions, such as interest and subsidies, must also be considered by private firms and by public agencies.

To obtain an accurate estimate of costs in the cash flow profile for the acquisition and operation of a project, it is necessary to specify the resources required to construct and operate the proposed physical facility, given the available technology and operating policy. Typically, each of the labor and material resources required by the facility is multiplied by its price, and the products are then summed to obtain the total costs. Private corporations generally ignore external social costs unless required by law to do so. In the public sector, externalities often must be properly accounted for. An example is the cost of property damage caused by air pollution from a new plant. In any case, the measurement of external costs is extremely difficult and somewhat subjective for lack of a market mechanism to provide even approximate answers to the appropriate value.

In the private sector, the benefits derived from a facility investment are often measured by the revenues generated from the operation of the facility. Revenues are estimated by the total of price times quantity purchased. The depreciation allowances and taxes on revenues must be deducted according to the prevailing tax laws. In the public sector, income may also be accrued to a public agency from the operation of the facility. However, several other categories of benefits may also be included in the evaluation of public projects. First, private benefits can be received by users of a facility or service in excess of costs such as user charges or price charged. After all, individuals only use a service or facility if their private benefit exceeds their cost. These private benefits or *consumers' surplus* represent a direct benefit to members of the public. In many public projects, it is difficult, impossible or impractical to charge for services received, so direct revenues equal zero and all user benefits appear as consumers' surplus. Examples are a park or roadways for which entrance is free. As a second special category of public benefit, there may be external or secondary beneficiaries of public projects, such as new jobs created and profits to private suppliers. Estimating these secondary benefits is extremely difficult since resources devoted to public projects might simply be displaced from private employment and thus represent no net benefit.

6.4 INTEREST RATES AND THE COSTS OF CAPITAL

Constructed facilities are inherently long-term investments with a deferred payoff. The cost of capital or MARR depends on the real interest rate (i.e., market interest rate less the inflation rate) over the period of investment. As the cost of capital rises, it becomes less and less attractive to invest in a large facility because of the opportunities forgone over a long period of time.

In Figure 6-1, the changes in the cost of capital from 1955 to 1985 are illustrated. This figure presents the market interest rate on a 20-year Treasury bond and the corresponding real interest rate over this period. The *real interest rate* is calculated as the market interest rate less the general rate of inflation. During the last decade in this figure, the real interest rate has varied substantially, ranging from 10 to −4 percent. The exceptional nature of the 1980 to 1985 years is dramatically evident: the real rate of interest reached remarkably high historic levels.

With these volatile interest rates, interest charges and the ultimate cost of projects are uncertain. Organizations and institutional arrangements capable of dealing with this uncertainty and able to respond to interest rate changes effectively would be quite valuable. For example, banks offer both fixed rate and variable rate mortgages.

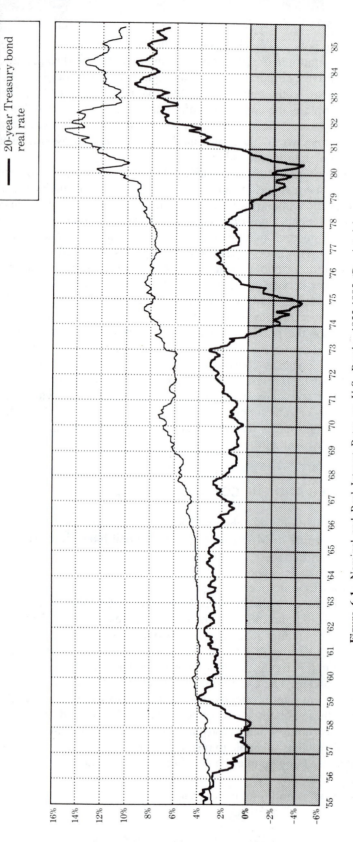

Figure 6-1 Nominal and Real Interest Rates on U.S. Bonds, 1955-1985 (Reprinted by permission of the *Wall Street Journal*,©Dow Jones & Company, Inc. 1985. All Rights Reserved.)

An owner who wants to limit its own risk may choose to take a fixed rate mortgage even though the ultimate interest charges may be higher. On the other hand, an owner who chooses a variable rate mortgage will have to adjust its annual interest charges according to the market interest rates.

In economic evaluation, a constant value of MARR over the planning horizon is often used to simplify the calculations. The use of a constant value for MARR is justified on the ground of long-term average of the cost of capital over the period of investment. If the benefits and costs over time are expressed in constant dollars, the constant value for MARR represents the average real interest rate anticipated over the planning horizon; if the benefits and costs over time are expressed in then-current dollars, the constant value for MARR reflects the average market interest rate anticipated over the planning horizon.

6.5 INVESTMENT PROFIT MEASURES

A *profit measure* is defined as an indicator of the desirability of a project from the standpoint of a decision maker. A profit measure may or may not be used as the basis for project selection. Since various profit measures are used by decision makers for different purposes, the advantages and restrictions for using these profit measures should be fully understood.

There are several profit measures that are commonly used by decision makers in both private corporations and public agencies. Each of these measures is intended to be an indicator of profit or net benefit for a project under consideration. Some of these measures indicate the size of the profit at a specific point in time; others give the rate of return per period when the capital is in use or when reinvestments of the early profits are also included. If a decision maker understands clearly the meaning of the various profit measures for a given project, there is no reason why one cannot use all of them for the restrictive purposes for which they are appropriate. With the availability of computer-based analysis and commercial software, it takes only a few seconds to compute these profit measures. However, it is important to define these measures precisely:

1. Net Future Value and Net Present Value. When an organization makes an investment, the decision maker looks forward to the gain over a planning horizon against what might be gained if the money were invested elsewhere. A minimum attractive rate of return is adopted to reflect this opportunity cost of capital. The MARR is used for compounding the estimated cash flows to the end of the planning horizon or for discounting the cash flow to the present. The profitability is measured by the net future value (NFV) which is the net return at the end of the planning horizon above what might have been gained by investing elsewhere at the MARR. The net present value (NPV) of the estimated cash flows over the planning horizon is the discounted value of the NFV to the present. A positive NPV for a project indicates the present value of the net gain corresponding to the project cash flows.

2. Equivalent Uniform Annual Net Value. The equivalent uniform annual net value (NUV) is a constant stream of benefits less costs at equally spaced time periods over the intended planning horizon of a project. This value can be calculated as the net present value multiplied by an appropriate "capital recovery factor." It is a measure of the net return of a project on an annualized or amortized basis. The equivalent uniform annual cost (EUAC) can be obtained by multiplying the present value of costs by an appropriate capital recovery factor. The use of EUAC alone presupposes that the discounted benefits of all potential projects over the planning horizon are identical and therefore only the discounted costs of various projects need be considered. Therefore, the EUAC is an indicator of the negative attribute of a project which should be minimized.

3. Benefit-Cost Ratio. The benefit-cost ratio (BCR), defined as the ratio of discounted benefits to the discounted costs at the same point in time, is a profitability index based on discounted benefits per unit of discounted costs of a project. It is sometimes referred to as the savings-to-investment ratio (SIR) when the benefits are derived from the reduction of undesirable effects. Its use also requires the choice of a planning horizon and a MARR. Since some savings may be interpreted as a negative cost to be deducted from the denominator or as a positive benefit to be added to the numerator of the ratio, the BCR or SIR is not an absolute numerical measure. However, if the ratio of the present value of benefit to the present value of cost exceeds 1, the project is profitable irrespective of different interpretations of such benefits or costs.

4. Internal Rate of Return. The internal rate of return (IRR) is defined as the discount rate which sets the net present value of a series of cash flows over the planning horizon equal to zero. If a project consists of a single outlay at the beginning and generates a stream of net benefits afterward, a unique value of IRR indicates the return over cost per period from funds remain invested in the project. However, the IRR does not take into consideration the external reinvestment opportunities related to the timing and intensity of the outlays and returns at the intermediate points over the planning horizon. For cash flows with two or more sign reversals of the cash flows in any period, there may exist multiple values of IRR; in such cases, the multiple values are subject to various interpretations.

5. Adjusted Internal Rate of Return. If the financing and reinvestment policies are incorporated into the evaluation of a project, an adjusted internal rate of return (AIRR) which reflects such policies may be a useful indicator of profitability under restricted circumstances. Because of the complexity of financing and reinvestment policies used by an organization over the life of a project, the AIRR seldom can reflect the reality of actual cash flows. However, it offers an approximate value of the yield on an investment for which two or more sign reversals in the cash flows would result in multiple values of IRR. The adjusted internal rate of return is usually calculated as the internal rate of return on the project cash flow modified so that all costs are discounted to the present and all benefits are compounded to the end of the planning horizon.

6. Return on Investment. When an accountant reports income in each year of a multiyear project, the stream of cash flows must be broken up into annual rates of return for those years. The return on investment (ROI) as used by accountants usually means the accountant's rate of return for each year of the project duration based on the ratio of the income (revenue less depreciation) for each year and the undepreciated asset value (investment) for that same year. Hence, the ROI is different from year to year, with a very low value at the early years and a high value in the later years of the project.

7. Payback Period. The payback period (PBP) refers to the length of time within which the benefits received from an investment can repay the costs incurred during the time in question while ignoring the remaining time periods in the planning horizon. Even the discounted payback period indicating the "capital recovery period" does not reflect the magnitude or direction of the cash flows in the remaining periods. However, if a project is found to be profitable by other measures, the payback period can be used as a secondary measure of the financing requirements for a project.

6.6 METHODS OF ECONOMIC EVALUATION

The objective of facility investment in the private sector is generally understood to be profit maximization within a specific time frame. Similarly, the objective in the public sector is the maximization of net social benefit which is analogous to profit maximization in private organizations. Given this objective, a method of economic analysis will be judged by the reliability and ease with which a correct conclusion may be reached in project selection.

The basic principle underlying the decision for accepting and selecting investment projects is that if an organization can lend or borrow as much money as it wishes at the MARR, the goal of profit maximization is best served by accepting all independent projects whose profit maximization based on the specified MARR are nonnegative, or by selecting the project with the maximum nonnegative net present value among a set of mutually exclusive proposals. The net present value criterion reflects this principle and is most straightforward and unambiguous when there is no budget constraint. Various methods of economic evaluation, when properly applied, will produce the same result if the profit maximization criterion is used as the basis for decision. For convenience of computation, a set of tables for the various compound interest factors is given in Appendix A.

Net Present Value Method

Let BPV_x be the present value of benefits of a project x and CPV_x be the present value of costs of the project x. Then, for MARR $= i$ over a planning horizon of n years,

$$\mathrm{BPV}_x = \sum_{t=0}^{n} B_{t,x}(1 + i)^{-t} = \sum_{t=0}^{n} B_{t,x}(P|F, i, t) \qquad (6.2)$$

$$CPV_x = \sum_{t=0}^{n} C_{t,x}(1 + i)^{-t} = \sum_{t=0}^{n} C_{t,x}(P|F, i, t) \qquad (6.3)$$

where the symbol $(P|F, i, t)$ is a discount factor equal to $(1 + i)^{-t}$ and reads as follows: "To find the present value P, given the future value $F = 1$, discounted at an annual discount rate i over a period of t years." When the benefit or cost in year t is multiplied by this factor, the present value is obtained. Then, the net present value of the project x is calculated as

$$NPV_x = BPV_x - CPV_x \qquad (6.4)$$

or

$$NPV_x = \sum_{t=0}^{n} (B_{t,x} - C_{t,x})(P|F, i, t) = \sum_{t=0}^{n} A_{t,x}(P|F, i, t) \qquad (6.5)$$

If there is no budget constraint, then all independent projects having net present values greater than or equal to zero are acceptable. That is, project x is acceptable as long as

$$NPV_x \geq 0 \qquad (6.6)$$

For mutually exclusive proposals $(x = 1, 2, \ldots, m)$, a proposal j should be selected if it has the maximum nonnegative net present value among all m proposals; that is,

$$NPV_j = \max_{x \in m}\{NPV_x\} \qquad (6.7)$$

provided that $NPV_j \geq 0$.

Net Future Value Method

Since the cash flow profile of an investment can be represented by its equivalent value at any specified reference point in time, the net future value (NFV_x) of a series of cash flows $A_{t,x}$ (for $t = 0, 1, 2, \ldots, n$) for project x is as good a measure of economic potential as the net present value. Equivalent future values are obtained by multiplying a present value by the compound interest factor $(F|P, i, n)$ which is $(1 + i)^n$. Specifically,

$$NFV_x = NPV_x(1 + i)^n = NPV_x(F|P, i, n) \qquad (6.8)$$

Consequently, if $NPV_x \geq 0$, it follows that $NFV_x \geq 0$, and vice versa.

Net Equivalent Uniform Annual Value Method

The *net equivalent uniform annual value* (NUV_x) refers to a uniform series over a planning horizon of n years whose net present value is that of a series of cash flow $A_{t,x}$ (for $t = 1, 2, \ldots, n$) representing project x. That is,

Economic Evaluation of Facility Investments   Chap. 6

$$\text{NUV}_x = \text{NPV}_x \frac{i(1 + i)^n}{(1 + i)^n - 1} = \text{NPV}_x(U|P, i, n) \tag{6.9}$$

where the symbol $(U|P, i, n)$ is referred to as the *capital recovery factor* and reads as follows: "To find the equivalent annual uniform amount U, given the present value $P = 1$, discounted at an annual discount rate i over a period of t years." Hence, if $\text{NPV}_x \geq 0$, it follows that $\text{NUV}_x \geq 0$, and vice versa.

Benefit-Cost Ratio Method

The benefit-cost ratio method is not as straightforward and unambiguous as the net present value method but, if applied correctly, will produce the same results as the net present value method. While this method is often used in the evaluation of public projects, the results may be misleading if proper care is not exercised in its application to mutually exclusive proposals.

The *benefit-cost ratio* is defined as the ratio of the discounted benefits to the discounted cost at the same point in time. In view of Eqs. (6.4) and (6.6), it follows that the criterion for accepting an *independent* project on the basis of the benefit-cost ratio is whether or not the benefit-cost ratio is greater than or equal to 1:

$$\frac{\text{BPV}_x}{\text{CPV}_x} \geq 1 \tag{6.10}$$

However, a project with the maximum benefit-cost ratio among a group of *mutually exclusive* proposals generally does not necessarily lead to the maximum net benefit. Consequently, it is necessary to perform incremental analysis through pairwise comparisons of such proposals in selecting the best in the group. In effect, pairwise comparisons are used to determine if incremental increases in costs between projects yields larger incremental increases in benefits. This approach is not recommended for use in selecting the best among mutually exclusive proposals.

Internal Rate of Return Method

The term *internal rate of return method* has been used by different analysts to mean somewhat different procedures for economic evaluation. The method is often misunderstood and misused, and its popularity among analysts in the private sector is undeserved even when the method is defined and interpreted in the most favorable light. The method is usually applied by comparing the MARR to the internal rate of return value(s) for a project or a set of projects.

A major difficulty in applying the internal rate of return method to economic evaluation is the possible existence of multiple values of IRR when there are two or more changes of sign in the cash flow profile $A_{t,x}$ (for $t = 0, 1, 2, \ldots, n$). When that happens, the method is generally not applicable either in determining the acceptance of independent projects or for selection of the best among a group of mutually exclusive proposals unless a set of well defined decision rules are introduced for incremental analysis. In any case, no advantage is gained by using this method since the procedure is cumbersome even if the method is correctly applied. This method is not recommended for use either in accepting independent projects or in selecting the best among mutually exclusive proposals.

Example 6-1: Evaluation of Four Independent Projects

The cash flow profiles of four independent projects are shown in Table (6-1). Using a MARR of 20 percent, determine the acceptability of each of the projects on the basis of the net present value criterion for accepting independent projects.

TABLE 6–1 CASH FLOW PROFILES OF FOUR INDEPENDENT PROJECTS

t	$A_{t,1}$	$A_{t,2}$	$A_{t,3}$	$A_{t,4}$
0	-77.0	-75.3	-39.9	18.0
1	0	28.0	28.0	10.0
2	0	28.0	28.0	-40.0
3	0	28.0	28.0	-60.0
4	0	28.0	28.0	30.0
5	235.0	28.0	-80.0	50.0

Using $i = 20\%$, we can compute NPV for $x = 1, 2, 3,$ and 4 from Eq. (6.5). Then, the acceptability of each project can be determined from Eq. (6.6). Thus,

$$[\text{NPV}_1]_{20\%} = -77 + (235)(P|F, 20\%, 5) = -77 + 94.4 = 17.4$$

$$[\text{NPV}_2]_{20\%} = -75.3 + (28)(P|U, 20\%, 5) = -75.3 + 83.7 = 8.4$$

$$[\text{NPV}_3]_{20\%} = -39.9 + (28)(P|U, 20\%, 4) - (80)(P|F, 20\%, 5)$$

$$= -39.9 + 72.5 - 32.2 = 0.4$$

$$[\text{NPV}_4]_{20\%} = 18 + (10)(P|F, 20\%, 1) - (40)(P|F, 20\%, 2)$$

$$-(60)(P|F, 20\%, 3) + (30)(P|F, 20\%, 4) + (50)(P|F, 20\%, 5)$$

$$= 18 + 8.3 - 27.8 - 34.7 + 14.5 + 20.1 = -1.6$$

Hence, the first three independent projects are acceptable, but the last project should be rejected.

It is interesting to note that if the four projects are mutually exclusive, the net present value method can still be used to evaluate the projects and, according to Eq. (6.7), the project ($x = 1$) that has the highest positive NPV should be selected. The use of the net equivalent uniform annual value or the net future value method will lead to the same conclusion. However, the project with the highest benefit-cost ratio is not necessarily the best choice among a group of mutually exclusive alternatives. Furthermore, the conventional internal rate of return method cannot be used to make a meaningful evaluation of these projects as the IRR for both $x = 1$ and $x = 2$ are found to be 25 percent while multiple values of IRR exist for both the $x = 3$ and $x = 4$ alternatives.

6.7 DEPRECIATION AND TAX EFFECTS

For private corporations, the cash flow profile of a project is affected by the amount of taxation. In the context of tax liability, *depreciation* is the amount allowed as a deduction due to capital expenses in computing taxable income and, hence, income tax in any year. Thus, depreciation results in a reduction in tax liabilities.

It is important to differentiate between the estimated useful life used in depreciation computations and the actual useful life of a facility. The former is often an arbitrary length of time, specified in the regulations of the U.S. Internal Revenue Service or a comparable organization. The depreciation allowance is a bookkeeping entry that does not involve an outlay of cash, but represents a systematic allocation of the cost of a physical facility over time.

There are various methods of computing depreciation which are acceptable to the U.S. Internal Revenue Service. The different methods of computing depreciation have different effects on the streams of annual depreciation charges, and hence on the stream of taxable income and taxes paid. Let P be the cost of an asset, S its estimated salvage value, and N the estimated useful life (depreciable life) in years. Furthermore, let D_t denote the depreciation amount in year t, T_t denote the accumulated depreciation up to year t, and B_t denote the book value of the asset at the end of year t, where $t = 1, 2, \ldots$, or n refers to the particular year under consideration. Then,

$$T_t = D_1 + D_2 + \cdots + D_t \tag{6.11}$$

and

$$B_t = P - T_t = B_{t-1} - D_t \tag{6.12}$$

The depreciation methods most commonly used to compute D_t and B_t are the straight-line method, sum-of-the-years'-digits (SOYD) method, and the double-declining-balance method. The U.S. Internal Revenue Service provides tables of acceptable depreciable schedules using these methods. Under straight-line depreciation, the net depreciable value resulting from the cost of the facility less salvage value is allocated uniformly to each year of the estimated useful life. Under the sum-of-the-years'-digits method, the annual depreciation allowance is obtained by multiplying the net depreciable value multiplied by a fraction, which has as its numerator the number of years of remaining useful life and its denominator the sum of all the digits from 1 to n. The annual depreciation allowance under the double-declining-balance method is obtained by multiplying the book value of the previous year by a constant depreciation rate $2/n$.

To consider tax effects in project evaluation, the most direct approach is to estimate the after-tax cash flow and then apply an evaluation method such as the net present value method. Since projects are often financed by internal funds representing the overall equity-debt mix of the entire corporation, the deductibility of interest on debt may be considered on a corporatewide basis. For specific project financing from internal funds, let *after-tax* cash flow in year t be Y_t. Then, for $t = 0, 1, 2, \ldots, n$,

$$Y_t = A_t - X_t(A_t - D_t) \tag{6.13}$$

where A_t is the net revenue before tax in year t, D_t is the depreciation allowable for year t and X_t is the marginal corporate income tax rate in year t.

Besides corporate income taxes, there are other provisions in the federal income tax laws that affect facility investments, such as tax credits for low-income housing. Since the tax laws are revised periodically, the estimation of tax liability in the future can only be approximate.

Example 6-2: Effects of Taxes on Investment

A company plans to invest $55,000 in a piece of equipment which is expected to produce a uniform annual net revenue before tax of $15,000 over the next 5 years. The equipment has a salvage value of $5,000 at the end of 5 years and the depreciation allowance is computed on the basis of the straight-line depreciation method. The marginal income tax rate for this company is 34 percent, and there is no expectation of inflation. If the after-tax MARR specified by the company is 8 percent, determine whether the proposed investment is worthwhile, assuming that the investment will be financed by internal funds.

Using Eqs.(6.11) and (6.13), the after-tax cash flow can be computed as shown in Table (6-2). Then, the net present value discounted at 8 percent is obtained from Eq.(6.5) as follows:

$$[\text{NPV}]_{8\%} = -55,000 + \sum_{t=1}^{5}(13,300)(P|F,\ 8\%,\ t)$$

$$+(5,000)(P|F,\ 8\%,\ 5) = \$1,510$$

The positive result indicates that the project is worthwhile.

TABLE 6-2 AFTER-TAX CASH FLOW COMPUTATION

Year t	Before-tax cash flow A_t	Straight-line depreciation D_t	Taxable income $A_t - D_t$	Income tax $X_t(A_t - D_t)$	After-tax cash flow Y_t
0	− $55,000				− $55,000
1–5 each	+ $15,000	$10,000	$5,000	$1,700	+ $13,300
5 only	+ $ 5,000				+ $ 5,000

6.8 PRICE-LEVEL CHANGES: INFLATION AND DEFLATION

In the economic evaluation of investment proposals, two approaches may be used to reflect the effects of future price-level changes due to inflation or deflation. The differences between the two approaches are primarily philosophical and can be succinctly stated as follows:

1. **The constant dollar approach**. The investor wants a specified MARR excluding inflation. Consequently, the cash flows should be expressed in terms of base-year or constant dollars, and a discount rate excluding inflation should be used in computing the net present value.

2. **The inflated dollar approach**. The investor includes an inflation component in the specified MARR. Hence, the cash flows should be expressed in terms of then-current or inflated dollars, and a discount rate including inflation should be used in computing the net present value.

If these approaches are applied correctly, they will lead to identical results.

Let i be the discount rate excluding inflation, i' be the discount rate including inflation, and j be the annual inflation rate. Then,

$$i' = i + j + ij \qquad (6.14)$$

and

$$i = \frac{i' - j}{1 + j} \qquad (6.15)$$

When the inflation rate j is small, these relations can be approximated by

$$i' = i + j \quad \text{or} \quad i = i' - j \qquad (6.16)$$

Note that inflation over time has a compounding effect on the price levels in various periods, as discussed in connection with the cost indices in Chapter 5.

If A_t denotes the cash flow in year t expressed in terms of constant (base-year) dollars, and A'_t denotes the cash flow in year t expressed in terms of inflated (then-current) dollars, then

$$\text{NPV} = A_0 + \sum_{t=1}^{n} A_t(1 + i)^{-t} \qquad (6.17)$$

or

$$\text{NPV} = A_0 + \sum_{t=1}^{n} A'_t(1 + i')^{-t} \qquad (6.18)$$

It can be shown that the results from these two equations are identical. Furthermore, the relationship applies to after-tax cash flow as well as to before-tax cash flow by replacing A_t and A'_t with Y_t and Y'_t, respectively, in Eqs.(6.17) and (6.18).

Example 6-3: Effects of Inflation

Suppose that, in the previous example, the inflation expectation is 5 percent per year, and the after-tax MARR specified by the company is 8 percent excluding inflation. Determine whether the investment is worthwhile.

In this case, the before-tax cash flow A_t in terms of constant dollars at base year 0 is inflated at $j = 5\%$ to then-current dollars A'_t for the computation of the taxable income $(A'_t - D_t)$ and income taxes. The resulting after-tax flow Y'_t in terms of then-current dollars is converted back to constant dollars. That is, for $X_t = 34\%$ and $D_t = \$10,000$. The annual depreciation charges D_t are not inflated to current dollars in conformity with the practice recommended by the U.S. Internal Revenue Service. Thus,

$$A'_t = A_t(1 + j)^t = A_t(1 + 0.05)^t$$

TABLE 6-3 AFTER-TAX CASH FLOW (CF) INCLUDING INFLATION

Time t	Constant \$ before-tax CF A_t	Current \$ before-tax DF A_t'	Current \$ depreciation D_t	Current \$ after depreciation $A_t' - D_t$	Current \$ income tax $X_t(A_t' - D_t)$	Current \$ after-tax CF Y_t'	Constant \$ after-tax CF Y_t
0	−\$55,000	+\$55,000				−\$55,000	−\$55,000
1	+ 15,000	+ 15,750	\$10,000	\$5,750	\$1,955	+ 13,795	+ 13,138
2	+ 15,000	+ 16,540	10,000	6,540	2,224	+ 14,316	+ 12,985
3	+ 15,000	+ 17,365	10,000	7,365	2,504	+ 14,861	+ 12,837
4	+ 15,000	+ 18,233	10,000	8,233	2,799	+ 15,434	+ 12,697
5	+ 15,000	+ 19,145	10,000	9,145	3,109	+ 16,036	+ 12,564
5	+ 5,000						+ 5,000

$$Y'_t = A'_t - X_t(A'_t - D_t) = A'_t - (34\%)(A'_t - \$10,000)$$

$$Y_t = Y'_t(1 + j)^{-t} = Y'_t(1 + 0.05)^{-t}$$

The detailed computation of the after-tax cash flow is recorded in Table 6-3. The net present value discounted at 8 percent, excluding inflation, is obtained by substituting Y_t for A_t in Eq. (6.17). Hence,

$$[\text{NPV}]_{8\%} = -\$55,000 + (\$13,138)(P|F, 8\%, 1) + (\$12,985)(P|F, 8\%, 2)$$

$$+ (\$12,837)(P|F, 8\%, 3) + (\$12,697)(P|F, 8\%, 4)$$

$$+ (\$12,564 + 5,000)(P|F, 8\%, 5)$$

$$= -\$227$$

With 5 percent inflation, the investment is no longer worthwhile because the value of the depreciation tax deduction is not increased to match the inflation rate.

6.9 UNCERTAINTY AND RISK

Since future events are always uncertain, all estimates of costs and benefits used in economic evaluation involve a degree of uncertainty. Probabilistic methods are often used in decision analysis to determine expected costs and benefits as well as to assess the degree of risk in particular projects.

In estimating benefits and costs, it is common to attempt to obtain the expected or average values of these quantities depending upon the different events which might occur. Statistical techniques such as regression models can be used directly in this regard to provide forecasts of average values. Alternatively, the benefits and costs associated with different events can be estimated and the expected benefits and costs calculated as the sum over all possible events of the resulting benefits and costs multiplied by the probability of occurrence of a particular event:

$$E[B_t] = \sum_{q=1}^{m} (B_{t|q}) \cdot Pr\{q\} \tag{6.19}$$

and

$$E[C_t] = \sum_{q=1}^{m} (C_{t|q}) \cdot Pr\{q\} \tag{6.20}$$

where $q = 1, \ldots, m$ represents possible events, $(B_{t|q})$ and $(C_{t|q})$ are benefits and costs, respectively, in period t due to the occurrence of q, $Pr\{q\}$ is the probability that q occurs, and $E[B_t]$ and $E[C_t]$ are, respectively, expected benefit and cost in period t. Hence, the expected net benefit in period t is given by

$$E[A_t] = E[B_t] - E[C_t] \tag{6.21}$$

For example, the average cost of a facility in an earthquake-prone site might be calculated as the sum of the cost of operation under normal conditions (multiplied by the probability of no earthquake) plus the cost of operation after an earthquake (multiplied by the probability of an earthquake). Expected benefits and costs can be used directly in the cash flow calculations described earlier.

In formulating objectives, some organizations wish to avoid risk so as to avoid the possibility of losses. In effect, a *risk-avoiding* organization might select a project with lower expected profit or net social benefit as long as it had a lower risk of losses . This preference results in a *risk premium* or higher desired profit for risky projects . A rough method of representing a risk premium is to make the desired MARR higher for risky projects. Let r_f be the risk-free market rate of interest as represented by the average rate of return of a safe investment such as U.S. government bonds. However, U.S. government bonds do not protect from inflationary changes or exchange rate fluctuations, but only ensure that the principal and interest will be repaid. Let r_p be the risk premium reflecting an adjustment of the rate of return for the perceived risk. Then, the risk-adjusted rate of return r is given by

$$r = r_f + r_p \qquad (6.22)$$

In using the risk-adjusted rate of return r to compute the net present value of an estimated net cash flow $A_t(t = 0, 1, 2, \ldots, n)$ over n years, it is tacitly assumed that the values of A_t become more uncertain as time goes on. That is,

$$[\text{NPV}]_r = \sum_{t=0}^{n} A_t(1 + r)^{-t} \qquad (6.23)$$

More directly, a decision maker may be confronted with the subjective choice among alternatives with different expected benefits of levels of risk such that at a given period t, the decision maker is willing to exchange an uncertain A_t, with a smaller but certain return $a_t A_t$, where a_t is less than 1. Consider the decision tree in Figure 6-2 in which the decision maker is confronted with a choice between the certain return of $a_t A_t$ and a gamble with possible outcomes $(A_t)_q$ and respective probabilities $Pr\{q\}$ for $q = 1, 2, \ldots, m$. Then, the net present value for the series of 'certainty equivalents' over n years may be computed on the basis of the risk-free rate. Hence,

$$[\text{NPV}]_{r_f} = \sum_{t=0}^{n} (a_t A_t)(1 + r_f)^{-t} \qquad (6.24)$$

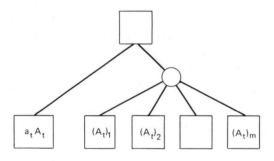

Figure 6-2 Determination of a Certainty Equivalent Value

Economic Evaluation of Facility Investments   Chap. 6

Note that if $r_f r_p$ is negligible in comparison with r, then

$$(1 + r_f)(1 + r_p) = 1 + r_f + r_p + r_f r_p = 1 + r$$

Hence, for Eq.(6.23)

$$A_t(1 + r)^{-t} = (a_t A_t/a_t)(1 + r_f)^{-t}(1 + r_p)^{-t}$$
$$= [(a_t A_t)(1 + r_f)^{-t}][(1 + r_p)^{-t}/a_t]$$

If $a_t = (1 + r_p)^{-t}$ for $t = 1, 2, \ldots, n$, then Eqs. (6.23) and (6.24) will be identical. Hence, the use of the risk-adjusted rate r for computing NPV has the same effect as accepting $a_t = (1 + r_p)^{-t}$ as a "certainty equivalent" factor in adjusting the estimated cash flow over time.

6.10 EFFECTS OF FINANCING ON PROJECT SELECTION

Selection of the best design and financing plans for capital projects is typically done separately and sequentially. Three approaches to facility investment planning most often adopted by an organization are

1. Need or demand driven. Public capital investments are defined and debated in terms of an absolute "need" for particular facilities or services. With a predefined "need," design and financing analysis then proceed separately. Even when investments are made on the basis of a demand or revenue analysis of the market, the separation of design and financing analysis is still prevalent.

2. Design driven. Designs are generated, analyzed, and approved prior to the investigation of financing alternatives, because projects are approved first and only then programmed for eventual funding.

3. Finance driven. The process of developing a facility within a particular budget target is finance driven since the budget is formulated prior to the final design. It is a common procedure in private developments and increasingly used for public projects.

Typically, different individuals or divisions of an organization conduct the analysis for the operating and financing processes. Financing alternatives are sometimes not examined at all since a single mechanism is universally adopted. An example of a single financing plan in the public sector is the use of pay-as-you-go highway trust funds. However, the importance of financial analysis is increasing with the increase of private ownership and private participation in the financing of public projects. The availability of a broad spectrum of new financing instruments has accentuated the needs for better financial analysis in connection with capital investments in both the public and private sectors. While simultaneous assessment of all design and financing alternatives is not always essential, more communication of information between the two evaluation processes would be advantageous to avoid the selection of inferior alternatives.

There is an ever-increasing variety of borrowing mechanisms available. First, the extent to which borrowing is tied to a particular project or asset may be varied.

Loans backed by specific, tangible, and fungible assets and with restrictions on that asset's use are regarded as less risky. In contrast, specific project finance may be more costly to arrange due to transactions costs than is general corporate or government borrowing. Also, backing by the full good faith and credit of an organization is considered less risky than are investments backed by generally immovable assets. Second, the options of fixed versus variable rate borrowing are available. Third, the repayment schedule and time horizon of borrowing may be varied. A detailed discussion of financing of constructed facilities will be deferred until the next chapter.

As a general rule, it is advisable to borrow as little as possible when borrowing rates exceed the minimum attractive rate of return. Equity or pay-as-you-go financing may be desirable in this case. It is generally preferable to obtain lower borrowing rates, unless borrowing associated with lower rates requires substantial transaction costs or reduces the flexibility for repayment and refinancing. In the public sector, it may be that increasing taxes or user charges to reduce borrowing involves economic costs in excess of the benefits of reduced borrowing costs of borrowed funds. Furthermore, since cash flow analysis is typically conducted on the basis of constant dollars and loan agreements are made with respect to current dollars, removing the effects of inflation will reduce the cost of borrowing. Finally, deferring investments until pay-as-you-go or equity financing are available may unduly defer the benefits of new investments.

It is difficult to conclude unambiguously that one financing mechanism is always superior to others. Consequently, evaluating alternative financing mechanisms is an important component of the investment analysis procedure. One possible approach to considering design and financing alternatives simultaneously is to consider each combination of design and financing options as a specific, mutually exclusive alternative. The cash flow of this combined alternative would be the sum of the economic or operating cash flow (assuming equity financing) and the financial cash flow over the planning horizon.

6.11 COMBINED EFFECTS OF OPERATING AND FINANCING CASH FLOWS

A general approach for obtaining the combined effects of operating and financing cash flows of a project is to make use of the additive property of net present values by calculating an adjusted net present value. The adjusted net present value (APV) is the sum of the net present value (NPV) of the operating cash flow plus the net present value of the financial cash flow due to borrowing or raising capital (FPV). Thus,

$$APV = [NPV]_i + [FPV]_i \qquad (6.25)$$

where each function is evaluated at $i = $ MARR if both the operating and the financing cash flows have the same degree of risk or if the risks are taken care of in other ways such as by the use of certainty equivalents. Then, project selection involving both design and financing alternatives is accomplished by selecting the combination which has the highest positive adjusted present value. The use of this adjusted net present value method will result in the same selection as an evaluation based on the net present value obtained from the combined cash flow of each alternative combination directly.

To be specific, let A_t be the net operating cash flow, $\overline{A}_t$ be the net financial cash flow resulting from debt financing, and AA_t be the combined net cash flow, all for year t before tax. Then

$$AA_t = A_t + \overline{A}_t \tag{6.26}$$

Similarly, let $\overline{Y}_t$ and YY_t be the corresponding cash flows after tax such that

$$YY_t = Y_t + \overline{Y}_t \tag{6.27}$$

The tax shields for interest on borrowing (for $t = 1, 2, \ldots, n$) are usually given by

$$\overline{Y}_t = \overline{A}_t + X_t I_t \tag{6.28}$$

where I_t is the interest paid in year t and X_t is the marginal corporate income tax rate in year t. In view of Eqs. (6.13), (6.27), and (6.28), we obtain

$$YY_t = A_t + \overline{A}_t - X_t(A_t - D_t - I_t) \tag{6.29}$$

When MARR $= i$ is applied to both the operating and the financial cash flows in Eqs. (6.13) and (6.28), respectively, in computing the net present values, the combined effect will be the same as the net present value obtained by applying MARR $= i$ to the combined cash flow in Eq. (6.29).

In many instances, a risk premium related to the specified type of operation is added to the MARR for discounting the operating cash flow. On the other hand, the MARR for discounting the financial cash flow for borrowing is often regarded as relatively risk free because debtors or holders of corporate bonds must be paid first before stockholders in case financial difficulties are encountered by a corporation. Then, the adjusted net present value is given by

$$\text{APV} = [\text{NPV}]_r + [\text{FPV}]_{r_f} \tag{6.30}$$

where NPV is discounted at r and FPV is obtained from the r_f rate. Note that the net present value of the financial cash flow includes not only tax shields for interest on loans and other forms of government subsidy, but also on transactions costs such as those for legal and financial services associated with issuing new bonds or stocks.

The evaluation of combined alternatives based on the adjusted net present value method should also be performed in dollar amounts which either consistently include or remove the effects of inflation. The MARR value used would reflect the inclusion or exclusion of inflation accordingly. Furthermore, it is preferable to use after-tax cash flows in the evaluation of projects for private firms since different designs and financing alternatives are likely to have quite different implications for tax liabilities and tax shields.

In theory, the corporate finance process does not necessarily require a different approach from that of the APV method discussed earlier. Rather than considering single projects in isolation, groups or sets of projects along with financing alternatives can be evaluated. The evaluation process would be to select that group of operating and financing plans which has the highest total APV. Unfortunately, the number of possible combinations to evaluate can become very large even though many combinations can be rapidly eliminated in practice because they are clearly inferior. More commonly, heuristic approaches are developed such as choosing projects with the highest benefit-cost ratio within a particular budget or financial constraint. These heuristic schemes will often involve the separation of the financing and design alternative evaluation. The typical result is design-driven or finance-driven planning in which one or the other process is conducted first.

Example 6-4: Combined Effects of Operating and Financing Plans

A public agency plans to construct a facility and is considering two design alternatives with different capacities. The operating net cash flows for both alternatives over a planning horizon of 5 years are shown in Table 6-4. For each design alternative, the project can be financed either through overdraft on bank credit or by issuing bonds spanning over the 5-year period, and the cash flow for each financing alternative is also shown in Table 6-4. The public agency has specified a MARR of 10 percent for discounting the operating and financing cash flows for this project. Determine the best combination of design and financing plan if (a) a design is selected before financing plans are considered or (b) the decision is made simultaneously rather than sequentially.

The net present values of all cash flows can be computed by Eq.(6-5), and the results are given at the bottom of Table 6-4. The adjusted net present value combining the operating cash flow of each design and an appropriate financing is obtained according to Eq. (6.25), and the results are also tabulated at the bottom of Table 6-4.

Under condition (a), design alternative 2 will be selected since NPV = $767,000

TABLE 6-4 DIFFERENT DESIGN AND FINANCING ALTERNATIVES (in $ thousands)

Year	Design alternative 1			Design alternative 2		
	Operating cash flow	Overdraft financing	Bond financing	Operating cash flow	Overdraft financing	Bond financing
0	−$1,000	$1,000	$3,653	−$2,500	$2,500	$3,805
1	− 2,500	2,500	− 418	− 1,000	1,000	− 435
2	1,000	− 1,000	− 418	1,000	− 1,000	− 435
3	1,500	− 1,500	− 418	1,500	− 1,500	− 435
4	1,500	− 1,500	− 418	1,500	− 1,500	− 435
5	1,700	− 921	− 4,217	1,930	− 1,254	− 4,392
NPV or FPV at 10%	761	− 277	− 290	767	− 347	− 301
APV = NPV + FPV		484	471		420	466

is the higher value when only operating cash flows are considered. Subsequently, bonds financing will be chosen because APV = $466,000 indicates that it is the best financing plan for design alternative 2.

Under condition (b), however, the choice will be based on the highest value of APV, that is APV = $484,000 for design alternative 1 in combination with overdraft financing. Thus, the simultaneous decision approach with yield the best results.

6.12 PUBLIC VERSUS PRIVATE OWNERSHIP OF FACILITIES

In recent years, various organizational ownership schemes have been proposed to raise the level of investment in constructed facilities. For example, independent authorities are assuming responsibility for some water and sewer systems, while private entrepreneurs are taking over the ownership of public buildings such as stadiums and convention centers in joint ventures with local governments. Such ownership arrangements not only can generate the capital for new facilities, but also will influence the management of the construction and operation of these facilities. In this section, we shall review some of these implications.

A particular organizational arrangement or financial scheme is not necessarily superior to all others in each case. Even for similar facilities, these arrangements and schemes may differ from place to place or over time. For example, U.S. water supply systems are owned and operated both by relatively large and small organizations in either the private or public sector. Modern portfolio theory suggests that there may be advantages in using a variety of financial schemes to spread risks. Similarly, small or large organizations may have different relative advantages with respect to personnel training, innovation, or other activities.

Differences in Required Rates of Return

A basic difference between public and private ownership of facilities is that private organizations are motivated by the expectation of profits in making capital investments. Consequently, private firms have a higher minimum attractive rate of return on investments than do public agencies. The MARR represents the desired return or profit for making capital investments. Furthermore, private firms often must pay a higher interest rate for borrowing than public agencies because of the tax-exempt or otherwise subsidized bonds available to public agencies. International loans also offer subsidized interest rates to qualified agencies or projects in many cases. With higher required rates of return, we expect that private firms will require greater receipts than would a public agency to make a particular investment desirable.

In addition to different minimum attractive rates of return, there is also an important distinction between public and private organizations with respect to their evaluation of investment benefits. For private firms, the returns and benefits to cover costs and provide profit are *monetary revenues*. In contrast, public agencies often consider *total* social benefits in evaluating projects. Total social benefits include monetary user payments plus users' surplus (e.g., the value received less costs incurred by users), external benefits (e.g., benefits to local businesses or property owners), and nonquantifiable factors (e.g., psychological support and unemployment relief). Generally, total social benefits will exceed monetary revenues.

While these different valuations of benefits may lead to radically different results with respect to the extent of benefits associated with an investment, they do not necessarily require public agencies to undertake such investments directly. First, many public enterprises must fund their investments and operating expenses from user-fees. Most public utilities fall into this category, and the importance of user fee financing is increasing for many civil works such as waterways. With user-fee financing, the required returns for the public and private firms to undertake the aforementioned investment are, in fact, limited to monetary revenues. As a second point, it is always possible for a public agency to contract with a private firm to undertake a particular project.

All other things being equal, we expect that private firms will require larger returns from a particular investment than would a public agency. From the users or taxpayers point of view, this implies that total payments would be *higher* to private firms for identical services. However, there are a number of mitigating factors to counterbalance this disadvantage for private firms.

Tax Implications of Public Versus Private Organizations

Another difference between public and private facility owners is in their relative liability for taxes. Public entities are often exempt from taxes of various kinds, whereas private facility owners incur a variety of income, property, and excise taxes. However, these private tax liabilities can be offset, at least in part, by tax deductions of various kinds.

For private firms, income taxes represent a significant cost of operation. However, taxable income is based on the gross revenues less all expenses and allowable deductions as permitted by the prevalent tax laws and regulations. The most significant allowable deductions are depreciation and interest. By selecting the method of depreciation and the financing plan which are most favorable, a firm can exert a certain degree of control on its taxable income and, thus, its income tax.

Another form of relief in tax liability is the *tax credit* which allows a direct deduction for income tax purposes of a small percentage of the value of certain newly acquired assets. Although the provisions for investment tax credit for physical facilities and equipment had been introduced at different times in the U.S. federal tax code, they were eliminated in the 1986 Tax Reformation Act except a tax credit for low-income housing.

Of course, a firm must have profits to take direct advantage of such tax shields; that is, tax deductions only reduce tax liabilities if before-tax profits exist. In many cases, investments in constructed facilities have net outlays or losses in the early years of construction. Generally, these losses in early years can be offset against profits occurring elsewhere or later in time. Without such offsetting profits, losses can be carried forward by the firm or merged with other firms' profits, but these mechanisms will not be reviewed here.

Effects of Financing Plans

Major investments in constructed facilities typically rely upon borrowed funds for a large portion of the required capital investments. For private organizations, these borrowed funds can be useful for leverage to achieve a higher return on the organizations' own capital investment.

For public organizations, borrowing costs which are larger than the MARR result in increased "cost" and higher required receipts. Incurring these costs may be essential if the investment funds are not otherwise available: capital funds must come from somewhere. But it is not unusual for the borrowing rate to exceed the MARR for public organizations. In this case, reducing the amount of borrowing lowers costs, whereas increasing borrowing lowers costs whenever the MARR is greater than the borrowing rate.

Although private organizations generally require a higher rate of return than do public bodies (so that the required receipts to make the investment desirable are higher for the private organization than for the public body), consideration of tax shields and introduction of a suitable financing plan may reduce this difference. The relative levels of the MARR for each group and their borrowing rates are critical in this calculation.

Effects of Capital Grant Subsidies

An important element in public investments is the availability of capital grant subsidies from higher levels of government. For example, interstate highway construction is eligible for federal capital grants for up to 90 percent of the cost. Other programs have different matching amounts, with 50/50 matching grants currently available for wastewater treatment plants and various categories of traffic systems improvement in the United States. These capital grants are usually made available solely for public bodies and for designated purposes.

While the availability of capital grant subsidies reduces the local cost of projects, the timing of investment can also be affected. In particular, public subsidies may be delayed or spread over a longer time period because of limited funds. To the extent that (discounted) benefits exceed costs for particular benefits, these funding delays can be costly. Consequently, private financing and investment may be a desirable alternative, even if some subsidy funds are available.

Implications for Design and Construction

Different perspectives and financial considerations also may have implications for design and construction choices. For example, an important class of design decisions arises relative to the trade-off between capital and operating costs. It is often the case that initial investment or construction costs can be reduced, but at the expense of higher operating costs or more frequent and extensive rehabilitation or repair expenditures. It is this trade-off which has led to the consideration of "life-cycle costs" of alternative designs. The financial schemes reviewed earlier can profoundly effect such evaluations.

For financial reasons, it would often be advantageous for a public body to select a more capital-intensive alternative which would receive a larger capital subsidy and, thereby, reduce the project's *local* costs. In effect, the capital grant subsidy would distort the trade-off between capital and operating costs in favor of more capital-intensive projects.

The various tax and financing considerations will also affect the relative merits of relatively capital-intensive projects. For example, as the borrowing rate increases, more capital-intensive alternatives become less attractive. Tax provisions such as the investment tax credit or accelerated depreciation are intended to stimulate investment and thereby make more capital-intensive projects relatively more desirable. In contrast, a higher minimum attractive rate of return tends to make more capital-intensive projects less attractive.

6.13 ECONOMIC EVALUATION OF DIFFERENT FORMS OF OWNERSHIP

While it is difficult to conclude definitely that one or another organizational or financial arrangement is always superior, different organizations have systematic implications for the ways in which constructed facilities are financed, designed, and constructed. Moreover, the selection of alternative investments for constructed facilities is likely to be affected by the type and scope of the decision-making organization.

As an example of the perspectives of public and private organizations, consider the potential investment on a constructed facility with a projected useful life of n years. Let $t = 0$ be the beginning of the planning horizon and $t = 1, 2, \ldots, n$ denote the end of each of the subsequent years. Furthermore, let C_0 be the cost of acquiring the facility at $t = 0$, and C_t be the cost of operation in year t. Then, the net receipts A_t in year t is given by $A_t = B_t - C_t$ in which A_t may be positive or negative for $t = 0, 1, 2, \ldots, n$.

Let the minimum attractive rate of return for the owner of the facility be denoted by i. Then, the net present value of a project as represented by the net cash flow discounted to the present time is given by

$$\text{NPV} = \sum_{t=0}^{n} A_t (1 + i)^{-t} = \sum_{t=0}^{n} B_t (1 + i)^{-t} - \sum_{t=0}^{n} C_t (1 + i)^{-t} \qquad (6.31)$$

Then, a project is acceptable if NPV ≥ 0. When the annual gross receipt is uniform, that is, $B_t = B$ for $t = 1, 2, \ldots, n$ and $B_0 = 0$, then, for NPV $= 0$,

$$B \sum_{t=1}^{n} (1 + i)^{-t} = \sum_{t=0}^{n} C_t (1 + i)^{-t} \qquad (6.32)$$

Thus, the minimum uniform annual gross receipt B which makes the project economically acceptable can be determined from Eq. (6.32), once the acquisition and operation costs C_t of the facility are known and the MARR is specified.

Example 6-5: Different MARRs for Public and Private Organizations

For the facility cost stream of a potential investment with $n = 7$ in Table 6-5, the required uniform annual gross receipts B are different for public and private ownerships since these two types of organizations usually choose different values of MARR. With a given value of MARR $= i$ in each case, the value of B can be obtained from Eq. (6.32). With a MARR of 10 percent, a public agency requires at least $B = \$184,000$. By contrast, a private firm using a 20 percent MARR before tax while neglecting other effects such as depreciation and tax deduction would require at least $B = \$219,000$. Then, according to Eq. (6.31), the gross receipt streams for both public and private ownerships in Table 6-5 will satisfy the condition NPV $= 0$ when each of them is netted from the cost stream and discounted at the appropriate value of MARR, that is 10 percent for a public agency and 20 percent (before tax) for a private firm. Thus, this case suggests that public provision of the facility has lower user costs.

TABLE 6-5 REQUIRED UNIFORM ANNUAL GROSS RECEIPTS FOR PUBLIC AND PRIVATE OWNERSHIP OF A FACILITY (in $ thousands)

		Public ownership		Private ownership	
Year t	(1) Facility cost, C_t	(2) Gross receipt, B_t	(3) Net receipt $A_t = B_t - C_t$	(4) Gross receipt B_t	(5) Net receipt $A_t = B_t - C_t$
0	$500	$ 0	−$500	$ 0	−$500
1	76	184	108	219	143
2	78	184	106	219	141
3	80	184	104	219	139
4	82	184	102	219	137
5	84	184	100	219	135
6	86	184	98	219	133
7	88	184	96	219	131

Example 6-6: Effects of Depreciation and Tax Shields for Private Firms

Using the same data as in Example 6-5, we now consider the effects of depreciation and tax deduction for private firms. Suppose that the marginal tax rate of the firm is 34 percent in each year of operation, and losses can always be offset by company-wide profits. Suppose further that the salvage value of the facility is zero at the end of seven years so that the entire amount of cost can be depreciated by means of the sum-of-the-years'-digits method. Thus, for the sum of digits 1 through 7 equal to 28, the depreciation allowances for years 1 to 7 are, respectively, 7/28, 6/28, . . . , 1/28 of the total depreciable value of $500,000, and the results are recorded in column 2 of Table 6-6. For a uniform annual gross receipt $B = \$219,000$, the net receipt before tax in column 5 of Table 6-5 in Example 6-5 can be used as the starting point for computing the after-tax cash flow according to Eq. (6.13), which is carried out step-by-step in Table 6-6. (Dollar amounts are given to the nearest $1,000.) By trial and error, it is found that an after-tax MARR $= 14.5\%$ will produce a zero value for

TABLE 6–6 EFFECTS OF DEPRECIATION AND TAX DEDUCTIONS FOR PRIVATE OWNERSHIP IN A FACILITY (in $ thousands)

Year t	(1) Net receipt before-tax A_t	(2) Depreciation (SOYD) D_t	(3) Taxable income $(A_t - D_t)$	(4) Income tax $X_t(A_t - D_t)$	(5) After-tax cash flow Y_t
0	−$500	$ 0	$ 0	$ 0	−$500
1	143	125	18	6	137
2	141	107	34	12	129
3	139	89	50	17	122
4	137	71	66	22	115
5	135	54	81	28	107
6	133	36	97	33	100
7	131	18	113	38	93

the net present value of the discounted after-tax flow at $t = 0$. In other words, the required uniform annual gross receipt for this project at 14.5 percent MARR after tax is also $B = $219,000$. It means that the MARR of this private firm must specify a 20 percent MARR before tax to receive the equivalent of 14.5 percent MARR after tax.

Example 6-7: Effects of Borrowing on Public Agencies

Suppose that the gross uniform annual receipt for public ownership is $B = $190,000$ instead of $184,000 for the facility with cost stream given in column 1 of Table 6-5. Suppose further that the public agency must borrow $400,000 (80 percent of the facility cost) at 12 percent annual interest, resulting in an annual uniform payment of $88,000 for the subsequent seven years. This information has been summarized in Table 6-7. The use of borrowed funds to finance a facility is referred to as debt financing or leveraged financing, and the combined cash flow resulting from operating and financial cash flows is referred to as the levered cash flow.

TABLE 6–7 EFFECTS OF BORROWING ON A PUBLICLY OWNED FACILITY (in $ thousands)

Year t	(1) Gross receipt B_t	(2) Facility cost C_t	(3) Net receipt (no loan) A_t	(4) Loan and payment (12% interest) $\overline{A}_t$	(5) Combined cash flow (12% interest) AA_t
0	$ 0	$500	−$500	+$400	−$100
1	190	76	114	− 88	26
2	190	78	112	− 88	24
3	190	80	110	− 88	22
4	190	82	108	− 88	20
5	190	84	106	− 88	18
6	190	86	104	− 88	16
7	190	88	102	− 88	14

To the net receipt A_t in column 3 of Table 6-7, which has been obtained from a uniform annual gross receipt of $190,000, we add the financial cash flow $\overline{A}_t$, which included a loan of $400,000 with an annual repayment of $88,000 corresponding to an interest rate of 12 percent. Then the resulting combined cash flow AA_t as computed according to Eq. (6.26) is shown in column 5 of Table 6-7. Note that for a loan at 12 percent interest, the net present value of the combined cash flow AA_t is zero when discounted at a 10 percent MARR for the public agency. This is not a coincidence, but several values of B have been tried until $B = \$190,000$ is found to satisfy NPV $= 0$ at 10 percent MARR. Hence, the minimum required uniform annual gross receipt is $B = \$190,000$.

Example 6-8: Effects of Leverage and Tax Shields for Private Organizations

Suppose that the uniform annual gross receipt for a private firm is also $B = \$190,000$ (the same as that for the public agency in Example 6-7). The salvage value of the facility is zero at the end of seven years so that the entire amount of cost can be depreciated by means of the sum-of-the-years'-digit method. The marginal tax rate of the firm is 34 percent in each year of operation, and losses can always be offset by companywide profits. Suppose further that the firm must borrow $400,000 (80 percent of the facility cost) at a 12 percent annual interest, resulting in an annual uniform payment of $88,000 for the subsequent seven years. The interest charge each year can be computed as 12 percent of the remaining balance of the loan in the previous year, and the interest charge is deductible from the tax liability.

For $B = \$190,000$ and a facility cost stream identical to that in Example 6-7, the net receipts before-tax A_t (operating cash flow with no loan) in Table 6-7 can be used as the starting point for analyzing the effects of financial leverage through borrowing. Thus, column 3 of Table 6-7 is reproduced in column 1 of Table 6-8.

The computation of the after-tax cash flow of the private firm including the effects of tax shields for interest is carried out in Table 6-8. The financial cash stream $\overline{A}_t$ in column 3 of Table 6-8 indicates a loan of $400,000 which is secured at $t = 0$ for an annual interest of 12 percent, and results in a series of uniform annual payments of $88,000 to repay the principal and interest. The levered after-tax cash flow YY_t can

TABLE 6–8 EFFECTS OF FINANCIAL LEVERAGE AND TAX SHIELDS ON PRIVATE OWNERSHIP OF A FACILITY (in $ thousands)

Year t	(1) Net receipt before tax (no loan) A_t	(2) Depreciation (SOYD) D_t	(3) Loan and scheduled payment $\overline{A}_t$	(4) Interest on loan I_t	(5) After-tax income tax (34% rate) $X_t(A_t - D_t - I_t)$	(6) cash flow (levered) YY_t
0	−$500	$ 0	$400	$ 0	$ 0	−$100
1	114	125	− 88	48	− 19	45
2	112	107	− 88	43	− 13	37
3	110	89	− 88	38	− 6	28
4	108	71	− 88	32	2	18
5	106	54	− 88	25	9	9
6	104	36	− 88	18	17	− 1
7	102	18	− 88	9	26	− 12

be obtained by Eq. (6.29), using the same investment credit, depreciation method and tax rate and is recorded in column 6 of Table 6-8. Since the net present value of YY_t in column 6 of Table 6-8 discounted at 14.5 percent happens to be zero, the minimum required uniform annual gross receipt for the potential investment is $190,000. By borrowing $400,000 (80 percent of the facility cost) at 12 percent annual interest, the investment becomes more attractive to the private firm. This is expected because of the tax shield for the interest and the 12 percent borrowing rate which is lower than the 14.5 percent MARR after-tax for the firm.

Example 6-9: Comparison of Public and Private Ownership.

In each of the analyses in Examples 6-5 through 6-8, a minimum required uniform annual gross receipt B is computed for each given condition whether the owner is a public agency or a private firm. By finding the value of B which will lead to NPV = 0 for the specified MARR for the organization in each case, various organizational effects with or without borrowing can be analyzed. The results are summarized in Table 6-9 for comparison. In this example, public ownership with an 80 percent loan and a 10 percent MARR has the same required benefit as private ownership with an identical 80 percent loan and a 14.5 percent after-tax MARR.

TABLE 6–9 SUMMARY EFFECTS OF FINANCIAL LEVERAGE AND TAX SHIELDS ON PRIVATE OWNERSHIP

Organizational condition	Financial arrangement	Minimum benefit required
Public, no tax (MARR = 10%)	No loan 80% loan at 12% interest	$184,000 190,000
Private, before tax (MARR = 20%)	No loan	219,000 219,000
Private, after tax (MARR = 14.5%)	No loan 80% loan at 12% interest	219,000 190,000

6.14 REFERENCES

6-1. Au, T., "Profit Measures and Methods of Economic Analysis for Capital Project Selection," *ASCE Journal of Management in Engineering,* Vol. 4, no. 3, 1988, pp.177–188.

6-2. Au, T., and T. P. Au, *Engineering Economics for Capital Investment Analysis*, Allyn & Bacon, Inc., Newton, MA, 1983.

6-3. Bierman, H., Jr., and S. Smidt, *The Capital Budgeting Decision*, 5th ed., Macmillan Publishing Company, New York, 1984.

6-4. Brealey, R., and S. Myers, *Principles of Corporate Finance,* 2nd ed., McGraw-Hill Book Company, New York, 1984.

6-5. Edwards, W. C. and J. F. Wong, "A Computer Model to Estimate Capital and Operating Costs," *Cost Engineering,* Vol. 29, no. 10, 1987, pp. 15–21.

6-6. Hendrickson, C., and T. Au, "Private Versus Public Ownership of Constructed Facilities," *ASCE Journal of Management in Engineering,* Vol. 1, no. 3, 1985, pp. 119–131.

6-7. Wohl, M., and C. Hendrickson, *Transportation Investment and Pricing Principles*, John Wiley and Sons, Inc., New York, 1984.

6.15 PROBLEMS

P6-1. The Salisbury Corporation is considering four mutually exclusive alternatives for a major capital investment project. All alternatives have a useful life of 10 years with no salvage value at the end. Straight-line depreciation will be used. The corporation pays federal and state tax at a rate of 34 percent, and expects an after-tax MARR of 10 percent. Determine which alternative should be selected, using the NPV method.

Alternatives	Initial cost (in $ millions)	Before-tax uniform annual net benefits (in $ millions)
1	$4.0	$1.5
2	3.5	1.1
3	3.0	1.0
4	3.7	1.3

P6-2. The operating cash flow for the acquisition and maintenance of a clamshell for excavation is given by A_t in the following table (no salvage value). Three financing plans, each charging a borrowing rate of 8 percent but having a different method of repayment, are represented by three different cash flows of $\bar{A}_t$. Find the net present value before tax for each of the three combined cash flows AA_t for operating and financing if the before-tax MARR is specified to be 8 percent.

Year t	Operating A_t	Financing $\bar{A}_t$ (a)	(b)	(c)
0	−$80,000	$40,000	$40,000	$40,000
1	30,000	− 10,020	− 3,200	− 13,200
2	30,000	− 10,020	− 3,200	− 12,400
3	30,000	− 10,020	− 3,200	− 11,600
4	30,000	− 10,020	− 3,200	− 10,800
5	30,000	− 10,020	− 43,200	0

P6-3. Find the net present value for each of the three cases in Problem P6-2 if the before-tax MARR is specified to be 5 percent.

P6-4. Find the net present value for each of the three cases in problem P6-2 if the before-tax MARR is specified to be 10 percent.

P6-5. An investment in a hauler will cost $40,000 and have no salvage value at the end of five years. The hauler will generate a gross income of $12,000 per year, but its operating cost will be $2,000 during the first year, increasing by $500 per year until it reaches $4,000 in the fifth year. The straight-line depreciation method is used.

The tax rate is 34 percent and the after-tax MARR is 10 percent. Determine the net present value of the hauler purchase for a five-year planning horizon.

P6-6. The Bailey Construction Company is considering the purchase of a diesel power shovel to improve its productivity. The shovel, which costs $80,000, is expected to produce a before-tax benefit of $36,000 in the first year and $4,000 less in each succeeding year for a total of five years (i.e., before-tax benefit of $32,000 in the second year, $28,000 in the third year, continuing to $20,000 in the fifth year). The salvage value of the equipment will be $5,000 at the end of five years. The firm uses the sum-of-years'-digits depreciation for the equipment and has an annual tax rate of 34 percent. If the MARR after tax is 10 percent, is the purchase worthwhile?

P6-7. The ABC Corporation is considering the purchase of a number of pipe-laying machines to facilitate the operation in a new pipeline project expected to last six years. Each machine will cost $24,000 and will have no salvage value after the project is complete. The firm uses the straight line depreciation method and pays annual income taxes on profits at the rate of 34 percent. If the firm's after-tax MARR is 8 percent, what is the minimum uniform annual net benefit before tax that must be generated by this machine in order to justify its purchase?

P6-8. The Springdale Corporation plans to purchase a demolition and wrecking machine to save labor costs. The machine costs $60,000 and has no salvage value at the end of five years. The machine is expected to be in operation for five years, and it will be depreciated by the straight-line method up to the salvage value. The corporation specifies an after-tax MARR, including inflation of 10 percent, and has an income tax rate of 34 percent. The annual inflation rate is expected to be 5 percent during the next five years. If the uniform annual net benefit before tax in terms of base-year dollars for the next five years is $20,000, is the new investment worthwhile?

P6-9. XYZ Company plans to invest $2 million in a new plant which is expected to produce a uniform annual net benefit before tax of $600,000 in terms of the base-year dollars over the next six years. The plant has a salvage value of $200,000 at the end of six years and the depreciation allowance is based on the straight-line depreciation method. The corporate tax rate is 34 percent, and the after-tax MARR specified by the firm is 10 percent excluding inflation. If the annual inflation rate during the next six years is expected to be 8 percent, determine whether the investment is worthwhile.

P6-10. A sewage treatment plant is being planned by a public authority. Two proposed designs require initial and annual maintenance costs as shown.

Year t	Design 1 (in $ thousands)	Design 2 (in $ thousands)
0	$1,000	$900
1–16 (each)	150	180

Both designs will last 16 years with no salvage value. There is no inflation. The federal government will subsidize 50 percent of the initial capital cost, and the state government has a policy to subsidize 10 percent of the annual maintenance cost. The local community intends to obtain a loan to finance 30 percent of the initial capital cost at a borrowing rate of 10 percent with 16 equal annual payments including principal and interest. The MARR for this type of project is 12 percent, for a public authority which is tax exempt. What is the uniform annual revenue that must be collected in the next 16 years to make each of the two designs worthwhile from the view of the local authority? Which design is better from this perspective?

P6-11. Suppose the clamshell in Problem P6-2 is purchased by a private firm that pays corporate taxes at a rate of 34 percent. Depreciation is based on the straight-line method with no salvage value at the end of five years. There is no inflation. If the after-tax MARR of the firm is 8 percent, find the net present value for each of the combined cash flows for operating and financing, including the interest deduction. The interest payments included in the annual repayments of each of the loans are 8 percent times the unpaid principal in each year, with the following values:

Year t	(a)	(b)	(c)
1	$3,200	$3,200	$3,200
2	2,656	3,200	2,400
3	2,064	3,200	1,600
4	1,428	3,200	800
5	740	3,200	0

7

Financing
of
Constructed Facilities

7.1 THE FINANCING PROBLEM

Investment in a constructed facility represents a cost in the short term that returns benefits only over the long-term use of the facility. Thus, costs occur earlier than the benefits, and owners of facilities must obtain the capital resources to finance the costs of construction. A project cannot proceed without adequate financing, and the cost of providing adequate financing can be quite large. For these reasons, attention to project finance is an important aspect of project management. Finance is also a concern to the other organizations involved in a project such as the general contractor and material suppliers. Unless an owner immediately and completely covers the costs incurred by each participant, these organizations face financing problems of their own.

At a more general level, project finance is only one aspect of the general problem of corporate finance. If numerous projects are considered and financed together, then the net cash flow requirements constitutes the corporate financing problem for capital investment. Whether project finance is performed at the project or at the corporate level does not alter the basic financing problem.

In essence, the project finance problem is to obtain funds to bridge the time between making expenditures and obtaining revenues. Based on the conceptual plan, the cost estimate, and the construction plan, the cash flow of costs and receipts for a project can be estimated. Normally, this cash flow will involve expenditures in early periods. Covering this negative cash balance in the most beneficial or cost-effective fashion is the project finance problem. During planning and design, expenditures of the owner are modest, whereas substantial costs are incurred during construction. Only after the facility is complete do revenues begin. In contrast, a contractor would receive periodic payments from the owner as construction proceeds. However, a contractor also may have a negative cash balance due to delays in payment and *retainage* of profits or cost reimbursements on the part of the owner.

Plans considered by owners for facility financing typically have both long- and short-term aspects. In the long term, sources of revenue include sales, grants, and tax revenues. Borrowed funds must be eventually paid back from these other sources. In the short term, a wider variety of financing options exist, including borrowing, grants, corporate investment funds, payment delays, and others. Many of these financing options involve the participation of third parties such as banks or bond underwriters. For private facilities such as office buildings, it is customary to have completely different financing arrangements during the construction period and during the period of facility use. During the latter period, mortgage or loan funds can be secured by the value of the facility itself. Thus, different arrangements of financing options and participants are possible at different stages of a project, so the practice of financial planning is often complicated.

On the other hand, the options for borrowing by contractors to bridge their expenditures and receipts during construction are relatively limited. For small- or medium-sized projects, overdrafts from bank accounts are the most common form of construction financing. Usually, a maximum limit is imposed on an overdraft account by the bank on the basis of expected expenditures and receipts for the duration of construction. Contractors who are engaged in large projects often own substantial assets and can make use of other forms of financing which have lower interest charges than overdrafting.

In this chapter, we will first consider facility financing from the owner's perspective, with due consideration for its interaction with other organizations involved in a project. Later, we discuss the problems of construction financing which are crucial to the profitability and solvency of construction contractors.

7.2 INSTITUTIONAL ARRANGEMENTS FOR FACILITY FINANCING

Financing arrangements differ sharply by type of owner and by the type of facility construction. As one example, many municipal projects are financed in the United States with *tax-exempt bonds* for which interest payments to a lender are exempt from income taxes. As a result, tax-exempt municipal bonds are available at lower interest charges. Different institutional arrangements have evolved for specific types of facilities and organizations.

A private corporation which plans to undertake large capital projects may use its retained earnings, seek equity partners in the project, issue bonds, offer new stocks in the financial markets, or seek borrowed funds in another fashion. Potential sources of funds would include pension funds, insurance companies, investment trusts, commercial banks, and others. Developers who invest in real estate properties for rental purposes have similar sources, plus quasi-governmental corporations such as urban development authorities. Syndicators for investment such as real estate investment trusts (REITs) as well as domestic and foreign pension funds represent relatively new entries to the financial market for building mortgage money.

Public projects may be funded by tax receipts, general revenue bonds, or special bonds with income dedicated to the specified facilities. General revenue bonds would be repaid from general taxes or other revenue sources, while special bonds would be redeemed either by special taxes or user fees collected for the project. Grants from higher levels of government are also an important source of funds for state, county, city, or other local agencies.

As an indication of the potential sources of financing, Table 7-1 shows the dollar amounts of borrowing in U.S. credit markets during 1985. Not all of these funds are used for construction, of course. Compared to the $1 trillion in borrowed funds shown in Table 7-1, the value of construction put in place is slightly more than a quarter of the total. Also, some construction is funded from other sources. Nevertheless, it is apparent that bonds, mortgages, and bank loans are all major sources of financing.

Despite the different sources of borrowed funds, there is a rough equivalence in the actual cost of borrowing money for particular types of projects. Because lenders can participate in many different financial markets, they tend to switch toward loans that return the highest yield for a particular level of risk. As a result, borrowed funds that can be obtained from different sources tend to have very similar costs, including interest charges and issuing costs.

As a general principle, however, the costs of funds for construction will vary inversely with the risk of a loan. Lenders usually require security for a loan

TABLE 7–1 FUNDS RAISED IN U.S. CREDIT MARKETS, 1985

Type		Amount ($ billions)
U.S. government securities		$ 324
State and local obligations		183
Corporate and foreign bonds		108
Mortgages		
Home mortgages	$156	
Multifamily residential mortages	26	
Commercial mortgages	61	
Farm mortgages	− 6	
Mortgages (total)		237
Consumer credit		97
Bank loans		42
Open market paper		53
Other		50
Total		$1,094

Source: *Federal Reserve Bulletin*, August 1986, Table 1.57, p.A42.

represented by a tangible asset. If for some reason the borrower cannot repay a loan, then the borrower can take possession of the loan security. To the extent that an asset used as security is of uncertain value, then the lender will demand a greater return and higher interest payments. Loans made for projects under construction represent considerable risk to a financial institution. If a lender acquires an unfinished facility, then it faces the difficult task of re-assembling the project team. Moreover, a default on a facility may result if a problem occurs such as foundation problems or anticipated unprofitability of the future facility. As a result of these uncertainties, construction lending for unfinished facilities commands a premium interest charge of several percentage points compared to mortgage lending for completed facilities.

Financing plans will typically include a reserve amount to cover unforeseen expenses, cost increases, or cash flow problems. This reserve can be represented by a special reserve or a contingency amount in the project budget. In the simplest case, this reserve might represent a borrowing agreement with a financial institution to establish a *line of credit* in case of need. For publicly traded bonds, specific reserve funds administered by a third party may be established. The cost of these reserve funds is the difference between the interest paid to bondholders and the interest received on the reserve funds plus any administrative costs.

Finally, arranging financing may involve a lengthy period of negotiation and review. Particularly for publicly traded bond financing, specific legal requirements in the issue must be met. A typical seven-month schedule to issue revenue bonds would include the various steps outlined in Table 7-2.[55] In many cases, the speed in which funds may be obtained will determine a project's financing mechanism.

---

[55] This table is adapted from A. J. Henkel, "The Mechanics of a Revenue Bond Financing: An Overview," *Infrastructure Financing*, Kidder, Peabody & Co., New York, 1984.

TABLE 7–2 ILLUSTRATIVE PROCESS AND TIMING FOR ISSUING REVENUE BONDS

Activities	Time of activities
Analysis of financial alternatives	Weeks 0–4
Preparation of legal documents	Weeks 1–17
Preparation of disclosure documents	Weeks 2–20
Forecasts of costs and revenues	Weeks 4–20
Bond ratings	Weeks 20–23
Bond marketing	Weeks 21–24
Bond closing and receipt of funds	Weeks 23–26

Example 7-1: Example of Financing Options

Suppose that you represent a private corporation attempting to arrange financing for a new headquarters building. These are several options that might be considered:

- **Use corporate equity and retained earnings.** The building could be financed by directly committing corporate resources. In this case, no other institutional parties would be involved in the finance. However, these corporate funds might be too limited to support the full cost of construction.

- **Construction loan and long-term mortgage.** In this plan, a loan is obtained from a bank or other financial institution to finance the cost of construction. Once the building is complete, a variety of institutions may be approached to supply mortgage or long-term funding for the building. This financing plan would involve both short- and long-term borrowing, and the two periods might involve different lenders. The long-term funding would have greater security since the building would then be complete. As a result, more organizations might be interested in providing funds (including pension funds), and the interest charge might be lower. Also, this basic financing plan might be supplemented by other sources such as corporate retained earnings or assistance from a local development agency.

- **Lease the building from a third party.** In this option, the corporation would contract to lease space in a headquarters building from a developer. This developer would be responsible for obtaining funding and arranging construction. This plan has the advantage of minimizing the amount of funds borrowed by the corporation. Under terms of the lease contract, the corporation still might have considerable influence over the design of the headquarters building even though the developer was responsible for design and construction.

7.3 EVALUATION OF ALTERNATIVE FINANCING PLANS

Since there are numerous different sources and arrangements for obtaining the funds necessary for facility construction, owners and other project participants require some mechanism for evaluating the different potential sources. The relative costs of different financing plans are certainly important in this regard. In addition, the flexibility of the plan and availability of reserves may be critical. As a project manager, it is important to assure adequate financing to complete a project. Alternative financing plans can be evaluated using the same techniques that are employed for the evaluation of investment alternatives.

As described in Chapter 6, the availability of different financing plans can affect the selection of alternative projects. A general approach for obtaining the combined effects of operating and financing cash flows of a project is to determine the adjusted net present value (APV) which is the sum of the net present value of the operating cash flow (NPV) and the net present value of the financial cash flow (FPV), discounted at their respective minimum attractive rates of return (MARR), that is,

$$APV = [NPV]_r + [FPV]_{r_f} \tag{7.1}$$

where r is the MARR reflecting the risk of the operating cash flow and r_f is the MARR representing the cost of borrowing for the financial cash flow. Thus,

$$APV = \sum_{t=0}^{n} \frac{A_t}{(1+r)^t} + \sum_{t=0}^{n} \frac{\bar{A}_t}{(1+r_f)^t} \tag{7.2}$$

where A_t and $\bar{A}_t$ are, respectively, the operating and financial cash flows in period t.

For the sake of simplicity, we shall emphasize in this chapter the evaluation of financing plans, with occasional references to the combined effects of operating and financing cash flows. In all discussions, we shall present various financing schemes with examples limiting to cases of before-tax cash flows discounted at a before-tax MARR of $r = r_f$ for both operating and financial cash flows. Once the basic concepts of various financing schemes are clearly understood, their application to more complicated situations involving depreciation, tax liability, and risk factors can be considered in combination with the principles for dealing with such topics enunciated in Chapter 6.

In this section, we shall concentrate on the computational techniques associated with the most common types of financing arrangements. More detailed descriptions of various financing schemes and the comparisons of their advantages and disadvantages will be discussed in later sections.

Typically, the interest rate for borrowing is stated in terms of *annual percentage rate* (APR), but the interest is accrued according to the rate for the interest period specified in the borrowing agreement. Let i_p be the nominal annual percentage rate and i be the interest rate for each of the p interest periods per year. By definition

$$i = \frac{i_p}{p} \tag{7.3}$$

If interest is accrued semiannually, that is, $p = 2$, the interest rate per period is $i_p/2$; similarly if the interest is accrued monthly, that is, $p = 12$, the interest rate per period is $i_p/12$. On the other hand, the effective annual interest rate i_e is given by

$$i_e = (1 + i)^p - 1 = \left(1 + \frac{i_p}{p}\right)^p - 1 \tag{7.4}$$

Note that the effective annual interest rate, i_e, takes into account compounding within the year. As a result, i_e is greater than i_p for the typical case of more than one compounding period per year.

For a coupon bond, the face value of the bond denotes the amount borrowed (called *principal*) which must be repaid in full at a maturity or due date, while each coupon designates the interest to be paid periodically for the total number of coupons covering all periods until maturity. Let Q be the amount borrowed, and I_p be the interest payment per period which is often six months for coupon bonds. If the coupon bond is prescribed to reach maturity in n years from the date of issue, the total number of interest periods will be $pn = 2n$. The semiannual interest payment is given by

$$I_p = iQ = i_p \frac{Q}{2} \tag{7.5}$$

In purchasing a coupon bond, a discount from or a premium above the face value may be paid.

An alternative loan arrangement is to make a series of uniform payments including both interest and part of the principal for a predefined number of repayment periods. In the case of uniform payments at an interest rate i for n repayment periods, the uniform repayment amount U is given by

$$U = Q \frac{i(1 + i)^n}{(1 + i)^n - 1} = Q(U|P, i, n) \tag{7.6}$$

where $(U|P, i, n)$ is a uniform series compound interest factor which reads "to find U, given $P = 1$, for an interest rate i over n periods." Compound interest factors are as tabulated in Appendix A. The number of repayment periods n will clearly influence the amounts of payments in this uniform payment case. Uniform payment bonds or mortgages are based on this form of repayment.

Usually, there is an origination fee associated with borrowing for legal and other professional services which is payable upon the receipt of the loan. This fee may appear in the form of issuance charges for revenue bonds or percentage point charges for mortgages. The borrower must allow for such fees in addition to the construction cost in determining the required original amount of borrowing. Suppose that a sum of P_0 must be reserved at $t = 0$ for the construction cost, and K is the origination fee. Then the original loan needed to cover both is

$$Q_0 = P_0 + K \tag{7.7}$$

If the origination fee is expressed as k percent of the original loan, that is, $K = kQ_0$, then

$$Q_0 = \frac{P_0}{1 - k} \tag{7.8}$$

Since interest and sometimes parts of the principal must be repaid periodically in most financing arrangements, an amount Q considerably larger than Q_0 is usually borrowed in the beginning to provide adequate reserve funds to cover interest payments, construction cost increases, and other unanticipated shortfalls. The net amount received from borrowing is deposited in a separate interest-bearing account from which funds will be withdrawn periodically for necessary payments. Let the borrowing rate per period be denoted by i and the interest for the running balance accrued to the project reserve account be denoted by h. Let A_t be the net operating cash flow for period t (negative for construction cost in period t) and $\bar{A}_t$ be the net financial cash flow in period t (negative for payment of interest or principal or a combination of both). Then, the running balance N_t of the project reserve account can be determined by noting that at $t = 0$,

$$N_0 = Q - K + A_0 \tag{7.9}$$

and at $t = 1, 2, \ldots, n$,

$$N_t = (1 + h)N_{t-1} + A_t + \bar{A}_t \tag{7.10}$$

where the value of A_t or $\bar{A}_t$ may be zero for some period(s). Eqs. (7.9) and (7.10) are approximate in that interest might be earned on intermediate balances based on the pattern of payments during a period instead of at the end of a period.

Because the borrowing rate i will generally exceed the investment rate h for the running balance in the project account and since the origination fee increases with the amount borrowed, the financial planner should minimize the amount of money borrowed under this finance strategy. Thus, there is an optimal value for Q such that all estimated shortfalls are covered, interest payments and expenses are minimized, and adequate reserve funds are available to cover unanticipated factors such as construction cost increases. This optimal value of Q can either be identified analytically or by trial and error.

Finally, variations in ownership arrangements may also be used to provide at least partial financing. Leasing a facility removes the need for direct financing of the facility. Sale-leaseback involves sale of a facility to a third party with a separate agreement involving use of the facility for a prespecified period of time. In one sense, leasing arrangements can be viewed as a particular form of financing. In return for obtaining the use of a facility or piece of equipment, the user (lessee) agrees to pay the owner (lessor) a lease payment every period for a specified number of periods. Usually, the lease payment is at a fixed level due every month, semiannually, or annually. Thus, the cash flow associated with the equipment or facility use is a series of uniform payments. This cash flow would be identical to a cash flow resulting from financing the facility or purchase with sufficient borrowed funds to cover initial construction (or purchase) and with a repayment schedule of uniform amounts. Of course, at the end of the lease period, the ownership of the facility or equipment would reside with the lessor. However, the lease terms may include a provision for transferring ownership to the lessee after a fixed period.

Example 7-2: A Coupon Bond Cash Flow and Cost

A private corporation wishes to borrow $10.5 million for the construction of a new building by issuing a 20-year coupon bond at an annual percentage interest rate of 10 percent to be paid semiannually, that is, 5 percent per interest period of six months. The principal will be repaid at the end of 20 years. The amount borrowed will cover the construction cost of $10.331 million and an origination fee of $169,000 for issuing the coupon bond.

The interest payment per period is $(5\%)(10.5) = \$0.525$ million over a lifetime of $(2)(20) = 40$ interest periods. Thus, the cash flow of financing by the coupon bond consists of a $10.5 million receipt at period 0, $-\$0.525$ million each for periods 1 through 40, and an additional $-\$10.5$ million for period 40. Assuming a MARR of 5 percent per period, the net present value of the financial cash flow is given by

$$[FPV]_{5\%} = 10.5 - (0.525)(P|U, 5\%, 40) - (10.5)(P|F, 5\%, 40) = 0$$

This result is expected since the corporation will be indifferent between borrowing and diverting capital from other uses when the MARR is identical to the borrowing rate. Note that the effective annual rate of the bond may be computed according to Eq. (7.4) as follows:

$$i_e = (1 + 0.05)^2 - 1 = 0.1025 = 10.25\%$$

If the interest payments were made only at the end of each year over 20 years, the annual payment should be

$$0.525(1 + 0.05) + 0.525 = 1.076$$

where the first term indicates the deferred payment at the midyear which would accrue interest at 5 percent until the end of the year, then

$$[FPV]_{10.25\%} = 10.5 - (1.076)(P|U, 10.25\%, 20) - (10.5)(P|F, 10.25\%, 20) = 0$$

In other words, if the interest is paid at 10.25 percent annually over 20 years of the loan, the result is equivalent to the case of semiannual interest payments at 5 percent over the same lifetime.

Example 7-3: An Example of Leasing Versus Ownership Analysis

Suppose that a developer offered a building to a corporation for an annual lease payment of $10 million over a 30-year lifetime. For the sake of simplicity, let us assume that the developer also offers to donate the building to the corporation at the end of 30 years or, alternatively, the building would then have no commercial value. Also, suppose that the initial cost of the building was $65.66 million. For the corporation, the lease is equivalent to receiving a loan with uniform payments over 30 years at an interest rate of 15 percent since the present value of the lease payments is equal to the initial cost at this interest rate:

$$\sum_{t=1}^{30} \frac{10}{(1.15)^t} = (\$10 \text{ million})(P|U, 15\%, 30) = \$65.66 \text{ million}$$

If the minimum attractive rate of return of the corporation is greater than 15 percent, this lease arrangement is advantageous as a financing scheme since the net present value of the leasing cash flow would be less than the cash flow associated with construction from retained earnings. For example, with MARR equal to 20 percent,

$$[FPV]_{20\%} = \$65.66 \text{ million} - (\$10 \text{ million})(P|U, 20\%, 30) = \$15.871 \text{ million}$$

On the other hand, with MARR equal to 10 percent,

$$[FPV]_{10\%} = \$65.66 \text{ million} - (\$10 \text{ million})(P|U, 10\%, 30) = -\$28.609 \text{ million}$$

and the lease arrangement is not advantageous.

Example 7-4: Example Evaluation of Alternative Financing Plans

Suppose that a small corporation wishes to build a headquarters building. The construction will require two years and cost a total of $12 million, assuming that $5 million is spent at the end of the first year and $7 million at the end of the second year. To finance this construction, several options are possible, including

- Investment from retained corporate earnings.
- Borrowing from a local bank at an interest rate of 11.2 percent with uniform annual payments over 20 years to pay for the construction costs. The shortfalls for repayments on loans will come from corporate earnings. An origination fee of 0.75 percent of the original loan is required to cover engineer's reports, legal issues, and so on.
- A 20 year coupon bond at an annual interest rate of 10.25 percent with interest payments annually, repayment of the principal in year 20, and a $169,000 origination fee.

The current corporate MARR is 15 percent, and short-term cash funds can be deposited in an account having a 10 percent annual interest rate.

The first step in evaluation is to calculate the required amounts and cash flows associated with these three alternative financing plans. First, investment using retained earnings will require a commitment of $5 million in year 1 and $7 million in year 2.

Second, borrowing from the local bank must yield sufficient funds to cover both years of construction plus the issuing fee. With the unused fund accumulating interest at a rate of 10 percent, the amount of dollars needed at the beginning of the first year for future construction cost payments is

$$P_0 = \frac{\$5 \text{ million}}{(1.1)} + \frac{\$7 \text{ million}}{(1.1)^2} = \$10.331 \text{ million}$$

Discounting at a 10 percent in this calculation reflects the interest earned in the intermediate periods. With a 10 percent annual interest rate, the accrued interests for the first two years from the project account of $10.331 million at $t=0$ will be

$$\text{Year 1: } I_1 = (10\%)(\$10.331 \text{ million}) = \$1.033 \text{ million}$$

$$\text{Year 2: } I_2 = (10\%)(\$10.331 \text{ million} + \$1.033 \text{ million}$$

$$-\$5.0 \text{ million}) = \$0.636 \text{ million}$$

Since the issuance charge is 0.75 percent of the loan, the amount borrowed from the bank at $t = 0$ to cover both the construction cost and the issuance charge is

$$Q_0 = \frac{\$10.331 \text{ million}}{1 - 0.0075} = \$10.409 \text{ million}$$

The issuance charge is $10.409 million − $10.331 million = $0.078 million, or $78,000. If this loan of 10.409 million is to be repaid by annual uniform payments from corporate earnings, the amount of each payment over the 20-year lifetime of the loan can be calculated by Eq.(7.6) as follows:

$$U = (\$10.409 \text{ million}) \frac{(0.112)(1.112)^{20}}{(1.112)^{20} - 1} = \$1.324 \text{ million}$$

Finally, the 20-year coupon bond would have to be issued in the amount of $10.5 million which will reflect a higher origination fee of $169,000. Thus, the amount for financing is

$$Q_0 = \$10.331 \text{ million} + \$0.169 \text{ million} = \$10.5 \text{ million}$$

With an annual interest charge of 10.25 percent over a 20-year lifetime, the annual payment would be $1.076 million except in year 20, when the sum of principal and interest would be $10.5 million + $1.076 million = $11.576 million. The computation for this case of borrowing has been given in Example 7-2.

Table 7-3 summarizes the cash flows associated with the three alternative financing plans. Note that annual incomes generated from the use of this building have not been included in the computation. The adjusted net present value of the combined operating and financial cash flows for each of the three plans discounted at the corporate MARR of 15 percent is also shown in the table. In this case, the coupon bond is the least expensive financing plan. Since the borrowing rates for both the bank loan and the coupon bond are lower than the corporate MARR, these results are expected.

TABLE 7–3 CASH FLOW ILLUSTRATION OF THREE ALTERNATIVE FINANCING PLANS (in $ millions)

Year	Source	Retained earnings	Bank loan	Coupon bond
0	Principal	—	$10.409	$10.500
0	Issuing cost	—	− 0.078	− 0.169
1	Earned interest	—	1.033	1.033
1	Contractor payment	−5.000	− 5.000	− 5.000
1	Loan repayment	—	− 1.324	− 1.076
2	Earned interest	—	0.636	0.636
2	Contractor payment	− 7.000	− 7.000	− 7.000
2	Loan repayment	—	− 1.324	− 1.076
3–19	Loan repayment	—	− 1.324	− 1.076
20	Loan repayment	—	− 1.324	− 11.576
$[APV]_{15\%}$		− 9.641	− 6.217	− 5.308

7.4 SECURED LOANS WITH BONDS, NOTES, AND MORTGAGES

Secured lending involves a contract between a borrower and lender, where the lender can be an individual, a financial institution, or a trust organization. Notes and mortgages represent formal contracts between financial institutions and owners. Usually, repayment amounts and timing are specified in the loan agreement. Public facilities are often financed by bond issues for either specific projects or for groups of projects. For publicly issued bonds, a trust company is usually designated to represent the diverse bondholders in case of any problems in the repayment. The borrowed funds are usually secured by granting the lender some rights to the facility or other assets in case of defaults on required payments. In contrast, corporate bonds such as debentures can represent loans secured only by the good faith and creditworthiness of the borrower.

Under the terms of many bond agreements, the borrower reserves the right to repurchase the bonds at any time before the maturity date by repaying the principal and all interest up to the time of purchase. The required repayment R_c at the end of period c is the net future value of the borrowed amount Q less the payment $\bar{A}_t$ made at intermediate periods compounded at the borrowing rate i to period c as follows:

$$R_c = Q(1 + i)^c - \sum_{t=1}^{c} \bar{A}_t (1 + i)^{c-t} \tag{7.11}$$

The required repayment R_c at the end of the period c can also be obtained by noting the net present value of the repayments in the remaining $(n\text{-}c)$ periods discounted at the borrowing rate i to $t = c$ as follows:

$$R_c = \sum_{t=1}^{n-c} \frac{\bar{A}_t}{(1 + i)^t} \tag{7.12}$$

For coupon bonds, the required repayment R_c after the redemption of the coupon at the end of period c is simply the original borrowed amount Q. For uniform payment bonds, the required repayment R_c after the last payment at the end of period c is

$$R_c = \sum_{t=1}^{n-c} \frac{U}{(1 + i)^t} = U(P|U, i, n - c) \tag{7.13}$$

Many types of bonds can be traded in a secondary market by the bondholder. As interest rates fluctuate over time, bonds will gain or lose in value. The actual value of a bond is reflected in the market discount or premium paid relative to the original principal amount (the face value). Another indicator of this value is the *yield to maturity* or *internal rate of return* of the bond. This yield is calculated by finding the interest rate that sets the (discounted) future cash flow of the bond equal to the current market price,

$$V_c = \sum_{t=1}^{n-c} \frac{\bar{A}_t}{(1 + r)^t} \tag{7.14}$$

where V_c is the current market value after c periods have lapsed since the issuance of the bond, $\bar{A}_t$ is the bond cash flow in period t, and r is the market yield. Since all the bond cash flows are positive after the initial issuance, only one value of the yield to maturity will result from Eq. (7.14).

Several other factors come into play in evaluation of bond values from the lender's point of view, however. First, the lender must adjust for the possibility that the borrower may default on required interest and principal payments. In the case of publicly traded bonds, special rating companies divide bonds into different categories of risk for just this purpose. Obviously, bonds that are more likely to default will have a lower value. Second, lenders will typically make adjustments to account for changes in the tax code affecting their after-tax return from a bond. Finally, expectations of future inflation or deflation as well as foreign exchange rates will influence market values.

Another common feature in borrowing agreements is to have a variable interest rate. In this case, interest payments would vary with the overall market interest rate in some prespecified fashion. From the borrower's perspective, this is less desirable since cash flows are less predictable. However, variable rate loans are typically available at lower interest rates because the lenders are protected in some measure from large increases in the market interest rate and the consequent decrease in value of their expected repayments. Variable rate loans can have floors and ceilings on the applicable interest rate or on rate changes in each year.

Example 7-5: Example of a Corporate Promissory Note

A corporation wishes to consider the option of financing the headquarters building in Example 7-4 by issuing a five-year promissory note which requires an origination fee of $25,000 for the note. Then a total borrowed amount needed at the beginning of the first year to pay for the construction costs and origination fee is $10.331 million + $0.025 million = $10.356 million. Interest payments are made annually at an annual rate of 10.8 percent with repayment of the principal at the end of the fifth year. Thus, the annual interest payment is (10.8%) ($10.356 million) = $1.118 million. With the data in Example 7-4 for construction costs and accrued interests for the first two years, the combined operating and and financial cash flows (in $ millions) can be obtained:

$$\text{Year } 0 : AA_0 = 10.356 - 0.025 = 10.331$$

$$\text{Year } 1 : AA_1 = 1.033 - 5.0 - 1.118 = -5.085$$

$$\text{Year } 2 : AA_2 = 0.636 - 7.0 - 1.118 = -7.482$$

$$\text{Year } 3 : AA_3 = -1.118$$

$$\text{Year } 4 : AA_4 = -1.118$$

$$\text{Year } 5 : AA_5 = -1.118 - 10.356 = -11.474$$

At the current corporate MARR of 15 percent,

$$[\text{APV}]_{15\%} = \sum_{t=0}^{5} \frac{AA_t}{(1.15)^t} = -6.828$$

which is inferior to the 20-year coupon bond analyzed in Table 7-3.

For this problem as well as for the financing arrangements in Example 7-4, the project account is maintained to pay the construction costs only, while the interest and principal payments are repaid from corporate earnings. Consequently, the A_t terms in Eq. (7.10) will disappear when the account balance in each period is computed for this problem (in $ millions):

At $t = 0$: $N_0 = 10.356 - 0.025 = 10.331$ million

At $t = 1$: $N_1 = (1 + 0.1)(10.331) - 5.0 = 6.364$

At $t = 2$: $N_2 = (1 + 0.1)(6.364) - 7.0 = 0$

Example 7-6: Bond Financing Mechanisms

Suppose that the net operating expenditures and receipts of a facility investment over a five-year time horizon are as shown in column 2 of Table 7-4 in which each period is six months. This is a hypothetical example with a deliberately short lifetime period to reduce the required number of calculations. Consider two alternative bond financing mechanisms for this project. Both involve borrowing $2.5 million at an issuing cost of 5 percent of the loan with semiannual repayments at a nominal annual interest rate of 10 percent, that is, 5 percent per period. Any excess funds can earn an interest of 4 percent each semiannual period. The coupon bond involves only interest payments in intermediate periods, plus the repayment of the principal at the end, whereas the uniform payment bond requires 10 uniform payments to cover both interests and the principal. Both bonds are subject to optional redemption by the borrower before maturity.

The operating cash flow in column 2 of Table 7-4 represents the construction expenditures in the early periods and rental receipts in later periods over the lifetime of the facility. By trial and error with Eqs. (7.9) and (7.10), it can be found that $Q = \$2.5$ million ($K = \$0.125$ million or 5 percent of Q) is necessary to ensure a nonnegative balance in the project account for the uniform payment bond, as shown in column 5 of Table 7-4. For the purpose of comparison, the same amount is borrowed for the coupon bond option even though a smaller loan will be sufficient for the construction expenditures in this case.

The financial cash flow of the coupon bond can easily be derived from $Q = \$2.5$ million and $K = \$0.125$ million. Using Eq. (7.5), $I_p = (5\%)(\$2.5$ million$) = \$0.125$ million, and the repayment in period 10 is $Q + I_p = \$2.625$ million as shown in column 2 of Table 7-4. The account balance for the coupon bond in column 3 is obtained from Eqs. (7.9) and (7.10). On the other hand, the uniform annual payment

TABLE 7–4 EXAMPLE OF TWO BORROWING CASH FLOWS (in $ thousands)

Period	(1) Operating cash flow	(2) Coupon cash flow	(3) Account balance	(4) Uniform cash flow	(5) Account balance
0	—	$2,375	$2,375	$2,375	$2,375
1	− $800	− 125	1,545	− 324	1,346
2	− 700	− 125	782	− 324	376
3	− 60	− 125	628	− 324	8
4	400	− 125	928	− 324	84
5	600	− 125	1,440	− 324	364
6	800	− 125	2,173	− 324	854
7	1,000	− 125	3,135	− 324	1,565
8	1,000	− 125	4,135	− 324	2,304
9	1,000	− 125	5,176	− 324	3,072
10	1,000	− 2,625	3,758	− 324	3,871

U = $0.324 million for the financial cash flow of the uniform payment bond (column 4) can be obtained from Eq. (7.6), and the bond account for this type of balance is computed by Eqs. (7.9) and (7.10).

Because of the optional redemption provision for both types of bonds, it is advantageous to redeem both options gradually at the end of period 3 to avoid interest payments resulting from i = 5% and h = 4% unless the account balance beyond period 3 is needed to fund other corporate investments. Corporate earnings are available for repurchasing the bonds at the end of period 3; the required repayment for the coupon bond after redeeming the last coupon at the end of period 3 is simply $2.625 million. In the case of the uniform payment bond, the required payment after the last uniform payment at the end of period 3 is obtained from Eq. (7-12) as

$$R_3 = (0.324)(P|U, 5\%, 7) = (0.324)(5.7864) = \$1.875 \text{ million}$$

Example 7-7: Provision of Reserve Funds

Typical borrowing agreements may include various required reserve funds.[56] Consider an 18-month project costing $5 million. To finance this facility, coupon bonds will be issued to generate revenues which must be sufficient to pay interest charges during the 18 months of construction, to cover all construction costs, to pay issuance expenses, and to maintain a debt service reserve fund. The reserve fund is introduced to assure bondholders of payments in case of unanticipated construction problems. It is estimated that a total amount of $7.4 million of bond proceeds is required, including a 2 percent discount to underwriters and an issuance expense of $100,000.

Three interest-bearing accounts are established with the bond proceeds to separate various categories of funds:

- A construction fund to provide payments to contractors, with an initial balance of $4,721,600. Including interest earnings, this fund will be sufficient to cover the $5,000,000 in construction expenses.
- A capitalized interest fund to provide interest payments during the construction period.
- A debt service reserve fund to be used for retiring outstanding debts after the completion of construction.

The total sources of funds (including interest from account balances) and uses of funds are summarized in Table 7-5.

Example 7-8: Variable Rate Revenue Bonds Prospectus

The information in Table 7-6 is abstracted from the prospectus for a new issue of revenue bonds for the Atwood City. This prospectus language is typical for municipal bonds. Notice the provision for variable rate after the initial interest periods. The borrower reserves the right to repurchase the bond before the date for conversion to variable rate takes effect to protect itself from declining market interest rates in the future so that the borrower can obtain other financing arrangements at lower rates.

---

[56] The calculations for this bond issue are adapted from a hypothetical example in F. H. Fuller, "Analyzing Cash Flows for Revenue Bond Financing," *Infrastructure Financing*, Kidder, Peabody & Co., Inc., New York, 1984, pp. 37–47.

TABLE 7–5   ILLUSTRATIVE SOURCES AND USES OF FUNDS
FROM REVENUE BONDS DURING CONSTRUCTION

Sources of funds	
Bond proceeds	$7,400,000
Interest earnings on construction fund	278,400
Interest earnings of capitalized interest fund	77,600
Interest earnings on debt service reserve fund	287,640
Total sources of funds	$8,043,640

Uses of funds	
Construction costs	$5,000,000
Interest payments	904,100
Debt service reserve fund	1,891,540
Bond discount (2.0%)	148,000
Issuance expense	100,000
Total uses of funds	$8,043,640

TABLE 7–6   PROVISION OF VARIABLE RATE FOR BONDS

First series of 1987: $12,000,000

Date: December 1, 1987   Due: November 1, 2017

The Bonds will be issued as fully registered bonds in the denomination of $5,000 or any multiple thereof. Principal or redemption price of the bonds will be payable upon surrender thereof. Interest on the Bonds will be payable on May 1, 1988, and semi-annually thereafter on November 1 and May 1 by check mailed to the Bondowners registered on the State Authority's books on the Record Date. The proceeds of the Bonds will be loaned to Atwood City under a loan agreement, dated as of November 1, 1987 between the State Authority and Gerald Bank as Trustee and Paying Agent. The Bonds will bear interest at a semi-annual fixed rate of 4% for the initial interest periods from December 1, 1987 through May 1, 1990, after which the Bonds may be converted to semi-annual variable mode at the option of Atwood City upon proper notice. If the bonds are so converted, such Bonds must be tendered for mandatory purchase at par, plus 1/8th of 1% of principal amount under certain circumstances and accrued interest to the Purchase Date (unless the Bondowner files a Non-tender Election). To be so purchased, Bonds must be delivered, accompanied by a notice of election to tender the Bonds, to the Paying Agent between the opening of business on the first day of the month preceding the effective rate date of the Bonds and 4:00 pm New York City time on the fifteenth day preceding such effective rate date for the Bonds.

7.5 OVERDRAFT ACCOUNTS

Overdrafts can be arranged with a banking institution to allow accounts to have either a positive or a negative balance. With a positive balance, interest is paid on the account balance, whereas a negative balance incurs interest charges. Usually, an overdraft account will have a maximum overdraft limit imposed. Also, the interest rate h available on positive balances is less than the interest rate i charged for borrowing.

Clearly, the effects of overdraft financing depend upon the pattern of cash flows over time. Suppose that the net cash flow for period t in the account is denoted by A_t which is the difference between the receipt P_t and the payment E_t in period t. Hence, A_t can either be positive or negative. The amount of overdraft at the end of period t is the cumulative net cash flow N_t which may also be positive or negative. If N_t is positive, a surplus is indicated and the subsequent interest would be paid to the borrower. Most often, N_t is negative during the early time periods of a project and becomes positive in the later periods when the borrower has received payments exceeding expenses.

If the borrower uses overdraft financing and pays the interest per period on the accumulated overdraft at a borrowing rate i in each period, then the interest per period for the accumulated overdraft N_{t-1} from the previous period $(t - 1)$ is $I_t = iN_{t-1}$ where I_t would be negative for a negative account balance N_{t-1}. For a positive account balance, the interest received is $I_t = hN_{t-1}$ where I_t would be positive for a positive account balance.

The account balance N_t at each period t is the sum of receipts P_t, payments E_t, interest I_t, and the account balance from the previous period N_{t-1}. Thus,

$$N_t = N_{t-1} + I_t + P_t - E_t \qquad (7.15)$$

where $I_t = iN_{t-1}$ for a negative N_{t-1} and $I_t = hN_{t-1}$ for a positive N_{t-1}. The net cash flow $A_t = P_t - E_t$ is positive for a net receipt and negative for a net payment. This equation is approximate in that the interest might be earned on intermediate balances based on the pattern of payments during the period instead of at the end of a period. The account balance in each period is of interest because there will always be a maximum limit on the amount of overdraft available.

For the purpose of separating project finances with other receipts and payments in an organization, it is convenient to establish a *credit* account into which receipts related to the project must be deposited when they are received, and all payments related to the project will be withdrawn from this account when they are needed. Since receipts typically lag behind payments for a project, this credit account will have a negative balance until such time when the receipts plus accrued interests are equal to or exceed payments in the period. When that happens, any surplus will not be deposited in the credit account, and the account is then closed with a zero balance. In that case, for negative N_{t-1}, Eq. (7.15) can be expressed as:

$$N_t = (1 + i)N_{t-1} + A_t \qquad (7.16)$$

and as soon as N_t reaches a positive value or zero, the account is closed.

Example 7-9: Overdraft Financing with Grants to a Local Agency

A public project which costs $61,525,000 is funded 80 percent by a federal grant and 20 percent from a state grant. The anticipated duration of the project is six years, with receipts from grant funds allocated at the end of each year to a local agency to cover partial payments to contractors for that year while the remaining payments to contractors will be allocated at the end of the sixth year. The end-of-year payments

TABLE 7–7 ILLUSTRATIVE PAYMENTS, RECEIPTS, AND OVERDRAFTS FOR A SIX-YEAR PROJECT (in $ millions)

Period t	Receipts P_t	Payments E_t	Interest I_t	Account N_t
0	0	0	0	0
1	$ 5.826	$ 6.473	0	−$0.647
2	8.401	9.334	−$0.065	− 1.645
3	12.013	13.348	− 0.165	− 3.145
4	15.149	16.832	− 0.315	− 5.143
5	13.984	15.538	− 0.514	− 7.211
6	6.152	0	− 0.721	− 1.780
Total	$61.525	$61.525	−$1.780	

are given in Table 7-7 in which $t = 0$ refers to the beginning of the project, and each period is one year.

If this project is financed with an overdraft at an annual interest rate $i = 10\%$, then the account balance are computed by Eq. (7.15) and the results are shown in Table 7-7.

In this project, the total grant funds to the local agency covered the cost of construction in the sense that the sum of receipts equaled the sum of construction payments of $61,525,000. However, the timing of receipts lagged payments, and the agency incurred a substantial financing cost, equal in this plan to the overdraft amount of $1,780,000 at the end of year 6 which must be paid to close the credit account. Clearly, this financing problem would be a significant concern to the local agency.

Example 7-10: Use of Overdraft Financing for a Facility

A corporation is contemplating an investment in a facility with the following before-tax operating net cash flow (in $ thousands) at year ends:

Year:	0	1	2	3	4	5	6	7
Cash Flow:	−500	110	112	114	116	118	120	122

The MARR of the corporation before tax is 15 percent. The corporation will finance the facility by using $200,000 from retained earnings and by borrowing the remaining $300,000 through an overdraft credit account which charges 14 percent interest for borrowing. Is this proposed project including financing costs worthwhile?

The results of the analysis of this project is shown in Table 7-8 (in $ thousands) as follows:

$$N_0 = -500 + 200 = -300$$

$$N_1 = (1.14)(-300) + 110 = -232$$

$$N_2 = (1.14)(-232) + 112 = -152.48$$

$$N_3 = (1.14)(-152.48) + 114 = -59.827$$

$$N_4 = (1.14)(-59.827) + 116 = +47.797$$

Since N_4 is positive, it is revised to exclude the net receipt of $116,000$ for this period. Then, the revised value for the last balance is

$$N'_4 = N_{4-116} = -68.203$$

The financial cash flow $\bar{A}_t$ resulting from using overdrafts and making repayments from project receipts will be

$$\bar{A}_0 = -N_0 = 300$$

$$\bar{A}_1 = -A_1 = -110$$

$$\bar{A}_2 = -A_2 = -112$$

$$\bar{A}_3 = -A_3 = -114$$

$$\bar{A}_4 = N_4 - A_4 = -68.203$$

The adjusted net present value of the combined cash flow discounted at 15 percent is $27,679$ as shown in Table 7-8. Hence, the project including the financing charges is worthwhile.

TABLE 7-8 EVALUATION OF FACILITY FINANCING USING OVERDRAFT (in $ thousands)

End of year t	Operating cash flow A_t	Overdraft balance N_t	Financing cash flow $\bar{A}_t$	Combined cash flow AA_t
0	-$500	-$300	$300	-$200
1	110	-232	-110	0
2	112	-152.480	-112	0
3	114	-59.827	-114	0
4	116	0	-68.203	47.797
5	118	0	0	118
6	120	0	0	120
7	122	0	0	122
$[PV]_{15\%}$	$ 21.971		$ 5.708	$ 27.679

7.6 REFINANCING OF DEBTS

Refinancing of debts has two major advantages for an owner. First, they allow refinancing at intermediate stages to save interest charges. If a borrowing agreement is made during a period of relatively high interest charges, then a repurchase agreement allows the borrower to refinance at a lower interest rate. Whenever the borrowing interest rate declines such that the savings in interest payments will cover any transaction expenses (for purchasing outstanding notes or bonds and arranging new financing), then it is advantageous to do so.

Another reason to repurchase bonds is to permit changes in the operation of a facility or new investments. Under the terms of many bond agreements, there may be restrictions on the use of revenues from a particular facility while any bonds are outstanding. These restrictions are inserted to insure bondholders that debts will be repaid. By repurchasing bonds, these restrictions are removed. For example, several bridge authorities had bonds that restricted any diversion of toll revenues to other transportation services such as transit. By repurchasing these bonds, the authority could undertake new operations. This type of repurchase may occur voluntarily even without a repurchase agreement in the original bond. The borrower may give bondholders a premium to retire bonds early.

Example 7-11: Refinancing a Loan

Suppose that the bank loan shown in Example 7-4 had a provision permitting the borrower to repay the loan without penalty at any time. Further, suppose that interest rates for new loans dropped to 9 percent at the end of year 6 of the loan. Issuing costs for a new loan would be $50,000. Would it be advantageous to refinance the loan at that time?

To repay the original loan at the end of year 6 would require a payment of the remaining principal plus the interest due at the end of year 6. This amount R_6 is equal to the present value of the remaining 14 payments discounted at the loan interest rate 11.2 percent to the end of year 6 as given in Eq. (7-13) as follows:

$$R_6 = \sum_{t=1}^{14} \frac{\$1.324 \text{ million}}{(1.112)^t} = \$9.152 \text{ million}$$

The new loan would be in the amount of $9.152 million plus the issuing cost of $0.05 million for a total of $9.202 million. Based on the new loan interest rate of 9 percent, the new uniform annual payment on this loan from years 7 to 20 would be

$$U' = (\$9.202 \text{ million})(U|P, 9\%, 14) = \$1.182 \text{ million}$$

The net present value of the financial cash flow for the new loan would be obtained by discounting at the corporate MARR of 15 percent to the end of year 6 as follows:

$$\text{FPV} = \sum_{t=1}^{t=14} \frac{\$1.182 \text{ million}}{(1.15)^t} = \$6.766 \text{ million}$$

Since the annual payment on the new loan is less than the existing loan ($1.182 million versus $1.324 million), the new loan is preferable.

7.7 PROJECT VERSUS CORPORATE FINANCE

We have focused so far on problems and concerns at the project level. While this is the appropriate viewpoint for project managers, it is always worth bearing in mind that projects must fit into broader organizational decisions and structures. This is particularly true for the problem of project finance, since it is often the case that financing is planned on a corporate or agency level, rather than a project level. Accordingly, project managers should be aware of the concerns at this level of decision making.

A construction project is only a portion of the general capital budgeting problem faced by an owner. Unless the project is very large in scope relative to the owner, a particular construction project is only a small portion of the capital budgeting problem. Numerous construction projects may be lumped together as a single category in the allocation of investment funds. Construction projects would compete for attention with equipment purchases or other investments in a private corporation.

Financing is usually performed at the corporate level using a mixture of long-term corporate debt and retained earnings. A typical set of corporate debt instruments would include the different bonds and notes discussed in this chapter. Variations would typically include different maturity dates, different levels of security interests, different currency denominations, and, of course, different interest rates.

Grouping projects together for financing influences the type of financing that might be obtained. As noted earlier, small and large projects usually involve different institutional arrangements and financing arrangements. For small projects, the fixed costs of undertaking particular kinds of financing may be prohibitively expensive. For example, municipal bonds require fixed costs associated with printing and preparation that do not vary significantly with the size of the issue. By combining numerous small construction projects, different financing arrangements become more practical.

While individual projects may not be considered at the corporate finance level, the problems and analysis procedures described earlier are directly relevant to financial planning for groups of projects and other investments. Thus, the net present values of different financing arrangements can be computed and compared. Since the net present values of different subsets of either investments or financing alternatives are additive, each project or finance alternative can be disaggregated for closer attention or aggregated to provide information at a higher decision-making level.

Example 7-12: Basic Types of Repayment Schedules for Loans

Coupon bonds are used to obtain loans which involve no payment of principal until the maturity date. By combining loans of different maturities, however, it is possible to achieve almost any pattern of principal repayments. However, the interest rates charged on loans of different maturities will reflect market forces such as forecasts of how interest rates will vary over time. As an example, Table 7-9 illustrates the cash flows of debt service for a series of coupon bonds used to fund a municipal construction project; for simplicity, not all years of payments are shown in the table.

In this financing plan, a series of coupon bonds was sold with maturity dates ranging from June 1988 to June 2012. Coupon interest payments on all outstanding bonds were to be paid every six months, on December 1 and June 1 of each year. The interest rate or "coupon rate" was larger on bonds with longer maturities, reflecting an assumption that inflation would increase during this period. The total principal obtained for construction was $26,250,000 from the sale of these bonds. This amount represented the gross sale amount before subtracting issuing costs or any sales discounts; the amount available to support construction would be lower. The maturity dates for bonds were selected to require relatively high repayment amounts until December 1995, with a declining repayment amount subsequently. By shifting the maturity dates and amounts of bonds, this pattern of repayments could be altered. The initial interest payment (of $819,760 on December 1, 1987), reflected a payment for only a portion of a six month period since the bonds were issued in late June 1987.

TABLE 7–9 ILLUSTRATION OF A 25-YEAR MATURITY SCHEDULE FOR BONDS

Date	Maturing principal	Corresponding interest rate	Interest due	Annual debt service
Dec. 1, 1987			$819,760	$ 819,760
June 1, 1988	$1,350,000	5.00%	894,429	
Dec. 1, 1988			860,540	3,184,830
June 1, 1989	1,450,000	5.25	860,540	
Dec. 1, 1989			822,480	3,133,010
June 1, 1990	1,550,000	5.50	822,480	
Dec. 1, 1990			779,850	3,152,330
June 1, 1991	1,600,000	5.80	779,850	
Dec. 1, 1991			733,450	3,113,300
June 1, 1992	1,700,000	6.00	733,450	
Dec. 1, 1992			682,450	3,115,900
June 1, 1993	1,800,000	6.20	682,450	
Dec. 1, 1993			626,650	3,109,100
.	.	.	.	.
.	.	.	.	.
.	.	.	.	.
June 1, 2011	880,000	8.00	68,000	
Dec. 1, 2011			36,000	964,000
June 1, 2012	96,000	8.00	36,000	
Dec. 1, 2012				936,000

7.8 SHIFTING FINANCIAL BURDENS

The different participants in the construction process have quite distinct perspectives on financing. In the realm of project finance, the revenues to one participant represent an expenditure to some other participant. Payment delays from one participant result in a financial burden and a cash flow problem to other participants. It is a common occurrence in construction to reduce financing costs by delaying payments in just this fashion. Shifting payment times does not eliminate financing costs, however, since the financial burden still exists.

Traditionally, many organizations have used payment delays both to shift financing expenses to others or to overcome momentary shortfalls in financial resources. From the owner's perspective, this policy may have short-term benefits, but it certainly has long-term costs. Since contractors do not have large capital assets, they typically do not have large amounts of credit available to cover payment delays. Contractors are also perceived as credit risks in many cases, so loans often require a premium interest charge. Contractors faced with large financing problems are likely to add premiums to bids or not bid at all on particular work. For example, A. Maevis noted [57]

[57] Maevis, A. C. "Construction Cost Control by the Owner," *ASCE Journal of the Construction Division*, Vol. 106, no. 4, December 1980, p. 444.

...there were days in New York City when city agencies had trouble attracting bidders; yet contractors were beating on the door to get work from Consolidated Edison, the local utility. Why? First, the city was a notoriously slow payer, COs (change orders) years behind, decision process chaotic, and payments made 60 days after close of estimate.

Con Edison paid on the 20th of the month for work done to the first of the month. Change orders negotiated and paid within 30 days–60 days. If a decision was needed, it came in 10 days.

The number of bids you receive on your projects are one measure of your administrative efficiency. Further, competition is bound to give you the lowest possible construction price.

Even after bids are received and contracts signed, delays in payments may form the basis for a successful claim against an agency on the part of the contractor.

The owner of a constructed facility usually has a better credit rating and can secure loans at a lower borrowing rate, but there are some notable exceptions to this rule, particularly for construction projects in developing countries. Under certain circumstances, it is advisable for the owner to advance periodic payments to the contractor in return for some concession in the contract price. This is particularly true for large-scale construction projects with long durations for which financing costs and capital requirements are high. If the owner is willing to advance these amounts to the contractor, the gain in lower financing costs can be shared by both parties through prior agreement.

Unfortunately, the choice of financing during the construction period is often left to the contractor who cannot take advantage of all available options alone. The owner is often shielded from participation through the traditional method of price quotation for construction contracts. This practice merely exacerbates the problem by excluding the owner from participating in decisions which may reduce the cost of the project.

Under conditions of economic uncertainty, a premium to hedge the risk must be added to the estimation of construction cost by both the owner and the contractor. The larger and longer the project is, the greater is the risk. For an unsophisticated owner who tries to avoid all risks and to place the financing burdens of construction on the contractor, the contract prices for construction facilities are likely to be increased to reflect the risk premium charged by the contractors. In dealing with small projects with short durations, this practice may be acceptable particularly when the owner lacks any expertise to evaluate the project financing alternatives or the financial stability to adopt innovative financing schemes. However, for large scale projects of long duration, the owner cannot escape the responsibility of participation if it wants to avoid catastrophes of runaway costs and expensive litigation. The construction of nuclear power plants in the private sector and the construction of transportation facilities in the public sector offer ample examples of such problems. If the responsibilities of risk sharing among various parties in a construction project can be clearly defined in the planning stage, all parties can be benefited to take advantage of cost saving and early use of the constructed facility.

Example 7-13: Effects of Payment Delays

Table 7-10 shows an example of the effects of payment timing on the general contractor and subcontractors. The total contract price for this project is $5,100,000, with scheduled payments from the owner shown in column 1. The general contractor's expenses in each period over the lifetime of the project are given in column 2, while the subcontractor's expenses are shown in column 3. If the general contractor must pay the subcontractor's expenses as well as its own at the end of each period, the net cash flow of the general contractor is obtained in column 4, and its cumulative cash flow in column 5.

TABLE 7–10 AN EXAMPLE OF THE EFFECTS OF PAYMENT TIMING

Period	(1) Owner payments	(2) General contractor's expenses	(3) Subcontractor's expenses	(4) General contractor's net cash flow	(5) Cumulative cash flow
1	—	$100,000	$ 900,000	−$1,000,000	−$1,000,000
2	$ 950,000	100,000	900,000	− 50,000	− 1,050,000
3	950,000	100,000	900,000	− 50,000	− 1,100,000
4	950,000	100,000	900,000	− 50,000	− 1,150,000
5	950,000	100,000	900,000	− 50,000	− 1,200,000
6	1,300,000	—	—	1,300,000	100,000
Total	$5,100,000	$500,000	$4,500,000	$ 100,000	

Note: Cumulative cash flow includes no financing charges.

In this example, the owner withholds a 5 percent retainage on cost as well as a payment of $100,000 until the completion of the project. This $100,000 is equal to the expected gross profit of the contractor without considering financing costs or cash flow discounting. Processing time and contractual agreements with the owner result in a delay of one period in receiving payments. The actual construction expenses from the viewpoint of the general contractor consist of $100,000 in each construction period plus payments due to subcontractors of $900,000 in each period. While the net cash flow without regard to discounting or financing is equal to a $100,000 profit for the general contractor, financial costs are likely to be substantial. With immediate payment to subcontractors, over $1,000,000 must be financed by the contractor throughout the duration of the project. If the general contractor uses borrowing to finance its expenses, a maximum borrowing amount of $1,200,000 in period 5 is required even without considering intermediate interest charges. Financing this amount is likely to be quite expensive and may easily exceed the expected project profit.

By delaying payments to subcontractors, the general contractor can substantially reduce its financing requirement. For example, Table 7-11 shows the resulting cash flows from delaying payments to subcontractors for one period and for two periods, respectively. With a one-period delay, a maximum amount of $300,000 (plus intermediate interest charges) would have to be financed by the general contractor. That is, from the data in Table 7-11, the net cash flow in period 1 is −$100,000, and the net cash flow for each of the periods 2 through 5 is given by

TABLE 7–11 AN EXAMPLE OF THE CASH FLOW EFFECTS OF DELAYED PAYMENTS

| | One-period payment delay | | Two-period payment delay | |
| | (1) Net cash flow | (2) Cumulative cash flow | (3) Net cash flow | (4) Cumulative cash flow |
Period				
1	−$100,000	−$100,000	−$100,000	−$ 100,000
2	− 50,000	− 150,000	850,000	750,000
3	− 50,000	− 200,000	− 50,000	700,000
4	− 50,000	− 250,000	− 50,000	650,000
5	− 50,000	− 300,000	− 50,000	600,000
6	400,000	100,000	400,000	1,000,000
7			− 900,000	100,000

$$\$950,000 - \$100,000 - \$900,000 = -\$50,000$$

Finally, the net cash flow for period 6 is

$$\$1,300,000 - \$900,000 = \$400,000$$

Thus, the cumulative net cash flow from periods 1 through 5 as shown in column 1 of Table 7-11 results in maximum shortfall of $300,000 in period 5 in column 2. For the case of a two-period payment delay to the subcontractors, the general contractor even runs a positive balance during construction as shown in column 4. The positive balance results from the receipt of owner payments prior to reimbursing the subcontractor's expenses. This positive balance can be placed in an interest-bearing account to earn additional revenues for the general contractor. Needless to say, however, these payment delays mean extra costs and financing problems to the subcontractors. With a two-period delay in payments from the general contractor, the subcontractors have an unpaid balance of $1,800,000, which would represent a considerable financial cost.

7.9 CONSTRUCTION FINANCING FOR CONTRACTORS

For a general contractor or subcontractor, the cash flow profile of expenses and incomes for a construction project typically follows the work-in-progress for which the contractor will be paid periodically. The markup by the contractor above the estimated expenses is included in the total contract price, and the terms of most contracts generally call for monthly reimbursements of work completed less retainage. At time period 0, which denotes the beginning of the construction contract, a considerable sum may have been spent in preparation. The contractor's expenses which occur more or less continuously for the project duration are depicted by a piecewise continuous curve while the receipts (such as progress payments from the owner) are represented by a step function as shown in Figure 7-1. The owner's payments for the work completed are assumed to lag one period behind expenses except that a withholding proportion or remainder is paid at the end of construction. This method

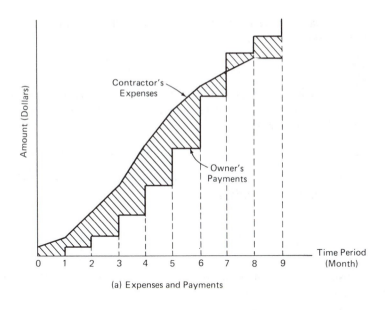

(a) Expenses and Payments

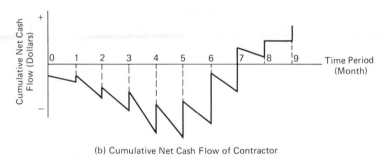

(b) Cumulative Net Cash Flow of Contractor

Figure 7-1 Contractor's Expenses and Owner's Payments

of analysis is applicable to realistic situations where a time period is represented by one month and the number of time periods is extended to cover delayed receipts as a result of retainage.

While the cash flow profiles of expenses and receipts are expected to vary for different projects, the characteristics of the curves depicted in Figure 7-1 are sufficiently general for most cases. Let E_t represent the contractor's expenses in period t, and P_t represent owner's payments in period t, for $t = 0, 1, 2, \ldots, n$ for $n = 5$ in this case. The net operating cash flow at the end of period t for $t \geq 0$ is given by

$$A_t = P_t - E_t \tag{7.17}$$

where A_t is positive for a surplus and negative for a shortfall.

The cumulative operating cash flow at the end of period t just before receiving payment P_t (for $t \geq 1$) is

$$F_t = N_{t-1} - E_t \tag{7.18}$$

where N_{t-1} is the cumulative net cash flows from year 0 to period $(t-1)$. Furthermore, the cumulative net operating cash flow after receiving payment P_t at the end of period t (for $t \geq 1$) is

$$N_t = F_t + P_t = N_{t-1} + A_t \tag{7.19}$$

The gross operating profit G for a n-period project is defined as net operating cash flow at $t = n$ and is given by:

$$G = \sum_{t=0}^{n} (P_t - E_t) = \sum_{t=0}^{n} A_t = N_n \tag{7.20}$$

The use of N_n as a measure of the gross operating profit has the disadvantage that it is not adjusted for the time value of money.

Since the net cash flow A_t (for $t = 0, 1, \ldots, n$) for a construction project represents the amount of cash required or accrued after the owner's payment is plowed back to the project at the end of period t, the internal rate of return (IRR) of this cash flow is often cited in the traditional literature in construction as a profit measure. To compute IRR, let the net present value of A_t discounted at a discount rate i per period be zero; that is,

$$\text{NPV} = \sum_{t=0}^{n} A_t (1 + i)^{-t} = 0 \tag{7.21}$$

The resulting i (if it is unique) from the solution of Eq. (7.21) is the IRR of the net cash flow A_t. Aside from the complications that may be involved in the solution of Eq. (7.21), the resulting $i = \text{IRR}$ has a meaning to the contractor only if the firm finances the entire project from its own equity. This is seldom if ever the case since most construction firms are highly *leveraged*; that is, they have relatively small equity in fixed assets such as construction equipment and depend almost entirely on borrowing in financing individual construction projects. The use of the IRR of the net cash flows as a measure of profit for the contractor is thus misleading. It does not represent even the IRR of the bank when the contractor finances the project through overdraft since the gross operating profit would not be given to the bank.

Since overdraft is the most common form of financing for small- or medium-sized projects, we shall consider the financing costs and effects on profit of the use of overdrafts. Let $\bar{F}_t$ be the cumulative cash flow before the owner's payment in period t *including interest* and $\bar{N}_t$ be the cumulative net cash flow in period t *including interest*. At $t = 0$ when there is no accrued interest, $\bar{F}_0 = F_0$ and $\bar{N}_0 = N_0$. For $t \geq 1$, the interest $\bar{I}_t$ in period t can be obtained by considering the contractor's expenses E_t to be dispersed uniformly during the period.

The inclusion of interest on contractor's expenses E_t during period t (for $t \geq 1$) is based on the rationale that the S-shaped curve depicting the contractor's expenses in Figure 7-1 is fairly typical of actual situations, where the owner's payments are typically made at the end of well-defined periods. Hence, interest on expenses during period t is approximated by one-half of the amount as if the expenses were paid at the beginning of the period. In fact, E_t is the accumulation of all expenses in period t and is treated as an expense at the end of the period. Thus, the interest per period $\bar{I}_t$ (for $t \geq 1$) is the combination of interest charge for N_{t-1} in period t and that for one-half of E_t in the same period t. If $\bar{N}_t$ is negative and i is the borrowing rate for the shortfall,

$$\bar{I}_t = i\bar{N}_{t-1} - \frac{iE_t}{2}$$ (7.22)

if $\bar{N}_t$ is positive and h is the investment rate for the surplus,

$$\bar{I}_t = h\bar{N}_{t-1} - \frac{iE_t}{2}$$ (7.23)

Hence, if the cumulative net cash flow $\bar{N}_t$ is negative, the interest on the overdraft for each period t is paid by the contractor at the end of each period. If N_t is positive, a surplus is indicated and the subsequent interest would be paid to the contractor. Most often, N_t is negative during the early time periods of a project and becomes positive in the later periods when the contractor has received payments exceeding expenses.

Including the interest accrued in period t, the cumulative cash flow at the end of period t just before receiving payment P_t (for $t \geq 1$) is

$$\bar{F}_t = \bar{N}_{t-1} + I_t - E_t$$ (7.24)

Furthermore, the cumulative net cash flow after receiving payment P_t at the end of period t (for $t \geq 1$) is

$$\bar{N}_t = \bar{F}_t + P_t = \bar{N}_t + \bar{I}_t - E_t + P_t$$ (7.25)

The gross operating profit $\bar{G}$ at the end of a n-period project including interest charges is

$$\bar{G} = \bar{N}_n$$ (7.26)

where $\bar{N}_n$ is the cumulative net cash flow for $t = n$.

Example 7-14: Contractor's Gross Profit from a Project

The contractor's expenses and owner's payments for a multiyear construction project are given in columns 1 and 2, respectively, of Table 7-12. Each time period is represented by one year, and the annual interest rate i is for borrowing 11 percent. The computation has been carried out in Table 7-12, and the contractor's gross profit G is found to be $N_5 = \$8.025$ million in the last column of the table.

TABLE 7–12 CONTRACTOR'S EXPENSES AND OWNER'S PAYMENTS (in $ millions)

Period t	(1) Contractor's expenses E_t	(2) Owner's payments P_t	(3) Net cash flow A_t	(4) Cumulative cash before payments F_t	(5) Cumulative net cash N_t
0	$ 3.782	$ 0	−$3.782	−$ 3.782	−$3.782
1	7.458	6.473	− 0.985	− 11.240	− 4.767
2	10.425	9.334	− 1.091	− 15.192	− 5.858
3	14.736	13.348	− 1.388	− 20.594	− 7.246
4	11.420	16.832	+ 5.412	− 18.666	− 1.834
5	5.679	15.538	+ 9.859	− 7.513	+ 8.025
Total	$53.500	$61.525	+$8.025		

The contractor's expenses and the owner's payments as well as the cumulative net cash flow in Table 7-12 can be plotted schematically as those for a similar case in Figure 7-1.

Example 7-15: Effects of Construction Financing

The computation of the cumulative cash flows including interest charges at $i = 11\%$ for Example 7-14 is shown in Table 7-13 with gross profit $\overline{G} = \overline{N}_5 = \$1.384$ million. The results of computation are also shown in Figure 7-2.

TABLE 7–13 CUMULATIVE CASH FLOWS INCLUDING INTERESTS FOR A CONTRACTOR (in $ millions)

Period (year) t	(1) Construction expenses E_t	(2) Owner's payments P_t	(3) Annual interest $\overline{I}_t$	(4) Cumulative net cash flow $\overline{F}_t$	(5) Cumulative net cash flow $\overline{N}_t$
0	$ 3.782	0	0	−$ 3.782	−$ 3.782
1	7.458	$ 6.473	−$0.826	− 12.066	− 5.593
2	10.425	9.334	− 1.188	− 17.206	− 7.872
3	14.736	13.348	− 1.676	− 24.284	− 10.936
4	11.420	16.832	− 1.831	− 24.187	− 7.354
5	5.679	15.538	− 1.121	− 14.154	+ 1.384

7.10 EFFECTS OF OTHER FACTORS ON A CONTRACTOR'S PROFITS

In times of economic uncertainty, the fluctuations in inflation rates and market interest rates affect profits significantly. The total contract price is usually a composite of expenses and payments in then-current dollars at different payment periods. In this case, estimated expenses are also expressed in then-current dollars.

During periods of high inflation, the contractor's profits are particularly vulnerable to delays caused by uncontrollable events for which the owner will not be responsible. Hence, the owner's payments will not be changed while the contractor's expenses will increase with inflation.

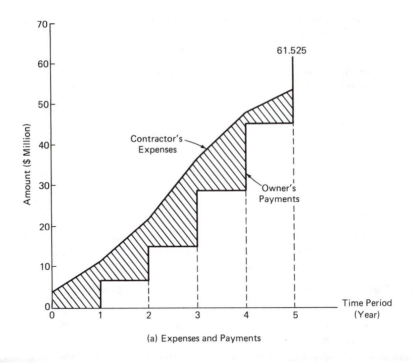

(a) Expenses and Payments

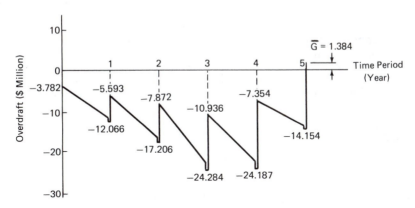

(b) Overdraft Including Interest Charges

Figure 7-2 Effects of Overdraft Financing

Example 7-16: Effects of Inflation

Suppose that both expenses and receipts for the construction project in the Example 7-14 are now expressed in then-current dollars (with annual inflation rate of 4 percent) in Table 7-14. The market interest rate reflecting this inflation is now 15 percent. In considering these expenses and receipts in then-current dollars and using an interest rate of 15 percent including inflation, we can recompute the cumulative net cash flow

TABLE 7-14 OVERDRAFT FINANCING BASED ON INFLATED DOLLARS
(in $ millions)

Period (year) *t*	(1) Construction expenses E_t	(2) Owner's payments P_t	(3) Annual interest $\bar{I}_t$	(4) Cumulative before payments $\bar{F}_t$	(5) Cumulative net cash flow $\bar{N}_t$
0	$ 3.782	0	0	-$ 3.782	-$ 3.782
1	7.756	$ 6.732	-$1.149	- 12.687	- 5.955
2	11.276	10.096	- 1.739	- 18.970	- 8.874
3	16.576	15.015	- 2.574	- 28.024	- 13.009
4	13.360	19.691	- 2.953	- 29.322	- 9.631
5	6.909	18.904	- 1.964	- 18.504	+ 0.400

(with interest). Thus, the gross profit less financing costs becomes $\bar{G} = \bar{N}_5 = \$0.4$ million. There will be a loss rather than a profit after deducting financing costs and adjusting for the effects of inflation with this project.

Example 7-17: Effects of Work Stoppage at Periods of Inflation

Suppose further that besides the inflation rate of 4 percent, the project in Example 7-16 is suspended at the end of year 2 due to a labor strike and resumed after one year. Also, assume that while the contractor will incur higher interest expenses due to the work stoppage, the owner will not increase the payments to the contractor. The cumulative net cash flows for the case and of operation and financing expenses are recomputed and tabulated in Table 7-15. The construction expenses and receipts

TABLE 7-15 EFFECTS OF WORK STOPPAGE AND INFLATION ON A CONTRACTOR
(in $ millions)

Period (year) *t*	(1) Construction expenses E_t	(2) Owner's payments P_t	(3) Annual interest $\bar{I}_t$	(4) Cumulative before payments $\bar{F}_t$	(5) Cumulative net cash flow $\bar{N}_t$
0	$ 3.782	0	0	-$ 3.782	-$ 3.782
1	7.756	$ 6.732	-$1.149	- 12.687	- 5.955
2	11.276	10.096	- 1.739	- 18.970	- 8.874
3	0	0	- 1.331	- 10.205	- 10.205
4	17.239	15.015	- 2.824	- 30.268	- 15.253
5	13.894	19.691	- 3.330	- 32.477	- 12.786
6	7.185	18.904	- 2.457	- 22.428	- 3.524

in then-current dollars resulting from the work stopping and the corresponding net cash flow of the project including financing (with annual interest accumulated in the overdraft to the end of the project) is shown in Figure 7-3. It is noteworthy that, with or without the work stoppage, the gross operating profit declines in value at the end of the project as a result of inflation, but with the work stoppage it has eroded further to a loss of $3.524 million as indicated by $\bar{N}_6 = -3.524$ in Table 7-15.

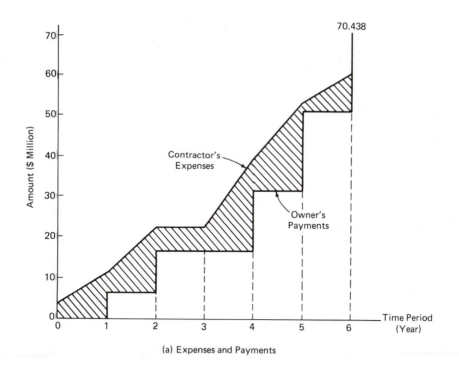

(a) Expenses and Payments

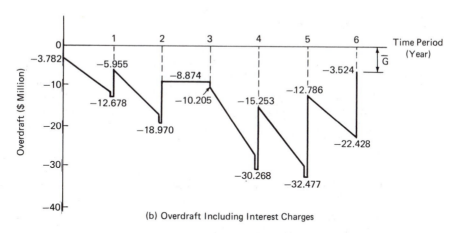

(b) Overdraft Including Interest Charges

Figure 7-3 Effects of Inflation and Work Stoppage

7.11 REFERENCES

7-1. Au, T., and C. Hendrickson, "Profit Measures for Construction Projects," *ASCE Journal of Construction Engineering and Management*, Vol. 112, no. CO-2, 1986, pp. 273–286.

7-2. Brealey, R., and S. Myers, *Principles of Corporate Finance*, 2nd ed., McGraw-Hill Book Company, 1984.

7-3. Collier, C. A. and D. A. Halperin, *Construction Funding: Where the Money Comes From*, 2nd ed., John Wiley and Sons, Inc., New York, 1984.

7-4. Dipasquale, D., and C. Hendrickson, "Options for Financing a Regional Transit Authority," *Transportation Research Record*, no. 858, 1982, pp. 29-35.

7-5. Goss, C. A., "Financing: The Contractor's Perspective," *Construction Contracting*, Vol. 62, no. 10, 1980, pp. 15–17.

7.12 PROBLEMS

P7-1. Compute the effective annual interest rate with a nominal annual percentage rate of 12 percent and compounding periods of

    a. Monthly
    b. Quarterly
    c. Semiannually (i.e., twice a year)

P7-2. A corporation is contemplating investment in a facility with the following before-tax operating cash flow (in thousands of constant dollars) at year ends:

Year:	0	1	2	3	4	5	6	7
Cash flow:	−$500	$110	$112	$114	$116	$118	$120	$122

The MARR of the corporation before tax is 10 percent. The corporation will finance the facility by using $200,000 from retained earning and by borrowing the remaining amount through one of the following two plans:

    a. A seven-year coupon bond with 5 percent issuance cost and 12 percent interest rate payable annually
    b. Overdraft from a bank at 13 percent interest

Which financing plan is preferable on the basis of before-tax analysis?

P7-3. Suppose that an overseas constructor proposed to build the facility in Problem P7-2 at a cost of $550,000 (rather than $500,000), but would also arrange financing with a 5 percent issuing charge and uniform payments over a seven-year period. This financing is available from an export bank with a special interest rate of 9 percent. Is this offer attractive on the basis of before-tax analysis?

P7-4. The original financing arrangement to obtain a $550,000 loan for a seven-year project with 5 percent issuing charge is to repay both the loan and issue charge through uniform annual payments with a 9 percent annual interest rate over the seven-year period. If this arrangement is to be refinanced after two years by coupon bonds that pay 8 percent nominal annual interest (4 percent per six-month period) for the remaining five years at the end of which the principal will be due, assuming an origination fee of 2 percent, determine the total amount of coupon bonds necessary for refinancing and the interest payment per period.

P7-5. A public agency is contemplating construction of a facility with the following operating cash flow (in thousands constant $) at year ends.

Year:	0	1	2	3	4	5
Cash flow:	−$400	−$195	$280	$300	$320	$340

The MARR of the agency is 10 percent. If the agency can finance this facility in one of the following two ways, which financing scheme is preferable?

a. Overdraft financing at an interest rate of 12 percent per annum.

b. Five-year coupon bonds issued at year 0 (so that all principal is repaid at the end of year 5) in the amount of $672,000 including an issuing cost of 5 percent and at 10 percent interest payable annually. The unused amount in year 0 will accumulate 10 percent interest so that there is sufficient to pay for the interest on coupon bond due in year 1.

P7-6. Suppose that the coupon bonds in Problem P7-5 are to be refinanced after two years by a uniform payment mortgage for the remaining three years, for an issuing cost of $10,000 in then-current dollars. If the mortgage is repaid with uniform monthly payments for 36 months and the monthly interest rate is 1 percent, determine the amount of monthly payment.

P7-7. Suppose the investment in a facility by a public agency results in a net operating cash flow at year ends (in $ thousands) as follows:

Year:	0	1	2	3	4	5	6
Cash flow:	−$850	$250	$250	$250	$450	$450	$450

The agency has a MARR of 9 percent and is not subject to tax. If the project can be financed in one of the two following ways, which financing scheme is prefer able?

a. Six-year uniform payment bonds at 11 percent interest rate for a total amount of borrowing of $875,000, which includes $25,000 of issuing cost

b. Five-year coupon bonds at 10 percent interest rate for a total amount of borrowing of $900,000 which includes $50,000 of issuing cost

P7-8. Suppose that the five-year coupon bond in Problem P7-7 is to be refinanced, *after* the payment of interest at the end of year 3, by a uniform mortgage which requires an issuance cost of 2 percent. If the annual interest rate is 9 percent, what is the uniform annual payment on the mortgage for another five years?

P7-9. A corporation plans to invest in a small project which costs a one-time expenditure of $700,000 and offers an annual return of $250,000 each in the next four years. It intends to finance this project by issuing a five-year promissory note which requires an origination fee of $10,000. Interest payments are made annually at 9 percent with the repayment of the principal at the end of five years. If the before tax MARR of the corporation is 11 percent, find the adjusted net present value of the investment in conjunction with the proposed financing.

P7-10. A local transportation agency is receiving a construction grant in annual installments from the federal and state governments for a construction project. However, it must make payments to the contractor periodically for construction expenditures. Consider two possible cases: (a) all receipts and expenditures (in $ millions) are made at year ends as shown, and (b) all expenditures are spread over each year uniformly but receipts are received at the end of each year only. Determine the overdraft at the end of year 5 if the project is financed with an overdraft at an annual interest rate of 10 percent for both cases (a) and (b).

Year:	0	1	2	3	4	5
Receipts:	0	$4.764	$7.456	$8.287	$6.525	$2.468
Expenditures:	$1.250	$6.821	$9.362	$7.744	$4.323	0

P7-11. The operating cash flows of contractor's expenses and the owner's payments for a construction project as stipulated in the contract agreement are shown in Table P7-11. The contractor has established a line of credit from the bank at a monthly interest rate of 1.5 percent, and the contractor is allowed to borrow the shortfall between expense and receipt at the end of each month but must deposit any excess of net operating cash flow to reduce the loan amount. Assuming that there is no inflation, determine (a) the cumulative net cash flow for operation only (excluding interest) and (b) the cumulative net cash flow including interest due to overdrafting. Also find the contractor's gross profit.

TABLE P7–11

End of month	Contractor's expenses	Owner's payments
0	– $200,000	0
1	– 250,000	$ 225,000
2	– 400,000	360,000
3	– 520,000	468,000
4	– 630,000	567.000
5	– 780,000	702,000
6	– 750,000	675,000
7	– 660,000	594,000
8	– 430,000	387,000
9	– 380,000	342,000
10	– 332,000	298,800
11	– 256,000	230,400
12	– 412,000	370,800
13	0	1,080,000
14	0	600,000
Total	$6,000,000	$6,900,000

P7-12. The contractor's construction expenses and owner's payments for a construction project are expressed in then-current inflated dollars in Table P7-12. The monthly interest rate required by the bank is 1.5 percent regardless of inflation. Suppose that the work is stopped for two months at the end of month 5 due to a labor strike while the monthly inflation rate is 0.5 percent. Under the terms of the contract between the owner and the contractor, suppose that the owner's payments will be delayed but not adjusted for inflation. Find the cumulative net cash flow with interest due to overdrafting for the following conditions: (a) if there were no labor strike and (b) when there is a strike for two months at the end of month 5.

P7-13. The contractor's construction expenses and the owner's payments for a construction project in then-current dollars as stipulated in the contract agreement are shown in Table P7-13. The contractor has established a line of credit from the bank at a monthly interest rate of 2 percent (based on then-current dollars), and the contractor is allowed to borrow the shortfalls between expense and receipt at the end of each month but must deposit any excess of net operating cash flow to reduce the loan amount. Determine the cumulative net cash flow including interest due to overdrafting. Also, find the contractor's gross profit.

TABLE P7–12

End of month	Contractor's expenses	Owner's payments
0	− $200,000	0
1	− 251,250	$ 225,000
2	− 404,000	360,000
3	− 527,852	468,000
4	− 642,726	567,000
5	− 799,734	702,000
6	− 772,800	675,000
7	− 683,430	594,000
8	− 447,501	387,000
9	− 397,442	342,000
10	− 348,965	298,800
11	− 270,438	230,400
12	− 437,420	370,800
13	0	1,080,000
14	0	600,000
Total	−$6,183,558	$6,900,000

TABLE P7–13

End of month	Contractor's expenses	Owner's payments
0	$ 50,000	0
1	85,000	$ 47,500
2	176,000	80,700
3	240,000	167,200
4	284,000	228,000
5	252,000	270,000
6	192,000	237,500
7	123,000	182,400
8	98,000	116,800
9	0	319,900
Total	$1,500,000	$1,650,000

P7-14. Suppose that both the contractor's expenses and owner's payments for a construction project are expressed in then-current dollars in Table P7-13 (Problem P7-13). The monthly interest rate required by the bank is 2.5 percent based on then-current dollars. Suppose that the work is stopped for three months at the end of month 4 due to a labor strike while the monthly inflation rate is 0.5 percent. The owner's payments will be delayed but not adjusted for inflation. Find the cumulative net cash flow expressed in then-current dollars, with interest compounded and accumulated to the end of the project.

8

Construction Pricing
and
Contracting

8.1 PRICING FOR CONSTRUCTED FACILITIES

Because of the unique nature of constructed facilities, it is almost imperative to have a separate price for each facility. The construction contract price includes the direct project cost, including field supervision expenses plus the markup imposed by contractors for general overhead expenses and profit. The factors influencing a facility price will vary by type of facility and location as well. Within each of the major categories of construction such as residential housing, commercial buildings, industrial complexes, and infrastructure, there are smaller segments which have very different environments with regard to price setting. However, all pricing arrangements have some common features in the form of the legal documents binding the owner and the supplier(s) of the facility. Without addressing special issues in various industry segments, the most common types of pricing arrangements can be described broadly to illustrate the basic principles.

Competitive Bidding

The basic structure of the bidding process consists of the formulation of detailed plans and specifications of a facility based on the objectives and requirements of the owner and the invitation of qualified contractors to bid for the right to execute the project. The definition of a qualified contractor usually calls for a minimal evidence of previous experience and financial stability. An owner may also require the prospective bidders to provide a form of surety bond for performing the contracted work. A contractor would submit a bid bond which guarantees that, if a contract is awarded, the contractor will provide a contract bond to protect the owner against defaults and other encumbrances. In the private sector, the owner has considerable latitude in selecting the bidders, ranging from open competition to the restriction of bidders to a few favored contractors. In the public sector, the rules are carefully delineated to place all qualified contractors on an equal footing for competition and strictly enforced to prevent collusion among contractors and unethical or illegal actions by public officials.

Detailed plans and specifications are usually prepared by an architectural/engineering firm which oversees the bidding process on behalf of the owner. The final bids are normally submitted on either a lump-sum or unit-price basis, as stipulated by the owner. A lump-sum bid represents the total price for which a contractor offers to complete a facility according to the detailed plans and specifications. Unit-price bidding is used in projects for which the quantity of materials or the amount of labor involved in some key tasks is particularly uncertain. In such cases, the contractor is permitted to submit a list of unit prices for those tasks. However, the total payment to the winning contractor will be based on the actual quantities multiplied by the respective quoted unit prices.

Negotiated Contracts

Instead of inviting competitive bidding, private owners often choose to award construction contracts with one or more selected contractors. A major reason for using negotiated contracts is the flexibility of this type of pricing arrangement, particularly for projects of large size and great complexity or for projects which substantially duplicate previous facilities sponsored by the owner. An owner may value the expertise and integrity of a particular contractor who has a good reputation or has worked successfully for the owner in the past. If it becomes necessary to meet a deadline for completion of the project, the construction of a project may proceed without waiting for the completion of the detailed plans and specifications with a contractor that the owner can trust. However, the owner's staff must be highly knowledgeable and competent in evaluating contractor proposals and monitoring subsequent performance.

Generally, negotiated contracts require the reimbursement of direct project cost plus the contractor's fee as determined by one of the following methods:

1. Cost plus fixed percentage
2. Cost plus fixed fee
3. Cost plus variable fee
4. Target estimate
5. Guaranteed maximum cost

The fixed percentage or fixed fee is determined at the outset of the project, while variable fee and target estimates are used as an incentive to reduce costs by sharing any cost savings. A guaranteed maximum cost arrangement imposes a penalty on a contractor for cost overruns and failure to complete the project on time.

Speculative Residential Construction

In residential construction, developers often build houses and condominiums in anticipation of the demand of home buyers. Because the basic needs of home buyers are very similar and home designs can be standardized to some degree, the probability of finding buyers of good housing units within a relatively short time is quite high. Consequently, developers are willing to undertake speculative building and lending institutions are also willing to finance such construction. The developer essentially set the price for each housing unit as the market will bear and can adjust the prices of remaining units at any given time according to the market trend.

Force-Account Construction

Some owners use in-house labor forces to perform a substantial amount of construction, particularly for addition, renovation, and repair work. Then, the total of the force-account charges including in-house overhead expenses will be the pricing arrangement for the construction.

8.2 CONTRACT PROVISIONS FOR RISK ALLOCATION

Provisions for the allocation of risk among parties to a contract can appear in numerous areas in addition to the total construction price. Typically, these provisions assign responsibility for covering the costs of possible or unforeseen occurrences. A partial list of responsibilities with concomitant risk that can be assigned to different parties would include

- Force majeure (i.e., payment for costs due to "acts of God" and other external events such as war or labor strikes)
- Indemnification (i.e., payment for losses and damages incurred by another party)
- Liens (i.e., assurances that third party claims are settled such as "mechanics liens" for worker wages)
- Labor laws (i.e., payments for any violation of labor laws and regulations on the job site)
- Differing site conditions (i.e., responsibility for extra costs due to unexpected site conditions)
- Delays and extensions of time
- Liquidated damages (i.e., payments for any facility defects with payment amounts agreed to in advance)
- Consequential damages (i.e., payments for actual damage costs assessed upon impact of facility defects)
- Occupational safety and health of workers
- Permits, licenses, laws, and regulations
- Equal employment opportunity regulations
- Termination for default by contractor
- Suspension of work
- Warranties and guarantees

The language used for specifying the risk assignments in these areas must conform to legal requirements and past interpretations which may vary in different jurisdictions or over time. Without using standard legal language, contract provisions may be unenforceable. Unfortunately, standard legal language for this purpose may be difficult to understand. As a result, project managers often have difficulty in interpreting their particular responsibilities. Competent legal counsel is required to advise the different parties to an agreement about their respective responsibilities.

Standard forms for contracts can be obtained from numerous sources, such as the American Institute of Architects (AIA) or the Associated General Contractors (AGC). These standard forms may include risk and responsibility allocations which are unacceptable to one or more of the contracting parties. In particular, standard forms may be biased to reduce the risk and responsibility of the originating organization or group. Parties to a contract should read and review all contract documents carefully.

The next three examples illustrate contract language resulting in different risk assignments between a contractor (CONTRACTOR) and an owner (COMPANY).

Each contract provision allocates different levels of indemnification risk to the contractor.[58]

Example 8-1: A Contract Provision Example with High Contractor Risk

"Except where the sole negligence of COMPANY is involved or alleged, CONTRACTOR shall indemnify and hold harmless COMPANY, its officers, agents, and employees, from and against any and all loss, damage, and liability and from any and all claims for damages on account of or by reason of bodily injury, including death, not limited to the employees of CONTRACTOR, COMPANY, and of any subcontractor or CONTRACTOR, and from and against any *and all damages to property, including property of COMPANY and third parties, direct and/or consequential,* caused by or arising out of, in whole or in part, or claimed to have been caused by or to have arisen out of, in whole or in part, an act of omission of CONTRACTOR or its agents, employees, vendors, or subcontractors, of their employees or agents in connection with the performance of the Contract Documents, *whether or not insured against*; and CONTRACTOR shall, at its own cost and expense, defend any claim, suit, action, or proceeding, whether groundless or not, which may be commenced against COMPANY by reason thereof or in connection therewith, and CONTRACTOR shall pay any and all judgments which may be recovered in such action, claim, proceeding or suit, and defray any and all expenses, including costs and attorney's fees which may be incurred by reason of such actions, claims, proceedings, or suits."

Comment: This is a very burdensome provision for the contractor. It makes the contractor responsible for practically every conceivable occurrence and type of damage, except when a claim for loss or damages is due to the *sole* negligence of the owner. As a practical matter, sole negligence on a construction project is very difficult to ascertain because the work is so intertwined. Since there is no dollar limitation to the contractor's exposure, sufficient liability coverage to cover worst scenario risks will be difficult to obtain. The best the contractor can do is to obtain as complete and broad excess liability insurance coverage as can be purchased. This insurance is costly, so the contractor should ensure that the contract price is sufficiently high to cover the expense.

Example 8-2: An Example Contract Provision with Medium Risk Allocation to Contractor

"CONTRACTOR shall protect, defend, hold harmless, and indemnify COMPANY from and against any loss, damage, claim, action, liability, or demand whatsoever (including, with limitation, costs, expenses, and attorney's fees, whether for appeals or otherwise, in connection therewith), arising out of any personal injury (including, without limitation, injury to any employee of COMPANY, CONTRACTOR or any subcontractor), arising out of any personal injury (including, without limitation, injury to any employee of COMPANY, CONTRACTOR, or any subcontractor), including

---

[58] These examples are taken directly from a construction industry cost-effectiveness project report, "Contractual Arrangements," The Business Roundtable, New York, Appendix D, 1982. Permission to quote this material from the Business Roundtable is gratefully acknowledged.

death resulting therefrom or out of any damage to or loss or destruction of property, real and or personal (including property of COMPANY, CONTRACTOR, and any subcontractor, and including tools and equipment whether owned, rented, or used by CONTRACTOR, any subcontractor, or any workman) in any manner based upon, occasioned by, or attributable or related to the performance, whether by the CONTRACTOR or any subcontractor, of the Work or any part thereof, and CONTRACTOR shall at its own expense defend any and all actions based thereon, except where said personal injury or property damage is caused by the negligence of COMPANY or COMPANY'S employees. Any loss, damage, cost expense or attorney's fees incurred by COMPANY in connection with the foregoing may, in addition to other remedies, be deducted from CONTRACTOR'S compensation, then due or thereafter to become due. *COMPANY shall effect for the benefit of CONTRACTOR a waiver of subrogation on the existing facilities, including consequential damages such as, but not by way of limitation, loss of profit and loss of product or plant downtime but excluding any deductibles which shall exist as at the date of this CONTRACT; provided, however, that said waiver of subrogation shall be expanded to include all said deductible amounts on the acceptance of the Work by COMPANY.*"

Comment: This clause provides the contractor considerable relief. He still has unlimited exposure for injury to all persons and third-party property but only to the extent caused by the contractor's negligence. The "sole" negligence issue does not arise. Furthermore, the contractor's liability for damages to the owner's property—a major concern for contractors working in petrochemical complexes, at times worth billions—is limited to the owner's insurance deductible, and the owner's insurance carriers have no right of recourse against the contractor. The contractor's limited exposure regarding the owner's facilities ends on completion of the work.

Example 8-3: An Example Contract Provision with Low Risk Allocation to Contractor

"CONTRACTOR hereby agrees to indemnify and hold COMPANY and/or any parent, subsidiary, or affiliate, or COMPANY and/or officers, agents, or employees of any of them, harmless from and against any loss or liability arising directly or indirectly out of any claim or cause of action for loss or damage to property including, but not limited to, CONTRACTOR'S property and COMPANY'S property and for injuries to or death of persons including but not limited to CONTRACTOR'S employees, caused by or resulting from the performance of the work by CONTRACTOR, its employees, agents, and subcontractors and shall, at the option of COMPANY, defend COMPANY at CONTRACTOR'S sole expense in any litigation involving the same regardless of whether such work is performed by CONTRACTOR, its employees, or by its subcontractors, their employees, or all or either of them. *In all instances, CONTRACTOR'S indemnity to COMPANY shall be limited to the proceeds of CONTRACTOR'S umbrella liability insurance coverage.*"

Comment: With respect to indemnifying the owner, the contractor in this provision has minimal out-of-pocket risk. Exposure is limited to whatever can be collected from the contractor's insurance company.

8.3 RISKS AND INCENTIVES ON CONSTRUCTION QUALITY

All owners want quality construction with reasonable costs, but not all are willing to share risks and/or provide incentives to enhance the quality of construction. In recent years, more owners recognize that they do not get the best quality of construction by squeezing the last dollar of profit from the contractor, and they accept the concept of risk sharing/risk assignment in principle in letting construction contracts. However, the implementation of such a concept in the past decade has received mixed results.

Many public owners have been the victims of their own schemes, not only because of the usual requirement in letting contracts of public works through competitive bidding to avoid favoritism, but at times because of the sheer weight of entrenched bureaucracy. Some contractors steer away from public works altogether; others submit bids at higher prices to compensate for the restrictive provisions of contract terms. As a result, some public authorities find that either there are few responsible contractors responding to their invitations to submit bids or the bid prices far exceed their engineers' estimates. Those public owners who have adopted the federal government's risk-sharing/risk-assignment contract concepts have found that while initial bid prices may have decreased somewhat, claims and disputes on contracts are more frequent than before, and notably more so than in privately funded construction. Some of these claims and disputes can no doubt be avoided by improving the contract provisions.[59]

Since most claims and disputes arise most frequently from lump-sum contracts for both public and private owners, the following factors associated with lump-sum contracts are particularly noteworthy:

- Unbalanced bids in unit prices on which periodic payment estimates are based
- Change orders subject to negotiated payments
- Changes in design or construction technology
- Incentives for early completion

An unbalanced bid refers to raising the unit prices on items to be completed in the early stage of the project and lowering the unit prices on items to be completed in the later stages. The purpose of this practice on the part of the contractor is to ease its burden of construction financing. It is better for owners to offer explicit incentives to aid construction financing in exchange for lower bid prices than to allow the use of hidden unbalanced bids. Unbalanced bids may also occur if a contractor feels some item of work was underestimated in amount, so that a high unit price on that item would increase profits. Since lump-sum contracts are awarded on the basis of low bids, it is difficult to challenge the low bidders on the validity of their unit prices except for flagrant violations. Consequently remedies should be sought by requesting the contractor to submit pertinent records of financial transactions to substantiate the

---

[59] See C. D. Sutliff and J. G. Zack, Jr., "Contract Provisions That Ensure Complete Cost Disclosures," *Cost Engineering*, Vol. 29, no. 10, October 1987, pp. 10–14.

expenditures associated with its monthly billings for payments of work completed during the period.

One of the most contentious issues in contract provisions concerns the payment for change orders. The owner and its engineer should have an appreciation of the effects of changes for specific items of work and negotiate with the contractor on the identifiable cost of such items. The owner should require the contractor to submit the price quotation within a certain period of time after the issuance of a change order and to assess whether the change order may cause delay damages. If the contract does not contain specific provisions on cost disclosures for evaluating change order costs, it will be difficult to negotiate payments for change orders and claim settlements later.

In some projects, the contract provisions may allow the contractor to provide alternative design and/or construction technology. The owner may impose different mechanisms for pricing these changes. For example, a contractor may suggest a design or construction method change that fulfills the performance requirements. Savings due to such changes may accrue to the contractor or the owner or may be divided in some fashion between the two. The contract provisions must reflect the owner's risk-reward objectives in calling for alternate design and/or construction technology. While innovations are often sought to save money and time, unsuccessful innovations may require additional money and time to correct earlier misjudgment. At worst, a failure could have serious consequences.

In spite of admonitions and good intentions for better planning before initiating a construction project, most owners want a facility to be in operation as soon as possible once a decision is made to proceed with its construction. Many construction contracts contain provisions of penalties for late completion beyond a specified deadline; however, unless such provisions are accompanied by similar incentives for early completion, they may be ruled unenforceable in court. Early completion may result in significant savings, particularly in rehabilitation projects in which the facility users are inconvenienced by the loss of the facility and the disruption due to construction operations.

Example 8-4: Arkansas Rice Growers Cooperative Association v. Alchemy Industries

A 1986 court case can illustrate the assumption of risk on the part of contractors and design professionals.[60] The Arkansas Rice Growers Cooperative contracted with Alchemy Industries, Inc., to provide engineering and construction services for a new facility intended to generate steam by burning rice hulls. Under the terms of the contract, Alchemy Industries guaranteed that the completed plant would be capable of "reducing a minimum of seven and one-half tons of rice hulls per hour to an ash and producing a minimum of 48 million BTU's per hour of steam at 200 pounds pressure." Unfortunately, the finished plant did not meet this performance standard, and the Arkansas Rice Growers Cooperative Association sued Alchemy Industries and its subcontractors for breach of warranty. Damages of almost $1.5 million were awarded to the association.

---

[60] *Arkansas Rice Growers* v. *Alchemy Industries, Inc.*, United States Court of Appeals, Eighth Circuit, 1986. The court decision appears in 797 Federal Reporter, 2d Series, pp. 565–574.

8.4 TYPES OF CONSTRUCTION CONTRACTS

While construction contracts serve as a means of pricing construction, they also structure the allocation of risk to the various parties involved. The owner has the sole power to decide what type of contract should be used for a specific facility to be constructed and to set forth the terms in a contractual agreement. It is important to understand the risks of the contractors associated with different types of construction contracts.

Lump-Sum Contract

In a lump-sum contract, the owner has essentially assigned all the risk to the contractor, who in turn can be expected to ask for a higher markup to take care of unforeseen contingencies. Beside the fixed lump-sum price, other commitments are often made by the contractor in the form of submittals such as a specific schedule, the management reporting system or a quality control program. If the actual cost of the project is underestimated, the underestimated cost will reduce the contractor's profit by that amount. An overestimate has an opposite effect, but may reduce the chance of being a low bidder for the project.

Unit-Price Contract

In a unit-price contract, the risk of inaccurate estimation of uncertain quantities for some key tasks has been removed from the contractor. However, some contractors may submit an "unbalanced bid" when it discovers large discrepancies between its estimates and the owner's estimates of these quantities. Depending on the confidence of the contractor on its own estimates and its propensity on risk, a contractor can slightly raise the unit prices on the underestimated tasks while lowering the unit prices on other tasks. If the contractor is correct in its assessment, it can increase its profit substantially since the payment is made on the actual quantities of tasks, and if the reverse is true, it can lose on this basis. Furthermore, the owner may disqualify a contractor if the bid appears to be heavily unbalanced. To the extent that an underestimate or overestimate is caused by changes in the quantities of work, neither error will affect the contractor's profit beyond the markup in the unit prices.

Cost Plus Fixed Percentage Contract

For certain types of construction involving new technology or extremely pressing needs, the owner is sometimes forced to assume all risks of cost overruns. The contractor will receive the actual direct job cost plus a fixed percentage and have little incentive to reduce job cost. Furthermore, if there are pressing needs to complete the project, overtime payments to workers are common and will further increase the job cost. Unless there are compelling reasons, such as the urgency in the construction of military installations, the owner should not use this type of contract.

Cost Plus Fixed Fee Contract

Under this type of contract, the contractor will receive the actual direct job cost plus a fixed fee and will have some incentive to complete the job quickly since its fee is fixed regardless of the duration of the project. However, the owner still assumes the risks of direct job cost overrun while the contractor may risk the erosion of its profits if the project is dragged on beyond the expected time.

Cost Plus Variable Percentage Contract

For this type of contract, the contractor agrees to a penalty if the actual cost exceeds the estimated job cost, or a reward if the actual cost is below the estimated job cost. In return for taking the risk on its own estimate, the contractor is allowed a variable percentage of the direct job cost for its fee. Furthermore, the project duration is usually specified and the contractor must abide by the deadline for completion. This type of contract allocates considerable risk for cost overruns to the owner, but also provides incentives to contractors to reduce costs as much as possible.

Target Estimate Contract

This is another form of contract which specifies a penalty or reward to a contractor, depending on whether the actual cost is greater than or less than the contractor's estimated direct job cost. Usually, the percentages of savings or overrun to be shared by the owner and the contractor are predetermined and the project duration is specified in the contract. Bonuses or penalties may be stipulated for different project completion dates.

Guaranteed Maximum-Cost Contract

When the project scope is well defined, an owner may choose to ask the contractor to take all the risks, both in terms of actual project cost and project time. Any work change orders from the owner must be extremely minor if at all, since performance specifications are provided to the owner at the outset of construction. The owner and the contractor agree to a project cost guaranteed by the contractor as maximum. There may be or may not be additional provisions to share any savings if any in the contract. This type of contract is particularly suitable for *turnkey* operation.

8.5 RELATIVE COSTS OF CONSTRUCTION CONTRACTS

Regardless of the type of construction contract selected by the owner, the contractor recognizes that the actual construction cost will never be identical to its own estimate because of imperfect information. Furthermore, it is common for the owner to place work change orders to modify the original scope of work for which the contractor will receive additional payments as stipulated in the contract. The contractor will use different markups commensurate with its market circumstances and with the risks involved in different types of contracts, leading to different contract prices at the time of bidding or negotiation. The type of contract agreed upon may also provide the contractor with greater incentives to try to reduce costs as much as possible. The contractor's gross profit at the completion of a project is affected by the type of contract, the accuracy of its original estimate, and the nature of work change orders. The owner's actual payment for the project is also affected by the contract and the nature of work change orders.

To illustrate the relative costs of several types of construction contracts, the pricing mechanisms for such construction contracts are formulated on the same direct job cost plus corresponding markups reflecting the risks. Let us adopt the following notation:

E = contractor's original estimate of the direct job cost at the time of contract award

M = amount of markup by the contractor in the contract

B = estimated construction price at the time of signing contract

A = contractor's actual cost for the original scope of work in the contract

U = underestimate of the cost of work in the original estimate (with negative value U denoting an overestimate)

C = additional cost of work due to change orders

P = actual payment to contractor by the owner

F = contractor's gross profit

R = basic percentage markup above the original estimate for fixed fee contract

R_i = premium percentage markup for contract type i such that the total percentage markup is $(R + R_i)$, for example, $(R + R_1)$ for a lump-sum contract, $(R + R_2)$ for a unit-price contract, and $(R + R_3)$ for a guaranteed maximum-cost contract

N = a factor in the target estimate for sharing the savings in cost as agreed upon by the owner and the contractor, with $0 \le N \le 1$

At the time of a contract award, the contract price is given by

$$B = E + M \tag{8.1}$$

The underestimation of the cost of work in the original contract is defined as

$$U = A - E \tag{8.2}$$

Then, at the completion of the project, the contractor's actual cost for the original scope of work is

$$A = E + U \tag{8.3}$$

For various types of construction contracts, the contractor's markup and the price for construction agreed to in the contract are shown in Table 8-1. Note that at the time of contract award, it is assumed that $A = E$, even though the effects of underestimation on the contractor's gross profits are different for various types

TABLE 8–1 ORIGINAL ESTIMATED CONTRACT PRICES

Type of contract	(1) Markup	(2) Contract price
1. Lump sum	$M = (R + R_1)E$	$B = (1 + R + R_1)E$
2. Unit price	$M = (R + R_2)E$	$B = (1 + R + R_2)E$
3. Cost plus fixed %	$M = RA = RE$	$B = (1 + R)E$
4. Cost plus fixed fee	$M = RE$	$B = (1 + R)E$
5. Cost plus variable %	$M = R(2E - A) = RE$	$B = (1 + R)E$
6. Target estimate	$M = RE + N(E - A) = RE$	$B = (1 + R)E$
7. Guaranteed max cost	$M = (R + R_3)E$	$B = (1 + R + R_3)E$

of construction contracts when the actual cost of the project is assessed upon its completion.

Payments of change orders are also different in contract provisions for different types of contracts. Suppose that payments for change orders agreed upon for various types of contracts are as shown in column 1 of Table 8-2. The owner's actual payments based on these provisions as well as the incentive provisions for various types of contracts are given in column 2 of Table 8-2. The corresponding contractor's profits under various contractual arrangements are shown in Table 8-3.

TABLE 8–2 OWNER'S ACTUAL PAYMENT WITH DIFFERENT CONTRACT PROVISIONS

Type of contract	(1) Change order payment	(2) Owner's payment
1. Lump sum	$C(1 + R + R_1)$	$P = B + C(1 + R + R_1)$
2. Unit price	$C(1 + R + R_2)$	$P = (1 + R + R_2)(A + C)$
3. Cost plus fixed %	$C(1 + R)$	$P = (1 + R)(A + C)$
4. Cost plus fixed fee	C	$P = RE + A + C$
5. Cost plus variable %	$C(1 + R)$	$P = R(2E - A + C) + A + C$
6. Target estimate	C	$P = RE + N(E - A) + A + C$
7. Guaranteed max cost	0	$P = B$

TABLE 8–3 CONTRACTOR'S GROSS PROFIT WITH DIFFERENT CONTRACT PROVISIONS

Type of contract	(1) Profit from change order	(2) Contractor's gross profit
1. Lump sum	$C(R + R_1)$	$F = E - A + (R + R_1)(E + C)$
2. Unit price	$C(R + R_2)$	$F = (R + R_2)(A + C)$
3. Cost plus fixed %	CR	$F = R(A + C)$
4. Cost plus fixed fee	0	$F = RE$
5. Cost plus variable %	CR	$F = R(2E - A + C)$
6. Target estimate	0	$F = RE + N(E - A)$
7. Guaranteed max cost	$-C$	$F = (1 + R + R_3)E - A - C$

It is important to note that the equations in Tables 8-1 through 8-3 are illustrative, subject to the simplified conditions of payments assumed under the various types of contracts. When the negotiated conditions of payment are different, the equations must also be modified.

Example 8-5: Contractor's Gross Profits Under Different Contract Arrangements

Consider a construction project for which the contractor's original estimate is $6,000,000. For various types of contracts, $R = 10\%$, $R_1 = 2\%$, $R_2 = 1\%$, $R_3 = 5\%$, and $N = 0.5$. The contractor is not compensated for change orders under the guaranteed maximum cost contract if the total cost for the change orders is within 6 percent ($360,000) of the original estimate. Determine the contractor's gross profit for each of the seven types of construction contracts for each of the following conditions.

(a) $U = 0$, $\quad C = 0$

(b) $U = 0$, $\quad C = 6\%$ $\quad E = \$360,000$

(c) $U = 4\%$, $\quad E = \$240,000$, $\quad C = 0$

(d) $U = 4\%$, $\quad E = \$240,000$, $\quad C = 6\%$ $E = \$360,000$

(e) $U = -4\%$, $\quad E = -\$240,000$, $\quad C = 0$

(f) $U = \quad 4\%$, $\quad E = -\$240,000$, $\quad C = 6\%$ $E = \$360,000$

In this example, the percentage markup for the cost plus fixed percentage contract is 10 percent which is used as the benchmark for comparison. The percentage markup for the lump-sum contract is 12 percent while that for the unit price contract is 11 percent, reflecting the degrees of higher risk. The fixed fee for the cost plus fixed fee is based on 10 percent of the estimated cost, which is comparable to the cost plus fixed percentage contract if there is no overestimate or underestimate in cost. The basic percentage markup is 10 percent for both the cost plus variable percentage contract and the target estimator contract, but they are subject to incentive bonuses and penalties that are built in the formulas for owners' payments. The percentage markup for the guaranteed maximum cost contract is 15 percent to account for the high risk undertaken by the contractor. The results of computation for all seven types of contracts under different conditions of underestimation U and change order C are shown in Table 8-4.

TABLE 8–4 CONTRACTOR'S GROSS PROFITS UNDER DIFFERENT CONDITIONS (in $ thousands)

Type of contract	(1) $U = 0$ $C = 0$	(2) $U = 0$ $C = 6\%E$	(3) $U = 4\%E$ $C = 0$	(4) $U = 4\%E$ $C = 6\%E$	(5) $U = -4\%E$ $C = 0$	(6) $U = -4\%E$ $C = 6\%E$
1. Lump sum	$720	$763	$480	$523	$ 960	$1,003
2. Unit price	660	700	686	726	634	674
3. Cost + fixed %	600	636	624	660	576	612
4. Cost + fixed fee	600	600	600	600	600	600
5. Cost + var %	600	636	576	616	624	660
6. Target estimate	600	600	480	480	720	720
7. Guaranteed max cost	900	540	660	300	1,140	780

TABLE 8–5 OWNER'S ACTUAL PAYMENTS UNDER DIFFERENT CONDITIONS (in $ thousands)

Type of contract	(1) $U = 0$ $C = 0$	(2) $U = 0$ $C = 6\%E$	(3) $U = 4\%E$ $C = 0$	(4) $U = 4\%E$ $C = 6\%E$	(5) $U = -4\%E$ $C = 0$	(6) $U = -4\%E$ $C = 6\%E$
1. Lump sum	$6,720	$7,123	$6,720	$7,123	$6,720	$7,123
2. Unit price	6,660	7,060	6,926	7,326	6,394	6,794
3. Cost + fixed %	6,600	6,996	6,864	7,260	6,336	6,732
4. Cost + fixed fee	6,600	6,960	6,840	7,200	6,360	6,720
5. Cost + var %	6,600	6,996	6,816	7,212	6,384	6,780
6. Target estimate	6,600	6,960	6,720	7,080	6,480	6,840
7. Guaranteed max cost	6,900	6,900	6,900	6,900	6,900	6,900

Example 8-6: Owner's Payments under Different Contract Arrangements

Using the data in Example 8-5, determine the owner's actual payment for each of the seven types of construction contracts for the same conditions of U and C. The results of computation are shown in Table 8-5.

8.6 PRINCIPLES OF COMPETITIVE BIDDING

Competitive bidding on construction projects involves decision making under uncertainty where one of the greatest sources of the uncertainty for each bidder is due to the unpredictable nature of his competitors. Each bid submitted for a particular job by a contractor will be determined by a large number of factors, including an estimate of the direct job cost, the general overhead, the confidence that the management has in this estimate, and the immediate and long-range objectives of management. So many factors are involved that it is impossible for a particular bidder to attempt to predict exactly what the bids submitted by its competitors will be.

It is useful to think of a bid as being made up of two basic elements: (1) the estimate of direct job cost, which includes direct labor costs, material costs, equipment costs, and direct filed supervision, and (2) the markup or return, which must be sufficient to cover a portion of general overhead costs and allow a fair profit on the investment. A large return can be assured simply by including a sufficiently high markup. However, the higher the markup, the less chance there will be of getting the job. Consequently, a contractor who includes a very large markup on every bid could become bankrupt from lack of business. Conversely, the strategy of bidding with very little markup to obtain high volume is also likely to lead to bankruptcy. Somewhere in between the two extreme approaches to bidding lies an "optimum markup" which considers both the return and the likelihood of being low bidder in such a way that, over the long run, the average return is maximized.

From all indications, most contractors confront uncertain bidding conditions by exercising a high degree of subjective judgment, and each contractor may give different weights to various factors. The decision on the bid price, if a bid is indeed submitted, reflects the contractor's best judgment on how well the proposed project fits into the overall strategy for the survival and growth of the company, as well as the contractor's propensity to risk greater profit versus the chance of not getting a contract.

Exogenous Economic Factors

Contractors generally tend to specialize in a submarket of construction and concentrate their work in particular geographic locations. The level of demand in a submarket at a particular time can influence the number of bidders and their bid prices. When work is scarce in the submarket, the average number of bidders for projects will be larger than at times of plenty. The net result of scarcity is likely to be the increase in the number of bidders per project and downward pressure on the bid price for each project in the submarket. At times of severe scarcity, some contractors may cross the line between segments to expand their activities or move into new geographic locations to get a larger share of the existing submarket. Either action will increase the risks incurred by such contractors as they move into less familiar segments or territories. The trend of market demand in construction and of the economy at large may also influence the bidding decisions of a contractor in other ways. If a contractor perceives drastic increases in labor wages and material prices as a result of recent labor contract settlements, it may take into consideration possible increases in unit prices for determining the direct project cost. Furthermore, the perceptions of increase in inflation rates and interest rates may also cause the contractor to use a higher markup to hedge the uncertainty. Consequently, at times of economic expansion and/or higher inflation rate, contractors are reluctant to commit themselves to long-term fixed price contracts.

Characteristics of Bidding Competition

All other things being equal, the probability of winning a contract diminishes as more bidders participate in the competition. Consequently, a contractor tries to find out as much information as possible about the number and identities of potential bidders on a specific project. Such information is often available in the *Dodge Bulletin*[61] or similar publications which provide data of potential projects and names of contractors who have taken out plans and specifications. For certain segments, potential competitors may be identified through private contacts, and bidders often confront the same competitor's project after project since they have similar capabilities and interests in undertaking the same type of work, including size, complexity, and geographical location of the projects. A general contractor may also obtain information of potential subcontractors from publications such as *Credit Reports*[62] published by Dun and Bradstreet, Inc. However, most contractors form an extensive network with a group of subcontractors with whom they have

---

[61] *Dodge Bulletin* (daily publication), F. W. Dodge Corp., New York, NY.

[62] *Credit Reports*, Building Construction Division, Dun and Bradstreet, Inc., New York, NY.

had previous business transactions. They usually rely on their own experience in soliciting subcontract bids before finalizing a bid price for the project.

Objectives of General Contractors in Bidding

The bidding strategy of some contractors are influenced by a policy of minimum percentage markup for general overhead and profit. However, the percentage markup may also reflect additional factors stipulated by the owner such as high retention and slow payments for completed work or perceptions of uncontrollable factors in the economy. The intensity of a contractor's efforts in bidding a specific project is influenced by the contractor's desire to obtain additional work. The winning of a particular project may be potentially important to the overall mix of work in progress or the cash flow implications for the contractor. The contractor's decision is also influenced by the availability of key personnel in the contractor organization. The company sometimes wants to reserve its resources for future projects or commits itself to the current opportunity for different reasons.

Contractor's Comparative Advantages

A final important consideration in forming bid prices on the part of contractors are the possible special advantages enjoyed by a particular firm. As a result of lower costs, a particular contractor may be able to impose a higher profit markup yet still have a lower total bid than competitors. These lower costs may result from superior technology, greater experience, better management, better personnel, or lower unit costs. A comparative cost advantage is the most desirable of all circumstances in entering a bid competition.

8.7 BIDDING SIMULATION: AN EXAMPLE

An example of simulating the bidding process is illustrated by a construction management game which has been programmed for use on a computer.[63] Teams of players are cast in the roles of managers in construction companies. Each company is a general contractor that subcontracts and coordinates all portions of a building construction project either to individual subcontractors or to its own operational divisions when awarded a general contract.

Each of the construction companies begins with a different amount of assets in the game. The simulated time of three years is divided into 12 three-month periods. At the beginning of each time period, a list of jobs available for bidding is produced by a mathematical equation depicting the market demand which is stored in the

[63] See T. Au, R. L. Bostleman, and E. W. Parti, "Construction Management Game—Deterministic Model," *ASCE Journal of Construction Division*, Vol. 95, 1969, pp. 25–38. A current version for operation on an IBM personal computer with the R-Base database package is available from the Department of Civil Engineering, Carnegie Mellon University, Pittsburgh, PA 15213, and was developed by D. R. George in 1987.

computer. Each general contractor will then make the necessary decisions to submit to the owner as represented by the computer. In some periods, the general contractor may request additional information at a cost. At the end of each time period the computer will process the input decisions according to the programmed game model and output a statement to each company indicating all contract awards, the cost of performing work, and its earnings. The company that shows the largest relative gain at the end of three years will be declared the winner.

Environment for the Game

Market demands.   The number of jobs available for bidding during various time periods 1 through 12 is given by a demand equation which can be modified easily if the administrator should desire to change the demand pattern of the game. The demand equation reflects the seasonal variation in construction activities and yet is not symmetrical or easily predictable. A typical example is shown in Figure 8-1.

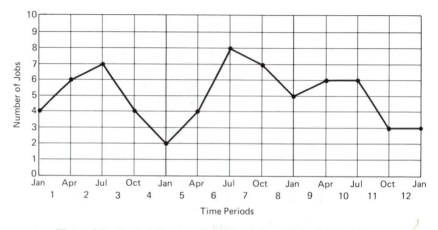

Figure 8-1   Typical Demand Curve for Projects in the Bidding Game

Geographical region of operation.   The construction companies in this game operate in a geographical region consisting of nine districts identified by consecutive numbers 1 through 9 as shown in Figure 8-2. The unit prices of labor and materials in a district are different from those in other districts, but within each one, the labor and material rates are constant.

The subcontractors and the proposed job sites are distributed throughout the region with each subcontractor and each job site located in a particular district. The distance units between districts are defined as follows: (1) zero units when both the subcontractor and the job site are in the same district, (2) one unit when the subcontractor's district is adjacent to the district of the job site, and (3) two units when there is one district between the subcontractor and the job site.

Subcontracting firms.   Four types of subcontractors, representing the four phases of the project (e.g., foundation excavation, foundation structure, superstruc-

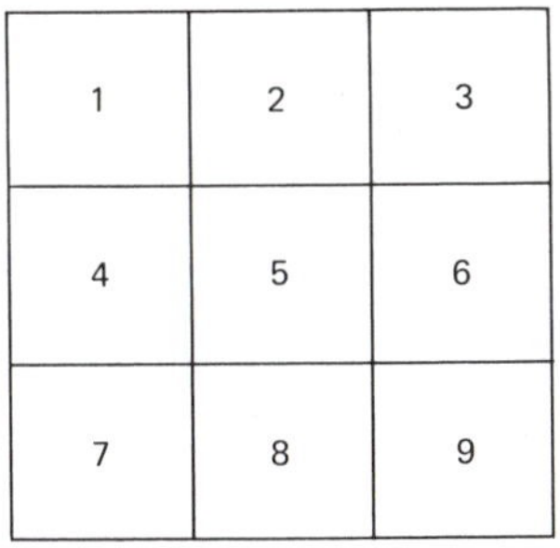

1	2	3
4	5	6
7	8	9

Figure 8-2 Geographical Locations of Districts for the Bidding Game

ture framing, and building closure), are required to complete any job. When a general contractor bids on a general contract, he must select one subcontractor of each type to perform the work. All behavior of the subcontractors is controlled by the computer.

Determination of Bid Prices

Subcontractor selection. For every job specified by the demand equation, 4 different subcontractors of each type will be selected internally by the computer from a pool of 40 subcontractors (10 of each type). Each job has its own requirement of labor and material units of each of the four types of work. The difference in bid prices submitted by the subcontractors for the same job is affected by (1) unit prices of labor and material in the different district, (2) transportation costs, (3) reliability factor, and (4) the desire for work. The unit prices used in any subcontract bid are those of the district in which the subcontractor is located. The relative transportation cost of a subcontractor is based on the distance between the job site and the location of the subcontractor. A reliability factor has been internally assigned to gauge each subcontractor on his performance at the end of each period. In general, other factors being equal, an unreliable subcontractor will be able to submit a bid lower than that of a reliable one because he is more willing to take risks. Finally, depending on his inclination to work, a variable factor representing a subcontractor's desire to work will be assigned by the computer. An upper limit is also placed on the work load that a subcontractor can take at any given time. If such a limit is reached, this subcontractor will be eliminated from the pool of subcontractors to be selected by the computer.

Information services. Two consulting services, the Construction Reports, Incorporated, and the Subcontractor Rating Service, are provided for obtaining additional information at a cost. These services are included to simulate existing services for the construction industry. An information request can be made only by the players during time period 1, period 4, period 7, and period 10. Therefore, a company must plan ahead and request any information it will need for the next three time periods.

Construction Reports, Incorporated, surveys the anticipated construction activities for each time period in three areas each comprising three districts, that is, districts 1-2-3, districts 4-5-6, and districts 7-8-9. At each of the time periods, period 1, period 4, period 7, and period 10, information may be requested for any of these areas in any of the next three successive time periods. Included in each report is a list of jobs anticipated to be let for bidding in the area specified during that time period requested, the location of each job site, and the approximate scope of each job in thousands of dollars.

The Subcontractor Rating Service rates any subcontractor on his overall reliability. The ratings are A = excellent, B = good, C = fair, and D = poor. At the beginning of the game, each general contractor is assumed to possess a backlog of information for some of the subcontractors available in the game. This backlog is simulated by providing each contractor with a partial set of the subcontractor's ratings prior to the start of game play. The information supplied to each contractor may or may not be the same. At the end of each period, the rating of each subcontractor will be reevaluated internally by the computer. Generally, a subcontractor's rating will improve if his work load has increased during the period, reflecting the confidence that has been placed upon this subcontractor by the general contractors. Since the Subcontractor Rating Services can be requested only in period 1, period 4, period 7, and period 10, the outputs represent the ratings at the beginning of the game and at the end of period 3, period 6, and period 9, respectively. In each consultation, the general contractor may request any number of individual ratings up to the entire list of 40 subcontractors.

Chance factors.   In any competitive game, risk and uncertainty play a major role in shaping the character of the environment. Generally speaking, the more that is known of a given situation, the less risky is a strategy for decision and the more certain is the outcome. Regardless of the precautions taken, however, there is always the chance that an undesirable event may occur. Many chance factors are therefore included in this game to produce a resemblance of reality. Each bid made by a general contractor will be influenced by the subcontractors allowed to bid on a job and by the magnitude of their bids. Both those factors are, to some extent, randomly controlled by the computer. Although the information services are expected to be generally helpful, their forecasts nevertheless are not perfect and must be viewed with a certain amount of distrust.

General Contractor Bidding and Award

Factors influencing bidding behavior.   In this game, the most important internal constraint on bidding behavior is a company's cash-on-hand which is comprised of liquid assets plus any outstanding loans. The cash-on-hand reflects the capacity of the general contractor to do work, since the cash-on-hand may be converted or transformed into other resources such as new equipment and personnel are both necessary to expand the company's operational base.

At the end of each time period when the bids are submitted, each general contractor's proposed work load is compared to his maximum allowable work load. The proposed work load is defined as the sum of the company's pending work from previously awarded construction contracts and the bids submitted at the current time period; the maximum allowable work load is defined as that work load which is equal to 40 times the cash-on-hand. If the proposed work load exceeds the maximum allowable work load, the general contractor will not be awarded any new contracts in spite of the fact that he may be the low bidder. In addition, bidding costs will be assessed for all attempted bids.

Should a general contractor wish to expand his operating base immediately, the only alternative within the framework of this game is to seek a loan. The contractor's capacity to do work will be increased by an amount that is 40 times the amount of the loan. However, the total amount of outstanding loans cannot exceed twice the company's liquid assets at a particular time period; otherwise, the request for loan will be denied. All loans are one-year notes at 6 percent interest per year. When a loan is approved, the company's account will be credited with the amount of the loan, and charged 1.5 percent interest in each of the four succeeding time periods. At the end of the four time periods, repayment of the loan is due and thus the amount is deducted from the company's account.

Contract awards, costs, and payments. Upon the submission of bids for the available jobs at the end of each time period, the contracts will be awarded. The cost of performing each job will be determined for the successful bidder, and a statement of earnings for each general contractor will be prepared. All general contractors will be notified of the successful bidder on each job and the amount of the contract; in addition, each successful bidder will be notified of the actual cost of his work.

In general the contract for each job will be awarded to the low bidder. However, this rule will be nullified should all bids exceed the maximum allowable bid for the particular job which is prestored in the computer or should the low bidder exceed the maximum allowable work load. In the first case all bids will be rejected and in the second case the individual bidder will be rejected.

The actual cost charged to the general contractor for performing work is computed by adjusting the base cost for the general contractor which is the sum of the subcontractors bids. This base cost is then modified according to the reliability of the subcontractors. Generally speaking, the probability of making a profit is directly related to the reliability of subcontractors selected.

Although the relation between the size of a job and its duration is not well defined, it is assumed that the number of time periods needed to complete a job is related to the size of the job and that the rate of progress of work is constant for these time periods. The general contractor will be reimbursed at the end of each time period for work done during that period. For example, if a job takes three time periods to complete, the contractor will be paid one-third of the total cost and realize one-third of his profit or loss in each of the next three time periods.

Measurement Performance

The performance of a company at the end of each time period is indicated by a statement of earnings output by the computer. The items in the statement refer to the transactions in the time period under consideration. The last item indicated the percentage of gain or loss up to the end of the period, which is the ratio of gain or loss to the amount of assets at the beginning of the game. The one that has the highest percentage of gain at the end of period 12 is the winner of the game.

Example 8-7: A Company's Performance in the Bidding Game

The bidding game described in this section has been programmed on a personal computer. Upon the submission of the required inputs, the corresponding outputs will be generated automatically. As an example, the measure of performance generated at period 4 for a team of players representing a construction company is shown in Table 8-6.

TABLE 8–6 A COMPANY'S PERFORMANCE IN A CONSTRUCTION MANAGEMENT GAME

Income statement	
A. Income from construction contracts	$412,510.00
Cost of contracts	
B. Subcontracts and supervision of subcontractors	347,891.00
C. Field overhead	2,063.00
D. Gross profit	$ 62,556.00
Administrative and general expenses	
E. Office operating cost	10,921.00
F. Information costs	650.00
G. Bidding costs	1,733.00
H. Interest on existing loans	900.00
I. Earnings before federal income taxes	$ 48,352.00
J. Federal income taxes	17,411.00
K. Net earnings	30,941.00
L. Retained earnings at beginning of period	208,422.00
M. Liquid assets	$239,363.00
Loans	
N. Existing loans	60,000.00
O. New loans (one year notes)	25,000.00
P. Loans due this time period	10,000.00
Q. Total cash-on-hand	314,363.00
R. Retained earnings at end of period	$239,363.00
S. Percentage gain or loss up to end of period	+19.7%

8.8 PRINCIPLES OF CONTRACT NEGOTIATION

Negotiation is another important mechanism for arranging construction contracts. Project managers often find themselves as participants in negotiations, either as principal negotiators or as expert advisors. These negotiations can be complex and often present important opportunities and risks for the various parties involved. For example, negotiation on work contracts can involve issues such as completion date, arbitration procedures, special work item compensation, contingency allowances, as well as the overall price. As a general rule, exogenous factors such as the history of a contractor and the general economic climate in the construction industry will determine the results of negotiations. However, the skill of a negotiator can affect the possibility of reaching an agreement, the profitability of the project, the scope of any eventual disputes, and the possibility for additional work among the participants. Thus, negotiations are an important task for many project managers. Even after a contract is awarded on the basis of competitive bidding, there are many occasions in which subsequent negotiations are required as conditions change over time.

In conducting negotiations between two parties, each side will have a series of objectives and constraints. The overall objective of each party is to obtain the most favorable, acceptable agreement. A two-party, one-issue negotiation illustrates this fundamental point. Suppose that a developer is willing to pay up to $500,000 for a particular plot of land, whereas the owner would be willing to sell the land for $450,000 or more. These maximum and minimum sales prices represent *constraints* on any eventual agreement. In this example, any purchase price between $450,000 and $500,000 is acceptable to both of the involved parties. This range represents a *feasible agreement space*. Successful negotiations would conclude in a sales price within this range. Which party receives the $50,000 in the middle range between $450,000 and $500,000 would typically depend upon the negotiating skills and special knowledge of the parties involved. For example, if the developer was a better negotiator, then the sales price would tend to be close to the minimum $450,000 level.

With different constraints, it might be impossible to reach an agreement. For example, if the owner was only willing to sell at a price of $550,000 while the developer remains willing to pay only $500,000, then there would be no possibility for an agreement between the two parties. Of course, the two parties typically do not know at the beginning of negotiations if agreements will be possible. But it is quite important for each party to the negotiation to have a sense of their own *reservation price*, such as the owner's minimum selling price or the buyer's maximum purchase price in the preceding example. This reservation price is equal to the value of the best alternative to a negotiated agreement.

Poor negotiating strategies adopted by one or the other party may also preclude an agreement even with the existence of a feasible agreement range. For example, one party may be so demanding that the other party simply breaks off negotiations. In effect, negotiations are not a well-behaved solution methodology for the resolution of disputes.

The possibility of negotiating failures in the land sale example highlights the importance of negotiating style and strategy with respect to revealing information. Style includes the extent to which negotiators are willing to seem reasonable, the type of arguments chosen, the forcefulness of language used, and so on. Clearly, different negotiating styles can be more or less effective. Cultural factors are also extremely important. American and Japanese negotiating styles differ considerably, for example. Revealing information is also a negotiating decision. In the land sale case, some negotiators would readily reveal their reserve or constraint prices, whereas others would conceal as much information as possible (i.e., "play their cards close to the vest") or provide misleading information.

In light of these tactical problems, it is often beneficial to all parties to adopt objective standards in determining appropriate contract provisions. These standards would prescribe a particular agreement or a method to arrive at appropriate values in a negotiation. Objective standards can be derived from numerous sources, including market values, precedent, professional standards, what a court would decide, and so on. By using objective criteria of this sort, personalities and disruptive negotiating tactics do not become impediments to reaching mutually beneficial agreements.

With additional issues, negotiations become more complex both in procedure and in result. With respect to procedure, the sequence in which issues are defined or considered can be very important. For example, negotiations may proceed on an issue-by-issue basis, and the outcome may depend upon the exact sequence of issues considered. Alternatively, the parties may proceed by proposing complete agreement packages and then proceed to compare packages. With respect to outcomes, the possibility of the parties having different valuations or weights on particular issues arises. In this circumstance, it is possible to trade off the outcomes on different issues to the benefit of both parties. By yielding on an issue of low value to himself but high value to the other party, concessions on other issues may be obtained.

The notion of Pareto optimal agreements can be introduced to identify negotiated agreements in which no change in the agreement can simultaneously make both parties better off. Figure 8-3 illustrates Pareto optimal agreements which can be helpful in assessing the result of multiple-issue negotiations. In this figure, the axes represent the satisfaction or desirability of agreements to the parties, denoted I and II. This representation assumes that one can place a dollar or utility value on various agreements reached in a multiple-issue negotiation between two parties. Points in the graph represent particular agreements on the different issues under consideration. A particular point may be obtained by more than one contract agreement. The curved line encloses the set of all feasible agreements; any point in this area is an acceptable agreement. Each party has a minimum acceptable satisfaction level in this graph. Points on the interior of this feasible area represent *inferior* agreements since

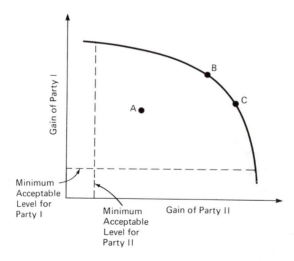

Figure 8-3 A Pareto Optimal Agreement Set

Construction Pricing and Contracting   Chap. 8

some other agreement is possible that benefits both parties. For example, point *B* represents a more desirable agreement than point *A*. In the previous land sale example, point *B* might represent a purchase price of $490,000 and an immediate purchase, whereas point *A* might represent a $475,000 sale price and a six-month delay. The feasible points that are not inferior constitute the set of Pareto optimal or efficient agreements; these points lie on the northeast quadrant of the feasible region as marked on the figure.

The definition of Pareto optimal agreements allows one to assess at least one aspect of negotiated outcomes. If two parties arrive at an inferior agreement (such as point *A* in Figure 8-3), then the agreement could be improved *to the benefit of both parties*. In contrast, different Pareto optimal agreements (such as points *B* and *C* in Figure 8-3) can represent widely different results to the individual parties but do not have the possibility for joint improvement.

Of course, knowledge of the concept of Pareto optimal agreements does not automatically give any guidance on what might constitute the best agreements. Much of the skill in contract negotiation comes from the ability to invent new options that represent mutual gains. For example, devising contract incentives for speedier completion of projects may result in benefits to both contractors and the owner.

Example 8-8: Effects of Different Value Perceptions

Suppose that the closing date for sale of the land in the previous case must also be decided in negotiation. The current owner would like to delay the sale for six months, which would represent rental savings of $10,000. However, the developer estimates that the cost of a six-month delay would be $20,000. After negotiation, suppose that a purchase price of $475,000 and a six month purchase delay are agreed upon. This agreement is acceptable but not optimal for both parties. In particular, both sides would be better off if the purchase price were increased by $15,000 and immediate closing instituted. The current owner would receive an additional payment of $15,000, incur a cost of $10,000, and have a net gain of $5,000. Similarly, the developer would pay $15,000 more for the land but save $20,000 in delay costs. While this superior result may seem obvious and easily achievable, recognizing such opportunities during a negotiation becomes increasingly difficult as the number and complexity of issues increases.

8.9 NEGOTIATION SIMULATION: AN EXAMPLE

This construction negotiation game simulates a contract negotiation between a utility, "CMG Gas," and a design/construct firm, "Pipeline Constructors, Inc."[64] The negotiation involves only two parties but multiple issues. Participants in the game are assigned to represent one party or the other and to negotiate with a designated partner. In a class setting, numerous negotiating partners are created. The following overview from the CMG Gas participants' instructions describes the setting for the game:

[64] This game is further described in W. Dudziak and C. Hendrickson, "A Negotiation Simulation Game," *ASCE Journal of Management in Engineering*, Vol. 4, no. 2, 1988, pp. 113–121.

CMG Gas has the opportunity to provide natural gas to an automobile factory under construction. Service will require a new 16-mile pipeline through farms and light forest. The terrain is hilly with moderate slopes, and equipment access is relatively good. The pipeline is to be buried 3 feet deep.

Construction of the pipeline itself will be contracted to a qualified design/construction firm, while required compression stations and ancillary work will be done by CMG Gas. As project manager for CMG Gas, you are about to enter negotiations with a local contractor, "Pipeline Constructors, Inc." This firm is the only local contractor qualified to handle such a large project. If a suitable contract agreement cannot be reached, then you will have to break off negotiations soon and turn to another company.

The Pipeline Constructors, Inc., instructions offer a similar overview.

To focus the negotiations, the issues to be decided in the contract are already defined:

- **Duration**

  The final contract must specify a required completion date.

- **Penalty for Late Completion**

  The final contract may include a daily penalty for late project completion on the part of the contractor.

- **Bonus for Early Completion**

  The final contract may include a daily bonus for early project completion.

- **Report Format**

  Contractor progress reports will either conform to the traditional CMG Gas format or to a new format proposed by the state.

- **Frequency of Progress Reports**

  Progress reports can be required daily, weekly, biweekly, or monthly.

- **Conform to Pending Legislation Regarding Pipeline Marking**

  State legislation is pending to require special markings and drawings for pipelines. The parties have to decide whether to conform to this pending legislation.

- **Contract Type**

  The construction contract may be a fixed fee, a cost plus a percentage profit, or a guaranteed maximum with cost plus a percentage profit below the maximum.

- **Amount of Fixed Fee**

  If the contract is a fixed fee, the dollar amount must be specified.

- **Percentage of Profit**

  If the contract involves a percentage profit, then the percentage must be agreed upon.

- **CMG Gas Clerk on Site**

  The contract may specify that a CMG Gas clerk may be on site and have access to all accounts or that only progress reports are made by Pipeline Constructors, Inc.

- **Penalty for Late Starting Date**

  CMG Gas is responsible for obtaining right-of-way agreements for the new pipeline. The parties may agree to a daily penalty if CMG Gas cannot obtain these agreements.

A final contract requires an agreement on each of these issues, represented on a form signed by both negotiators.

As a further aid, each participant is provided with additional information and a scoring system to indicate the relative desirability of different contract agreements. Additional information includes items such as estimated construction cost and expected duration as well as company policies such as desired reporting formats or work arrangements. This information may be revealed or withheld from the other party depending upon an individual's negotiating strategy. The numerical scoring system includes point totals for different agreements on specific issues, including interactions among the various issues. For example, the amount of points received by Pipeline Constructors, Inc., for a bonus for early completion *increases* as the completion date becomes *later*. An earlier completion becomes more likely with a later completion date, and hence the probability of receiving a bonus increases, so the resulting point total likewise increases.

The two firms have differing perceptions of the desirability of different agreements. In some cases, their views will be directly conflicting. For example, increases in a flat fee imply greater profits for Pipeline Constructors, Inc., and greater costs for CMG Gas. In some cases, one party may feel strongly about a particular issue, whereas the other is not particularly concerned. For example, CMG Gas may want a clerk on site, while Pipeline Constructors, Inc., may not care. As described in the previous section, these differences in the evaluation of an issue provide opportunities for negotiators. By conceding an unimportant issue to the other party, a negotiator may trade for progress on an issue that is more important to his or her firm. Examples of instructions to the negotiators follow.

Instructions to the Pipelines Constructors, Inc., Representative

After examining the project site, your company's estimators are convinced that the project can be completed in 36 weeks. In bargaining for the duration, keep two things in mind: the longer past 36 weeks the contract duration is, the more money that can be made off the "bonuses for being early" and the chances of being late are reduced. That reduces the risk of paying a "penalty for lateness."

Throughout the project the gas company will want progress reports. These reports take time to compile and therefore the fewer you need to submit, the better. In addition, state law dictates that the Required Standard Report be used unless the contractor and the owner agree otherwise. These standard reports are even more time consuming to produce than are more traditional reports.

The state legislature is considering a law that requires accurate drawings and markers of all pipelines by all utilities. You would prefer not to conform to this uncertain set of requirements, but this is negotiable.

What type of contract and the amount your company will be paid are two of the most important issues in negotiations. In the fixed-fee contract, your company will receive an agreed amount from CMG Gas. Therefore, when there are any delay or cost overruns, it will be the full responsibility of your company. With this type of contract, your company assumes all the risk and will in turn want a higher price. Your estimators believe a cost and contingency amount of $4,500,000. You would like a higher fee, of course.

With the cost plus contract, the risk is shared by the gas company and your company. With this type of contract, your company will bill CMG Gas for all its costs *plus* a specified percentage of those costs. In this case, cost overruns will be paid by the gas company. Not only does the percentage above cost have to be decided upon but also whether or not your company will allow a field clerk from the gas company to be at the job site to monitor reported costs. Whether or not he is around is of no concern to your company since its policy is not to inflate costs. This point can be used as a bargaining weapon.

Finally, your company is worried whether the gas company will obtain the land rights to lay the pipe. Therefore, you should demand a penalty for the potential delay of the project starting date.

Instructions to the CMG Gas Company Representative

To satisfy the auto manufacturer, the pipeline must be completed in 40 weeks. An earlier completion date will not result in receiving revenue any earlier. Thus, the only reason to bargain for shorter duration is to feel safer about having the project done on time. If the project does exceed the 40-week maximum, a penalty will have to be paid to the auto manufacturer. Consequently, if the project exceeds the agreed-upon duration, the contractor should pay you a penalty. The penalty for late completion might be related to the project duration. For example, if the duration is agreed to be 36 weeks, then the penalty for being late need not be so severe. Also, it is normal that the contractor get a bonus for early completion. Of course, completion before 40 weeks doesn't yield any benefit other than your own peace of mind. Try to keep the early bonus as low as possible.

Throughout the project you will want progress reports. The more often these reports are received, the better to monitor the progress. State law dictates that the Required Standard Report be used unless the contractor and the owner agree otherwise. These reports are very detailed and time consuming to review. You would prefer to use the traditional CMG Gas reports.

The state legislature is considering a law that requires accurate drawings and markers of all pipelines by all utilities. For this project it will cost an additional $250,000 to do this now, or $750,000 to do this when the law is passed.

One of the most important issues is the type of contract, and the amount to be paid. The fixed-fee contract means that CMG Gas will pay the contractor a set amount. Therefore, when there are delays and cost overruns, the contractor assumes full responsibility for the individual costs. However, this evasion of risk has to be paid for and results in a higher price. If fixed fee is chosen, only the contract price is to be determined. Your company's estimators have determined that the project should cost about $5,000,000.

The cost-plus-percent contract may be cheaper, but the risk is shared. With this type of contract, the contractor will bill the gas company for all costs, plus a specified percentage of those costs. In this case, cost overruns will be paid by the gas company. If this type of contract is chosen, not only must the profit percentage be chosen, but also whether or not a gas company representative will be allowed on site all of the time acting as a field clerk, to ensure that a proper amount of material and labor is billed. The usual percentage agreed upon is about 10 percent.

Contractors also have a concern whether or not they will receive a penalty if the gas right-of-way is not obtained in time to start the project. In this case, CMG Gas has already secured the rights-of-way. But, if the penalty is too high, this is a dangerous precedent for future negotiations. However, you might try to use this as a bargaining tool.

Example 8-9: An Example of a Negotiated Contract

A typical contract resulting from a simulation of the negotiation between CMG Gas and Pipeline Constructors, Inc., appears in Table 8-7. An agreement with respect to each pre-defined issue is included, and the resulting contract signed by both negotiators.

TABLE 8–7 A NEGOTIATED CONTRACT BETWEEN CMG GAS AND PIPELINE CONSTRUCTORS, INC.

Duration	38 weeks
Penalty for late completion	$6,800 per day
Bonus for early completion	$0 per day
Report format	Traditional CMG form
Frequency of progress reports	Weekly
Conform to pending pipeline marking legislation	Yes
Contract type	Fixed fee
Amount of fixed fee	$5,050,000.
Percentage of profit	Not applicable
CMG Gas clerk on site	Yes
Penalty for late starting date	$3,000 per day
Signed:	

CMG Gas representative

Pipeline Constructors, Inc.

Example 8-10: Scoring Systems for the Negotiated Contract Games

To measure the performance of the negotiators in the previous example, a scoring system is needed for the representative of Pipeline Constructors, Inc., and another scoring system for the representative of CMG Gas. These scoring systems for the companies associated with the issues described earlier are designated as system A.

To make the negotiating game viable for classroom use, another set of instructions for each company is described in this example, and the associated scoring systems for the two companies are designated as system B. In each game play, the instructor may choose a different combination of instructions and negotiating teams, leading to four possible combinations of scoring systems for Pipeline Constructors, Inc., and CMG Gas.[65]

Instruction to the Pipeline Constructors, Inc., Representative

Your boss has left you with a scoring table for all the issues and alternatives. Two different scoring systems are listed here; you will be assigned to use one or the other. Instructions for scoring system A appear earlier. The instructions for scoring system B are as follows:

After examining the site, your estimator believes that the project will require 38 weeks. You are happy to conform with any reporting or pipeline marking system, since your computer-based project control and design systems can easily produce these submissions. You would prefer to delay the start of the contract as long as possible, since your forces are busy on another job; hence, you do not want to impose a penalty for late start. Try to maximize the amount of points, as they reflect profit brought into your company, or a cost savings. In parts 3 and 4, be sure to use the project duration agreed upon to calculate your score. Finally, do not discuss your scoring system with the CMG Gas representative; this is proprietary information!

SCORING FOR PIPELINE CONSTRUCTORS, INC.

1. COMPLETION DATE

	System A	System B
Under 36 weeks	NA	NA
36 weeks	0	NA
37 weeks	+ 5	−10
38 weeks	+10	0
39 weeks	+20	+10
40 weeks	+40	+20

2. REPORTS

Required standard report	−20	0
Agreed reports	− 5	0

3. PENALTY FOR LATENESS ($ PER DAY)

Duration (Weeks)				
Scoring system A 36	37	38	39	40
Scoring system B 37	38	39	40	41
0– 999 −1	−1	−1	0	0
1,000–1,999 −2	−2	−2	−1	0
2,000–2,999 −4	−3	−3	−2	−1
3,000–3,999 −6	−5	−4	−3	−1

[65] To undertake this exercise, the instructor needs to divide students into negotiating teams, with each individual assigned scoring system A or B. Negotiators will represent Pipeline Constructors, Inc., or CMG Gas. Negotiating pairs should not be told which scoring system their counterpart is assigned.

4,000–4,999	− 8	− 7	− 5	−4	−2
5,000–5,999	−11	− 9	− 7	−5	−2
6,000–6,999	−14	−12	− 9	−6	−3
7,000–7,999	−18	−14	−11	−7	−3
Over 8,000	NA	NA	NA	NA	NA

4. BONUS FOR BEING EARLY ($ PER DAY)

Scoring system A	**36**	**37**	**38**	**39**	**40**
Scoring system B	**37**	**38**	**39**	**40**	**41**
0– 999	0	0	0	0	2
1,000–1,999	0	0	2	2	2
2,000–2,999	0	2	4	4	4
3,000–3,999	1	4	6	6	8
4,000–4,999	2	6	8	10	12
5,000–5,999	3	8	10	14	16
6,000–6,999	4	10	14	18	22
7,000–7,999	5	12	18	24	28
8,000–8,999	6	14	22	28	36
9,000–9,999	7	16	26	32	40
Over 10,000	8	18	30	36	45

5. CONFORM TO PENDING LEGISLATION (MARKING PIPELINES)

	A	B
Yes	+ 5	+10
No	+15	+10

6. HOW OFTEN FOR THE PROGRESS REPORTS

	A	B
Daily	NA	0
Weekly	−20	0
Bi-weekly	−10	0
Monthly	− 6	0

7. CONTRACT TYPE

	A	B
Fixed fee	5	5
Cost plus $X\%$	+25	+25

If fixed fee, do part 8 and skip parts 9 and 10.
If cost plus $X\%$, do parts 9 and 10 and skip part 8.

8. FIXED FEE

	A	B
Below 4,500,000	NA	−15 for each 10,000
Over 4,500,000	+ 1 for each 10,000	+2 for each 10,000

9. IF COST PLUS $X\%$

	A	B
Below 6%	NA	NA
6%	+250	NA
7%	+375	+300
8%	+450	+330
9%	+475	+360

10%	+500	+400
11%	+525	+440
12%	+550	+480
13%	+600	+540
14%	+725	+600
Over 14%	+900	+800

10. GAS CO. FIELD CLERK ON SITE

	A	B
Yes	0	0
No	0	+10

11. PENALTY FOR DELAYED STARTING DATE DUE TO GAS COMPANY ERROR ($ PER DAY)

	A	B
0– 499	NA	NA
500–1,499	−6	−10
1,500–2,499	−4	− 7
2,500–3,499	−2	− 5
3,500–4,499	−1	− 3
4,500–5,499	0	− 1
5,500–6,499	+1	0
6,500–7,499	+2	+ 3
7,500 or more	+4	+ 6

Instructions to the CMG Gas Company Representative

Your boss has left you with a scoring table for all the issues and alternatives. Two different scoring systems are listed here; you will be assigned to use one or the other. Instructions for scoring system A appear earlier. The instructions for scoring system B are described as follows:

Your contract with the automobile company provides an incentive for completion of the pipeline earlier than 38 weeks and a penalty for completion after 38 weeks. To ensure timely completion of the project, you would like to receive detailed project reports as often as possible.

Try to maximize the number of points from the final contract provisions; this corresponds to minimizing costs. Do not discuss your scoring systems with Pipeline Constructors, Inc.

SCORING SYSTEM FOR CMG GAS

1. DURATION	POINTS*	
	A	B
Over 40 weeks	NA	−40
40 weeks	0	−10
39 weeks	+2	+ 2

*Note: NA means not acceptable and the deal will not be approved by your boss with any of these provisions. If you can't negotiate a contract your score will be +450. Also, the alternatives listed are the only ones in the context of this problem; no other alternatives are acceptable.

38 weeks	+4	+ 8
37 weeks	+5	+14
0 – 36 weeks	+6	+14

2. REPORTS

	A	B
Required standard report	+ 2	0
"Traditional" CMG gas reports	+10	0

3. PENALTY FOR LATENESS ($PER DAY)

DURATION (WEEKS)

Scoring system A	36	37	38	39	40
Scoring system B	38	39	40	41	42
0 – 999	NA	NA	NA	NA	NA
1,000 – 1,999	9	7	6	3	0
2,000 – 2,999	10	9	8	5	2
3,000 – 3,999	11	10	9	6	4
4,000 – 4,999	12	11	10	7	5
5,000 – 5,999	13	12	11	8	6
6,000 – 6,999	14	13	12	9	7
7,000 – 7,999	15	15	13	11	8
8,000 – 8,999	16	15	14	12	9
9,000 – 9,999	17	16	15	13	10
10,000 or more	18	16	15	13	11

4. BONUS FOR BEING EARLY ($ PER DAY)

	A	B
8,000 or more	NA	− 5
7,000 – 7,999	+ 3	− 2
6,000 – 6,999	+ 6	− 1
5,000 – 5,999	+ 8	0
4,000 – 4,999	+10	+ 5
3,000 – 3,999	+12	+ 7
2,000 – 2,999	+13	+ 9
1,000 – 1,999	+14	+13
0 – 999	+15	+17

5. CONFORM TO PENDING LEGISLATION (MARKING PIPELINES)

	A	B
Yes	+25	0
No	−25	NA

6. HOW OFTEN FOR THE PROGRESS REPORTS

	A	B
Daily	+45	+50
Weekly	+50	+30
Bi-weekly	+30	+10
Monthly	NA	+ 5

7. CONTRACT TYPE

	A	B
Fixed fee	25	25
Cost plus $X\%$	0	0

If fixed fee, do part 8 and skip parts 9 and 10.
If cost plus $X\%$, do parts 9 and 10 and skip part 8.

8. FIXED FEE

	A	B
Over $5,500,000	NA	NA
0–5,000,000	+ 1 for each 10,000 below 10,000,000	+1 for each 10,000 below 10,000,000

9. IF COST PLUS $X\%$

	A	B
Below 5%	+950	+700
5%	+800	+660
6%	+700	+620
7%	+600	+590
8%	+550	+570
9%	+525	+550
10%	+500	+535
11%	+475	+500
12%	+450	+440
13%	+400	+380
14%	+300	+300
15%	+200	+100
Over 15%	NA	+ 10

10. GAS CO. FIELD CLERK ON SITE

	A	B
Yes	+20	+10
No	+ 5	+ 0

11. PENALTY FOR DELAYED STARTING DATE DUE TO UNAVAILABLE RIGHT OF WAYS ($ PER DAY)

	A	B
0 – 1,999	+10	+3
2,000 – 3,999	+ 8	+2
4,000 – 5,999	+ 6	+1
6,000 – 7,999	+ 4	0
8,000 – 9,999	+ 2	−10
10,000+	NA	−20

8.10 RESOLUTION OF CONTRACT DISPUTES

Once a contract is reached, a variety of problems may emerge during the course of work. Disputes may arise over quality of work, over responsibility for delays, over appropriate payments due to changed conditions, or over a multitude of other considerations. Resolution of contract disputes is an important task for project managers. The mechanism for contract dispute resolution can be specified in the original contract or, less desirably, decided when a dispute arises.

The most prominent mechanism for dispute resolution is adjudication in a court of law. This process tends to be expensive and time consuming since it involves legal representation and waiting in queues of cases for available court times. Any party to a contract can bring a suit. In adjudication, the dispute is decided by a neutral third party with no necessary specialized expertise in the disputed subject. After all, it is not a prerequisite for judges to be familiar with construction procedures! Legal procedures are highly structured with rigid, formal rules for presentations and fact finding. On the positive side, legal adjudication strives for consistency and predictability of results. The results of previous cases are published and can be used as precedents for resolution of new disputes.

Negotiation among the contract parties is a second important dispute resolution mechanism. These negotiations can involve the same sorts of concerns and issues as with the original contracts. Negotiation typically does not involve third parties such as judges. The negotiation process is usually informal, unstructured, and relatively inexpensive. If an agreement is not reached between the parties, then adjudication is a possible remedy.

A third dispute resolution mechanism is the resort to arbitration or mediation and conciliation. In these procedures, a third party serves a central role in the resolution. These outside parties are usually chosen by mutual agreement of the parties involved and will have specialized knowledge of the dispute subject. In arbitration, the third party may make a decision which is binding on the participants. In mediation and conciliation, the third party serves only as a facilitator to help the participants reach a mutually acceptable resolution. Like negotiation, these procedures can be informal and unstructured.

Finally, the high cost of adjudication has inspired a series of nontraditional dispute resolution mechanisms that have some of the characteristics of judicial proceedings. These mechanisms include

- **Private judging** in which the participants hire a third-party judge to make a decision.
- **Neutral expert fact finding** in which a third party with specialized knowledge makes a recommendation.
- **Minitrial** in which legal summaries of the participants' positions are presented to a jury comprised of principals of the affected parties.

Some of these procedures may be court sponsored or are required for particular types of disputes.

While these various disputes resolution mechanisms involve varying costs, it is important to note that the most important mechanism for reducing costs and problems in dispute resolution is the reasonableness of the initial contract among the parties as well as the competence of the project manager.

8.11 REFERENCES

8-1. Au, T., R. L. Bostleman, and E. W. Parti, "Construction Management Game-Deterministic Model," *ASCE Journal of the Construction Division*, Vol. 95, 1969, pp. 25–38.

8-2. Building Research Advisory Board, *Exploratory Study on Responsibility, Liability and Accountability for Risks in Construction*, National Academy of Sciences, Washington, D.C., 1978.

8-3. Construction Industry Cost Effectiveness Project, "Contractual Arrangements," Report A-7, The Business Roundtable, New York, October 1982.

8-4. Dudziak, W., and C. Hendrickson, "A Negotiating Simulation Game," *ASCE Journal of Management in Engineering*, Vol. 4, no. 2, 1988, pp.113–121.

8-5. Graham, P. H., "Owner Management of Risk in Construction Contracts," *Current Practice in Cost Estimating and Cost Control*, Proceedings of an ASCE Conference, Austin, TX, April 1983, pp. 207–215.

8-6. Green, E. D., "Getting Out of Court—Private Resolution of Civil Disputes," *Boston Bar Journal*, May–June 1986, pp. 11–20.

8-7. Park, William R., *The Strategy of Contracting for Profit*, Prentice Hall, Englewood Cliffs, NJ, 1966.

8-8. Raiffa, Howard, *The Art and Science of Negotiation*, Harvard University Press, Cambridge, MA, 1982.

8-9. Walker, N., E. N. Walker, and T. K. Rohdenburg, *Legal Pitfalls in Architecture, Engineering and Building Construction*, 2nd ed., McGraw-Hill Book Company, New York, 1979.

8.12 PROBLEMS

P8-1. Suppose that in Example 8-5, the terms for the guaranteed maximum-cost contract are such that change orders will not be compensated if their total cost is within 3 percent of the original estimate, but will be compensated in full for the amount beyond 3 percent of the original estimate. If all other conditions remain unchanged, determine the contractor's profit and the owner's actual payment under this contract for the following conditions of U and C:

a. $U = 0,$ $\qquad C = 6\%E$

b. $U = 4\%E,$ $\qquad C = 6\%E$

c. $U = -4\%E,$ $\quad C = 6\%E$

P8-2. Suppose that in Example 8-5, the terms of the target estimate contract call for $N = 0.3$ instead of $N = 0.5$, meaning that the contractor will receive 30 percent of the savings. If all other conditions remain unchanged, determine the contractor's profit and the owner's actual payment under this contract for the given conditions of U and C.

P8-3. Suppose that in Example 8-5, the terms of the cost plus variable percentage contract allow an incentive bonus for early completion and a penalty for late completion of the project. Let D be the number of days early, with negative value denoting D days late. The bonus per day early or the penalty per day late with be T dollars. The agreed formula for owner's payment is

$$P = R(2E - A + C) + A + C + DT(1 + 0.4C/E)$$

The value of T is set at \$5,000 per day, and the project is completed 30 days behind schedule. If all other conditions remain unchanged, find the contractor's profit and the owner's actual payment under this contract for the given conditions of U and C.

P8-4. Consider a construction project for which the contractor's estimate is $3,000,000. For various types of contracts, $R = 10\%$, $R_1 = 3\%$, $R_2 = 1.5\%$, $R_3 = 6\%$ and $N = 0.6$. The contractor is not compensated for change orders under the guaranteed maximum cost contract if the total cost for the change order is within 5 percent ($150,000) of the original estimate. Determine the contractor's gross profit for each of the seven types of construction contracts for each of the following conditions of U and C:

    a. $U = 0$, $C = 0$

    b. $U = 0$, $C = 4\% E = \$120,000$

    c. $U = 5\% E = \$150,000$, $C = 0$

    d. $U = 5\% E = \$150,000$, $C = 4\% E = \$120,000$

    e. $U = 2\% E = \$60,000$, $C = 0$

    f. $U = 2\% E = \$60,000$, $C = 4\% E = \$120,000$

P8-5. Using the data in Problem P8-4, determine the owner's actual payment for each of the seven types of construction contracts for the same conditions of U and C.

P8-6. Suppose that in Problem P8-4, the terms of the guaranteed maximum-cost contract are such that change orders will not be compensated if their total cost is within 3 percent of the original estimate, but will be compensated in full for the amount beyond 3 percent of the original estimate. If all conditions remained unchanged, determine the contractor's profit and the owner's actual payment under this contract for the following conditions of U and C:

    a. $U = 0$, $C = 5\% E$

    b. $U = 2\%$, $C = 5\% E$

    c. $U = -2\%$, $C = 5\% E$

P8-7. Suppose that in Problem P8-4, the terms of the target estimate contract call for $N = 0.7$ instead of $N = 0.6$, meaning that the contractor will receive 70 percent of the savings. If all other conditions remain unchanged, determine the contractor's profit and the owner's actual payment under this contract for the given conditions of U and C.

P8-8. Suppose that in Problem P8-4, the terms of the cost plus variable percentage contract allow an incentive bonus for early completion and a penalty for late completion of the project. Let D be the number of days early, with negative value denoting D days late. The bonus per days early or the penalty per day late will be T dollars. The agreed formula for owner's payment is

$$P = R(2E - A + C) + A + C + DT(1 + 0.2C/E)$$

The value of T is set at $10,000 per day, and the project is completed 20 days ahead schedule. If all other conditions remain unchanged, find the contractor's profit and the owner's actual payment under this contract for the given conditions of U and C.

P8-9. The bidding game described in Section 8-7 is operational on an IBM personal computer with the R-base database and the Lotus 1-2-3 packages. Your instructor may divide the class into 5 teams or groups of 5 students, each group representing a separate market for competition. Although the computer program can accommodate up to 20 different teams, 5 is a good number of competitors to have in each bidding simulation. Your instructor may choose to play 4, 8, or 12 periods. Based on your instructor's intention, you should formulate a strategy to win the game accordingly.

P8-10. In playing the construction negotiating game described in Section 8-9, your instructor may choose one of the following combinations of companies and issues leading to different combinations of the scoring systems:

	Pipeline Constructors, Inc.	CMG Gas
a.	System A	System A
b.	System A	System B
c.	System B	System A
d.	System B	System B

Since the scoring systems are confidential information, your instructor will not disclose the combination used for the assignment. Your instructor may divide the class into pairs of two students, each pair acting as negotiators representing the two companies in the game. To keep the game interesting and fair, do not try to find out the scoring system of your negotiating counterpart. To seek insider information is unethical and illegal!

9

Construction Planning

9.1 BASIC CONCEPTS IN THE DEVELOPMENT OF CONSTRUCTION PLANS

Construction planning is a fundamental and challenging activity in the management and execution of construction projects. It involves the choice of technology, the definition of work tasks, the estimation of the required resources and durations for individual tasks, and the identification of any interactions among the different work tasks. A good construction plan is the basis for developing the budget and the schedule for work. Developing the construction plan is a critical task in the management of construction, even if the plan is not written or otherwise formally recorded. In addition to these technical aspects of construction planning, it may also be necessary to make organizational decisions about the relationships between project participants and even which organizations to include in a project. For example, the extent to which subcontractors will be used on a project is often determined during construction planning.

Forming a construction plan is a highly challenging task. As Sherlock Holmes noted,

> Most people, if you describe a train of events to them, will tell you what the result would be. They can put those events together in their minds, and argue from them that something will come to pass. There are few people, however, who, if you told them a result, would be able to evolve from their own inner consciousness what the steps were which led up to that result. This power is what I mean when I talk of reasoning backward.[66]

Like a detective, a planner begins with a result (i.e., a facility design) and must synthesize the steps required to yield this result. Essential aspects of construction planning include the *generation* of required activities, *analysis* of the implications of these activities, and *choice* among the various alternative means of performing activities. In contrast to a detective discovering a single train of events, however, construction planners also face the normative problem of choosing the best among numerous alternative plans. Moreover, a detective is faced with an observable result, whereas a planner must imagine the final facility as described in the plans and specifications.

In developing a construction plan, it is common to adopt a primary emphasis on either cost control or on schedule control as illustrated in Figure 9-1. Some projects are primarily divided into expense categories with associated costs. In these cases, construction planning is cost or expense oriented. Within the categories of expenditure, a distinction is made between costs incurred directly in the performance of an activity and indirectly for the accomplishment of the project. For example, borrowing expenses for project financing and overhead items are commonly treated as indirect costs. For other projects, scheduling of work activities over time is critical and is emphasized in the planning process. In this case, the planner ensures that the proper precedences among activities are maintained and that efficient scheduling

---

[66] A. C. Doyle, "A Study in Scarlet," *The Complete Sherlock Holmes*, Doubleday & Co., Garden City, N.Y., 1930, p. 83.

of the available resources prevails. Traditional scheduling procedures emphasize the maintenance of task precedences (resulting in *critical path scheduling procedures*) or efficient use of resources over time (resulting in *job shop scheduling* procedures). Finally, most complex projects require consideration of both cost and scheduling over time, so that planning, monitoring, and record keeping must consider both dimensions. In these cases, the integration of schedule and budget information is a major concern.

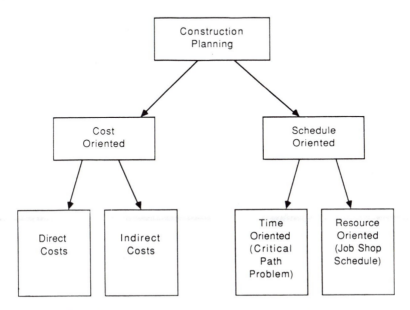

Figure 9-1 Alternative Emphases in Construction Planning

In this chapter, we shall consider the functional requirements for construction planning such as technology choice, work breakdown, and budgeting. Construction planning is not an activity which is restricted to the period after the award of a contract for construction. It should be an essential activity during the facility design. Also, if problems arise during construction, replanning is required.

9.2 CHOICE OF TECHNOLOGY AND CONSTRUCTION METHOD

As in the development of appropriate alternatives for facility design, choices of appropriate technology and methods for construction are often ill structured yet critical ingredients in the success of the project. For example, a decision whether to pump or to transport concrete in buckets will directly affect the cost and duration of tasks involved in building construction. A decision between these two alternatives should consider the relative costs, reliabilities, and availability of equipment for the two transport methods. Unfortunately, the exact implications of different methods depend upon numerous considerations for which information may be sketchy during the planning phase, such as the experience and expertise of workers or the particular underground condition at a site.

In selecting among alternative methods and technologies, it may be necessary to formulate a number of construction plans based on alternative methods or assumptions. Once the full plan is available, then the cost, time, and reliability impacts of the alternative approaches can be reviewed. This examination of several alternatives is often made explicit in bidding competitions in which several alternative designs may be proposed or *value engineering* for alternative construction methods may be permitted. In this case, potential constructors may wish to prepare plans for each alternative design using the suggested construction method as well as to prepare plans for alternative construction methods which would be proposed as part of the value engineering process.

In forming a construction plan, a useful approach is to simulate the construction process either in the imagination of the planner or with a formal computer-based simulation technique.[67] By observing the result, comparisons among different plans or problems with the existing plan can be identified. For example, a decision to use a particular piece of equipment for an operation immediately leads to the question of whether or not there is sufficient access space for the equipment. Three-dimensional geometric models in a computer-aided design (CAD) system may be helpful in simulating space requirements for operations and for identifying any interferences. Similarly, problems in resource availability identified during the simulation of the construction process might be effectively forestalled by providing additional resources as part of the construction plan.

Example 9-1: A Roadway Rehabilitation

An example from a roadway rehabilitation project in Pittsburgh, PA, can serve to illustrate the importance of good construction planning and the effect of technology choice. In this project, the decks on overpass bridges as well as the pavement on the highway itself were to be replaced. The initial construction plan was to work outward from each end of the overpass bridges while the highway surface was replaced below the bridges. As a result, access of equipment and concrete trucks to the overpass bridges was a considerable problem. However, the highway work could be staged so that each overpass bridge was accessible from below at prescribed times. By pumping concrete up to the overpass bridge deck from the highway below, costs were reduced and the work was accomplished much more quickly.

Example 9-2: Laser Leveling

An example of technology choice is the use of laser leveling equipment to improve the productivity of excavation and grading.[68] In these systems, laser surveying equipment is erected on a site so that the relative height of mobile equipment is known exactly.

---

[67] See, for example, B. C. Paulson, S. A. Douglas, A. Kalk, A. Touran and G. A. Victor, "Simulation and Analysis of Construction Operations," *ASCE Journal of Technical Topics in Civil Engineering*, Vol. 109 no. 2, August, 1983, p. 89, or R. I. Carr, "Simulation of Construction Project Duration," *ASCE Journal of the Construction Division*, Vol. 105 no. 2, June 1979, pp. 117–128.

This height measurement is accomplished by flashing a rotating laser light on a level plane across the construction site and observing exactly where the light shines on receptors on mobile equipment such as graders. Since laser light does not disperse appreciably, the height at which the laser shines anywhere on the construction site gives an accurate indication of the height of a receptor on a piece of mobile equipment. In turn, the receptor height can be used to measure the height of a blade, excavator bucket, or other piece of equipment. Combined with electrohydraulic control systems mounted on mobile equipment such as bulldozers, graders, and scrapers, the height of excavation and grading blades can be precisely and automatically controlled in these systems. This automation of blade heights has reduced costs in some cases by over 80 percent and improved quality in the finished product, as measured by the desired amount of excavation or the extent to which a final grade achieves the desired angle. These systems also permit the use of smaller machines and less skilled operators. However, the use of these semiautomated systems require investments in the laser surveying equipment as well as modification to equipment to permit electronic feedback control units. Still, laser leveling appears to be an excellent technological choice in many instances.

9.3 DEFINING WORK TASKS

At the same time that the choice of technology and general method are considered, a parallel step in the planning process is to define the various work tasks that must be accomplished. These work tasks represent the necessary framework to permit *scheduling* of construction activities, along with estimating the *resources* required by the individual work tasks, and any necessary *precedences* or required sequence among the tasks. The terms work "tasks" or "activities" are often used interchangeably in construction plans to refer to specific, defined items of work. In job shop or manufacturing terminology, a project would be called a "job" and an activity called an "operation," but the sense of the terms is equivalent.[69] The *scheduling problem* is to determine an appropriate set of activity start times, resource allocations, and completion times that will result in completion of the project in a timely and efficient fashion. Construction planning is the necessary forerunner to scheduling. In this planning, defining work tasks, technology, and construction method is typically done either simultaneously or in a series of iterations.

The definition of appropriate work tasks can be a laborious and tedious process, yet it represents the necessary information for application of formal scheduling procedures. Since construction projects can involve thousands of individual work tasks, this definition phase can also be expensive and time consuming. Fortunately, many tasks may be repeated in different parts of the facility or past facility construction plans can be used as general models for new projects. For example, the

[68] For a description of a laser leveling system, see B. C. Paulson, Jr., "Automation and Robotics for Construction," *ASCE Journal of Construction Engineering and Management*, Vol. 111 no. 3, 1985, pp. 190–207.

[69] See K. R. Baker, *Introduction to Sequencing and Scheduling*, John Wiley and Sons, Inc., New York, 1974, for an introduction to scheduling in manufacturing.

tasks involved in the construction of a building floor may be repeated with only minor differences for each of the floors in the building. Also, standard definitions and nomenclatures for most tasks exist. As a result, the individual planner defining work tasks does not have to approach each facet of the project entirely from scratch.

While repetition of activities in different locations or reproduction of activities from past projects reduces the work involved, there are very few computer aids for the process of defining activities. Databases and information systems can assist in the storage and recall of the activities associated with past projects as described in Chapter 14. For the scheduling process itself, numerous computer programs are available. But for the important task of defining activities, reliance on the skill, judgment, and experience of the construction planner is likely to continue. In the next few decades, however, more powerful computer aids may become available for this problem; an example is described in Chapter 15.

More formally, an *activity* is any subdivision of project tasks. The set of activities defined for a project should be *comprehensive* or completely *exhaustive* so that all necessary work tasks are included in one or more activities. Typically, each design element in the planned facility will have one or more associated project activities. Execution of an activity requires time and resources, including manpower and equipment, as described in the next section. The time required to perform an activity is called the *duration* of the activity. The beginning and the end of activities are signposts or *milestones,* indicating the progress of the project. Occasionally, it is useful to define activities which have no duration to mark important events. For example, receipt of equipment on the construction site may be defined as an activity since other activities would depend upon the equipment availability and the project manager might appreciate formal notice of the arrival. Similarly, receipt of regulatory approvals would also be specially marked in the project plan.

The extent of work involved in any one activity can vary tremendously in construction project plans. Indeed, it is common to begin with fairly coarse definitions of activities and then to subdivide tasks further as the plan becomes better defined. As a result, the definition of activities evolves during the preparation of the plan. A result of this process is a natural *hierarchy* of activities with large, abstract functional activities repeatedly subdivided into more and more specific subtasks. For example, the problem of placing concrete on site would have subactivities associated with placing forms, installing reinforcing steel, pouring concrete, finishing the concrete, removing forms, and others. Even more specifically, subtasks such as removal and cleaning of forms after concrete placement can be defined. Even further, the subtask "clean concrete forms" could be subdivided into the various operations:

- Transport forms from on-site storage and unload onto the cleaning station.
- Position forms on the cleaning station.
- Wash forms with water.
- Clean concrete debris from the form's surface.
- Coat the form surface with an oil release agent for the next use.
- Unload the form from the cleaning station and transport to the storage location.

This detailed task breakdown of the activity "clean concrete forms" would not generally be done in standard construction planning, but it is essential in the process of programming or designing a *robot* to undertake this activity since the various specific tasks must be well defined for a robot implementation.[70]

It is generally advantageous to introduce an explicit *hierarchy* of work activities for the purpose of simplifying the presentation and development of a schedule. For example, the initial plan might define a single activity associated with "site clearance." Later, this single activity might be subdivided into "relocating utilities," "removing vegetation," "grading", etc. However, these activities could continue to be identified as subactivities under the general activity of "site clearance." This hierarchical structure also facilitates the preparation of summary charts and reports in which detailed operations are combined into aggregate or "super"-activities.

More formally, a hierarchical approach to work task definition decomposes the work activity into component parts in the form of a tree. Higher levels in the tree represent decision nodes or summary activities, while branches in the tree lead to smaller components and work activities. A variety of constraints among the various nodes may be defined or imposed, including precedence relationships among different tasks as defined shortly. Technology choices may be *decomposed* to decisions made at particular nodes in the tree. For example, choices on plumbing technology might be made without reference to choices for other functional activities.

Of course, numerous different activity hierarchies can be defined for each construction plan. For example, upper-level activities might be related to facility components such as foundation elements, and then lower-level activity divisions into the required construction operations might be made. Alternatively, upper-level divisions might represent general types of activities such as electrical work, while lower work divisions represent the application of these operations to specific facility components. As a third alternative, initial divisions might represent different spatial locations in the planned facility. The choice of a hierarchy depends upon the desired scheme for summarizing work information and on the convenience of the planner. In computerized databases, multiple hierarchies can be stored so that different aggregations or views of the work breakdown structure can be obtained.

The number and detail of the activities in a construction plan is a matter of judgment or convention. Construction plans can easily range from less than a hundred to many thousand defined tasks, depending on the planner's decisions and the scope of the project. If subdivided activities are too refined, the size of the network becomes unwieldy and the cost of planning excessive. Sub-division yields no benefit if reasonably accurate estimates of activity durations and the required resources cannot be made at the detailed work breakdown level. On the other hand, if the specified activities are too coarse, it is impossible to develop realistic schedules and details of resource requirements during the project. More detailed task definitions

[70] See M. J. Skibniewski and C. T. Hendrickson, "Evaluation Method for Robotics Implementation: Application to Concrete Form Cleaning," *Proc. Second Intl. Conf. on Robotics in Construction*, Carnegie Mellon University, Pittsburgh, 1985, for more detail on the work process design of a concrete form cleaning robot.

permit better control and more realistic scheduling. It is useful to define separate work tasks for

- Those activities that involve different resources or
- Those activities that do not require continuous performance

For example, the activity "prepare and check shop drawings" should be divided into a task for preparation and a task for checking since different individuals are involved in the two tasks and there may be a time lag between preparation and checking.

In practice, the proper level of detail will depend upon the size, importance, and difficulty of the project as well as the specific scheduling and accounting procedures which are adopted. However, it is generally the case that most schedules are prepared with too little detail than too much. It is important to keep in mind that task definition will serve as the basis for scheduling, for communicating the construction plan and for construction monitoring. Completion of tasks will also often serve as a basis for progress payments from the owner. Thus, more detailed task definitions can be quite useful. But more detailed task breakdowns are only valuable to the extent that the resources required, durations, and activity relationships are realistically estimated for each activity. Providing detailed work task breakdowns is not helpful without a commensurate effort to provide realistic resource requirement estimates. As more powerful, computer-based scheduling and monitoring procedures are introduced, the ease of defining and manipulating tasks will increase, and the number of work tasks can reasonably be expected to expand.

Example 9-3: Task Definition for a Road Building Project

As an example of construction planning, suppose that we wish to develop a plan for a road construction project including two culverts.[71] Initially, we divide project activities into three categories as shown in Figure 9-2: structures, roadway, and general. This division is based on the major types of design elements to be constructed. Within the roadway work, a further subdivision is into earthwork and pavement. Within these subdivisions, we identify clearing, excavation, filling, and finishing (including seeding and sodding) associated with earthwork, and we define watering, compaction, and paving subactivities associated with pavement. Finally, we note that the roadway segment is fairly long, and so individual activities can be defined for different physical segments along the roadway path. In Figure 9-2, we divide each paving and earthwork activity into activities specific to each of two roadway segments. For the culvert construction, we define the subdivisions of structural excavation, concreting, and reinforcing. Even more specifically, structural excavation is divided into excavation itself and the required backfill and compaction. Similarly, concreting is divided into placing concrete forms, pouring concrete, stripping forms, and curing the concrete. As a final step in the structural planning, detailed activities are defined for reinforcing each of the two culverts. General work activities are defined for move-in, general supervision, and clean up. As a result of this planning, over 30 different detailed activities have been defined.

[71] This example is adapted from R. Aras and J. Surkis, "PERT and CPM Techniques in Project Management," *ASCE Journal of the Construction Division,* Vol. 90, no. CO1, March 1964.

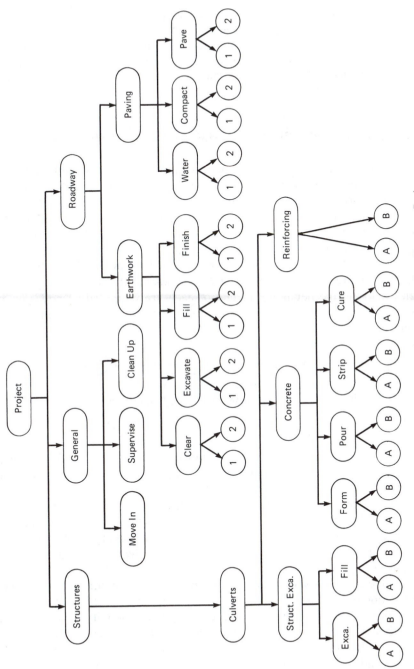

Figure 9-2 Hierarchical Activity Divisions for a Roadway Project

At the option of the planner, additional activities might also be defined for this project. For example, materials ordering or lane striping might be included as separate activities. It might also be the case that a planner would define a different hierarchy of work breakdowns than that shown in Figure 9-2. For example, placing reinforcing might have been a subactivity under concreting for culverts. One reason for separating reinforcement placement might be to emphasize the different material and resources required for this activity. Also, the division into separate roadway segments and culverts might have been introduced early in the hierarchy. With all these potential differences, the important aspect is to ensure that all necessary activities are included somewhere in the final plan.

9.4 DEFINING PRECEDENCE RELATIONSHIPS AMONG ACTIVITIES

Once work activities have been defined, the relationships among the activities can be specified. *Precedence* relations between activities signify that the activities must take place in a particular sequence. Numerous natural sequences exist for construction activities due to requirements for structural integrity, regulations, and other technical requirements. For example, design drawings cannot be checked before they are drawn. Diagrammatically, precedence relationships can be illustrated by a *network* or *graph* in which the activities are represented by arrows as in Figure 9-3. The arrows in Figure 9-3 are called *branches* or *links* in the *activity network*, while the circles marking the beginning or end of each arrow are called *nodes* or *events*. In this figure, links represent particular activities, while the nodes represent milestone events.

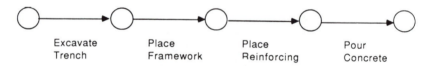

| Excavate | Place | Place | Pour |
| Trench | Framework | Reinforcing | Concrete |

Figure 9-3 Four Activities with Precedences

More complicated precedence relationships can also be specified. For example, one activity might not be able to start for several days after the completion of another activity. As a common example, concrete might have to cure (or set) for several days before formwork is removed. This restriction on the removal of forms activity is called a *lag* between the completion of one activity (i.e., pouring concrete in this case) and the start of another activity (i.e., removing formwork in this case). Many computer-based scheduling programs permit the use of a variety of precedence relationships.

Three mistakes should be avoided in specifying predecessor relationships for construction plans. First, a circle of activity precedences will result in an impossible plan. For example, if activity A precedes activity B, activity B precedes activity C, and activity C precedes activity A, then the project can never be started or completed! Figure 9-4 illustrates the resulting activity network. Fortunately, formal scheduling methods and good computer scheduling programs will find any such errors in the logic of the construction plan.

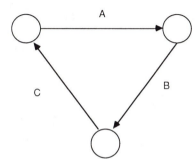

Figure 9-4 An Impossible Work Plan

Forgetting a necessary precedence relationship can be more insidious. For example, suppose that installation of dry wall should be done prior to floor finishing. Ignoring this precedence relationship may result in both activities being scheduled at the same time. Corrections on the spot may result in increased costs or problems of quality in the completed project. Unfortunately, there are few ways in which precedence omissions can be found other than with checks by knowledgeable managers or by comparison to comparable projects. One other possible but little used mechanism for checking precedences is to conduct a physical or computer-based simulation of the construction process and observe any problems.

Finally, it is important to realize that different types of precedence relationships can be defined and that each has different implications for the schedule of activities:

- Some activities have a necessary technical or physical relationship that cannot be superseded. For example, concrete pours cannot proceed before formwork and reinforcement are in place.
- Some activities have a necessary precedence relationship over a continuous space rather than as discrete work task relationships. For example, formwork may be placed in the first part of an excavation trench even as the excavation equipment continues to work further along in the trench. Formwork placement cannot proceed further than the excavation, but the two activities can be started and stopped independently within this constraint.
- Some "precedence relationships" are not technically necessary but are imposed due to implicit decisions within the construction plan. For example, two activities may require the same piece of equipment so a precedence relationship might be defined between the two to ensure that they are not scheduled for the same time period. Which activity is scheduled first is arbitrary. As a second example, reversing the sequence of two activities may be technically possible but more expensive. In this case, the precedence relationship is not physically necessary but only applied to reduce costs as perceived at the time of scheduling.

In revising schedules as work proceeds, it is important to realize that different types of precedence relationships have quite different implications for the flexibility and cost of changing the construction plan. Unfortunately, many formal scheduling systems do not possess the capability of indicating this type of flexibility. As a result, the burden is placed upon the manager of making such decisions and ensuring realistic and effective schedules. With all the other responsibilities of a project manager, it is no surprise that preparing or revising the formal, computer-based construction plan is a low priority to a manager in such cases. Nevertheless, formal construction plans may be essential for good management of complicated projects.

Example 9-4: Precedence Definition for Site Preparation and Foundation Work

Suppose that a site preparation and concrete slab foundation construction project consists of nine different activities:

A. Site clearing (of brush and minor debris)

B. Removal of trees

C. General excavation

D. Grading general area

E. Excavation for utility trenches

F. Placing formwork and reinforcement for concrete

G. Installing sewer lines

H. Installing other utilities

I. Pouring concrete

Activities A (site clearing) and B (tree removal) do not have preceding activities since they depend on none of the other activities. We assume that activities C (general excavation) and D (general grading) are preceded by activity A (site clearing). It might also be the case that the planner wished to delay any excavation until trees were removed, so that B (tree removal) would be a precedent activity to C (general excavation) and D (general grading). Activities E (trench excavation) and F (concrete preparation) cannot begin until the completion of general excavation and grading, since they involve subsequent excavation and trench preparation. Activities G (install lines) and H (install utilities) represent installation in the utility trenches and cannot be attempted until the trenches are prepared, so that activity E (trench excavation) is a preceding activity. We also assume that the utilities should not be installed until grading is completed to avoid equipment conflicts, so activity D (general grading) is also preceding activities G (install sewers) and H (install utilities). Finally, activity I (pour concrete) cannot begin until the sewer line is installed and formwork and reinforcement are ready, so activities F and G are preceding. Other utilities may be routed over the slab foundation, so activity H (install utilities) is not necessarily a preceding activity for activity I (pour concrete). The result of our planning are the immediate precedences shown in Table 9-1.

With this information, the next problem is to represent the activities in a network diagram and to determine all the precedence relationships among the activities. One network representation of these nine activities is shown in Figure 9-5, in which the activities appear as branches or links between nodes. The nodes represent milestones of possible beginning and starting times. This representation is called an *activity-on-branch* diagram. Note that an initial event beginning activity is defined (node 0 in Figure 9-5), while node 5 represents the completion of all activities.

Alternatively, the nine activities could be represented by nodes and predecessor relationships by branches or links, as in Figure 9-6. The result is an *activity-on-node*

TABLE 9–1 PRECEDENCE RELATIONS FOR A NINE-ACTIVITY PROJECT EXAMPLE

Activity	Description	Predecessors
A	Site clearing	—
B	Removal of trees	—
C	General excavation	A
D	Grading general area	A
E	Excavation for utility trenches	B, C
F	Placing formwork and reinforcement for concrete	B, C
G	Installing sewer lines	D, E
H	Installing other utilites	D, E
I	Pouring concrete	F, G

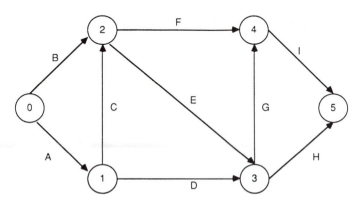

Figure 9-5   Activity-on-Branch Representation of a Nine-Activity Project

diagram. In Figure 9-6, new activity nodes representing the beginning and the end of construction have been added to mark these important milestones.

These network representations of activities can be very helpful in visualizing the various activities and their relationships for a project. Whether activities are represented as branches (as in Figure 9-5) or as nodes (as in Figure 9-6) is largely a matter of

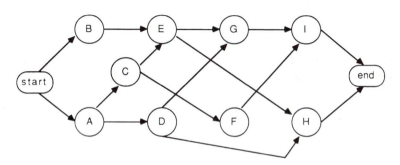

Figure 9-6   Activity-on-Node Representation of a Nine Activity Project

organizational or personal choice. Some considerations in choosing one form or another are discussed in Chapter 10.

It is also notable that Table 9-1 lists only the *immediate* predecessor relationships. Clearly, there are other precedence relationships which involve more than one activity. For example, "installing sewer lines" (activity G) cannot be undertaken before "site clearing" (activity A) is complete since the activity "grading general area" (activity D) must precede activity G and must follow activity A. Table 9-1 is an *implicit* precedence list since only immediate predecessors are recorded. An explicit predecessor list would include *all* the preceding activities for activity G. Table 9-2 shows all such predecessor relationships implied by the project plan. This table can be produced by tracing all paths through the network back from a particular activity and can be performed algorithmically.[72] For example, inspecting Figure 9-6 reveals that each activity except for activity B depends upon the completion of activity A.

TABLE 9–2 ALL ACTIVITY PRECEDENCE RELATIONSHIPS FOR A NINE-ACTIVITY PROJECT

Predecessor activity	Direct successor activities	All successor activities	All predecessor activities
A	C, D	E, F, G, H, I	—
B	E, F	G, H, I	—
C	E, F	G, H, I	A
D	G, H	I	A
E	G, H	I	A, B, C
F	I	—	A, B, C
G	I	—	A, B, C, D, E
H	—	—	A, B, C, D, E
I	—	—	A, B, C, D, E, F, G

9.5 ESTIMATING ACTIVITY DURATIONS

In most scheduling procedures, each work activity has an associated time duration. These durations are used extensively in preparing a schedule. For example, suppose that the durations shown in Table 9-3 were estimated for the project diagrammed in Figure 9-3. The entire set of activities would then require at least three days, since the activities follow one another directly and require a total of $1.0 + 0.5 + 0.5 + 1.0 = 3$ days. If another activity proceeded in *parallel* with this sequence, the three day minimum duration of these four activities is unaffected. More than three days would be required for the sequence if there were a delay or a lag between the completion of one activity and the start of another.

All formal scheduling procedures rely upon estimates of the durations of the

[72] For a discussion of network reachability and connectivity computational algorithms, see Chapters 2 and 7 in N. Christofides, *Graph Theory: An Algorithmic Approach*, Academic Press, London, 1975, or any other text on graph theory.

TABLE 9–3 DURATIONS AND PREDECESSORS FOR A FOUR-ACTIVITY PROJECT ILLUSTRATION

Activity	Predecessor	Duration (days)
Excavate trench	—	1.0
Place formwork	Excavate trench	0.5
Place reinforcing	Place formwork	0.5
Pour concrete	Place reinforcing	1.0

various project activities as well as the definitions of the predecessor relationships among tasks. The variability of an activity's duration may also be considered. Formally, the *probability distribution* of an activity's duration as well as the expected or most likely duration may be used in scheduling. A probability distribution indicates the chance that a particular activity duration will occur. In advance of actually doing a particular task, we cannot be certain exactly how long the task will require.

A straightforward approach to the estimation of activity durations is to keep historical records of particular activities and rely on the average durations from this experience in making new duration estimates. Since the scope of activities are unlikely to be identical between different projects, unit productivity rates are typically employed for this purpose. For example, the duration of an activity D_{ij} such as concrete formwork assembly might be estimated as

$$D_{ij} = \frac{A_{ij}}{P_{ij} N_{ij}} \tag{9.1}$$

where A_{ij} is the required formwork area to assemble (in square yards), P_{ij} is the average productivity of a standard crew in this task (measured in square yards per hour), and N_{ij} is the number of crews assigned to the task. In some organizations, unit production time, T_{ij}, is defined as the time required to complete a unit of work by a standard crew (measured in hours per square yards) is used as a productivity measure such that T_{ij} is a reciprocal of P_{ij}.

A formula such as Eq. (9. 1) can be used for nearly all construction activities. Typically, the required quantity of work, A_{ij} is determined from detailed examination of the final facility design. This *quantity takeoff* to obtain the required amounts of materials, volumes, and areas is a very common process in bid preparation by contractors. In some countries, specialized quantity surveyors provide the information on required quantities for all potential contractors and the owner. The number of crews working, N_{ij}, is decided by the planner. In many cases, the number or amount of resources applied to particular activities may be modified in light of the resulting project plan and schedule. Finally, some estimate of the expected work productivity, P_{ij}, must be provided to apply Eq. (9.1). As with cost factors, commercial services can provide average productivity figures for many standard activities of this sort. Historical records in a firm can also provide data for estimation of productivities.

The calculation of a duration as in Equation (9.1) is only an approximation to the actual activity duration for a number of reasons. First, it is usually the case that peculiarities of the project make the accomplishment of a particular activity more or less difficult. For example, access to the forms in a particular location may be difficult; as a result, the productivity of assembling forms may be *lower* than the average value for a particular project. Often, adjustments based on engineering judgment are made to the calculated durations from Equation (9.1) for this reason.

In addition, productivity rates may vary in both systematic and random fashions from the average. An example of systematic variation is the effect of *learning* on productivity. As a crew becomes familiar with an activity and the work habits of the crew, their productivity will typically improve. Figure 9-7 illustrates the type of productivity increase that might occur with experience; this curve is called a *learning curve*. The result is that productivity P_{ij} is a function of the duration of an activity or project. A common construction example is that the assembly of floors in a building might go faster at higher levels due to improved productivity even though the transportation time up to the active construction area is longer. Again, historical records or subjective adjustments might be made to represent learning curve variations in average productivity.[73]

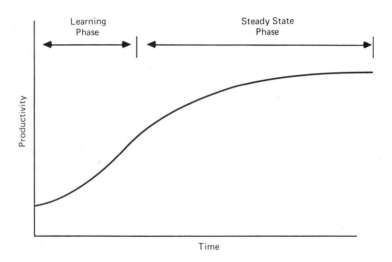

Figure 9-7 Productivity Changes due to Learning

Random factors will also influence productivity rates and make estimation of activity durations uncertain. For example, a scheduler will typically not know at the time of making the initial schedule how skillful the crew and manager will be that are assigned to a particular project. The productivity of a skilled designer may be

[73] See H. R. Thomas, C. T. Matthews, and J. G. Ward, "Learning Curve Models of Construction Productivity," *ASCE Journal of Construction Engineering and Management*, Vol. 112, no. 2, June 1986, pp. 245–258.

many times that of an inexperienced engineer. In the absence of specific knowledge, the estimator can only use average values of productivity.

Weather effects are often very important and thus deserve particular attention in estimating durations. Weather has both systematic and random influences on activity durations. Whether or not a rainstorm will come on a particular day is certainly a random effect that will influence the productivity of many activities. However, the likelihood of a rainstorm is likely to vary systematically from one month or one site to the next. Adjustment factors for inclement weather as well as meteorological records can be used to incorporate the effects of weather on durations. As a simple example, an activity might require 10 days in perfect weather, but the activity could not proceed in the rain. Furthermore, suppose that rain is expected 10 percent of the days in a particular month. In this case, the expected activity duration is 11 days, including 1 expected rain day.

Finally, the use of average productivity factors themselves cause problems in the calculation presented in Eq. (9.1). The expected value of the multiplicative reciprocal of a variable is not exactly equal to the reciprocal of the variable's expected value. For example, if productivity on an activity is either six in good weather (i.e., $P = 6$) or two in bad weather (i.e., $P = 2$) and good or bad weather is equally likely, then the expected productivity is $E[P] = (6)(0.5) + (2)(0.5) = 4$, and the reciprocal of expected productivity is 1/4. However, the expected reciprocal of productivity is $E[1/P] = (0.5)/6 + (0.5)/2 = 1/3$. The reciprocal of expected productivity is 33 percent greater than the expected value of the reciprocal in this case! By representing only two possible productivity values, this example represents an extreme case, but it is always true that the use of average productivity factors in Eq. (9.1) will result in *optimistic* estimates of activity durations. The use of actual averages for the reciprocals of productivity or small adjustment factors may be used to correct for this nonlinearity problem.

The simple duration calculation shown in Eq. (9.1) also assumes an inverse linear relationship between the number of crews assigned to an activity and the total duration of work. While this is a reasonable assumption in situations for which crews can work independently and require no special coordination, it need not always be true. For example, design tasks may be divided among numerous architects and engineers, but delays to ensure proper coordination and communication increase as the number of workers increase. As another example, ensuring a smooth flow of material to all crews on a site may be increasingly difficult as the number of crews increase. In these latter cases, the relationship between activity duration and the number of crews is unlikely to be inversely proportional as shown in Eq. (9.1). As a result, adjustments to the estimated productivity from Eq. (9.1) must be made. Alternatively, more complicated functional relationships might be estimated between duration and resources used in the same way that nonlinear preliminary or. conceptual cost estimate models are prepared.

One mechanism to formalize the estimation of activity durations is to employ a hierarchical estimation framework. This approach decomposes the estimation problem into component parts in which the higher levels in the hierarchy represent attributes that depend upon the details of lower-level adjustments and calculations. For example, Figure 9-8 represents various levels in the estimation of the duration of masonry construction.[74] At the lowest level, the maximum productivity for the activity is estimated based upon general work conditions. Table 9-4 illustrates some possible maximum productivity values that might be employed in this estimation. At the next higher level, adjustments to these maximum productivities are made to account for special site conditions and crew compositions; Table 9-5 illustrates some possible adjustment rules. At the highest level, adjustments for overall effects such as weather are introduced. Also shown in Figure 9-8 are nodes to estimate down or unproductive time associated with the masonry construction activity. The formalization of the estimation process illustrated in Figure 9-8 permits the development of computer aids for the estimation process (as described in Chapter 15) or can serve as a conceptual framework for a human estimator.

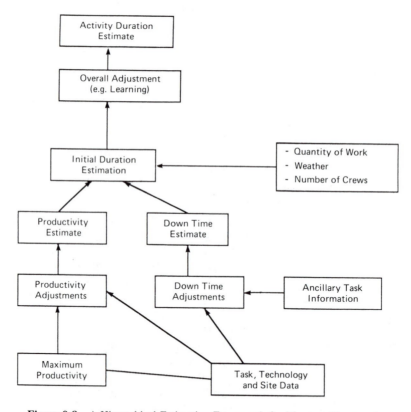

Figure 9-8 A Hierarchical Estimation Framework for Masonry Construction

[74] For a more extensive discussion and description of this estimation procedure, see C. Hendrickson, D. Martinelli, and D. Rehak, "Hierarchical Rule-Based Activity Duration Estimation," *ASCE Journal of Construction Engineering and Management*, Vol. 113, no. 2, 1987, pp. 288–301.

TABLE 9–4 MAXIMUM PRODUCTIVITY ESTIMATES FOR MASONRY WORK

Masonry unit size	Condition(s)	Maximum productivity achievable
8 inch block	None	400 units/day/mason
6 inch	Wall is "long."	430 units/day/mason
6 inch	Wall is not "long."	370 units/day/mason
12 inch	Labor is nonunion.	300 units/day/mason
4 inch	Wall is "long." Weather is "warm and dry" or high-strength mortar is used.	480 units/day/mason
4 inch	Wall is not "long." Weather is "warm and dry" or high-strength mortar is used.	430 units/day/mason
4 inch	Wall is "long." Weather is not "warm and dry" or high-strength mortar is not used.	370 units/day/mason
4 inch	Wall is not "long." Weather is not "warm and dry" or high-strength mortar is not used.	320 units/day/mason
8 inch	There is support from existing wall.	1,000 units/day/mason
8 inch	There is no support from existing wall.	750 units/day/mason
12 inch	There is support from existing wall.	700 units/day/mason
12 inch	There is no support from existing wall.	550 units/day/mason

TABLE 9–5 POSSIBLE ADJUSTMENTS TO MAXIMUM PRODUCTIVITIES FOR MASONRY CONSTRUCTION

Impact	Condition(s)	Adjustment magnitude (% of maximum)
Crew type	Crew type is nonunion. Job is "large."	15%
Crew type	Crew type is union. Job is "small."	10%
Supporting labor	There are less than two laborers per crew.	20%
Supporting labor	There are more than two masons/laborers.	10%
Elevation	Steel frame building with masonry exterior wall has "insufficient" support labor.	10%
Elevation	Solid masonry building with work on exterior wall uses nonunion labor.	12%
Visibility	Block is not covered.	7%
Temperature	Temperature is below 45° F.	15%
Temperature	Temperature is above 85° F.	10%
Brick texture	Bricks are baked high. Weather is cold or moist.	10%

In addition to the problem of estimating the expected duration of an activity, some scheduling procedures explicitly consider the uncertainty in activity duration estimates by using the probabilistic distribution of activity durations. That is, the duration of a particular activity is assumed to be a random variable that is distributed in a particular fashion. For example, an activity duration might be assumed to be distributed as a normal or a beta distributed random variable as illustrated in Figure 9-9. This figure shows the probability or chance of experiencing a particular activity duration based on a probabilistic distribution. The beta distribution is often used to characterize activity durations, since it can have an absolute minimum and an absolute maximum of possible duration times. The normal distribution is a good approximation to the beta distribution in the center of the distribution and is easy to work with, so it is often used as an approximation.

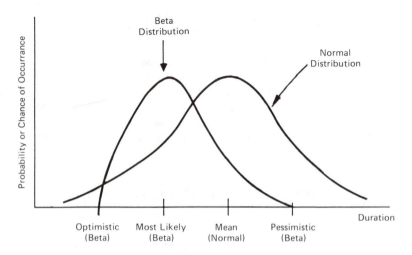

Figure 9-9   Beta and Normally Distributed Activity Durations

If a standard random variable is used to characterize the distribution of activity durations, then only a few parameters are required to calculate the probability of any particular duration. Still, the estimation problem is increased considerably since more than one parameter is required to characterize most of the probabilistic distribution used to represent activity durations. For the beta distribution, three or four parameters are required, depending on its generality, whereas the normal distribution requires two parameters.

As an example, the normal distribution is characterized by two parameters, μ and σ representing the average duration and the standard deviation of the duration, respectively. Alternatively, the *variance* of the distribution σ^2 could be used to describe or characterize the variability of duration times; the variance is the value of the standard deviation multiplied by itself. From historical data, these two parameters can be estimated as

$$\mu \approx \bar{x} = \sum_{k=1}^{n} \frac{x_k}{n} \tag{9.2}$$

$$\sigma^2 \approx \sum_{k=1}^{n} \frac{(x_k - \bar{x})^2}{n-1} \tag{9.3}$$

where we assume that n different observations x_k of the random variable x are available. This estimation process might be applied to activity durations directly (so that x_k would be a record of an activity duration D_{ij} on a past project).

If the distribution of productivities is used to estimate durations, Equations (9.2) and (9.3) would be used to estimate the mean and standard deviation of the reciprocal of productivity to avoid non-linear effects. Hence, x_k would be a distribution of $T_{i_j} = 1/P_{i_j}$ (derived from a record of the productivity P_{i_j} on a past project.) Then, the standard deviation of activity duration would be calculated as

$$\sigma_{ij} \approx \frac{A_{ij}\, \sigma_{1/P}}{N_{ij}} \tag{9.4}$$

where $\sigma_{1/P}$ is the estimated standard deviation of the reciprocal of productivity that is calculated from Eq. (9.3), and A_{ij} and N_{ij} are defined for Eq. (9.1).

9.6 ESTIMATING RESOURCE REQUIREMENTS FOR WORK ACTIVITIES

In addition to precedence relationships and time durations, *resource requirements* are usually estimated for each activity. Since the work activities defined for a project are comprehensive, the total resources required for the project are the sum of the resources required for the various activities. By making resource requirement estimates for each activity, the requirements for particular resources during the course of the project can be identified. Potential bottlenecks can thus be identified and schedule, resource allocation, or technology changes made to avoid problems.

Many formal scheduling procedures can incorporate constraints imposed by the availability of particular resources. For example, the unavailability of a specific piece of equipment or crew may prohibit activities from being undertaken at a particular time. Another type of resource is space. A planner typically will schedule only one activity in the same location at the same time. While activities requiring the same space may have no necessary technical precedence, simultaneous work might not be possible. Computational procedures for these various scheduling problems will be described in Chapters 10 and 11. In this section, we shall discuss the estimation of required resources.

The initial problem in estimating resource requirements is to decide the extent and number of resources that might be defined. At a very aggregate level, resources categories might be limited to the amount of labor (measured in worker-hours or in dollars), the amount of materials required for an activity, and the total cost of the activity. At this aggregate level, the resource estimates may be useful for purposes of project monitoring and cash flow planning. For example, actual expenditures on an activity can be compared with the estimated required resources to reveal any problems that are being encountered during the course of a project. Monitoring procedures of this sort are described in Chapter 12. However, this aggregate definition of resource use would not reveal bottlenecks associated with particular types of equipment or workers.

More detailed definitions of required resources would include the number and type of both workers and equipment required by an activity as well as the amount and types of materials. Standard resource requirements for particular activities can be recorded and adjusted for the special conditions of particular projects. As a result, the resources types required for particular activities may already be defined. Reliance on historical or standard activity definitions of this type requires a standard coding system for activities.

In making adjustments for the resources required by a particular activity, most of the problems encountered in forming duration estimations described in the previous section are also present. In particular, resources such as labor requirements will vary in proportion to the work productivity, P_{ij}, used to estimate activity durations in Eq. (9.1). Mathematically, a typical estimating equation would be

$$R_{ij}^k = D_{ij} N_{ij} U_{ij}^k \qquad (9.5)$$

where R_{ij}^k are the resources of type k required by activity ij, D_{ij} is the duration of activity ij, N_{ij} is the number of standard crews allocated to activity ij, and U_{ij}^k is the amount of resource type k used per standard crew per unit of time. For example, if an activity required 8 hours with two crews assigned and each crew required three workers, the effort would be $R = 8 \times 2 \times 3 = 48$ labor-hours.

From the planning perspective, the important decisions in estimating resource requirements are to determine the type of technology and equipment to employ and the number of crews to allocate to each task. Clearly, assigning additional crews might result in faster completion of a particular activity. However, additional crews might result in congestion and coordination problems, so that work productivity might decline. Further, completing a particular activity earlier might not result in earlier completion of the entire project, as discussed in Chapter 10.

Example 9-5: Resource Requirements for Block Foundations

In placing concrete block foundation walls, a typical crew would consist of three bricklayers and two bricklayer helpers. If sufficient space were available on the site, several crews could work on the same job at the same time, thereby speeding up completion of the activity in proportion to the number of crews. In more restricted sites, multiple crews might interfere with one another. For special considerations such as complicated scaffolding or large blocks (such as 12 inch block), a bricklayer helper for each bricklayer might be required to ensure smooth and productive work. In general, standard crew composition depends upon the specific construction task and the equipment or technology employed. These standard crews are then adjusted in response to special characteristics of a particular site.

Example 9-6: Pouring Concrete Slabs

For large concrete pours on horizontal slabs, it is important to plan the activity so that the slab for a full block can be completed continuously in a single day. Resources required for pouring the concrete depend upon the technology used. For example, a standard crew for pumping concrete to the slab might include a foreman, five laborers, one finisher, and one equipment operator. Related equipment would be vibrators and the concrete pump itself. For delivering concrete with a chute directly from the delivery truck, the standard crew might consist of a foreman, four laborers, and a finisher. The number of crews would be chosen to ensure that the desired amount of concrete could be placed in a single day. In addition to the resources involved in the actual placement, it would also be necessary to ensure a sufficient number of delivery trucks and availability of the concrete itself.

9.7 CODING SYSTEMS

One objective in many construction planning efforts is to define the plan within the constraints of a universal *coding system* for identifying activities. Each activity defined for a project would be identified by a predefined code specific to that activity. The use of a common nomenclature or identification system is basically motivated by the desire for better integration of organizational efforts and improved information flow. In particular, coding systems are adopted to provide a numbering system to replace verbal descriptions of items. These codes reduce the length or complexity of the information to be recorded. A common coding system within an organization also aids consistency in definitions and categories between projects and among the various parties involved in a project. Common coding systems also aid in the retrieval of historical records of cost, productivity, and duration on particular activities. Finally, electronic data storage and retrieval operations are much more efficient with standard coding systems, as described in Chapter 14.

In North America, the most widely used standard coding system for constructed facilities is the MASTERFORMAT system developed by the Construction Specifications Institute (CSI) of the United States and Construction Specifications of Canada.[75] After development of separate systems, this combined system was originally introduced as the Uniform Construction Index (UCI) in 1972 and was subsequently adopted for use by numerous firms, information providers, professional societies, and trade organizations. The term MASTERFORMAT was introduced with the 1978 revision of the UCI codes. MASTERFORMAT provides a standard identification code for nearly all the elements associated with building construction.

MASTERFORMAT involves a hierarchical coding system with multiple levels plus keyword text descriptions of each item. In the numerical coding system, the

[75] Information on the MASTERFORMAT coding system can be obtained from The Construction Specifications Institute, 601 Madison St., Alexandria, VA 22314.

first two digits represent 1 of the 16 divisions for work; a seventeenth division is used to code conditions of the contract for a constructor. In the latest version of the MASTERFORMAT, a third digit is added to indicate a subdivision within each division. Each division is further specified by a three-digit extension indicating another level of subdivisions. In many cases, these subdivisions are further divided with an additional three digits to identify more specific work items or materials. For example, the code 16-950-960, "Electrical Equipment Testing" are defined as within Division 16 (Electrical) and Subdivision 950 (Testing). The keywords "Electrical Equipment Testing" is a standard description of the activity. The 17 major divisions in the UCI/CSI MASTERFORMAT system are shown in Table 9-6. As an example, site-work second-level divisions and some third-level divisions according to the 3rd edition of this code (1983) are shown in Table 9-7.

While MASTERFORMAT provides a very useful means of organizing and communicating information, it has some obvious limitations as a complete project coding system. First, more specific information such as location of work or responsible organization might be required for project cost control. Code extensions are then added in addition to the digits in the basic MASTERFORMAT codes. For example, a typical extended code might have the following elements:

$$0534.02220.21.A.00.cf34$$

The first four digits indicate the project for this activity; this code refers to an activity on project number 0534. The next five digits refer to the MASTERFORMAT secondary division; according to Table 9-7, this activity would be 02220, "Excavating, Backfilling, and Compacting." The next two digits refer to specific activities defined within this MASTERFORMAT code; the digits 21 in this example might refer to excavation of column footings. The next character refers to the *block* or general area on the site that the activity will take place; in this case, block A is indicated. The digits 00 could be replaced by a code to indicate the responsible organization for the activity. Finally, the characters cf34 refer to the particular design element number for which this excavation is intended; in this case, column footing number 34 is intended. Thus, this activity is to perform the excavation for column footing number 34 in block A on the site. Note that a number of additional activities would be associated with column footing 34, including formwork and concreting. Additional fields in the coding systems might also be added to indicate the respon-

TABLE 9–6 MAJOR DIVISIONS IN THE UNIFORM CONSTRUCTION INDEX

0 Conditions of the contract	9 Finishes
1 General requirements	10 Specialties
2 Site work	11 Equipment
3 Concrete	12 Furnishings
4 Masonry	13 Special construction
5 Metals	14 Conveying system
6 Wood and plastics	15 Mechanical
7 Thermal and moisture prevention	16 Electrical
8 Doors and windows	

TABLE 9–7 SECONDARY DIVISIONS IN MASTERFORMAT FOR SITE WORK

02-010	Subsurface investigation	02-350	Piles and caissons
02-012	Standard penetration tests	02-355	Pile driving
02-016	Seismic investigation	02-360	Driven piles
		02-370	Bored/augered piles
02-050	Demolition	02-380	Caissons
02-060	Building demolition		
02-070	Selective demolition	02-450	Railroad work
02-075	Concrete removal		
02-080	Asbestos removal	02-480	Marine work
02-100	Site preparation	02-500	Paving and surfacing
02-110	Site clearing	02-510	Walk, road and parking paving
02-115	Selective clearing	02-515	Unit Pavers
02-120	Structure moving	02-525	Curbs
		02-530	Athletic paving and surfacing
02-140	Dewatering	02-540	Synthetic surfacing
		02-545	Surfacing
02-150	Shoring and underpinning	02-550	Highway Paving
		02-560	Airfield paving
02-160	Excavation supporting system	02-575	Pavement repair
		02-580	Pavement marking
02-170	Cofferdams	02-600	Piped utility materials
02-200	Earthwork		
02-210	Grading	02-660	Water distribution
02-220	Excavating, backfilling and compaction	02-680	Fuel distribution
02-230	Base Course		
02-240	Soil stabilization	02-700	Sewage and drainage
02-250	Vibro-floatation		
02-270	Slope protection	02-760	Restoration of underground pipelines
02-280	Soil treatment		
02-290	Earth dams	02-770	Ponds and reservoirs
02-300	Tunneling	02-700	Power and Communications
02-305	Tunnel ventilation		
02-310	Tunnel excavating	02-880	Site improvements
02-320	Tunnel lining		
02-330	Tunnel grouting	02-900	Landscaping
02-340	Tunnel support Systems		

Source: *MASTERFORMAT: Master List of Section Titles and Numbers*, 1983 Edition, The Construction Specifications Institute, Alexandria, VA, 1983.

sible crew for this activity or to identify the specific location of the activity on the site (defined, for example, as x, y, and z coordinates with respect to a base point).

As a second problem, the MASTERFORMAT system was originally designed for building construction activities, so it is difficult to include various construction activities for other types of facilities or activities associated with planning or design. Different coding systems have been provided by other organizations in particular subfields such as power plants or roadways. Nevertheless, MASTERFORMAT provides a useful starting point for organizing information in different construction domains.

In devising organizational codes for project activities, there is a continual tension between adopting systems that are convenient or expedient for one project or for one project manager and systems appropriate for an entire organization. As a general rule, the record-keeping and communication advantages of standard systems are excellent arguments for their adoption. Even in small projects, however, ad hoc or haphazard coding systems can lead to problems as the system is revised and extended over time.

9.8 REFERENCES

9-1. Baracco-Miller E. "Planning for Construction," unpublished MS thesis, Department of Civil Engineering, Carnegie Mellon University, Pittsburgh, 1987.

9-2. Construction Specifications Institute, *MASTERFORMAT—Master List of Section Titles and Numbers,* The Construction Specifications Institute, Alexandria, VA, 1983.

9-3. Jackson M. J. *Computers in Construction Planning and Control,* Allen & Unwin, London, 1986.

9-4. Sacerdoti E. D. *A Structure for Plans and Behavior,* Elsevier North-Holland, New York, 1977.

9-5. Zozaya-Gorostiza C., C. Hendrickson and D.R. Rehak, *Knowledge-Based Process Planning for Construction and Manufacturing,* Academic Press, Cambridge MA, 1989.

9.9 PROBLEMS

P9-1. Develop an alternative work breakdown for the activities shown in Figure 9-2 (Example 9-3). Begin first with a spatial division on the site (i.e., by roadway segment and structure number), and then include functional divisions to develop a different hierarchy of activities.

P9-2. Consider a cold-weather structure built by inflating a special rubber tent, spraying water on the tent, letting the water freeze, and then de-flating and removing the tent. Develop a work breakdown for this structure and precedence relationships . Assume that the tent is 20 feet by 15 feet by 8 feet tall.

P9-3. Develop a work breakdown and activity network for the project of designing a tower to support a radio transmission antenna on the ground. Use less than 15 activities.

P9-4. Select a vacant site in your vicinity and define the various activities and precedences among these activities that would be required to prepare the site for the placement of prefabricated residences.

P9-5. Develop precedence relationships for the roadway project activities appearing in Figure 9-2 (Example 9-3) for one roadway segment including a culvert.

P9-6. Suppose that you have a robot capable of performing two tasks in manipulating blocks on a large tabletop:

- PLACE BLOCK X ON BLOCK Y: This action places the block x on top of the block y. Preconditions for applying this action are that both block x and block y have clear tops (so there is no block on top of x or y). The robot will automatically locate the specified blocks.
- CLEAR BLOCK X: This action removes any block from the top of block x. A necessary precondition for this action is that block x has one and only one block on top. The block removed is placed on the table top.

For this robot, answer the following questions:

a. Using only the two types of robot actions described above, specify a sequence of robot actions to take the five blocks shown in Figure P9-6(a) to the position shown in Figure P9-6(b) in five or six robot actions.

b. Specify a sequence of robot actions to move the blocks from position (b) to position (c) in Figure P9-6 in six moves.

c. Develop an activity network for the robot actions in moving from position (b) to position (c) in Figure P9-6. Prepare both activity-on-node and activity-on-branch representations. Are there alternative sequences of activities that the robot might perform to accomplish the desired position?

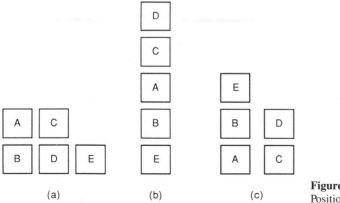

(a)   (b)   (c)

Figure P9-6 Illustrative Block
Positions for Robot Motion Planning

P9-7. In Problem P9-6, suppose that switching from the PLACE BLOCK action to the CLEAR BLOCK action or vice versa requires an extra ten seconds. Movements themselves require 8 seconds. What is the sequence of actions of shortest duration to go from position (b) to position (a) in Figure P9-6?

P9-8. Develop an activity network for the movement in 5 actions from position (a) to position (c) in Figure P9-6. Prepare both activity-on-node and activity-on-branch representations.

P9-9. Repeat Problem P9-7 for the movement in 5 actions from position (a) to position (c) in Figure P9-6 instead of movement from position (b) to position (a).

P9-10. Suppose that you have an enhanced robot with two additional commands capabilities:

- CARRY BLOCKS X-Y to BLOCK Z: This action moves blocks X-Y to the top of block Z. Blocks X-Y may involve any number of blocks as long as X is on the bottom and Y is on the top. This move assumes that Z has a clear top.
- CLEAR ALL BLOCK X TO BLOCK Z: This action moves all blocks on top of block X to the top of block Z. If a block Z is not specified, then the blocks are moved to the table top.

Assume that any switch in command type requires 10 seconds, find the sequence of actions with the shortest duration for moving the blocks in Figure P9-6 if the movement is

(i) from position (a) to position (b)

(ii) from position (b) to position (c)

P9-11. The productivities P of a standard crew for assembling concrete formwork under five different weather conditions together with the probabilities of their occurrences have been observed as indicated below. The corresponding time T required to complete a unit of work by a standard crew under each weather condition is defined as the reciprocal of P. Show that the expected value of P is 23 yd^2/hr and the reciprocal of the expected value of T is 22.93 yd^2/hr.

Weather	Probability	P(yd^2/hr)	T (hr/yd^2)
Excellent	0.15	25	1/25
Good	0.20	24	1/24
Fair	0.30	23	1/23
Poor	0.20	22	1/22
Very bad	0.15	21	1/21

P9-12. If the probabilities in Problem P9-11 represent the results from a total of 100 observations, i.e., 15 times each for excellent or very bad weather, 20 times each for good or poor weather and 30 times for fair weather, find the estimated standard deviation of the reciprocal of productivity.

P9-13. A building project requires the assembly of 10,00 yd^2 of concrete for framework. If the average productivity of a standard crew for performing the task is 23 yd^2/hr and the number of crews assigned to the task is 5, what is the estimated duration of this task?

P9-14. If the standard deviation of the reciprocal of productivity obtained in Problem P9-12 is found to be 0.0024 hr/yd^2, find the standard deviation of the duration of a task requiring the assembly of 10,000 yd^2 of concrete framework with 5 crews assigned to the task.

10

Fundamental Scheduling Procedures

10.1 RELEVANCE OF CONSTRUCTION SCHEDULES

In addition to assigning dates to project activities, project scheduling is intended to match the resources of equipment, materials, and labor with project work tasks over time. Good scheduling can eliminate problems due to production bottlenecks, facilitate the timely procurement of necessary materials, and otherwise ensure the completion of a project as soon as possible. In contrast, poor scheduling can result in considerable waste as laborers and equipment wait for the availability of needed resources or the completion of preceding tasks. Delays in the completion of an entire project due to poor scheduling can also create havoc for owners who are eager to start using the constructed facilities.

Attitudes toward the formal scheduling of projects are often extreme. Many owners require detailed construction schedules to be submitted by contractors as a means of monitoring the work progress. The actual work performed is commonly compared to the schedule to determine if construction is proceeding satisfactorily. After the completion of construction, similar comparisons between the planned schedule and the actual accomplishments may be performed to allocate the liability for project delays due to changes requested by the owner, worker strikes, or other unforeseen circumstances.

In contrast to these instances of reliance upon formal schedules, many field supervisors disdain and dislike formal scheduling procedures. In particular, the *critical path method* of scheduling is commonly required by owners and has been taught in universities for over two decades, but is often regarded in the field as irrelevant to actual operations and a time-consuming distraction. The result is "seat-of-the-pants" scheduling that can be good or that can result in grossly inefficient schedules and poor productivity. Progressive construction firms use formal scheduling procedures whenever the complexity of work tasks is high and the coordination of different workers is required.

With the continued development of easy-to-use computer programs and improved methods of presenting schedules, many of the practical problems associated with formal scheduling mechanisms are being overcome. But problems with the use of scheduling techniques will continue until managers understand their proper use and limitations.

A basic distinction exists between *resource-oriented* and *time-oriented* scheduling techniques. For resource oriented scheduling, the focus is on using and scheduling particular resources in an effective fashion. For example, the project manager's main concern on a highrise building site might be to ensure that cranes are used effectively for moving materials; without effective scheduling in this case, delivery trucks might queue on the ground and workers wait for deliveries on upper floors. For time-oriented scheduling, the emphasis is on determining the completion time of the project given the necessary precedence relationships among activities. Hybrid techniques for resource-leveling or resource-constrained scheduling in the presence of precedence relationships also exist.

This chapter will introduce the fundamentals of scheduling methods. Our discussion will generally assume that computer-based scheduling programs will be applied. Consequently, the wide variety of manual or mechanical scheduling techniques will not be discussed in any detail. These manual methods are not as capable or as convenient as computer-based scheduling. With the availability of these computer-based scheduling programs, it is important for managers to understand the basic operations performed by scheduling programs. Moreover, even if formal methods are not applied in particular cases, the conceptual framework of formal scheduling methods provides a valuable reference for a manager. Accordingly, examples involving hand calculations will be provided throughout the chapter to facilitate understanding.

10.2 THE CRITICAL PATH METHOD

The most widely used scheduling technique is the critical path method (CPM) for scheduling, often referred to as *critical path scheduling*. This method calculates the minimum completion time for a project along with the possible start and finish times for the project activities. Indeed, many texts and managers regard critical path scheduling as the only usable and practical scheduling procedure. Computer programs and algorithms for critical path scheduling are widely available and can efficiently handle projects with thousands of activities.

The *critical path* itself represents the set or sequence of predecessor/successor activities that will take the longest time to complete. The duration of the critical path is the sum of the activities' durations along the path. Thus, the critical path can be defined as the longest possible path through the "network" of project activities, as described in Chapter 9. The duration of the critical path represents the minimum time required to complete a project. Any delays along the critical path would imply that additional time would be required to complete the project. There may be more than one critical path among all the project activities, so completion of the entire project could be delayed by delaying activities along any one of the critical paths.

Formally, critical path scheduling assumes that a project has been divided into activities of fixed duration and well-defined predecessor relationships. No resource constraints other than those implied by precedence relationships are recognized. To use critical path scheduling in practice, construction planners often attempt to represent a *resource constraint* by a precedence relation. A *constraint* is simply a restriction on the options available to a manager, and a *resource constraint* is a constraint deriving from the limited availability of some resource of equipment, material, space, or labor. For example, one of two activities requiring the same piece of equipment might be arbitrarily assumed to precede the other activity. This artificial precedence constraint ensures that the two activities requiring the same resource will not be scheduled at the same time. Also, most critical path scheduling algorithms impose restrictions on the generality of the activity relationships or network geometries which are used. In essence, these restrictions imply that the construction plan can be represented by a network plan in which activities appear as links or "branches" in a network, as in Figure 9-5, or activities appear as nodes in a network, as in Figure 9-6. In the first representation, nodes in the network represent events or milestones. Nodes are numbered, and no two nodes can have the same number or designation. Activities themselves are usually referenced by their predecessor and successor node numbers. Two nodes are introduced to represent the start and completion of the project itself.

The actual computer representation of the project schedule generally consists of a list of activities along with their associated durations, required resources, and predecessor activities. Graphical network representations rather than a list are helpful for visualization of the plan and for ensuring that mathematical requirements are met. The actual input of the data to a computer program may be accomplished by filling in blanks on a screen menu, reading an existing datafile, or typing data directly to the program with identifiers for the type of information being provided.

With an activity-on-branch network, dummy activities may be introduced for the purposes of providing unique activity designations and maintaining the correct sequence of activities. A *dummy activity* is assumed to have no time duration and can be graphically represented by a dashed line in a network. Several cases in which dummy activities are useful are illustrated in Figure 10-1. In Figure 10-1(a), the elimination of activity C would mean that both activities B and D would be identified as being between nodes 1 and 3. However, if a dummy activity X is introduced, as shown in part (b) of the figure, the unique designations for activity B (node 1 to 2) and D (node 2 to 3) will be preserved. Furthermore, if the problem in part (a) is changed so that activity E cannot start until both C and D are completed but that F can start after D alone is completed, the order in the new sequence can be indicated by the addition of a dummy activity Y, as shown in part (c). In general, dummy activities may be necessary to meet the requirements of specific computer

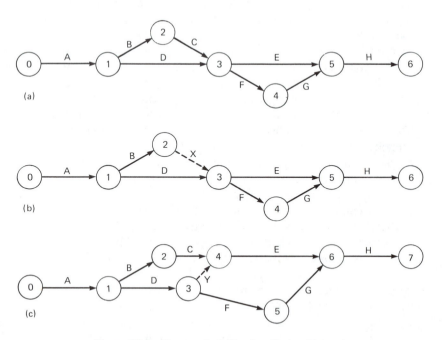

Figure 10-1 Dummy Activities in a Project Network

scheduling algorithms, but it is important to limit the number of such dummy link insertions to the extent possible.

Example 10-1: Formulating a Network Diagram

Suppose that we wish to form an activity network for a seven-activity network with the following precedences:

Activity	Predecessors
A	—
B	—
C	A, B
D	C
E	C
F	D
G	D, E

Forming an activity-on-branch network for this set of activities might begin by drawing activities A, B, and C as shown in Figure 10-2(a). At this point, we note that two activities (A and B) lie between the same two event nodes; for clarity, we insert a

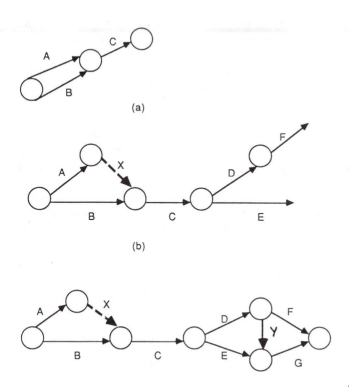

(a)

(b)

(c)

Figure 10-2 An Activity-on-Branch Network for Critical Path Scheduling

dummy activity X and continue to place other activities as in Figure 10-2(b). Placing activity G in the figure presents a problem, however, since we wish both activity D and activity E to be predecessors. Inserting an additional dummy activity Y along with activity G completes the activity network, as shown in Figure 10-2(c). A comparable activity-on-node representation is shown in Figure 10-3, including project start and finish nodes. Note that dummy activities are not required for expressing precedence relationships in activity-on-node networks.

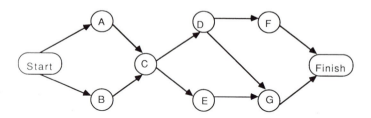

Figure 10-3   Example of an Activity-on-Node Network for Critical Path Scheduling

10.3 CALCULATIONS FOR CRITICAL PATH SCHEDULING

With the background provided by the previous sections, we can formulate the critical path scheduling mathematically. We shall present an algorithm or set of instructions for critical path scheduling assuming an activity-on-branch project network. We also assume that all precedences are of a finish-to-start nature, so that a succeeding activity cannot start until the completion of a preceding activity. In a later section, we present a comparable algorithm for activity-on-node representations with multiple precedence types.

Suppose that our project network has $n + 1$ nodes, the initial event being 0 and the last event being n. Let the time at which node events occur be $x_1, x_2, \ldots, x_n$, respectively. The start of the project at x_0 will be defined as time 0. Nodal event times must be consistent with activity durations, so that an activity's successor node event time must be larger than an activity's predecessor node event time plus its duration. For an activity defined as starting from event i and ending at event j, this relationship can be expressed as the inequality constraint, $x_j \geq x_i + D_{ij}$ where D_{ij} is the duration of activity (i,j). This same expression can be written for every activity and must hold true in any feasible schedule. Mathematically, then, the critical path scheduling problem is to minimize the time of project completion (x_n) subject to the constraints that each node completion event cannot occur until each of the predecessor activities has been completed:

Minimize $$z = x_n \tag{10.1}$$

subject to

$$x_0 = 0$$

$$x_j - x_i - D_{ij} \geq 0 \text{ for each activity } (i,j)$$

Fundamental Scheduling Procedures   Chap. 10

This is a linear programming problem since the objective value to be minimized and each of the constraints is a linear equation.[76]

Rather than solving the critical path scheduling problem with a linear programming algorithm (such as the simplex method), more efficient techniques are available that take advantage of the network structure of the problem. These solution methods are very efficient with respect to the required computations, so that very large networks can be treated even with small microcomputers. These methods also give some very useful information about possible activity schedules. The programs can compute the earliest and latest possible starting times for each activity which are consistent with completing the project in the shortest possible time. This calculation is of particular interest for activities which are not on the critical path (or paths), since these activities might be slightly delayed or rescheduled over time as a manager desires without delaying the entire project.

An efficient solution process for critical path scheduling based upon node labeling is shown in Table 10-1. Three algorithms appear in the table. The *event numbering algorithm* numbers the nodes (or events) of the project such that the beginning event has a lower number than the ending event for each activity. Technically,

---

TABLE 10–1 CRITICAL PATH SCHEDULING ALGORITHMS (ACTIVITY-ON-BRANCH REPRESENTATION)

Event numbering algorithm

Step 1: Give the starting event number 0.

Step 2: Give the next number to any unnumbered event whose predecessor events are each already numbered.

Repeat step 2 until all events are numbered.

Earliest event time algorithm

Step 1: Let $E(0) = 0$.

Step 2: For $j = 1, 2, 3, \ldots, n$ (where n is the last event), let
$$E(j) = \text{maximum} \left\{ E(i) + D_{ij} \right\}$$
  where the maximum is computed over all activities (i, j) that have j as the ending event.

Latest event time algorithm

Step 1: Let $L(n)$ equal the required completion time of the project. Note: $L(n)$ must equal or exceed $E(n)$.

Step 2: For $i = n - 1, n - 2, \ldots, 0$, let
$$L(i) = \text{minimum} \left\{ L(j) - D_{ij} \right\}$$
  where the minimum is computed over all activities (i, j) that have i as the starting event.

---

[76] See T. Au, *Introduction to Systems Engineering, Deterministic Models*, Addison-Wesley Publishing Co., Inc., Reading, MA, 1973, for a detailed description of linear programming as a form of mathematical optimization.

this algorithm accomplishes a "topological sort" of the activities. The project start node is given number 0. As long as the project activities fulfill the conditions for an activity-on-branch network, this type of numbering system is always possible. Some software packages for critical path scheduling do not have this numbering algorithm programmed, so that the construction project planners must ensure that appropriate numbering is done.

The *earliest event time algorithm* computes the earliest possible time, $E(i)$, at which each event, i, in the network can occur. Earliest event times are computed as the maximum of the earliest start times plus activity durations for each of the activities immediately preceding an event. The earliest start time for each activity (i,j) is equal to the earliest possible time for the preceding event $E(i)$:

$$ES(i,j) = E(i) \tag{10.2}$$

The earliest finish time of each activity (i,j) can be calculated by:

$$EF(i,j) = E(i) + D_{ij} \tag{10.3}$$

Activities are identified in this algorithm by the predecessor node (or event) i and the successor node j. The algorithm simply requires that each event in the network should be examined in turn beginning with the project start (node 0).

The *latest event time algorithm* computes the latest possible time, $L(j)$, at which each event j in the network can occur, given the desired completion time of the project, $L(n)$ for the last event n. Usually, the desired completion time will be equal to the earliest possible completion time, so that $E(n) = L(n)$ for the final node n. The procedure for finding the latest event time is analogous to that for the earliest event time except that the procedure begins with the final event and works backward through the project activities. Thus, the earliest event time algorithm is often called a *forward pass* through the network, whereas the latest event time algorithm is the *backward pass* through the network. The latest finish time consistent with completion of the project in the desired time frame of $L(n)$ for each activity (i,j) is equal to the latest possible time $L(j)$ for the succeeding event:

$$LF(i,j) = L(j) \tag{10.4}$$

The latest start time of each activity (i,j) can be calculated by

$$LS(i,j) = L(j) - D_{ij} \tag{10.5}$$

The earliest start and latest finish times for each event are useful pieces of information in developing a project schedule. Events which have equal earliest and latest times, $E(i) = L(i)$, lie on the critical path or paths. An activity (i,j) is a critical activity if it satisfies all of the following conditions:

$$E(i) = L(i) \tag{10.6}$$

$$E(j) = L(j) \tag{10.7}$$

$$E(i) + D_{ij} = L(j) \tag{10.8}$$

Hence, activities between critical events are also on a critical path as long as the activity's earliest start time equals its latest start time, $ES(i,j) = LS(i,j)$. To avoid delaying the project, all the activities on a critical path should begin as soon as possible, so each critical activity (i,j) must be scheduled to begin at the earliest possible start time, $E(i)$.

Example 10-2: Critical Path Scheduling Calculations

Consider the network shown in Figure 10-4 in which the project start is given number 0. Then, the only event that has each predecessor numbered is the successor to activity A, so it receives number 1. After this, the only event that has each predecessor numbered is the successor to the two activities B and C, so it receives number 2. The other event numbers resulting from the algorithm are also shown in the figure. For this simple project network, each stage in the numbering process found only one possible event to number at any time. With more than one feasible event to number, the choice of which to number next is arbitrary. For example, if activity C did not exist in the project for Figure 10-4, the successor event for activity A or for activity B could have been numbered 1.

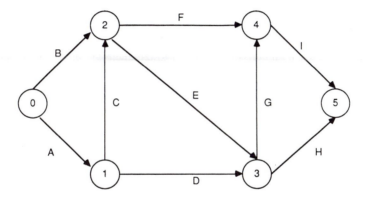

Figure 10-4   A Nine-Activity Project Network

For the network in Figure 10-4 with activity durations in Table 10-2, the earliest event time calculations proceed as follows:

$$\text{Step 1} \rightarrow \quad E(0) = 0$$

Step 2

$$j = 1 \rightarrow \quad E(1) = \max \{E(0) + D_{01}\}$$
$$= \max \{0 + 4\} = 4$$

$$j = 2 \rightarrow \quad E(2) = \max \{E(0) + D_{02}; E(1) + D_{12}\}$$
$$= \max \{0 + 3; 4 + 8\} = 12$$

$$j = 3 \rightarrow \quad E(3) = \max \{E(1) + D_{13}; E(2) + D_{23}\}$$
$$= \max \{4 + 7; 12 + 9\} = 21$$

$$j = 4 \rightarrow \quad E(4) = \max \{E(2) + D_{24}; \; E(3) + D_{34}\}$$

$$= \max \{12 + 12; \; 21 + 2\} = 24$$

$$j = 5 \rightarrow \quad E(5) = \max \{E(3) + D_{35}; \; E(4) + D_{45}\}$$

$$= \max \{21 + 5; \; 24 + 6\} = 30$$

TABLE 10-2 PRECEDENCE RELATIONS AND DURATIONS FOR A NINE-ACTIVITY PROJECT EXAMPLE

Activity	Description	Predecessors	Duration
A	Site clearing	—	4
B	Removal of trees	—	3
C	General excavation	A	8
D	Grading general area	A	7
E	Excavation for trenches	B, C	9
F	Placing formwork and reinforcement for concrete	B, C	12
G	Installing sewer lines	D, E	2
H	Installing other utilities	D, E	5
I	Pouring concrete	F, G	6

Thus, the minimum time required to complete the project is 30 since $E(5) = 30$. In this case, each event had at most two predecessors.

For the "backward pass", the latest event time calculations are

$$\text{Step 1} \rightarrow \quad L(5) = E(5) = 30$$

Step 2

$$j = 4 \rightarrow \quad L(4) = \min \{L(5) - D_{45}\}$$

$$= \min \{30 - 6\} = 24$$

$$j = 3 \rightarrow \quad L(3) = \min \{L(5) - D_{35}; \; L(4) - D_{34}\}$$

$$= \min \{30 - 5; \; 24 - 2\} = 22$$

$$j = 2 \rightarrow \quad L(2) = \min \{L(4) - D_{24}; \; L(3) - D_{23}\}$$

$$= \min \{24 - 12; \; 22 - 9\} = 12$$

$$j = 1 \rightarrow \quad L(1) = \min \{L(3) - D_{13}; \; L(2) - D_{12}\}$$

$$= \min \{22 - 7; \; 12 - 8\} = 4$$

$$j = 0 \rightarrow \quad L(0) = \min \{L(2) - D_{02}; \; L(1) - D_{01}\}$$

$$= \min \{12 - 3; \; 4 - 4\} = 0$$

In this example, $E(0) = L(0), E(1) = L(1), E(2) = L(2), E(4) = L(4)$, and $E(5) = L(5)$. As a result, all nodes but node 3 are in the critical path. Activities on the critical path include C (1, 2), F (2, 4), and I (4, 5) as shown in Table 10-3.

TABLE 10–3 IDENTIFICATION OF ACTIVITIES ON THE CRITICAL PATH FOR A NINE-ACTIVITY PROJECT

Activity	Duration $D_{i,j}$	Earliest start time $E(i) = ES(ij)$	Latest finish time $L(j) = LF(ij)$	Latest start time $LS(i,j)$
A (0, 1)	4	0*	4*	0
B (0, 2)	3	0	12	9
C (1, 2)	8	4*	12*	4
D (1, 3)	7	4	22	15
E (2, 3)	9	12	22	13
F (2, 4)	12	12*	24*	12
G (3, 4)	2	21	24	22
H (3, 5)	5	21	30	25
I (4, 5)	6	24	30*	24

*Activity on a critical path since $E(i) + D_{i,j} = L(j)$.

10.4 ACTIVITY FLOAT AND SCHEDULES

A number of different activity schedules can be developed from the critical path scheduling procedure described in the previous section. An *earliest time* schedule would be developed by starting each activity as soon as possible, at $ES(i,j)$. Similarly, a *latest time* schedule would delay the start of each activity as long as possible but still finish the project in the minimum possible time. This late schedule can be developed by setting each activity's start time to $LS(i,j)$.

Activities that have different early and late start times (i.e., $ES(i,j) < LS(i,j)$) can be scheduled to start anytime between $ES(i,j)$ and $LS(i,j)$ as shown in Figure 10-5. The concept of *float* is to use part or all of this allowable range to schedule an activity without delaying the completion of the project. An activity that has the earliest time for its predecessor and successor nodes differing by more than its duration possesses a "float" in which it can be scheduled. That

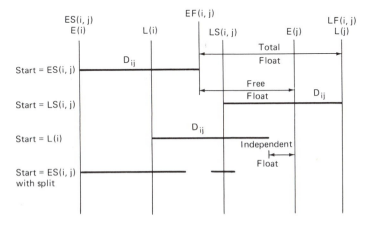

Figure 10-5 Activity Float

is, if $E(i) + D_{ij} < L(j)$, then some float is available in which to schedule this activity.

Float is a very valuable concept since it represents the scheduling flexibility or "maneuvering room" available to complete particular tasks. Activities on the critical path do not provide any flexibility for scheduling or leeway in case of problems. For activities with some float, the actual starting time might be chosen to balance work loads over time, to correspond with material deliveries, or to improve the project's cash flow.

Of course, if one activity is allowed to float or change in the schedule, then the amount of float available for other activities may decrease. Three separate categories of float are defined in critical path scheduling:

1. *Free float* is the amount of delay that can be assigned to any one activity without delaying subsequent activities. The free float, $FF(i,j)$, associated with activity (i,j) is

$$FF(i,j) = E(j) - E(i) - D_{ij} \qquad (10.9)$$

2. *Independent float* is the amount of delay that can be assigned to any one activity without delaying subsequent activities or restricting the scheduling of preceding activities. Independent float, $IF(i,j)$, for activity (i,j) is calculated as

$$IF(i,j) = \max \begin{Bmatrix} 0 \\ E(j) - L_{(i)} - D_{ij} \end{Bmatrix} \qquad (10.10)$$

3. *Total float* is the maximum amount of delay which can be assigned to any activity without delaying the entire project. The total float, $TF(i,j)$, for any activity (i,j) is calculated as

$$TF(i,j) = L(j) - E(i) - D_{(ij)} \qquad (10.11)$$

Each of these floats indicates an amount of flexibility associated with an activity. In all cases, total float equals or exceeds free float, while independent float is always less than or equal to free float. Also, any activity on a critical path has all three values of float equal to zero. The converse of this statement is also true, so any activity which has zero total float can be recognized as being on a critical path.

The various categories of activity float are illustrated in Figure 10-5 in which the activity is represented by a bar which can move back and forth in time depending upon its scheduling start. Three possible scheduled starts are shown, corresponding to the cases of starting each activity at the earliest event time, $E(i)$, the latest activity start time $LS(i,j)$, and at the latest event time $L(i)$. The three categories of float can be found directly from this figure. Finally, a fourth bar is included in the figure to illustrate the possibility that an activity might start, be temporarily halted, and then restart. In this case, the temporary halt was sufficiently short that it was less than the independent float time and thus would not interfere with other activities. Whether or not such work splitting is possible or economical depends upon the nature of the activity.

As shown in Table 10-5, activity D (1, 3) has free and independent floats of 10 for the project shown in Figure 10-4. Thus, the start of this activity could be scheduled anytime between time 4 and 14 after the project began without interfering with the schedule of other activities or with the earliest completion time of the project. As the total float of 11 units indicates, the start of activity D could also be delayed until time 15, but this would require that the schedule of other activities be restricted. For example, starting activity D at time 11 would required that activity G would begin as soon as activity D was completed. However, if this schedule was maintained, the overall completion date of the project would not be changed.

Example 10-3: Critical Path for a Fabrication Project

As another example of critical path scheduling, consider the seven activities associated with the fabrication of a steel component shown in Table 10-4. Figure 10-6 shows the network diagram associated with these seven activities. Note that an additional dummy activity X has been added to ensure that the correct precedence relationships are maintained for activity E. A simple rule to observe is that if an activity has more than one immediate predecessor and another activity has at least one but not all of these predecessor activity as a predecessor, a dummy activity will be required to maintain precedence relationships. Thus, in the figure, activity E has activities B and C as predecessors, while activity D has only activity C as a predecessor. Hence, a dummy activity is required. Node numbers have also been added to this figure using the procedure outlined in Table 10-1. Note that the node numbers on nodes 1 and 2 could have been exchanged in this numbering process since after numbering node 0, either node 1 or node 2 could be numbered next.

TABLE 10-4 PRECEDENCES AND DURATIONS FOR A SEVEN-ACTIVITY PROJECT

Activity	Description	Predecessors	Duration
A	Preliminary design	—	6
B	Evaluation of design	A	1
C	Contract negotiation	—	8
D	Preparation of fabrication plant	C	5
E	Final design	B, C	9
F	Fabrication of product	D, E	12
G	Shipment of product to owner	F	3

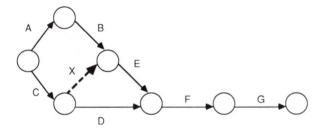

Figure 10-6 A Seven-Activity Project Network

The results of the earliest and latest event time algorithms (appearing in Table 10-1) are shown in Table 10-5. The minimum completion time for the project is 32 days. In this small project, all of the event nodes except node 1 are on the critical path. Table 10-6 shows the earliest and latest start times for the various activities including the different categories of float. Activities C,E,F,G and the dummy activity X are seen to lie on the critical path.

TABLE 10–5 EVENT TIMES FOR A SEVEN-ACTIVITY PROJECT

Node	Earliest time $E(i)$	Latest time $L(j)$
0	0	0
1	6	7
2	8	8
3	8	8
4	17	17
5	29	29
6	32	32

TABLE 10–6 EARLIEST START, LATEST START, AND ACTIVITY FLOATS FOR A SEVEN-ACTIVITY PROJECT

Activity	Earliest start time $ES(i,j)$	Latest start time $LS(i,j)$	Free float	Independent float	Total float
A(0, 1)	0	1	0	0	1
B(1, 3)	6	7	1	0	1
C(0, 2)	0	0	0	0	0
D(2, 4)	8	12	4	4	4
E(3, 4)	8	8	0	0	0
F(4, 5)	17	17	0	0	0
G(5, 6)	29	29	0	0	0
X(2, 3)	8	8	0	0	0

10.5 PRESENTING PROJECT SCHEDULES

Communicating the project schedule is a vital ingredient in successful project management. A good presentation will greatly ease the manager's problem of understanding the multitude of activities and their interrelationships. Moreover, numerous individuals and parties are involved in any project, and they have to understand their assignments. *Graphical* presentations of project schedules are particularly useful since it is much easier to comprehend a graphical display of numerous pieces of information than it is to sift through a large table of numbers. Early computer scheduling systems were particularly poor in this regard since they produced pages and pages of numbers without aids to the manager for understanding them. A short example appears in Tables 10-5 and 10-6; in practice, a project summary table would be much longer. It is extremely tedious to read a table of activity numbers, durations, schedule times, and floats and thereby gain an understanding and appreciation of a project schedule. In practice, producing diagrams manually has been a common prescription to the lack of automated drafting facilities. Indeed, it has been common to use computer programs to perform critical path scheduling and then to produce bar charts of detailed activity schedules and resource assignments manually. With the availability of computer graphics, the cost and effort of producing graphical presentations has been significantly reduced and the production of presentation aids can be automated.

Network diagrams for projects have already been introduced. These diagrams provide a powerful visualization of the precedences and relationships among the various project activities. They are a basic means of communicating a project plan among the participating planners and project monitors. Project planning is often conducted by producing network representations of greater and greater refinement until the plan is satisfactory.

A useful variation on project network diagrams is to draw a *time-scaled* network. The activity diagrams shown in the previous section were topological networks in that only the relationship between nodes and branches were of interest. The actual diagram could be distorted in any way desired as long as the connections between nodes were not changed. In time-scaled network diagrams, activities on the network are plotted on a horizontal axis measuring the time since project commencement. Figure 10-7 gives an example of a time-scaled activity-on-branch diagram for the nine activity project in Figure 10-4. In this time-scaled diagram, each node is shown at its earliest possible time. By looking over the horizontal axis, the time at which activity can begin can be observed. Obviously, this time-scaled diagram is produced as a display after activities are initially scheduled by the critical path method.

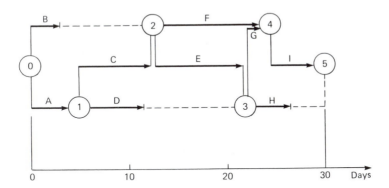

Figure 10-7 A Time Scaled Network Diagram with Nine Activities

Another useful graphical representation tool is a bar or Gantt chart illustrating the scheduled time for each activity. The bar chart lists activities and shows their scheduled start, finish, and duration. An illustrative bar chart for the nine-activity project appearing in Figure 10-4 is shown in Figure 10-8. Activities are listed in the vertical axis of this figure, while time since project commencement is shown along the horizontal axis. During the course of *monitoring* a project, useful additions to the basic bar chart include a vertical line to indicate the current time plus small marks

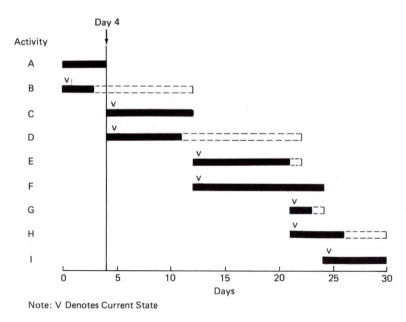

Figure 10-8 Bar Chart for a Nine-Activity Project

to indicate the current state of work on each activity. In Figure 10-8, a hypothetical project state after four periods is shown. The small "v" marks on each activity represent the current state of each activity.

Bar charts are particularly helpful for communicating the current state and schedule of activities on a project. As such, they have found wide acceptance as a project representation tool in the field. For planning purposes, bar charts are not as useful since they do not indicate the precedence relationships among activities. Thus, a planner must remember or record separately that a change in one activity's schedule may require changes to successor activities. There have been various schemes for mechanically linking activity bars to represent precedences, but it is now easier to use computer-based tools to represent such relationships.

Other graphical representations are also useful in project monitoring. Time and activity graphs are extremely useful in portraying the current status of a project as well as the existence of activity float. For example, Figure 10-9 shows two possible schedules for the nine activity project described in Table 9-1 and shown in the previous figures. The first schedule would occur if each activity was scheduled at its earliest start time, $ES(i,j)$ consistent with completion of the project in the minimum possible time. With this schedule, Figure 10-9 shows the percentage of project activity completed versus time. The second schedule in Figure 10-9 is based on latest possible start times for each activity, $LS(i,j)$. The horizontal time difference between the two feasible schedules gives an indication of the extent of possible float. If the project goes according to plan, the actual percentage completion at different times should fall between these curves. In practice, a vertical axis representing cash expenditures rather than percentage completed is often used in

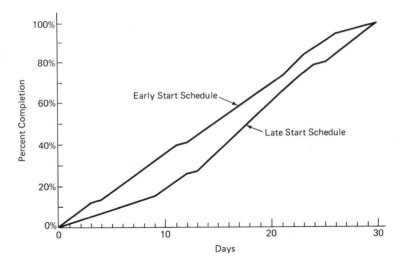

Figure 10-9 Percentage-of-Completion Versus Time for Alternative Schedules with a Nine-Activity Project

developing a project representation of this type. For this purpose, activity cost estimates are used in preparing a time versus completion graph. Separate "S curves" may also be prepared for groups of activities on the same graph, such as separate curves for the design, procurement, foundation, or particular subcontractor activities.

Time versus completion curves are also useful in project monitoring. Not only the history of the project can be indicated, but the future possibilities for earliest and latest start times. For example, Figure 10-10 illustrates a project that is 40 percent

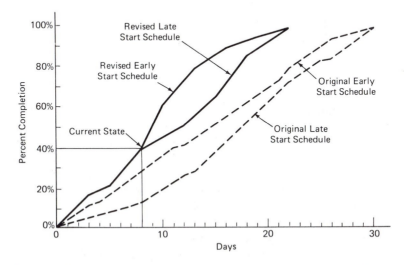

Figure 10-10 Actual Percentage-of-Completion Versus Time for a Nine-Activity Project Underway

complete after eight days for the nine-activity example. In this case, the project is well ahead of the original schedule; some activities were completed in less than their expected durations. The possible earliest and latest start time schedules from the current project status are also shown in the figure.

Graphs of resource use over time are also of interest to project planners and managers. An example of resource use is shown in Figure 10-11 for the resource of total employment on the site of a project. This graph is prepared by summing the resource requirements for each activity at each time period for a particular project schedule. With limited resources of some kind, graphs of this type can indicate when the competition for a resource is too large to accommodate; in cases of this kind, resource-constrained scheduling may be necessary as described in Section 10.9. Even without fixed resource constraints, a scheduler tries to avoid extreme fluctuations in the demand for labor or other resources since these fluctuations typically incur high costs for training, hiring, transportation, and management. Thus, a planner might alter a schedule through the use of available activity floats so as to level or smooth out the demand for resources. Resource graphs such as Figure 10-11 provide an invaluable indication of the potential trouble spots and the success that a scheduler has in avoiding them.

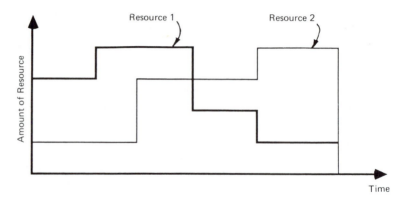

Figure 10-11   Resource Use over Time for a Nine-Activity Project

A common difficulty with project network diagrams is that too much infor-mation is available for easy presentation in a network. In a project with, say, 500 activities, drawing activities so that they can be seen without a microscope requires a considerable expanse of paper. A large project might require the wall space in a room to include the entire diagram. On a computer display, a typical restriction is that less than 20 activities can be successfully displayed at the same time. The problem of displaying numerous activities becomes particularly acute when acces-sory information such as activity identifying numbers or phrases, durations, and resources are added to the diagram.

One practical solution to this representation problem is to define sets of activi-ties that can be represented together as a single activity. That is, for display purposes, network diagrams can be produced in which one "activity" would represent a number

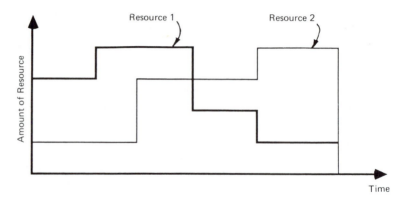

of real subactivities. For example, an activity such as "foundation design" might be inserted in summary diagrams. In the actual project plan, this one activity could be subdivided into numerous tasks with their own precedences, durations and other attributes. These subgroups are sometimes termed *fragnets* for fragments of the full network. The result of this organization is the possibility of producing diagrams that summarize the entire project as well as detailed representations of particular sets of activities. The hierarchy of diagrams can also be introduced to the production of reports so that summary reports for groups of activities can be produced. Thus, detailed representations of particular activities such as plumbing might be prepared with all other activities either omitted or summarized in larger, aggregate activity representations. The MASTERFORMAT activity definition codes described in Chapter 9 provide a widely adopted example of a hierarchical organization of this type. Even if summary reports and diagrams are prepared, the actual scheduling would use detailed activity characteristics, of course.

An example figure of a subnetwork appears in Figure 10-12. Summary displays would include only a single node A to represent the set of activities in the subnetwork. Note that precedence relationships shown in the master network would have to be interpreted with care since a particular precedence might be due to an activity that would not commence at the start of activity on the subnetwork.

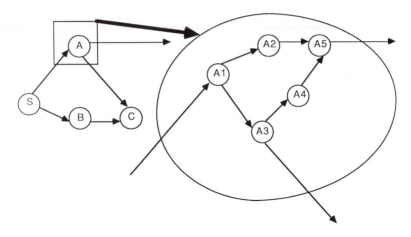

Figure 10-12   A Subnetwork in a Summary Diagram

The use of graphical project representations is an important and extremely useful aid to planners and managers. Of course, detailed numerical reports may also be required to check the peculiarities of particular activities. But graphs and diagrams provide an invaluable means of rapidly communicating or understanding a project schedule. With computer based storage of basic project data, graphical output is readily obtainable and should be used whenever possible.

Finally, the scheduling procedure described in Section 10.3 simply counted days from the initial starting point. Practical scheduling programs include a calendar conversion to provide calendar dates for scheduled work as well as the number of days from the initiation of the project. This conversion can be accomplished by establishing a one-to-one correspondence between project dates and calendar dates. For example, project day 2 would be May 4 if the project began at time 0 on May 2 and no holidays intervened. In this calendar conversion, weekends and holidays would be excluded from consideration for scheduling, although the planner might overrule this feature. Also, the number of work shifts or working hours in each day could be defined, to provide consistency with the time units used is estimating activity durations. Project reports and graphs would typically use actual calendar days.

10.6 CRITICAL PATH SCHEDULING WITH LEADS, LAGS, AND WINDOWS

Building on the critical path scheduling calculations described in the previous sections, some additional capabilities are useful. Desirable extensions include the definition of allowable *windows* for activities and the introduction of more complicated precedence relationships among activities. For example, a planner may wish to have an activity of removing formwork from a new building component *follow* the concrete pour by some predefined lag period to allow setting. This delay would represent a required gap between the completion of a preceding activity and the start of a successor. The scheduling calculations to accommodate these complications will be described in this section. Again, the standard critical path scheduling assumptions of fixed activity durations and unlimited resource availability will be made here, although these assumptions will be relaxed in later sections.

A capability of many scheduling programs is to incorporate types of activity interactions in addition to the straightforward predecessor finish to successor start constraint used in Section 10.3. Incorporation of additional categories of interactions is often called *precedence diagramming*.[77] For example, it may be the case that installing concrete forms in a foundation trench might begin a few hours after the start of the trench excavation. This would be an example of a start-to-start constraint with a lead: the start of the trench-excavation activity would lead the start of the concrete-form-placement activity by a few hours. Eight separate categories of precedence constraints can be defined, representing greater than (leads) or less than (lags) time constraints for each of four different interactivity relationships. These relationships are summarized in Table 10-7. Typical precedence relationships would be

- **Direct or finish-to-start leads**
  The successor activity cannot start until the preceding activity is complete by at least the prescribed lead time *(FS)*. Thus, the earliest start of a successor activity must exceed the latest finish of the preceding activity by at least *FS*.

[77] See K. C. Crandall, "Project Planning with Precedence Lead/Lag Factors," *Project Management Quarterly*, Vol. 4, no. 3, September 1973, pp. 18–27, or J. J. Moder, C. R. Phillips, and E. W. Davis, *Project Management with CPM, PERT and Precedence Diagramming*, 3rd ed., Van Nostrand Reinhold Co., New York, 1983, Chapter 4.

- **Start-to-start leads**

  The successor activity cannot start until work on the preceding activity has been underway by at least the prescribed lead time *(SS)*.

- **Finish-to-finish lags**

  The successor activity must have at least *FF* periods of work remaining at the completion of the preceding activity.

- **Start-to-finish lags**

  The successor activity must have at least *SF* periods of work remaining at the start of the preceding activity.

TABLE 10–7 EIGHT POSSIBLE ACTIVITY PRECEDENCE RELATIONSHIPS

Relationship	Explanation
Finish-to-start lead	
	Latest finish of predecessor $\geq$ earliest start of successor $+$ *FS*
Finish-to-start lag	
	Latest finish of predecessor $\leq$ earliest start of successor $+$ *FS*
Start-to-start lead	
	Earliest start of predecessor $\geq$ earliest start of successor $+$ *SS*
Start-to-start lag	
	Earliest start of predecessor $\leq$ earliest start of successor $+$ *SS*
Finish-to-finish lead	
	Latest finish of predecessor $\geq$ earliest finish of successor $+$ *FF*
Finish-to-finish lag	
	Latest finish of predecessor $\leq$ earliest finish of successor $+$ *FF*
Start-to-finish lead	
	Earliest start of predecessor $\geq$ earliest finish of successor $+$ *SF*
Start-to-finish lag	
	Earliest start of predecessor $\leq$ earliest finish of successor $+$ *SF*

While the eight precedence relationships in Table 10-7 are all possible, the most common precedence relationship is the straightforward direct precedence between the finish of a preceding activity and the start of the successor activity with no required gap (so $FS = 0$).

The computations with these lead and lag constraints are somewhat more complicated variations on the basic calculations defined in Table 10-1 for critical path scheduling. For example, a start-to-start lead would modify the calculation of the earliest start time to consider whether or not the necessary lead constraint was met:

$$E(j) = \max \{E(i) + D_{ij}; E(i) + SS_{ij}\} \qquad (10.12)$$

where SS_{ij} represents a start-to-start lead between activity (i,j) and any of the activities starting at event j.

The possibility of interrupting or *splitting* activities into two work segments can be particular important to ensure feasible schedules in the case of numerous lead or lag constraints. With activity splitting, an activity is divided into two subactivities with a possible gap or idle time between work on the two subactivities. The computations for scheduling treat each sub-activity separately after a split is made. Splitting is performed to reflect available scheduling flexibility or to allow the development of a feasible schedule. For example, splitting may permit scheduling the early finish of a successor activity at a date *later* than the earliest start of the successor plus its duration. In effect, the successor activity is split into two segments with the later segment scheduled to finish after a particular time. Most commonly, this occurs when a constraint involving the finish time of two activities determines the required finish time of the successor. When this situation occurs, it is advantageous to split the successor activity into two so the first part of the successor activity can start earlier but still finish in accordance with the applicable finish-to-finish constraint.

Finally, the definition of activity *windows* can be extremely useful. An activity window defines a permissible period in which a particular activity may be scheduled. To impose a window constraint, a planner could specify an earliest possible start time for an activity *(WES)* or a latest possible completion time *(WLF)*. Latest possible starts *(WLS)* and earliest possible finishes *(WEF)* might also be imposed. In the extreme, a required start time might be ensured by setting the earliest and latest window start times equal *(WES = WLS)*. These window constraints would be in addition to the time constraints imposed by precedence relationships among the various project activities. Window constraints are particularly useful in enforcing milestone completion requirements on project activities. For example, a milestone activity may be defined with no duration but a latest possible completion time. Any activities preceding this milestone activity cannot be scheduled for completion after the milestone date. Window constraints are actually a special case of the other precedence constraints summarized: windows are constraints in which the predecessor activity is the project start. Thus, an earliest possible start time window *(WES)* is a start-to-start lead.

One related issue is the selection of an appropriate network representation. Generally, the activity-on-branch representation will lead to a more compact diagram and is also consistent with other engineering network representations of structures or circuits.[78] For example, the nine activities shown in Figure 10-4 result in an activity-on-branch network with 6 nodes and 9 branches. In contrast, the comparable activity-on-node network shown in Figure 9-6 has 11 nodes (with the addition of a node for project start and completion) and 15 branches. The activity-on-node diagram is more complicated and more difficult to draw, particularly since branches must be drawn crossing one another. Despite this larger size, an important practical reason to select activity-on-node diagrams is that numerous types of precedence relationships are easier to represent in these diagrams. For example, different symbols might be used on each of the branches in Figure 9-6 to represent direct precedences, start-to-start precedences, start-to-finish precedences, and so on. Alternatively, the beginning and end points of the precedence links can indicate the type of lead or lag precedence relationship. Another advantage of activity-on-node representations

[78] See C. T. Hendrickson and B. N. Janson, "A Common Network Formulation of Several Civil Engineering Problems," *Civil Engineering Systems*, Vol. 1, no. 4, 1984, pp. 195–203.

is that the introduction of dummy links as in Figure 10-1 is not required. Either representation can be used for the critical path scheduling computations described earlier. In the absence of lead and lag precedence relationships, it is more common to select the compact activity-on-branch diagram, although a unified model for this purpose is described in Chapter 11. Of course, one reason to pick activity-on-branch or activity-on-node representations is that particular computer scheduling programs available at a site are based on one representation or the other. Since both representations are in common use, project managers should be familiar with either network representation.

Many commercially available computer scheduling programs include the necessary computational procedures to incorporate windows and many of the various precedence relationships described. Indeed, the term "precedence diagramming" and the calculations associated with these lags seems to have first appeared in the user's manual for a computer scheduling program.[79]

If the construction plan suggests that such complicated lags are important, then these scheduling algorithms should be adopted. In the next section, the various computations associated with critical path scheduling with several types of leads, lags, and windows are presented.

10.7 CALCULATIONS FOR SCHEDULING WITH LEADS, LAGS, AND WINDOWS

Table 10-8 contains an algorithmic description of the calculations required for critical path scheduling with leads, lags, and windows. This description assumes an *activity-on-node* project network representation, since this representation is much easier to use with complicated precedence relationships. The possible precedence relationships accommodated by the procedure contained in Table 10-8 are finish-to-start leads, start-to-start leads, finish-to-finish lags, and start-to-finish lags. Windows for earliest starts or latest finishes are also accommodated. Incorporating other precedence and window types in a scheduling procedure is also possible as described in Chapter 11. With an activity-on-node representation, we assume that an initiation and a termination activity are included to mark the beginning and end of the project. The set of procedures described in Table 10-8 does not provide for automatic splitting of activities.

The first step in the scheduling algorithm is to sort activities such that no higher-numbered activity precedes a lower-numbered activity. With numbered activities, durations can be denoted $D(k)$, where k is the number of an activity. Other activity information can also be referenced by the activity number. Note that node events used in *activity-on-branch* representations are not required in this case.

The forward pass calculations compute an earliest start time $(ES(k))$ and an earliest finish time $(EF(k))$ for each activity in turn (Table 10-8). In computing the earliest start time of an activity k, the earliest start window time *(WES)*, the earliest

[79] See IBM, *Project Management System, Application Description Manual*, (H20-0210), IBM, 1968.

TABLE 10–8 CRITICAL PATH SCHEDULING ALGORITHMS WITH LEADS, LAGS, AND WINDOWS (ACTIVITY-ON-NODE REPRESENTATIONS)

Activity Numbering Algorithm

Step 1: Give the starting activity number 0.

Step 2: Give the next number to any unnumbered activity whose predecessor activities are each already numbered.

Repeat step 2 until all activities are numbered, $k = 0, 1, 2, \ldots, m$

Forward Pass

Step 0: Set the earliest start and the earliest finish of the initial activity to zero, $E(0) = EF(0) = 0$.

Repeat the following steps for each activity $k = 1, 2, \ldots, m$:

Step 1: Compute the earliest start time $(ES(k))$ of activity k:

$ES(k) = \max \{ 0;\ WES(k)$ for the earliest start window time,
$WEF(k) - D(k)$ for the earliest finish window time,
$EF(i) + FS(i, k)$ for each preceding activity with a FS constraint,
$ES(i) + SS(i, k)$ for each preceding activity with a SS constraint,
$EF(i) + FF(i, k) - D(k)$ for each preceding activity with a FF constraint,
$ES(i) + SF(i, k) - D(k)$ for each preceding activity with a SF constraint$\}$

Step 2: Compute the earliest finish time $EF(k)$ of activity k;

$EF(k) = ES(k) + D(k)$

Backward Pass

Step 0: Set the latest finish and latest start of the terminal activity to the early start time:

$LF(m) = LS(m) = ES(m) = EF(m)$

Repeat the following steps for each activity in reverse order, $k = m - 1, m - 2, \ldots, 2, 1, 0$:

Step 1: Compute the latest finish time for activity k:

$LF(k) = \min \{ LF(m), WLF(k)$ for the latest finish window time,
$WLS(k) + D(k)$ for the latest start window time,
$LS(j) - FS(k, j)$ for each succeeding activity with a FS constraint,
$LF(j) - FF(k, j)$ for each succeeding activity with a FF constraint,
$LS(j) - SS(k, j) + D(k)$ for each succeeding activity with a SS constraint,
$LF(j) - SF(k, j) + D(k)$ for each succeeding activity with a SF constraint$\}$

Step 2: Compute the latest start time for activity k;

$LS(k) = LF(k) - D(k)$

---

finish window time *(WEF)*, and each of the various precedence relationships must be considered. Constraints on finish times are included by identifying minimum finish times and then subtracting the activity duration. A default earliest start time of day 0 is also ensured for all activities. A second step in the procedure is to identify each activity's earliest finish time $(EF(k))$.

The backward pass calculations proceed in a manner very similar to those of the forward pass (Table 10-8). In the backward pass, the latest finish and the latest start times for each activity are calculated. In computing the latest finish time, the latest start time is identified which is consistent with precedence constraints on an activity's starting time. This computation requires a minimization over applicable window times and all successor activities. A check for a feasible activity schedule can also be imposed at this point: if the late start time is less than the early start time $(LS(k) < ES(k))$, then the activity schedule is not possible.

The result of the forward and backward pass calculations are the earliest start time, the latest start time, the earliest finish time, and the latest finish time for each activity. The activity float is computed as the latest start time less the earliest start time. Note that window constraints may be instrumental in setting the amount of float, so that activities without any float may either lie on the critical path or be constrained by an allowable window.

To consider the possibility of activity splitting, the various formulas for the forward and backward passes in Table 10-8 must be modified. For example, the possibility of activity splitting due to finish-to-start (FS) and start-to-start lead (SS) precedences must be considered. Considering start-to-start precedence relationships are somewhat complicated since it is important to ensure that the preceding activity has been underway for at least the required lead period of $SF(i,k)$. If the preceding activity was split and the first subactivity was not underway for a sufficiently long period, then the following activity cannot start until the first plus the second sub-activities have been underway for a period equal to $SF(i,k)$. Thus, in setting the earliest start time for an activity, the calculation takes into account the duration of the first subactivity $(DA(i))$ for preceding activities involving a start-to-start lead. Algebraically, the term in the earliest start time calculation pertaining to start-to-start precedence constraints $(ES(i) + SS(i,k))$ has two parts with the possibility of activity splitting:

$$ES(i) + SS(i,k) \text{ for non-split preceding activities}$$
$$\text{or when } DA(i) > SS(i,k) \tag{10.13}$$

$$EF(i) - D(i) + SS(i,k) \text{ for split preceding activities}$$
$$\text{with } DA(i) < SS(i,k) \tag{10.14}$$

where $DA(i)$ is the duration of the first subactivity of the preceding activity.

The computation of earliest finish time involves similar considerations, except that the finish-to-finish and start-to-finish lag constraints are involved. In this case, a maximization over the following terms is required:

$$EF(k) = \max \{ES(k) + D(k)$$

$$EF(i) + FF(i,k) \text{ for each preceding activity with a } FF \text{ precedence},$$

$$ES(i) + SF(i,k) \text{ for each preceding activity with a } SF \text{ precedence}$$
$$\text{and which is not split or has } DA(i) > SF(i,k),$$

$$EF(i) - D(i) + SF(i,k) \text{ for each preceding activity with a}$$
$$SF \text{ precedence and which is split and has } DA(i) < SF(i,k)\}$$

$$\tag{10.15}$$

Finally, the necessity to split an activity is also considered. If the earliest possible finish time is greater than the earliest start time plus the activity duration, then the activity must be split.

Another possible extension of the scheduling computations in Table 10-8 would be to include a duration modification capability during the forward and backward passes. This capability would permit alternative work calendars for different activities or for modifications to reflect effects of time of the year on activity durations. For example, the duration of outside work during winter months would be increased. As another example, activities with weekend work permitted might have their weekday durations shortened to reflect weekend work accomplishments.

Example 10-4: Impacts of Precedence Relationships and Windows

To illustrate the impacts of different precedence relationships and windows, consider a project consisting of only two activities in addition to the start and finish. The start is numbered activity 0, the first activity is number 1, the second activity is number 2, and the finish is activity 3. Each activity is assumed to have a duration of five days. With a direct finish-to-start precedence relationship without a lag, the critical path calculations reveal

$$ES\,(0) = 0$$

$$ES\,(1) = 0$$

$$EF\,(1) = ES\,(1) + D(1) \quad = 0 + 5 = 5$$

$$ES\,(2) = EF\,(1) + FS(1,2) = 5 + 0 = 5$$

$$EF\,(2) = ES\,(2) + D(2) \quad = 5 + 5 = 10$$

$$ES\,(3) = EF\,(2) + FS(2,3) = 10 + 0 = 10 = EF\,(3)$$

So the earliest project completion time is 10 days.

With a start-to-start precedence constraint with a two-day lead, the scheduling calculations are

$$ES\,(0) = 0$$
$$ES\,(1) = 0$$
$$EF\,(1) = ES(1) + D(1) = 0 + 5 = 5$$
$$ES\,(2) = ES(1) + SS(1,2) = 0 + 2 = 2$$
$$EF\,(2) = ES(2) + D(2) = 2 + 5 = 7$$
$$ES\,(3) = EF\,(2) + FS(2,3) = 7 + 0 = 7$$

In this case, activity 2 can begin two days after the start of activity 1 and proceed in parallel with activity 1. The result is that the project completion date drops from 10 days to 7 days.

Finally, suppose that a finish-to-finish precedence relationship exists between activity 1 and activity 2 with a two-day lag. The scheduling calculations are

$$ES\,(0) = 0 = EF\,(0)$$
$$ES\,(1) = EF\,(0) + FS(0,1) = 0 + 0 = 0$$
$$ES\,(1) = ES\,(1) + D\quad(1) = 0 + 5 = 5$$

$$ES\,(2) \;=\; EF\,(1) + FF(1,2) - D(2) = 5 + 2 - 5 = 2$$

$$EF\,(2) \;=\; ES\,(2) + D(2) \;\; = 2 + 5 = 7$$

$$ES\,(3) \;=\; EF\,(2) + FS(2,3) = 7 + 0 = 7 = EF\,(3)$$

In this case, the earliest finish for activity 2 is on day 7 to allow the necessary 2-day lag from the completion of activity 1. The minimum project completion time is again seven days.

Example 10-5: Scheduling in the Presence of Leads, Lags, and Windows

As a second example of the scheduling computations involved in the presence of leads, lags, and windows, we shall perform the calculations required for the project shown in Figure 10-13. Start and end activities are included in the project diagram, making a total of 11 activities. The various windows and durations for the activities are summarized in Table 10-9 and the precedence relationships appear in Table 10-10. Only earliest

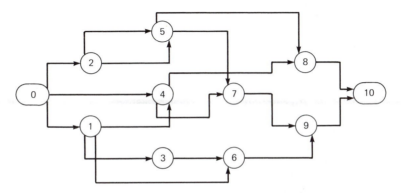

Figure 10-13   Project Network with Lead and Lag Precedences

TABLE 10–9   PREDECESSORS, SUCCESSORS, WINDOWS, AND DURATIONS FOR A SAMPLE PROJECT

Activity number	Predecessors	Successors	Earliest start window	Latest finish window	Activity duration
0	—	1, 2, 4	—	—	0
1	0	3, 4, 6	—	—	2
2	0	3, 4, 6	—	—	5
3	1	6	2	—	4
4	0	7, 8	—	—	3
5	2, 2	7, 8	—	16	5
6	1, 3	9	6	16	6
7	4, 5	9	—	—	2
8	4, 5	10	—	—	4
9	6, 7	10	—	16	5
10	8, 9	—	—	—	0

TABLE 10–10 PRECEDENCES IN AN ELEVEN-ACTIVITY PROJECT EXAMPLE

Predecessor	Successor	Type	Lead or lag
0	1	FS	0
0	2	FS	0
0	4	FS	0
1	3	SS	1
1	4	SF	1
1	6	FS	2
2	5	SS	2
2	5	FF	2
3	6	FS	0
4	7	SS	2
4	8	FS	0
5	7	FS	1
5	8	SS	3
6	9	FF	4
7	9	FS	0
8	10	FS	0
9	10	FS	0

start *(WES)* and latest finish *(WLF)* window constraints are included in this example problem. All four types of precedence relationships are included in this project. Note that two activities may have more than one type of precedence relationship at the same time; in this case, activities 2 and 5 have both SS and FF precedences. In Figure 10-13, the different precedence relationships are shown by links connecting the activity nodes. The type of precedence relationship is indicated by the beginning or end point of each arrow. For example, start-to-start precedences go from the left portion of the preceding activity to the left portion of the following activity. Application of the activity sorting algorithm (Table 10-8) reveals that the existing activity numbers are appropriate for the critical path algorithm. These activity numbers will be used in the forward and backward pass calculations.

During the forward pass calculations (Table 10-8), the earliest start and earliest finish times are computed for each activity. The relevant calculations are

$$ES(0) = EF(0) = 0$$

$$ES(1) = \max\{0; EF(0) + FS(0,1)\} = \max\{0; 0 + 0\} = 0$$

$$EF(1) = ES(1) + D(1) = 0 + 2 = 2$$

$$ES(2) = \max\{0; EF(0) + FS(0,1)\} = \max\{0; 0 + 0\} = 0$$

$$EF(2) = ES(2) + D(2) = 0 + 5 = 5$$

$$ES(3) = \max\{0; WES(3); ES(1) + SS(1,3)\} = \max\{0; 2; 0 + 1\} = 2$$

$$EF(3) = ES(3) + D(3) = 2 + 4 = 6$$

Note that in the calculation of the earliest start for activity 3, the start was delayed to be consistent with the earliest start time window.

$$ES\,(4) \;=\; \max\,\{0; ES\,(0) + FS\,(0,1)\} = \max\,\{0; 0 + 0\} = 0$$
$$EF\,(4) \;=\; ES\,(4) + D(4) = 0 + 3 = 3$$
$$ES\,(5) \;=\; \max\,\{0; ES\,(2) + SS\,(2,5); EF\,(2) + FF\,(2,5) - D(5)\}$$
$$\;=\; \max\,\{0; 0 + 2; 5 + 2 - 5\} = 2$$
$$EF\,(5) \;=\; ES\,(5) + D(5) = 2 + 5 = 7$$

$$ES\,(6) \;=\; \max\,\{0; W\,ES\,(6); EF\,(1) + FS\,(1,6); EF\,(3) + FS\,(3,6)\}$$
$$\;=\; \max\,\{0; 6; 2 + 2; 6 + 0\} = 6$$
$$EF\,(6) \;=\; ES\,(6) + D(6) = 6 + 6 = 12$$

$$ES\,(7) \;=\; \max\,\{0; ES\,(4) + SS\,(4,7); EF\,(5) + FS\,(5,7)\}$$
$$\;=\; \max\,\{0; 0 + 2; 7 + 1\} = 8$$
$$EF\,(7) \;=\; ES\,(7) + D(7) = 8 + 2 = 10$$

$$ES\,(8) \;=\; \max\,\{0; EF\,(4) + FS\,(4,8); ES\,(5) + SS\,(5,8)\}$$
$$\;=\; \max\,\{0; 3 + 0; 2 + 3\} = 5$$
$$EF\,(8) \;=\; ES\,(8) + D(8) = 5 + 4 = 9$$

$$ES\,(9) \;=\; \max\,\{0; EF\,(7) + FS\,(7,9); EF\,(6) + FF\,(6,9) - D(9)\}$$
$$\;=\; \max\,\{0; 10 + 0; 12 + 4 - 5\} = 11$$
$$EF\,(9) \;=\; ES\,(9) + D(9) = 11 + 5 = 16$$

$$ES(10) \;=\; \max\,\{0; EF\,(8) + FS\,(8,10); EF\,(9) + FS\,(9,10)\}$$
$$\;=\; \max\,\{0; 9 + 0; 16 + 0\} = 16$$
$$EF(10) \;=\; ES(10) + D(10) = 16$$

As the result of these computations, the earliest project completion time is found to be 16 days.

The backward pass computations result in the latest finish and latest start times for each activity. These calculations are

$$LF(10) = LS(10) = ES(10) = EF\,(10) = 16$$

$$LF\,(9) = \min\,\{LF\,(10); LS(16) - FS\,(9,10)\} = \min\,\{16; 16 - 0\} = 16$$
$$LS\,(9) = LF\,(9) - D(9) = 16 - 5 = 11$$

$$LF\,(8) = \min\,\{LF\,(10); LS(16) - FS\,(8,10)\} = \min\,\{16; 16 - 0\} = 16$$
$$LS\,(8) = LF\,(8) - D(8) = 16 - 4 = 12$$

$$LF\,(7) = \min\,\{LF\,(10); LS(9) - FS\,(7,9)\} = \min\,\{16; 11 - 0\} = 11$$
$$LS\,(7) = LF\,(7) - D(7) = 11 - 2 = 9$$

$$LS\,(6) = \min\,\{LF\,(10); W\,LF\,(6); LF\,(9) - FF\,(6,9)\}$$
$$= \min\,\{16; 16; 16 - 4\} = 12$$
$$LS\,(6) = LF\,(6) - D(6) = 12 - 6 = 6$$

$$LF\ (5) = \min\ \{LF\ (10); WLF\ (10);$$
$$LS\,(7) - FS(5,7); LS(8) - SS(5,8) + D(8)\}$$
$$= \min\ \{16; 16; 9 - 1; 12 - 3 + 4\} = 8$$
$$LS\ (5) = LF\ (5) - D(5) = 8 - 5 = 3$$

$$LF\ (4) = \min\ \{LF\,(10); LS(8) - FS(4,8); LS(7) - SS(4,7) + D(7)\}$$
$$= \min\ \{16; 12 - 0; 9 - 2 + 2\} = 9$$
$$LS\ (4) = LF\ (4) - D(4) = 9 - 3 = 6$$

$$LF\ (3) = \min\ \{LF\,(10); LS(6) - FS(3,6)\} = \min\ \{16; 6 - 0\} = 6$$
$$LS\ (3) = LF\ (3) - D(3) = 6 - 4 = 2$$

$$LF\ (2) = \min\ \{LF\,(10); LF\,(5) - FF\,(2,5); LS(5) - SS(2,5) + D(5)\}$$
$$= \min\ \{16; 8 - 2; 3 - 2 + 5\} = 6$$
$$LS\ (2) = LF\ (2) - D(2) = 6 - 5 = 1$$

$$LF\ (1) = \min\ \{LF\,(10); LS(6) - FS(1,6); LS(3) - SS(1,3) + D(3);$$
$$LF\,(4) - SF\,(1,4) + D(4)\}$$
$$LS\ (1) = LF\ (1) - D(1) = 2 - 2 = 0$$

$$LF\ (0) = \min\ \{LF\,(10); LS(1) - FS(0,1);$$
$$LS(2) - FS(0,2); LS(4) - FS(0,4)\}$$
$$= \min\ \{16; 0 - 0; 1 - 0; 6 - 0\} = 0$$
$$LS\ (0) = LF\ (0) - D(0) = 0$$

The earliest and latest start times for each of the activities are summarized in Table 10-11. Activities without float are 0, 1, 6, 9, and 10. These activities also constitute the critical path in the project. Note that activities 6 and 9 are related by a finish-to-finish precedence with a four-day lag. Decreasing this lag would result in a reduction in the overall project duration.

TABLE 10–11 SUMMARY OF ACTIVITY START AND FINISH TIMES FOR A SAMPLE PROBLEM

Activity	Earliest start	Latest start	Float
0	0	0	0
1	0	0	0
2	0	1	1
3	0	2	2
4	0	6	6
5	2	3	1
6	6	6	0
7	8	9	1
8	5	12	7
9	11	11	0
10	16	16	0

10.8 RESOURCE-ORIENTED SCHEDULING

Resource-constrained scheduling should be applied whenever there are limited resources available for a project and the competition for these resources among the project activities is keen. In effect, delays are liable to occur in such cases as activities must wait until common resources become available. To the extent that resources are limited and demand for the resource is high, this waiting may be considerable. In turn, the congestion associated with these waits represents increased costs, poor productivity, and, in the end, project delays. Schedules made without consideration for such bottlenecks can be completely unrealistic.

Resource-constrained scheduling is of particular importance in managing multiple projects with fixed resources of staff or equipment. For example, a design office has an identifiable staff which must be assigned to particular projects and design activities. When the work-load is heavy, the designers may fall behind on completing their assignments. Government agencies are particularly prone to the problems of fixed staffing levels, although some flexibility in accomplishing tasks is possible through the mechanism of contracting work to outside firms. Construction activities are less susceptible to this type of problem since it is easier and less costly to hire additional personnel for the (relatively) short duration of a construction project. Overtime or double shift work also provides some flexibility.

Resource-oriented scheduling also is appropriate in cases in which unique resources are to be used. For example, scheduling excavation operations when only one excavator is available is simply a process of assigning work tasks or job segments on a day-by-day basis while ensuring that appropriate precedence relationships are maintained. Even with more than one resource, this manual assignment process may be quite adequate. However, a planner should be careful to ensure that necessary precedences are maintained.

Resource-constrained scheduling represents a considerable challenge and source of frustration to researchers in mathematics and operations research. While algorithms for optimal solutions of the resource-constrained problem exist, they are generally too computationally expensive to be practical for all but small networks (of less than about 100 nodes).[80] The difficulty of the resource-constrained project scheduling problem arises from the combinatorial explosion of different resource assignments which can be made and the fact that the decision variables are integer values representing all-or-nothing assignments of a particular resource to a particular activity. In contrast, simple critical path scheduling deals with continuous time variables. Construction projects typically involve many activities, so optimal solution techniques for resource allocation are not practical.

One possible simplification of the resource-oriented scheduling problem is

---

[80] A variety of mathematical programming techniques have been proposed for this problem. For a review and comparison, see J. H. Patterson, "A Comparison of Exact Approaches for Solving the Multiple Constrained Resource Project Scheduling Problem," *Management Science*, Vol. 30, no. 7, 1984, pp. 854–867.

to ignore precedence relationships. In some applications, it may be impossible or unnecessary to consider precedence constraints among activities. In these cases, the focus of scheduling is usually on efficient utilization of project resources. To ensure minimum cost and delay, a project manager attempts to minimize the amount of time that resources are unused and to minimize the waiting time for scarce resources. This resource-oriented scheduling is often formalized as a problem of "job shop" scheduling in which numerous tasks are to be scheduled for completion and a variety of discrete resources need to perform operations to complete the tasks. Reflecting the original orientation toward manufacturing applications, tasks are usually referred to as "jobs" and resources to be scheduled are designated "machines." In the provision of constructed facilities, an analogy would be an architectural/engineering design office in which numerous design related tasks are to be accomplished by individual professionals in different departments. The scheduling problem is to ensure efficient use of the individual professionals (i.e., the resources) and to complete specific tasks in a timely manner.

The simplest form of resource-oriented scheduling is a reservation system for particular resources. In this case, competing activities or users of a resource prearrange use of the resource for a particular time period. Since the resource assignment is known in advance, other users of the resource can schedule their activities more effectively. The result is less waiting or "queuing" for a resource. It is also possible to inaugurate a preference system within the reservation process so that high-priority activities can be accommodated directly.

In the more general case of multiple resources and specialized tasks, practical resource-constrained scheduling procedures rely on heuristic procedures to develop good but not necessarily optimal schedules. While this is the occasion for considerable anguish among researchers, the heuristic methods will typically give fairly good results. An example heuristic method is provided in the next section. Manual methods in which a human scheduler revises a critical path schedule in light of resource-constraints can also work relatively well. Given that much of the data and the network representation used in forming a project schedule are uncertain, the results of applying heuristic procedures may be quite adequate in practice.

Example 10-6: A Reservation System [81]

A recent construction project for a highrise building complex in New York City was severely limited in the space available for staging materials for hauling up the building. On the four-building site, 38 separate cranes and elevators were available, but the number of movements of men, materials, and equipment was expected to keep the equipment very busy. With numerous subcontractors desiring the use of this equipment, the potential for delays and waiting in the limited staging area was considerable. By implementing a crane reservation system, these problems were nearly entirely avoided. The reservation system required contractors to telephone one or more days in advance

---

[81] This example is adapted from H. Smallowitz, "Construction by Computer," *Civil Engineering*, June 1986, pp. 71–73.

to reserve time on a particular crane. Time slots were available on a first-come, first-served basis (i.e., first call, first choice of available slots). Penalties were imposed for making an unused reservation. The reservation system was also computerized to permit rapid modification and updating of information as well as the provision of standard reservation schedules to be distributed to all participants.

Example 10-7: Heuristic Resource Allocation

Suppose that a project manager has 11 pipe sections for which necessary support structures and materials are available in a particular week. To work on these 11 pipe sections, five crews are available. The allocation problem is to assign the crews to the eleven pipe sections. This allocation would consist of a list of pipe sections allocated to each crew for work plus a recommendation on the appropriate sequence to undertake the work. The project manager might make assignments to minimize completion time, to ensure continuous work on the pipeline (so that one section on a pipeline run is not left incomplete), to reduce travel time between pipe sections, to avoid congestion among the different crews, and to balance the work-load among the crews. Numerous trial solutions could be rapidly generated, especially with the aid of an electronic spreadsheet. For example, if the nine sections had estimated work durations for each of the fire crews as shown in Table 10-12, then the allocations shown in Figure 10-14 would result in a minimum completion time.

TABLE 10–12 ESTIMATED REQUIRED TIME FOR EACH WORK TASK IN A RESOURCE ALLOCATION PROBLEM

Section	Work duration
A	9
B	9
C	8
D	8
E	7
F	7
G	6
H	6
I	5
J	5
K	5

Example 10-8: Algorithms for Resource Allocation with Bottleneck Resources

In the previous example, suppose that a mathematical model and solution were desired. For this purpose, we define a binary (i.e., 0 or 1 valued) decision variable for each pipe section and crew, x_{ij}, where $x_{ij} = 1$ implies that section i was assigned to crew j and $x_{ij} = 0$ implied that section i was not assigned to crew j. The time required to complete each section is t_j. The overall time to complete the nine sections is denoted z. In this case, the problem of minimizing overall completion time is

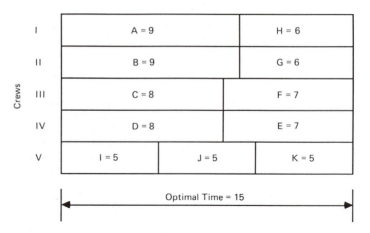

Figure 10-14 Allocation of Crews to Work Tasks

minimize z = maximum $\left(\sum_{i=1}^{11} t_i x_{i1}; \sum_{i=1}^{11} t_i x_{i2}; \sum_{i=1}^{11} t_i x_{i3}; \sum_{i=1}^{11} t_i x_{i4}; \sum_{i=1}^{11} t_i x_{i5} \right)$

subject to the constraints

$$\sum_{j=1}^{5} x_{ij} = 1 \text{ for each section } i$$

$$x_{ij} \text{ is 0 or 1}$$

where the constraints simply ensure that each section is assigned to one and only one crew. A modification permits a more conventional mathematical formulation, resulting in a generalized bottleneck assignment problem:

Minimize z

subject to the constraints

$$z \geq \sum_{i=1}^{11} t_i x_{ij} \text{ for each crew } j$$

$$\sum_{j=1}^{5} x_{ij} = 1 \text{ for each section } i$$

$$x_{ij} \text{ is 0 or 1}$$

This problem can be solved as an integer programming problem, although at considerable computational expense. A common extension to this problem would occur with differential productivities for each crew, so that the time to complete an activity, t_{ij}, would be defined for each crew. Another modification to this problem would substitute a cost factor, c_j, for the time factor, t_j, and attempt to minimize overall costs rather than completion time.

10.9 SCHEDULING WITH RESOURCE CONSTRAINTS AND PRECEDENCES

The previous section outlined resource-oriented approaches to the scheduling problem. In this section, we shall review some general approaches to integrating both concerns in scheduling.

Two problems arise in developing a resource-constrained project schedule. First, it is not necessarily the case that a critical path schedule is feasible. Because one or more resources might be needed by numerous activities, it can easily be the case that the shortest project duration identified by the critical path scheduling calculation is impossible. The difficulty arises because critical path scheduling assumes that no resource availability problems or bottlenecks will arise. Finding a feasible or possible schedule is the first problem in resource-constrained scheduling. Of course, there may be numerous possible schedules which conform with time and resource constraints. As a second problem, it is also desirable to determine schedules which have low costs or, ideally, the lowest cost.

Numerous heuristic methods have been suggested for resource-constrained scheduling. Many begin from critical path schedules which are modified in light of the resource constraints. Others begin in the opposite fashion by introducing resource constraints and then imposing precedence constraints on the activities. Still others begin with a ranking or classification of activities into priority groups for special attention in scheduling.[82] One type of heuristic may be better than another for different types of problems. Certainly, projects in which only an occasional resource constraint exists might be best scheduled starting from a critical path schedule. At the other extreme, projects with numerous important resource constraints might be best scheduled by considering critical resources first. A mixed approach would be to proceed simultaneously considering precedence and resource constraints.

A simple modification to critical path scheduling has been shown to be effective for a number of scheduling problems and is simple to implement. For this heuristic procedure, critical path scheduling is applied initially. The result is the familiar set of possible early and late start times for each activity. Scheduling each activity to begin at its earliest possible start time may result in more than one activity requiring a particular resource at the same time. Hence, the initial schedule may not be feasible. The heuristic proceeds by identifying cases in which activities compete for a resource and selecting one activity to proceed. The start time of other activities are then shifted later in time. A simple rule for choosing which activity has priority is to select the activity with the earliest CPM late start time (calculated as $LS(i,j) = L(j) - D_{ij}$) among those activities that are both feasible (in that all their precedence requirements

---

[82] For discussions and comparisons of alternative heuristic algorithms, see E. M. Davies, "An Experimental Investigation of Resource Allocation in Multiactivity Projects," *Operational Research Quarterly*, Vol. 24, no. 11, July 1976, pp. 1186–1194; J. D. Wiest and F. K. Levy, *A Management Guide to PERT/CPM*, Prentice Hall, Englewood Cliffs, NJ, 1977; or S. R. Lawrence, *A Computational Comparison of Heuristic Scheduling Techniques*, Technical Report, Graduate School of Industrial Administration, Carnegie Mellon University, Pittsburgh, 1985.

are satisfied) and competing for the resource. This decision rule is applied from the start of the project until the end for each type of resource in turn.

The order in which resources are considered in this scheduling process may influence the ultimate schedule. A good heuristic to employ in deciding the order in which resources are to be considered is to consider more important resources first. More important resources are those that have high costs or that are likely to represent an important bottleneck for project completion. Once important resources are scheduled, other resource allocations tend to be much easier. The resulting scheduling procedure is described in Table 10-13.

The late start time heuristic described in Table 10-13 is only one of many possible scheduling rules. It has the advantage of giving priority to activities which must start sooner to finish the project on time. However, it is *myopic* in that it doesn't consider trade-offs among resource types or the changes in the late start time that will be occurring as activities are shifted later in time. More complicated rules can be devised to incorporate broader knowledge of the project schedule. These complicated rules require greater computational effort and may or may not result in scheduling improvements in the end.

TABLE 10-13 A RESOURCE-ORIENTED SCHEDULING PROCEDURE

Step 1: Rank all resources from the most important to the least
    important, and number the resources $i = 1, 2, 3, \ldots, m$.

Step 2: Set the scheduled start time for each activity to the earliest start time.
    For each resource $i = 1, 2, 3, \ldots, m$ in turn:

Step 3: Start at the project beginning, so set $t = 0$.

Step 4: Compute the demand for resource i at time t by summing up the requirements
    for resource i for all activities scheduled to be underway at time t.

    If demand for resource i in time t is greater than the resource availability, then
      select the activity with the greatest late start time requiring
      resource i at time t, and shift its scheduled start time to time $t + 1$.

    Repeat step 4 until the resource constraint at time t for resource i is satisfied.

Step 5: Repeat step 4 for each project period in turn, setting $t = t + 1$.

Example 10-9: Resource-constrained Scheduling with Nine Activities

As an example of resource-constrained scheduling, we shall reexamine the nine-activity project discussed in Section 10.3. To begin, suppose that four workers and two pieces of equipment such as backhoes are available for the project. The required resources for each of the nine project activities are summarized in Table 10-14. Graphs of resource requirements over the 30-day project duration are shown in Figure 10-15. Equipment availability in this schedule is not a problem. However, on two occasions, more than the four available workers are scheduled for work. Thus, the existing project schedule is infeasible and should be altered.

The first resource problem occurs on day 21 when activity F is underway and activities G and H are scheduled to start. Applying the latest start time heuristic to decide which activity should start, the manager should reschedule activity H since it

TABLE 10–14

TABLE 10–14 RESOURCES REQUIRED AND STARTING TIMES FOR A NINE-ACTIVITY PROJECT

Activity	Workers required	Equipment required	Earliest start time	Latest start time	Duration
A	2	0	0	0	4
B	2	1	0	9	3
C	2	1	4	4	8
D	2	1	4	15	7
E	2	1	12	13	9
F	2	0	12	12	12
G	2	1	21	22	2
H	2	1	21	25	5
I	4	1	24	24	6

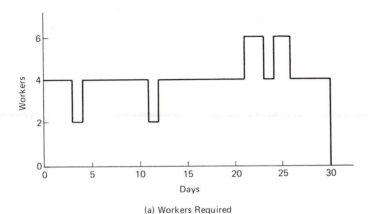

(a) Workers Required

(b) Equipment Required

Figure 10-15 Resources Required over Time for a Nine-Activity Project: Schedule I

has a later value of $LS(i,j)$, that is, day 25 versus day 22 as seen in Table 10-14. Two workers become available on day 23 after the completion of activity G. Since activity H is the only activity which is feasible at that time, it is scheduled to begin. Two workers also become available on day 24 at the completion of activity F. At this point, activity I is available for starting. If possible, it would be scheduled to begin with only two workers until the completion of activity H on day 28. If all four workers were definitely required, then activity I would be scheduled to begin on day 28. In this latter case, the project duration would be 34 days, representing a 4-day increase due to the limited number of workers available.

Example 10-10: Additional Resource Constraints

As another example, suppose that only one piece of equipment was available for the project. As seen in Figure 10-15, the original schedule would have to be significantly modified in this case. Application of the resource-constrained scheduling heuristic proceeds as follows as applied to the original project schedule:

1. On day 4, activities D and C are both scheduled to begin. Since activity D has a larger value of late start time, it should be rescheduled.
2. On day 12, activities D and E are available for starting. Again based on a later value of late start time (15 versus 13), activity D is deferred.
3. On day 21, activity E is completed. At this point, activity D is the only feasible activity, and it is scheduled for starting.
4. On day 28, the planner can start either activity G or activity H. Based on the later start time heuristic, activity G is chosen to start.
5. On completion of activity G at day 30, activity H is scheduled to begin.

The resulting profile of resource use is shown in Figure 10-16. Note that activities F and I were not considered in applying the heuristic since these activities did not require the special equipment being considered. In the figure, activity I is scheduled after the completion of activity H due to the requirement of four workers for this activity. As a

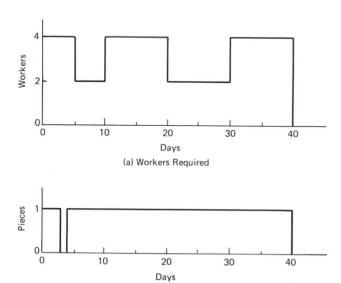

(a) Workers Required

(b) Equipment Required

Figure 10-16 Resources Required over Time for Nine Activity Project: Schedule II

result, the project duration has increased to 41 days. During much of this time, all four workers are not assigned to an activity. At this point, a prudent planner would consider whether or not it would be cost effective to obtain an additional piece of equipment for the project.

10.10 REFERENCES

10-1. Au, T. *Introduction to Systems Engineering–Deterministic Models*, Addison-Wesley, Publishing Co., Reading, MA, 1973, Chapter 8.

10-2. Baker, K., *An Introduction to Sequencing and Scheduling*, John Wiley and Sons, Inc., New York, 1974.

10-3 Jackson, M. J., *Computers in Construction Planning and Control*, Allen & Unwin, London, 1986.

10-4. Moder, J., C. Phillips and E. Davis, *Project Management with CPM, PERT and Precedence Diagramming*, 3rd ed., Van Nostrand Reinhold Co., Inc., New York, 1983.

10-5. Willis, E. M., *Scheduling Construction Projects*, John Wiley and Sons, Inc., New York, 1986.

10.11 PROBLEMS

P10-1 to
P10-4. Construct an activity-on-branch network from the precedence relationships of activities in the project given in the table for the problem, Tables P10-1 to P10-4.

TABLE P10–1

Activity	Predecessors	Duration
A	—	6
B	A	7
C	A	1
D	—	14
E	B	5
F	C, D	8
G	C, D	9
H	D	3
I	H	5
J	F	3
K	E, J	4
L	F	12
M	G, I	6
N	G, I	2
O	L, N	7

TABLE P10–2

Activity	Predecessors	Duration
A	—	5
B	A	6
C	B	3
D	C	4
E	D, G	5
F	A	8
G	F, J	3
H	—	3
I	H	2
J	I	7
K	F, J	2
L	H	7
M	L	4
N	K, M	3

TABLE P10–3

Activity	Predecessors	Duration
A	—	6
B	—	12
C	—	16
D	A	5
E	B	3
F	C	10
G	B, D	9
H	C, E	4
I	F	5
J	F	3
K	E, G, I	10
L	H, J	6

TABLE P10–4

Activity	Predecessors	Duration
A	—	3
B	—	6
C	—	2
D	C	3
E	C	8
F	B, E	5
G	A, F	7
H	B, E	10
I	B, E	6
J	B, E	6
K	D, J	8
L	G, H	3
M	I, K, L	4

P10-5 to

P10-8. Determine the critical path and all floats (total, free and independent) for the projects in Tables P10-1 to P10-4.

P10-9. Suppose that the precedence relationships for Problem P10-1 in Table P10-1 are all direct finish-to-start relationships with no lags except for the following:

- B to E : SS with a lag of 2
- D to H : FF with a lag of 3
- F to L : SS with a lag of 2
- G to N : SS with a lag of 1
- G to M : SS with a lag of 2

Formulate an activity-on-node network representation and recompute the critical path with these precedence relationships.

P10-10. Suppose that the precedence relationships for Problem P10-2 in Table P10-2 are all direct finish-to-start relationships with no lags except for the following:

- C to D : SS with a lag of 1
- D to E : FF with a lag of 3
- A to F : SS with a lag of 2
- H to I : FF with a lag of 4
- L to M : SS with a lag of 1

Formulate an activity-on-node network representation and recompute the critical path with these precedence relationships.

P10-11 to

P10-12. For the projects described in Tables P10-11 and P10-12, respectively, suggest a project schedule that would complete the project in minimum time and result in relatively constant or level requirements for labor over the course of the project.

TABLE P10–11

Activity	Predecessors	Duration	Workers per day
A	—	3	9
B	—	5	6
C	—	1	4
D	A	1	10
E	B	7	16
F	B	6	9
G	C	4	5
H	C	3	8
I	D, E	6	2
J	F, G	4	3
K	H	3	7

TABLE P10–12

Activity	Predecessors	Duration	Workers per Day
A	—	5	0
B	—	1	3
C	—	7	0
D	A	2	9
E	B	6	5
F	B	4	4
G	C	3	2
H	D, E	2	14
I	A	4	10
J	D, E	3	4
K	A	5	1
L	F, G, H	1	2
M	I, J	4	7
N	K, L	5	3

P10-13. Develop an example of a project network with three critical paths.

P10-14. For the project defined in Table P10-11, suppose that you are limited to a maximum of 20 workers at any given time. Determine a desirable schedule for the project, using the late start time heuristic described in Section 10.9.

P10-15. For the project defined in Table P10-12, suppose that you are limited to a maximum of 15 workers at any given time. Determine a desirable schedule for the project, using the late start time heuristic described in Section 10.9.

P10-16. The examples and problems presented in this chapter generally make use of activity duration and project durations as measured in working days from the beginning of the project. (a) Outline the procedures by which time measured in working days would be converted into calendar days with single- or double-shift work. (b) Could your procedure be modified to allow some but not all activities to be underway on weekends?

11

Advanced
Scheduling Techniques

11.1 USE OF ADVANCED SCHEDULING TECHNIQUES

Construction project scheduling is a topic that has received extensive research over a number of decades. The previous chapter described the fundamental scheduling techniques widely used and supported by numerous commercial scheduling systems. A variety of special techniques have also been developed to address specific circumstances or problems. With the availability of more powerful computers and software, the use of advanced scheduling techniques is becoming easier and of greater relevance to practice. In this chapter, we survey some of the techniques that can be employed in this regard. These techniques address some important practical problems, such as

- Scheduling in the face of uncertain estimates on activity durations
- Integrated planning of scheduling and resource allocation
- Scheduling in unstructured or poorly formulated circumstances

A final section in the chapter describes some possible improvements in the project scheduling process. In Chapter 14, we consider issues of computer-based implementation of scheduling procedures, particularly in the context of integrating scheduling with other project management procedures.

11.2 A UNIFIED ACTIVITY NETWORK REPRESENTATION

As described in Chapter 10, the activity-on-node (or precedence diagram) and the activity-on-branch (or arrow diagram) network models are alternative activity network representations. Numerous commercial scheduling software systems allow users to input network information and to view network graphs employing either representation. Virtually any graphic illustration of an activity network (arrow diagram, bar chart, etc.) can be generated from either network model, as described in Section 10.5. However, solution methods, network topology, and types of allowable precedences differ in the two methods.

In this section, a unified activity network model is presented in which each activity is represented by a start node, a finish node, and an intervening link. Precedence relationships and activity window constraints are also represented by links. Project milestones can be modeled as nodes in the activity network. This representation originated in work supporting the generation of project plans so that partial plans and plans at different levels of abstraction could be more easily represented. Even without consideration of the plan generation problem, the unified representation model has some distinct advantages.

The basic unified activity network method is identical in form to a basic critical path model (CPM) with activities on branches. Nodes represent events, including a project start and a project completion node. Links are characterized by a duration and the preceding event time plus the duration must be less than the succeeding event time for each link.

While the CPM and unified model structures are similar, the interpretation of network elements is different. Figure 11-1 illustrates a small unified network with two activities i and j. In this model, nodes represent project milestone events (such as the project start PS and project finish PF nodes). Links represent activity durations (such as i and j), activity precedences, or window constraints (which are precedences defined with respect to project milestones). In particular, the precedences in Figure 11-1 are

1. The project start must precede the start of activity i by at least D_1.
2. The project start must precede the finish of activity j by at least D_2.
3. The start of activity i must precede the start of activity j by at least D_3.
4. The start of activity i must precede the finish of activity j by at least D_4.
5. The finish of activity i must precede the start of activity j by at least D_5.
6. The finish of activity i must precede the finish of activity j by at least D_6.
7. The finish of activity j must precede the project finish by at least D_7.
8. The start of activity i must precede the project finish by at least D_8.

These eight links represent four precedence relationships and four window constraint types (numbers 1, 2, 7, and 8) of a minimum or greater than type.

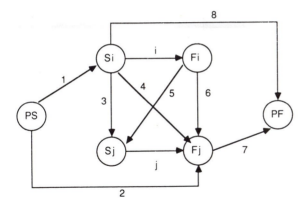

Figure 11-1 A Two-Activity Network with Eight Precedence and Window Constraint Types

Permitting negative link durations allows an additional eight constraint types to be represented. With a negative link duration, a maximum precedence lead is imposed. If event k must occur within a prescribed time period ($|D|$) time units after event h, then a link from k to h with negative duration D_{kh} requires that the time of event k, E_k, must be less than or equal to the time of event h plus a prespecified lead $|D_{kh}|$:

$$E_k + D_{kh} \leq E_h$$

or

$$E_k \leq E_h + |D_{kh}|$$

for

$$D_{kh} \leq 0$$

As shown in the partial network in Figure 11-2, the additional links 9 to 16 represent the following constraints:

9. The start of activity i must be within $|D_9|$ of the project start.
10. The finish of activity j must be within $|D_{10}|$ of the project start.
11. The start of activity j must be within $|D_{11}|$ of the start of activity i.
12. The finish of activity j must be within $|D_{12}|$ of the start of activity i.
13. The start of activity j must be within $|D_{13}|$ of the finish of activity i.
14. The finish of activity j must be within $|D_{14}|$ of the finish of activity i.
15. The project finish must be within $|D_{15}|$ of the finish of activity j .
16. The project finish must be within $|D_{16}|$ of the start of activity i.

Again, eight different precedence and window constraint types exist for greater than constraints. Unfortunately, positive cycles may be introduced in the network by allowing the negative links, so the longest-path solution algorithms become more complicated than the algorithm presented in Section 10.2.

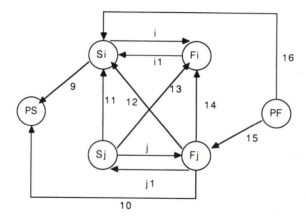

Figure 11-2 A Two-Activity Network with Eight Maximum Duration Links

The possibility of activity splitting also deserves mention. In Figure 11-1, activities are implicitly assumed to be amenable to splitting: the only constraint is that the activity start time does not precede the start node event time and the activity finish occurs by the finish node event time. Activity *splitting* implies that an activity can be started, stopped, and then restarted without penalty. To prohibit the possibility of splitting, an activity can be represented by a positive and a negative link as in Figure 11-2. In this case, the activity start and finish node event times are separated by exactly the activity duration so that no splitting can occur.

In the absence of negative link durations, the unified model can be solved with the familiar CPM longest-path algorithms involving both forward and backward passes. Applying a node-labeling algorithm such as the algorithm in Table 10-1 yields the critical path and float times for all nodes (including activity start and finishes).

Allowing negative link durations permits a greater variety of precedence relationships, but also complicates the scheduling calculations. For this situation, a variety of solution algorithms are possible. Table 11-1 summarizes one such algorithm based on a modification of the shortest-path algorithm due originally to Dijkstra.[83] This algorithm makes a distinction between the longest path to a node found during the course of the algorithm and the actual longest path to a particular node. The longest path to a node can be altered during the application of the algorithm, so the same node may be evaluated numerous times.

The use of a solution method such as the algorithm in Table 11-1 imposes a considerable additional computational burden. As a result, it may be efficient to apply a longest-path algorithm initially without considering negative duration links. If the resulting schedule is feasible with respect to the maximum lead constraints (i.e., links with negative duration), then a more complicated solution algorithm is not required.

In the unified model, node and link floats may be computed directly. Node floats represent the amount of time that an *event* (e.g., the start or finish of an

TABLE 11–1 CALCULATIONS FOR THE UNIFIED NETWORK MODEL WITH NEGATIVE LINK DURATIONS

Forward Pass:

Step 1: Set $PL(i) = -\infty$ and $TL(i) = -\infty$, where ∞ is a number larger than any link duration.

Set $TL(PS) = 0$

where PS = the project start node
$PL(i)$ = the maximum distance from PS to node i
$TL(i)$ = the maximum distance from PS to node i found at intermediate stages

Step 2: Select node i for which $TL(i)$ is the maximum among all nodes.

Set $PL(i) = TL(i)$ and $TL(i) = -\infty$

For each link originating at node i,

If $PL(j) = -\infty$ and $PL(i) + D(i,j) > TL(j)$,
then set $TL(j) = PL(i) + D(i,j)$.

If $PL(j) = -\infty$ and $PL(i) + D(i,j) \leq TL(j)$,
then do not change the labels on j.

If $PL(j) > -\infty$ and $PL(i) + D(i,j) > PL(j)$,
then set $PL(j) = -\infty$ and $TL(j) = PL(i) + D(i,j)$.

If $PL(j) > -\infty$ and $PL(i) + D(i,j) > PL(j)$,
then do not change the labels on j.

Step 3: Repeat step 2 until $PL(PF) > -\infty$, where PF is the project finish node.

Step 4: Set the earliest event time for each node, $E(i) = PL(i)$.

Backward Pass: Repeat application of the algorithm with the following changes:

1. Reverse each link direction.
2. Start with the project finish node PF with $TL(PF) = 0$.
3. At the end of step 3, set the latest event time, $L(i) = E(PF) - PL(i)$ for all nodes i.

[83] See E. Minieka, *Optimization Algorithms for Networks and Graphs*, Marcel Dekker, Inc., New York, 1978, pp. 41-51.

activity) can be delayed without affecting the total duration of the project and are computed by subtracting latest event times $L(i)$ from their corresponding earliest event times $E(i)$. Link floats for both activities and constraints are obtained by using the following definitions (see Chapter 10):

- *Total float* is the maximum amount of delay that can be assigned to any one activity or constraint without delaying the entire project. The total float is calculated as $TF(i,j) = L(j) - E(i) - D_{i,j}$ for any link (i,j).
- *Free float* is the amount of delay that can be assigned to any one activity or constraint without delaying subsequent activities. The quantity $FF(i,j) = E(j) - E(i) - D_{i,j}$ is the free float associated with any link (i,j).
- *Independent float* is the amount of delay that can be assigned to any one activity without delaying subsequent activities or restricting the scheduling of preceding activities. Independent float, $IF(i,j)$ for link (i,j) is equal to the maximum of zero or the value of $E(j) - L(i) - D_{i,j}$.

By reducing the number of required link types and special computational rules, the unified model of activity networks can be a useful simplification. The network representation also makes activity relationships immediately apparent. Sixteen different window or precedence relationships can be accommodated in the model with only one link type. The disadvantages of the unified model stem from the increased network model size. Nevertheless, the increasing computational speed and memory capacity of computers used for project management reduces the effective cost of this size increase.

Example 11-1: Scheduling for a Small Unified Network Model with All Positive Durations

Figure 11-3 shows an application of the basic unified model to a project with 5 activities and 12 precedence links. In the absence of negative link durations and

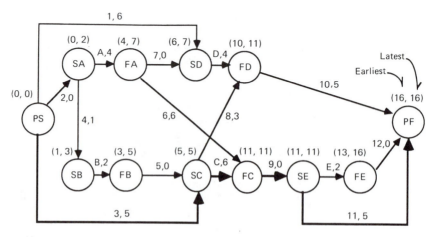

Figure 11-3 A Small Unified Network Model

assuming that all activities are amenable to splitting, the unified model can be solved with the familiar CPM longest-path algorithms involving both forward and backward passes shown in Table 10-1.

The critical path for this example is $PS \rightarrow SC \rightarrow FC \rightarrow SE \rightarrow PF$. The following observations are directly obtained from the results of the solution algorithms:

- Both the *start* and *finish* times of activity C are critical (i.e., they cannot be delayed without delaying the completion time of the project).
- Only the *start* of activity E is critical. The *finish* time of activity E can be delayed three days. Thus, activity E can have an overall duration between two and five days (e.g., by splitting its execution) without affecting the completion time of the project.
- All other activity events are noncritical.

Table 11-2 shows the values of the three floats for constraints and activities. Some observations are the following:

- Activity C has no total float (i.e., it is a *critical* activity) because both its start time and its finish time are critical events. The duration of this activity cannot be increased without delaying the project.
- Activity E has three units of total float even though its start cannot be delayed. These three units could be distributed to increase the duration of the activity in the period between time units 12 and 16.
- The precedence constraint $SC \rightarrow FD$ could be increased by three time units without delaying the project.

TABLE 11–2 FLOATS FOR CONSTRAINTS AND ACTIVITIES FOR EXAMPLE 11-1

Link (i, j)	$E(i)$	$L(i)$	$E(j)$	$L(j)$	$D(i,j)$	Floats Independent	Free	Total
A	0	2	4	7	4	0	0	3
B	1	3	3	5	2	0	0	2
C	5	5	11	11	6	0	0	0
D	6	7	10	11	4	0	0	1
E	11	11	13	16	2	0	0	3
1	0	0	6	7	6	0	0	1
2	0	0	0	2	0	0	0	2
3	0	0	5	5	5	0	0	0
4	0	2	1	3	1	0	0	2
5	3	5	5	5	0	0	2	2
6	4	7	11	11	6	0	1	1
7	4	7	6	7	0	0	2	3
8	5	5	10	11	3	2	2	3
9	11	11	11	11	0	0	0	0
10	10	11	16	16	5	0	1	1
11	11	11	16	16	5	0	0	0
12	13	16	16	16	0	0	3	3

Example 11-2: Application of the Unified Model with Some Negative Link Durations

A common example application of the unified model with maximum durations occurs when activity splitting is restricted. Figure 11-4 shows the solution to a modified version of the example of Figure 11-3 for the case in which no activities are amenable to splitting (i.e., their durations are fixed). In this second example, the *start* of activity D has been constrained to be exactly equal to the *finish* of activity A. With these assumptions, the total duration of the project is 17 time units, and the critical path becomes $PS \rightarrow SD \rightarrow FA \rightarrow FC \rightarrow SE \rightarrow PF$. The early start of activity A has been set to two units even though there is no window constraint imposed on this event. The reason is that the finish time of activity A is critical and its duration is fixed.

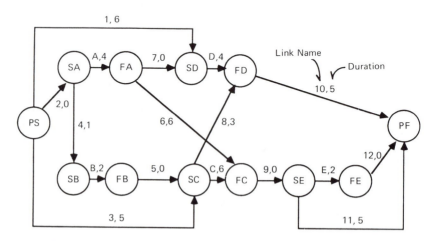

Figure 11-4 Solution to the Unified Model with Maximum Durations

11.3 SCHEDULING WITH UNCERTAIN DURATIONS

Section 10.3 described the application of *critical path scheduling* for the situation in which activity durations are fixed and known. Unfortunately, activity durations are estimates of the actual time required, and there is liable to be a significant amount of uncertainty associated with the actual durations. During the preliminary planning stages for a project, the uncertainty in activity durations is particularly large since the scope and obstacles to the project are still undefined. Activities that are outside of the control of the owner are likely to be more uncertain. For example, the time required to gain regulatory approval for projects may vary tremendously. Other external events such as adverse weather, trench collapses, or labor strikes make duration estimates particularly uncertain.

Two simple approaches to dealing with the uncertainty in activity durations warrant some discussion before introducing more formal scheduling procedures to deal with uncertainty. First, the uncertainty in activity durations may simply be ignored and scheduling done using the expected or most likely time duration for each activity. Since only one duration estimate needs to be made for each activity, this approach reduces the required work in setting up the original schedule.

Formal methods of introducing uncertainty into the scheduling process require more work and assumptions. While this simple approach might be defended, it has two drawbacks. First, the use of expected activity durations typically results in overly optimistic schedules for completion; a numerical example of this optimism appears shortly. Second, the use of single-activity durations often produces a rigid, inflexible mind set on the part of schedulers. As field managers appreciate, activity durations vary considerably and can be influenced by good leadership and close attention. As a result, field managers may lose confidence in the realism of a schedule based upon fixed activity durations. Clearly, the use of fixed activity durations in setting up a schedule makes a continual process of monitoring and updating the schedule in light of actual experience imperative. Otherwise, the project schedule is rapidly outdated.

A second simple approach to incorporating uncertainty also deserves mention. Many managers recognize that the use of expected durations may result in overly optimistic schedules, so they include a contingency allowance in their estimate of activity durations. For example, an activity with an expected duration of 2 days might be scheduled for a period of 2.2 days, including a 10 percent contingency. Systematic application of this contingency would result in a 10 percent increase in the expected time to complete the project. While the use of this rule of thumb or heuristic contingency factor can result in more accurate schedules, it is likely that formal scheduling methods that incorporate uncertainty more formally are useful as a means of obtaining greater accuracy or in understanding the effects of activity delays.

The most common formal approach to incorporate uncertainty in the scheduling process is to apply the critical path scheduling process (as described in Section 10.3) and then analyze the results from a probabilistic perspective. This process is usually referred to as the PERT scheduling or evaluation method.[84] As noted earlier, the duration of the critical path represents the minimum time required to complete the project. Using expected activity durations and critical path scheduling, a critical path of activities can be identified. This critical path is then used to analyze the duration of the project incorporating the uncertainty of the activity durations along the critical path. The expected project duration is equal to the sum of the expected durations of the activities along the critical path. Assuming that activity durations are independent random variables, the variance or variation in the duration of this critical path is calculated as the sum of the variances along the critical path. With the mean and variance of the identified critical path known, the distribution of activity durations can also be computed.

The mean and variance for each activity duration are typically computed from estimates of "optimistic" $(a_{i,j})$, "most likely" $(m_{i,j})$, and "pessimistic" $(b_{i,j})$ activity durations using the formulas:

$$\mu(i,j) = \frac{1}{6}(a_{i,j} + 4m_{i,j} + b_{i,j}) \qquad (11.1)$$

---

[84] See D. G. Malcolm, J. H. Rosenbloom, C. E. Clark, and W. Fazar, "Applications of a Technique for R and D Program Evaluation," *Operations Research*, Vol. 7, no. 5, 1959, pp. 646–669.

and

$$\sigma^2(i,j) = \frac{1}{36}(b_{i,j} - a_{i,j})^2 \tag{11.2}$$

where $\mu(i,j)$ and $\sigma^2(i,j)$ are the mean duration and its variance, respectively, of an activity (i,j). Three activity durations estimates (i.e., optimistic, most likely, and pessimistic durations) are required in the calculation. The use of these optimistic, most likely, and pessimistic estimates stems from the fact that these are thought to be easier for managers to estimate subjectively. The formulas for calculating the mean and variance are derived by assuming that the activity durations follow a probabilistic beta distribution under a restrictive condition.[85] The probability density function of a beta distribution for a random variable x is given by

$$f(x) = k(x-a)^\alpha (b-x)^\beta \qquad a \le x \le b; \quad \alpha, \beta > -1 \tag{11.3}$$

where k is a constant that can be expressed in terms of α and β. Several beta distributions for different sets of values of α and β are shown in Figure 11-5. For a beta distribution in the interval $a \le x \le b$ having a modal value m, the mean is given by

$$\mu = \frac{a + (\alpha + \beta)m + b}{\alpha + \beta + 2} \tag{11.4}$$

If $\alpha + \beta = 4$, then Eq. (11.4) will result in Eq. (11.1). Thus, the use of Eqs. (11.1) and (11.2) impose an additional condition on the beta distribution. In particular, the restriction that $\sigma = (b-a)/6$ is imposed.

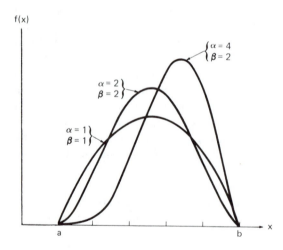

Figure 11-5 Several Beta Distributions

[85] See M. W. Sasieni, "A Note on PERT Times," *Management Science*, Vol. 32, no. 12, 1986, pp. 1652–1653, and T. K. Littlefield and P. H. Randolph, "An Answer to Sasieni's Question on PERT Times," *Management Science*, Vol. 33, no. 10, 1987, pp. 1357–1359. For a general discussion of the beta distribution, see N. L. Johnson and S. Kotz, *Continuous Univariate Distributions-2*, John Wiley and Sons, Inc., New York, 1970, Chapter 24.

Since absolute limits on the optimistic and pessimistic activity durations are extremely difficult to estimate from historical data, a common practice is to use the ninety-fifth percentile of activity durations for these points. Thus, the optimistic time would be such that there is only a 1 in 20 (5 percent) chance that the actual duration would be less than the estimated optimistic time. Similarly, the pessimistic time is chosen so that there is only a 5 percent chance of exceeding this duration. Thus, there is a 90 percent chance of having the actual duration of an activity fall between the optimistic and pessimistic duration time estimates. With the use of ninety-fifth percentile values for the optimistic and pessimistic activity duration, the calculation of the expected duration according to Eq. (11.1) is unchanged but the formula for calculating the activity variance becomes

$$\sigma^2(i,j) = \frac{1}{10}(b_{i,j}^{95\%} - a_{i,j}^{95\%})^2 \tag{11.5}$$

The difference between Eqs. (11.2) and (11.5) comes only in the value of the divisor, with 36 used for absolute limits and 10 used for 95 percentile limits. This difference might be expected since the difference between $b_{i,j}$ and $a_{i,j}$ would be *larger* for absolute limits than for the ninety-fifth percentile limits.

While the PERT method has been made widely available, it suffers from three major problems. First, the procedure focuses upon a single critical path, when many paths might become critical due to random fluctuations. For example, suppose that the critical path with longest expected time happened to be completed early. Unfortunately, this does not necessarily mean that the project is completed early since another path or sequence of activities might take longer. Similarly, a longer than expected duration for an activity not on the critical path might result in that activity suddenly becoming critical. As a result of the focus on only a single path, the PERT method typically *underestimates* the actual project duration.

As a second problem with the PERT procedure, it is incorrect to assume that most construction activity durations are independent random variables. In practice, durations are *correlated* with one another. For example, if problems are encountered in the delivery of concrete for a project, this problem is likely to influence the expected duration of numerous activities involving concrete pours on a project. Positive correlations of this type between activity durations imply that the PERT method *underestimates* the variance of the critical path and thereby produces overly optimistic expectations of the probability of meeting a particular project completion deadline.

Finally, the PERT method requires three duration estimates for each activity rather than the single estimate developed for critical path scheduling. Thus, the difficulty and labor of estimating activity characteristics is multiplied threefold.

As an alternative to the PERT procedure, a straightforward method of obtaining information about the *distribution* of project completion times (as well as other schedule information) is through the use of Monte Carlo simulation. This technique calculates sets of artificial (but realistic) activity duration times and then applies a deterministic scheduling procedure to each set of durations. Numerous calculations are required in this process since simulated activity durations must be calculated and the scheduling procedure applied many times. For realistic project networks, 40 to 1,000 separate sets of activity durations might be used in a single scheduling simulation. The calculations associated with Monte Carlo simulation are described in the following section.

A number of different indicators of the project schedule can be estimated from the results of a Monte Carlo simulation:

- Estimates of the expected time and variance of the project completion.
- An estimate of the distribution of completion times, so that the probability of meeting a particular completion date can be estimated.
- The probability that a particular activity will lie on the critical path. This is of interest since the longest or critical path through the network may change as activity durations change.

The disadvantage of Monte Carlo simulation results from the additional information about activity durations that is required and the computational effort involved in numerous scheduling applications for each set of simulated durations. For each activity, the distribution of possible durations as well as the parameters of this distribution must be specified. For example, durations might be assumed or estimated to be uniformly distributed between a lower and upper value. In addition, *correlations* between activity durations should be specified. For example, if two activities involve assembling forms in different locations and at different times for a project, then the time required for each activity is likely to be closely related. If the forms pose some problems, then assembling them on both occasions might take longer than expected. This is an example of a positive correlation in activity times. In application, such correlations are commonly ignored, leading to errors in results. As a final problem and discouragement, easy to use software systems for Monte Carlo simulation of project schedules are not generally available when correlations between activity durations are desired.

Another approach to the simulation of different activity durations is to develop specific scenarios of events and determine the effect on the overall project schedule. This is a type of "what-if" problem solving in which a manager simulates events that might occur and sees the result. For example, the effects of different weather patterns on activity durations could be estimated and the resulting schedules for the different weather patterns compared. One method of obtaining information about the range of possible schedules is to apply the scheduling procedure using all optimistic, all most likely, and then all pessimistic activity durations. The result is three project schedules representing a range of possible outcomes. This process of "what-if" analysis is similar to that undertaken during the process of construction planning.

Example 11-3: Scheduling Activities with Uncertain Time Durations.

Suppose that the nine-activity example project shown in Table 10-2 and Figure 10-4 of Chapter 10 was thought to have very uncertain activity time durations. As a result, project scheduling considering this uncertainty is desired. All three methods (PERT, Monte Carlo simulation, and "what-if" simulation) will be applied.

Table 11-3 shows the estimated optimistic, most likely and pessimistic durations for the nine activities. From these estimates, the mean, variance, and standard deviation are calculated. In this calculation, ninety-fifth percentile estimates of optimistic and pessimistic duration times are assumed, so that Eq. (11.5) is applied. The critical path for this project ignoring uncertainty in activity durations consists of activities A, C, F, and I as found in Table 10-3 (Section 10.3). Applying the PERT analysis procedure suggests that the duration of the project would be approximately normally distributed. The sum of the means for the critical activities is $4.0 + 8.0 + 12.0 + 6.0 = 30.0$ days, and the sum of the variances is $0.4 + 1.6 + 1.6 + 1.6 = 5.2$ leading to a standard deviation of 2.3 days.

With a normally distributed project duration, the probability of meeting a project deadline is equal to the probability that the standard normal distribution is less than or equal to $(PD - \mu_D)|\sigma_D$, where PD is the project deadline, μ_D is the expected duration and σ_D is the standard deviation of project duration. For example, the probability of project completion within 35 days is

$$Pr\{D \le PD\} = Pr\left\{z \le \frac{PD - \mu_D}{\sigma_D}\right\} = Pr\left\{z \le \frac{35 - 30.0}{2.3}\right\} = Pr\{z \le 2.17\}$$

where z is the standard normal distribution tabulated value of the cumulative standard distribution appears in Table B.1 of Appendix B, and the probability is found to be 0.985.

Monte Carlo simulation results provide slightly different estimates of the project duration characteristics. Assuming that activity durations are independent and approximately normally distributed random variables with the mean and variances shown in Table 11-3, a simulation can be performed by obtaining simulated duration realization for each of the nine activities and applying critical path scheduling to the resulting network. Applying this procedure 500 times, the average project duration is found to be 30.9 days with a standard deviation of 2.5 days. The PERT result is less than this estimate by 0.9 days or 3 percent. Also, the critical path considered in the PERT procedure (consisting of activities A, C, F, and I) is found to be the critical path in the simulated networks less than half the time.

If there are correlations among the activity durations, then significantly different results can be obtained. For example, suppose that activities C, E, G, and H are all positively correlated random variables with a correlation of 0.5 for each pair of

TABLE 11-3 ACTIVITY DURATION ESTIMATES FOR A NINE-ACTIVITY PROJECT

Activity	Optimistic duration	Most likely duration	Pessimistic duration	Mean	Variance
A	3	4	5	4.0	0.4
B	2	3	5	3.2	0.9
C	6	8	10	8.0	1.6
D	5	7	8	6.8	0.9
E	6	9	14	9.3	6.4
F	10	12	14	12.0	1.6
G	2	2	4	2.3	0.4
H	4	5	8	5.3	1.6
I	4	6	8	6.0	1.6

variables. Applying Monte Carlo simulation using 500 activity network simulations results in an average project duration of 36.5 days and a standard deviation of 4.9 days. This estimated average duration is 6.5 days or 20 percent longer than the PERT estimate or the estimate obtained ignoring uncertainty in durations. If correlations like this exist, these methods can seriously underestimate the actual project duration.

Finally, the project durations obtained by assuming all optimistic and all pessimistic activity durations are 23 and 41 days, respectively. Other "what-if" simulations might be conducted for cases in which peculiar soil characteristics might make excavation difficult; these soil peculiarities might be responsible for the correlations of excavation activity durations described.

Results from the different methods are summarized in Table 11-4. Note that positive correlations among some activity durations results in relatively large increases in the expected project duration and variability.

11.4 CALCULATIONS FOR MONTE CARLO SCHEDULE SIMULATION

In this section, we outline the procedures required to perform Monte Carlo simulation for the purpose of schedule analysis. These procedures presume that the various steps involved in forming a network plan and estimating the characteristics of the probability distributions for the various activities have been completed. Given a plan and the activity duration distributions, the heart of the Monte Carlo simulation procedure is the derivation of a *realization* or synthetic outcome of the relevant activity durations. Once these realizations are generated, standard scheduling techniques can be applied. We shall present the formulas associated with the generation of normally distributed activity durations and then comment on the requirements for other distributions in an example.

TABLE 11-4 PROJECT DURATION RESULTS FROM VARIOUS TECHNIQUES AND ASSUMPTIONS FOR AN EXAMPLE

Procedure and assumptions	Project duration (days)	Standard deviation of project duration (days)
Critical path method	30.0	NA
PERT method	30.0	2.3
Monte Carlo simulation		
No duration correlations	30.9	2.5
Positive duration correlations	36.5	4.9
"What-if" simulations		
Optimistic	23.0	NA
Most likely	30.0	NA
Pessimistic	41.0	NA

To generate normally distributed realizations of activity durations, we can use a two-step procedure. First, we generate uniformly distributed random variables, u_i in the interval from 0 to 1. Numerous techniques can be used for this purpose. For example, a general formula for random number generation can be of the form

$$u_i = \text{fractional part of } [(\pi + u_{i-1})^5] \tag{11.6}$$

where $\pi = 3.14159265$ and u_{i-1} was the previously generated random number or a pre-selected beginning or seed number. For example, a seed of $u_0 = 0.215$ in Eq. (11.6) results in $u_1 = 0.0820$, and by applying this value of u_1, the result is $u_2 = 0.1029$. This formula is a special case of the mixed congruential method of random number generation. While Eq. (11.6) will result in a series of numbers that have the appearance and the necessary statistical properties of true random numbers, we should note that these are actually pseudo-random numbers since the sequence of numbers will repeat given a long enough time.

With a method of generating uniformly distributed random numbers, we can generate normally distributed random numbers using two uniformly distributed realizations with the equations:[86]

$$x_k = \mu_x + s \sin t \tag{11.7}$$

with

$$s = \sigma_x \sqrt{-2 \ln u_1}$$

$$t = 2\pi u_2$$

where x_k is the normal realization, μ_x is the mean of x, σ_x is the standard deviation of x, and u_1 and u_2 are the two uniformly distributed random variable realizations. For the case in which the mean of an activity is 2.5 days and the standard deviation of the duration is 1.5 days, a corresponding realization of the duration is $s = 2.2365$, $t = 0.6465$ and $x_k = 2.525$ days, using the two uniform random numbers generated from a seed of 0.215.

Correlated random number realizations may be generated making use of conditional distributions. For example, suppose that the duration of an activity d is normally distributed and correlated with a second normally distributed random variable x which may be another activity duration or a separate factor such as a weather effect. Given a realization x_k of x, the conditional distribution of d is still normal, but it is a function of the value x_k. In particular, the conditional mean $(\mu'_d \mid x = x_k)$ and standard deviation $(\sigma'_d \mid x = x_k)$ of a normally distributed variable given a realization of the second variable is

$$\{\mu'_d \mid x = x_k\} = \rho_{dx}(\sigma_d/\sigma_x)(x_k - \mu_x) + \mu_d$$

$$\{\sigma'_d \mid x = x_k\} = \sigma_d \sqrt{1 - \rho_{dx}} \tag{11.8}$$

where ρ_{dx} is the correlation coefficient between d and x. Once x_k is known, the conditional mean and standard deviation can be calculated from Eq. (11.8) and then a realization of d obtained by applying Eq. (11.7).

Correlation coefficients indicate the extent to which two random variables will tend to vary together. Positive correlation coefficients indicate one random variable will tend to exceed its mean when the other random variable does the same. From

---

[86] See T. Au, R. M. Shane, and L. A. Hoel, *Fundamentals of Systems Engineering — Probabilistic Models*, Addison-Wesley Publishing Co., Reading, MA, 1972.

a set of n historical observations of two random variables, x and y, the correlation coefficient can be estimated as

$$\rho_{xy} = \frac{n\sum_{i=1}^{n} x_i y_i - \sum_{i=1}^{n} x_i \sum_{i=1}^{n} y_i}{\left(n\sum_{i=1}^{n} x_i^2 - \left(\sum_{i=1}^{n} x_i\right)^2\right)^{1/2}\left(n\sum_{i=1}^{n} y_i^2 - \left(\sum_{i=1}^{n} y_i\right)^2\right)^{1/2}} \qquad (11.9)$$

The value of ρ_{xy} can range from 1 to -1, with values near 1 indicating a positive, near linear, relationship between the two random variables.

It is also possible to develop formulas for the conditional distribution of a random variable correlated with numerous other variables; this is termed a multi-variate distribution.[87] Random number generations from other types of distributions are also possible.[88] Once a set of random variable distributions is obtained, then the process of applying a scheduling algorithm is required as described in previous sections.

Example 11-4: A Three-Activity Project Example

Suppose that we wish to apply a Monte Carlo simulation procedure to a simple project involving three activities in series. As a result, the critical path for the project includes all three activities. We assume that the durations of the activities are normally distributed with the following parameters:

Activity	Mean (days)	Standard Deviation (days)
A	2.5	1.5
B	5.6	2.4
C	2.4	2.0

To simulate the schedule effects, we generate the duration realizations shown in Table 11-5 and calculate the project duration for each set of three-activity duration realizations.

For the 12 sets of realizations shown in the table, the mean and standard deviation of the project duration can be estimated to be 10.49 days and 4.06 days, respectively. In this simple case, we can also obtain an analytic solution for this duration, since it is only the sum of three independent normally distributed variables. The actual project duration has a mean of 10.5 days, and a standard deviation of $\sqrt{(1.5)^2 + (2.4)^2 + (2.0)^2} = 3.5$ days. With only a limited number of simulations, the mean obtained from simulations is close to the actual mean, while the estimated standard deviation from the simulation differs significantly from the actual value. This latter difference can be attributed to the nature of the set of realizations used in the simulations; using a larger number of simulated durations would result in a more accurate estimate of the standard deviation.

---

[87] See N. L. Johnson and S. Kotz, *Distributions in Statistics: Continuous Multivariate Distributions*, John Wiley and Sons, Inc., New York, 1973.

[88] See, for example, P. Bratley, B. L. Fox, and L. E. Schrage, *A Guide to Simulation*, Springer-Verlag, New York, 1983.

TABLE 11–5 DURATION REALIZATIONS FOR A MONTE CARLO SCHEDULE SIMULATION

Simulation number	Activity A	Activity B	Activity C	Project duration
1	1.53	6.94	1.04	9.51
2	2.67	4.83	2.17	9.66
3	3.36	6.86	5.56	15.78
4	0.39	7.65	2.17	10.22
5	2.50	5.82	1.74	10.06
6	2.77	8.71	4.03	15.51
7	3.83	2.05	1.10	6.96
8	3.73	10.57	3.24	17.53
9	1.06	3.68	2.47	7.22
10	1.17	0.86	1.37	3.40
11	1.68	9.47	0.13	11.27
12	0.37	6.66	1.70	8.72

Estimated mean project duration = 10.49

Estimated standard deviation of project duration = 4.06

Note: All durations in days.

Example 11-5: Generation of Realizations from Triangular Distributions

To simplify calculations for Monte Carlo simulation of schedules, the use of a triangular distribution is advantageous compared to the normal or the beta distributions. Triangular distributions also have the advantage relative to the normal distribution that negative durations cannot be estimated. As illustrated in Figure 11-6, the triangular distribution can be skewed to the right or left and has finite limits like the beta distribution. If a is the lower limit, b the upper limit and m the most likely value, then the mean and standard deviation of a triangular distribution are

$$\mu = \frac{a + b + m}{3} \tag{11.10}$$

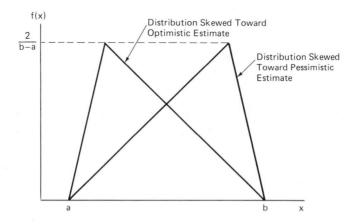

Figure 11-6 Two Triangular-Activity Duration Distributions

$$\sigma = \sqrt{(a^2 + b^2 + m^2 + ab + am + mb)/18} \qquad (11.11)$$

The cumulative probability function for the triangular distribution is

$$F(x) = \begin{cases} \dfrac{(x-a)^2}{(b-a)(m-a)} & \text{for } a \le x \le m \\[2ex] 1 - \dfrac{(b-x)^2}{(b-a)(b-m)} & \text{for } m \le x \le b \end{cases} \qquad (11.12)$$

where $F(x)$ is the probability that the random variable is less than or equal to the value of x.

Generating a random variable from this distribution can be accomplished with a single uniform random variable realization using the inversion method. In this method, a realization of the cumulative probability function, $F(x)$, is generated and the corresponding value of x is calculated. Since the cumulative probability function varies from 0 to 1, the density function realization can be obtained from the uniform value random number generator, Eq. (11.6). The calculation of the corresponding value of x is obtained from inverting Eq. (11.12):

$$x_k = \begin{cases} a + \sqrt{u_k(b-a)(m-a)} & \text{if } u_k \le \dfrac{m-a}{b-a} \\[2ex] b - \sqrt{(1-u_k)(b-a)(b-m)} & \text{if } u_k \ge \dfrac{m-a}{b-a} \end{cases} \qquad (11.13)$$

For example, if $a = 3.2$, $m = 4.5$ and $b = 6.0$, then $\mu_x = 4.8$ and $\sigma_x = 2.7$. With a uniform realization of $u = 0.215$, then for $(m - a)/(b - a) \ge 0.215$, x will lie between a and m and is found to have a value of 4.1 from Eq. (11.13).

11.5 CRASHING AND TIME-COST TRADE-OFFS

The previous sections discussed the duration of activities as either fixed or random numbers with known characteristics. However, activity durations can often vary depending upon the type and amount of resources that are applied. Assigning more workers to a particular activity will normally result in a shorter duration.[89] Greater speed may result in higher costs and lower quality, however. In this section, we shall consider the impacts of time, cost, and quality trade-offs in activity durations. In this process, we shall discuss the procedure of *project crashing*.

A simple representation of the possible relationship between the duration of an activity and its direct costs appears in Figure 11-7. Considering only this activity in isolation and without reference to the project completion deadline, a manager would undoubtedly choose a duration which implies minimum direct cost, represented by D_{ij} and C_{ij} in the figure. Unfortunately, if each activity were scheduled for the

---

[89] There are exceptions to this rule, though. More workers may also mean additional training burdens and more problems of communication and management. Some activities cannot be easily broken into tasks for numerous individuals; some aspects of computer programming provide notable examples. Indeed, software programming can be so perverse that examples exist of additional workers resulting in slower project completion. See F. P. Brooks, Jr., *The Mythical Man-Month*, Addison Wesley Publishing Co., Reading, MA, 1975.

duration that resulted in the minimum direct cost in this way, the time to complete the entire project might be too long and substantial penalties associated with the late project start-up might be incurred. This is a small example of *suboptimization*, in which a small component of a project is optimized or improved to the detriment of the entire project performance. Avoiding this problem of suboptimization is a fundamental concern of project managers.

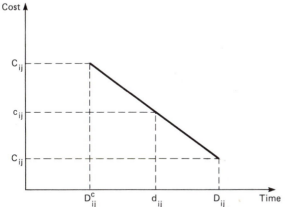

Figure 11-7 A Linear Time-Cost Trade-off for an Activity

At the other extreme, a manager might choose to complete the activity in the minimum possible time, D_{ij}^c, but at a higher cost C_{ij}^c. This minimum completion time is commonly called the activity *crash* time. The linear relationship shown in the figure between these two points implies that any intermediate duration could also be chosen. It is possible that some intermediate point may represent the ideal or optimal trade-off between time and cost for this activity.

What is the reason for an increase in direct cost as the activity duration is reduced? A simple case arises in the use of overtime work. By scheduling weekend or evening work, the completion time for an activity as measured in calendar days will be reduced. However, premium wages must be paid for such overtime work, so the cost will increase. Also, overtime work is more prone to accidents and quality problems that must be corrected, so indirect costs may also increase. More generally, we might not expect a *linear* relationship between duration and direct cost, but some convex function such as the nonlinear curve or the step function shown in Figure 11-8. A linear function may be a good approximation to the actual curve, however, and results in considerable analytical simplicity.[90]

With a linear relationship between cost and duration, the critical path time-cost trade-off problem can be defined as a linear programming optimization problem. In particular, let R_{ij} represent the rate of change of cost as duration is decreased, illustrated by the absolute value of the slope of the line in Figure 11-7. Then, the direct cost of completing an activity is

---

[90] For a discussion of solution procedures and analogies of the general function time-cost trade-off problem, see C. Hendrickson and B. N. Janson, "A Common Network Flow Formulation for Several Civil Engineering Problems," *Civil Engineering Systems*, Vol. 1, no. 4, 1984, pp. 195–203.

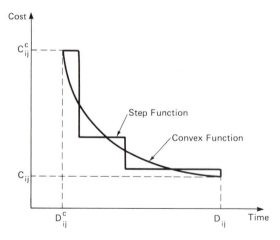

Figure 11-8 Nonlinear Time-Cost Trade-offs for an Activity

$$c_{ij} = C_{ij} + R_{ij}(D_{ij} - d_{ij}) \tag{11.14}$$

where the lowercase c_{ij} and d_{ij} represent the scheduled duration and resulting cost of the activity ij. The actual duration of an activity must fall between the minimum cost time (D_{ij}) and the crash time (D_{ij}^c). Also, precedence constraints must be imposed as described earlier for each activity. Finally, the required completion time for the project or, alternatively, the costs associated with different completion times must be defined. Thus, the entire scheduling problem is to minimize total cost (equal to the sum of the c_{ij} values for all activities) subject to constraints arising from (1) the desired project duration, PD, (2) the minimum and maximum activity duration possibilities, and (3) constraints associated with the precedence or completion times of activities. Algebraically, this is

$$\text{Minimize } z = \sum\nolimits_{\text{all}(i,j)} c_{ij}$$
$$= \sum\nolimits_{\text{all}(i,j)} \left[(C_{ij} + R_{ij}(D_{ij} - d_{ij})) \right] \tag{11.15}$$

subject to the constraints

$$x(n) \leq PD$$

$$x(i) + d_{ij} \leq x(j) \quad \text{for all activities}(ij)$$

$$D_{ij}^c \leq d_{ij} \leq D_{ij} \quad \text{for all activities}(ij)$$

where the notation is as defined above and the decision variables are the activity durations $d_{i,j}$ and event times $x(k)$. The appropriate schedules for different project durations can be found by repeatedly solving this problem for different project durations PD. The entire problem can be solved by linear programming or more efficient algorithms which take advantage of the special network form of the problem constraints.

One solution to the time-cost trade-off problem is of particular interest and deserves mention here. The minimum time to complete a project is called the *project crash time*. This minimum completion time can be found by applying critical path scheduling with all activity durations set to their minimum values (D_{ij}^c). This minimum completion time for the project can then be used in the time-cost scheduling problem described earlier to determine the minimum *project crash cost*. Note that the project crash cost is not found by setting each activity to its crash duration and summing up the resulting costs; this solution is called the *all-crash cost*. Since there are some activities not on the critical path that can be assigned longer duration without delaying the project, it is advantageous to change the all-crash schedule and thereby reduce costs.

Heuristic approaches are also possible to the time-cost trade-off problem. In particular, a simple approach is first to apply critical path scheduling with all activity durations assumed to be at minimum cost (D_{ij}). Next, the planner can examine activities on the critical path and reduce the scheduled duration of activities which have the lowest resulting increase in costs. In essence, the planner develops a list of activities on the critical path ranked in accordance with the unit change in cost for a reduction in the activity duration. The heuristic solution proceeds by shortening activities in the order of their lowest impact on costs. As the duration of activities on the shortest path is shortened, the project duration is also reduced. Eventually, another path becomes critical, and a new list of activities on the critical path must be prepared. By manual or automatic adjustments of this kind, good but not necessarily optimal schedules can be identified. Optimal or best schedules can only be assured by examining changes in combinations of activities as well as changes to single activities. However, by alternating between adjustments in particular activity durations (and their costs) and a critical path scheduling procedure, a planner can fairly rapidly devise a shorter schedule to meet a particular project deadline or, in the worst case, find that the deadline is impossible of accomplishment.

This type of heuristic approach to time-cost trade-offs is essential when the time-cost trade-offs for each activity are not known in advance or in the case of resource constraints on the project. In these cases, heuristic explorations may be useful to determine if greater effort should be spent on estimating time-cost trade-offs or if additional resources should be retained for the project. In many cases, the basic time-cost trade-off might not be a smooth curve as shown in Figure 11-8, but only a series of particular resource and schedule combinations which produce particular durations. For example, a planner might have the option of assigning either one or two crews to a particular activity; in this case, there are only two possible durations of interest.

Example 11-6: Time-Cost Trade-offs

The construction of a permanent transitway on an expressway median illustrates the possibilities for time-cost trade-offs in construction work.[91] One section of 10 miles of transitway was built in 1985 and 1986 to replace an existing contraflow lane system (in which one lane in the expressway was reversed each day to provide additional capacity in the peak flow direction). Three engineers' estimates for work time were prepared:

[91] This example was abstracted from work performed in Houston and reported in U. Officer, "Using Accelerated Contracts with Incentive Provisions for Transitway Construction in Houston," paper presented at the January 1986 Transportation Research Board Annual Conference, Washington, D. C.

- 975 calendar days, based on 750 working days at 5 days/week and 8 hours/day of work plus 30 days for bad weather, weekends, and holidays.
- 702 calendar days, based on 540 working days at 6 days/week and 10 hours/day of work.
- 360 calendar days, based on 7 days/week and 24 hours/day of work.

The savings from early completion due to operating savings in the contraflow lane and contract administration costs were estimated to be $5,000 per day.

In accepting bids for this construction work, the owner required both a dollar amount and a completion date. The bidder's completion date was required to fall between 360 and 540 days. In evaluating contract bids, a $5,000 credit was allowed for each day less than 540 days that a bidder specified for completion. In the end, the successful bidder completed the project in 270 days, receiving a bonus of $5,000 × (540 − 270) = $450,000 in the $8,200,000 contract. However, the contractor experienced 15 to 30 percent higher costs to maintain the continuous work schedule.

Example 11-7: Time-cost Trade-offs and Project Crashing

As an example of time-cost trade-offs and project crashing, suppose that we needed to reduce the project completion time for a seven-activity product delivery project first analyzed in Section 10.3 as shown in Table 10-4 and Figure 10-6. Table 11-6 gives information pertaining to possible reductions in time which might be accomplished for the various activities. Using the minimum cost durations (as shown in column 1 of Table 11-6), the critical path includes activities C, E, F, G, plus a dummy activity X. The project duration is 32 days in this case, and the project cost is $70,000.

Examining the unit change in cost, R_{ij} shown in column 5 of Table 11-6, the lowest rate of change occurs for activity E. Accordingly, a good heuristic strategy might be to begin by crashing this activity. The result is that the duration of activity E goes from 9 days to 5 days, and the total project cost increases by $8,000. After making this change, the project duration drops to 28 days and two critical paths exist: (1) activities C, X, E, F, and G and (2) activities C, D, F, and G.

Examining the unit changes in cost again, activity F has the lowest value of R_{ij}. Crashing this activity results in an additional time savings of 6 days in the project duration, an increase in project cost of $16,000, but no change in the critical paths. The activity on the critical path with the next lowest unit change in cost is activity

TABLE 11–6 ACTIVITY DURATIONS AND COSTS FOR A SEVEN-ACTIVITY PROJECT

Activity	(1) Minimum cost	(2) Normal duration	(3) Crash cost	(4) Crash duration	(5) Change in cost per day
A	8	6	14	4	3
B	4	1	4	1	—
C	8	8	24	4	4
D	10	5	24	3	7
E	10	9	18	5	2
F	20	12	36	6	2.7
G	10	3	18	2	8

Note: Dollar amounts in thousands; time durations in days.

C. Crashing this activity to its minimum completion time would reduce its duration by 4 days at a cost increase of $16,000. However, this reduction does not result in a reduction in the duration of the project by 4 days. After activity C is reduced to 7 days, the alternate sequence of activities A and B lie on the critical path and further reductions in the duration of activity C alone do not result in project time savings. Accordingly, our heuristic corrections might be limited to reducing activity C by only 1 day, thereby increasing costs by $4,000 and reducing the project duration by 1 day.

At this point, our choices for reducing the project duration are fairly limited. We can either reduce the duration of activity G or, alternatively, reduce activity C and either activity A or activity B by an identical amount. Inspection of Table 11-6 and Figure 10-4 suggest that reducing activity A and activity C is the best alternative. Accordingly, we can shorten activity A to its crash duration (from 6 days to 4 days) and shorten the duration of activity C (from 7 days to 5 days) at an additional cost of $6,000 + $8,000 = $14,000. The result is a reduction in the project duration of 2 days.

Our last option for reducing the project duration is to crash activity G from 3 days to 2 days at an increase in cost of $8,000. No further reductions are possible in this time since each activity along a critical path (comprised of activities A, B, E, F, and G) are at minimum durations. At this point, the project duration is 18 days and the project cost is $120,000, representing a 50 percent reduction in project duration and a 70 percent increase in cost. Note that not all the activities have been crashed. Activity C has been reduced in duration to 5 days (rather than its 4-day crash duration), while activity D has not been changed at all. If all activities had been crashed, the total project cost would have been $138,000, representing a useless expenditure of $18,000. The change in project cost with different project durations is shown graphically in Figure 11-9.

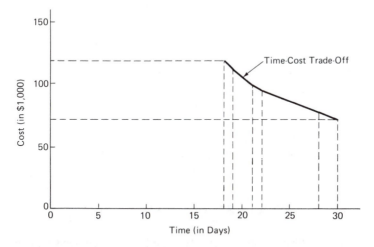

Figure 11-9 Project Cost Versus Time for a Seven-Activity Project

Example 11-8: Mathematical Formulation of Time-Cost Trade-offs

The same results obtained in the previous example could be obtained using a formal optimization program and the data appearing in Tables 10-4 and 11-6. In this case, the heuristic approach used above has obtained the optimal solution at each stage. Using

Eq. (11.15), the linear programming problem formulation would be

$$\text{Minimize } z = \sum_{k=1}^{7} c_k$$

$$= \lceil 8 + 3(6 - d_A) \rceil + \lceil 4 \rceil + \lceil 8 + 4(8 - d_C) \rceil + \lceil 10 + 7(5 - d_D) \rceil$$
$$+ \lceil 10 + 2(9 - d_E) \rceil + \lceil 20 + 2.7(9 - d_F) \rceil + \lceil 10 + 2(3 - d_G) \rceil$$

subject to the constraints

$$x(6) = PD$$
$$x(0) + d_A \le x(2)$$
$$x(0) + d_C \le x(1)$$
$$x(1) \qquad \le x(3)$$
$$x(2) + d_B \le x(4)$$
$$x(1) + d_D \le x(4)$$
$$x(3) + d_E \le x(4)$$
$$x(4) + d_F \le x(5)$$
$$x(5) + d_G \le x(6)$$
$$x(0) = 0$$
$$4 \le d_A \le 6$$
$$1 \le d_B \le 1$$
$$4 \le d_C \le 8$$
$$3 \le d_D \le 5$$
$$5 \le d_E \le 9$$
$$6 \le d_F \le 12$$
$$2 \le d_G \le 3$$

which can be solved for different values of project duration PD using a linear programming algorithm or a network flow algorithm. Note that even with only seven activities, the resulting linear programming problem is fairly large.

11.6 SCHEDULING IN POORLY STRUCTURED PROBLEMS

The previous discussion of activity scheduling suggested that the general structure of the construction plan was known in advance. With previously defined activities, relationships among activities, and required resources, the scheduling problem could be represented as a mathematical optimization problem. Even in the case in which durations are uncertain, we assumed that the underlying probability distribution of durations is known and applied analytical techniques to investigate schedules.

While these various scheduling techniques have been exceedingly useful, they do not cover the range of scheduling problems encountered in practice. In particular, there are many cases in which costs and durations depend upon other activities due to congestion on the site. In contrast, the scheduling techniques discussed previously assume that durations of activities are generally independent of each other. A second problem stems from the complexity of construction technologies. In the course of resource allocations, numerous additional constraints or objectives may exist that are difficult to represent analytically. For example, different workers may have specialized in one type of activity or another. With greater experience, the work efficiency for particular crews may substantially increase. Unfortunately, representing such effects in the scheduling process can be very difficult. Another case of complexity occurs when activity durations and schedules are negotiated among the different parties in a project so there is no single overall planner.

A practical approach to these types of concerns is to ensure that all schedules are reviewed and modified by experienced project managers before implementation. This manual review permits the incorporation of global constraints or consideration of peculiarities of workers and equipment. Indeed, interactive schedule revision to accommodate resource constraints is often superior to any computer-based heuristic. With improved graphic representations and information availability, man-machine interaction is likely to improve as a scheduling procedure.

More generally, the solution procedures for scheduling in these more complicated situations cannot be reduced to mathematical algorithms. The best solution approach is likely to be a "generate-and-test" cycle for alternative plans and schedules. In this process, a possible schedule is hypothesized or generated. This schedule is tested for feasibility with respect to relevant constraints (such as available resources or time horizons) and desirability with respect to different objectives. Ideally, the process of evaluating an alternative will suggest directions for improvements or identify particular trouble spots. These results are then used in the generation of a new test alternative. This process continues until a satisfactory plan is obtained.

Two important problems must be borne in mind in applying a "generate-and-test" strategy. First, the number of possible plans and schedules is enormous, so considerable insight to the problem must be used in generating reasonable alternatives. Second, evaluating alternatives also may involve considerable effort and judgment. As a result, the number of actual cycles of alternative testing that can be accommodated is limited. One hope for computer technology in this regard is that the burdensome calculations associated with this type of planning may be assumed by the computer, thereby reducing the cost and required time for the planning effort. Some mechanisms along these lines are described in Chapter 15.

Example 11-9: Man-Machine Interactive Scheduling

An interactive system for scheduling with resource constraints might have the following characteristics:[92]

[92] This description is based on an interactive scheduling system developed at Carnegie Mellon University and described in C. Hendrickson, C. Zozaya-Gorostiza, D. Rehak, E. Baracco-Miller, and P. Lim, "An Expert System for Construction Planning," *ASCE Journal of Computing*, Vol. 1, no. 4, 1987, pp. 253–269.

- Graphic displays of bar charts, resource use over time, activity networks, and other graphic images available in different windows of a screen simultaneously
- Descriptions of particular activities, including allocated resources and chosen technologies available in windows as desired by a user
- A three-dimensional animation of the construction process that can be stopped to show the progress of construction on the facility at any time
- Easy-to-use methods for changing start times and allocated resources
- Utilities to run relevant scheduling algorithms such as the critical path method at any time

Figure 11-10 shows an example of a screen for this system. In Figure 11-10, a bar chart appears in one window, a list of critical activities in another window, and a

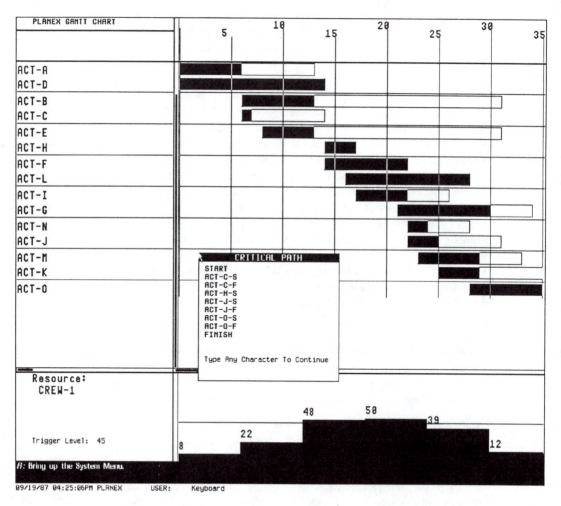

Figure 11-10 A Bar Chart and Other Windows for Interactive Scheduling

graph of the use of a particular resource over time appears in a third window. These different "windows" appear as sections on a computer screen displaying different types of information. With these capabilities, a project manager can call up different pictures of the construction plan and make changes to accommodate objectives or constraints that are not formally represented. With rapid response to such changes, the effects can be immediately evaluated.

11.7 IMPROVING THE SCHEDULING PROCESS

Despite considerable attention by researchers and practitioners, the process of construction planning and scheduling still presents problems and opportunities for improvement. The importance of scheduling in ensuring the effective coordination of work and the attainment of project deadlines is indisputable. For large projects with many parties involved, the use of formal schedules is indispensable.

The network model for representing project activities has been provided as an important conceptual and computational framework for planning and scheduling. Networks not only communicate the basic precedence relationships between activities, they also form the basis for most scheduling computations.

As a practical matter, most project scheduling is performed with the critical path scheduling method, supplemented by heuristic procedures used in project crash analysis or resource-constrained scheduling. Many commercial software programs are available to perform these tasks. Probabilistic scheduling or the use of optimization software to perform time-cost trade-offs is rather more infrequently applied, but there are software programs available to perform these tasks if desired.

Rather than concentrating upon more elaborate solution algorithms, the most important innovations in construction scheduling are likely to appear in the areas of data storage, ease of use, data representation, estimation, communication, and diagnostic or interpretation aids. Integration of scheduling information with accounting and design information through the means of database systems is one beneficial innovation; many scheduling systems do not provide such integration of information. The techniques discussed in Chapter 14 are particularly useful in this regard.

With regard to ease of use, the introduction of interactive scheduling systems, graphical output devices, and automated data acquisition should produce a very different environment than has existed. In the past, scheduling was performed as a batch operation with output contained in lengthy tables of numbers. Updating of work progress and revising activity durations were time-consuming manual tasks. It is no surprise that managers viewed scheduling as extremely burdensome in this environment. The lower costs associated with computer systems as well as improved software make "user-friendly" environments a real possibility for field operations on large projects.

Finally, information representation is an area which can result in substantial improvements. While the network model of project activities is an extremely useful device to represent a project, many aspects of project plans and activity interrelationships cannot or have not been represented in network models. For example, the similarity of processes among different activities is usually unrecorded in the formal project representation. As a result, updating a project network in response to new information about a process such as concrete pours can be tedious. What is needed is a much more flexible and complete representation of project information. Some avenues for change along these lines are discussed in Chapter 15.

11.8 REFERENCES

11-1. Bratley, P., Bennett L. Fox, and Linus E. Schrage, *A Guide to Simulation*, Springer-Verlag, New York, 1973.

11-2. Elmaghraby, S. E., *Activity Networks: Project Planning and Control by Network Models*, John Wiley and Sons, Inc., New York, 1977.

11-3. Jackson, M. J., *Computers in Construction Planning and Control*, Allen & Unwin, London, 1986.

11-4. Moder, J., C. Phillips and E. Davis, *Project Management with CPM, PERT and Precedence Diagramming*, 3rd ed., Van Nostrand Reinhold Co., New York, 1983.

11.9 PROBLEMS

P11-1. For the project defined in Problem P10-1 (in Chapter 10), suppose that the early, most likely, and late time schedules are desired. Assume that the activity durations are approximately normally distributed with means as given in Table P10-1 and the following standard deviations: A, 4; B, 10; C, 1; D, 15; E, 6; F, 12; G, 9; H, 2; I, 4; J, 5; K, 1; L, 12; M, 2; N, 1; O, 5. (a) Find the early start time and the latest possible start time schedules for each activity, and (b) estimate the probability that the project requires at least 25 percent more time than the expected duration.

P11-2. For the project defined in Problem P10-2 (in Chapter 10), suppose that the early, most likely, and late time schedules are desired. Assume that the activity durations are approximately normally distributed with means as given in Table 10-2 and the following standard deviations, A, 2; B, 2; C, 1; D, 0; E, 0; F, 2; G, 0; H, 0; I, 0; J, 3; K, 0; L, 3; M, 2; N, 1. (a) Find the early start time and the latest possible start time schedules for each activity, and (b) estimate the probability that the project requires at least 25 percent more time than the expected duration.

P11-3 to
P11-6. The time-cost trade-off data corresponding to each of the Problems P10-1 to P10-4 (in Chapter 10), respectively, are given in the table for the problem (Tables P11-3 to P11-6). Determine the all-crash and the project crash durations and cost based on the early time schedule for the project. Also, suggest a combination of activity durations which will lead to a project completion time equal to three days longer than the project crash time but would result in the (approximately) maximum savings. Assume that no activities will extend beyond their normal completion times.

TABLE P11–3

Activity	Shortest possible completion time	Normal completion time cost	Change in cost per day earlier completion
A	3	150	20
B	5	250	30
C	1	80	Infinity
D	10	400	15
E	4	220	20
F	6	300	25
G	6	260	10
H	2	120	35
I	4	200	20
J	3	180	Infinity
K	3	220	25
L	9	500	15
M	2	100	30
N	2	120	Infinity
O	5	240	10

TABLE P11–4

Activity	Shortest possible completion time	Normal completion time cost	Crash completion time cost
A	2	400	460
B	4	450	510
C	1	200	250
D	3	300	350
E	3	350	430
F	5	550	640
G	2	250	300
H	1	180	250
I	2	150	150
J	6	480	520
K	1	120	150
L	4	500	560
M	3	280	320
N	2	220	260

TABLE P11–5

Activity	Shortest possible completion time	Normal completion time cost	Crash completion time cost
A	4	70	90
B	8	150	210
C	11	200	250
D	4	60	80
E	1	40	60
F	9	120	140
G	6	100	130
H	2	50	70
I	3	70	90
J	2	60	80
K	7	120	150
L	3	70	100

TABLE P11–6

Activity	Shortest possible completion time	Normal completion time cost	Change in cost per day earlier completion
A	3	50	Infinity
B	5	150	50
C	2	90	Infinity
D	2	125	40
E	5	300	30
F	3	240	20
G	5	80	15
H	6	270	30
I	6	120	Infinity
J	4	600	40
K	5	300	50
L	2	80	40
M	2	140	40

P11-7 to
P11-10. Develop a project completion time versus cost trade-off curve for the projects in Problems P11-3 to P11-6. (Note: A linear programming computer program or more specialized programs can reduce the calculating work involved in these problems!)

P11-11. Suppose that the project described in Problem P10-5 proceeds normally on an earliest time schedule with all activities scheduled for their normal completion time. However, suppose that activity G requires 20 days rather than the expected 9. What is the new schedule? Prepare bar charts for the original and current schedules.

P11-12. For the project defined in Problem P10-1 (in Chapter 10), suppose that a Monte Carlo simulation with 5 repetitions is desired. Suppose further that the activity durations have triangular distributions with the following lower and upper bounds, A: 4, 8; B: 4, 9, C: 0.5, 2; D: 10, 20; E: 4, 7; F: 7, 10; G: 6, 12; H: 2, 4; I: 4, 7; J: 2, 4; K: 2, 6; L: 10, 15; M: 2, 9; N: 1, 4; O: 4, 11.

  a. Calculate the value of m for each activity given the upper and lower bounds and the expected duration shown in Table P10-1.

  b. Generate a set of realizations for each activity and calculate the resulting project duration.

  c. Repeat part (b) five times and estimate the mean and standard deviation of the project duration.

12

Cost Control, Monitoring, and Accounting

12.1 THE COST-CONTROL PROBLEM

During the execution of a project, procedures for project control and record keeping become indispensable tools to managers and other participants in the construction process. These tools serve the dual purpose of recording the financial transactions that occur as well as giving managers an indication of the progress and problems associated with a project. The problems of project control are aptly summed up in an old definition of a project as "any collection of vaguely related activities that are ninety percent complete, over budget and late."[93] The task of project control systems is to give a fair indication of the existence and the extent of such problems.

In this chapter, we consider the problems associated with resource utilization, accounting, monitoring, and control during a project. In this discussion, we emphasize the project management uses of accounting information. Interpretation of project accounts is generally not straightforward until a project is completed, and then it is too late to influence project management. Even after completion of a project, the accounting results may be confusing. Hence, managers need to know how to interpret accounting information for the purpose of project management. In the process of considering management problems, however, we shall discuss some of the common accounting systems and conventions, although our purpose is not to provide a comprehensive survey of accounting procedures.

The limited objective of project control deserves emphasis. Project control procedures are primarily intended to identify deviations from the project plan rather than to suggest possible areas for cost savings. This characteristic reflects the advanced stage at which project control becomes important. The time at which major cost savings can be achieved is during planning and design for the project. During the actual construction, changes are likely to delay the project and lead to inordinate cost increases. As a result, the focus of project control is on fulfilling the original design plans or indicating deviations from these plans, rather than on searching for significant improvements and cost savings. It is only when a rescue operation is required that major changes will normally occur in the construction plan.

Finally, the issues associated with integration of information will require some discussion. Project management activities and functional concerns are intimately linked, yet the techniques used in many instances do not facilitate comprehensive or integrated consideration of project activities. For example, schedule information and cost accounts are usually kept separately. As a result, project managers themselves must synthesize a comprehensive view from the different reports on the project plus their own field observations. In particular, managers are often forced to infer the cost impacts of schedule changes, rather than being provided with aids for this process. Communication or integration of various types of information can serve a number of useful purposes, although it does require special attention in the establishment of project control procedures.

---

[93] Cited in P. F. Zoll, "Database Structures for Project Management," *Proceedings of the Seventh Conference on Electronic Computation*, ASCE, St. Louis, MO, 1979.

12.2 THE PROJECT BUDGET

For cost control on a project, the construction plan and the associated cash flow estimates can provide the baseline reference for subsequent project monitoring and control. For schedules, progress on individual activities and the achievement of milestone completions can be compared with the project schedule to monitor the progress of activities. Contract and job specifications provide the criteria by which to assess and assure the required quality of construction. The final or detailed cost estimate provides a baseline for the assessment of financial performance during the project. To the extent that costs are within the detailed cost estimate, then the project is thought to be under *financial control*. Overruns in particular cost categories signal the possibility of problems and give an indication of exactly what problems are being encountered. Expense-oriented construction planning and control focuses upon the categories included in the final cost estimation. This focus is particularly relevant for projects with few activities and considerable repetition such as grading and paving roadways.

For control and monitoring purposes, the original detailed cost estimate is typically converted to a *project budget*, and the project budget is used subsequently as a guide for management. Specific items in the detailed cost estimate become job cost elements. Expenses incurred during the course of a project are recorded in specific job cost accounts to be compared with the original cost estimates in each category. Thus, individual job cost accounts generally represent the basic unit for cost control. Alternatively, job cost accounts may be disaggregated or divided into *work elements* which are related both to particular scheduled activities and to particular cost accounts. Work element divisions will be described in Section 12-8.

In addition to cost amounts, information on material quantities and labor inputs within each job account is also typically retained in the project budget. With this information, actual materials usage and labor employed can be compared to the expected requirements. As a result, cost overruns or savings on particular items can be identified as due to changes in unit prices, labor productivity, or the amount of material consumed.

The number of cost accounts associated with a particular project can vary considerably. For constructors, on the order of 400 separate cost accounts might be used on a small project.[94] These accounts record all the transactions associated with a project. Thus, separate accounts might exist for different types of materials, equipment use, payroll, project office, and so on. Both physical and nonphysical resources are represented, including overhead items such as computer use or interest charges. Table 12-1 summarizes a typical set of cost accounts that might be used

---

[94] Thomas Gibb reports a median number of 400 cost accounts for a $2 million project in a sample of 30 contractors in 1975. See T. W. Gibb, Jr., "Building Construction in Southeastern United States," School of Civil Engineering, Georgia Institute of Technology, 1975, reported in D. W. Halpin, *Financial and Cost Concepts for Construction Management*, John Wiley and Sons, Inc., New York, 1985.

TABLE 12–1 ILLUSTRATIVE SET OF PROJECT COST ACCOUNTS

201	Clearing and preparing site
202	Substructure
202.1	Excavation and shoring
202.2	Piling
202.3	Concrete masonry
202.31	Mixing and placing
202.32	Formwork
202.33	Reinforcing
203	Outside utilities (water, gas, sewer, etc.)
204	Superstructure
204.1	Masonry construction
204.2	Structural steel
204.3	Wood framing, partitions, etc.
204.4	Exterior finishes (brickwork, terra cotta, cut stone, etc.)
204.5	Roofing, drains, gutters, flashing, etc.
204.6	Interior finish and trim
204.61	Finish flooring, stairs, doors, trim
204.62	Glass, windows, glazing
204.63	Marble, tile, terrazo
204.64	Lathing and plastering
204.65	Soundproofing and insulation
204.66	Finish hardware
204.67	Painting and decorating
204.68	Waterproofing
204.69	Sprinklers and fire protection
204.7	Service work
204.71	Electrical work
204.72	Heating and ventilating
204.73	Plumbing and sewage
204.74	Air conditioning
204.75	Fire alarm, telephone, security, miscellaneous
205	Paving, curbs, walks
206	Installed equipment (elevators, revolving doors, mail chutes, etc.)
207	Fencing

in building construction.[95] Note that this set of accounts is organized hierarchically, with seven major divisions (accounts 201 to 207) and numerous subdivisions under each division. This hierarchical structure facilitates aggregation of costs into predefined categories; for example, costs associated with the superstructure (account 204) would be the sum of the underlying subdivisions (204.1, 204.2, etc.) or finer levels of detail (204.61, 204.62, etc.). The subdivision accounts in Table 12-1 could be further divided into personnel, material, and other resource costs for the purpose of financial accounting, as described in Section 12.4.

In developing or implementing a system of cost accounts, an appropriate numbering or coding system is essential to facilitate communication of information and

[95] This illustrative set of accounts was adapted from an ASCE Manual of Practice, *Construction Cost Control*, Task Committee on Revision of Construction Cost Control Manual, ASCE, New York, 1985.

proper aggregation of cost information. Particular cost accounts are used to indicate the expenditures associated with specific projects and to indicate the expenditures on particular items throughout an organization. These are examples of different *perspectives* on the same information, in which the same information may be summarized in different ways for specific purposes. Thus, more than one aggregation of the cost information and more than one application program can use a particular cost account. Separate identifiers of the type of cost account and the specific project must be provided for project cost accounts or for financial transactions. As a result, a standard set of cost codes such as the MASTERFORMAT codes described in Chapter 9 may be adopted to identify cost accounts along with project identifiers and extensions to indicate organization or job-specific needs. Similarly the use of databases or, at a minimum, intercommunicating applications programs facilitate access to cost information, as described in Chapter 14.

Converting a final cost estimate into a project budget compatible with an organization's cost accounts is not always a straightforward task. As described in Chapter 5, cost estimates are generally disaggregated into appropriate *functional* or *resource-based* project categories. For example, labor and material quantities might be included for each of several physical components of a project. For cost accounting purposes, labor and material quantities are aggregated by type no matter for which physical component they are employed. For example, particular types of workers or materials might be used on numerous different physical components of a facility. Moreover, the categories of cost accounts established within an organization may bear little resemblance to the quantities included in a final cost estimate. This is particularly true when final cost estimates are prepared in accordance with an external reporting requirement rather than in view of the existing cost accounts within an organization.

One particular problem in forming a project budget in terms of cost accounts is the treatment of contingency amounts. These allowances are included in project cost estimates to accommodate unforeseen events and the resulting costs. However, in advance of project completion, the source of contingency expenses is not known. Realistically, a budget accounting item for *contingency allowance* should be established whenever a contingency amount was included in the final cost estimate.

A second problem in forming a project budget is the treatment of inflation. Typically, final cost estimates are formed in terms of real dollars and an item reflecting inflation costs is added on as a percentage or lump sum. This inflation allowance would then be allocated to individual cost items in relation to the actual expected inflation over the period for which costs will be incurred.

Example 12-1: Project Budget for a Design Office

An example of a small project budget is shown in Table 12-2. This budget might be used by a design firm for a specific design project. While this budget might represent all the work for this firm on the project, numerous other organizations would be involved with their own budgets. In Table 12-2, a summary budget is shown as well as a detailed listing of costs for individuals in the Engineering Division. For the purpose of consistency with cost accounts and managerial control, labor costs are aggregated into three groups: the engineering, architectural, and environmental

TABLE 12–2 A SMALL PROJECT BUDGET
FOR A DESIGN FIRM

	Budget summary
Personnel	
Architectural division	$ 67,251.00
Engineering	45,372.00
Environmental division	28,235.00
Total	$140,858.00
Other direct expenses	
Travel	2,400.00
Supplies	1,500.00
Communication	600.00
Computer services	1,200.00
Total	$ 5,700.00
Overhead	175,869.60
Contingency and profit	95,700.00
Total	$418,127.60
	Engineering personnel detail
Senior engineer	$ 11,562.00
Associate engineer	21,365.00
Engineer technician	12,654.00
Total	$ 45,372.00

divisions. The detailed budget shown in Table 12-2 applies only to the engineering division labor; other detailed budget amounts for categories such as supplies and the other work divisions would also be prepared. Note that the salary costs associated with individuals are aggregated to obtain the total labor costs in the engineering group for the project. To perform this aggregation, some means of identifying individuals within organizational groups is required. Accompanying a budget of this nature, some estimate of the actual hours of labor required by project task would also be prepared. Finally, this budget might be used for internal purposes alone. In submitting financial bills and reports to the client, overhead and contingency amounts might be combined with the direct labor costs to establish an aggregate billing rate per hour. In this case, the overhead, contingency and profit would represent *allocated costs* based on the direct labor costs.

Example 12-2: Project Budget for a Constructor

Table 12-3 illustrates a summary budget for a constructor. This budget is developed from a project to construct a wharf. As with the design office budget, costs are divided into direct and indirect expenses. Within direct costs, expenses are divided into material, subcontract, temporary work, and machinery costs. This budget indicates aggregate amounts for the various categories. Cost details associated with particular cost accounts would supplement and support the aggregate budget shown in Table 12-3. A profit and a contingency amount might be added to the basic budget of $1,715,147 shown in Table 12-3 for completeness.

TABLE 12–3 A PROJECT BUDGET FOR A WHARF PROJECT
(Amounts in Thousands of Dollars)

	Material cost	Subcontract work	Temporary work	Machinery cost	Total cost
Steel piling	$292,172	$129,178	$16,389	$ 0	$437,739
Tie-rod	88,233	29,254	0	0	117,487
Anchor wall	130,281	60,873	0	0	191,154
Backfill	242,230	27,919	0	0	300,149
Coping	42,880	22,307	13,171	0	78,358
Dredging	0	111,650	0	0	111,650
Fender	48,996	10,344	0	1,750	61,090
Other	5,000	32,250	0	0	37,250
Subtotal	$849,800	$423,775	$29,560	$1,750	$1,304,885

Summary

Total of direct cost	$1,304,885
Indirect cost	
Common temporary work	19,320
Common machinery	80,934
Transportation	15,550
Office operating costs	294,458
Total	410,262
Total project cost	$1,715,147

12.3 FORECASTING FOR ACTIVITY COST CONTROL

For the purpose of project management and control, it is not sufficient to consider only the past record of costs and revenues incurred in a project. Good managers should focus upon future revenues, future costs, and technical problems. For this purpose, traditional financial accounting schemes are not adequate to reflect the dynamic nature of a project. Accounts typically focus on recording routine costs and past expenditures associated with activities.[96] Generally, past expenditures represent *sunk costs* that cannot be altered in the future and may or may not be relevant in the future. For example, after the completion of some activity, it may be discovered that some quality flaw renders the work useless. Unfortunately, the resources expended on the flawed construction will generally be *sunk* and cannot be recovered for reconstruction (although it may be possible to change the burden of who pays for these resources by financial withholding or charges; owners will typically attempt to have constructors or designers pay for changes due to quality flaws). Since financial accounts are historical in nature, some means of forecasting or projecting the future course of a project is essential for management control. In this section, some methods for cost control and simple forecasts are described.

[96] For a fuller exposition of this point, see W. H. Lucas and T. L. Morrison, "Management Accounting for Construction Contracts," *Management Accounting*, 1981, pp. 59–65.

An example of forecasting used to assess the project status is shown in Table 12-4. In this example, costs are reported in five categories, representing the sum of all the various cost accounts associated with each category:

- **Budgeted Cost**

  The budgeted cost is derived from the detailed cost estimate prepared at the start of the project. Examples of project budgets were presented in Section 12.2. The factors of cost would be referenced by cost account and by a prose description.

- **Estimated Total Cost**

  The estimated or forecast total cost in each category is the current best estimate of costs based on progress and any changes since the budget was formed. Estimated total costs are the sum of cost to date, commitments, and exposure. Methods for estimating total costs are described subsequently.

- **Cost Committed and Cost Exposure**

  Estimated cost to completion in each category in divided into firm commitments and estimated additional cost or *exposure*. Commitments may represent material orders or subcontracts for which firm dollar amounts have been committed.

- **Cost to Date**

  The actual cost incurred to date is recorded in column 5 and can be derived from the financial record keeping accounts.

- **Over (or Under)**

  A final column in Table 12-4 indicates the amount over or under the budget for each category. This column is an indicator of the extent of variance from the project budget; items with unusually large overruns would represent a particular managerial concern. Note that *variance* is used in the terminology of project control to indicate a difference between budgeted and actual expenditures. The term is defined and used quite differently in statistics or mathematical analysis. In Table 12-4, labor costs are running higher than expected, whereas subcontracts are less than expected.

The current status of the project is a forecast budget overrun of $5,950 with 23 percent of the budgeted project costs incurred to date.

TABLE 12–4 A JOB STATUS REPORT

Factor	(1) Budgeted cost	(2) Estimated total cost	(3) Cost committed	(4) Cost exposure	(5) Cost to date	(6) Over or (under)
Labor	$ 99,406	$102,342	$49,596	–	$ 52,746	$2,936
Material	88,499	88,499	42,506	45,993	–	0
Subcontracts	198,458	196,323	83,352	97,832	15,139	(2,135)
Equipment	37,543	37,543	23,623	–	13,920	0
Other	72,693	81,432	49,356	–	32,076	8,739
Total	496,509	506,139	248,433	143,825	113,881	5,950

For project control, managers would focus particular attention on items indicating substantial deviation from budgeted amounts. In particular, the cost overruns in the labor and in the "other expense" category would be worthy of attention by a project manager in Table 12–4. A next step would be to look in greater detail at the various components of these categories. Overruns in cost might be due to lower than expected productivity, higher than expected wage rates, higher than expected material costs, or other factors. Even further, low productivity might be caused by inadequate training, lack of required resources such as equipment or tools, or inordinate amounts of re-work to correct quality problems. Review of a job status report is only the first step in project control.

The job status report illustrated in Table 12–4 employs explicit estimates of ultimate cost in each category of expense. These estimates are used to identify the actual progress and status of an expense category. Estimates might be made from simple linear extrapolations of the productivity or cost of the work to date on each project item. Algebraically, a linear estimation formula is generally in one of two forms. Using a linear extrapolation of costs, the forecast total cost, C_f, is

$$C_f = \frac{C_t}{p_t} \qquad (12.1)$$

where C_t is the cost incurred to time t and p_t is the proportion of the activity completed at time t. For example, an activity which is 50 percent complete with a cost of \$40,000 would be estimated to have a total cost of \$40,000/0.5 = \$80,000. More elaborate methods of forecasting costs would disaggregate costs into different categories, with the total cost the sum of the forecast costs in each category.

Alternatively, the use of measured unit cost amounts can be used for forecasting total cost. The basic formula for forecasting cost from unit costs is

$$C_f = Wc_t \qquad (12.2)$$

where C_f is the forecast total cost, W is the total units of work, and c_t is the average cost per unit of work experienced up to time t. If the average unit cost is \$50 per unit of work on a particular activity and 1,600 units of work exist, then the expected cost is (1,600)(\$50) = \$80,000 for completion.

The unit cost in Eq. (12.2) may be replaced with the hourly productivity and the unit cost per hour (or other appropriate time period), resulting in the equation

$$C_f = Wh_t u_t \qquad (12.3)$$

where the cost per work unit, c_t, is replaced by the time per unit, h_t, multiplied by the cost per unit of time, u_t.

More elaborate forecasting systems might recognize peculiar problems associated with work on particular items and modify these simple proportional cost estimates. For example, if productivity is improving as workers and managers become more familiar with the project activities, the estimate of total costs for an item might be revised downward. In this case, the estimating equation would become

$$C_f = C_t + (W - W_t)c_t \qquad (12.4)$$

where forecast total cost, C_f, is the sum of cost incurred to date, C_t, and the cost resulting from the remaining work $(W - W_t)$ multiplied by the expected cost per unit time period for the remainder of the activity, c_t.

As a numerical example, suppose that the average unit cost has been $50 per unit of work, but the most recent figure during a project is $45 per unit of work. If the project manager were assured that the improved productivity could be maintained for the remainder of the project (consisting of 800 units of work out of a total of 1,600 units of work), the cost estimate would be ($50)(800) + ($45)(800) = $76,000 for completion of the activity. Note that this forecast uses the actual average productivity achieved on the first 800 units and uses a forecast of productivity for the remaining work. Historical changes in productivity might also be used to represent this type of nonlinear changes in work productivity on particular activities over time.

In addition to changes in productivities, other components of the estimating formula can be adjusted or more detailed estimates substituted. For example, the change in unit prices due to new labor contracts or material supplier's prices might be reflected in estimating future expenditures. In essence, the same problems encountered in preparing the detailed cost estimate are faced in the process of preparing exposure estimates, although the number and extent of uncertainties in the project environment decline as work progresses. The only exception to this rule is the danger of quality problems in completed work which would require reconstruction.

Each of the estimating methods described requires current information on the state of work accomplishment for particular activities. There are several possible methods to develop such estimates, including [97]

- **Units of Work Completed**
  For easily measured quantities the actual proportion of completed work amounts can be measured. For example, the linear feet of piping installed can be compared to the required amount of piping to estimate the percentage of piping work completed.

- **Incremental Milestones**
  Particular activities can be subdivided or "decomposed" into a series of milestones, and the milestones can be used to indicate the percentage of work complete based on historical averages. For example, the work effort involved with installation of standard piping might be divided into four milestones:

    Spool in place: 20 percent of work and 20 percent of cumulative work

    Ends welded: 40 percent of work and 60 percent of cumulative work

    Hangars and trim complete: 30 percent of work and 90 percent of cumulative work

    Hydrotested and installation complete: 10 percent of work and 100 percent of cumulative work

---

[97] For a description of these methods and examples as used by a sample of construction companies, see L. S. Riggs, *Cost and Schedule Control in Industrial Construction*, Report to the Construction Industry Institute, December, 1986.

Thus, a pipe section for which the ends have been welded would be reported as 60 percent complete.

- **Opinion**

  Subjective judgments of the percentage complete can be prepared by inspectors, supervisors or project managers themselves. Clearly, this estimated technique can be biased by optimism, pessimism or inaccurate observations. Knowledgeable estimators and adequate field observations are required to obtain sufficient accuracy with this method.

- **Cost Ratio**

  The cost incurred to date can also be used to estimate the work progress. For example, if an activity were budgeted to cost $20,000. and the cost incurred at a particular date were $10,000, then the estimated percentage complete under the cost ratio method would be $10,000/$20,000 = 0.5 or 50 percent. This method provides no independent information on the actual percentage complete or any possible errors in the activity budget: the cost forecast will always be the budgeted amount. Consequently, managers must use the estimated costs to complete an activity derived from the cost ratio method with extreme caution.

Systematic application of these different estimating methods to the various project activities enables calculation of the percentage complete or the productivity estimates used in preparing job status reports.

In some cases, automated data acquisition for work accomplishments might be instituted. For example, transponders might be moved to the new work limits after each day's activity and the new locations automatically computed and compared with project plans. These measurements of actual progress should be stored in a central database and then processed for updating the project schedule. The use of database management systems in this fashion is described in Chapter 14.

Example 12-3: Estimated Total Cost to Complete an Activity

Suppose that we wish to estimate the total cost to complete piping construction activities on a project. The piping construction involves 1,000 linear feet of piping which has been divided into 50 sections for management convenience. At this time, 400 linear feet of piping has been installed at a cost of $40,000 and 500 hours of labor. The original budget estimate was $90,000 with a productivity of 1 ft per worker-hour, a unit cost of $60 per worker-hour, and a total material cost of $30,000. Firm commitments of material delivery for the $30,000 estimated cost have been received.

The first task is to estimate the proportion of work completed. Two estimates are readily available. First, 400 Lf(linear feet) of pipe is in place out of a total of 1,000 Lf, so the proportion of work completed is 400/1,000 = 0.4 or 40 percent. This is the "units of work completed" estimation method. Second, the cost ratio method would estimate the work complete as the cost to date divided by the cost estimate or $40,000/$90,000 = 0.44 or 44 percent. Third, the "incremental milestones" method would be applied by examining each pipe section and estimating a percentage complete and then aggregating to determine the total percentage complete. For example, suppose the following quantities of piping fell into four categories of completeness:

Complete (100%)	380 ft
Hangars and trim complete (90%)	20 ft
Ends welded (60%)	5 ft
Spool in place (20%)	0 ft

Then using the incremental milestones shown, the estimate of completed work would be 380 + (20)(0.9) + (5)(0.6) + 0 = 401 ft and the proportion complete would be 401 ft/1,000 ft = 0.401 or 40 percent after rounding.

Once an estimate of work completed is available, then the estimated cost to complete the activity can be calculated. First, a simple linear extrapolation of cost results in an estimate of $40,000/0.4 = $100,000 for the piping construction using the 40 percent estimate of work completed. This estimate projects a cost overrun of $100,000 − $90,000 = $10,000.

Second, a linear extrapolation of productivity results in an estimate of (1,000 ft)(500 hr/400 ft)($60/hr) + $30,000 = $105,000. for completion of the piping construction. This estimate suggests a variance of $105,000 − $90,000 = $15,000 above the activity estimate. In making this estimate, labor and material costs were entered separately, whereas the two were implicitly combined in the simple linear cost forecast. The source of the variance can also be identified in this calculation: compared to the original estimate, the labor productivity is 1.25 hours per foot or 25 percent higher than the original estimate.

Example 12-4: Estimated Total Cost for Completion

The forecasting procedures just described assumed linear extrapolations of future costs, based either on the complete experience on the activity or the recent experience. For activities with good historical records, it can be the case that a typically nonlinear profile of cost expenditures and completion proportions can be estimated. Figure 12-1 illustrates one possible nonlinear relationship derived from experience in some

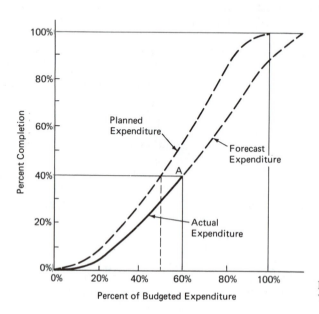

Figure 12-1 Proportion Completion Versus Expenditure for an Activity

Cost Control, Monitoring, and Accounting   Chap. 12

particular activity. The progress on a new job can be compared to this historical record. For example, point A in Figure 12-1 suggests a higher expenditure than is normal for the completion proportion. This point represents 40 percent of work completed with an expenditure of 60 percent of the budget. Since the historical record suggests only 50 percent of the budget should be expended at time of 40 percent completion, a 60% − 50% = 10% overrun in cost is expected even if work efficiency can be increased to historical averages. If comparable cost overruns continue to accumulate, then the cost to complete will be even higher.

12.4 FINANCIAL ACCOUNTING SYSTEMS AND COST ACCOUNTS

The cost accounts described in the previous sections provide only one of the various components in a financial accounting system. Before further discussing the use of cost accounts in project control, the relationship of project and financial accounting deserves mention. Accounting information is generally used for three distinct purposes:

- Internal reporting to project managers for day-to-day planning, monitoring, and control
- Internal reporting to managers for aiding strategic planning
- External reporting to owners, government, regulators, and other outside parties

External reports are constrained to particular forms and procedures by contractual reporting requirements or by generally accepted accounting practices. Preparation of such external reports is referred to as *financial accounting*. In contrast, *cost* or *managerial* accounting is intended to aid internal managers in their responsibilities of planning, monitoring, and control.

Project costs are always included in the system of financial accounts associated with an organization. At the heart of this system, all expense transactions are recorded in a general ledger. The general ledger of accounts forms the basis for management reports on particular projects as well as the financial accounts for an entire organization. Other components of a financial accounting system include

- **The accounts payable** journal is intended to provide records of bills received from vendors, material suppliers, subcontractors, and other outside parties. Invoices of charges are recorded in this system as are checks issued in payment. Charges to individual cost accounts are relayed or *posted* to the general ledger.
- **Accounts receivable journals** provide the opposite function to that of accounts payable. In this journal, billings to clients are recorded as well as receipts. Revenues received are relayed to the general ledger.
- **Job cost ledgers** summarize the charges associated with particular projects, arranged in the various cost accounts used for the project budget.
- **Inventory records** are maintained to identify the amount of materials available at any time.

In traditional bookkeeping systems, day-to-day transactions are first recorded in journals. With double-entry bookkeeping, each transaction is recorded as both a debit and a credit to particular accounts in the ledger. For example, payment of a supplier's bill represents a debit or increase to a project cost account and a credit or reduction to the company's cash account. Periodically, the transaction information is summarized and transferred to ledger accounts. This process is called *posting* and may be done instantaneously or daily in computerized systems.

In reviewing accounting information, the concepts of *flows* and *stocks* should be kept in mind. Daily transactions typically reflect flows of dollar amounts entering or leaving the organization. Similarly, use or receipt of particular materials represent flows from or to inventory. An account balance represents the *stock* or cumulative amount of funds resulting from these daily flows. Information on both flows and stocks are needed to give an accurate view of an organization's state. In addition, forecasts of future changes are needed for effective management.

Information from the general ledger is assembled for the organization's financial reports, including balance sheets and income statements for each period. These reports are the basic products of the financial accounting process and are often used to assess the performance of an organization. Table 12-5 shows a typical income statement for a small construction firm, indicating a net profit of $330,000 after taxes. This statement summarizes the flows of transactions within a year. Table 12-6 shows the comparable balance sheet, indicating a net increase in retained earnings equal to the net profit. The balance sheet reflects the effects of income flows during the year on the overall worth of the organization.

TABLE 12–5 AN ACCOUNTING STATEMENT OF INCOME

Income Statement
for the year ended December 31, 19xx

Gross project revenues	$7,200,000
Direct project costs on contracts	5,500,000
Depreciation of equipment	200,000
Estimating	150,000
Administrative and other expenses	650,000
Subtotal of cost and expenses	$6,500,000
Operating income	700,000
Interest expense, net	150,000
Income before taxes	$ 550,000
Income tax	220,000
Net income after tax	$ 330,000
Cash dividends	100,000
Retained earnings, current year	$ 230,000
Retention at beginning of year	650,000
Retained earnings at end of year	$ 880,000

In the context of private construction firms, particular problems arise in the treatment of uncompleted contracts in financial reports. Under the "completed-contract" method, income is reported only for completed projects. Work on projects underway is only reported on the balance sheet, representing an asset if contract billings exceed costs or a liability if costs exceed billings. When a project is completed, the total net profit (or loss) is reported in the final period as income. Under the "percentage-of-completion" method, actual costs are reported on the income statement plus a proportion of all project revenues (or billings) equal to the proportion of work completed during the period. The proportion of work completed is computed as the ratio of costs incurred to date and the total estimated cost of the project. Thus, if 20 percent of a project were completed in a particular period at a direct cost of $180,000 and on a project with expected revenues of $1,000,000, then the contract revenues earned would be calculated as $1,000,000(0.2) = $200,000. This figure represents a profit and contribution to overhead of $200,000 − $180,000 = $20,000 for the period. Note that billings and actual receipts might be in excess or less than the calculated revenues of $200,000. On the balance sheet of an organization using the percentage-of-completion method, an asset is usually reported to reflect billings and the estimated or calculated earnings in excess of actual billings.

As another example of the difference in the "percentage-of-completion" and the "completed-contract" methods, consider a three-year project to construct a plant with the following cash flow for a contractor:

TABLE 12–6 AN ACCOUNTING BALANCE SHEET

Balance Sheet

December 31, 19xx

Assets	Amount
Cash	$ 150,000
Payments receivable	750,000
Work in progress, not claimed	700,000
Work in progress, retention	200,000
Equipment at cost less accumulated depreciation	1,400,000
Total	$3,200,000

Liabilities and Equity

Liabilities	
Accounts payable	$ 950,000
Other items payable (taxes, wages, etc.)	50,000
Long-term debts	500,000
Subtotal	1,500,000
Shareholders' funds	
40,000 shares of common stock	
(Including paid-in capital)	900,000
Retained earnings	800,000
Subtotal	1,700,000
Total liabilities and equity	$3,200,000

Year	Contract Expenses	Payments Received
1	$700,000	$900,000
2	180,000	250,000
3	320,000	150,000
Total	$1,200,000	$1,300,000

The supervising architect determines that 60 percent of the facility is complete in year 1 and 75 percent in year 2. Under the "percentage-of-completion" method, the net income in year 1 is $780,000 (60% of $1,300,000) less the $700,000 in expenses or $80,000. Under the "completed-contract" method, the entire profit of $100,000 would be reported in year 3.

The percentage-of-completion method of reporting period earnings has the advantage of representing the actual estimated earnings in each period. As a result, the income stream and resulting profits are less susceptible to precipitate swings on the completion of a project as can occur with the completed-contract method of calculating income. However, the percentage of completion has the disadvantage of relying upon estimates which can be manipulated to obscure the actual position of a company or which are difficult to reproduce by outside observers. There are also subtleties such as the deferral of all calculated income from a project until a minimum threshold of the project is completed. As a result, interpretation of the income statement and balance sheet of a private organization is not always straightforward. Finally, there are tax disadvantages from using the percentage of completion method since corporate taxes on expected profits may become due during the project rather than being deferred until the project completion. As an example of tax implications of the two reporting methods, a study of 47 construction firms conducted by the General Accounting Office found that $280 million in taxes were deferred from 1980 to 1984 through use of the completed-contract method.[98]

It should be apparent that percentage-of-completion accounting provides only a rough estimate of the actual profit or status of a project. Also, the completed contract method of accounting is entirely retrospective and provides no guidance for management. This is only one example of the types of allocations that are introduced to correspond to generally accepted accounting practices, yet may not further the cause of good project management. Another common example is the use of equipment depreciation schedules to allocate equipment purchase costs. Allocations of costs or revenues to particular periods within a project may cause severe changes in particular indicators, but have no real meaning for good management or profit over the entire course of a project. As Johnson and Kaplan argue:[99]

[98] As reported in *The Wall Street Journal*, February 19, 1986, p. A1, c. 4.

[99] H. T. Johnson and R. S. Kaplan, *Relevance Lost, The Rise and Fall of Management Accounting*, Harvard Business School Press, Boston, 1987, p. 1.

Today's management accounting information, driven by the procedures and cycle of the organization's financial reporting system, is too late, too aggregated and too distorted to be relevant for managers' planning and control decisions. . . .

Management accounting reports are of little help to operating managers as they attempt to reduce costs and improve productivity. Frequently, the reports decrease productivity because they require operating managers to spend time attempting to understand and explain reported variances that have little to do with the economic and technological reality of their operations. . . .

The managagement accounting system also fails to provide accurate product costs. Cost are distributed to products by simplistic and arbitrary measures, usually direct labor based, that do not represent the demands made by each product on the firm's resources.

As a result, complementary procedures to those used in traditional financial accounting are required to accomplish effective project control, as described in the preceding and following sections. While financial statements provide consistent and essential information on the condition of an entire organization, they need considerable interpretation and supplementation to be useful for project management.

Example 12-5: Calculating Net Profit

As an example of the calculation of net profit, suppose that a company began six jobs in a year, completing three jobs and having three jobs still underway at the end of the year. Details of the six jobs are shown in Table 12-7. What would be the company's net profit under, first, the percentage-of-completion and, second, the completed-contract method accounting conventions?

TABLE 12–7 FINANCIAL RECORDS OF PROJECTS

Net Profit on Completed Contracts (in $ thousands)

Job 1	$1,436		
Job 2	356		
Job 3	− 738		
Total net profit on completed jobs	$1,054		

Status of Jobs Underway	Job 4	Job 5	Job 6
Original contract price	$4,200	$3,800	$5,630
Contract changes (change orders, etc.)	400	600	− 300
Total cost to date	3,600	1,710	620
Payments received or due to date	3,520	1,830	340
Estimated cost to complete	500	2,300	5,000

As shown in Table 12-7, a net profit of $1,054,000 was earned on the three completed jobs. Under the completed-contract method, this total would be total profit. Under the percentage-of-completion method, the year's expected profit on the projects underway would be added to this amount. For job 4, the expected profits (in $ thousands) are calculated as follows:

$$\text{Current contract price} = \text{original contract price} + \text{contract changes}$$
$$= \$4,200 + \$400 = \$4,600$$
$$\text{Credit or debit to date} = \text{payments received or due to date}$$
$$-\text{total costs to date}$$
$$= \$3,520 - \$3,600 = -\$80$$
$$\text{Contract value of uncompleted work} = \text{current contract price}$$
$$-\text{payments received or due}$$
$$= \$4,600 - \$3,520 = \$1,080$$
$$\text{Credit or debit to come} = \text{contract value of uncompleted work}$$
$$-\text{estimated cost to complete}$$
$$= \$1,080 - \$500 = \$580$$
$$\text{Estimated final gross profit} = \text{credit or debit to date}$$
$$+\text{credit or debit to come}$$
$$= -\$80 + \$580 = \$500$$
$$\text{Estimated total project costs} = \text{contract price} - \text{gross profit}$$
$$= \$4,600 - \$500 = \$4,100$$
$$\text{Estimated profit to date} = \text{estimated final gross profit}$$
$$\times \text{proportion of work complete}$$
$$= \$500(\$3,600/\$4,100)) = \$439$$

Similar calculations for the other jobs underway indicate estimated profits to date of $161,000 for job 5 and −$42,000 for job 6. As a result, the net profit using the percentage-of-completion method would be $1,612,000 for the year. Note that this figure would be altered in the event of multiyear projects in which net profits on projects completed or underway in this year were claimed in earlier periods.

12.5 CONTROL OF PROJECT CASH FLOWS

Section 12.3 described the development of information for the control of project costs with respect to the various functional activities appearing in the project budget. Project managers also are involved with assessment of the overall status of the project, including the status of activities, financing, payments, and receipts. These various items comprise the project and financing cash flows described in earlier chapters. These components include costs incurred, billings and receipts, billings to owners (for contractors), payable amounts to suppliers and contractors, financing plan cash flows (for bonds or other financial instruments), and so on.

As an example of cash flow control, consider the report shown in Table 12-8. In this case, costs are not divided into functional categories as in Table 12-4, such as labor, material, or equipment. Table 12-8 represents a summary of the project status as viewed from *different components of the accounting system*. Thus, the aggregation of different kinds of cost exposure or cost commitment shown in Table 12-4 has not been performed. The elements in Table 12-8 include

- **Costs**

  This is a summary of charges as reflected by the job cost accounts, including expenditures and estimated costs. This row provides an aggregate summary of the detailed activity cost information described in the previous section. For this example, the total costs as of July 2 (7/02) were $8,754,516, and the original cost estimate was $65,863,092, so the approximate percentage complete was $8,754,516/$65,863,092 or 13.292 percent. However, the project manager now projects a cost of $66,545,263 for the project, representing an increase of $682,171 over the original estimate. This new estimate would reflect the actual percentage of work completed as well as other effects such as changes in unit prices for labor or materials. Needless to say, this increase in expected costs is not a welcome change to the project manager.

- **Billings**

  This row summarizes the state of cash flows with respect to the owner of the facility; this row would not be included for reports to owners. The contract amount was $67,511,602, and a total of $9,276,621 or 13.741 percent of the contract has been billed. The amount of allowable billing is specified under the terms of the contract between an owner and an engineer, architect, or constructor. In this case, total billings have exceeded the estimated project completion proportion. The final column includes the currently projected net earnings of $966,339. This figure is calculated as the contract amount less projected costs: $67,511,602 − $66,545,263 = $966,339. Note that this profit figure does not reflect the time value of money or discounting.

- **Payables**

  The payables row summarizes the amount owed by the contractor to material suppliers, labor or subcontractors. At the time of this report, $6,719,103 had been paid to subcontractors, material suppliers, and others. Invoices of $1,300,089 have accumulated but have not yet been paid. A retention of $391,671 has been imposed on subcontractors, and $343,653 in direct labor expenses have been occurred. The total of payables is equal to the total project expenses shown in the first row of costs.

- **Receivables**

  This row summarizes the cash flow of receipts from the owner. Note that the actual receipts from the owner may differ from the amounts billed due to delayed payments or retainage on the part of the owner. The net billed equals the gross billed less retention by the owner. In this case, gross billed is $9,276,621 (as shown in the billings row), the net billed is $8,761,673 and the retention is $514,948. Unfortunately, only $7,209,344 has been received from the owner, so the open receivable amount is a (substantial !) $2,067,277 due from the owner.

- **Cash Position**

  This row summarizes the cash position of the project as if all expenses and receipts for the project were combined in a single account. The actual expenditures have been $7,062,756 (calculated as the total costs of $8,754,516 less subcontractor retentions of $391,671 and unpaid bills of $1,300,089) and $7,209,344 has been received from the owner. As a result, a net cash balance of $146,588 exists which can be used in an interest earning bank account or to finance deficits on other projects.

Each of the rows shown in Table 12-8 would be derived from different sets of financial accounts. Additional reports could be prepared on the financing cash flows for bonds or interest charges in an overdraft account.

The overall status of the project requires synthesizing the different pieces of information summarized in Table 12-8. Each of the different accounting systems contributing to this table provides a different view of the status of the project. In this example, the budget information indicates that costs are higher than expected, which could be troubling. However, a profit is still expected for the project. A substantial amount of money is due from the owner, and this could turn out to be a problem if the owner continues to lag in payment. Finally, the positive cash position for the project is highly desirable since financing charges can be avoided.

TABLE 12–8   A CASH FLOW STATUS REPORT ($)

Costs	Charges	Estimated	% Complete	Projected	Change
7/02	8,754,516	65,863,092	13.292	66,545,263	682,171
Billings	Contract	Gross bill	% Billed	Profit	
7/01	67,511,602	9,276,621	13.741	966,339	
Payables	Paid	Open	Retention	Labor	**Total**
7/01	6,719,103	1,300,089	391,671	343,653	8,754,516
Receivable	Net bill	Received	Retention	Open	
7/02	8,761,673	7,209,344	514,948	2,067,277	
Cash position	Paid	Received	Position		
	7,062,756	7,209,344	146,588		

The job status reports illustrated in this and the previous sections provide a primary tool for project cost control. Different reports with varying amounts of detail and item reports would be prepared for different individuals involved in a project. Reports to upper management would be summaries, reports to particular staff individuals would emphasize their responsibilities (purchasing, payroll, etc.), and detailed reports would be provided to the individual project managers. Coupled with scheduling reports described in Chapter 10, these reports provide a snapshot view of how a project is doing. Of course, these schedule and cost reports would have to be tempered by the actual accomplishments and problems occurring in the field. For example, if work already completed is of substandard quality, these reports would not reveal such a problem. Even though the reports indicated a project on time and on budget, the possibility of rework or inadequate facility performance due to quality problems would quickly reverse that rosy situation.

12.6 SCHEDULE CONTROL

In addition to cost control, project managers must also give considerable attention to monitoring schedules. Construction typically involves a deadline for work completion, so contractual agreements will force attention to schedules. More generally, delays in construction represent additional costs due to late facility occupancy or other factors. Just as costs incurred are compared to budgeted costs, actual activity durations may be compared to expected durations. In this process, forecasting the time to complete particular activities may be required.

The methods used for forecasting completion times of activities are directly analogous to those used for cost forecasting. For example, a typical estimating formula might be

$$D_f = Wh_t \qquad (12.5)$$

where D_f is the forecast duration, W is the amount of work, and h_t is the observed productivity to time t. As with cost control, it is important to devise efficient and cost-effective methods for gathering information on actual project accomplishments. Generally, observations of work completed are made by inspectors and project managers and then work completed is estimated as described in Section 12.3. Once estimates of work complete and time expended on particular activities is available, deviations from the original duration estimate can be estimated. The calculations for making duration estimates are quite similar to those used in making cost estimates in Section 12.3.

For example, Figure 12-2 shows the originally scheduled project progress versus the actual progress on a project. This figure is constructed by summing up the percentage of each activity which is complete at different points in time; this summation can be weighted by the magnitude of effort associated with each activity. In Figure 12-2, the project was ahead of the original schedule for a period including point A, but is now late at point B by an amount equal to the horizontal distance between the planned progress and the actual progress observed to date.

Schedule adherence and the current status of a project can also be represented on geometric models of a facility. For example, an animation of the construction sequence can be shown on a computer screen, with different colors or other coding scheme indicating the type of activity underway on each component of the facility. Deviations from the planned schedule can also be portrayed by color coding. The result is a mechanism to both indicate work in progress and schedule adherence specific to individual components in the facility.

In evaluating schedule progress, it is important to bear in mind that some activities possess float or scheduling leeway, whereas delays in activities on the critical path will cause project delays. In particular, the delay in planned progress at time t may be soaked up in activities' float (thereby causing no overall delay in the project completion) or may cause a project delay. As a result of this ambiguity,

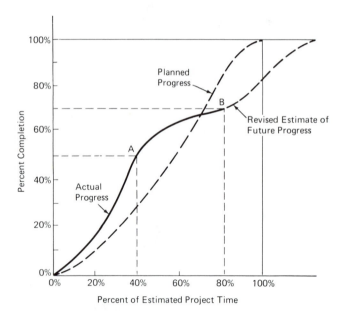

Figure 12-2 Planned Versus Actual Progress over Time on a Project

it is preferable to update the project schedule to devise an accurate protrayal of the schedule adherence. After applying a scheduling algorithm, a new project schedule can be obtained. For cash flow planning purposes, a graph or report similar to

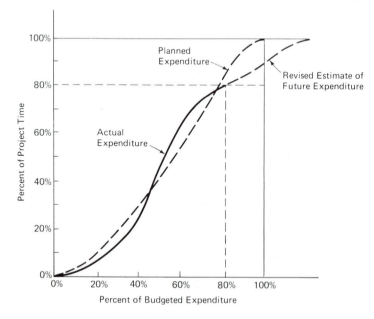

Figure 12-3 Planned Versus Actual Expenditures on a Project

that shown in Figure 12-3 can be constructed to compare actual expenditures to planned expenditures at any time. This process of rescheduling to indicate the schedule adherence is only one of many instances in which schedule and budget updating may be appropriate, as discussed in the next section.

12.7 SCHEDULE AND BUDGET UPDATES

Scheduling and project planning is an activity that continues throughout the lifetime of a project. As changes or discrepancies between the plan and the realization occur, the project schedule and cost estimates should be modified and new schedules devised. Too often, the schedule is devised once by a planner in the central office, and then revisions or modifications are done incompletely or only sporadically. The result is the lack of effective project monitoring and the possibility of eventual chaos on the project site.

On "fast-track" projects, initial construction activities are begun even before the facility design is finalized. In this case, special attention must be placed on the coordinated scheduling of design and construction activities. Even in projects for which the design is finalized before construction begins, *change orders* representing changes in the "final" design are often issued to incorporate changes desired by the owner.

Periodic updating of future activity durations and budgets is especially important to avoid excessive optimism in projects experiencing problems. If one type of activity experiences delays on a project, then related activities are also likely to be delayed unless managerial changes are made. Construction projects normally involve numerous activities which are closely related due to the use of similar materials, equipment, workers, or site characteristics. Expected cost changes should also be propagated thoughout a project plan. In essence, duration and cost estimates for future activities should be revised in light of the actual experience on the job. Without this updating, project schedules slip more and more as time progresses. To perform this type of updating, project managers need access to original estimates and estimating assumptions.

Unfortunately, most project cost-control and scheduling systems do not provide many aids for such updating. What is required is a means of identifying discrepancies, diagnosing the cause, forecasting the effect, and propagating this effect to all related activities. While these steps can be undertaken manually, computers aid to support interactive updating or even automatic updating would be helpful.[100]

Beyond the direct updating of activity durations and cost estimates, project managers should have mechanisms available for evaluating any type of schedule change. Updating activity duration estimations, changing scheduled start times, modifying the estimates of resources required for each activity, and even changing

[100] One experimental program directed at this problem is a knowledge-based expert system described in R. E. Levitt and J. C. Kunz, "Using Knowledge of Construction and Project Management for Automated Schedule Updating," *Project Management Journal*, Vol. 16, 1985, pp. 57–76. Expert systems and related developments are described in Chapter 15.

the project network logic (by inserting new activities or other changes) should all be easily accomplished. In effect, scheduling aids should be directly available to project managers.[101] Fortunately, local computers are commonly available on site for this purpose.

Example 12-6: Schedule Updates in a Small Project

As an example of the type of changes that might be required, consider the nine activity project described in Section 10.3 and appearing in Figure 12-4. Also, suppose that

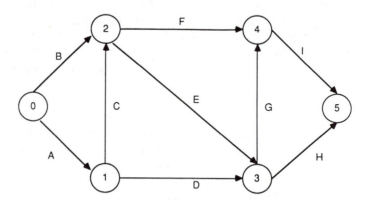

Figure 12-4 A Nine-Activity Example Project

the project is four days underway, with the current activity schedule and progress as shown in Figure 12-5. A few problems or changes that might be encountered include the following:

1. An underground waterline that was previously unknown was ruptured during the fifth day of the project. An extra day was required to replace the ruptured section, and another day will be required for clean-up. What is the impact on the project duration?

   • To analyze this change with the critical path scheduling procedure, the manager has the options of (1) changing the expected duration of activity C, General Excavation, to the new expected duration of 10 days or (2) splitting activity C into two tasks (corresponding to the work done prior to the waterline break and that to be done after) and adding a new activity representing repair and clean-up from the waterline break. The second approach has the advantage that any delays to other activities (such as activities D and E) could also be indicated by precedence constraints.

---

[101] For an example of a prototype interactive project management environment that includes graphical displays and scheduling algorithms, see R. Kromer, "Interactive Activity Network Analysis Using a Personal Computer," unpublished MS thesis, Department of Civil Engineering, Carnegie Mellon University, Pittsburgh, 1984.

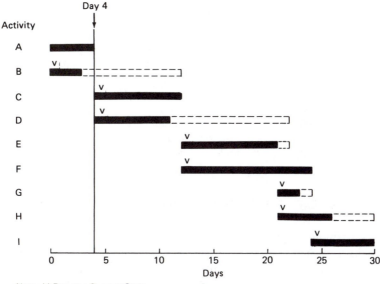

Figure 12-5 Current Schedule for an Example Project Presented as a Bar Chart

- Assuming that no other activities are affected, the manager decides to increase the expected duration of activity C to 10 days. Since activity C is on the critical path, the project duration also increases by 2 days. Applying the critical path scheduling procedure would confirm this change and also give a new set of earliest and latest starting times for the various activities.

2. After 8 days on the project, the owner asks that a new drain be installed in addition to the sewer line scheduled for activity G. The project manager determines that a new activity could be added to install the drain in parallel with activity G and requiring 2 days. What is the effect on the schedule?

   - Inserting a new activity in the project network between nodes 3 and 4 violates the activity-on-branch convention that only one activity can be defined between any two nodes. Hence, a new node and a dummy activity must be inserted in addition to the drain installation activity. As a result, the nodes must be renumbered and the critical path schedule developed again. Performing these operations reveals that no change in the project duration would occur and the new activity has a total float of 1 day.

   - To avoid the labor associated with modifying the network and renumbering nodes, suppose that the project manager simply redefined activity G as installation of sewer and drain lines requiring 4 days. In this case, activity G would appear on the critical path and the project duration would increase. Adding an additional crew so that the two installations could proceed in parallel might reduce the duration of activity G back to 2 days and thereby avoid the increase in the project duration.

3. At day 12 of the project, the excavated trenches collapse during activity E. An additional 5 days will be required for this activity. What is the effect on

the project schedule? What changes should be made to ensure meeting the completion deadline?

- Activity E has a total float of only 1 day. With the change in this activity's duration, it will lie on the critical path and the project duration will increase.
- Analysis of possible time savings in subsequent activities is now required, using the procedures described in Section 10.9.

As can be imagined, it is not at all uncommon to encounter changes during the course of a project that require modification of durations, changes in the network logic of precedence relationships, or additions and deletions of activities. Consequently, the scheduling process should be readily available as the project is underway.

12.8 RELATING COST AND SCHEDULE INFORMATION

The previous sections focused upon the identification of the budgetary and schedule status of projects. Actual projects involve a complex interrelationship between time and cost. As projects proceed, delays influence costs and budgetary problems may in turn require adjustments to activity schedules. Trade-offs between time and costs were discussed in Section 10.9 in the context of project planning in which additional resources applied to a project activity might result in a shorter duration but higher costs. Unanticipated events might result in increases in both time and cost to complete an activity. For example, excavation problems may easily lead to much lower than anticipated productivity on activities requiring digging.

While project managers implicitly recognize the interplay between time and cost on projects, it is rare to find effective project-control systems which include both elements. Usually, project costs and schedules are recorded and reported by separate application programs. Project managers must then perform the tedious task of relating the two sets of information.

The difficulty of integrating schedule and cost information stems primarily from the level of detail required for effective integration. Usually, a single project activity will involve numerous cost account categories. For example, an activity for the preparation of a foundation would involve laborers, cement workers, concrete forms, concrete, reinforcement, transportation of materials, and other resources. Even a more disaggregated activity definition such as erection of foundation forms would involve numerous resources such as forms, nails, carpenters, laborers, and material transportation. Again, different cost accounts would normally be used to record these various resources. Similarly, numerous activities might involve expenses associated with particular cost accounts. For example, a particular material such as standard piping might be used in numerous different schedule activities. To integrate cost and schedule information, the disaggregated charges for specific activities and specific cost accounts must be the basis of analysis.

A straightforward means of relating time and cost information is to define individual *work elements* representing the resources in a particular cost category associated with a particular project activity. Work elements would represent an element in a two-dimensional matrix of activities and cost accounts as illustrated in Figure 12-6. A numbering or identifying system for work elements would include both the relevant cost account and the associated activity. In some cases, it might also be desirable to identify work elements by the responsible organization or individual. In this case, a three-dimensional representation of work elements is required, with the third dimension corresponding to responsible individuals.[102] More generally, modern computerized databases can accommodate a flexible structure of data representation to support aggregation with respect to numerous different perspectives; this type of system will be discussed in Chapter 14.

With this organization of information, a number of management reports or views could be generated. In particular, the costs associated with specific activities could be obtained as the sum of the work elements appearing in any row in Figure 12-6. These costs could be used to evaluate alternate technologies to accomplish particular activities or to derive the expected project cash flow over time as the schedule changes. From a management perspective, problems developing from particular activities could be rapidly identified since costs would be accumulated at such a disaggregated level. As a result, project control becomes at once more precise and detailed.

Unfortunately, the development and maintenance of a work element database can represent a large data collection and organization effort. As noted earlier, 400 separate cost accounts and 400 activities would not be unusual for a construction project. The result would be up to $400 \times 400 = 160,000$ separate work elements. Of course, not all activities involve each cost account. However, even a density of 2 percent (so there would be 400 cost accounts and each account would have 8 associated activities on the average) would involve a total of 3,200 work elements. Initially preparing this database represents a considerable burden, but it is also the case that project bookkeepers must record project events within each of these various work elements. Implementations of the "work element" project-

Project Activity Group	Cost Amount for Superstructure					
	204.1	204.2	204.3	204.4	204.5	204.6
First Floor	X	X		X		X
Second Floor		X		X		X
Third Floor		X	X	X		X
Fourth Floor		X	X			X
Fifth Floor		X	X		X	X

Figure 12-6 A Cost Account and Project Activity Matrix

[102] A three-dimensional work element definition was proposed by J. M. Neil, "A System for Integrated Project Management," *Proceedings of the Conference on Current Practice in Cost Estimating and Cost Control, ASCE*, Austin, TX, April 1983, pp. 138–146.

control systems have typically foundered on the burden of data collection, storage, and bookkeeping.

Until data collection is better automated, the use of work elements to control activities in large projects is likely to be difficult to implement. However, certain segments of project activities can profit tremendously from this type of organization. In particular, material requirements can be tracked in this fashion. Materials involve only a subset of all cost accounts and project activities, so the burden of data collection and control is much smaller than for an entire system. Moreover, the benefits from integration of schedule and cost information are particularly noticeable in materials control since delivery schedules are directly affected and bulk order discounts might be identified. Consequently, materials control systems can reasonably encompass a "work element" accounting system.

In the absence of a work element accounting system, costs associated with particular activities are usually estimated by summing expenses in all cost accounts directly related to an activity plus a proportion of expenses in cost accounts used jointly by two or more activities. The basis of cost allocation would typically be the level of effort or resource required by the different activities. For example, costs associated with supervision might be allocated to different concreting activities on the basis of the amount of work (measured in cubic yards of concrete) in the different activities. With these allocations, cost estimates for particular work activities can be obtained.

12.9 REFERENCES

12-1. American Society of Civil Engineers, *Construction Cost Control,* ASCE Manuals and Reports of Engineering Practice No. 65, rev. ed., New York, 1985.

12-2. Coombs, W. E. and W. J. Palmer, *Construction Accounting and Financial Management*, McGraw-Hill Book Company, New York, 1977.

12-3. Halpin, D. W., *Financial and Cost Concepts for Construction Management*, John Wiley and Sons, Inc., New York, 1985.

12-4. Johnson, H. Thomas, and Robert S. Kaplan, *Relevance Lost, The Rise and Fall of Management Accounting*, Harvard Business School Press, Boston, 1987.

12-5. Mueller, F. W. *Integrated Cost and Schedule Control for Construction Projects*, Van Nostrand Reinhold Co., New York, 1986.

12-6. Tersine, R. J., *Principles of Inventory and Materials Management*, North Holland, New York, 1982.

12.10 PROBLEMS

12-1. Suppose that the expected expenditure of funds in a particular category was expected to behave in a piecewise linear fashion over the course of the project. In particular, the following points have been established from historical records for the percentage of completion versus the expected expenditure (as a percentage of the budget):

Percentage of completion	Expected expenditure
0%	0%
20%	10%
40%	25%
60%	55%
80%	90%
100%	100%

a. Graph the relationship between percentage complete and expected expenditure.

b. Develop a formula or set of formulas for forecasting the ultimate expenditure on this activity given the percentage of completion. Assume that any over or under expenditure will continue to grow proportionately during the course of the project.

c. Using your formula, what is the expected expenditure as a percentage of the activity budget if

 i. 15 percent of funds have been expended and 15 percent of the activity is complete.

 ii. 30 percent of funds have been expended and 30 percent of the activity is complete.

 iii. 80 percent of funds have been expended and 80 percent of the activity is complete.

12-2. Repeat Problem P12-1 parts (b) and (c) assuming that any over- or under-expenditure will not continue to grow during the course of the project.

12-3. Suppose that you have been asked to take over as project manager on a small project involving installation of 5,000 Lf of metal ductwork in a building. The job was originally estimated to take 10 weeks, and you are assuming your duties after six weeks on the project. The original estimate assumed that each linear foot of ductwork would cost $10, representing $6 in labor costs and $4 in material cost. The expected production rate was 500 Lf of ductwork per week. The data concerning this project available from your firm's job control information system are the following:

	Weekly unit costs ($/Lf)			Quantity placed (Lf)		Total cost	
Week	Labor	Materials	Total	Week	To date	Week	To date
1	12.00	4.00	16.00	250	250	4000	4000
2	8.57	4.00	12.57	350	600	4400	8400
3	6.67	4.00	10.67	450	1050	4800	13200

a. Based on an extrapolation using the average productivity and cost for all three weeks, forecast the completion time, cost, and variance from original estimates.

b. Suppose that you assume that the productivity achieved in week 3 would continue for the remainder of the project. How would this affect your forecasts in (a)? Prepare new forecasts based on this assumption.

12-4. What criticisms could you make of the job status report in the previous problem from the viewpoint of good project management?

12-5. Suppose that the following estimate was made for excavation of 120,000 cubic yards on a site:

Resource	Quantity	Cost
Machines	1,200 hours	$ 60,000
Labor	6,000 hours	150,000
Trucks	2,400 hours	75,000
Total		$285,000

After 95,000 cubic yards of excavation was completed, the following expenditures had been recorded:

Resource	Quantity	Cost
Machines	1,063 hours	$ 47,835
Labor	7,138 hours	142,527
Trucks	1,500 hours	46,875
Total		$237,237

a. Calculate estimated and experienced productivity (cubic yards per hour) and unit cost (cost per cubic yard) for each resource.

b. Based on straight line extrapolation, do you see any problem with this activity? If so, can you suggest a reason for the problem based on your findings in (a)?

12-6. Suppose the following costs and units of work completed were recorded on an activity involving 800 work units:

Month	Monthly expenditure	Number of work units completed
1	$1,200	30
2	1,250	32
3	1,260	38
4	1,280	42
5	1,290	42
6	1,280	42

Answer the following questions:

a. For each month, determine the cumulative cost, the cumulative work completed, the average cumulative cost per unit of work, and the monthly cost per unit of work.

b. For each month, prepare a forecast of the eventual cost to complete the activity based on the proportion of work completed.

c. For each month, prepare a forecast of the eventual cost to complete the activity based on the average productivity experienced on the activity.

d. For each month, prepare a forecast of the eventual cost to complete the activity based on the productivity experienced in the current month.

12-7. Repeat Problem P12-6 for the following expenditure pattern:

Month	Monthly expenditure	Number of work units completed
1	$1,200	30
2	1,250	35
3	1,260	45
4	1,280	48
5	1,290	52
6	1,300	54

12-8. Why is it difficult to integrate scheduling and cost accounting information in project records?

12-9. Suppose that the following 10 activities were agreed upon in a contract between an owner and an engineer.

Original work plan information			
Activity	Duration (months)	Predecessors	Estimated cost ($ thousands)
A	2	—	7
B	5	—	9
C	5	B	8
D	2	C	4
E	3	B	1
F	8	—	7
G	4	E, F	6
H	4	E, F	5
I	11	B	10
J	2	E, F	7

Original contract information	
Total direct cost	$ 64
Overhead	64
Total direct and overhead	128
Profit	12.8
Total contract amount	$140.8

First year cash flow	
Expenditures including overhead	$56,000
Receipts from owner	$60,800

The markup on the activities' costs included 100 percent overhead and a profit of 10 percent on all costs (including overhead). This job was suspended for one year after completion of activities A, B, C, and D, and the owner paid a total of $60,800 to the engineer. Now the owner wishes to recommence the job and finish as soon as possible. However, general inflation has increased costs by ten percent in the intervening year. The engineer's discount rate is 15 percent per year (in current year dollars). For simplicity, you may assume that all cash transactions occur at the end of the year in making discounting calculations in answering the following questions:

a. How long will the remaining six activities require?

b. Suppose that the owner agrees to make a lump-sum payment of the remaining original contract at the completion of the project. Would the engineer still make a profit on the job? If so, how much?

c. Given that the engineer would receive a lump-sum payment at the end of the project, what amount should he request to earn 10 percent profit on all costs?

d. What is the net future value of the entire project at the end, assuming that the lump-sum payment you calculated in (c) is obtained?

13

Quality Control
and
Safety During Construction

13.1 QUALITY AND SAFETY CONCERNS IN CONSTRUCTION

Quality control and safety represent increasingly important concerns for project managers. Defects or failures in constructed facilities can result in very large costs. Even with minor defects, reconstruction may be required and facility operations impaired. Increased costs and delays are the result. In the worst case, failures may cause personal injuries or fatalities. Accidents during the construction process can similarly result in personal injuries and large costs. Indirect costs of insurance, inspection, and regulation are increasing rapidly due to these increased direct costs. Good project managers try to ensure that the job is done right the first time and that no major accidents occur on the project.

As with cost control, the most important decisions regarding the quality of a completed facility are made during the design and planning stages rather than during construction. It is during these preliminary stages that component configurations, material specifications, and functional performance are decided. Quality control during construction consists largely of ensuring *conformance* to these original design and planning decisions.

While conformance to existing design decisions is the primary focus of quality control, there are exceptions to this rule. First, unforeseen circumstances, incorrect design decisions or changes desired by an owner in the facility function may require reevaluation of design decisions during the course of construction. While these changes may be motivated by the concern for quality, they represent occasions for redesign with all the attendant objectives and constraints. As a second case, some designs rely upon informed and appropriate decision making during the construction process itself. For example, some tunneling methods make decisions about the amount of shoring required at different locations based upon observation of soil conditions during the tunneling process. Since such decisions are based on better information concerning actual site conditions, the facility design may be more cost effective as a result. Any special case of redesign during construction requires the various considerations discussed in Chapter 3.

With the attention to conformance as the measure of quality during the construction process, the specification of quality requirements in the design and contract documentation becomes extremely important. Quality requirements should be clear and verifiable, so that all parties in the project can understand the requirements for conformance. Much of the discussion in this chapter relates to the development and the implications of different quality requirements for construction as well as the issues associated with ensuring conformance.

Safety during the construction project is also influenced in large part by decisions made during the planning and design process. Some designs or construction plans are inherently difficult and dangerous to implement, whereas other, comparable plans may considerably reduce the possibility of accidents. For example, clear separation of traffic from construction zones during roadway rehabilitation can greatly reduce the possibility of accidental collisions. Beyond these design decisions, safety largely depends upon education, vigilance, and cooperation during the construction process. Workers should be constantly alert to the possibilities of accidents and avoid taking unnecessary risks.

13.2 ORGANIZING FOR QUALITY AND SAFETY

A variety of different organizations are possible for quality and safety control during construction. One common model is to have a group responsible for quality assurance and another group primarily responsible for safety within an organization. In large organizations, departments dedicated to quality assurance and to safety might assign specific individuals to assume responsibility for these functions on particular projects. For smaller projects, the project manager or an assistant might assume these and other responsibilities. In either case, ensuring safe and quality construction is a concern of the project manager in overall charge of the project in addition to the concerns of personnel, cost, time, and other management issues.

Inspectors and quality assurance personnel will be involved in a project to represent a variety of different organizations. Each of the parties directly concerned with the project may have their own quality and safety inspectors, including the owner, the engineer/architect, and the various constructor firms. These inspectors may be contractors from specialized quality assurance organizations. In addition to on-site inspections, samples of materials will commonly be tested by specialized laboratories to ensure compliance. Inspectors to ensure compliance with regulatory requirements will also be involved. Common examples are inspectors for the local government's building department, for environmental agencies, and for occupational health and safety agencies.

The U. S. Occupational Safety and Health Administration (OSHA) routinely conducts site visits of work places in conjunction with approved state inspection agencies. OSHA inspectors are required by law to issue citations for all standard violations observed. Safety standards prescribe a variety of mechanical safeguards and procedures; for example, ladder safety is covered by over 140 regulations. In cases of extreme noncompliance with standards, OSHA inspectors can stop work on a project. However, only a small fraction of construction sites are visited by OSHA inspectors, and most construction-site accidents are not caused by violations of existing standards. As a result, safety is largely the responsibility of the managers and workers on site rather than that of public inspectors.

While the multitude of participants involved in the construction process require the services of inspectors, it cannot be emphasized too strongly that inspectors are only a formal check on quality control. Quality control should be a primary objective for all the members of a project team. Managers should take responsibility for maintaining and improving quality control. Employee participation in quality control should be sought and rewarded, including the introduction of new ideas. Most important of all, quality improvement can serve as a catalyst for improved productivity. By suggesting new work methods, by avoiding rework, and by avoiding long-term problems, good quality control can pay for itself. Owners should promote good quality control and seek out contractors who maintain such standards.

In addition to the various organizational bodies involved in quality control, issues of quality control arise in virtually all the functional areas of construction activities. For example, ensuring accurate and useful information is an important part of maintaining quality performance. Other aspects of quality control include document control (including changes during the construction process), procurement, field inspection and testing, and final checkout of the facility.

13.3 WORK AND MATERIAL SPECIFICATIONS

Specifications of work quality are an important feature of facility designs. Specifications of required quality and components represent part of the necessary documentation to describe a facility. Typically, this documentation includes any special provisions of the facility design as well as references to generally accepted specifications to be used during construction.

General specifications of work quality are available in numerous fields and are issued in publications of organizations such as the American Society for Testing and Materials (ASTM), the American National Standards Institute (ANSI), or the Construction Specifications Institute (CSI). Distinct specifications are formalized for particular types of construction activities, such as welding standards issued by the American Welding Society, or for particular facility types, such as the *Standard Specifications for Highway Bridges* issued by the American Association of State Highway and Transportation Officials. These general specifications must be modified to reflect local conditions, policies, available materials, local regulations, and other special circumstances.

Construction specifications normally consist of a series of instructions or prohibitions for specific operations. For example, the following passage illustrates a typical specification, in this case for excavation for structures:

> Conform to elevations and dimensions shown on plan within a tolerance of plus or minus 0.10 foot, and extending a sufficient distance from footings and foundations to permit placing and removal of concrete formwork, installation of services, other construction, and for inspection. In excavating for footings and foundations, take care not to disturb bottom of excavation. Excavate by hand to final grade just before concrete reinforcement is placed. Trim bottoms to required lines and grades to leave solid base to receive concrete.

This set of specifications requires judgment in application since some items are not precisely specified. For example, excavation must extend a "sufficient" distance to permit inspection and other activities. Obviously, the term "sufficient" in this case may be subject to varying interpretations. In contrast, a specification that tolerances are within plus or minus a tenth of a foot is subject to direct measurement. However, specific requirements of the facility or characteristics of the site may make the standard tolerance of a tenth of a foot inappropriate. Writing specifications typically requires a trade-off between assuming reasonable behavior on the part of all the parties concerned in interpreting words such as "sufficient" versus the effort and possible inaccuracy in prespecifying all operations.

In recent years, *performance specifications* have been developed for many construction operations. Rather than specifying the required construction *process*, these specifications refer to the required performance or quality of the finished facility. The exact method by which this performance is obtained is left to the construction contractor. For example, traditional specifications for asphalt pavement specified the composition of the asphalt material, the asphalt temperature during paving, and compacting procedures. In contrast, a performance specification for asphalt would detail the desired performance of the pavement with respect to impermeability, strength, et cetera. How the desired performance level was attained would be up to the paving contractor. In some cases, the payment for asphalt paving might increase with better quality of asphalt beyond some minimum level of performance.

Example 13-1: Concrete Pavement Strength

Concrete pavements of superior strength result in cost savings by delaying the time at which repairs or reconstruction is required. In contrast, concrete of lower quality will necessitate more frequent overlays or other repair procedures. Contract provisions with adjustments to the amount of a contractor's compensation based on pavement quality have become increasingly common in recognition of the cost savings associated with higher-quality construction. Even if a pavement does not meet the "ultimate" design standard, it is still worth using the lower-quality pavement and resurfacing later rather than completely rejecting the pavement. Based on these life-cycle cost considerations, a typical pay schedule might be[103]

Load Ratio	Pay Factor
< 0.50	Reject
0.50–0.69	0.90
0.70–0.89	0.95
0.90–1.09	1.00
1.10–1.29	1.05
1.30–1.49	1.10
> 1.50	1.12

In this table, the load ratio is the ratio of the actual pavement strength to the desired design strength and the pay factor is a fraction by which the total pavement contract amount is multiplied to obtain the appropriate compensation to the contractor. For example, if a contractor achieves concrete strength 20 percent greater than the design specification, then the load ratio is 1.20 and the appropriate pay factor is 1.05, so the contractor receives a 5 percent bonus. Load factors are computed after tests on the concrete actually used in a pavement. Note that a 90 percent pay factor exists in this case with even pavement quality only 50 percent of that originally desired. This

[103] This illustrative pay factor schedule is adapted from R. M. Weed, "Development of Multicharacteristic Acceptance Procedures for Rigid Pavement," *Transportation Research Record 885*, 1982, pp. 25–36.

high pay factor even with weak concrete strength might exist since much of the cost of pavements are incurred in preparing the pavement foundation. Concrete strengths of less than 50 percent are cause for complete rejection in this case.

13.4 TOTAL QUALITY CONTROL

Quality control in construction typically involves ensuring compliance with minimum standards of material and workmanship to ensure the performance of the facility according to the design. These minimum standards are contained in the specifications described in the previous section. For the purpose of ensuring compliance, random samples and statistical methods are commonly used as the basis for accepting or rejecting work completed and batches of materials. Rejection of a batch is based on nonconformance or violation of the relevant design specifications. Procedures for this quality control practice are described in the following sections.

An implicit assumption in these traditional quality control practices is the notion of an *acceptable quality level* which is an allowable fraction of defective items. Materials obtained from suppliers or work performed by an organization is inspected and passed as acceptable if the estimated defective percentage is within the acceptable quality level. Problems with materials or goods are corrected after delivery of the product.

In contrast to this traditional approach of quality control is the goal of *total quality control*. In this system, no defective items are allowed anywhere in the construction process. While the zero defects goal can never be permanently attained, it provides a goal so that an organization is never satisfied with its quality control program even if defects are reduced by substantial amounts year after year. This concept and approach to quality control was first developed in manufacturing firms in Japan and Europe, but has since spread to many construction companies.

Total quality control is a commitment to quality expressed in all parts of an organization and typically involves many elements. Design reviews to ensure safe and effective construction procedures are a major element. Other elements include extensive training for personnel, shifting the responsibility for detecting defects from quality control inspectors to workers, and continually maintaining equipment. Worker involvement in improved quality control is often formalized in *quality circles* in which groups of workers meet regularly to make suggestions for quality improvement. Material suppliers are also required to ensure zero defects in delivered goods. Initially, all materials from a supplier are inspected and batches of goods with any defective items are returned. Suppliers with good records can be certified and not subject to complete inspection subsequently.

The traditional microeconomic view of quality control is that there is an "optimum" proportion of defective items. Trying to achieve greater quality than this optimum would substantially increase costs of inspection and reduce worker productivity. However, many companies have found that commitment to total quality control has substantial economic benefits that had been unappreciated in traditional approaches. Expenses associated with inventory, rework, scrap, and warranties were reduced. Worker enthusiasm and commitment improved. Customers often appreciated higher-quality work and would pay a premium for good quality. As a result, improved quality control became a competitive advantage.

Of course, total quality control is difficult to apply, particularly in construction. The unique nature of each facility, the variability in the work force, the multitude of subcontractors, and the cost of making necessary investments in education and procedures make programs of total quality control in construction difficult. Nevertheless, a commitment to improved quality even without endorsing the goal of zero defects can pay real dividends to organizations.

Example 13-2: Experience with Quality Circles

Quality circles represent a group of 5 to 15 workers who meet on a frequent basis to identify, discuss, and solve productivity and quality problems. A circle leader acts as liaison between the workers in the group and upper levels of management. The following are some examples of reported quality circle accomplishments in construction:[104]

1. On a highway project under construction by Taisei Corporation, it was found that the loss rate of ready-mixed concrete was too high. A quality circle composed of cement masons found out that the most important reason for this was due to an inaccurate checking method. By applying the circle's recommendations, the loss rate was reduced by 11.4 percent.

2. In a building project by Shimizu Construction Company, many cases of faulty reinforced concrete work were reported. The iron workers quality circle examined their work thoroughly and soon the faulty workmanship disappeared. A 10 percent increase in productivity was also achieved.

13.5 QUALITY CONTROL BY STATISTICAL METHODS

An ideal quality control program might test all materials and work on a particular facility. For example, nondestructive techniques such as x-ray inspection of welds can be used throughout a facility. An on-site inspector can witness the appropriateness and adequacy of construction methods at all times. Even better, individual craftsmen can perform continuing inspection of materials and their own work. Exhaustive or 100 percent testing of all materials and work by inspectors can be exceedingly expensive, however. In many instances, testing requires the destruction of a material sample, so exhaustive testing is not even possible. As a result, small samples are used to establish the basis of accepting or rejecting a particular work item or shipment of materials. Statistical methods are used to interpret the results of tests on a small sample to reach a conclusion concerning the acceptability of an entire *lot* or batch of materials or work products.

The use of statistics is essential in interpreting the results of testing on a small sample. Without adequate interpretation, small sample testing results can be quite

[104] B. A. Gilly, A. Touran, and T. Asai, "Quality Control Circles in Construction," *ASCE Journal of Construction Engineering and Management*, Vol. 113, no. 3, 1987, p. 432.

misleading. As an example, suppose that there are 10 defective pieces of material in a lot of 100. In taking a sample of five pieces, the inspector might not find *any* defective pieces or might have *all* sample pieces defective. Drawing a direct inference that none or all pieces in the population are defective on the basis of these samples would be incorrect. Due to this random nature of the sample selection process, testing results can vary substantially. It is only with statistical methods that issues such as the chance of different levels of defective items in the full lot can be fully analyzed from a small sample test.

There are two types of statistical sampling which are commonly used for the purpose of quality control in batches of work or materials:

1. The acceptance or rejection of a lot is based on the number of defective (bad) or nondefective (good) items in the sample. This is referred to as *sampling by attributes*.
2. Instead of using defective and nondefective classifications for an item, a quantitative quality measure or the value of a measured variable is used as a quality indicator. This testing procedure is referred to as *sampling by variables*.

Whatever sampling plan is used in testing, it is always assumed that the samples are representative of the entire population under consideration. Samples are expected to be chosen randomly so that each member of the population is equally likely to be chosen. Convenient sampling plans such as sampling every twentieth piece, choosing a sample every two hours, or picking the top piece on a delivery truck may be adequate to ensure a random sample if pieces are randomly mixed in a stack or in use. However, some convenient sampling plans can be inappropriate. For example, checking only easily accessible joints in a building component is inappropriate since joints that are hard to reach may be more likely to have erection or fabrication problems.

Another assumption implicit in statistical quality control procedures is that the quality of materials or work is expected to vary from one piece to another. This is certainly true in the field of construction. While a designer may assume that all concrete is exactly the same in a building, the variations in material properties, manufacturing, handling, pouring, and temperature during setting ensure that concrete is actually heterogeneous in quality. Reducing such variations to a minimum is one aspect of quality construction. Ensuring that the materials actually placed achieve some minimum quality level with respect to average properties or fraction of defectives is the task of quality control.

13.6 STATISTICAL QUALITY CONTROL WITH SAMPLING BY ATTRIBUTES

Sampling by attributes is a widely applied quality control method. The procedure is intended to determine whether or not a particular group of materials or work products is acceptable. In the literature of statistical quality control, a group of materials or work items to be tested is called a *lot* or *batch*. An assumption in the procedure is that each item in a batch can be tested and classified as either acceptable or deficient based upon mutually acceptable testing procedures and acceptance criteria. Each lot is tested to determine if it satisfies a minimum acceptable quality level (AQL) expressed as the maximum percentage of defective items in a lot or process.

In its basic form, sampling by attributes is applied by testing a predefined number of sample items from a lot. If the number of defective items is greater than a trigger level, then the lot is rejected as being likely to be of unacceptable quality. Otherwise, the lot is accepted. Developing this type of *sampling plan* requires consideration of probability, statistics, and acceptable risk levels on the part of the supplier and consumer of the lot. Refinements to this basic application procedure are also possible. For example, if the number of defectives is greater than some predefined number, then additional sampling may be started rather than immediate rejection of the lot. In many cases, the trigger level is a single defective item in the sample. In the remainder of this section, the mathematical basis for interpreting this type of sampling plan is developed.

More formally, a lot is defined as acceptable if it contains a fraction p_1 or less defective items. Similarly, a lot is defined as unacceptable if it contains a fraction p_2 or more defective units. Generally, the acceptance fraction is less than or equal to the rejection fraction, $p_1 \leq p_2$, and the two fractions are often equal so that there is no ambiguous range of lot acceptability between p_1 and p_2. Given a sample size and a trigger level for lot rejection or acceptance, we would like to determine the probabilities that acceptable lots might be incorrectly rejected (termed *producer's risk*) or that deficient lots might be incorrectly accepted (termed *consumer's risk*).

Consider a lot of finite number N, in which m items are defective (bad) and the remaining $(N - m)$ items are nondefective (good). If a random sample of n items is taken from this lot, then we can determine the probability of having different numbers of defective items in the sample. With a predefined acceptable number of defective items, we can then develop the probability of accepting a lot as a function of the sample size, the allowable number of defective items, and the actual fraction of defective items. This derivation is as follows.

The number of different samples of size n that can be selected from a finite population N is termed a mathematical *combination* and is computed as

$$\binom{N}{n} = \frac{N(N-1)\cdots(N-n+1)}{n!} = \frac{N!}{n!(N-n)!} \tag{13.1}$$

where a factorial, *n!* is $n \cdot (n-1) \cdot (n-2)\cdots(1)$ and 0 factorial (0!) is 1 by convention. The number of possible samples with exactly x defectives is the combination associated with obtaining x defectives from m possible defective items and $n - x$ good items from $N - m$ good items:

$$\binom{m}{x}\binom{N-m}{n-x} = \frac{m!}{x!(m-x)!} \times \frac{(N-m)!}{(n-x)!(N-m-n+x)!} \tag{13.2}$$

Given these possible numbers of samples, the probability of having exactly x defective items in the sample is given by the ratio as the hypergeometric series:

$$P(X = x) = \frac{\binom{m}{x}\binom{N-m}{n-x}}{\binom{N}{n}} \qquad x = 1, 2, \ldots, m \qquad (13.3)$$

With this function, we can calculate the probability of obtaining different numbers of defectives in a sample of a given size.

Suppose that the actual fraction of defectives in the lot is p and the actual fraction of nondefectives is q, then p plus q is 1, resulting in $m = Np$ and $N - m = Nq$. Then, a function $g(p)$ representing the probability of having r or less defective items in a sample of size n is obtained by substituting m and N into Eq. (13.3) and summing over the acceptable defective number of items:

$$g(p) = \sum_{x=0}^{r} P(X = x) = \sum_{x=0}^{r} \frac{\binom{Np}{x}\binom{Nq}{n-x}}{\binom{N}{n}} \qquad (13.4)$$

If the number of items in the lot, N, is large in comparison with the sample size n, then the function $g(p)$ can be approximated by the binomial distribution

$$g(p) = \sum_{x=0}^{r} \binom{n}{x} p^x q^{n-x} \qquad (13.5)$$

or

$$g(p) = 1 - \sum_{x=r+1}^{n} \binom{n}{x} p^x q^{n-x} \qquad (13.6)$$

The function $g(p)$ indicates the probability of accepting a lot, given the sample size n and the number of allowable defective items in the sample r. The function $g(p)$ can be represented graphically for each combination of sample size n and number of allowable defective items r, as shown by an example for $n = 15$ in Figure 13-1. Each curve corresponding to a sample size n is referred to as the operating characteristic curve (OC curve). For the special case of a single sample ($n = 1$), the function $g(p)$ can be simplified,

$$g(p) = \binom{1}{0} p^0 q^1 = q \qquad (13.7)$$

so that the probability of accepting a lot is equal to the fraction of acceptable items in the lot. For example, there is a probability of 0.5 that the lot may be accepted from a single sample test even if 50 percent of the lot is defective.

For any combination of n and r, we can read off the value of $g(p)$ for a given p from the corresponding OC curve. For example, $n = 15$ is specified in Figure

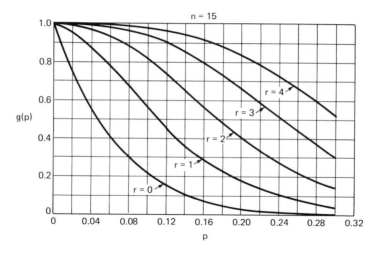

Figure 13-1 Operating Characteristic Curves Indicating Probability of Lot Acceptance

13-1. Then, for various values of r, we find:

$$
\begin{aligned}
r &= 0 \quad p = 24\% \quad g(p) \approx 2\% \\
r &= 0 \quad p = \ 4\% \quad g(p) \approx 54\% \\
r &= 1 \quad p = 24\% \quad g(p) \approx 10\% \\
r &= 1 \quad p = \ 4\% \quad g(p) \approx 88\%
\end{aligned}
$$

The producer's and consumer's risk can be related to various points on an operating characteristic curve. Producer's risk is the chance that an otherwise *acceptable* lot fails the sampling plan (i.e., there are more defective items than the allowable number in the sample) solely due to random fluctuations in the selection of the sample. In contrast, consumer's risk is the chance that an *unacceptable* lot passes the sampling plan (i.e., there are less defective items than the allowable number in the sample) due to a better than average quality in the sample. For example, suppose that a sample size of 15 is chosen with a trigger level for rejection of one item. With a 4 percent acceptable level and a greater than 4 percent defective fraction, the consumer's risk is at most 88 percent. In contrast, with a 4 percent acceptable level and less than 4 percent defective fraction, the producer's risk is at most $1 - 0.88 = 0.12$ or 12 percent.

In specifying the sampling plan implicit in the operating characteristic curve, the supplier and consumer of materials or work must agree on the levels of risk acceptable to themselves. If the lot is of acceptable quality, the supplier would like to minimize the chance or risk that a lot is rejected solely on the basis of a lower than average quality sample. Similarly, the consumer would like to minimize the risk of accepting under the sampling plan a deficient lot. In addition, both parties presumably would like to minimize the costs and delays associated with testing. Devising an acceptable sampling plan requires trading off the objectives of risk minimization among the parties involved and the cost of testing.

Example 13-3: Acceptance Probability Calculation

Suppose that the sample size is 5 ($n = 5$) from a lot of 100 items ($N = 100$). The lot of materials is to be rejected if any of the 5 samples are defective ($r = 0$). In this case, the probability of acceptance as a function of the actual number of defective items can be computed by noting that for $r = 0$, only one term ($x = 0$) need be considered in Eq. (13.4). Thus, for $N = 100$ and $n = 5$;

$$g(p) = \frac{\binom{100p}{0}\binom{100q}{5}}{\binom{100}{5}}$$

For a 2 percent defective fraction ($p = 0.02$), the resulting acceptance value is

$$g(p) = \frac{\binom{2}{0}\binom{98}{5}}{\binom{100}{5}} = \frac{\frac{98!}{93! \cdot 5!}}{\frac{100!}{95! \cdot 5!}} = \frac{98! \cdot 95!}{93! \cdot 100!} = 0.9020$$

Using the binomial approximation in Eq. (13.5), the comparable calculation would be

$$g(p) \approx \binom{5}{0} p^0 q^5 = q^5 = (0.98)^5 = 0.9039$$

which is a difference of 0.0019 or 0.21 percent from the actual value of 0.9020 found earlier.

If the acceptable defective proportion is 2 percent (so $p_1 = p_2 = 0.02$), then the chance of an incorrect rejection (or producer's risk) is $1 - g(0.02) = 1 - 0.9 = 0.1$ or 10 percent. Note that a prudent producer should ensure better than minimum quality products to reduce the probability or chance of rejection under this sampling plan. If the actual proportion of defectives were 1 percent, then the producer's risk would be only 5 percent with this sampling plan.

Example 13-4: Designing a Sampling Plan

Suppose that an owner (or product "consumer" in the terminology of quality control) wishes to have zero defective items in a facility with 5,000 items of a particular kind. What would be the different amounts of consumer's risk for different sampling plans?

With an acceptable quality level of no defective items (so $p_1 = 0$), the allowable defective items in the sample is zero (so $r = 0$) in the sampling plan. Using the binomial approximation, the probability of accepting the 5,000 items as a function of the fraction of actual defective items and the sample size is

$$g(p) = (1 - p)^n$$

To ensure a 90 percent chance of rejecting a lot with an actual percentage defective of 1 percent ($p = 0.01$), the required sample size would be calculated as

$$g(p) = 1 - 0.90 = 0.1 = (1 - 0.01)^n$$

Then,

$$n = \frac{\ln(0.1)}{\ln(0.99)} = \frac{-2.30}{-0.01} \approx 229$$

As can be seen, large sample sizes are required to ensure relatively large probabilities of zero defective items.

Example 13-5: Military Standard 105

Beginning in 1945, the U. S. Department of Defense has issued standard procedures for acceptance sampling by attribute. The procedures appeared as MIL-STD-105 or, equivalently, ABC-STD-105, and have been widely adopted and applied in industry.[105] The procedures appearing in MIL-STD-105 are also similar to the procedures adopted by the International Organization for Standardization as ISO 2859. In its simplest form, MIL-STD-105 requires specification of a desired inspection level and an acceptable quality level (AQL). The desired inspection level permits greater or lesser precision in making acceptance decisions by varying the sample size. Implicit in the application of MIL-STD-105 is the assumption that samples are random and that each item can be classified as having zero, one, or multiple defects. The procedures can be applied to the percentage of defective items or to the percentage of defects in the lot, with the latter defined as the number of defects divided by the number of items in the lot. The difference between defects and defective items is readily seen by noting that a deficient item may have one or more defects.

Table 13-1 shows the sample size code levels for different lot sizes and for different inspection levels. Inspection level II is generally prescribed in applications, while inspection levels I and III represent tighter and more lenient inspection levels.

TABLE 13–1 SAMPLE SIZE CODES FOR MIL-STD-105

Lot or batch size	Special Inspection Levels				General Inspection Levels		
	S-1	S-2	S-3	S-4	I	II	III
2–8	A	A	A	A	A	A	B
9–15	A	A	A	A	A	B	C
16–25	A	A	B	B	B	C	D
26–50	A	B	B	C	C	D	E
51–90	B	B	C	C	C	E	F
91–150	B	B	C	D	D	F	G
151–280	B	C	D	E	E	G	H
281–500	B	C	D	E	F	H	J
501–1,200	C	C	E	F	G	J	K
1,201–3,200	C	D	E	G	H	K	L
3,201–10,000	C	D	F	G	J	L	M
10,001–35,000	C	D	F	H	K	M	N
35,001–150,000	D	E	G	J	L	N	P
150,001–500,000	D	E	G	J	M	P	Q
500,001 and over	D	E	H	K	N	Q	R

Source: U.S. Department of Defense, *Sampling Procedures and Tables for Inspection by Attributes*, (Military Standard 105D), U.S. Government Printing Office, Washington DC, 1963.

[105] Documentation for MIL-STD-105 can be obtained from the National Technical Information Service, Washington DC 20402.

Special inspection levels are used when testing is very expensive or destructive, and prescribe lower sample sizes.

Table 13-2 shows the trigger level for different sample sizes and acceptable quality levels. As an illustration, suppose that the normal inspection level II is desired for a lot of size 700. Using Table 13-1, the appropriate sample size code letter is J in this case. Referring to Table 13-2, this code letter implies a sample size of 80 out of the lot. For an acceptable quality level of 1.5 percent, the appropriate trigger level is 4 defective items. If 4 or more items in the 80-item sample are defective, then the lot should be rejected.

Selection of the appropriate inspection level and acceptable quality level in the application of MIL-STD-105 requires the same sort of trade-offs discussed between

TABLE 13–2 MASTER SAMPLING PLAN TABLE FOR MIL-STD-105

Sample size code letter	Sample size	Acceptable quality levels (normal inspection)										
		0.010	0.015	0.025	0.040	0.065	0.10	0.15	0.25	0.40	0.65	1.0
		Ac Re	Ac Re	Ac Re	Ac Re	Ac Re	Ac Re	Ac Re	Ac Re	Ac Re	Ac Re	Ac Re
A	2											
B	3											
C	5											
D	8											↓
E	13										↓	0 1
F	20									↓	0 1	↑
G	32								↓	0 1	↑	↓
H	50							↓	0 1	↑	↓	1 2
J	80						↓	0 1	↑	↓	1 2	2 3
K	125					↓	0 1	↑	↓	1 2	2 3	3 4
L	200				↓	0 1	↑	↓	1 2	2 3	3 4	5 6
M	315				0 1	↑	↓	1 2	2 3	3 4	5 6	7 8
N	500			0 1	↑	↓	1 2	2 3	3 4	5 6	7 8	10 11
P	800	↓	0 1	↑	↓	1 2	2 3	3 4	5 6	7 8	10 11	14 15
Q	1,250	0 1	↑	↓	1 2	2 3	3 4	5 6	7 8	10 11	14 15	21 22
R	2,000	↑		1 2	2 3	3 4	5 6	7 8	10 11	14 15	21 22	↑

Note: Ac = Accept; Re = Reject.

Source: U.S. Department of Defense, *Sampling Procedures and Tables for Inspection by Attributes*, (Military Standard 105D), U.S. Government Printing Office, Washington DC, 1963.

the cost of testing, the importance of item quality, the producer's risk, and the consumer's risk. The full documentation of MIL-STD-105 includes graphs of operating characteristic curves for the different sampling plans, so these risk levels can be examined. For example, Figure 13-2 contains operating characteristic curves for single, double and multiple sampling with sampling plan K and average quality level AQL = 1.0 under normal inspection. In this figure, it can be seen that the single, double, and multiple sampling plans result in approximately the same levels of risk. Using this figure, the producer's risk at a 0.5 defective rate is approximately 1 percent, whereas the consumer's risk for a 3 percent defective rate is about 40 percent.

MIL-STD-105 also provides procedures for more complicated sampling plans. First, provisions for normal, tightened, and reduced inspection can be accommodated.

Acceptable quality levels (normal inspection)														
1.5	2.5	4.0	6.5	10	15	25	40	65	100	150	250	400	650	1,000
Ac Re	Ac Re	Ac Re	Ac Re	Ac Re	Ac Re	Ac Re	Ac Re	Ac Re	Ac Re	Ac Re	Ac Re	Ac Re	Ac Re	Ac Re
↓	↓	↓	0 1	↑	↓	1 2	2 3	3 4	5 6	7 8	10 11	14 15	21 22	30 31
	↓	0 1	↑	↓	1 2	2 3	3 4	5 6	7 8	10 11	14 15	21 22	30 31	44 45
↓	0 1	↑	↓	1 2	2 3	3 4	5 6	7 8	10 11	14 15	21 22	30 31	44 45	↑
0 1	↑	↓	1 2	2 3	3 4	5 6	7 8	10 11	14 15	21 22	30 31	44 45	↑	
↑	↓	1 2	2 3	3 4	5 6	7 8	10 11	14 15	21 22	↑				
↓	1 2	2 3	3 4	5 6	7 8	10 11	14 15	21 22	↑					
1 2	2 3	3 4	5 6	7 8	10 11	14 15	21 22	↑						
2 3	3 4	5 6	7 8	10 11	14 15	21 22	↑							
3 4	5 6	7 8	10 11	14 15	21 22	↑								
5 6	7 8	10 11	14 15	21 22	↑									
7 8	10 11	14 15	21 22	↑										
10 11	14 15	21 22	↑											
14 15	21 22	↑												
21 22	↑													
↑	↑													

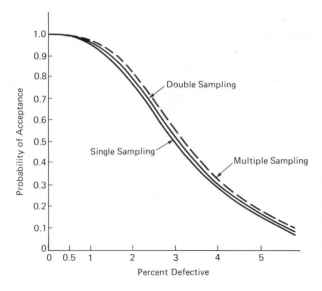

Figure 13-2 Operating Characteristic Curves for a MIL-STD-105 Sampling Plan (Source: U.S. Department of Defense, *Sampling Procedures and Tables for Inspection by Attributes*, [Military Standard 105D], U.S. Government Printing Office, Washington D.C., 1963.)

These are relevant in situations in which a continuing series of material or work lots are received to be tested. If some lots are found to have a large number of deficient items, then a tightened sampling plan involving larger sample sizes or smaller trigger levels may be used to ensure adequate quality. Conversely, reduced inspection provides lower trigger levels and increased consumer risk. Second, double and multiple sampling plans are possible. These may be useful when testing can be performed rapidly so that additional samples can be taken before the lot items are approved or used. From the initial sample, three outcomes may occur in these plans: (1) the number of defectives may be sufficiently low that the lot is accepted, (2) the number of defectives may be sufficiently high that the lot is rejected, or (3) the number of defectives may be in an ambiguous range in which further sampling and testing is prescribed.

13.7 STATISTICAL QUALITY CONTROL WITH SAMPLING BY VARIABLES

As described in the previous section, sampling by attributes is based on a classification of items as *good* or *defective*. Many work and material attributes possess continuous properties, such as strength, density, or length. With the sampling by attributes procedure, a particular level of a variable quantity must be defined as acceptable quality. More generally, two items classified as *good* might have quite different strengths or other attributes. Intuitively, it seems reasonable that some "credit" should be provided for exceptionally good items in a sample. Sampling by variables was developed for application to continuously measurable quantities of this type. The procedure uses measured values of an attribute in a sample to determine the overall acceptability of a batch or lot. Sampling by variables has the advantage of using more information from tests since it is based on actual measured values rather than a simple classification. As a result, acceptance sampling by variables can be more efficient than sampling by attributes in the sense that fewer samples are required to obtain a desired level of quality control.

In applying sampling by variables, an acceptable lot quality can be defined with respect to an upper limit U, a lower limit L, or both. With these boundary conditions, an acceptable quality level can be defined as a maximum allowable fraction of defective items, M. In Figure 13-3, the probability distribution of item attribute x is illustrated. With an upper limit U, the fraction of defective items is equal to the area under the distribution function to the right of U (so that $x \geq U$). This fraction of defective items would be compared to the allowable fraction M to determine the acceptability of a lot. With both a lower and an upper limit on acceptable quality, the fraction defective would be the fraction of items greater than the upper limit or less than the lower limit. Alternatively, the limits could be imposed upon the acceptable *average* level of the variable.

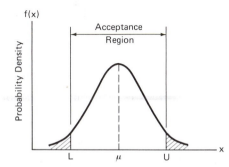

Figure 13-3 Variable Probability Distributions and Acceptance Regions

In sampling by variables, the fraction of defective items is estimated by using measured values from a sample of items. As with sampling by attributes, the procedure assumes a random sample of a given size is obtained from a lot or batch. In the application of sampling by variables plans, the measured characteristic is virtually always assumed to be *normally distributed* as illustrated in Figure 13-3. The probabilities of a normal distribution are given by Table B.1 in Appendix B. The normal distribution is likely to be a reasonably good assumption for many measured characteristics such as material density or degree of soil compaction. The central limit theorem in probability theory provides a general support for the assumption: if the source of variations is a large number of small and independent random effects, then the resulting distribution of values will approximate the normal distribution. If the distribution of measured values is not likely to be approximately normal, then sampling by attributes should be adopted. Deviations from normal distributions may appear as *skewed* or nonsymmetric distributions or as distributions with fixed upper and lower limits.

The fraction of defective items in a sample or the chance that the population average has different values is estimated from two statistics obtained from the sample: the sample mean and standard deviation. Mathematically, let n be the number of items in the sample and x_i, $i = 1, 2, 3, \ldots, n$, be the measured values of the variable characteristic x. Then an estimate of the overall population mean μ is the sample mean $\bar{x}$:

$$\mu \approx \bar{x} = \frac{1}{n} \sum_{i=1}^{n} x_i \qquad (13.8)$$

An estimate of the population standard deviation is s, the square root of the sample variance statistic:

$$\sigma^2 \approx s^2 = \frac{1}{n-1} \sum_{i=1}^{n} (x_i - \bar{x})^2 = \frac{1}{n-1} \left(\sum_{i=1}^{n} x_i^2 - n\bar{x}^2 \right) \qquad (13.9)$$

Based on these two estimated parameters and the desired limits, the various fractions of interest for the population can be calculated.

The probability that the average value of a population is greater than a particular lower limit is calculated from the test statistic:

$$t_L = \frac{\bar{x} - L}{s/\sqrt{n}} = \frac{(\bar{x} - L)\sqrt{n}}{s} \qquad (13.10)$$

which is t-distributed with $n - 1$ degrees of freedom. If the population standard deviation is known in advance, then this known value is substituted for the estimate s and the resulting test statistic would be normally distributed. The t-distribution is similar in appearance to a standard normal distribution, although the spread or variability in the function *decreases* as the degrees of freedom parameter *increases*. As the number of degrees of freedom becomes very large, the t-distribution coincides with the normal distribution. Tables of the t-distribution appear in Appendix B. Note that the two t-distribution tables appearing in Appendix B represent the same information, but one is a lookup by t value (Table B.2) and the other is a lookup by probability value (Table B.3). For example, if $\bar{x} = 4.5$, $L = 4.0$, $s = 3.0$, and $n = 5$, the test statistic value t is $(4.5 - 4.0)(\sqrt{5})/3.0 = 0.37$. Using table B.2, this value corresponds to a 36.7 percent chance that the actual lot average is less than the lower limit value, $L = 4.0$. That is, by interpolating between the t-values of 0.2 and 0.4 for the test value $t = 0.37$ with $\nu = n - 1 = 4$ degrees of freedom (DF), the probability of exceeding the test value is found to be

$$Pr\{t \geq 0.37\} = 0.426 - \left| \frac{0.37 - 0.2}{0.4 - 0.2} \right| (0.426 - 0.355)$$

$$= 0.367 \text{ or } 36.7 \text{ percent}$$

Alternatively, using Table B.3, the test value $t = 0.37$ lies between the t-values of 0.271 and 0.569 for $\nu = 4$ DF, corresponding to probabilities 0.6 and 0.7. By interpolation,

$$Pr\{t \le 0.37\} = 0.6 + \left| \frac{0.37 - 0.271}{0.569 - 0.271} \right| (0.7 - 0.6)$$

$$= 0.633 \text{ or } 63.3 \text{ percent}$$

That is, the test value $t = 0.37$ corresponds to a 63.3 percent chance that the actual lot average is greater than the lower limit value $L = 4.0$.

With an upper limit, the calculations are similar, and the probability that the average value of a population is less than a particular upper limit can be calculated from the test statistic:

$$t_U = \frac{U - \bar{x}}{s/\sqrt{n}} = \frac{(U - \bar{x})\sqrt{n}}{s} \tag{13.11}$$

With both upper and lower limits, the sum of the probabilities of being above the upper limit or below the lower limit can be calculated.

The calculations to estimate the fraction of items above an upper limit or below a lower limit are very similar to those for the population average. The only difference is that the square root of the number of samples does not appear in the test statistic formulas,

$$t_{AL} = \frac{\bar{x} - L}{s} \tag{13.12}$$

and

$$t_{AU} = \frac{U - \bar{x}}{s} \tag{13.13}$$

where t_{AL} is the test statistic for all items with a lower limit and t_{AU} is the test statistic for all items with an upper limit. For example, the test statistic for items above an upper limit of 5.5 with $\bar{x} = 4.0, s = 3.0,$ and $n = 5$ is $t_{AU} = (8.5 - 4.0)/3.0 = 1.5$ with $\nu = n - 1 = 4$ degrees of freedom. Referring to Table B.2 in Appendix B, the corresponding probability value or fraction of items greater than 5.5 is seen to lie between 0.117 and 0.092 corresponding to $t = 1.4$ and $t = 1.6$. By interpolation, the probability $Pr\{t \ge 1.5\}$ is found to be 0.105 or 10.5 percent.

Instead of using sampling plans that specify an allowable fraction of defective items, it saves computations simply to write specifications in terms of the allowable test statistic values themselves. This procedure is equivalent to requiring that the sample average be at least a prespecified number of standard deviations away from an upper or lower limit. For example, with $\bar{x} = 4.0, U = 8.5, s = 3.0,$ and $n = 41,$ the sample mean is only about $(8.5 - 4.0)/3.0 = 1.5$ standard deviations away from the upper limit.

To summarize, the application of sampling by variables requires the specification of a sample size, the relevant upper or lower limits and either (1) the allowable fraction of items falling outside the designated limits or (2) the allowable probability that the population average falls outside the designated limit. Random samples are drawn from a predefined population and tested to obtained measured values of a variable attribute. From these measurements, the sample mean, standard deviation, and quality control test statistic are calculated. Finally, the test statistic is compared to the allowable trigger level and the lot is either accepted or rejected. It is also possible to apply sequential sampling in this procedure, so that a batch may be subjected to additional sampling and testing to refine the test statistic values further.

With sampling by variables, it is notable that a producer of material or work can adopt two general strategies for meeting the required specifications. First, a producer may ensure that the average quality level is quite high, even if the variability among items is high. This strategy is illustrated in Figure 13-4 as a "high-quality-average" strategy. Second, a producer may meet a desired quality target by reducing the *variability* within each batch. In Figure 13-4, this is labeled the "low-variability" strategy. In either case, a producer should maintain high standards to avoid rejection of a batch.

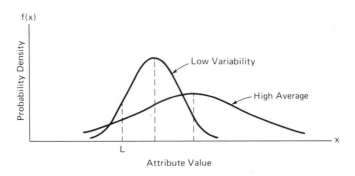

Figure 13-4 Alternative Production Strategies to Meet Quality Specifications

Example 13-6: Testing for Defective Component Strengths

Suppose that an inspector takes eight strength measurements with the following results:

$$4.3, \ 4.8, \ 4.6, \ 4.7, \ 4.4, \ 4.6, \ 4.7, \ 4.6$$

In this case, the sample mean and standard deviation can be calculated using Eqs. (13.8) and (13.9):

$$\bar{x} = \frac{1}{8}(4.3 + 4.8 + 4.6 + 4.7 + 4.4 + 4.6 + 4.7 + 4.6)$$

$$= 4.59$$

$$s^2 = \frac{1}{8-1}((4.3 - 4.59)^2 + (4.8 - 4.59)^2 + (4.6 - 4.59)^2 + (4.7 - 4.59)^2$$

$$+ (4.4 - 4.59)^2 + (4.6 - 4.59)^2 + (4.7 - 4.59)^2 + (4.6 - 4.59)^2)$$

$$= 0.16$$

The percentage of items below a lower quality limit of $L = 4.3$ is estimated from the test statistic t_{AL} in Eq. (13.12):

$$t_{AL} = \frac{4.59 - 4.3}{0.16} = 1.81$$

Referring to Table B.2 in Appendix B, the fraction of items with strength below 4.3 is found to be approximately 0.057 or 5.7 percent for $t_{AL} = 1.81$ with degrees of freedom $\nu = 8 - 1 = 7$.

Example 13-7: Military Standard 414

As with sampling by attributes, a number of testing standards exist for sampling by variables. Examples include Military Standard 414 (MIL-STD-414) developed by the U. S. Department of Defense or ISO-3951 provided by the International Standards Organization. In MIL-STD-414, sampling plans are chosen based on the prespecified acceptable quality level, defined as the maximum percentage defective that is acceptable in a process. Inherent in the sampling plans in MIL-STD-414 are the assumptions that the measured attribute of interest is normally distributed, designated samples are chosen randomly, and measurements are made without appreciable error.

Figure 13-5 illustrates the operating characteristic (OC) curves used in MIL-STD-414. Different curves are shown for seven separate AQL values ranging from 1 percent to 15 percent. The OC curves indicate the percentage of lots expected to be accepted as a function of the quality of submitted lots (represented by the percentage of defective items in an average lot).

Table 13-3 illustrates the type of sampling plan prescribed by MIL-STD-414. For example, suppose that sample size K (corresponding to 35 sample items) and a AQL value of 1 percent were desired. Appropriate sample sizes are based on desired inspection levels and lot sizes as in MIL-STD-105 (for sampling by attributes) shown in Table 13-1. In this case, the designated k value is 1.89 as shown in Table 13-3. This value is compared to the sample *quality index*. For example, with an upper level quality specification (U), the quality index is computed as

$$Q_U = \frac{U - x}{s} \qquad (13.14)$$

where the sample mean $\bar{x}$ and sample standard deviation, s, are computed from Eqs. (13.8) and (13.9). If the quality index (Q_U) exceeds the value k, then the lot is acceptable.

As with other sampling-by-variable standards, MIL-STD-414 has a number of user options in the development of a sampling plan, including

- Whether the standard deviation of the process is known or is to estimated from the sample data
- Whether upper, lower, or both upper and lower quality limits are specified
- Different levels of inspection
- Shifts to tightened or reduced inspection procedures based on the quality of preceding lots

As a result of all these options, the number of tables and OC curves associated with MIL-STD-414 is large.

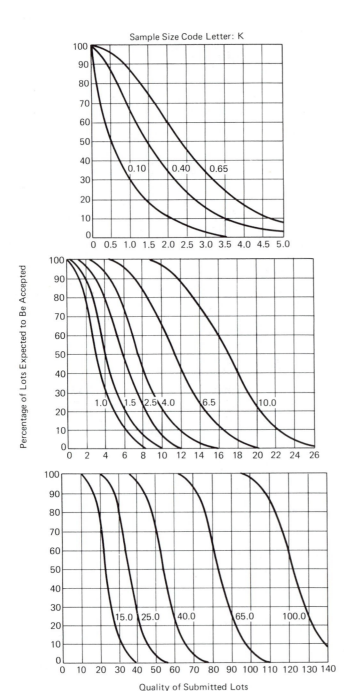

Figure 13-5 Operating Characteristic Curves in MIL-STD-414 (Source: U.S. Department of Defense, *Sampling Procedures and Tables for Inspection by Variables*, [Military Standard 414], U.S. Government Printing Office, Washington, D.C., 1957)

TABLE 13–3 TABLE OF MASTER SAMPLING PLANS FOR MIL-STD-414

Sample size code letter	Sample size	Acceptable quality levels (normal inspection)													
		0.04	0.065	0.10	0.15	0.25	0.40	0.65	1.00	1.50	2.50	4.00	6.50	10.00	15.00
		k	k	k	k	k	k	k	k	k	k	k	k	k	k
B	3	↓	↓	↓	↓	↓	↓	↓	↓	↓	1.12	0.958	0.765	0.566	0.341
C	4	↓	↓	↓	↓	↓	↓	↓	1.45	1.34	1.17	1.01	0.814	0.617	0.393
D	5	↓	↓	↓	↓	↓	↓	1.65	1.53	1.40	1.24	1.07	0.874	0.675	0.455
E	7	↓	↓	↓	↓	↓	1.88	1.75	1.62	1.50	1.33	1.15	0.955	0.755	0.536
F	10	↓	↓	↓	2.24	2.11	1.98	1.84	1.72	1.58	1.41	1.23	1.03	0.828	0.611
G	15	2.64	2.53	2.42	2.32	2.20	2.06	1.91	1.79	1.65	1.47	1.30	1.09	0.886	0.664
H	20	2.69	2.58	2.47	2.36	2.24	2.11	1.96	1.82	1.69	1.51	1.33	1.12	0.917	0.695
I	25	2.72	2.61	2.50	2.40	2.26	2.14	1.98	1.85	1.72	1.53	1.35	1.14	0.936	0.712
J	30	2.73	2.61	2.51	2.41	2.28	2.15	2.00	1.86	1.73	1.55	1.36	1.15	0.946	0.723
K	35	2.77	2.65	2.54	2.45	2.31	2.18	2.03	1.89	1.76	1.57	1.39	1.18	0.969	0.745
L	40	2.77	2.66	2.55	2.44	2.31	2.18	2.03	1.89	1.76	1.58	1.39	1.18	0.971	0.746
M	50	2.83	2.71	2.60	2.50	2.35	2.22	2.08	1.93	1.80	1.61	1.42	1.21	1.00	0.774
N	75	2.90	2.77	2.66	2.55	2.41	2.27	2.12	1.98	1.84	1.65	1.46	1.24	1.03	0.804
O	100	2.92	2.80	2.69	2.58	2.43	2.29	2.14	2.00	1.86	1.67	1.48	1.26	1.05	0.819
P	150	2.96	2.84	2.73	2.61	2.47	2.33	2.18	2.03	1.89	1.70	1.51	1.29	1.07	0.841
Q	200	2.97	2.85	2.73	2.62	2.47	2.33	2.18	2.04	1.89	1.70	1.51	1.29	1.07	0.845
		0.065	0.10	0.15	0.25	0.40	0.65	1.00	1.50	2.50	4.00	6.50	10.00	15.00	
		Acceptable quality levels (tightened inspection)													

Source: U.S. Department of Defense, *Sampling Procedures and Tables for Inspection by Variables*, (Military Standard 414), U.S. Government Printing Office, Washington DC, 1957.

13.8 SAFETY DURING CONSTRUCTION

Construction is a relatively hazardous undertaking. As Table 13-4 illustrates, there are significantly more injuries and lost workdays due to injuries or illnesses in construction than in virtually any other industry. These work-related injuries and illnesses are exceedingly costly. The *Construction Industry Cost Effectiveness Project* estimated that accidents cost $8.9 billion or nearly 7 percent of the $137 billion (in 1979 dollars) spent annually for industrial, utility, and commercial construction in the United States.[106] Included in this total are direct costs (medical costs, premiums for workers' compensation benefits, liability, and property losses) as well as indirect costs (reduced worker productivity, delays in projects, administrative time, and damage to equipment and the facility). In contrast to most industrial accidents, innocent bystanders may also be injuried by construction accidents. Several crane collapses from highrise buildings under construction have resulted in fatalities to passersby. Prudent project managers and owners would like to reduce accidents, injuries, and illnesses as much as possible.

TABLE 13-4 OCCUPATIONAL INJURY AND ILLNESS INCIDENCE RATES

Industry	Total Cases	Lost Workdays
Agriculture, forestry, fishing	7.7	86.0
Mining	10.5	137.3
Construction	14.6	115.7
Manufacturing	10.2	75.0
Transportation, utilities	8.5	96.7
Wholesale and retail trade	7.2	45.5
Finance, insurance, real estate	2.0	13.2
Services	4.9	35.8

Note: Data represent total number of cases and lost workdays per 100 workers in U.S. industries in 1982.

Source: U.S. Dept. of Commerce, *Statistical Abstract of the United States, 1985*, Government Printing Office, Washington, DC, 1985, Table No. 713, p. 426, 1985.

As with all the other costs of construction, it is a mistake for owners to ignore a significant category of costs such as injury and illnesses. While contractors may pay insurance premiums directly, these costs are reflected in bid prices or contract amounts. Delays caused by injuries and illnesses can present significant opportunity costs to owners. In the long run, the owners of constructed facilities must pay all the costs of construction. For the case of injuries and illnesses, this general principle might be slightly qualified since significant costs are borne by workers themselves or society at large. However, court judgments and insurance payments compensate for individual losses and are ultimately borne by the owners.

[106] See *Improving Construction Safety Performance*, Report A-3, The Business Roundtable, New York, NY, January 1982.

The causes of injuries in construction are numerous. Table 13-5 lists the reported causes of accidents in Britain in 1976. A similar catalog of causes would exist for the United States or other countries. The largest single category for both injuries and fatalities are individual falls. Handling goods is also a significant cause of injuries. From a management perspective, however, these reported causes do not really provide a useful prescription for safety policies. An individual fall may be caused by a series of coincidences: a railing might not be secure, a worker might be inattentive, the footing may be slippery. Removing any one of these compound causes might serve to prevent any particular accident. However, it is clear that conditions such as unsecured railings will normally increase the risk of accidents.

TABLE 13–5 REPORTED ACCIDENTS IN CONSTRUCTION IN BRITAIN, 1976

All accidents		Fatal accidents	
Cause	Percentage	Cause	Percentage
Falls of persons	30.0%	Falls of persons	48.1%
Handling of goods	24.8	Fall of materials	11.7
Falls of materials	8.0	Transport	11.7
Transport	5.4	Lifting equipment	8.4
Lifting equipment	1.6	Electricity	5.2
Excavation and tunneling	0.6	Excavation and tunneling	4.5
Miscellaneous	29.5	Miscellaneous	10.4

Source: Department of Employment, "Reported Accidents in Construction," *Health and Safety Executive*, Her Majesty's Stationary Office, London, April 1978.

Various measures are available to improve job-site safety in construction. Several of the most important occur before construction is undertaken. These include design, choice of technology, and education. By altering facility designs, particular structures can be safer or more hazardous to construct.

Choice of technology can also be critical in determining the safety of a job site. Safeguards built into machinery can notify operators of problems or prevent injuries. For example, simple switches can prevent equipment from being operating when protective shields are not in place. With the availability of on-board electronics (including computer chips) and sensors, the possibilities for sophisticated machine controllers and monitors has greatly expanded for construction equipment and tools. Materials and work process choices also influence the safety of construction. For example, substitution of alternative materials for asbestos can reduce or eliminate the prospects of long-term illnesses such as *asbestiosis*.

Educating workers and managers in proper procedures and hazards can have a direct impact on job site safety. The realization of the large costs involved in construction injuries and illnesses provides a considerable motivation for awareness and education.

Prequalification of contractors and subcontractors with regard to safety is another important avenue for safety improvement. If contractors are only invited to bid or enter negotiations if they have an acceptable record of safety (as well as quality performance), then a direct incentive is provided to ensure adequate safety on the part of contractors.

During the construction process itself, the most important safety-related measures are to ensure vigilance and cooperation on the part of managers, inspectors, and workers. Vigilance involves considering the risks of different working practices. It also involves maintaining temporary physical safeguards such as barricades, braces, guylines, railings, toeboards, and the like.

While eliminating accidents and work-related illnesses is a worthwhile goal, it will never be attained. Construction has a number of characteristics making it inherently hazardous. Large forces are involved in many operations. The job-site is continually changing as construction proceeds. Workers do not have fixed work sites and must move around a structure under construction. The tenure of a worker on a site is short, so the worker's familiarity and the employer-employee relationship are less settled than in manufacturing settings. Despite these peculiarities and as a result of exactly these special problems, improving work-site safety is a very important project management concern.

Example 13-8: Trench Collapse [107]

To replace 1,200 ft of a sewer line, a trench of between 12.5 and 18 ft deep was required down the center of a four-lane street. The contractor chose to begin excavation of the trench from the shallower end, requiring a 12.5 ft deep trench. Initially, the contractor used a 9 ft high, 4 ft wide steel trench box for soil support. A trench box is a rigid steel frame consisting of two walls supported by welded struts with open sides and ends. This method had the advantage that traffic could be maintained in at least two lanes during the reconstruction work.

In the shallow parts of the trench, the trench box seemed to support the excavation adequately. However, as the trench got deeper, more soil was unsupported below the trench box. Intermittent soil collapses in the trench began to occur. Eventually, an old parallel 6-inch water main collapsed, thereby saturating the soil and leading to massive soil collapse at the bottom of the trench. Replacement of the water main was added to the initial contract. At this point, the contractor began sloping the sides of the trench, thereby requiring the closure of the entire street.

The initial use of the trench box was convenient, but it was clearly inadequate and unsafe. Workers in the trench were in continuing danger of accidents stemming from soil collapse. Disruption to surrounding facilities such as the parallel water main was highly likely. Adoption of a tongue and groove vertical sheeting system over the full height of the trench or, alternatively, the sloping excavation eventually adopted are clearly preferable.

13.9 REFERENCES

13-1. Ang, A. H. S. and W. H. Tang, *Probability Concepts in Engineering Planning and Design: Volume I–Basic Principles*, John Wiley and Sons, Inc., New York, 1975.

[107] This example was adapted from E. Elinski, *External Impacts of Reconstruction and Rehabilitation Projects with Implications for Project Management,* unpublished MS thesis, Department of Civil Engineering, Carnegie Mellon University, Pittsburgh, 1985.

13-2. Au, T., R. M. Shane, and L. A. Hoel, *Fundamentals of Systems Engineering: Probabilistic Models*, Addison-Wesley Publishing Co., Reading, MA, 1972.

13-3. Bowker, A. H., and G. J. Liebermann, *Engineering Statistics*, Prentice-Hall, Englewood Cliffs, NJ, 1972.

13-4. Fox, A. J. and H. A. Cornell (editors), *Quality in the Constructed Project,* American Society of Civil Engineers, New York, 1984.

13-5. International Organization for Standardization, "Sampling Procedures and Charts for Inspection by Variables for Percent Defective, ISO 3951–1981 (E)," *Statistical Methods*, ISO Standard Handbook 3, International Organization for Standardization, Paris, France, 1981.

13-6. Skibniewski, M., and C. Hendrickson, *Methods to Improve the Safety Performance of the U. S. Construction Industry,* Technical Report, Department of Civil Engineering, Carnegie Mellon University, Pittsburgh, 1983.

13-7. U. S. Department of Defense, *Sampling Procedures and Tables for Inspection by Variables* (Military Standard 414), U. S. Government Printing Office, Washington DC, 1957.

13-8. U. S. Department of Defense, *Sampling Procedures and Tables for Inspection by Attributes*, (Military Standard 105D), U. S. Government Printing Office, Washington DC, 1963.

13.10 PROBLEMS

P13-1. Consider the following specification for mixing and curing concrete. Would you consider it to be a process or performance specification? Why?

> Water used in mixing or curing shall be reasonably clean and free of oil, salt, acid, alkali, sugar, vegetable, or other substance injurious to the finished product. Water known to be potable quality may be used without test. Where the source of water is relatively shallow, the intake shall be so enclosed as to exclude silt, mud, grass, or other foreign materials.[108]

P13-2. Suppose that a sampling plan calls for a sample of size $n = 5$ from a population of size $N = 50$. To be acceptable, only one or zero items in the sample can be defective. Estimate the probability of accepting the lot if the defective percentage is (a) 20 percent, (b) 10 percent, or (c) 2 percent. Do not use an approximation in this calculation.

P13-3. Repeat Problem 13-2 using the binomial approximation.

P13-4. Suppose that a project manager tested the strength of one tile out of a lot of 3,000 to be used on a building. This one sample measurement was compared with the design specification and, in this case, the sampled tile's strength exceeded that of the specification. On this basis, the project manager accepted the tile shipment. If the sampled tile was defective (with a strength less than the specification), the project manager would have rejected the lot. Suppose that 90 percent of the tiles in the lot are

---

[108] American Association of State Highway and Transportation Officials, *Guide Specifications for Highway Construction*, AASHTO, Washington, DC, 1984, Section 714.01, p. 244.

defective, even though the project manager's sample gave a satisfactory result. What is the chance of accepting the lot under this cicumstance? Sketch out the operating characteristic curve for this sampling plan as a function of the actual fraction of defective tiles.

P13-5. Repeat Problem P13-4 for sample sizes of (a) 5, (b) 10, and (c) 20.

P13-6. Suppose that a sampling-by-attributes plan is specified in which 10 samples are taken at random from a large lot ($N = 100$) and at most one sample item is allowed to be defective for the lot to be acceptable.

    a. If the actual percentage defective is 5 percent, what is the probability of lot acceptance? (Note: You may use relevant approximations in this calculation.)

    b. What is the consumer's risk if an acceptable quality level is 15 percent defective?

    c. What is the producer's risk with this sampling plan if an 8 percent defective percentage is acceptable?

P13-7. The yield stress of a random sample of 26 pieces of steel was measured, yielding a mean of 52,800 psi and an estimated standard deviation of $s = 4,600$ psi.

    a. What is the probability that the population mean is less than 50,000 psi?

    b. What is the estimated fraction of pieces with yield strength less than 50,000 psi?

    c. Is this sampling procedure sampling by attributes or sampling by variable?

P13-8. Suppose that a contract specifies a sampling-by-attributes plan in which a normal inspection based on MIL-STD-105 is imposed on a lot of size 30.

    a. What is the appropriate sample size code?

    b. If an acceptable quality level is 2.5 percent defective, how many defective items are allowed?

P13-9. Suppose that we wish to adopt sampling plan D with normal sampling and a 1.5 AQL in MIL-STD-414 and an upper bound constraint on the fraction defective.

    a. What is the appropriate test value k?

    b. Suppose that the upper bound is 47.0 and the five sample measurements were 48.3, 46.5, 45.2, 45.6, and 46.0, respectively. Should this lot be accepted?

    c. Based on the five sample values, estimate the fraction of items above the upper bound of 47.0.

P13-10. In a random sample of 41 blocks chosen from a production line, the mean length was 10.63 inches and the estimated standard deviation was 0.4 inch. Between what lengths can it be said that 98 percent of block lengths will lie?

14

Organization
and
Use of Project Information

14.1 TYPES OF PROJECT INFORMATION

Construction projects inevitably generate enormous and complex sets of information. Effectively managing this bulk of information to ensure its availability and accuracy is an important managerial task. Poor or missing information can readily lead to project delays, uneconomical decisions, or even the complete failure of the desired facility. Pity the project manager who suddenly discovers on the expected delivery date that important facility components have not yet been fabricated and cannot be delivered for six months! With better information, the problem could have been identified earlier, so that alternative suppliers might have been located or schedules arranged. Both project design and control are crucially dependent upon accurate and timely information, as well as the ability to use this information effectively. At the same time, too much unorganized information presented to managers can result in confusion and paralysis of decision making.

As a project proceeds, the types and extent of the information used by the various organizations involved will change. A listing of the most important information sets would include

- Cash flow and procurement accounts for each organization
- Intermediate analysis results during planning and design
- Design documents, including drawings and specifications
- Construction schedules and cost estimates
- Quality control and assurance records
- Chronological files of project correspondence and memorandum
- Construction field activity and inspection logs
- Legal contracts and regulatory documents

Some of these sets of information evolve as the project proceeds. The financial accounts of payments over the entire course of the project is an example of overall growth. The passage of time results in steady additions in these accounts, whereas the addition of a new actor such as a contractor leads to a sudden jump in the number of accounts. Some information sets are important at one stage of the process but may then be ignored. Common examples include planning or structural analysis databases which are not ordinarily used during construction or operation. However, it may be necessary at later stages in the project to redo analyses to consider desired changes. In this case, archival information storage and retrieval become important. Even after the completion of construction, an historical record may be important for use during operation, for assessing responsibilities in case of facility failures, or for planning similar projects elsewhere.

While there may be substantial costs due to inaccurate or missing information, there are also significant costs associated with the generation, storage, transfer, retrieval, and other manipulation of information. In addition to the costs of clerical work and providing aids such as computers, the organization and review of information command an inordinate amount of the attention of project managers, which may be the scarcest resource on any construction project. It is useful, therefore, to understand the scope and alternatives for organizing project information.

14.2 ACCURACY AND USE OF INFORMATION

Numerous sources of error are expected for project information. While numerical values are often reported to the nearest cent or values of equivalent precision, it is rare that the actual values are so accurately known. Living with some uncertainty is an inescapable situation, and a prudent manager should have an understanding of the uncertainty in different types of information and the possibility of drawing misleading conclusions.

We have already discussed the uncertainty inherent in making forecasts of project costs and durations sometime in the future. Forecast uncertainty also exists in the short term. For example, consider estimates of work completed. Every project manager is familiar with situations in which the final few bits of work for a task take an inordinate amount of time. Unforeseen problems, inadequate quality on already completed work, lack of attention, accidents, or postponing the most difficult work problems to the end can all contribute to making the final portion of an activity actually require far more time and effort than expected. The net result is that estimates of the actual proportion of work completed are often inaccurate.

Some inaccuracy in reports and estimates can arise from conscious choices made by workers, foremen, or managers. If the value of ensuring accuracy is thought to be low or nonexistent, then a rational worker will not expend effort or time to gather or to report information accurately. Many project scheduling systems flounder on exactly this type of nonreporting or misreporting. The original schedule can quickly become extremely misleading without accurate updating! Only if all parties concerned have specific mandates or incentives to report accurately will the data be reliable.

Another source of inaccuracy comes from transcription errors of various sorts. Typographical errors, incorrect measurements from reading equipment, or other recording and calculation errors may creep into the sets of information which are used in project management. Despite intensive efforts to check and eliminate such errors, their complete eradication is virtually impossible.

One method of indicating the relative accuracy of numerical data is to report ranges or expected deviations of an estimate or measurement. For example, a measurement might be reported as 198 ft $\pm$ 2 ft. There are two common interpretations of these deviations. First, a range (such as $\pm$ 2) might be chosen so that the actual value is *certain* to be within the indicated range. In the case given, the actual length would be somewhere between 196 and 200 ft with this convention. Alternatively, this deviation might indicate the *typical* range of the estimate or measurement in the statistical sense. Then, the example given might imply that there is, say, a two-thirds chance that the actual length is between 196 and 200.

When the absolute range of a quantity is very large or unknown, the use of a statistical standard deviation as a measure of uncertainty may be useful. If a quantity is measured n times resulting is a set of values $x_i (i = 1, 2, \ldots, n)$, then the average or mean value μ is estimated by the sample mean $\bar{x}$, i.e., $\mu \approx \bar{x}$, where

$$\bar{x} = \sum_{i=1}^{n} \frac{x_i}{n} \qquad (14.1)$$

The standard deviation σ can be estimated as the square root s of the sample variance s^2, i.e., $\sigma \approx s$, where

$$s^2 = \frac{\sum_{i=1}^{n} (x_i - \bar{x})^2}{n-1} \qquad (14.2)$$

The standard deviation σ is a direct indicator of the spread or variability in a measuremēnt, in the same units as the measurement itself. Higher values of the standard deviation indicate greater and greater uncertainty about the exact value of the measurement. For the commonly encountered *normal distribution* of a random variable, the average value plus or minus one standard deviation, $\mu \pm \sigma$, will include about two-thirds of the actual occurrences. A related measure of random variability is the coefficient of variation, defined as the ratio of the standard deviation to the mean:

$$c = \frac{\sigma}{\mu} \qquad (14.3)$$

Thus, a coefficient of variation indicates the variability as a proportion of the expected value. A coefficient of variation equal to 1 ($c = 1$) represents substantial uncertainty, whereas a value such as $c = 0.1$ or 10 percent indicates much smaller variability.

More generally, even information which is gathered and reported correctly may be interpreted incorrectly. While the actual information might be correct within the terms of the data gathering and recording system, it may be quite misleading for managerial purposes. A few examples can illustrate the problems which may arise in naively interpreting recorded information without involving any conceptual understanding of how the information is actually gathered, stored, and recorded or how work on the project actually proceeds.

Example 14-1: Sources of Delay and Cost Accounts

It is common in construction activity information to make detailed records of costs incurred and work progress. It is less common to keep detailed records of delays and their causes, even though these delays may be the actual cause of increased costs and lower productivity.[109] Paying exclusive attention to *cost* accounts in such situations may be misleading. For example, suppose that the accounts for equipment and material inventories show cost savings relative to original estimates, whereas the costs associated with particular construction activities show higher than estimated expenditures. In this situation, it is not necessarily the case that the inventory function is performing well, or the field workers are the cause of cost overrun problems. It may be that construction

[109] See D. F. Rogge, "Delay Reporting Within Cost Accounting System," *ASCE Journal of Construction Engineering and Management,* Vol. 110, no. 2, 1984, pp. 289-292.

activities are delayed by lack of equipment or materials, thus causing cost increases. Keeping a larger inventory of materials and equipment might increase the inventory account totals but lead to lower overall costs on the project. Better yet, more closely matching demands and supplies might reduce delay costs without concurrent inventory cost increases. Thus, simply examining cost account information may not lead to a correct diagnosis of a problem or to the correct managerial responses.

Example 14-2: Interest Charges

Financial or interest charges are usually accumulated in a separate account for projects, while the accounts associated with particular activities represent actual expenditures. For example, planning activities might cost $10,000 for a small project during the first year of a two-year project. Since dollar expenditures have a time value, this $10,000 cost in year 1 is *not* equivalent in value to a $10,000 cost in year 2. In particular, financing the early $10,000 involves payment of interest or, similarly, the loss of investment opportunities. If the borrowing rate is 10 percent, then financing the first-year $10,000 expenditure would require $10,000 x 0.10 = $1,000 and the value of the expenditure by the end of the second year of the project would be $11,000. Thus, some portion of the overall interest charges represents a cost associated with planning activities. Recognizing the true value of expenditures made at different periods of time is an important element in devising rational planning and management strategies.

14.3 COMPUTERIZED ORGANIZATION AND USE OF INFORMATION

Numerous formal methods and possible organizations exist for the information required for project management. Before discussing the details of computations and information representation, it will be useful to describe a record-keeping implementation, including some of the practical concerns in design and implementation. In this section, we shall describe a computer-based system to provide construction yard and warehouse management information from the point of view of the system users.[110] In the process, the usefulness of computerized databases can be illustrated.

A yard or warehouse is used by most construction firms to store equipment and to provide an inventory of materials and parts needed for projects. Large firms may have several warehouses at different locations so as to reduce transit time between project sites and materials supplies. In addition, local "yards" or "equipment sheds" are commonly provided on the job site. Examples of equipment in a yard would be drills, saws, office trailers, graders, back hoes, concrete pumps, and cranes. Material items might include nails, plywood, wire mesh, forming lumber, et cetera.

In typical construction warehouses, written records are kept by warehouse clerks to record transfer or return of equipment to job sites, dispatch of material to jobs, and maintenance histories of particular pieces of equipment. In turn, these records are used as the basis for billing projects for the use of equipment and materials. For example, a daily charge would be made to a project for using a concrete pump. During the course of a month, the concrete pump might spend

---

[110] The system is based loosely upon a successful construction yard management system originally developed for Mellon-Stuart Company, Pittsburgh, in 1983. The authors are indebted to A. Pasquale for providing the information and operating experience of the system.

several days at different job sites, so each project would be charged for its use. The record-keeping system is also used to monitor materials and equipment movements between sites so that equipment can be located.

One common mechanism to organize record keeping is to fill out cards recording the transfer of items to or from a job site. Table 14-1 illustrates one possible transfer record. In this case, seven items were requested for the Carnegie Mellon job site (project number 83–1557). These seven items would be loaded on a delivery truck, along with a copy of the transfer record. Shown in Table 14-1 a code number identifying each item (0609.02, 0609.03, etc.), the quantity of each item requested, an item description, and a unit price. For equipment items, an equipment number identifying the individual piece of equipment used is also recorded, such as grinder No. 4517 in Table 14-1; a unit price is not specified for equipment, but a daily rental charge might be imposed.

Transfer sheets are numbered (such as No. 100311 in Table 14-1), with the date and the preparer identified to facilitate control of the record-keeping process. During the course of a month, numerous transfer records of this type are accumulated. At the end of a month, each of the transfer records is examined to compile the various items or equipment used at a project and the appropriate charges. Constructing these bills would be a tedious manual task. Equipment movements would have to be tracked individually, days at each site counted, and the daily charge accumulated for each project. For example, Table 14-1 records the transfer of grinder No. 4517 to a job site. This project would be charged a daily rental rate until the grinder was returned. Hundreds or thousands of individual item transfers would have to be examined, and the process of preparing bills could easily require a week or two of effort.

In addition to generating billing information, a variety of reports would be useful in the process of managing a company's equipment and individual projects. Records of the history of use of particular pieces of equipment are useful for planning maintenance and deciding on the sale or scrapping of equipment. Reports on the cumulative amount of materials and equipment delivered to a job site would be of obvious benefit to project managers. Composite reports on the amount, location, and use of pieces of equipment of particular types are also useful in making decisions

TABLE 14-1 A CONSTRUCTION WAREHOUSE TRANSFER RECORD

TRANSFER SHEET NUMBER 100311

Deliver to: Carnegie Mellon   Job No. 83-1557
Received from: Pittsburgh Warehouse   Job No. 99-PITT

ITEM NO.	EQ. NO.	QTY	DESCRIPTION	UNIT PRICE
0609.02		200	Hilti pins NK27	$ 0.36
0609.03		200	Hilti pins NK27	0.36
0188.21		1	Kiel, box of 12	6.53
0996.01		3	Paint, spray	5.57
0607.03		4	Plywood, $4 \times 8 \times \frac{1}{4}''$	11.62
0172.00	4517	1	Grinder	
0181.53		1	Grinding wheel, 6'' cup	14.97
Preparer: Vicki		Date: x/xx/xx		

about the purchase of new equipment, inventory control, or for project planning. Unfortunately, producing each of these reports requires manually sifting through a large number of transfer cards. Alternatively, record keeping for these specific projects could have to proceed by keeping multiple records of the same information. For example, equipment transfers might be recorded on (1) a file for a particular piece of equipment and (2) a file for a particular project, in addition to the basic transfer form illustrated in Table 14-1. Even with these redundant records, producing the various desired reports would be time consuming.

Organizing this inventory information in a computer program is a practical and desirable innovation. In addition to speeding up billing (and thereby reducing borrowing costs), application programs can readily provide various reports or *views* of the basic inventory information described. Information can be entered directly to the computer program as needed. For example, the transfer record shown in Table 14-1 is based upon an input screen to a computer program, which, in turn, had been designed to duplicate the manual form used prior to computerization. Use of the computer also allows some interactive aids in preparing the transfer form. This type of aid follows a simple rule: "Don't make the user provide information that the system already knows."[111] In using the form shown in Table 14-1, a clerk need only enter the code and quantity for an item; the verbal description and unit cost of the item then appear automatically. A copy of the transfer form can be printed locally, while the data are stored in the computer for subsequent processing. As a result, preparing transfer forms and record keeping are rapidly and effectively performed.

More dramatically, the computerized information allows warehouse personnel both to ask questions about equipment management and to generate readily the requisite data for answering such questions. The records of transfers can be readily processed by computer programs to develop bills and other reports. For example, proposals to purchase new pieces of equipment can be rapidly and critically reviewed after summarizing the actual usage of existing equipment. Ultimately, good organization of information will typically lead to the desire to store new types of data and to provide new views of this information as standard managerial tools.

Of course, implementing an information system such as the warehouse inventory database requires considerable care to ensure that the resulting program is capable of accomplishing the desired task. In the warehouse inventory system, a variety of details are required to make the computerized system an acceptable alternative to a long-standing, manual, record-keeping procedure. Coping with these details makes a big difference in the system's usefulness. For example, changes to the status of equipment are generally made by recording transfers as illustrated in Table 14-1. However, a few status changes are not accomplished by physical movement. One example is a charge for air conditioning in field trailers: even though the air conditioners may be left in the field, the construction project should not be charged for the air conditioner after it has been turned off during the cold weather months. A special status change report may be required for such details. Other details of record keeping require similar special controls.

[111] Attributed to R. Lemons in J. Bentley, "Programming Pearls," *Communications of the ACM*, Vol.28, no.9, 1985, pp. 896–899.

Even with a capable program, simplicity of design for users is a critical factor affecting the successful implementation of a system. In the warehouse inventory system just described, input forms and initial reports were designed to duplicate the existing manual, paper-based records. As a result, warehouse clerks could readily understand what information was required and its ultimate use. A good rule to follow is the "principle of least astonishment:" make communications with users as consistent and predictable as possible in designing programs.

Finally, flexibility of systems for changes is an important design and implementation concern. New reports or views of the data are a common requirement as the system is used. For example, the introduction of a new accounting system would require changes in the communications procedure from the warehouse inventory system to record changes and other cost items.

In sum, computerizing the warehouse inventory system could save considerable labor, speed up billing, and facilitate better management control. Against these advantages must be placed the cost of introducing computer hardware and software in the warehouse.

14.4 ORGANIZING INFORMATION IN DATABASES

Given the bulk of information associated with construction projects, formal organization of the information is essential so as to avoid chaos. Virtually all major firms in the arena of project management have computer-based organization of cost accounts and other data. With the advent of microcomputer database managers, it is possible to develop formal, computerized databases for even small organizations and projects. In this section, we will discuss the characteristics of such formal databases. Equivalent organization of information for *manual* manipulation is possible but tedious. Computer-based information systems also have the significant advantage of rapid retrieval for immediate use and, in most instances, lower overall costs. For example, computerized specifications writing systems have resulted in well-documented savings. These systems have records of common specification phrases or paragraphs that can be tailored to specific project applications.[112]

Formally, a database is a collection of stored operational information used by the management and application systems of some particular enterprise.[113] This stored information has explicit associations or relationships depending upon the content and definition of the stored data, and these associations may themselves be considered to be part of the database. Figure 14-1 illustrates some of the typical elements of a database. The *internal model* is the actual location and representation of the stored data. At some level of detail, it consists of the strings of "bits" which are stored in a computer's memory, on the tracks of a recording disk, on a tape, or on some other storage device.

[112] See R. W. Wilkinson, "Computerized Specifications on a Small Project," *ASCE Journal of Construction Engineering and Management*, Vol. 110, no. CO3, 1984, pp. 337–345.

[113] See C. J. Date, *An Introduction to Database Systems*, 3rd ed., Addison-Wesley Publishing Co., Reading, MA, 1981.

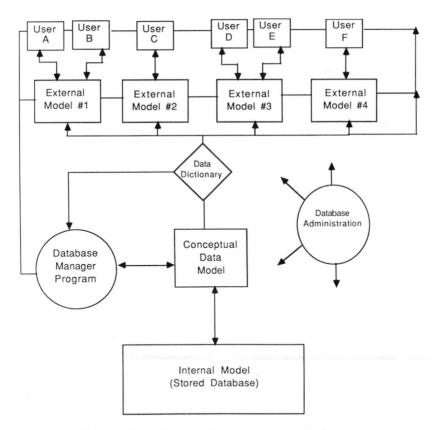

Figure 14-1 A Database Management System Architecture

A manager need not be concerned with the details of data storage since this internal representation and manipulation is regulated by the *Database Manager Program (DBM)*. The DBM is the software program that directs the storage, maintenance, manipulation, and retrieval of data. Users retrieve or store data by issuing specific requests to the DBM. The objective of introducing a DBM is to free the user from the detail of exactly how data are stored and manipulated. At the same time, many different users with a wide variety of needs can use the same database by calling on the DBM. Usually the DBM will be available to a user by means of a special query language. For example, a manager might ask a DBM to report on all project tasks which are scheduled to be underway on a particular date. The desirable properties of a DBM include the ability to provide the user with ready access to the stored data and to maintain the integrity and security of the data. Numerous commercial DBM exist which provide these capabilities and can be readily adopted to project management applications.

While the actual storage of the information in a database will depend upon the particular machine and storage media employed, a *Conceptual Data Model* exists which provides the user with an idea or abstract representation of the data organization. (More formally, the overall configuration of the information in the database is called the *conceptual schema*). For example, a piece of data might be viewed as a particular value within a *record* of a datafile. In this conceptual model, a datafile for an application system consists of a series of records with predefined variables within each record. A record is simply a sequence of variable values, which may be text characters or numerals. This datafile model is one of the earliest and most important data organization structures. But other views of data organization exist and can be exceedingly useful. The next section describes one such general model, called the relational model.

Continuing with the elements in Figure 14-1, the *data dictionary* contains the definitions of the information in the database. In some systems, data dictionaries are limited to descriptions of the items in the database. More general systems employ the data dictionary as the information source for anything dealing with the database systems. It documents the design of the database: what data are stored, how the data are related, what are the allowable values for data items, et cetera. The data dictionary may also contain user authorizations specifying who may have access to particular pieces of information. Another important element of the data dictionary is a specification of allowable ranges for pieces of data; by prohibiting the input of erroneous data, the accuracy of the database improves.

External models are the means by which the users view the database. Of all the information in the database, one particular user's view may be just a subset of the total. A particular view may also require specific translation or manipulation of the information in the database. For example, the *external model* for a paycheck-writing program might consist solely of a list of employee names and salary totals, even if the underlying database would include employee hours and hourly pay rates. As far as that program is concerned, no other data exist in the database. The DBM provides a means of translating particular external models or views into the overall data model. Different users can *view* the data in quite distinct fashions, yet the data itself can be centrally stored and need not be copied separately for each user. External models provide the format by which any specific information needed is retrieved. Database "users" can be human operators or other application programs such as the paycheck writing program just mentioned.

Finally, the *Database Administrator* is an individual or group charged with the maintenance and design of the database, including approving access to the stored information. The assignment of the database administrator should not be taken lightly. Especially in large organizations with many users, the database administrator is vital to the success of the database system. For small projects, the database administrator might be an assistant project manager or even the project manager.

14.5 RELATIONAL MODEL OF DATABASES

As an example of how data can be organized conceptually, we shall describe the *relational data model*. In this conceptual model, the data in the database is viewed as being organized into a series of *relations* or tables of data which are associated in ways defined in the data dictionary. A relation consists of rows of data with columns containing particular attributes. The term "relational" derives from the mathematical theory of relations which provides a theoretical framework for this type of data model. Here, the terms "relation" and data "table" will be used interchangeably. Table 14-2 defines one possible relation to record unit cost data associated with particular activities. Included in the database would be one row (or *tuple*) for each of the various items involved in construction or other project activities. The unit cost information associated with each item is then stored in the form of the relation defined in Table 14-2.

TABLE 14–2 A RELATION DESCRIPTION: UNIT-PRICE INFORMATION ATTRIBUTES

Attribute name	Attribute description	Attribute type	Key
ITEM__CODE	Item code number	Predefined code	Yes
DESCRIPTION	Item description	Text	No
WORK__UNIT	Standard unit of work for the item	Text (restricted to allowable units)	No
CREW__CODE	Standard crew code for activity	Predefined code	No
OUTPUT	Average productivity of crew	Numerical	No
TIME__UNIT	Standard unit of OUTPUT	Text	No
MATL__UNIT__COST	Material unit cost	Numerical ($)	No
DATEMCOS	Date of MATL__UNIT__COST	Date text	No
INSTCOST	Installation unit cost	Numerical ($)	No
DATEICOS	Date of INSTCOST	Date text	No

Using Table 14-2, a typical unit cost entry for an activity in construction might be

```
ITEM_CODE: 04.2-66-025
DESCRIPTION:  common brick masonry,
              12" thick wall, 19.0 bricks per Square Foot
WORK_UNIT: 1000 bricks
CREW_CODE: 04.2-3
OUTPUT: 1.9
TIME_UNIT: Shift
MATL_UNIT_COST: 124
DATEMCOS: June-09-79
INSTCOST: 257
DATEICOS: August-23-79
```

This entry summarizes the unit costs associated with construction of 12″ thick brick masonry walls, as indicated by the item DESCRIPTION. The ITEM_CODE is a numerical code identifying a particular activity. This code might identify general categories as well; in this case, 04.2 refers to general masonry work. ITEM_CODE might be based on the MASTERFORMAT or other coding scheme. The CREW_CODE entry identifies the standard crew which would be involved in the activity. The actual composition of the standard crew would be found in a CREW RELATION under the entry 04.2-3, which is the third standard crew involved in masonry work (04.2). This ability to *point* to other relations reduces the *redundancy* or duplication of information in the database. In this case, standard crew number 04.2-3 might be used for numerous masonry construction tasks, but the definition of this crew need only appear once.

WORK_UNIT, OUTPUT, and TIME_UNIT summarize the expected output for this task with a standard crew and define the standard unit of measurement for the item. In this case, costs are given per thousand bricks per shift. Finally, material (MATL_UNIT_COST) and installation (INSTCOSTS) costs are recorded along with the date (DATEMCOS and DATEICOS) at which the prices were available and entered in the database. The date of entry is useful to ensure that any inflation in costs can be considered during use of the data.

The data recorded in each row could be obtained by survey during bid preparations, from past project experience or from commercial services. For example, the data recorded in the Table 14-2 relation could be obtained as nationwide averages from commercial sources.

An advantage of the relational database model is that the number of attributes and rows in each relation can be expanded as desired. For example, a manager might wish to divide material costs (MATL_UNIT_COST) into attributes for specific materials such as cement, aggregate, and other ingredients of concrete in the unit cost relation defined in Table 14-2. As additional items are defined or needed, their associated data can be entered in the database as another row (or tuple) in the unit cost relation. Also, new relations can be defined as the need arises. Hence, the relational model of database organization can be quite flexible in application. In practice, this is a crucial advantage. Application systems can be expected to change radically over time, and a flexible system is highly desirable.

With a relational database, it is straightforward to issue queries for particular data items or to combine data from different relations. For example, a manager might wish to produce a report of the crew composition needed on a site to accomplish a given list of tasks. Assembling this report would require accessing the unit price information to find the standard crew and then combining information about the construction activity or item (e.g., quantity desired) with crew information. However, to accomplish this type of manipulation effectively requires the definition of a "key" in each relation.

In Table 14-2, the ITEMCODE provides a unique identifier or *key* for each row. No other row should have the same ITEMCODE in any one relation. Having a unique key reduces the *redundancy* of data, since only one row is included in the database for each activity. It also avoids error. For example, suppose one queried the database to find the material cost entered on a particular date. This response might be misleading since more than one material cost could have been entered on the same date. Similarly, if there are multiple rows with the same ITEMCODE value, then a query might give erroneous responses if one of the rows was out of date. Finally, each row has only a single entry for each attribute.[114]

---

[114] This is one example of a normalization in relational databases. For more formal discussions of the *normalizations* of relational databases and the explicit algebra which can be used on such relations, see ibid.

The ability to combine or separate relations into new arrangements permits the definition of alternative *views* or external models of the information. Since there are usually a number of different users of databases, this can be very useful. For example, the payroll division of an organization would normally desire a quite different organization of information about employees than would a project manager. By explicitly defining the type and organization of information a particular user group or application requires, a specific view or subset of the entire database can be constructed. This organization is illustrated in Figure 14-1 with the DATA DICTIONARY serving as a translator between the external data models and the database management system.

Behind the operations associated with querying and manipulating relations is an explicit algebraic theory. This algebra defines the various operations that can be performed on relations, such as union (consisting of all rows belonging to one or the other of two relations), intersection (consisting of all rows belonging to both of two relations), minus (consisting of all rows belonging to one relation and not another), or projection (consisting of a subset of the attributes from a relation). The algebraic underpinnings of relational databases permits rigorous definitions and confidence that operations will be accomplished in the desired fashion.[115]

Example 14-3: A Subcontractor Relation

As an illustration of the preceding discussion, consider the problem of developing a database of possible subcontractors for construction projects. This database might be desired by the cost estimation department of a general contractor to identify subcontractors to ask to bid on parts of a project. Appropriate subcontractors appearing in the database could be contacted to prepare bids for specific projects. Table 14-3 lists the various attributes which might be required for such a list and an example entry,

TABLE 14–3 SUBCONTRACTOR RELATION EXAMPLE

Attribute	Example
NAME	XYZ Electrical Co.
CONTACT	Betty XYZ
PHONE	(412) xxx-xxxx
STREET	xxx Mulberry St.
CITY	Pittsburgh
STATE	PA
ZIPCODE	152xx
SIZE	large
CONCRETE	no
ELECTRICAL	yes
MASONRY	no
etc.	

[115] For a discussion of relational algebra, see E. F. Codd, "Relational Completeness of Data Base Sublanguages," *Courant Computer Science Symposia Series*, Vol. 6, Prentice Hall, Englewood Cliffs, NJ, 1972.

including the subcontractor's name, contact person, address, size (large, medium, or small), and capabilities.

To use this relation, a cost estimator might be interested in identifying large, electrical subcontractors in the database. A query typed into the DBM such as

```
SELECT from SUBCONTRACTORS
where SIZE = Large and ELECTRICAL = Yes
```

would result in the selection of all large subcontractors performing electrical work in the subcontractor's relation. More specifically, the estimator might want to find subcontractors in a particular state:

```
SELECT from SUBCONTRACTORS
where SIZE = Large and ELECTRICAL = Yes
and STATE = VI
```

In addition to providing a list of the desired subcontractors' names and addresses, a utility application program could also be written which would print mailing labels for the selected firms.

Other portions of the general contracting firm might also wish to use this list. For example, the accounting department might use this relation to record the addresses of subcontractors for payment of invoices, thereby avoiding the necessity to maintain duplicate files. In this case, the accounting code number associated with each subcontractor might be entered as an additional attribute in the relation, and the accounting department could find addresses directly.

Example 14-4: Historical Bridge Work Relation

As another simple example of a data table, consider the relation shown in Table 14-4 which might record historical experience with different types of bridges accumulated by a particular agency. The actual instances or rows of data in Table 14-4 are hypothetical. The attributes of this relation are

- PROJECT NUMBER—a six-digit code identifying the particular project.
- TYPE OF BRIDGE—a text field describing the bridge type. (For retrieval purposes, a numerical code might also be used to describe bridge type to avoid any differences in terminology to describe similar bridges.)
- LOCATION—The location of the project.
- CROSSING—What the bridge crosses over, e.g., a river.
- SITE CONDITIONS—A brief description of the site peculiarities.
- ERECTION TIME—Time required to erect a bridge, in months.
- SPAN—Span of the bridge in feet.
- DATE—Year of bridge completion.
- ACTUAL-ESTIMATED COSTS—Difference of actual from estimated costs.

These attributes could be used to answer a variety of questions concerning construction experience useful during preliminary planning.

TABLE 14–4 EXAMPLE OF BRIDGE WORK RELATION

Project number	Bridge type	Location	Crossing	Site conditions	Erection time (months)	Span (ft)	Estimated less actual cost
169137	Steel plate girder	Altoona	Railroad	200' valley Limestone	5	240	−$50,000
170145	Concrete arch	Pittsburgh	River	250' high Sandy Loam	7	278	− 27,500
197108	Steel truss	Allentown	Highway	135' deep Pile foundation	8	256	35,000

As an example, suppose that a bridge is to be built with a span of 250 ft, located in Pittsburgh, and crossing a river with limestone substrata. In initial or preliminary planning, a designer might query the database four separate times as follows:

- SELECT from BRIDGEWORK, where SPAN > 200 and SPAN < 300 and where CROSSING = "river"
- SELECT from BRIDGEWORK, where SPAN > 200 and SPAN < 300 and where SITE CONDITIONS = "Limestone"
- SELECT from BRIDGEWORK, where TYPE OF BRIDGE = "Steel Plate Girder" and LOCATION = "PA"
- SELECT from BRIDGEWORK, where SPAN < 300 and SPAN > 200 and ESTIMATED LESS ACTUAL COST < 100,000

Each SELECT operation would yield the bridge examples in the database which corresponds to the desired selection criteria. In practice, an input/output interpreter program should be available to translate these inquiries to and from the DBM and an appropriate problem-oriented language.

The four queries may represent subsequent thoughts of a designer faced with these problem conditions. He or she may first ask, "What experience have we had with bridges of this span over rivers?" "What experience have we had with bridges of this span with these site conditions? What is our experience with steel girder bridges in Pennsylvania? For bridges of this span, how many and which were erected without a sizable cost overrun?" We could pose many more questions of this general type using only the small data table shown in Table 14-4.

14.6 OTHER CONCEPTUAL MODELS OF DATABASES

While the relational model offers a considerable amount of flexibility and preserves considerable efficiency, there are several alternative models for organizing databases, including network and hierarchical models. The hierarchical model is a tree structure in which information is organized as branches and nodes from a particular base.[116] As an example, Figure 14-2 illustrates a hierarchical structure for rented equipment costs. In this case, each piece of equipment belongs to a particular supplier and has a cost which might vary by the duration of use. To find the cost of a particular piece of equipment from a particular supplier, a query would first find the supplier, then the piece of equipment and then the relevant price.

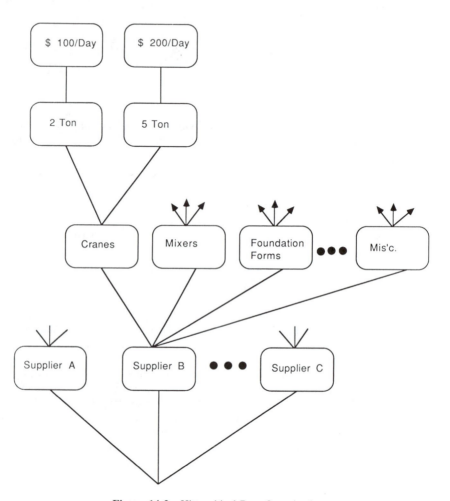

Figure 14-2 Hierarchical Data Organization

The hierarchical model has the characteristic that each item has a single predecessor and a variable number of subordinate data items. This structure is natural for many applications, such as the equipment cost information just described. However,

[116] See D. C. Trichritzis and F. H. Lochovsky, "Hierarchical Data-Base Management," *ACM Computing Surveys*, Vol. 8, no. 1, 1976, pp. 105–123.

it might be necessary to construct similar hierarchies for each project to record the equipment used or for each piece of equipment to record possible suppliers. Otherwise, generating these lists of assignments from the database illustrated in Figure 14-2 would be difficult. For example, finding the least expensive supplier of a crane might involve searching every supplier and every equipment node in the database to find all crane prices.

The network model or database organization retains the organization of information on branches and nodes, but does not require a tree of structure such as the one in Figure 14-2.[117] This gives greater flexibility but does not necessarily provide ease of access to all data items. For example, Figure 14-3 shows a portion of a network model database for a building. The structural member shown in the figure is related to four adjoining members, data on the joints designed for each end, an assembly related to a room, and an aggregation for similar members to record member specifications.

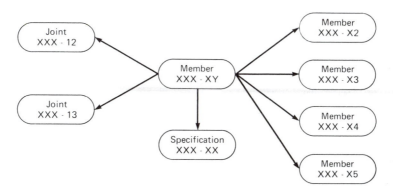

Figure 14-3   A Network Data Model

While the early, large databases were based on the hierarchical or network organizations, the relational model is now preferred in many applications due to its flexibility and conceptual simplicity.

More recently, some new forms of organized databases have appeared, spurred in part by work in artificial intelligence. For example, Figure 14-4 illustrates a *frame* data structure used to represent a building design element. This frame describes the location, type, cost, material, scheduled work time, et cetera., for a particular concrete footing. A frame is a general-purpose data representation scheme in which information is arranged in *slots* within a named frame. Slots may contain lists, values, text, procedural statements (such as calculation rules), pointers, or other entities. Frames can be interconnected so that information may be *inherited* between

[117] For a more extensive comparison, see A. S. Michaels, B. Mittman, and C. R. Carlson, "A Comparison of Relational and CODASYL Approaches to Data-Base Management," *ACM Computing Surveys*, Vol. 8, no. 1, 1976, pp. 125–157.

SLOT	VALUE	UNITS
part-of	foundation	---
is-a	DE	---
name	footing	---
name-code	60	---
shape	rectangular	---
material	concrete	---
material-code	01	---
multiplier	24	---
construction-type	---	cast-in-place
concrete-type	4000	psi
psteel	......	---
grade	......	---
P-dead	......	kips
P-live	......	kips
Mmax-X	......	k-in
Mmax-Y	......	k-in
xl-dimension	3	ft
yl-dimension	2	ft
zl-dimension	14	ft
element-numbers	(foot-1 foot-2 ...)	---
x1	(......)	---
x2	(......)	---
y1	(......)	---
y2	(......)	---
xg-coordinates	(10 50 ...)	ft
yg-coordinates	(25 34 ...)	ft
zg-coordinates	(20 20 ....)	ft
material-cost	......	$
crew-cost	......	$
start-time	......	month-day-year
finish-time	......	month-date-year

Figure 14-4 Data Stored in a Frame

slots. Figure 14-5 illustrates a set of interconnected frames used to describe a building design and construction plan.[118] *Object-oriented* data representation is similar in that very flexible local arrangements of data are permitted. While these types of data storage organizations are active areas of research, commercial database systems based on these organizations are not yet available.

---

[118] This organization is used for the central data store in an integrated building design environment. See S. Fenves, U. Flemming, C. Hendrickson, M. Maher, and G. Schmitt, "An Integrated Software Environment for Building Design and Construction," *Proceedings of the Fifth ASCE Conference on Computing in Civil Engineering*, Alexandria, Va., 1987.

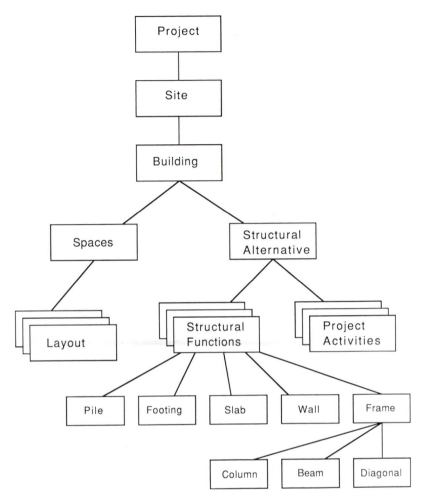

Figure 14-5 Frame Based Data Storage Hierarchy

14.7 CENTRALIZED DATABASE MANAGEMENT SYSTEMS

Whichever conceptual model or database management system is adopted, the use of a central database management system has a number of advantages and some costs compared to the commonly employed special-purpose datafiles. A datafile consists of a set of records arranged and defined for a single application system. Relational information between items in a record or between records is not explicitly described or available to other application systems. For example, a file of project activity durations and scheduled times might be assembled and manipulated by a project scheduling system. This datafile would not necessarily be available to the accounting system or to corporate planners. A centralized DBM has several advantages over such stand-alone systems:[119]

- **Reduced redundancy.** Good planning can allow duplicate or similar data stored in different files for different applications to be combined and stored only once.
- **Improved availability.** Information may be made available to any application program through the use of the DBM.
- **Reduced inconsistency.** If the same data is stored in more than one place, then updating in one place and not everywhere can lead to inconsistencies in the database.
- **Enforced data security.** Authorization to use information can be centralized.

For the purpose of project management, the issue of improved availability is particularly important. Most application programs create and *own* particular datafiles in the sense that information is difficult to obtain directly for other applications. Common problems in attempting to transfer data between such special-purpose files are missing data items, unusable formats, and unknown formats.

As an example, suppose that the purchasing department keeps records of equipment rental costs on each project underway. These data are arranged so that payment of invoices can be handled expeditiously and project accounts are properly debited. The records are arranged by individual suppliers for this purpose. These records might not be particularly useful for the purpose of preparing cost estimates since

- Some suppliers might not exist in the historical record.
- Finding the lowest-cost supplier for particular pieces of equipment would be exceedingly tedious since every record would have to be read to find the desired piece of equipment and the cost.
- No direct way of abstracting the equipment codes and prices might exist.

An alternative arrangement might be to separately record equipment rental costs in (1) the purchasing department records, (2) the cost estimating division, and (3) the company warehouse. While these multiple databases might each be designed for individual use, they represent considerable redundancy and could easily result in inconsistencies as prices change over time. With a central DBM, desired views for each of these three users could be developed from a single database of equipment costs.

A manager need not conclude from this discussion that initiating a formal database will be a panacea. Life is never so simple. Installing and maintaining databases is a costly and time-consuming endeavor. A single database is particularly vulnerable to equipment failure. Moreover, a central database system may be so expensive and cumbersome that it becomes ineffective; we will discuss some possi-

---

[119] For a discussion, see D. R. Rehak and L. A. Lopez, *Computer Aided Engineering Problems and Prospects*, Civil Engr. Systems Lab., University of Illinois at Urbana-Champaign, 1981.

bilities for transferring information between databases in a later section. But lack of good information and manual information management can also be expensive.

One might also contrast the operation of a formal, computerized database with that of a manual filing system. For the equipment supplier example cited, an experienced purchasing clerk might be able immediately to find the lowest-cost supplier of a particular piece of equipment. Making this identification might well occur in spite of the formal organization of the records by supplier organization. The experienced clerk will have his own subjective, conceptual model of the available information. This subjective model can be remarkably powerful. Unfortunately, the mass of information required, the continuing introduction of new employees, and the need for consistency on large projects make such manual systems less effective and reliable.

14.8 DATABASES AND APPLICATIONS PROGRAMS

The usefulness of a database organization is particularly evident in integrated design or management environments. In these systems, numerous applications programs share a common store of information. Data are drawn from the central database as needed by individual programs. Information requests are typically performed by including predefined function calls to the database management system within an application program. Results from one program are stored in the database and can be used by subsequent programs without specialized translation routines. Additionally, a *user interface* usually exists by which a project manager can directly make queries to the database. Figure 14-6 illustrates the role of an integrated database in this regard as the central data store.

An architectural system for design can provide an example of an integrated system.[120] First, a database can serve the role of storing a library of information on standard architectural features and component properties. These standard components

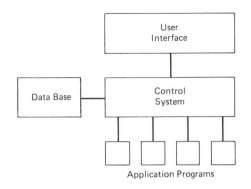

Figure 14-6   An Integrated Applications System

[120] See W. J. Mitchell, *Computer-Aided Architectural Design,* Van Nostrand Reinhold Co., New York, 1977.

can be called from the database library and introduced into a new design. The database can also store the description of a new design, such as the number, type, and location of individual building components. The design itself can be composed using an interactive graphics program. This program would have the capability to store a new or modified design in the database. A graphics program typically has the capability to compose numerous, two- or three-dimensional views of a design, to introduce shading (to represent shadows and provide greater realism to a perspective), and to allow editing (including moving, replicating, or sizing individual components). Once a design is completed and its description stored in a database, numerous analysis programs can be applied, such as

- Structural analysis
- Daylight contour programs to produce plots of available daylight in each room
- A heat-loss computation program
- Area, volume, and materials quantities calculations

Production information can also be obtained from the integrated system, such as

- Dimensioned plans, sections, and elevations
- Component specifications
- Construction detail specifications
- Electrical layout
- System isometric drawings
- Bills of quantities and materials

The advantage of an integrated system of this sort is that each program need only be designed to communicate with a single database. Accomplishing appropriate transformations of data between each pair of programs would be much more difficult. Moreover, as new applications are required, they can be added into an integrated system without extensive modifications to existing programs. For example, a library of specifications language or a program for joint design might be included in the design system described. Similarly, a construction planning and cost estimating system might also be added; an example is described in Chapter 15.

The use of integrated systems with open access to a database is not common for construction activities at the current time. Typically, commercial systems have a closed architecture with simple datafiles or a "captive," inaccessible database management system. However, the benefits of an open architecture with an accessible database are considerable as new programs and requirements become available over time.

Example 14-5: An Integrated System Design

As an example, Figure 14-7 illustrates the computer-aided engineering (CAE) system envisioned for the knowledge and information-intensive construction industry of the

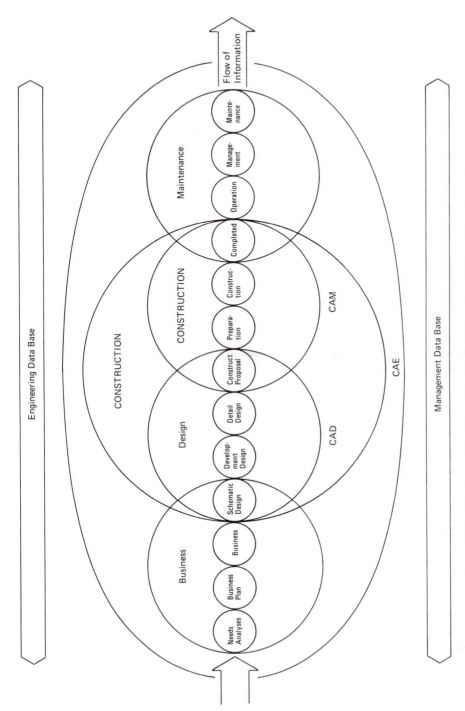

Figure 14-7 Computer-Aided Engineering in the Construction Industry (Reprinted with permission from Y. Ohaski and M. Mikumo, "Computer-Aided Engineering in the Construction Industry," *Engineering with Computers, Vol.1 no.2, 1985.*)

future.[121] In this system, comprehensive engineering and "business" databases support different functions throughout the lifetime of a project. The construction phase itself includes overlapping design and construction functions. During this construction phase, computer-aided design (CAD) and computer-aided manufacturing (CAM) aids are available to the project manager. Databases recording the "as-built" geometry and specifications of a facility as well as the subsequent history can be particularly useful during the use and maintenance life cycle phase of the facility. As changes or repairs are needed, plans for the facility can be accessed from the database.

14.9 INFORMATION TRANSFER AND FLOW

The previous sections outlined the characteristics of a computerized database. In an overabundance of optimism or enthusiasm, it might be tempting to conclude that all information pertaining to a project might be stored in a single database. This has never been achieved and is both unlikely to occur and undesirable in itself. Among the difficulties of such excessive centralization are

- **Existence of multiple firms or agencies involved in any project.** Each organization must retain its own records of activities, whether or not other information is centralized.
- **Advantages of distributed processing.** Current computer technology suggests that using a number of computers at the various points that work is performed is more cost effective than is using a single, centralized mainframe computer. Personal computers not only have cost and access advantages, they also provide a degree of desired redundancy and increased reliability.
- **Dynamic changes in information needs.** As a project evolves, the level of detail and the types of information required will vary greatly.
- **Database diseconomies of scale.** As any database gets larger, it becomes less and less efficient to find desired information.
- **Incompatible user perspectives.** Defining a single data organization involves trade-offs between different groups of users and application systems. A good organization for one group may be poor for another.

In addition to these problems, there will always be a set of untidy information which cannot be easily defined or formalized to the extent necessary for storage in a database.

While a single database may be undesirable, it is also apparent that it is desirable to structure independent application systems or databases so that measurement information need only be manually recorded once and communication between the databases might exist. Consider the following examples illustrating the desirability of

---

[121] This figure was reproduced with permission from Y. Ohsaki and M. Mikumo, "Computer-Aided Engineering in the Construction Industry," *Engineering with Computers*, Vol. 1, no. 2, 1985, pp. 87–102.

communication between independent application systems or databases. While some progress has occurred, the level of integration and existing mechanisms for information flow in project management is fairly primitive. By and large, information flow relies primarily on talking, written texts of reports and specifications and drawings.

Example 14-6: Time Cards

Time card information of labor is used to determine the amount which employees are to be paid and to provide records of work performed by activity. In many firms, the system of payroll accounts and the database of project management accounts (i.e., expenditure by activity) are maintained independently. As a result, the information available from time cards is often recorded twice in mutually incompatible formats. This repetition increases costs and the possibility of transcription errors. The use of a preprocessor system to check for errors and inconsistencies and to format the information from each card for the various systems involved is likely to be a significant improvement (Figure 14-8). Alternatively, a communications facility between two databases of payroll and project management accounts might be developed.

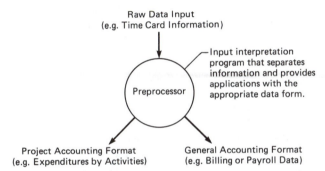

Figure 14-8 Application of an Input Preprocessor

Example 14-7: Final Cost Estimation, Scheduling, and Monitoring

Many firms maintain essentially independent systems for final cost estimation and project activity scheduling and monitoring. As a result, the detailed breakdown of the project into specific job-related activities must be completely redone for scheduling and monitoring. By providing a means of *rolling-over* or transferring the final cost estimate, some of this expensive and time-consuming planning effort could be avoided.

Example 14-8: Design Representation

In many areas of engineering design, the use of computer analysis tools applied to facility models has become prevalent and remarkably effective. However, these computer-based facility models are often separately developed or encoded by each firm involved in the design process. Thus, the architect, structural engineer, mechanical engineer, steel fabricator, construction manager, and others might all have separate computer-based representations of a facility. Communication by means of reproduced facility plans and prose specifications is traditional among these groups. While transfer of this information in a form suitable for direct computer processing is difficult, it offers obvious advantages in avoiding repetition of work, delays, and transcription errors.

14.10 REFERENCES

14-1. Au, T., C. Hendrickson, and A. Pasquale, "Introduction of a Relational Database Within a Cost Estimating System," *Transportation Research Record* 1050, 1986, pp. 57–62.

14-2. Bosserman, B.E. and M.E. Ford, "Development of Computerized Specifications," *ASCE Journal of Construction Engineering and Management,* Vol. 110, no. CO3, 1984, pp. 375–384.

14-3. Date, C. J., *An Introduction to Database Systems*, 3rd ed., Addison-Wesley Publishing Co., Reading, MA, 1981.

14-4. Kim, W., "Relational Database Systems," *ACM Computing Surveys*, Vol. 11, no. 3, 1979, pp. 185–211.

14-5. Mitchell, William J., *Computer Aided Architectural Design*, Van Nostrand Reinhold Co., New York, 1977.

14-6. Vieceli, A. M., "Communication and Coding of Computerized Construction Project Information," unpublished MS thesis, Department of Civil Engineering, Carnegie Mellon University, Pittsburgh, 1984.

14-7. Wilkinson, R.W., "Computerized Specifications on a Small Project," *ASCE Journal of Construction Engineering and Management,* Vol. 110, no. 3, 1984, pp. 337–345.

14.11 PROBLEMS

P14-1. Suppose we wish to develop a database consisting of contractor names, addresses, and particular specialties as in Table 14-3.

    a. Suggest two *hierarchical* organizations of these data.

    b. Suggest an alternative *relational* organization for these data.

    c. Which organization would you recommend for implementation of a database?

P14-2. Suggest four reports which could be obtained from the warehouse inventory system described in Section 14.3 and describe what each report might be used for and by whom.

P14-3. Suppose that a general contractor wished to keep an historical database of the results of bid competitions. Suggest (a) the information that might be stored and (b) a possible organization of this information.

P14-4. Describe a relational database that would be useful in storing the beginning, ending and all intermediate stages for blockworld robot movements as described in Problem P9-6 in Chapter 9.

P14-5. Describe a relational database that would be appropriate for maintaining activity scheduling information during project monitoring. Be explicit about what relations would be defined, the attributes in each relation, and allowable ranges of values.

15

Knowledge-Based
Expert Systems
in Project Management

15.1 COMPUTER AIDS FOR PROJECT MANAGEMENT

As described in earlier chapters, computer aids available for project management include project scheduling, accounting, and computer-aided design. Chapter 14 described the implementation of computerized databases and information systems intended to support a broad range of such applications for project management. Our attention on computer aids reflects the increasing usefulness of these systems to a project manager. With the introduction of less expensive computers and more capable, easier-to-use application programs, the use of computers to aid project management has taken off. Now, it is common to find microcomputers to aid managers even on construction sites. The computer revolution has reached the *practice* of project management, and project managers should be prepared to take full advantage of these automated tools. It is this potential which has motivated the attention on computer-based aids in this text.

Even with the expansion of computer uses in project management, most applications are restricted to formal numerical analysis of well-defined problems. In this chapter, some new types of computer-based aids for project management will be described. These are *knowledge-based expert systems*, which were originally developed as an outgrowth of research in *artificial intelligence*. Knowledge-based expert systems are often called *knowledge-based systems* or, more simply, *expert systems*. These systems are computer programs which were originally intended to mimic the performance of a human expert in a limited problem domain. By avoiding some of the restrictions associated with conventional programs, these systems have the potential for greatly expanding the range of available computer aids for a project manager. More generally, *artificial intelligence* is the study of models of complex information processing and simulation of human cognitive processes. Expert systems apply "artificial" problem-solving strategies to practical problems in limited problem domains.

Expert systems use specific knowledge of an application area (or *domain*) and *heuristic* problem solving methods to perform functions normally reserved for a human expert. Heuristic methods are techniques which may not be complete for all possible conditions or yield good results in all cases. For example, a heuristic rule in scheduling the sequence of repairs on a number of vehicles would be "schedule the vehicles which are easiest to repair first." The result is to minimize the number of vehicles waiting for repair, but to increase the amount of time that vehicles needing major repairs must wait. This is a simple scheduling heuristic that could be used in a variety of applications. "Domain-specific knowledge" in this vehicle repair example would consist of rules indicating the ease with which particular repairs could be undertaken. Other expert system applications would have quite different domain-specific information, even if the same scheduling heuristic were used. For example, a warehouse scheduling system might give priority to "easy" orders which require less handling time.

The success of any expert system depends mainly on the system developer's ability to formalize and to represent the knowledge and problem-solving procedures employed by a particular expert. In some cases, this expertise may consist of the ability to recognize a particular situation or pattern in the environment out of the many thousands of possible situations. This *pattern recognition* expertise is difficult to formalize in a computer program. In other cases, a limited number of rules or organizational patterns may be sufficient for good problem solving. Practical expert systems exist with a few dozen to many thousand rules. In either case, experts typically have difficulty formalizing the methods they employ to reach conclusions, so the development of an expert system is largely a matter of slowly experimenting and expanding known bits of information relevant to the domain.

An important side benefit of this process of expert system development is the formal organization of information that was previously unexpressed. As knowledge and problem-solving strategies are formalized in the expert system, this information, which had been available only to the domain expert, can be recorded for use elsewhere, validated, or generalized for new situations. It is also possible that the process of developing an heuristic expert system may reveal the potential for an optimization or analytic algorithmic solution, thereby making the problem better understood, easier to solve, and amenable to a conventional computer aid.

15.2 WHAT IS AN EXPERT SYSTEM?

Early research in artificial intelligence concentrated upon the general representation and manipulation of symbols, especially in an effort to duplicate human learning and problem-solving techniques. Early systems began with only general-purpose problem-solving strategies such as a structured search process and no specific knowledge about the domain. The performance of these "general-purpose" systems was disappointing. The first generation of expert systems emerged when these general problem-solving strategies were intimately combined with specific domain knowledge. The results were systems that could solve practical problems in limited domains such as geological prospecting or molecular genetics experimentation. The next major development occurred when problem-solving techniques and domain-specific knowledge were separated, permitting the combination of new domain knowledge with existing problem-solving frameworks. These problem-solving frameworks became *expert system shells* or *environments* in which system developers only needed to add domain specific knowledge to create a new expert system.

Reflecting this history, a usual characteristic of expert systems is the separation of the knowledge base, the problem-solving control strategy, and the description of a particular problem. Consequently, a simple *production* expert system consists of three central components: (1) a *knowledge base*, expressed in a series of rules specific to a particular domain; (2) the *context*, which describes the known or deduced information about a particular problem; and (3) an *inference engine*, or *inference machine*, which is an operator to apply the knowledge base rules to modify the contents of the context. As illustrated in Figure 15-1, the knowledge

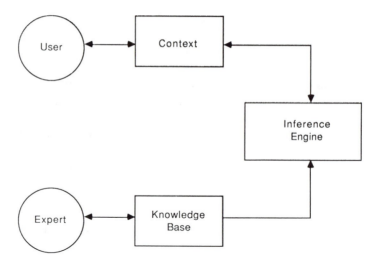

Figure 15-1 Central Components of a Rule-Based Expert System

base is extracted from an expert, and the problem presented by a user is represented in the context. The problem description, the steps used in the solution process, and conclusions are communicated to the user. In solving a problem, the inference engine decides what to do next to alter the problem description in the context. A typical simple production consists of an "if-then" rule stating the preconditions and corresponding actions. Applying or *firing* a rule occurs only if the preconditions are true and the result is an implementation of the actions specified by the rule.

As a simple example, suppose that the context included scheduling information and the knowledge base included a rule of the following form:

IF: activity has no total float time ($TF = 0$)

THEN: activity is on the critical path.

In this case, the *inference engine* could select this rule, apply it to a particular activity for which the precondition is true (in this case, the precondition is that the total float time of the activity is zero), and record the conclusion that the activity is on the critical path. The *context* description of the activity would be altered to indicate that this activity was on the critical path. After this, additional rules might be used to suggest adding resources to critical activities to reduce their duration, to reschedule noncritical activities, or other actions. These additional rules would be selected by the *inference engine* as the rules' preconditions became true (such as a precondition identifying at least one activity on the critical path).

Of course, the three components shown in Figure 15-1 do not make a full system: some additional facilities are required. First, an expert system should have the capability of explaining conclusions or the reasoning employed on a particular problem interactively (Figure 15-2). This dialogue is intended to aid users and to provide a check on the performance of the system. Since explanations are made of

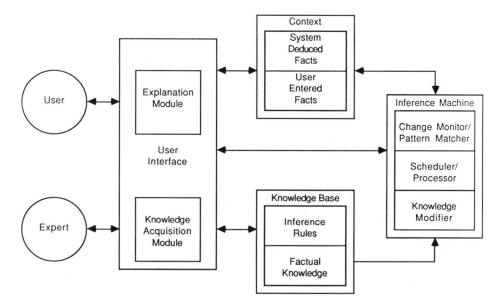

Figure 15-2 Complete Facilities of a Rule-Based Expert System

the specific problem at hand and of the problem-solving actions actually undertaken, an expert system's *explanation facility* is quite different from the on-line "help" facilities provided in many programs or the complete absence of explanations in some conventional, "black box" application programs. The dialogue between a user and an expert system is conducted by means of a *user interface* which can have a multitude of forms including keyboards, drawings, or selection menus.

Another component in a full expert system is the *knowledge acquisition facility* shown in Figure 15-2. Initially, this component permits the entry and editing of domain knowledge from the expert for the creation of a new system. As expert system frameworks have developed, this initial knowledge entry has become easier. Originally, knowledge was entered in special computer languages such as *PROLOG* or *LISP*. Improved expert system frameworks permit different kinds of input, including some systems in which natural languages or examples can be used to input rules. More important, this facility permits incremental expansion of the system as new rules are added. As a result, new knowledge can be represented or the system can be tailored to an individual user's objectives and tastes. This incremental growth is quite different from conventional systems in which patchwork corrections and modifications can be extremely difficult. By separating the knowledge base from the control mechanism and by using "if-then" rule productions or similar atomic information representations, expert systems readily lend themselves to modification over time.

It is also useful to reflect on the characteristics of a human expert that typical expert systems lack. An expert system has very limited senses and virtually no "common sense." An expert system knows only what it is told; it has no independent means of obtaining information. In contrast, humans can observe widely on a site and notice peculiarities that might never be reported to a computer system. Expert systems are designed to operate in a limited problem domain, and they usually will know nothing about commonsense requirements. For example, unless an expert system is explicitly "told" that worker rest breaks are required, it would not plan for such breaks. In addition to cognitive problem-solving skills, more advanced expert systems might also include other human qualities such as the ability to adapt and to learn in the face of new circumstances or as experience accumulates. While most existing expert systems do not possess automatic abilities of this type, it is possible to envision mechanisms by which learning can be introduced.

Modeling of human cognition provided much of the early impetus for expert system development. Early researchers in the area were interested in capturing the actual processes used by human experts. While this artificial intelligence research is still a fruitful analogy and source of new concepts, it is not essential to maintain that all expert systems must incorporate or mimic human thinking and problem solving. In particular, expert systems represent a useful computer system development environment for many applications, whether or not they represent a realistic model of human cognition. In many cases, "expert system" environments represent the most convenient programming and problem-solving environment, regardless of their similarity or dissimilarity to human thinking.

The principal distinction between expert systems and algorithmic programs lies in the use of knowledge. A conventional algorithmic application program is organized into data and program. Data manipulation is repetitive and fully specified in advance. An expert system is organized to represent and use knowledge best. It is not guaranteed to reach a correct solution nor is the course of problem-solving predictable in advance. As a result, the organization and content of expert systems can be quite different from conventional programs.

Reflecting the different style of an expert system, a common difference between expert systems and conventional programs is the separation of the knowledge base from the control mechanism. In Figure 15-1, this separation is represented by the separate box around the inference engine component. By maintaining this separation, expert systems can use complex rules and handle difficult problem domains without becoming bogged down in the problem of program control.

A second distinguishing characteristic of an expert system is the *self-knowledge* inherent in the program. A true expert system can examine its own reasoning and explain its operation during execution. Conventional "help" facilities do not provide this level of dialogue transparency since these facilities are separate from the actual program execution.

A third characteristic of an expert system is the identifiable expertise in the program. Ideally, this expertise should be sufficient to permit expert performance in a limited domain. The expertise should also be readable, understandable, and capable of manipulation (i.e., displaying, searching, modifying) apart from application of the system.

A final characteristic of an expert system is the ability for incremental expansion without major changes to the control strategy. By permitting modification over time, expert systems can be customized to particular users or updated to reflect new situations.

Of course, none of these characteristics provides an acid test for classifying an expert system. Generally, the boundaries between conventional and expert system programs are fuzzy, with expert systems recognized as much by intent as by style. The line between conventional programs and expert systems is likely to become even more difficult to draw as better expert system environments in conventional programming languages (e.g., FORTRAN, Pascal, or C) are developed and as richer integration of expert systems and conventional programs appear.

15.3 DEVELOPING EXPERT SYSTEMS

Expert systems are appearing in many application areas. Of course, not all tasks are amenable to this type of system. The range of possible applications is growing, however, as users become more familiar with the capabilities of expert systems, the software environments for expert systems improve, and new problem-solving and data representation strategies are devised. A partial list of criteria to evaluate promising potential applications would include the following:

- There are recognized experts in the field whose performance is significantly better than that of novices.
- The factual component of domain knowledge is routinely taught to neophytes who become experts by developing their own rules and empirical associations.
- Typical tasks are performed by an expert in a few minutes to several hours.
- Tasks are primarily cognitive, requiring reasoning at multiple levels of abstraction.
- Algorithmic solutions are either impractical or result in overly constrained or specialized programs.
- There are substantial benefits possible from the expert system either through the importance of each decision made (as in nuclear reactor evaluation) or due to the large volume of decisions to be made (as in monitoring purchase orders for materials within a large organization).

A variety of problems encountered by project managers or by other participants in the provision of constructed facilities meet these criteria. As a result, the range of potential expert system applications is correspondingly large. Table 15-1 summarizes some possible systems, progressing from *derivative* or *interpretive* problems to more complicated *formative* or *generative* problems.

The process of building an expert system is similar in nature to producing a plan of work or a facility design. Typical steps include *problem identification, system design, knowledge acquisition, implementation, testing,* and *revision.* Problem identification requires the development of a well-defined problem and domain for application as well as the overall goals for the system. System design involves the

TABLE 15–1 SOME POSSIBLE EXPERT SYSTEM APPLICATIONS IN PROJECT
MANAGEMENT

Interpretation	An interpretation system takes observed data and explains its meaning. Possible applications include interpretation of site core boring data, accounting or scheduling results, or quality control monitors such as embedded strain gauges.
Prediction	Starting with a given situation, a prediction system infers likely consequences. Possible applications include warning systems of possible equipment malfunction, of cost or time overruns on projects, and of safety risks.
Diagnosis	These systems infer malfunctions or system state from observed irregularities and interpretation of data. Possible applications include equipment diagnosis and repair or structural system diagnosis.
Monitoring	A monitor observes system behavior and compares the observations to the planned behavior to determine flaws in the plan or potential malfunctions of the system. Possible applications include real-time evaluation of structural strains or the efficiency of equipment.
Design	Design is the process of developing an artificial configuration of a physical object to satisfy existing constraints and objectives. Systems to aid in preliminary structural design or in the detailed design of system connections are possible examples.
Planning	Planning is a design process that recommends a set of actions to reach a desired outcome. Overall construction planning of activities or detailed planning of robot actions are potential applications.

selection of the overall structure or architecture of the expert system, including data representation and appropriate problem-solving strategies. After the design is formalized, knowledge is acquired through interviews and interaction with a domain expert as part of the knowledge acquisition process. Ideally, the domain expert himself or herself might serve as the system developer, so the communication required in this step is minimized. A useful strategy in the process of knowledge acquisition is to produce simple systems that are refined through the use of example problem solving. Encoding the system design and knowledge is accomplished in the implementation phase. By taking advantage of the various tools that are available for building expert systems, implementation of the system can be greatly simplified. Testing and revision of the resulting program are essential steps in the process. Indeed, the typical development of an expert system requires the testing and modification of numerous prototype systems in an iterative fashion.

The goals of developing expert systems are generally threefold: usefulness, performance, and transparency. In essence, the expert system must be capable of performing a useful, problem-solving function. It should have an acceptably high level of performance over the desired range of applications. Ideally, it should utilize the specialized knowledge that separates human experts from novices to accomplish the desired performance level. Finally, the expert system should be capable of explaining its actions and reasoning to a user. In practice, expert systems are often used as assistants to human users, so adequate explanations are essential.

The interaction of conventional programs and expert systems is likely to lead to rapid development in the future. Originally, expert systems were developed as

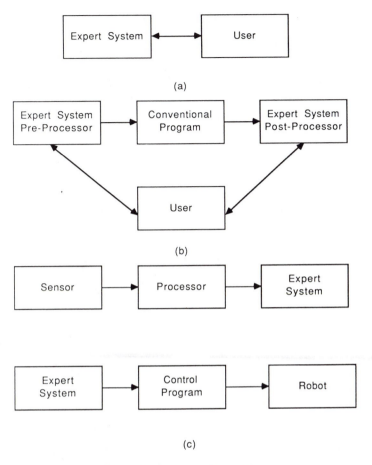

Figure 15-3 Expert System Uses

stand-alone programs to assist a human user (Figure 15-3(a)). More recently, the capabilities of expert systems for formulating problems, checking the reasonableness of data, or providing explanations and interpretations sparked considerable interest in expert system as preprocessors or postprocessors for conventional programs (Figure 15-3(b)). The feature extraction and strategic planning capabilities of expert systems provide incentives for the introduction of expert systems into sensor systems and robots (Figure 15-3(c)). Finally, there is the possibility that expert systems can interact with external databases or other application programs (Figure 15-2). For project management applications, this interaction is extremely important since extensive data exist about projects and a number of existing application programs provide extremely useful results, such as critical path scheduling. As a result, expert systems need not be used or developed as independent programs, but can operate in concert with other programs.

As an outgrowth of research in artificial intelligence, full-blown expert systems might be expected to duplicate the existing problem-solving performance of an expert but also to have the capability to adapt, learn, and invent in a fashion similar to humans. This capability does not yet exist in practical expert systems, and there are some observers who believe that artificial intelligence programs will never exhibit these human characteristics. Even without these dimensions, expert systems offer a means to deal with a variety of the ill-structured aspects of project management. They represent an important new tool in the repertoire of good project managers.

15.4 PROBLEM-SOLVING STRATEGIES IN EXPERT SYSTEMS

In rule-based expert systems, the most common solution strategies are forward chaining, backward chaining, or a mixture of the two. Rule-based expert systems represent knowledge as a series of *productions* with a premise (an *if* clause) and a conclusion (a *then* clause).

In the forward-chaining approach, the system works from an initial state of known facts and draws inferences until a final goal state is reached. With a forward-chaining strategy, the user inputs known information, and rules are then applied to draw conclusions. Intermediate conclusions can be used to decide which rules to apply next, so the problem-solving strategy may be *event driven* during applications. This problem-solving strategy is particularly useful if there are a large number of possible conclusions and few input data.

A forward-chaining strategy is illustrated in Figure 15-4 for a simple expert system containing four rules in the knowledge base.[122] For this example, a rule such as

$$F \text{ and } W \rightarrow Z$$

is interpreted as "If F is true and W is true, then Z is true. " "Truth" might represent the literal correctness of the fact Z or the existence of a calculated value for a previously unknown variable Z; application of a rule might include calculation instructions for the variable value. The overall system goal in this small example is to establish the truth of Z if possible. Initially, the context contains the facts represented by the variables A, B, C, E, G, and H (Figure 15-4). Given these facts, the inference engine works to apply the rules in the knowledge base.

In step 1 of the forward-chaining solution (Figure 15-4), the inference engine identifies rule 3 as available for execution. This identification is based on a comparison of the premise conditions for each rule with the available facts in the context; in this case, only the premises for rule 3 are satisfied. Executing or *firing* rule 3 requires the inference engine to modify the context to include the result D.

In step 2 of the forward-chaining solution, the inference engine identifies two applicable or *active* rules, 2 and 4. Rule 3 is excluded from consideration since it has

---

[122] This example has been adapted from D. A. Waterman, *A Guide to Expert Systems*, Addison-Wesley Publishing Co., Reading, MA, 1986.

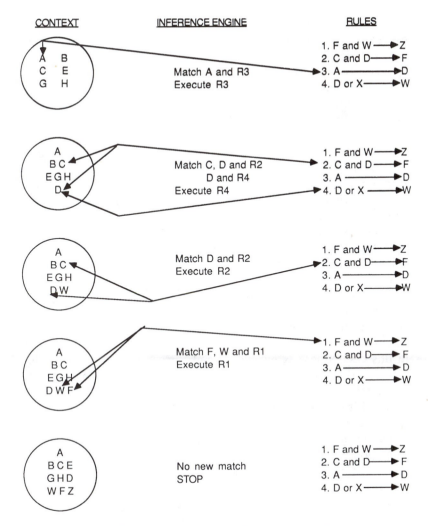

Figure 15-4 A Forward-Chaining Problem-Solving Strategy

already been applied. Some mechanism for choosing which rule to fire is required at this stage; in this example, we will choose to fire the rule with the smaller number of required premises. Applying this rule leads to the execution of rule 4 and the addition of fact W to the context. Obviously, numerous other schemes for selection of the next rule to fire could be adopted.

At the next stage, only rule 2 is active, and execution results in the addition of fact F to the context. Finally, the inference engine identifies rule 1 as executable. Firing rule 1 results in the addition of fact Z to the context. No further new matches are possible, and the system has achieved a desired goal, so execution of the program stops.

A simple mechanism for explanation exists by tracing back these rule executions. For example, suppose a user wishes to know why the fact Z was asserted or concluded. The direct answer is because facts F and W are true and rule 1 was applied. Tracing back farther would identify the rules and data used in asserting the facts F and W or other variables used in the inference process. This process of retracing rule executions provides considerable scope for user review of the program execution and the knowledge applied.

Backward chaining is an alternative problem-solving technique in rule-based systems. In this strategy, calculation or inference of particular attributes are expressed as a system goal to be satisfied. A backward-chaining system works by identifying the final goal and working backward to identify the necessary steps to reach the final goal. This backward-chaining problem-solving strategy is widely employed in diagnostic or interpretive expert systems in which a limited number of conclusions can be obtained.

Figure 15-5 illustrates a backward-chaining strategy for the same problem and knowledge base shown in Figure 15-4. In this case, a set of active goals to be satisfied is recorded in the context in addition to known variable values. Initially, the goal to "find Z" is active. This goal can be fulfilled by applying rule 1, which requires values for F and W. The first step in the problem-solving strategy is to define subgoals to find F and W (See Figure 15-5). No rule can be fired to directly obtain the values of Z, F, or W, so the next step is to generate additional subgoals. In this case, rule 2 is evaluated, and a new subgoal D is derived. Note that C is already known to be true, so no subgoal is required for this case. At this point, the set of desired goals include values for Z, F, W, and D. The value of D can be obtained from rule 3 at this point, and the next step in the program execution would be to fire or execute rule 3. After updating the context, D is added as a known fact and removed as a goal to be fulfilled. In step 4, another match is available with rule 2 and goal F. At this point, rule 4 can be executed to obtain a value for W. Finally, rule 1 can be fired to fulfill the final goal Z.

Backward chaining requires the development of the set of goals and subgoals to be pursued in problem solving, and it results in a more complicated and lengthy solution process in this case. However, by focusing on the particular goals that are required for a specific problem, backward chaining can often reduce the number of rule firings and thereby improve problem-solving efficiency in an expert system. Either forward-chaining or backward-chaining problem-solving strategy can report the series of rule activations and intermediate results used in deriving a final conclusion. Thus, either strategy can support an interactive explanation facility.

With different types of knowledge representation or with more complicated expert systems, some additional problem strategies become useful. These strategies include

- **Means-Ends Analysis**. By analyzing the difference between the existing state of the problem solution and the desired final goal, a desirable set of rule applications or process changes can be identified. This is an *active* strategy for control of problem solving.

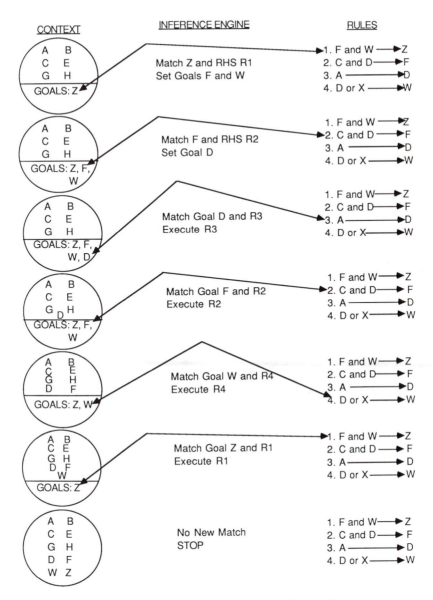

Figure 15-5 A Backward-Chaining Problem-Solving Strategy

- **Blackboard Communication.** A *blackboard* provides a mechanism for an expert system to place a message to be read by other programs. This mechanism permits the development of cooperating yet independent knowledge bases to work on a problem. For example, expert systems could be developed for different subproblems with communication of necessary information handled on a blackboard.

Another dimension for problem-solving strategies is the type of knowledge representation employed. The foregoing examples pertained to rule-based systems in which the context information is generally available to any rule. In different types of expert systems, the explicit relationships among items in the context are of interest. For example, *frame representations* provide facilities for storing information about a particular entity as well as links among the different entities. This stored information may include procedural instructions for calculations, default values, allowable ranges for values, explanations, pointers to related objects, or other information.

15.5 AN EXAMPLE EXPERT SYSTEM FOR ESTIMATING ACTIVITY DURATIONS: MASON

MASON is a rule-based expert system used in the estimation of masonry construction activities.[123] The MASON knowledge base was developed from interviews with several experienced masons. The system provides facilities for estimating the duration of masonry construction, explaining the various calculations made, and making recommendations for alternative crew compositions and technologies. The estimation strategy employed by MASON is illustrated in Figure 15-6 as a hierarchy of estimation tasks. Based on general job characteristics, the maximum productivity that might be obtained is calculated. This maximum productivity is modified to reflect special characteristics of the job such as height or weather. An overall duration is calculated based on the estimated productivity and the amount of work. Finally, general modifications may be introduced to capture effects such as differing productivities due to learning on the job. These estimation steps are organized in a hierarchical fashion. Once an estimation is formed, the type and allocation of resources can be critiqued using the same rules used for estimation.

As originally implemented, MASON employs a *backward-chaining* problem solving approach in which calculation of particular attributes or quantities is expressed as a system goal to be satisfied. For example, an important system goal is to estimate an activity duration. Before this can be accomplished, subgoals associated with the estimation of crew productivity and idle time must be fulfilled. MASON could also have been implemented as a *forward chaining* system. In this case, a description of the masonry site would be input, and the MASON would apply all applicable rules to obtain a duration estimate.

Examples of the knowledge rules included in MASON appear in Chapter 9. These rules pertain to the estimation of maximum productivities achievable as well as modifications in this optimistic projection for peculiar sites, ancillary requirements (such as installing tie-backs), and external impacts such as weather. An example of

---

[123] MASON is further described in C. Hendrickson, D. Martinelli, and D. Rehak, "Hierarchical Rule-Based Activity Duration Estimation," *ASCE Journal. of Construction Engineering and Management*, Vol. 113, no. 2, 1987, pp. 288–301.

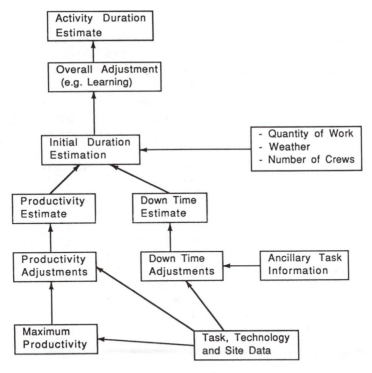

Figure 15-6 MASON's Hierarchical Estimation Framework

a full rule is

> *IF* the maximum productivity assessment is desired
>
> *AND* an 8-inch block is to be used on the activity
>
> *THEN* the maximum productivity on the activity is 400 units
> per day per mason
>
> *AND* a maximum productivity assessment is no longer desired

This rule can be applied when the goal to "find maximum productivity" is active (i.e., desired) and the site characteristics match the premises (i.e., 8-inch block). The conclusion reflects the maximum productivity that might be obtained and a deactivation of the goal to "find maximum productivity." Over 100 rules appear in MASON for productivity estimation under various conditions.

In addition to the estimation procedures, MASON also includes a series of rules intended to make recommendations concerning appropriate crew compositions and technologies. These recommendations are based on a strategy of overcoming the reductions imposed on the maximum productivity due to site conditions or the crew composition. In essence, if a particular rule was used to modify (reduce) the productivity, then a recommendation that would reverse this modification might be possible. For example, if there are too few laborers assigned to the crew, then a rule reduces the productivity accordingly. However a recommendation to add more laborers to the crew can be made, yielding an improvement in productivity.

Upon each recommendation, the user may respond *yes* to accept, thus implementing the recommendation, *no* to reject it, or *why* to be given an explanation of why the suggested recommendation will lead to the estimated improvement. The appropriate explanation of a recommendation depends on the specific job and activity conditions and may vary from session to session. If the user has asked *why*, he will again be given the option of accepting or rejecting the recommendation following the explanation. If the user wishes to accept the recommendation, the productivity and the resulting activity duration is adjusted for the improvement. If it is rejected, the productivity remains the same.

Example 15-1: Example Expert System Dialogue: MASON

To illustrate the operation of MASON and the hierarchical approach to duration estimation, a sample estimation session with MASON follows. Note that MASON provides duration estimates through an assessment of the productivity and downtime inefficiencies at both the project and activity levels. The system queries the user and determines if there exist possible productivity impacts or downtime events that could have a bearing on the duration. In such cases, the user is usually asked follow-up questions to make assessments of these impacts and events. Thus, a session with MASON includes input, recommendation, and explanation phases as well as the estimation of durations and productivities. In what follows, user responses are italicized, and menu-based queries from MASON are omitted; notes are included in regular font.

This example illustrates the interactive, explanatory characteristics of MASON that would be quite useful in application. Graphic displays to improve interaction and more sophisticated input control to avoid unnecessary questions would enhance the usefulness of the system.

Welcome to MASON.

What is the name of the job?
Martinelli's

What type of job is it?
Steel-frame

Is this job large or small?
Large

Is this an addition for an existing building?
No

What would you like to call this activity?
First

What is the expected temperature level during this activity?
Low (Note: "Low" implies a temperature under 50^0 F.)

And the precipitation level?
High (Note: More sophisticated input control would omit this question for interior jobs.)

Where on the job is this activity located?
Interior Wall

How many crews are you putting on this activity?
1

How many laborers are on each crew?
2

And how many masons?
6

Are you using union or nonunion labor?
Union

I need to know how many openings there are?
9

Will this wall be insulated?
No

What type of material is being laid?
Block

And how many orders of this material were placed?
1

What thickness of block was ordered for this activity [inches]?
4 inch

Will high-strength mortar be used?
No

What type of finishing will be placed over the block?
Drywall

What is the average length of the wall(s) [feet]?
50

Will FIRST take place on more than one floor? [yes,no]
No

On what floor will FIRST take place? [0 for foundation]
4

What is the average width of the opening(s) [feet]?
2

And the height?
3

How much areas to be covered [sq ft]?
10,000

How will strap anchors be attached to steel?
Shoot with hildy guns

Input is now complete.
THE DURATION OF ACTIVITY: FIRST IS 16.4 DAYS
THE PRODUCTIVITY IS 176.0 UNITS PER DAY PER BRICKLAYER
THE TOTAL DOWNTIME IS 5.7 DAYS
Would you like recommendations to improve productivity?
Yes

You can increase the productivity on FIRST by 32.0 BLOCK per bricklayer per day if at least one laborer is added to each crew.
Would you like to increase the number of laborers by one?
Why

Supporting laborers are needed to mix mortar, keep the bricklayer stocked, as well as assist him in laying out corners, and so on. If there are more than two bricklayers for every laborer, then it is said that the laborers cannot keep up and that the bricklayers will have to slow down.

Also, because FIRST is on floor 4, the added labor is necessary to transport the materials and tools efficiently to the high-elevation activity site. Because you plan to use six bricklayers, you should add one laborer to each crew. By doing this, the bricklayers will not have to be delayed.

You can increase the productivity on FIRST by 32.0 BLOCK per bricklayer per day if at least one laborer is added to each crew.
Would you like to increase the number of laborers by one?
Yes

Your increase in the number of laborers in each crew is confirmed.
You can increase the productivity on FIRST by 41.0 units per day per mason if high-strength mortar is used.
Do you wish to switch to high-strength mortar?
Why

When working with regular-strength mortar in the cool and damp conditions expected for activity FIRST, the block does not set as fast. This situation has significant impact on productivity when using 4-inch block. This is because the thinner 4-inch blocks, in general, are more difficult to balance than blocks of other thicknesses.

You can increase the productivity on FIRST by 41.0 units per day per mason if high-strength mortar is used.
Do you wish to switch to high-strength mortar?
Yes

Revised duration estimation is complete.
THE DURATION OF ACTIVITY: FIRST IS 13.2 DAYS
THE PRODUCTIVITY IS 249.0 UNITS PER DAY PER BRICKLAYER
THE TOTAL DOWNTIME IS 5.7 DAYS
Would you like to know the factors considered in calculating the productivity?
Yes

The low temperatures expected for this activity have given rise to a 12 percent (of the maximum) reduction in the productivity.

15.6 AN EXPERT SYSTEM FOR RETAINING WALL DIAGNOSIS
AND DESIGN: RETAIN

The design of emergency repairs and the growing inventory of failing retaining walls present a considerable practical problem. Time and budget constraints are pressing, especially for repair work. The available expertise is limited and often dispersed among numerous individuals, so extensive consultation may be required. RETAIN was developed to provide an expert system assistant in such situations. RETAIN can diagnose causes of failure and make recommendations concerning suitable repair or reconstruction strategies.[124] A database management program stores information on unit costs and will also store a description of particular sites and designs. Thus, RETAIN contains modules to accomplish failure diagnosis, generation of alternatives, and evaluation as illustrated in Figure 15-7. Each module has a separate set of inference rules and a separate problem-solving strategy. RETAIN can be used by an engineer called upon to evaluate a retaining wall failure, to conduct a survey of existing walls, or to design a rehabilitation or new construction strategy for a wall.

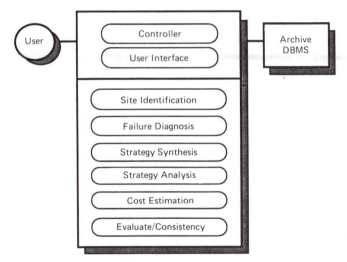

Figure 15-7 Architecture of the RETAIN Expert System

Diagnosing a failing retaining wall involves evaluating the wall's structural stability and failure characteristics to determine the influencing mechanisms. The first step is problem identification. A complete description of the retaining wall, the surrounding site, and the loading conditions is collected. Examples of problem attributes are the wall type, construction material and geometry, bearing and backfill soil properties, and surcharge load types and magnitude. The identification phase

[124] For further detail on the RETAIN system, see T. M. Adams, C. Hendrickson, and P. Christiano, *An Expert System Architecture for Retaining Wall Design,* Technical Report, Department of Civil Engineering, Carnegie Mellon University, Pittsburgh, 1987.

contains knowledge for assigning soil properties based on soil characteristics and for assigning appropriate models for various surcharge load types. Engineering knowledge, including equations and algorithms for computing earth pressures and surcharge load pressures is applied in the analysis step. The pressure loads are combined to determine resultant wall loads, bearing pressure, and factors of safety against problems such as overturning or sliding. While analysis computations are for the most part straightforward substitutions into equations and algorithms, they are not independent of wall type. For instance, computing the bending capacities of various cantilever wall types such as soldier piles and lagging or cast-in-place reinforced concrete follow different algorithms. The final step in the diagnosis phase is the application of a diagnostic network model to the failing retaining wall. Diagnostic models contain heuristic knowledge on failure possibilities.

Synthesis of alternative rehabilitation strategies follows the *generate and test* problem-solving strategy in RETAIN. In this strategy, possible solution alternatives are formulated and then tested for feasibility. In its pure form, generate and test would generate all possible solutions for consideration. A common variation on the generate and test strategy is to *plan, generate, and test,* where the planning phase seeks out reasonable combinations before synthesis of individual alternatives. Given the set of conditions that establish the state of a specific wall, the retained backfill and the constraints on the access of construction equipment, RETAIN will generate and test all remedial actions. The scope of retaining wall rehabilitation strategies includes reducing loads, underpinning, installing tie-backs, buttressing, removing (then regrading), and rebuilding or resurfacing. Some example rehabilitation alternatives are illustrated in Figure 15-8. For example, rock or soil anchors are possible tie-back strategies for repairing an existing wall.

A prerequisite for testing rehabilitation strategies is the preliminary design of each strategy. Preliminary designs include wall and footing dimensions, drainage characteristics, approximate spacing of tie-backs and anchors, amount of excavation, and so on. Each strategy has associated knowledge regarding conditions under which they are technically feasible or infeasible. In the course of the testing phase these conditions are checked. For example, the following list includes a selection of conditions under which replacement by soldier piles and lagging may be technically feasible:

- Height of wall is greater than 10 feet, and length is greater than 100 feet.
- Soil beneath the base of wall has sufficient strength (specified by the expert system for the given type and height of backfill).
- Access exists for pile driving or drilling equipment.
- Operation of construction equipment creates no unacceptable disturbance (such as vibrations or diversion of traffic) to the environment.
- If rock exists at a depth below the base of the wall equal to one-half the height of the wall, this rock must be corable.
- Subsidence-sensitive structures are located above the wall at a horizontal distance greater than the height of the wall, et cetera.

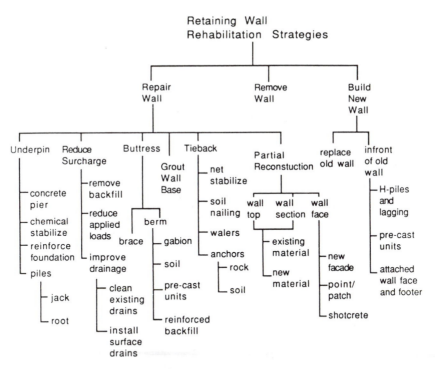

Figure 15-8 A Hierarchical Network of Possible Retaining Wall Rehabilitation Strategies

In the recommendation phase, all feasible rehabilitation strategies are ranked according to how well they fulfill project objectives such as cost, availability of materials, minimizing construction time, and minimizing disruptions to traffic and other structures. Cost estimation is handled by a rule-based expert system, with algorithmic computational functions, which queries a database for specific unit cost factors. Output from the recommendation phase include the conditions leading to failure, what circumstances caused rehabilitation alternatives to be considered infeasible, and the overall evaluation and ranking of feasible rehabilitation alternatives.

Example 15-2: A Probabilistic Inference Network for Failure Diagnosis

In assessing possible failures, RETAIN applies a series of inference networks recognizing the uncertainty of input information and causal relationships. An example of an inference network used in RETAIN appears in Figure 15-9. This network illustrates the information used to reach a conclusion regarding the cause of forward tilting failures in a cast-in-place concrete wall. Three possible causes are included in the figure: toe settlement, overturning, or bearing capacity failure, as illustrated in Figure 15-10.

The inference network in Figure 15-9 is traversed from the bottom to the top. Three types of nodes are included in the figure: (1) inputs from computations or field observations that may be uncertain to some degree, (2) inference rules, and (3) AND or OR combinations of results. For example, if field observation reveals a soil bulge

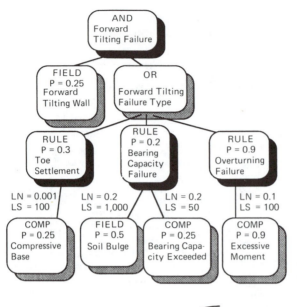

Figure 15-9 A Small Failure Diagnosis Inference Network

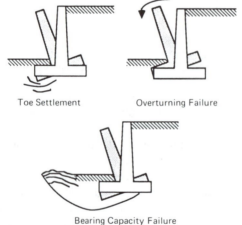

Figure 15-10 Forward Tilting Failures of Cast-in-Place Concrete Walls

and a computation on other inputs suggests that the bearing capacity is exceeded, then the conclusion may be reached that a bearing capacity failure is likely. The inference networks in RETAIN assign a certainty factor to such a conclusion. In Figure 15-9, each relationship has two associated likelihood values. The *sufficiency measure LS* is the degree of support of a hypothesis given positive evidence, while the *necessity measure LN* is the degree of refutation when evidence is lacking. With these values, an inference rule actually has two forms:

> *If* evidence E exists,
> *Then* hypothesis H is true to degree LS
> *If* evidence E does not exist,
> *Then* hypothesis H is not true to degree LN

Application of rules of this sort can also take into account the probability that evidence E actually exists. In addition, each node has an associated prior or base probability. Given particular inputs and their associated certainties, the result of applying these likelihood values and evidence probabilities is some probability of existence for each possible conclusion.

15.7 AN EXPERT SYSTEM FOR CONSTRUCTION PLANNING: CONSTRUCTION PLANEX

CONSTRUCTION PLANEX is a knowledge-intensive expert system for construction project planning. The system generates project activity networks, cost estimates, and schedules, including the definition of activities, specification of precedences, selection of appropriate technologies, and estimation of durations and costs.[125] PLANEX involves interpretation of a final design plan, prediction of durations, and the formation of the construction plan itself. As a result, PLANEX is a fairly large system involving both expert system operators and algorithmic processes for functions such as scheduling or animation of the construction process.

In the initial creation of a construction plan, PLANEX would perform the following operations:

- **Create element activities** for design elements. This operation only identifies the set of element activities required to construct each design element.

- **Group element activities** of common characteristics to have a hierarchy of element activities similar to that of the MASTERFORMAT described in Chapter 9.

- **Determine quantities of work** for element activities. Geometric information is inherited from design element information for this calculation.

- **Select units of measure** for element activities. Crew productivities or material quantities may be expressed in different units (e.g., days instead of hours). In these cases, the system performs appropriate unit conversions.

- **Determine material packages** for element activities. Material packages should satisfy design specifications.

- **Create project activities** that aggregate element activities and are used for scheduling.

- **Select technologies** for project activities. For this operation the system uses heuristics related to soil and site information, resource productivity information and other factors (such as weather). Dependent choices are expressed by creating auxiliary frames pointing to several project activities.

[125] See C. Hendrickson, C. Zozaya-Gorostiza, D. Rehak, E. Baracco-Miller, and P. Lim, "Expert System for Construction Planning," *ASCE Journal of Computing in Civil Engineering,* Vol. 1, no. 4, 1987, pp. 253–269.

- **Estimate durations** for project and element activities. Standard productivities of selected resources are adjusted to estimate the duration of construction activities.
- **Determine precedences** for project activities. Project activities can be then structured into a conventional *project activity network*.
- **Estimate lags** for project activities. Element activities of several project activities are structured into an *element activity subnetwork*. A simple CPM algorithm is used to determine scheduling information in this subnetwork. This information can be analyzed to compute lags between aggregated project activities.
- **Schedule** project activities using critical path (CPM), resource allocation, and constraint satisfaction algorithms.
- **Estimate costs** by computing activity costs and project costs using unit costs and scheduling information.

Similar to other knowledge-based expert systems, CONSTRUCTION PLANEX has three essential parts, as illustrated in Figure 15-11. The *context* contains information on the particular project being considered, including the design, site characteristics, the planning decisions made, and the current project plan. The *operator module* contains operators that create, delete, or modify the information stored in the context. Operators are used for different tasks such as technology choice, activity synthesis, duration estimation, and others. The *knowledge base* contains distinct *knowledge sources* of tables and rules specific to particular technology choices, activity durations, or other considerations. In addition to these three components, CONSTRUCTION PLANEX contains a menu-driven interface used to control the execution of the operators and a *Knowledge Source Acquisition Module* used to modify the contents of the knowledge base.

In the *context*, information is stored in a series of hierarchically organized *frames*. Each frame is linked to parent or children frames from which information can be inherited. Frames are named and contain various slots to record information. For example, *element activity* frames record information on classification, location, geometry, and specifications of the activity. These different frames are organized to represent the current project plan, decisions made during the planning process, and different aggregation schemes. Figure 15-12 shows the general structure of the context. On top of the hierarchy there are frames used to store information at the *project, sector, block*, and *floor* levels. Below them, there are trees for *design elements*, *element activities*, and *project activities*. Element activities are linked to design elements, to element activity groups, and to project activities. Decisions and computations undertaken during the planning process can be stored in any of the frames of this hierarchy and inherited by element activities. Furthermore, inherited values can be overridden by local decisions for particular cases. Thus, the set of project activities can form a conventional project network while the system context contains a more extensive network which also records the planning process and other information.

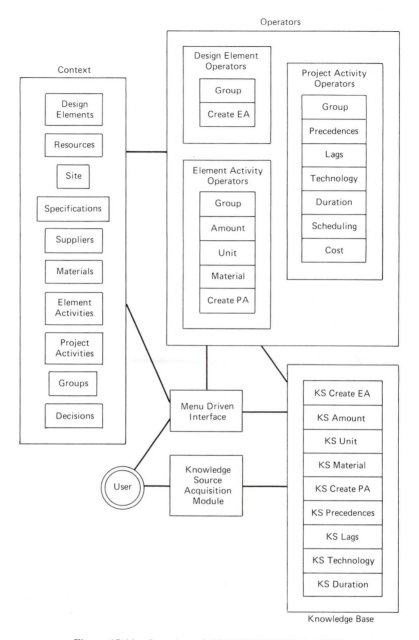

Figure 15-11 Overview of CONSTRUCTION PLANEX

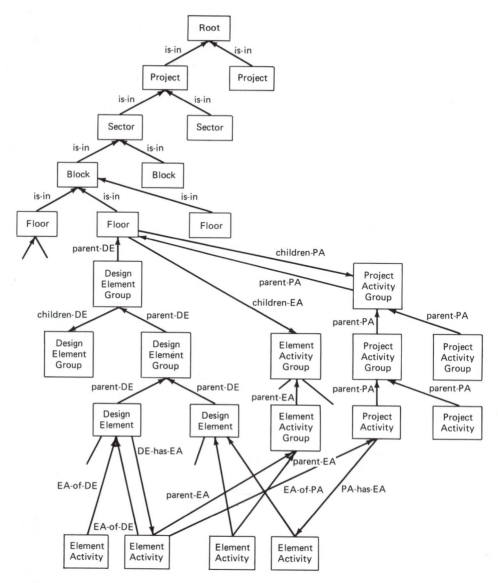

Figure 15-12 The CONSTRUCTION PLANEX Context

The operator modules alter the system context by creating frames or modifying attributes. The exact modifications made are found by evaluating relevant *knowledge sources* in the knowledge base.

The knowledge base is organized into a set of *knowledge sources (KS)* that represent rules, heuristics, and calculation functions. These knowledge sources can best be pictured as decision tables, although they are actually written as frames and production rules. A KS functions as a small expert system, in a fashion similar to the MASON activity duration estimating system described earlier.

Example 15-3: A PLANEX Knowledge Source

An example of a knowledge source appears in Figure 15-13. This KS contains two conditions, three rules, and three possible actions. The first rule indicates that if the *soil type* is *hard* and the result of evaluating *KS water level* is not *wet*, then the appropriate technology is *power shovel* (machine-1 in Table 15-13). The second rule indicates that if the *soil type* is not *hard* and the result of evaluating *KS water level* is *wet*, then the appropriate technology is *clamshell* (machine-2). Finally, the third rule indicates that if neither of the previous two rules were fired, the appropriate technology is *special machine* (machine-3). Knowledge sources can involve recursion, binding of attributes, functional calculations, and other operations.

Object	Slot	Op	Value	RULES		
soil-characteristics	soil-type	is	soft	t	i	i
soil-characteristics	water	is	wet	t	t	i
None	exc-vol	<	vol-x	f	t	i
machine-1				x		
machine-2					x	
machine-3						x

Figure 15-13 A CONSTRUCTION PLANEX Knowledge Source

15.8 AN INTEGRATED BUILDING DESIGN ENVIRONMENT

Architectural design, structural engineering, and construction planning for buildings are typically performed by separate organizations with communication relying upon drawings and specifications. In Chapter 14, we described the possibility of integrating disparate processes through means of a central database of information used by numerous application programs. The integrated building design environment is an experimental prototype to provide just this type of integration.[126] In addition, a specialized *blackboard architecture* and centralized *agenda control* provided a means of overall control on the design process.

The integrated building design environment includes the following processes (Figure 15-14):

- *Architectural Planner*: A knowledge-based expert system to aid an architect in developing the architectural plan and layout of the building.
- *Preliminary Structural Designer*: A knowledge-based expert system to configure and evaluate alternative structural systems.

---

[126] This environment is described in S. J., Fenves, U. Flemming, C. Hendrickson, M. L. Maher, and G. Schmitt, *An Integrated Software Environment for Building Design and Construction,* Technical Report, Engineering Design Research Center, Carnegie Mellon University, Pittsburgh, 1987.

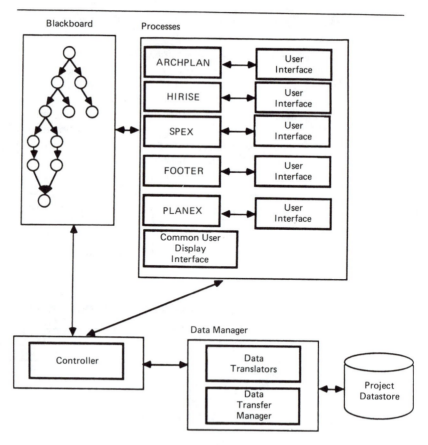

Figure 15-14 Architecture of an Integrated Building Design Environment

- *Component Designer*: An expert system to design strutural components either for preliminary or detailed design.
- *Foundation Designer*: An expert system to generate feasible preliminary foundation designs.
- *Construction Planner*: A knowledge-based expert system for planning the construction schedule and preparing the cost estimate. This component was the CONSTRUCTION PLANEX system described in the previous section.
- *Graphic User Interface*: The user interface includes indications of the state of the processes and a geometric design representation, including a capability for animation of the construction process.

These different processes can run on different computers, with communication and data transfer taking place over a network. In automatic mode, requirements for a building can be entered originally and the system will then develop a building design and construction plan. Alternatively, each of the processes can be monitored and decisions reviewed as they are made.

In addition to the central data store, the blackboard architecture and agenda control for message passing were critical components of the integrated system. A *blackboard* provides a mechanism for a computer program to place a message that can be read by other programs. Once a process finishes a particular task, an appropriate message is posted on the blackboard. The central controller in the design environment monitors the system blackboard for such messages. If a particular process completes a task successfully, then the central controller posts a message for a subsequent process to commence. The sequence of processes to be invoked, including alternative courses of action in case of process failure, is also determined by the central controller.

While this integrated building design is an experimental system, it illustrates a number of features required for a new generation of computer aids in project management. The central database is extended to provide a richer representation of the building design and construction plan. This extended information can support knowledge-based expert system applications. A flexible controller permits automation of the entire process and modifications over time in the number and type of processes in the system. At the same time, existing processes such as graphic displays of construction progress can be maintained.

15.9 REFERENCES

15-1. Fenves, S. J., "What Is an Expert System," in C. Kostem and M. Maher, eds., *Expert Systems in Civil Engineering*, American Society of Civil Engineers, New York, 1986, pp. 1–6.

15-2. Harmon, Paul, and David King, *Expert Systems: Artificial Intelligence in Business*, John Wiley and Sons, Inc., New York, 1985.

15-3. Hendrickson, C., C. Zozaya-Gorostiza, D. Rehak, E. Baracco-Miller, and P. Lim, "Expert System for Construction Planning," *ASCE Journal of Computing*, Vol. 1, no. 4, 1987, pp. 253-269.

15-4. Maher, M. L. (ed.), *Expert Systems for Civil Engineers: Technology and Application*, American Society of Civil Engineers, New York, 1987.

15-5. Waterman, D. A., *A Guide to Expert Systems*, Addison-Wesley Publishing Co., Reading, MA, 1986.

16

Construction Automation and Robotics

16.1 INTRODUCTION

While many construction tasks have been mechanized, construction has seen little automation. Construction remains a labor-intensive industry which has been resistant to the introduction of new technology. Regulatory restrictions and the fragmentation of the construction industry present severe organizational restraints on the implementation of new technology. Technically, the unstructured environment of construction sites and the difficulty of transporting large, prefabricated components have also hindered the large-scale introduction of automated processes. Recent advances in robotic technology and the related experience in manufacturing industries suggests that greater automation may be extremely beneficial for constructed facilities. In addition, construction in hazardous environments may be greatly expanded by the use of construction robots. In this chapter, we shall examine the possibilities for greater automation in the construction industry. The overall purpose of this review is to suggest the scope of technological possibilities that will be influencing construction in the next decades.

There are several means by which construction automation and robotics might repay the additional equipment and development costs associated with high-technology investments. First, robotics offers opportunities for extending the scope of practical construction activities into hazardous environments, including outer space, nuclear reactors, or undersea construction. Even standard construction sites represent hazardous environments as suggested by the large number of industrial accidents associated with construction. Second, robotics may permit the practical introduction and broader use of nonhuman senses and capabilities on construction sites. For example, robotic technology permits construction activities within highly constrained spaces such as pipelines. As another example, robots can use extraordinary senses of radar or sonar to perceive operational opportunities during a construction process. Third, automation and robotics may permit the expansion of construction operations over time. Continuous operation of construction processes and shorter construction times might be more easily achieved by tireless robot workers. Fourth, it may be possible to achieve improved quality in the finished product by means of automation and robots. With automated control, the work tasks in a construction project might be achieved with greater consistency and precision. This greater precision may in itself lead to greater productivity. For example, one advantage cited for automated tunnel boring equipment is the greater precision of drilling, and consequent faster progress in tunneling. Finally, the introduction of automation and robots may result in cost savings due to the direct elimination of labor.

Achieving these potential benefits is an extremely challenging task. Construction involves a wide variety of tasks in a constantly changing, hostile environment. Construction robots must be hardened for extreme conditions of vibration and environmental distress. After all, many existing manufacturing robots would be ruined if they sat out in the rain! In addition to the technical problems, institutional and organizational impediments to the introduction of automation might be expected from existing workers and managers. Nevertheless, the benefits of automation can be so large that some form of automation and robotization is inevitable in many activities.

In considering construction automation and robotics, it is difficult to draw firm lines between advanced mechanized equipment and true robotics. Clearly, machines that look like humans and can undertake many manual tasks would be classified as robots. However, anthropomorphic machines of this type are unlikely to be used in construction in the foreseeable future. More likely is the adoption of specialized equipment that can perform a number of tasks of particular kinds. For example, surveying robots may look like small tractors rather than human surveying parties. Moreover, mobility might not even be a crucial characteristic of important construction robots. Adoption of flexible manufacturing with immovable robots in factories or in assembly plants on a construction site may make prefabrication of components increasingly attractive and significantly reduce construction costs.

16.2 TYPES OF ROBOTS AND AUTOMATION

A common definition of a robot is a reprogrammable, multifunctional manipulator designed to move material, parts, tools, or specialized devices through various programmed motions for the performance of a variety of tasks.[127] This definition reflects the present predominance of manufacturing robots in that the necessity of coping with unstructured environments, mobility, and large-scale forces as required in construction robotics are omitted. Also, the entire class of remote or teleoperated machines is omitted from this definition since they are not necessarily programmable; many organizations define and treat teleoperated machines as robots even though these devices are limited in capability and scope. For construction applications, each of the three major categories of robots can fulfill a role: (1) *teleoperated robots* in hazardous or inaccessible environments, (2) *programmed robots* as commonly seen in industrial applications, and (3) *cognitive* or *intelligent robots* that can sense, model the world, plan, and act to achieve working goals.

Robots form an important ingredient in modern automation since the multifunctional capability and flexibility of a robot permits a wider scope than does stationary automated equipment. These capabilities will be especially important in attacking the many ill-structured tasks in a construction environment. However, the economic impact of automated plants *without* robots should not be ignored. Process plants for producing construction materials such as concrete have already been automated in many instances.

In manufacturing industries, robots have found permanent employment in a variety of tasks, including machine tool processing, welding, palletizing, paint spraying, inspection, assembly, casting, loading, and unloading. While mobile robots exist in manufacturing plants, they are usually restricted to tasks associated

---

[127]See V. D. Hunt, *Industrial Robotics Handbook*, Industrial Press Inc., New York, 1983.

with the movement of materials. Robots used for manipulation or assembly are usually stationary, with raw materials and product components brought to them. As a result, complicated problems of motion and stability are avoided by most industrial robots. In addition, locational problems are reduced since industrial robots can always reference their position with respect to their fixed base. A second characteristic of most industrial robots is the reliance on programmed, repetitive task performance. Since manufacturing often requires the repetition of the same task on different components (such as paint spraying the side of numerous automobiles being assembled), the use of programmed robot control is often effective. In contrast, construction tasks usually involve at least displacement from place to place if not modification to account for changes in the environment. For example, bricklaying operations change when openings for doors and windows are required. Finally, many industrial robots need not apply large-scale forces in work tasks. For example, an extremely successful application of industrial robotics is assembly of small electronic components. In contrast, construction materials are usually bulky and heavy, requiring greater force in assembly and manipulation.

This description of manufacturing sector robots suggests prefabrication as an immediate use for construction robotics. If facility components can be fabricated in a controlled, factory environment, then existing industrial robot technology can be employed. Possible prefabricated components might include wall sections, small rooms, HVAC machinery, transportation equipment (such as elevators), and others. For example, large prestressed concrete blocks are now made in several automated production facilities. Automated fabrication might be accomplished in a central factory or in a temporary facility close to a construction site. One difficulty with this application stems from the limited number of repetitions for many facility components: there are far fewer identical units used in construction than in manufacturing. However, as system programming becomes easier and industrial robots more flexible, the economic feasibility of small production lots increases correspondingly.

Even on the construction site, there exist numerous tasks that are relatively well structured and sufficiently repetitive to warrant robotization. A prime example would be surface finishing works involving spraying, scraping, blasting, or similar activities. These activities are often required for large areas and involve repetition of simple tasks. In most cases, only small forces are required to effect the desired changes: in sand blasting, for example, a robot would only have to position and move existing sand blasting equipment properly. By locating the geometric limits of work manually or through some sensing mechanism, the basic work tasks of this type can be accomplished by conventional programmed control. Existing prototypes of this type of robot include insulation sprayers and painting robots. One existing spray robot applies insulation faster and as accurately as a human worker. The robot also avoids exposing a human to a dirty, uncomfortable environment.

At the highest level, there is also the potential for introducing robots with the ability to plan, act, and respond to changing conditions on their own. This type of robot is the most difficult to develop, yet offers the greatest potential for impact on the construction site. An example would be a robot excavator that would be given only the location and dimensions of a desired excavation. From that point on, the robot excavator would plan the excavation activity, sense the environment, react to changes as excavation proceeds, and accomplish the desired excavation without human intervention.

16.3 SOME ILLUSTRATIVE CONSTRUCTION ROBOTS

Experimental or production robots have been developed for a variety of construction tasks. In this section, we shall give some examples of existing robots.[128] This discussion will be organized by functional applications, including materials handling, tunneling and excavation, finishing, and inspection. Our discussion is only intended to introduce the range of possible construction robots; we will not survey all existing robots or all possible robot applications.

Material Handling

Material handling is a pervasive activity on construction sites and in factories. It includes moving material between locations, placing materials in specific arrangements, and positioning large objects at a specific location and orientation. Material handling applications often require mobility and the ability to apply large lifting forces.

Example 16-1: Shotcrete Robot

Spraying concrete can be a laborious, expensive, and hazardous task. It also requires considerable expertise to regulate properly the amount of concrete to be sprayed and the quality of the hardening agent to be applied. In applications such as the new Austrian tunneling method that employs extensive shotcrete, concrete spraying can take as much as 30 percent of the total. To improve and speed up the shotcreting process, Kajima Company developed a computer-controlled applicator. This machine can be remote controlled (as a teleoperated robot), semiautomatically controlled (involving both computer and operator inputs), or used to play back specific sets of movements. The machine resembles a conventional track-propelled excavator but with a flexible manipulator holding a nozzle.

Example 16-2: Reinforcement Placing Robot

Kajima Company's reinforcing bar placing robot can carry up to 20 bars and automatically place these bars in preselected patterns in both floors and walls. The equipment has achieved 40 to 50 percent savings in labor and 10 percent savings in time on several Japanese projects. Rebars in these applications can be long and heavy, so the rebar placing robot can exert considerable force as required.

---

[128] Unless otherwise noted, the examples in this section have been adapted from I. J. Oppenheim and M. J. Skibniewski, "Robots in Construction," *Encyclopedia of Robotics,* John Wiley and Sons, Inc., New York, 1988.

Tunneling and Excavation

Tunneling and excavation are common tasks in construction. It is an interesting robot application since the nature and disposition of the material being excavated is usually only partially known during the tunneling or excavation process. Robots must respond to changes in the material being excavated. In the extreme, robots should be able to sense and recognize unforeseen obstacles such as pipes or large boulders.

Example 16-3: REX

A prototype robotic excavator (REX) developed at Carnegie Mellon University to uncover buried utility pipes as shown in Figure 16-1. This application is of particular interest in the hazardous process of excavating leaking gas pipes. REX mapped the excavation site using magnetic vision, planned the digging operations, and controlled the excavation equipment. Thus, REX is an example of an autonomous construction robot. The excavation tool used by REX was an air jet.

Figure 16-1 REX, a Robot Excavator (Photo courtesy of Robotics Institute, Carnegie-Mellon University. Copyright ©, 1987.)

Example 16-4: Five-Boom Drilling Robot

Kajima Company has developed and used a drilling robot with up to five active booms. This machine can be used for drilling, blasting, mucking, and shotcreting operations in tunnel bores. The company reports increased efficiency with the machine and increased accuracy in drilling and tunneling.

Surface Finishing

Surface finishing is a widespread construction task that is particularly amenable to automation. Typical finishing activities involve surface treatment (such as grinding, brushing, or smoothing) and surface coating (with fireproofing, paint, plaster, mortar, etc.). Numerous robots and mechanized aids have been developed for this application, such as the two robots described next.

Example 16-5: Slab Finishing Robot

Smoothing the rough surface of a cast-in-place concrete slab is a laborious yet common procedure. Since the process is confined to a flat, two-dimensional surface, simple robotic machines may be applied. Kajima Company has used a computer-controlled applicator involving a mobile platform equipped with mechanical trowels. By means of a gyro compass and a linear distance sensor, the machine navigates throughout a prespecified slab area. The machine was designed to replace at least six skilled workers.

Example 16-6: Fireproofing Spray Robot

Typical materials for fireproofing are rock wool and cement slurry. Rock wool can be sprayed in wool-permeated air. Performing this operation is laborious and can be hazardous, although it is a necessary operation in many highrise buildings. Shimizu Company has developed several robots for this purpose. As illustrated in Figure 16-2, one robot model has a mobile base, hydraulic stabilizers, an articulated robot arm, and a rock wool nozzle. This robot can spray faster than a human worker, but requires time for transportation and set up.[129]

Inspection

Inspection is a required construction task in many applications to ensure adequate quality of materials and work. Robot inspectors can have the advantage of using superhuman senses such as magnetic vision as well as reaching inaccessible spots. However, robots do not have the flexibility and intelligence of human inspectors, so their autonomous role in inspection may be limited.

Example 16-7: Wall Climbing Inspection Robot

Nordmed Shipyards of Dunkerque, France, developed a wall climbing robot called RM3 for tasks such as video inspections of ship hulls, gamma-ray inspection of structural welds, and high-pressure washing, deburring, painting, shotblasting, and barnacle removal. The RM3 weighs 206 lb and has three legs, one arm, and two bodies. Magnetic cups on its hydraulic actuated legs allow the RM3 to ascend a vertical steel plate, such as a ship's hull, at a speed of 8.2 ft/min. (150 m/hr). RM3 has a cleaning rate of 53,800 ft^2/day (5,000 m^2 per day) and a 320-ft range.

---

[129] The authors are indebted to Tetsuji Yoshida of Shimizu Corporation for providing this photo.

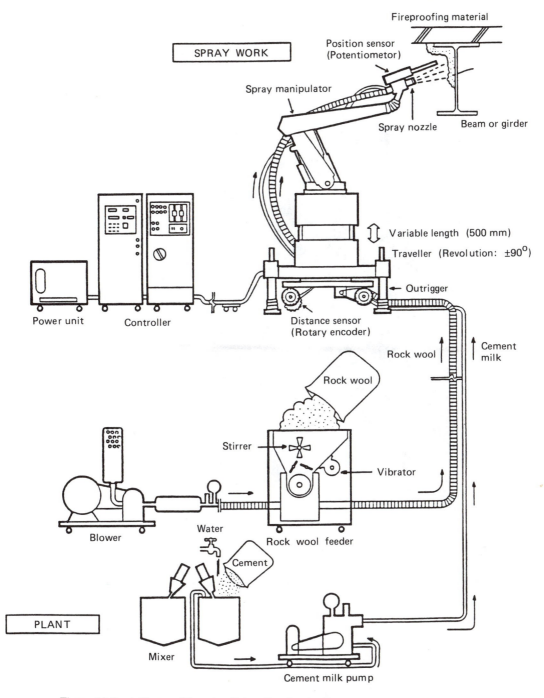

Figure 16-2 A Fireproof Spraying Robot (Reprinted with permission from Shimizu Corporation.)

Example 16-8: Robotic Core Boring and Reconnaissance

Carnegie Mellon University developed a roving, teleoperated vehicle used in the radioactively contaminated areas at the Three Mile Island (TMI) nuclear power plant in Pennsylvania. One special-purpose tool mounted on the roving reconnaissance vehicle was a remotely controlled concrete core-boring tool to provide samples of contamination (Figure 16-3).

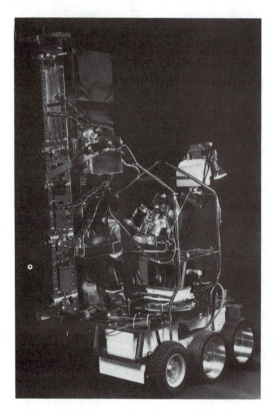

Figure 16-3 A Remotely Controlled Reconnaissance and Core-Boring Robot (Photo courtesy of Robotics Institute, Carnegie Mellon University. Copyright ©, 1987.)

16.4 CONSTRUCTION ROBOT TECHNOLOGY

By their very nature, robotics and automation borrow heavily from developments in related areas such as computer hardware, tooling, navigation algorithms, robotic vision, and software control procedures. Knowledge-based expert systems are examples of a new technology developed in an independent area (in this case, artificial intelligence research) which has filled an important requirement in the control of advanced robot systems. Since construction robotic applications are in their infancy, existing technologies used in industrial settings are also a fertile source of relevant construction automation technology. In this section, we briefly review some of the more important pieces of technology required for successful implementation of construction robots.

Manipulators

Manipulators comprising robot arms are a useful starting point in the discussion of robot technology. Stationary robots with flexible, articulated arms represent the most common form of industrial robot. These industrial robots are in a sense extremely limited: a comparable human would be someone who is blind, deaf, dumb, one-armed, and with feet set in concrete. Nevertheless, the tireless nature and flexibility of robot arms make them effective workers in industrial environments.

The essential role of a robot arm is to move a tool or *effector* into the proper orientation relative to a workpiece. To achieve necessary flexibility, arms typically require six axis of movement (or *degrees of freedom*): three translational movements (right/left, forward/back, up/down) and three rotational movements (pitch, roll, and yaw). Various movements can be accommodated with quite different robot architectures. For example, Figure 16-4(a) shows a robot arm that works in rectangular coordinate axes similar to a gantry crane. Three directions of movement are shown in the figure, corresponding to movements along the three rectangular coordinates. In contrast, the manipulator in Figure 16-4(b) works in a cylindrical space with two extension joints and one rotational joint. In Figure 16-4(c), a manipulator configured to work in spherical coordinates is shown. Finally, the manipulators shown in Figure 16-4(d) and (e) more closely duplicate human arm or wrist movements.

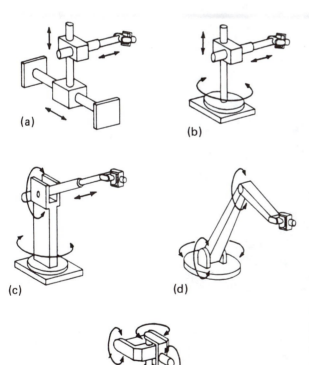

(a)

(b)

(c)

(d)

(e)

Figure 16-4 Typical Configurations of Industrial Robots: (a) Rectangular, (b) Cylindrical, (c) Spherical, (d) Jointed, (e) Wrist (Reprinted with permission from A. Warszawski and D. A. Sangrey, *ASCE Journal of Construction Engineering and Management*, Vol.111, no.3, 1985.)

Movement of robot arms require drive mechanisms able to influence the various degrees of movements. Typical mechanisms used in practice include hydraulic cylinders and electric drives. Special consideration must be given to precise control over the speed and extent of all the possible movements. Accuracy and repeatability of movements are greatly influenced by the accuracy and reliability of the drive mechanism. Transmissions to convert drive movements into appropriate speeds and directions may also be required.

Robot Effectors

Perched on a robot arm manipulator, a variety of tools or effectors may be employed. Sprayers, scrappers, grippers, sensors, and other tools would be typically used for construction tasks. These tools could be identical to those used by human workers or specially designed for easier control and manipulation by machine. In Figure 16-5, for example, a teleoperated robot is shown operating a gripping tool. Integrated

Figure 16-5 A Gripping Robot Effector (Photo courtesy of Robotics Institute, Carnegie Mellon University. Copyright ©, 1987.)

effectors may be sophisticated robotic machines in themselves, involving sensors and control algorithms. An example of a sophisticated effector would be a wrench capable of sensing torque and elongation of bolts and automatically shutting off the turning force at the proper degree of tightness. Another example is the development of robot effectors capable of either spot or arc welding.

Mobility Systems

On construction sites themselves, mobility and locomotion are extremely desirable characteristics for robots. In many cases, work must be performed in situ, so a stationary robot has a quite limited usefulness. Fortunately, a variety of mobile platforms can be used to support particular manipulators. Indeed, mobile platforms may be identical to those used for existing mechanized equipment except for the control system and the payload. Thus, numerous wheeled or tracked platforms are commercially available.

Unfortunately, construction sites are not always accessible for wheeled or tracked vehicles. A research topic of considerable interest is the development of climbing or walking robots capable of general movement about a construction site. Cable-supported robots are also of interest. In these systems, a robot would be supported and moved by a remote crane. More specialized robots to crawl along beams or flat surfaces are also possible.

Robot Control

Robot control is the most important distinction between a robot and a piece of mechanized equipment, although there is no general agreement on exactly where to draw the line between robots and other machines. All robot controllers possess mechanisms for controlling the position and movement of robot arms and effectors. These control programs will typically have memory available so that a sequence of movements can be "taught" and played back as required. At a higher level of abstraction, a robot controller may be able to plan movements and sequences of actions given a desired goal.

Computer-based controllers can work at each level of abstraction. *Actuator level* languages were the first to be developed and include commands for movements of particular joints in a robot manipulator. For each desired movement, a programmer must specify individual movements and positions for each joint in the manipulator arm. At a higher level of abstraction, *manipulator level* or *end effector* languages exist. These languages include commands specifying desired movements or positions of the end effector of a robot manipulator. When such a command is issued, the software must determine what actuator level commands are required to achieve the desired final position. Finally, at the highest level are languages and control systems that can plan manipulator movements in response to goal statements or sensor information. These languages are often called *object level* since they include commands related to objects in the robot's world. Knowledge-based expert systems are one possibility for an object-level command system.

Sensors

Sensors are also components of all but primitive robots. A sensor is any device or transducer that converts an environmental condition into an electrical signal. An environmental condition might be mechanical, optical, electrical, acoustic, magnetic, or other physical effect. A simple example is a microswitch installed on an end effector that will go on when an object is touched. In this case, the microswitch sensor sends an on (i.e., "contact") or off (i.e., "no contact") signal to the robot controller. More complicated sensors make measurements of desired parameters, such as flow rates in an air supply or the current position of the robot manipulator. These measurements are used to control robot movements and, in advanced robots, to plan operations.

While measuring different physical effects can be achieved in a variety of fashions, interpreting sensor information for the purpose of robot control is a very difficult and computer-intensive process. Consequently, most existing robots have only limited capabilities to sense the environment. As with control languages, different levels of interpretation exist. At the lowest level, mechanisms for receiving each sensor signal must be implemented, so sensor-level programs are required. Direct sensor measurements are converted into parameters describing the physical effect being considered. Finally, parameter values are integrated into a world model of the robot environment at the object level. Since performing all these different interpretation operations is computationally burdensome, there has been considerable attention devoted to *smart sensors* in which the calculation of parameters is handled internally. As a result, the robot controller computer does not have to devote time to polling and interpreting direct sensor signals. Since robots require *real-time* interpretation to guide robot movements, this form of parallel or distributed processing can be very helpful.

Artificial vision represents an extreme example of sensor and interpretation complexity. In essence, vision is an information processing task in which two-dimensional arrays of brightness values received by a camera or other type of sensor are manipulated to form a two- or three-dimensional model of a scene. This process may involve inferring the types of objects or material characteristics present in a scene. Figure 16-6 illustrates the image processing used in a magnetic vision system. In this case, the scene consists of two reinforcing bars crossing at right angles. The initial brightness pattern shown in Figure 16-6 represents intensity readings from a magnetic sensor moving over the scene. These intensity readings are digitized and manipulated to accomplish the extraction of features, mapping the likely location of reinforcing bars, and classifying the size and depth of the bars in the scene. Figure 16-6 shows the progressive interpretation of the original scene. As might be imagined, vision is extremely computationally intensive, with each bit in the scene requiring considerable interpretation. In this example, magnetic sensing permits mapping of reinforcing bars embedded in a material such as concrete.

Integrating sensor information and robot control can be accomplished at various levels of abstraction. At the lowest level, tactile or proximity sensors may be added to a robot to react to imminent collisions. At higher levels, sensors provide the information required to construct a *world model* of a robot's surroundings. This

Figure 16-6 Robot Vision: Raw Intensity Data and Progressive Interpretation of Crossing Reinforcing Bars (Photo courtesy of Robotics Institute, Carnegie Mellon University. Copyright ©, 1987.)

world model is then used to plan robot movements to accomplish some prescribed goal. It is this overall integration that distinguishes cognitive robots that are able to sense, interpret, and plan activities.

16.5 A SANDBLASTING ROBOT EXAMPLE

The various types of sandblasting work on structures are usually performed by highly specialized and small- or medium-sized contracting firms. For example, a firm specialized in masonry restoration sandblasting would not be prepared to perform rust removal from the bearing elements of a highway steel bridge, and a steel container sandblasting contractor would usually not perform blasting of concrete or brick walls. The work styles, due to somewhat different occurrences and intensities of health and safety hazards, are also different, since the surfaces and environment in which laborers work differ considerably.

The sandblasting process involves only a few relatively very simple work tasks, lending themselves to partial or full performance by an automated machine. These tasks include:

- Determining and following the work range path.
- Determining and following the work surface.
- Applying a uniform jet stream onto the surface.
- Control of work parameters (e.g., flow of abrasive, air pressure).
- Parallel control of blasting effect.

Each of these tasks can be performed with currently available robotic technology and have been attempted with success for other applications in the manufacturing industries.

The productivity and work quality of sandblasting is largely affected by human factors. Eliminating some of the human limitations and drawbacks could decrease the labor cost and possibly increase the quality of work considerably. For example, existing work rules require one worker to watch the sand hopper while the others are operating the blast nozzles. Every 3 hours a rotation is mandatory. Each sandblaster is also entitled to 4 hours of rest after performing 4 hours of work at the nozzle. Experience indicates that on a typical job site, due to workers' partial exhaustion, up to 70 percent of day's production is normally completed between 8 and 12 A. M. Also, the overall day's productivity is down by about 20 percent if the air temperature is over 75° F. Operating conditions are often arduous, and in addition with the operator working on scaffolding or in tanks, his tiredness will grow rapidly if he works too long without rest. Apart from wearing cumbersome clothing and a compressed–air–fed helmet, his vision will gradually be impaired as the visor becomes dimmed with abrasive action and dust. This often precludes satisfactory control of the blast outcome on the surface during the work itself, and later corrections of previous work are often costly and cumbersome.

Expected cost savings on labor are partially a direct result of eliminating the same factors that affect productivity. Reorganization of the sandblasting crew to meet the needs of the robotic sandblaster would require the elimination of the operator and assistant work tasks. Instead, technical supervision of robotized equipment would be necessary.

The following robot features are necessary for successful performance of the sandblasting task. A diagram of a possible design appears in Figure 16-7.

- **Mobility and Maneuverability:** It can be provided by a tether or light emitting diode (LED) guided mobile platform constituting a base for a robot sandblaster mounted on top, with a positioning accuracy of ±1 in. A commercially available platform could be used for this purpose.
- **Robot Arm Characteristics:** The robot arm should be extendable up to 8 ft. There is one end effector and three sensors mounted on the arm: a blast gun, a sonar for surface proximity measurement, LED direction sensor, and a surface reflectivity meter. The arm would have four degrees of freedom: one at the base and one each at the elbow, pitch, and yaw.

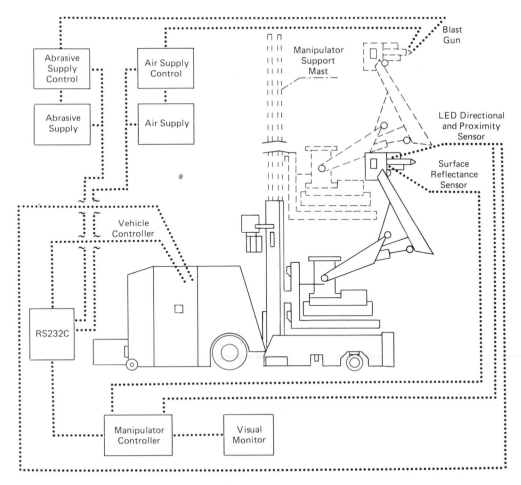

Figure 16-7 General Setup of the Sandblasting System

- **End Effector:** The only end effector applicable to the surface sandblasting would be the blast gun. Its basic design and function remains similar to the gun used in manual sandblasting operation.
- **Motion Control System:** The control system would be provided by a set of microprocessors mounted next to the arm sensors and an on-board computer managing all the individual functions of the robot. The control of the following motion functions are considered:
    - Sensory information processing (from LED, sonar, and reflectometer) for the motion command initiation
    - Speed and direction of platform travel
    - Speed and direction of the robot arm move
- **Environment Sensing:** This work would be performed by three types of sensors.
    - The light beams generated by the LEDs mounted on the corners of the

work surface would be sensed by a light sensor capable of detecting the distance and the direction from which the light beam is emitted. Data obtained from these sensors would serve to determine the spatial position of the robot with respect to the work surface.

- A sonar mounted on the robot arm would provide for short-range proximity sensing, enabling the arm to position itself closely to the work surface.
- A surface reflectivity meter would inspect the effect of the blasting process continuously and provide the information through its microprocessor to the on-board computer.

- **Material Feed and Flow Control:** A continuous, uninterrupted feed of sand and compressed air would be assured by microprocessors mounted in critical locations of the feeding system. The following sensors and microprocessors are considered:
  - *Dampness meter*. To measure the dampness of sand stored in the hopper. Dampness above a critical value would be reported by microprocessor to the host computer for decision making and appropriate action.
  - *Air flow sensor*. To measure the flow of air from the compressor to the blast nozzle. Any deviation from the regular flow quantity would be signaled to the on-board computer by the flow sensor and considered for appropriate action.
  - *Pressure sensor*. To be mounted near the blast nozzle to monitor the air pressure in the air/sand mixture. Any deviations detected by sensor's microprocessor would be reported to the computer.

The robotic components necessary for the construction of the autonomous sandblasting machine are available on the commercial market in the United States and/or other industrialized countries. Most of them already constitute elements or segments of existing industrial robotics. With respect to the components specified, there are in most cases several options from which to select the desired hardware and controls. Manufacturers' catalogs contain an overview of selected commercially available components applicable to the subsystems of the considered sandblasting robot.

The sandblasting robot would consist of the following components:

- *Mobile robotic platform*. An autonomously guided vehicle available on the commercial market and subjected to slight modifications would be implemented.
- *Robot manipulator*. A stationary industrial robot should prove suitable for the sandblasting task. The robot would be mounted on an extendable steel frame mast fixed on the mobile platform. The manipulator would consist of a blasting gun as the end effector, a light sensor as a surface shape orientation and proximity sensing device, and surface reflectometer as the work quality control device.
- *Power supply*. A standard AC/DC power supply of approximately one kilowatt

should be sufficient to drive the manipulator mechanisms and the mobile platform. It is assumed that in most cases an on-site power supply connection would be available. In other cases, a 48-V, 6-hr battery for the operation of the electric engine should be feasible.

- *Sand and air pressure supply.* A standard air compressor used in the manual sandblasting process would be implemented. Sand would be supplied by means of a traditional hopper into the pressure vessel.
- *Electronic controls.* Six types of controls, supplied with microprocessors, would be used: sand dampness meter and control, sand supply control, air pressure control, vehicle position control, manipulator position control, and surface condition control.
- *System state displays.* The displays would inform the operator about the parameters of the work process underway. They should include display of the vehicle position with respect to the work site layout, manipulator position with respect to work surface, air pressure, sand supply, and electric power supply values.

The sandblasting robot would perform a continuous task of applying a stream of pressurized sand onto the cleaned surface. To accomplish this objective, the following steps are required:

- Light emitting diodes are mounted on the characteristic corners and other locations of the work area. Their signals are received by directional light sensors placed on the robotic vehicle carrying the sandblasting arm. The on-board computer uses this information to determine the relative location between the work surface and the robotic vehicle.
- The vehicle approaches the work surface and stops at its initial work position. The sonar sensor mounted on the robot arm determines the relative position of the nozzle with respect to the work surface. The arm moves at its initial work location.
- The air and sand flow is activated at a given "ready" signal. After applying the jet stream to the given location, surface "cleanliness" measurement is assessed by means of a reflectivity meter and a microprocessor. The assessment signal is sent to the on-board computer for the decision making. The decision is sent back to the blast nozzle actuator and the blast action is repeated at the same location or the arm moved to the next area. The blast areas would slightly overlap to ensure proper blasting effect on the area between the nozzle moves.
- The blasting process repeats, and after a positive surface assessment the nozzle moves to the next location. At the completion of blasting the last location, the stop signal is issued, and the vehicle is removed from the work area.

The robot system mechanical setup must be particularly rugged to withstand typical and unforeseen work-site conditions. However, no large external forces exerted on the machine are anticipated. The manipulator arm frame could even be be made of lightweight metal material.

16.6 FUTURE PROSPECTS FOR AUTOMATION AND ROBOTICS IN CONSTRUCTION

Robots certainly have considerable limitations relative to human workers. The limited capabilities of existing industrial robots would not be particularly useful on existing, uncontrolled construction sites. However, robots are rapidly becoming more capable. Moreover, it is often possible to structure environments or particular tasks so that robots are technically feasible. And the various superhuman senses and tireless work of robots can be quite useful in many applications. Consequently, robots for construction are likely to be inevitable developments in the future.

The development of capable software and computation power is particularly important for construction robotics. Currently, high-level controllers and sensing programs require considerable programming and engineering expertise. The development of more capable and user-friendly programming environments should be of great benefit. Cheaper computation hardware would also play a role in enhancing robot capabilities.

Initially, one can expect robots to be used in hazardous environments such as nuclear reactor maintenance and demolition. Robots designed to assist human operators are also likely to be the rule in the next decades. These robots would be teleoperated or have only limited autonomous intelligence. An example general-purpose, teleoperated robot called the *Workhorse* is shown in Figure 16-8.[130] This

Figure 16-8 The Workhorse Teleoperated Robot (Photo courtesy of Robotics Institute, Carnegie Mellon University. Copyright ©, 1987.)

[130] See W. Whittaker, J. Bares, and L. Champeny, "Three Remote Systems for TMI-2 Basement Recovery," *International Conference on CAD and Robotics in Architecture and Construction,* Marseilles, France, 1986.

machine can collapse to fit through doorways, extend to reach high workplaces, exert large forces (including sufficient force to lift itself up), and operate numerous effector tools. The Workhorse was designed to operate in radioactive environments. Stationary robots will also be a trend in that numerous construction operations can be performed in a factory either off-site or near a construction site. Improvements in work quality or reduction in worker hazard are likely to be the most important incentives for automation.

16.7 REFERENCES

16-1. Oppenheim, I. J. and M. J. Skibniewski, "Robots in Construction," *Encyclopedia of Robotics*, John Wiley and Sons Inc., New York, 1988.

16-2. Paulson, B. C., "Automation and Robotics for Construction," *ASCE Journal of Construction Engineering and Management*, Vol. 111, no. 3, 1985, pp. 190–207.

16-3. Skibniewski, M. J. and C. Hendrickson, "Analysis of Robotic Surface Finishing Work on the Construction Site," *ASCE Journal of Construction Engineering and Management,* Vol. 115, no. CO2, 1988.

16-4. Warszawski, A. and D. A. Sangrey, "Robotics in Building Construction," *ASCE Journal of Construction Engineering and Management*, Vol. 111, no. 3, 1985, pp. 260–280.

16-5. Whittaker, W. L. , "Cognitive Robots for Construction," *Annual Research Review,* The Robotics Institute, Carnegie Mellon University, Pittsburgh, 1986, pp. 6-17.

Appendix A
Compound Interest Tables

Source: All compound interest tables are reprinted from T. Au and T.P. Au, *Engineering Economics for Capital Investment Analysis*, Allyn & Bacon, Inc., Newton, MA, 1983, with permission of the publisher.

TABLE A.1 COMPOUND INTEREST TABLE, $i = 0.5\%$

	COMPOUND AMOUNT FACTOR	DISCOUNT AMOUNT FACTOR	COMPOUND UNIFORM SERIES FACTOR	SINKING FUND FACTOR	DISCOUNT UNIFORM SERIES FACTOR	CAPITAL RECOVERY FACTOR	DISCOUNT GRADIENT FACTOR
n	(F|P,i,n)	(P|F,i,n)	(F|U,i,n)	(U|F,i,n)	(P|U,i,n)	(U|P,i,n)	(P|G,i,n)
1	1.0050	0.9950	1.0000	1.0000	0.9950	1.0050	0.0000
2	1.0100	0.9901	2.0050	0.4988	1.9851	0.5038	0.9893
3	1.0151	0.9851	3.0150	0.3317	2.9702	0.3367	2.9589
4	1.0202	0.9802	4.0301	0.2481	3.9505	0.2531	5.8992
5	1.0253	0.9754	5.0502	0.1980	4.9259	0.2030	9.8003
6	1.0304	0.9705	6.0755	0.1646	5.8964	0.1696	14.6522
7	1.0355	0.9657	7.1059	0.1407	6.8621	0.1457	20.4456
8	1.0407	0.9609	8.1414	0.1228	7.8229	0.1278	27.1712
9	1.0459	0.9561	9.1821	0.1089	8.7790	0.1139	34.8193
10	1.0511	0.9513	10.2280	0.0978	9.7304	0.1028	43.3813
11	1.0564	0.9466	11.2791	0.0887	10.6770	0.0937	52.8469
12	1.0617	0.9419	12.3355	0.0811	11.6189	0.0861	63.2069
13	1.0670	0.9372	13.3972	0.0746	12.5561	0.0796	74.4536
14	1.0723	0.9326	14.4642	0.0691	13.4887	0.0741	86.5757
15	1.0777	0.9279	15.5365	0.0644	14.4166	0.0694	99.5659
16	1.0831	0.9233	16.6142	0.0602	15.3399	0.0652	113.4152
17	1.0885	0.9187	17.6973	0.0565	16.2586	0.0615	128.1139
18	1.0939	0.9141	18.7857	0.0532	17.1727	0.0582	143.6539
19	1.0994	0.9096	19.8797	0.0503	18.0823	0.0553	160.0257
20	1.1049	0.9051	20.9791	0.0477	18.9874	0.0527	177.2214
21	1.1104	0.9006	22.0840	0.0453	19.8879	0.0503	195.2325
22	1.1160	0.8961	23.1944	0.0431	20.7840	0.0481	214.0491
23	1.1216	0.8916	24.3103	0.0411	21.6756	0.0461	233.6642
24	1.1272	0.8872	25.4319	0.0393	22.5628	0.0443	254.0688
25	1.1328	0.8828	26.5590	0.0377	23.4456	0.0427	275.2549
26	1.1385	0.8784	27.6918	0.0361	24.3240	0.0411	297.2139
27	1.1442	0.8740	28.8303	0.0347	25.1980	0.0397	319.9378
28	1.1499	0.8697	29.9744	0.0334	26.0676	0.0384	343.4179
29	1.1556	0.8653	31.1243	0.0321	26.9330	0.0371	367.6473
30	1.1614	0.8610	32.2799	0.0310	27.7940	0.0360	392.6160
35	1.1907	0.8398	38.1453	0.0262	32.0353	0.0312	528.2935
40	1.2208	0.8191	44.1587	0.0226	36.1721	0.0276	681.3133
45	1.2516	0.7990	50.3240	0.0199	40.2071	0.0249	850.7396
50	1.2832	0.7793	56.6450	0.0177	44.1427	0.0227	1035.6700
55	1.3156	0.7601	63.1256	0.0158	47.9813	0.0208	1235.2395
60	1.3488	0.7414	69.7698	0.0143	51.7254	0.0193	1448.6141
70	1.4178	0.7053	83.5658	0.0120	58.9393	0.0170	1913.6063
80	1.4903	0.6710	98.0674	0.0102	65.8022	0.0152	2424.6044
90	1.5666	0.6383	113.3105	0.0088	72.3311	0.0138	2976.0311
100	1.6467	0.6073	129.3333	0.0077	78.5425	0.0127	3562.7440

TABLE A.2 COMPOUND INTEREST TABLE, $i = 1.0\%$

	COMPOUND AMOUNT FACTOR	DISCOUNT AMOUNT FACTOR	COMPOUND UNIFORM SERIES FACTOR	SINKING FUND FACTOR	DISCOUNT UNIFORM SERIES FACTOR	CAPITAL RECOVERY FACTOR	DISCOUNT GRADIENT FACTOR
n	(F|P,i,n)	(P|F,i,n)	(F|U,i,n)	(U|F,i,n)	(P|U,i,n)	(U|P,i,n)	(P|G,i,n)
1	1.0100	0.9901	1.0000	1.0000	0.9901	1.0100	0.0000
2	1.0201	0.9803	2.0100	0.4975	1.9704	0.5075	0.9803
3	1.0303	0.9706	3.0301	0.3300	2.9410	0.3400	2.9214
4	1.0406	0.9610	4.0604	0.2463	3.9020	0.2563	5.8043
5	1.0510	0.9515	5.1010	0.1960	4.8534	0.2060	9.6101
6	1.0615	0.9420	6.1520	0.1625	5.7955	0.1725	14.3203
7	1.0721	0.9327	7.2135	0.1386	6.7282	0.1486	19.9165
8	1.0829	0.9235	8.2857	0.1207	7.6517	0.1307	26.3809
9	1.0937	0.9143	9.3685	0.1067	8.5660	0.1167	33.6956
10	1.1046	0.9053	10.4622	0.0956	9.4713	0.1056	41.8431
11	1.1157	0.8963	11.5668	0.0865	10.3676	0.0965	50.8063
12	1.1268	0.8874	12.6825	0.0788	11.2551	0.0888	60.5682
13	1.1381	0.8787	13.8093	0.0724	12.1337	0.0824	71.1121
14	1.1495	0.8700	14.9474	0.0669	13.0037	0.0769	82.4215
15	1.1610	0.8613	16.0969	0.0621	13.8650	0.0721	94.4803
16	1.1726	0.8528	17.2579	0.0579	14.7179	0.0679	107.2726
17	1.1843	0.8444	18.4304	0.0543	15.5622	0.0643	120.7827
18	1.1961	0.8360	19.6147	0.0510	16.3983	0.0610	134.9949
19	1.2081	0.8277	20.8109	0.0481	17.2260	0.0581	149.8941
20	1.2202	0.8195	22.0190	0.0454	18.0455	0.0554	165.4655
21	1.2324	0.8114	23.2392	0.0430	18.8570	0.0530	181.6940
22	1.2447	0.8034	24.4716	0.0409	19.6604	0.0509	198.5653
23	1.2572	0.7954	25.7163	0.0389	20.4558	0.0489	216.0648
24	1.2697	0.7876	26.9735	0.0371	21.2434	0.0471	234.1789
25	1.2824	0.7798	28.2432	0.0354	22.0231	0.0454	252.8934
26	1.2953	0.7720	29.5256	0.0339	22.7952	0.0439	272.1944
27	1.3082	0.7644	30.8209	0.0324	23.5596	0.0424	292.0690
28	1.3213	0.7568	32.1291	0.0311	24.3164	0.0411	312.5034
29	1.3345	0.7493	33.4504	0.0299	25.0658	0.0399	333.4850
30	1.3478	0.7419	34.7849	0.0287	25.8077	0.0387	355.0007
35	1.4166	0.7059	41.6603	0.0240	29.4086	0.0340	470.1567
40	1.4889	0.6717	48.8863	0.0205	32.8347	0.0305	596.8543
45	1.5648	0.6391	56.4810	0.0177	36.0945	0.0277	733.7017
50	1.6446	0.6080	64.4631	0.0155	39.1961	0.0255	879.4155
55	1.7285	0.5785	72.8524	0.0137	42.1472	0.0237	1032.8123
60	1.8167	0.5504	81.6696	0.0122	44.9550	0.0222	1192.8036
70	2.0068	0.4983	100.6763	0.0099	50.1685	0.0199	1528.6446
80	2.2167	0.4511	121.6714	0.0082	54.8882	0.0182	1879.8739
90	2.4486	0.4084	144.8632	0.0069	59.1609	0.0169	2240.5641
100	2.7048	0.3697	170.4812	0.0059	63.0289	0.0159	2605.7721

TABLE A.3 COMPOUND INTEREST TABLE, i = 2.0%

n	COMPOUND AMOUNT FACTOR (F|P,i,n)	DISCOUNT AMOUNT FACTOR (P|F,i,n)	COMPOUND UNIFORM SERIES FACTOR (F|U,i,n)	SINKING FUND FACTOR (U|F,i,n)	DISCOUNT UNIFORM SERIES FACTOR (P|U,i,n)	CAPITAL RECOVERY FACTOR (U|P,i,n)	DISCOUNT GRADIENT FACTOR (P|G,i,n)
1	1.0200	0.9804	1.0000	1.0000	0.9804	1.0200	0.0000
2	1.0404	0.9612	2.0200	0.4950	1.9416	0.5150	0.9611
3	1.0612	0.9423	3.0604	0.3268	2.8839	0.3468	2.8457
4	1.0824	0.9238	4.1216	0.2426	3.8077	0.2626	5.6173
5	1.1041	0.9057	5.2040	0.1922	4.7135	0.2122	9.2402
6	1.1262	0.8880	6.3081	0.1585	5.6014	0.1785	13.6800
7	1.1487	0.8706	7.4343	0.1345	6.4720	0.1545	18.9033
8	1.1717	0.8535	8.5830	0.1165	7.3255	0.1365	24.8777
9	1.1951	0.8368	9.7546	0.1025	8.1622	0.1225	31.5718
10	1.2190	0.8203	10.9497	0.0913	8.9826	0.1113	38.9549
11	1.2434	0.8043	12.1687	0.0822	9.7868	0.1022	46.9975
12	1.2682	0.7885	13.4121	0.0746	10.5753	0.0946	55.6709
13	1.2936	0.7730	14.6803	0.0681	11.3484	0.0881	64.9472
14	1.3195	0.7579	15.9739	0.0626	12.1062	0.0826	74.7996
15	1.3459	0.7430	17.2934	0.0578	12.8493	0.0778	85.2017
16	1.3728	0.7284	18.6393	0.0537	13.5777	0.0737	96.1284
17	1.4002	0.7142	20.0121	0.0500	14.2919	0.0700	107.5550
18	1.4282	0.7002	21.4123	0.0467	14.9920	0.0667	119.4577
19	1.4568	0.6864	22.8405	0.0438	15.6785	0.0638	131.8134
20	1.4859	0.6730	24.2974	0.0412	16.3514	0.0612	144.5998
21	1.5157	0.6598	25.7833	0.0388	17.0112	0.0588	157.7954
22	1.5460	0.6468	27.2990	0.0366	17.6580	0.0566	171.3789
23	1.5769	0.6342	28.8449	0.0347	18.2922	0.0547	185.3303
24	1.6084	0.6217	30.4218	0.0329	18.9139	0.0529	199.6299
25	1.6406	0.6095	32.0303	0.0312	19.5234	0.0512	214.2587
26	1.6734	0.5976	33.6709	0.0297	20.1210	0.0497	229.1981
27	1.7069	0.5859	35.3443	0.0283	20.7069	0.0483	244.4305
28	1.7410	0.5744	37.0512	0.0270	21.2813	0.0470	259.9386
29	1.7758	0.5631	38.7922	0.0258	21.8444	0.0458	275.7057
30	1.8114	0.5521	40.5681	0.0246	22.3964	0.0446	291.7158
35	1.9999	0.5000	49.9944	0.0200	24.9986	0.0400	374.8819
40	2.2080	0.4529	60.4019	0.0166	27.3555	0.0366	461.9923
45	2.4379	0.4102	71.8927	0.0139	29.4902	0.0339	551.5643
50	2.6916	0.3715	84.5793	0.0118	31.4236	0.0318	642.3596
55	2.9717	0.3365	98.5864	0.0101	33.1748	0.0301	733.3516
60	3.2810	0.3048	114.0514	0.0088	34.7609	0.0288	823.6965
70	3.9996	0.2500	149.9778	0.0067	37.4986	0.0267	999.8332
80	4.8754	0.2051	193.7718	0.0052	39.7445	0.0252	1166.7856
90	5.9431	0.1683	247.1564	0.0040	41.5869	0.0240	1322.1690
100	7.2446	0.1380	312.2319	0.0032	43.0983	0.0232	1464.7516

TABLE A.4 COMPOUND INTEREST TABLE, i = 3.0%

n	COMPOUND AMOUNT FACTOR $(F|P,i,n)$	DISCOUNT AMOUNT FACTOR $(P|F,i,n)$	COMPOUND UNIFORM SERIES FACTOR $(F|U,i,n)$	SINKING FUND FACTOR $(U|F,i,n)$	DISCOUNT UNIFORM SERIES FACTOR $(P|U,i,n)$	CAPITAL RECOVERY FACTOR $(U|P,i,n)$	DISCOUNT GRADIENT FACTOR $(P|G,i,n)$
1	1.0300	0.9709	1.0000	1.0000	0.9709	1.0300	0.0000
2	1.0609	0.9426	2.0300	0.4926	1.9135	0.5226	0.9426
3	1.0927	0.9151	3.0909	0.3235	2.8286	0.3535	2.7729
4	1.1255	0.8885	4.1836	0.2390	3.7171	0.2690	5.4383
5	1.1593	0.8626	5.3091	0.1884	4.5797	0.2184	8.8887
6	1.1941	0.8375	6.4684	0.1546	5.4172	0.1846	13.0761
7	1.2299	0.8131	7.6625	0.1305	6.2303	0.1605	17.9547
8	1.2668	0.7894	8.8923	0.1125	7.0197	0.1425	23.4805
9	1.3048	0.7664	10.1591	0.0984	7.7861	0.1284	29.6119
10	1.3439	0.7441	11.4639	0.0872	8.5302	0.1172	36.3087
11	1.3842	0.7224	12.8078	0.0781	9.2526	0.1081	43.5329
12	1.4258	0.7014	14.1920	0.0705	9.9540	0.1005	51.2481
13	1.4685	0.6810	15.6178	0.0640	10.6350	0.0940	59.4195
14	1.5126	0.6611	17.0863	0.0585	11.2961	0.0885	68.0140
15	1.5580	0.6419	18.5989	0.0538	11.9379	0.0838	77.0001
16	1.6047	0.6232	20.1569	0.0496	12.5611	0.0796	86.3475
17	1.6528	0.6050	21.7616	0.0460	13.1661	0.0760	96.0278
18	1.7024	0.5874	23.4144	0.0427	13.7535	0.0727	106.0135
19	1.7535	0.5703	25.1169	0.0398	14.3238	0.0698	116.2786
20	1.8061	0.5537	26.8704	0.0372	14.8775	0.0672	126.7985
21	1.8603	0.5375	28.6765	0.0349	15.4150	0.0649	137.5495
22	1.9161	0.5219	30.5368	0.0327	15.9369	0.0627	148.5092
23	1.9736	0.5067	32.4529	0.0308	16.4436	0.0608	159.6564
24	2.0328	0.4919	34.4265	0.0290	16.9355	0.0590	170.9709
25	2.0938	0.4776	36.4592	0.0274	17.4131	0.0574	182.4334
26	2.1566	0.4637	38.5530	0.0259	17.8768	0.0559	194.0258
27	2.2213	0.4502	40.7096	0.0246	18.3270	0.0546	205.7307
28	2.2879	0.4371	42.9309	0.0233	18.7641	0.0533	217.5317
29	2.3566	0.4243	45.2188	0.0221	19.1885	0.0521	229.4134
30	2.4273	0.4120	47.5754	0.0210	19.6004	0.0510	241.3610
35	2.8139	0.3554	60.4621	0.0165	21.4872	0.0465	301.6264
40	3.2620	0.3066	75.4012	0.0133	23.1148	0.0433	361.7497
45	3.7816	0.2644	92.7198	0.0108	24.5187	0.0408	420.6322
50	4.3839	0.2281	112.7968	0.0089	25.7298	0.0389	477.4800
55	5.0821	0.1968	136.0715	0.0073	26.7744	0.0373	531.7408
60	5.8916	0.1697	163.0533	0.0061	27.6756	0.0361	583.0523
70	7.9178	0.1263	230.5939	0.0043	29.1234	0.0343	676.0866
80	10.6409	0.0940	321.3627	0.0031	30.2008	0.0331	756.0863
90	14.3005	0.0699	443.3485	0.0023	31.0024	0.0323	823.6300
100	19.2186	0.0520	607.2871	0.0016	31.5989	0.0316	879.8538

TABLE A.5 COMPOUND INTEREST TABLE, $i = 4.0\%$

n	COMPOUND AMOUNT FACTOR (F|P,i,n)	DISCOUNT AMOUNT FACTOR (P|F,i,n)	COMPOUND UNIFORM SERIES FACTOR (F|U,i,n)	SINKING FUND FACTOR (U|F,i,n)	DISCOUNT UNIFORM SERIES FACTOR (P|U,i,n)	CAPITAL RECOVERY FACTOR (U|P,i,n)	DISCOUNT GRADIENT FACTOR (P|G,i,n)
1	1.0400	0.9615	1.0000	1.0000	0.9615	1.0400	0.0000
2	1.0816	0.9246	2.0400	0.4902	1.8861	0.5302	0.9246
3	1.1249	0.8890	3.1216	0.3203	2.7751	0.3603	2.7026
4	1.1699	0.8548	4.2465	0.2355	3.6299	0.2755	5.2670
5	1.2167	0.8219	5.4163	0.1846	4.4518	0.2246	8.5547
6	1.2653	0.7903	6.6330	0.1508	5.2421	0.1908	12.5063
7	1.3159	0.7599	7.8983	0.1266	6.0021	0.1666	17.0658
8	1.3686	0.7307	9.2142	0.1085	6.7327	0.1485	22.1806
9	1.4233	0.7026	10.5828	0.0945	7.4353	0.1345	27.8013
10	1.4802	0.6756	12.0061	0.0833	8.1109	0.1233	33.8814
11	1.5395	0.6496	13.4864	0.0741	8.7605	0.1141	40.3772
12	1.6010	0.6246	15.0258	0.0666	9.3851	0.1066	47.2477
13	1.6651	0.6006	16.6268	0.0601	9.9856	0.1001	54.4546
14	1.7317	0.5775	18.2919	0.0547	10.5631	0.0947	61.9618
15	1.8009	0.5553	20.0236	0.0499	11.1184	0.0899	69.7355
16	1.8730	0.5339	21.8245	0.0458	11.6523	0.0858	77.7441
17	1.9479	0.5134	23.6975	0.0422	12.1657	0.0822	85.9581
18	2.0258	0.4936	25.6454	0.0390	12.6593	0.0790	94.3498
19	2.1068	0.4746	27.6712	0.0361	13.1339	0.0761	102.8934
20	2.1911	0.4564	29.7781	0.0336	13.5903	0.0736	111.5647
21	2.2788	0.4388	31.9692	0.0313	14.0292	0.0713	120.3414
22	2.3699	0.4220	34.2480	0.0292	14.4511	0.0692	129.2024
23	2.4647	0.4057	36.6179	0.0273	14.8568	0.0673	138.1284
24	2.5633	0.3901	39.0826	0.0256	15.2470	0.0656	147.1012
25	2.6658	0.3751	41.6459	0.0240	15.6221	0.0640	156.1040
26	2.7725	0.3607	44.3117	0.0226	15.9828	0.0626	165.1213
27	2.8834	0.3468	47.0842	0.0212	16.3296	0.0612	174.1385
28	2.9987	0.3335	49.9676	0.0200	16.6631	0.0600	183.1424
29	3.1187	0.3207	52.9663	0.0189	16.9837	0.0589	192.1206
30	3.2434	0.3083	56.0849	0.0178	17.2920	0.0578	201.0619
35	3.9461	0.2534	73.6522	0.0136	18.6646	0.0536	244.8768
40	4.8010	0.2083	95.0255	0.0105	19.7928	0.0505	286.5303
45	5.8412	0.1712	121.0294	0.0083	20.7200	0.0483	325.4028
50	7.1067	0.1407	152.6671	0.0066	21.4822	0.0466	361.1639
55	8.6464	0.1157	191.1592	0.0052	22.1086	0.0452	393.6890
60	10.5196	0.0951	237.9907	0.0042	22.6235	0.0442	422.9967
70	15.5716	0.0642	364.2905	0.0027	23.3945	0.0427	472.4789
80	23.0498	0.0434	551.2451	0.0018	23.9154	0.0418	511.1162
90	34.1193	0.0293	827.9835	0.0012	24.2673	0.0412	540.7369
100	50.5050	0.0198	1237.6239	0.0008	24.5050	0.0408	563.1249

TABLE A.6 COMPOUND INTEREST TABLE, $i = 5.0\%$

n	COMPOUND AMOUNT FACTOR (F|P,i,n)	DISCOUNT AMOUNT FACTOR (P|F,i,n)	COMPOUND UNIFORM SERIES FACTOR (F|U,i,n)	SINKING FUND FACTOR (U|F,i,n)	DISCOUNT UNIFORM SERIES FACTOR (P|U,i,n)	CAPITAL RECOVERY FACTOR (U|P,i,n)	DISCOUNT GRADIENT FACTOR (P|G,i,n)
1	1.0500	0.9524	1.0000	1.0000	0.9524	1.0500	0.0000
2	1.1025	0.9070	2.0500	0.4878	1.8594	0.5378	0.9070
3	1.1576	0.8638	3.1525	0.3172	2.7232	0.3672	2.6347
4	1.2155	0.8227	4.3101	0.2320	3.5460	0.2820	5.1028
5	1.2763	0.7835	5.5256	0.1810	4.3295	0.2310	8.2369
6	1.3401	0.7462	6.8019	0.1470	5.0757	0.1970	11.9680
7	1.4071	0.7107	8.1420	0.1228	5.7864	0.1728	16.2321
8	1.4775	0.6768	9.5491	0.1047	6.4632	0.1547	20.9699
9	1.5513	0.6446	11.0266	0.0907	7.1078	0.1407	26.1268
10	1.6289	0.6139	12.5779	0.0795	7.7217	0.1295	31.6520
11	1.7103	0.5847	14.2068	0.0704	8.3064	0.1204	37.4988
12	1.7959	0.5568	15.9171	0.0628	8.8633	0.1128	43.6240
13	1.8856	0.5303	17.7130	0.0565	9.3936	0.1065	49.9879
14	1.9799	0.5051	19.5986	0.0510	9.8986	0.1010	56.5538
15	2.0789	0.4810	21.5786	0.0463	10.3797	0.0963	63.2880
16	2.1829	0.4581	23.6575	0.0423	10.8378	0.0923	70.1597
17	2.2920	0.4363	25.8404	0.0387	11.2741	0.0887	77.1404
18	2.4066	0.4155	28.1324	0.0355	11.6896	0.0855	84.2043
19	2.5269	0.3957	30.5390	0.0327	12.0853	0.0827	91.3275
20	2.6533	0.3769	33.0659	0.0302	12.4622	0.0802	98.4884
21	2.7860	0.3589	35.7192	0.0280	12.8212	0.0780	105.6672
22	2.9253	0.3418	38.5052	0.0260	13.1630	0.0760	112.8461
23	3.0715	0.3256	41.4305	0.0241	13.4886	0.0741	120.0086
24	3.2251	0.3101	44.5020	0.0225	13.7986	0.0725	127.1402
25	3.3864	0.2953	47.7271	0.0210	14.0939	0.0710	134.2275
26	3.5557	0.2812	51.1134	0.0196	14.3752	0.0696	141.2585
27	3.7335	0.2678	54.6691	0.0183	14.6430	0.0683	148.2225
28	3.9201	0.2551	58.4026	0.0171	14.8981	0.0671	155.1101
29	4.1161	0.2429	62.3227	0.0160	15.1411	0.0660	161.9126
30	4.3219	0.2314	66.4388	0.0151	15.3725	0.0651	168.6225
35	5.5160	0.1813	90.3203	0.0111	16.3742	0.0611	200.5806
40	7.0400	0.1420	120.7997	0.0083	17.1591	0.0583	229.5451
45	8.9850	0.1113	159.7001	0.0063	17.7741	0.0563	255.3145
50	11.4674	0.0872	209.3479	0.0048	18.2559	0.0548	277.9147
55	14.6356	0.0683	272.7125	0.0037	18.6335	0.0537	297.5104
60	18.6792	0.0535	353.5836	0.0028	18.9293	0.0528	314.3431
70	30.4264	0.0329	588.5283	0.0017	19.3427	0.0517	340.8409
80	49.5614	0.0202	971.2283	0.0010	19.5965	0.0510	359.6460
90	80.7303	0.0124	1594.6064	0.0006	19.7523	0.0506	372.7488
100	131.5012	0.0076	2610.0236	0.0004	19.8479	0.0504	381.7492

TABLE A.7 COMPOUND INTEREST TABLE, $i = 6.0\%$

n	COMPOUND AMOUNT FACTOR (F|P,i,n)	DISCOUNT AMOUNT FACTOR (P|F,i,n)	COMPOUND UNIFORM SERIES FACTOR (F|U,i,n)	SINKING FUND FACTOR (U|F,i,n)	DISCOUNT UNIFORM SERIES FACTOR (P|U,i,n)	CAPITAL RECOVERY FACTOR (U|P,i,n)	DISCOUNT GRADIENT FACTOR (P|G,i,n)
1	1.0600	0.9434	1.0000	1.0000	0.9434	1.0600	0.0000
2	1.1236	0.8900	2.0600	0.4854	1.8334	0.5454	0.8900
3	1.1910	0.8396	3.1836	0.3141	2.6730	0.3741	2.5692
4	1.2625	0.7921	4.3746	0.2286	3.4651	0.2886	4.9455
5	1.3382	0.7473	5.6371	0.1774	4.2124	0.2374	7.9345
6	1.4185	0.7050	6.9753	0.1434	4.9173	0.2034	11.4593
7	1.5036	0.6651	8.3938	0.1191	5.5824	0.1791	15.4497
8	1.5938	0.6274	9.8975	0.1010	6.2098	0.1610	19.8416
9	1.6895	0.5919	11.4913	0.0870	6.8017	0.1470	24.5768
10	1.7908	0.5584	13.1808	0.0759	7.3601	0.1359	29.6023
11	1.8983	0.5268	14.9716	0.0668	7.8869	0.1268	34.8702
12	2.0122	0.4970	16.8699	0.0593	8.3838	0.1193	40.3368
13	2.1329	0.4688	18.8821	0.0530	8.8527	0.1130	45.9629
14	2.2609	0.4423	21.0151	0.0476	9.2950	0.1076	51.7128
15	2.3966	0.4173	23.2760	0.0430	9.7122	·0.1030	57.5545
16	2.5404	0.3936	25.6725	0.0390	10.1059	0.0990	63.4592
17	2.6928	0.3714	28.2129	0.0354	10.4773	0.0954	69.4011
18	2.8543	0.3503	30.9056	0.0324	10.8276	0.0924	75.3569
19	3.0256	0.3305	33.7600	0.0296	11.1581	0.0896	81.3061
20	3.2071	0.3118	36.7856	0.0272	11.4699	0.0872	87.2304
21	3.3996	0.2942	39.9927	0.0250	11.7641	0.0850	93.1135
22	3.6035	0.2775	43.3923	0.0230	12.0416	0.0830	98.9411
23	3.8197	0.2618	46.9958	0.0213	12.3034	0.0813	104.7007
24	4.0489	0.2470	50.8156	0.0197	12.5504	0.0797	110.3812
25	4.2919	0.2330	54.8645	0.0182	12.7834	0.0782	115.9731
26	4.5494	0.2198	59.1564	0.0169	13.0032	0.0769	121.4684
27	4.8223	0.2074	63.7058	0.0157	13.2105	0.0757	126.8600
28	5.1117	0.1956	68.5281	0.0146	13.4062	0.0746	132.1420
29	5.4184	0.1846	73.6398	0.0136	13.5907	0.0736	137.3096
30	5.7435	0.1741	79.0582	0.0126	13.7648	0.0726	142.3588
35	7.6861	0.1301	111.4348	0.0090	14.4982	0.0690	165.7427
40	10.2857	0.0972	154.7619	0.0065	15.0463	0.0665	185.9568
45	13.7646	0.0727	212.7435	0.0047	15.4558	0.0647	203.1096
50	18.4201	0.0543	290.3358	0.0034	15.7619	0.0634	217.4574
55	24.6503	0.0406	394.1719	0.0025	15.9905	0.0625	229.3222
60	32.9877	0.0303	533.1280	0.0019	16.1614	0.0619	239.0428
70	59.0759	0.0169	967.9318	0.0010	16.3845	0.0610	253.3271
80	105.7959	0.0095	1746.5991	0.0006	16.5091	0.0606	262.5493
90	189.4644	0.0053	3141.0735	0.0003	16.5787	0.0603	268.3946
100	339.3019	0.0029	5638.3647	0.0002	16.6175	0.0602	272.0471

TABLE A.8 COMPOUND INTEREST TABLE, $i = 7.0\%$

n	COMPOUND AMOUNT FACTOR $(F|P,i,n)$	DISCOUNT AMOUNT FACTOR $(P|F,i,n)$	COMPOUND UNIFORM SERIES FACTOR $(F|U,i,n)$	SINKING FUND FACTOR $(U|F,i,n)$	DISCOUNT UNIFORM SERIES FACTOR $(P|U,i,n)$	CAPITAL RECOVERY FACTOR $(U|P,i,n)$	DISCOUNT GRADIENT FACTOR $(P|G,i,n)$
1	1.0700	0.9346	1.0000	1.0000	0.9346	1.0700	0.0000
2	1.1449	0.8734	2.0700	0.4831	1.8080	0.5531	0.8734
3	1.2250	0.8163	3.2149	0.3111	2.6243	0.3811	2.5060
4	1.3108	0.7629	4.4399	0.2252	3.3872	0.2952	4.7947
5	1.4026	0.7130	5.7507	0.1739	4.1002	0.2439	7.6467
6	1.5007	0.6663	7.1533	0.1398	4.7665	0.2098	10.9784
7	1.6058	0.6227	8.6540	0.1156	5.3893	0.1856	14.7149
8	1.7182	0.5820	10.2598	0.0975	5.9713	0.1675	18.7889
9	1.8385	0.5439	11.9780	0.0835	6.5152	0.1535	23.1404
10	1.9672	0.5083	13.8164	0.0724	7.0236	0.1424	27.7156
11	2.1049	0.4751	15.7836	0.0634	7.4987	0.1334	32.4665
12	2.2522	0.4440	17.8885	0.0559	7.9427	0.1259	37.3506
13	2.4098	0.4150	20.1406	0.0497	8.3577	0.1197	42.3302
14	2.5785	0.3878	22.5505	0.0443	8.7455	0.1143	47.3718
15	2.7590	0.3624	25.1290	0.0398	9.1079	0.1098	52.4461
16	2.9522	0.3387	27.8881	0.0359	9.4466	0.1059	57.5271
17	3.1588	0.3166	30.8402	0.0324	9.7632	0.1024	62.5923
18	3.3799	0.2959	33.9990	0.0294	10.0591	0.0994	67.6220
19	3.6165	0.2765	37.3790	0.0268	10.3356	0.0968	72.5991
20	3.8697	0.2584	40.9955	0.0244	10.5940	0.0944	77.5091
21	4.1406	0.2415	44.8652	0.0223	10.8355	0.0923	82.3393
22	4.4304	0.2257	49.0057	0.0204	11.0612	0.0904	87.0793
23	4.7405	0.2109	53.4361	0.0187	11.2722	0.0887	91.7201
24	5.0724	0.1971	58.1767	0.0172	11.4693	0.0872	96.2545
25	5.4274	0.1842	63.2490	0.0158	11.6536	0.0858	100.6765
26	5.8074	0.1722	68.6765	0.0146	11.8258	0.0846	104.9814
27	6.2139	0.1609	74.4838	0.0134	11.9867	0.0834	109.1656
28	6.6488	0.1504	80.6977	0.0124	12.1371	0.0824	113.2264
29	7.1143	0.1406	87.3465	0.0114	12.2777	0.0814	117.1622
30	7.6123	0.1314	94.4608	0.0106	12.4090	0.0806	120.9718
35	10.6766	0.0937	138.2369	0.0072	12.9477	0.0772	138.1353
40	14.9745	0.0668	199.6351	0.0050	13.3317	0.0750	152.2928
45	21.0025	0.0476	285.7493	0.0035	13.6055	0.0735	163.7559
50	29.4570	0.0339	406.5290	0.0025	13.8007	0.0725	172.9051
55	41.3150	0.0242	575.9286	0.0017	13.9399	0.0717	180.1243
60	57.9464	0.0173	813.5204	0.0012	14.0392	0.0712	185.7677
65	81.2729	0.0123	1146.7552	0.0009	14.1099	0.0709	190.1452
70	113.9894	0.0088	1614.1343	0.0006	14.1604	0.0706	193.5185
75	159.8760	0.0063	2269.6576	0.0004	14.1964	0.0704	196.1035
80	224.2344	0.0045	3189.0629	0.0003	14.2220	0.0703	198.0748

TABLE A.9 COMPOUND INTEREST TABLE, $i = 8.0\%$

	COMPOUND AMOUNT FACTOR	DISCOUNT AMOUNT FACTOR	COMPOUND UNIFORM SERIES FACTOR	SINKING FUND FACTOR	DISCOUNT UNIFORM SERIES FACTOR	CAPITAL RECOVERY FACTOR	DISCOUNT GRADIENT FACTOR
n	(F|P,i,n)	(P|F,i,n)	(F|U,i,n)	(U|F,i,n)	(P|U,i,n)	(U|P,i,n)	(P|G,i,n)
1	1.0800	0.9259	1.0000	1.0000	0.9259	1.0800	0.0000
2	1.1664	0.8573	2.0800	0.4808	1.7833	0.5608	0.8573
3	1.2597	0.7938	3.2464	0.3080	2.5771	0.3880	2.4450
4	1.3605	0.7350	4.5061	0.2219	3.3121	0.3019	4.6501
5	1.4693	0.6806	5.8666	0.1705	3.9927	0.2505	7.3724
6	1.5869	0.6302	7.3359	0.1363	4.6229	0.2163	10.5233
7	1.7138	0.5835	8.9228	0.1121	5.2064	0.1921	14.0242
8	1.8509	0.5403	10.6366	0.0940	5.7466	0.1740	17.8061
9	1.9990	0.5002	12.4876	0.0801	6.2469	0.1601	21.8081
10	2.1589	0.4632	14.4866	0.0690	6.7101	0.1490	25.9768
11	2.3316	0.4289	16.6455	0.0601	7.1390	0.1401	30.2657
12	2.5182	0.3971	18.9771	0.0527	7.5361	0.1327	34.6339
13	2.7196	0.3677	21.4953	0.0465	7.9038	0.1265	39.0463
14	2.9372	0.3405	24.2149	0.0413	8.2442	0.1213	43.4723
15	3.1722	0.3152	27.1521	0.0368	8.5595	0.1168	47.8857
16	3.4259	0.2919	30.3243	0.0330	8.8514	0.1130	52.2640
17	3.7000	0.2703	33.7502	0.0296	9.1216	0.1096	56.5883
18	3.9960	0.2502	37.4502	0.0267	9.3719	0.1067	60.8425
19	4.3157	0.2317	41.4463	0.0241	9.6036	0.1041	65.0134
20	4.6610	0.2145	45.7620	0.0219	9.8181	0.1019	69.0898
21	5.0338	0.1987	50.4229	0.0198	10.0168	0.0998	73.0629
22	5.4365	0.1839	55.4567	0.0180	10.2007	0.0980	76.9256
23	5.8715	0.1703	60.8933	0.0164	10.3711	0.0964	80.6726
24	6.3412	0.1577	66.7647	0.0150	10.5288	0.0950	84.2997
25	6.8485	0.1460	73.1059	0.0137	10.6748	0.0937	87.8041
26	7.3964	0.1352	79.9544	0.0125	10.8100	0.0925	91.1841
27	7.9881	0.1252	87.3507	0.0114	10.9352	0.0914	94.4390
28	8.6271	0.1159	95.3388	0.0105	11.0511	0.0905	97.5687
29	9.3173	0.1073	103.9659	0.0096	11.1584	0.0896	100.5738
30	10.0627	0.0994	113.2832	0.0088	11.2578	0.0888	103.4558
35	14.7853	0.0676	172.3168	0.0058	11.6546	0.0858	116.0920
40	21.7245	0.0460	259.0564	0.0039	11.9246	0.0839	126.0422
45	31.9204	0.0313	386.5055	0.0026	12.1084	0.0826	133.7331
50	46.9016	0.0213	573.7699	0.0017	12.2335	0.0817	139.5928
55	68.9138	0.0145	848.9228	0.0012	12.3186	0.0812	144.0064
60	101.2570	0.0099	1253.2127	0.0008	12.3766	0.0808	147.3000
65	148.7798	0.0067	1847.2471	0.0005	12.4160	0.0805	149.7387
70	218.6063	0.0046	2720.0785	0.0004	12.4428	0.0804	151.5326
75	321.2043	0.0031	4002.5542	0.0002	12.4611	0.0802	152.8448
80	471.9545	0.0021	5886.9316	0.0002	12.4735	0.0802	153.8001

TABLE A.10 COMPOUND INTEREST TABLE, $i = 9.0\%$

n	COMPOUND AMOUNT FACTOR $(F|P,i,n)$	DISCOUNT AMOUNT FACTOR $(P|F,i,n)$	COMPOUND UNIFORM SERIES FACTOR $(F|U,i,n)$	SINKING FUND FACTOR $(U|F,i,n)$	DISCOUNT UNIFORM SERIES FACTOR $(P|U,i,n)$	CAPITAL RECOVERY FACTOR $(U|P,i,n)$	DISCOUNT GRADIENT FACTOR $(P|G,i,n)$
1	1.0900	0.9174	1.0000	1.0000	0.9174	1.0900	0.0000
2	1.1881	0.8417	2.0900	0.4785	1.7591	0.5685	0.8417
3	1.2950	0.7722	3.2781	0.3051	2.5313	0.3951	2.3860
4	1.4116	0.7084	4.5731	0.2187	3.2397	0.3087	4.5113
5	1.5386	0.6499	5.9847	0.1671	3.8897	0.2571	7.1110
6	1.6771	0.5963	7.5233	0.1329	4.4859	0.2229	10.0924
7	1.8280	0.5470	9.2004	0.1087	5.0330	0.1987	13.3746
8	1.9926	0.5019	11.0285	0.0907	5.5348	0.1807	16.8877
9	2.1719	0.4604	13.0210	0.0768	5.9952	0.1668	20.5711
10	2.3674	0.4224	15.1929	0.0658	6.4177	0.1558	24.3728
11	2.5804	0.3875	17.5603	0.0569	6.8052	0.1469	28.2481
12	2.8127	0.3555	20.1407	0.0497	7.1607	0.1397	32.1590
13	3.0658	0.3262	22.9534	0.0436	7.4869	0.1336	36.0731
14	3.3417	0.2992	26.0192	0.0384	7.7862	0.1284	39.9633
15	3.6425	0.2745	29.3609	0.0341	8.0607	0.1241	43.8069
16	3.9703	0.2519	33.0034	0.0303	8.3126	0.1203	47.5849
17	4.3276	0.2311	36.9737	0.0270	8.5436	0.1170	51.2821
18	4.7171	0.2120	41.3013	0.0242	8.7556	0.1142	54.8860
19	5.1417	0.1945	46.0185	0.0217	8.9501	0.1117	58.3868
20	5.6044	0.1784	51.1601	0.0195	9.1285	0.1095	61.7770
21	6.1088	0.1637	56.7645	0.0176	9.2922	0.1076	65.0509
22	6.6586	0.1502	62.8733	0.0159	9.4424	0.1059	68.2048
23	7.2579	0.1378	69.5319	0.0144	9.5802	0.1044	71.2359
24	7.9111	0.1264	76.7898	0.0130	9.7066	0.1030	74.1433
25	8.6231	0.1160	84.7009	0.0118	9.8226	0.1018	76.9265
26	9.3992	0.1064	93.3240	0.0107	9.9290	0.1007	79.5863
27	10.2451	0.0976	102.7231	0.0097	10.0266	0.0997	82.1241
28	11.1671	0.0895	112.9682	0.0089	10.1161	0.0989	84.5419
29	12.1722	0.0822	124.1353	0.0081	10.1983	0.0981	86.8422
30	13.2677	0.0754	136.3075	0.0073	10.2737	0.0973	89.0280
35	20.4140	0.0490	215.7107	0.0046	10.5668	0.0946	98.3590
40	31.4094	0.0318	337.8824	0.0030	10.7574	0.0930	105.3762
45	48.3273	0.0207	525.8586	0.0019	10.8812	0.0919	110.5561
50	74.3575	0.0134	815.0834	0.0012	10.9617	0.0912	114.3251
55	114.4082	0.0087	1260.0915	0.0008	11.0140	0.0908	117.0362

TABLE A.11 COMPOUND INTEREST TABLE, $i = 10.0\%$

n	COMPOUND AMOUNT FACTOR (F|P,i,n)	DISCOUNT AMOUNT FACTOR (P|F,i,n)	COMPOUND UNIFORM SERIES FACTOR (F|U,i,n)	SINKING FUND FACTOR (U|F,i,n)	DISCOUNT UNIFORM SERIES FACTOR (P|U,i,n)	CAPITAL RECOVERY FACTOR (U|P,i,n)	DISCOUNT GRADIENT FACTOR (P|G,i,n)
1	1.1000	0.9091	1.0000	1.0000	0.9091	1.1000	0.0000
2	1.2100	0.8264	2.1000	0.4762	1.7355	0.5762	0.8264
3	1.3310	0.7513	3.3100	0.3021	2.4869	0.4021	2.3291
4	1.4641	0.6830	4.6410	0.2155	3.1699	0.3155	4.3781
5	1.6105	0.6209	6.1051	0.1638	3.7908	0.2638	6.8618
6	1.7716	0.5645	7.7156	0.1296	4.3553	0.2296	9.6842
7	1.9487	0.5132	9.4872	0.1054	4.8684	0.2054	12.7631
8	2.1436	0.4665	11.4359	0.0874	5.3349	0.1874	16.0287
9	2.3579	0.4241	13.5795	0.0736	5.7590	0.1736	19.4214
10	2.5937	0.3855	15.9374	0.0627	6.1446	0.1627	22.8913
11	2.8531	0.3505	18.5312	0.0540	6.4951	0.1540	26.3963
12	3.1384	0.3186	21.3843	0.0468	6.8137	0.1468	29.9012
13	3.4523	0.2897	24.5227	0.0408	7.1034	0.1408	33.3772
14	3.7975	0.2633	27.9750	0.0357	7.3667	0.1357	36.8005
15	4.1772	0.2394	31.7725	0.0315	7.6061	0.1315	40.1520
16	4.5950	0.2176	35.9497	0.0278	7.8237	0.1278	43.4164
17	5.0545	0.1978	40.5447	0.0247	8.0216	0.1247	46.5819
18	5.5599	0.1799	45.5992	0.0219	8.2014	0.1219	49.6395
19	6.1159	0.1635	51.1591	0.0195	8.3649	0.1195	52.5827
20	6.7275	0.1486	57.2750	0.0175	8.5136	0.1175	55.4069
21	7.4002	0.1351	64.0025	0.0156	8.6487	0.1156	58.1095
22	8.1403	0.1228	71.4027	0.0140	8.7715	0.1140	60.6893
23	8.9543	0.1117	79.5430	0.0126	8.8832	0.1126	63.1462
24	9.8497	0.1015	88.4973	0.0113	8.9847	0.1113	65.4813
25	10.8347	0.0923	98.3470	0.0102	9.0770	0.1102	67.6964
26	11.9182	0.0839	109.1817	0.0092	9.1609	0.1092	69.7940
27	13.1100	0.0763	121.0999	0.0083	9.2372	0.1083	71.7772
28	14.4210	0.0693	134.2099	0.0075	9.3066	0.1075	73.6495
29	15.8631	0.0630	148.6309	0.0067	9.3696	0.1067	75.4146
30	17.4494	0.0573	164.4940	0.0061	9.4269	0.1061	77.0766
35	28.1024	0.0356	271.0243	0.0037	9.6442	0.1037	83.9871
40	45.2592	0.0221	442.5924	0.0023	9.7791	0.1023	88.9525
45	72.8904	0.0137	718.9045	0.0014	9.8628	0.1014	92.4544
50	117.3908	0.0085	1163.9079	0.0009	9.9148	0.1009	94.8889
55	189.0590	0.0053	1880.5903	0.0005	9.9471	0.1005	96.5619

TABLE A.12 COMPOUND INTEREST TABLE, $i = 11.0\%$

n	COMPOUND AMOUNT FACTOR (F|P,i,n)	DISCOUNT AMOUNT FACTOR (P|F,i,n)	COMPOUND UNIFORM SERIES FACTOR (F|U,i,n)	SINKING FUND FACTOR (U|F,i,n)	DISCOUNT UNIFORM SERIES FACTOR (P|U,i,n)	CAPITAL RECOVERY FACTOR (U|P,i,n)	DISCOUNT GRADIENT FACTOR (P|G,i,n)
1	1.1100	0.9009	1.0000	1.0000	0.9009	1.1100	0.0000
2	1.2321	0.8116	2.1100	0.4739	1.7125	0.5839	0.8116
3	1.3676	0.7312	3.3421	0.2992	2.4437	0.4092	2.2740
4	1.5181	0.6587	4.7097	0.2123	3.1024	0.3223	4.2502
5	1.6851	0.5935	6.2278	0.1606	3.6959	0.2706	6.6240
6	1.8704	0.5346	7.9129	0.1264	4.2305	0.2364	9.2972
7	2.0762	0.4817	9.7833	0.1022	4.7122	0.2122	12.1872
8	2.3045	0.4339	11.8594	0.0843	5.1461	0.1943	15.2246
9	2.5580	0.3909	14.1640	0.0706	5.5370	0.1806	18.3520
10	2.8394	0.3522	16.7220	0.0598	5.8892	0.1698	21.5217
11	3.1518	0.3173	19.5614	0.0511	6.2065	0.1611	24.6945
12	3.4985	0.2858	22.7132	0.0440	6.4924	0.1540	27.8388
13	3.8833	0.2575	26.2116	0.0382	6.7499	0.1482	30.9290
14	4.3104	0.2320	30.0949	0.0332	6.9819	0.1432	33.9449
15	4.7846	0.2090	34.4054	0.0291	7.1909	0.1391	36.8709
16	5.3109	0.1883	39.1899	0.0255	7.3792	0.1355	39.6953
17	5.8951	0.1696	44.5008	0.0225	7.5488	0.1325	42.4094
18	6.5436	0.1528	50.3959	0.0198	7.7016	0.1298	45.0074
19	7.2633	0.1377	56.9395	0.0176	7.8393	0.1276	47.4856
20	8.0623	0.1240	64.2028	0.0156	7.9633	0.1256	49.8423
21	8.9492	0.1117	72.2651	0.0138	8.0751	0.1238	52.0771
22	9.9336	0.1007	81.2143	0.0123	8.1757	0.1223	54.1912
23	11.0263	0.0907	91.1479	0.0110	8.2664	0.1210	56.1864
24	12.2392	0.0817	102.1741	0.0098	8.3481	0.1198	58.0656
25	13.5855	0.0736	114.4133	0.0087	8.4217	0.1187	59.8322
26	15.0799	0.0663	127.9988	0.0078	8.4881	0.1178	61.4900
27	16.7386	0.0597	143.0786	0.0070	8.5478	0.1170	63.0433
28	18.5799	0.0538	159.8173	0.0063	8.6016	0.1163	64.4965
29	20.6237	0.0485	178.3972	0.0056	8.6501	0.1156	65.8542
30	22.8923	0.0437	199.0208	0.0050	8.6938	0.1150	67.1210
35	38.5748	0.0259	341.5895	0.0029	8.8552	0.1129	72.2538
40	65.0009	0.0154	581.8259	0.0017	8.9511	0.1117	75.7789
45	109.5302	0.0091	986.6383	0.0010	9.0079	0.1110	78.1551
50	184.5648	0.0054	1668.7707	0.0006	9.0417	0.1106	79.7340
55	311.0024	0.0032	2818.2034	0.0004	9.0617	0.1104	80.7712

TABLE A.13 COMPOUND INTEREST TABLE, $i = 12.0\%$

n	COMPOUND AMOUNT FACTOR (F|P,i,n)	DISCOUNT AMOUNT FACTOR (P|F,i,n)	COMPOUND UNIFORM SERIES FACTOR (F|U,i,n)	SINKING FUND FACTOR (U|F,i,n)	DISCOUNT UNIFORM SERIES FACTOR (P|U,i,n)	CAPITAL RECOVERY FACTOR (U|P,i,n)	DISCOUNT GRADIENT FACTOR (P|G,i,n)
1	1.1200	0.8929	1.0000	1.0000	0.8929	1.1200	0.0000
2	1.2544	0.7972	2.1200	0.4717	1.6901	0.5917	0.7972
3	1.4049	0.7118	3.3744	0.2963	2.4018	0.4163	2.2208
4	1.5735	0.6355	4.7793	0.2092	3.0373	0.3292	4.1273
5	1.7623	0.5674	6.3528	0.1574	3.6048	0.2774	6.3970
6	1.9738	0.5066	8.1152	0.1232	4.1114	0.2432	8.9302
7	2.2107	0.4523	10.0890	0.0991	4.5638	0.2191	11.6443
8	2.4760	0.4039	12.2997	0.0813	4.9676	0.2013	14.4714
9	2.7731	0.3606	14.7757	0.0677	5.3282	0.1877	17.3563
10	3.1058	0.3220	17.5487	0.0570	5.6502	0.1770	20.2541
11	3.4785	0.2875	20.6546	0.0484	5.9377	0.1684	23.1288
12	3.8960	0.2567	24.1331	0.0414	6.1944	0.1614	25.9523
13	4.3635	0.2292	28.0291	0.0357	6.4235	0.1557	28.7024
14	4.8871	0.2046	32.3926	0.0309	6.6282	0.1509	31.3624
15	5.4736	0.1827	37.2797	0.0268	6.8109	0.1468	33.9202
16	6.1304	0.1631	42.7533	0.0234	6.9740	0.1434	36.3670
17	6.8660	0.1456	48.8837	0.0205	7.1196	0.1405	38.6973
18	7.6900	0.1300	55.7497	0.0179	7.2497	0.1379	40.9080
19	8.6128	0.1161	63.4397	0.0158	7.3658	0.1358	42.9979
20	9.6463	0.1037	72.0524	0.0139	7.4694	0.1339	44.9676
21	10.8038	0.0926	81.6987	0.0122	7.5620	0.1322	46.8188
22	12.1003	0.0826	92.5026	0.0108	7.6446	0.1308	48.5543
23	13.5523	0.0738	104.6029	0.0096	7.7184	0.1296	50.1776
24	15.1786	0.0659	118.1552	0.0085	7.7843	0.1285	51.6929
25	17.0001	0.0588	133.3339	0.0075	7.8431	0.1275	53.1046
26	19.0401	0.0525	150.3339	0.0067	7.8957	0.1267	54.4177
27	21.3249	0.0469	169.3740	0.0059	7.9426	0.1259	55.6369
28	23.8839	0.0419	190.6989	0.0052	7.9844	0.1252	56.7674
29	26.7499	0.0374	214.5827	0.0047	8.0218	0.1247	57.8141
30	29.9599	0.0334	241.3327	0.0041	8.0552	0.1241	58.7821
35	52.7996	0.0189	431.6634	0.0023	8.1755	0.1223	62.6052
40	93.0510	0.0107	767.0913	0.0013	8.2438	0.1213	65.1159
45	163.9876	0.0061	1358.2298	0.0007	8.2825	0.1207	66.7342
50	289.0021	0.0035	2400.0178	0.0004	8.3045	0.1204	67.7624
55	509.3205	0.0020	4236.0043	0.0002	8.3170	0.1202	68.4082

TABLE A.14 COMPOUND INTEREST TABLE, $i = 15.0\%$

n	COMPOUND AMOUNT FACTOR (F|P,i,n)	DISCOUNT AMOUNT FACTOR (P|F,i,n)	COMPOUND UNIFORM SERIES FACTOR (F|U,i,n)	SINKING FUND FACTOR (U|F,i,n)	DISCOUNT UNIFORM SERIES FACTOR (P|U,i,n)	CAPITAL RECOVERY FACTOR (U|P,i,n)	DISCOUNT GRADIENT FACTOR (P|G,i,n)
1	1.1500	0.8696	1.0000	1.0000	0.8696	1.1500	0.0000
2	1.3225	0.7561	2.1500	0.4651	1.6257	0.6151	0.7561
3	1.5209	0.6575	3.4725	0.2880	2.2832	0.4380	2.0712
4	1.7490	0.5718	4.9934	0.2003	2.8550	0.3503	3.7864
5	2.0114	0.4972	6.7424	0.1483	3.3522	0.2983	5.7751
6	2.3131	0.4323	8.7537	0.1142	3.7845	0.2642	7.9368
7	2.6600	0.3759	11.0668	0.0904	4.1604	0.2404	10.1924
8	3.0590	0.3269	13.7268	0.0729	4.4873	0.2229	12.4807
9	3.5179	0.2843	16.7858	0.0596	4.7716	0.2096	14.7548
10	4.0456	0.2472	20.3037	0.0493	5.0188	0.1993	16.9795
11	4.6524	0.2149	24.3493	0.0411	5.2337	0.1911	19.1289
12	5.3503	0.1869	29.0017	0.0345	5.4206	0.1845	21.1849
13	6.1528	0.1625	34.3519	0.0291	5.5831	0.1791	23.1352
14	7.0757	0.1413	40.5047	0.0247	5.7245	0.1747	24.9725
15	8.1371	0.1229	47.5804	0.0210	5.8474	0.1710	26.6930
16	9.3576	0.1069	55.7175	0.0179	5.9542	0.1679	28.2960
17	10.7613	0.0929	65.0751	0.0154	6.0472	0.1654	29.7828
18	12.3755	0.0808	75.8364	0.0132	6.1280	0.1632	31.1565
19	14.2318	0.0703	88.2118	0.0113	6.1982	0.1613	32.4213
20	16.3665	0.0611	102.4436	0.0098	6.2593	0.1598	33.5822
21	18.8215	0.0531	118.8101	0.0084	6.3125	0.1584	34.6448
22	21.6447	0.0462	137.6316	0.0073	6.3587	0.1573	35.6150
23	24.8915	0.0402	159.2764	0.0063	6.3988	0.1563	36.4988
24	28.6252	0.0349	184.1678	0.0054	6.4338	0.1554	37.3023
25	32.9190	0.0304	212.7930	0.0047	6.4641	0.1547	38.0314
26	37.8568	0.0264	245.7120	0.0041	6.4906	0.1541	38.6918
27	43.5353	0.0230	283.5688	0.0035	6.5135	0.1535	39.2890
28	50.0656	0.0200	327.1041	0.0031	6.5335	0.1531	39.8283
29	57.5755	0.0174	377.1697	0.0027	6.5509	0.1527	40.3146
30	66.2118	0.0151	434.7451	0.0023	6.5660	0.1523	40.7526

TABLE A.15 COMPOUND INTEREST TABLE, $i = 20.0\%$

n	COMPOUND AMOUNT FACTOR (F|P,i,n)	DISCOUNT AMOUNT FACTOR (P|F,i,n)	COMPOUND UNIFORM SERIES FACTOR (F|U,i,n)	SINKING FUND FACTOR (U|F,i,n)	DISCOUNT UNIFORM SERIES FACTOR (P|U,i,n)	CAPITAL RECOVERY FACTOR (U|P,i,n)	DISCOUNT GRADIENT FACTOR (P|G,i,n)
1	1.2000	0.8333	1.0000	1.0000	0.8333	1.2000	0.0000
2	1.4400	0.6944	2.2000	0.4545	1.5278	0.6545	0.6944
3	1.7280	0.5787	3.6400	0.2747	2.1065	0.4747	1.8519
4	2.0736	0.4823	5.3680	0.1863	2.5887	0.3863	3.2986
5	2.4883	0.4019	7.4416	0.1344	2.9906	0.3344	4.9061
6	2.9860	0.3349	9.9299	0.1007	3.3255	0.3007	6.5806
7	3.5832	0.2791	12.9159	0.0774	3.6046	0.2774	8.2551
8	4.2998	0.2326	16.4991	0.0606	3.8372	0.2606	9.8831
9	5.1598	0.1938	20.7989	0.0481	4.0310	0.2481	11.4335
10	6.1917	0.1615	25.9587	0.0385	4.1925	0.2385	12.8871
11	7.4301	0.1346	32.1504	0.0311	4.3271	0.2311	14.2330
12	8.9161	0.1122	39.5805	0.0253	4.4392	0.2253	15.4667
13	10.6993	0.0935	48.4966	0.0206	4.5327	0.2206	16.5883
14	12.8392	0.0779	59.1959	0.0169	4.6106	0.2169	17.6008
15	15.4070	0.0649	72.0351	0.0139	4.6755	0.2139	18.5095
16	18.4884	0.0541	87.4421	0.0114	4.7296	0.2114	19.3208
17	22.1861	0.0451	105.9305	0.0094	4.7746	0.2094	20.0419
18	26.6233	0.0376	128.1167	0.0078	4.8122	0.2078	20.6805
19	31.9480	0.0313	154.7400	0.0065	4.8435	0.2065	21.2439
20	38.3376	0.0261	186.6880	0.0054	4.8696	0.2054	21.7395
21	46.0051	0.0217	225.0256	0.0044	4.8913	0.2044	22.1742
22	55.2061	0.0181	271.0307	0.0037	4.9094	0.2037	22.5546
23	66.2474	0.0151	326.2368	0.0031	4.9245	0.2031	22.8867
24	79.4968	0.0126	392.4842	0.0025	4.9371	0.2025	23.1760
25	95.3962	0.0105	471.9810	0.0021	4.9476	0.2021	23.4276
26	114.4754	0.0087	567.3772	0.0018	4.9563	0.2018	23.6460
27	137.3705	0.0073	681.8527	0.0015	4.9636	0.2015	23.8353
28	164.8446	0.0061	819.2232	0.0012	4.9697	0.2012	23.9991
29	197.8136	0.0051	984.0678	0.0010	4.9747	0.2010	24.1406
30	237.3763	0.0042	1181.8814	0.0008	4.9789	0.2008	24.2628

TABLE A.16 COMPOUND INTEREST TABLE, $i = 25.0\%$

n	COMPOUND AMOUNT FACTOR (F|P,i,n)	DISCOUNT AMOUNT FACTOR (P|F,i,n)	COMPOUND UNIFORM SERIES FACTOR (F|U,i,n)	SINKING FUND FACTOR (U|F,i,n)	DISCOUNT UNIFORM SERIES FACTOR (P|U,i,n)	CAPITAL RECOVERY FACTOR (U|P,i,n)	DISCOUNT GRADIENT FACTOR (P|G,i,n)
1	1.2500	0.8000	1.0000	1.0000	0.8000	1.2500	0.0000
2	1.5625	0.6400	2.2500	0.4444	1.4400	0.6944	0.6400
3	1.9531	0.5120	3.8125	0.2623	1.9520	0.5123	1.6640
4	2.4414	0.4096	5.7656	0.1734	2.3616	0.4234	2.8928
5	3.0518	0.3277	8.2070	0.1218	2.6893	0.3718	4.2035
6	3.8147	0.2621	11.2588	0.0888	2.9514	0.3388	5.5142
7	4.7684	0.2097	15.0735	0.0663	3.1611	0.3163	6.7725
8	5.9605	0.1678	19.8419	0.0504	3.3289	0.3004	7.9469
9	7.4506	0.1342	25.8023	0.0388	3.4631	0.2888	9.0207
10	9.3132	0.1074	33.2529	0.0301	3.5705	0.2801	9.9870
11	11.6415	0.0859	42.5661	0.0235	3.6564	0.2735	10.8460
12	14.5519	0.0687	54.2077	0.0184	3.7251	0.2684	11.6020
13	18.1899	0.0550	68.7596	0.0145	3.7801	0.2645	12.2617
14	22.7374	0.0440	86.9495	0.0115	3.8241	0.2615	12.8334
15	28.4217	0.0352	109.6868	0.0091	3.8593	0.2591	13.3260
16	35.5271	0.0281	138.1085	0.0072	3.8874	0.2572	13.7482
17	44.4089	0.0225	173.6357	0.0058	3.9099	0.2558	14.1085
18	55.5112	0.0180	218.0446	0.0046	3.9279	0.2546	14.4147
19	69.3889	0.0144	273.5558	0.0037	3.9424	0.2537	14.6741
20	86.7362	0.0115	342.9447	0.0029	3.9539	0.2529	14.8932
21	108.4202	0.0092	429.6809	0.0023	3.9631	0.2523	15.0777
22	135.5253	0.0074	538.1011	0.0019	3.9705	0.2519	15.2326
23	169.4066	0.0059	673.6263	0.0015	3.9764	0.2515	15.3625
24	211.7582	0.0047	843.0329	0.0012	3.9811	0.2512	15.4711
25	264.6978	0.0038	1054.7912	0.0009	3.9849	0.2509	15.5618
26	330.8722	0.0030	1319.4890	0.0008	3.9879	0.2508	15.6373
27	413.5903	0.0024	1650.3612	0.0006	3.9903	0.2506	15.7002
28	516.9879	0.0019	2063.9515	0.0005	3.9923	0.2505	15.7524
29	646.2348	0.0015	2580.9394	0.0004	3.9938	0.2504	15.7957
30	807.7935	0.0012	3227.1742	0.0003	3.9950	0.2503	15.8316

Appendix B
Statistical Tables

TABLE B.1 SIGNIFICANCE LEVELS OF THE NORMAL DISTRIBUTION

z +	0.00	0.01	0.02	0.03	0.04	0.05	0.06	0.07	0.08	0.09
0.0	0.5000	0.5040	0.5080	0.5120	0.5160	0.5199	0.5239	0.5279	0.5319	0.5359
0.1	0.5398	0.5438	0.5478	0.5517	0.5557	0.5596	0.5636	0.5675	0.5714	0.5753
0.2	0.5793	0.5832	0.5871	0.5910	0.5948	0.5987	0.6026	0.6064	0.6103	0.6141
0.3	0.6179	0.6217	0.6255	0.6293	0.6331	0.6368	0.6406	0.6443	0.6480	0.6517
0.4	0.6554	0.6591	0.6628	0.6664	0.6700	0.6736	0.6772	0.6808	0.6844	0.6879
0.5	0.6915	0.6950	0.6985	0.7019	0.7054	0.7088	0.7123	0.7157	0.7190	0.7224
0.6	0.7257	0.7291	0.7324	0.7357	0.7389	0.7422	0.7454	0.7486	0.7517	0.7549
0.7	0.7580	0.7611	0.7642	0.7673	0.7704	0.7734	0.7764	0.7794	0.7823	0.7852
0.8	0.7881	0.7910	0.7939	0.7967	0.7995	0.8023	0.8051	0.8078	0.8106	0.8133
0.9	0.8159	0.8186	0.8212	0.8238	0.8264	0.8289	0.8315	0.8340	0.8365	0.8389
1.0	0.8413	0.8438	0.8461	0.8485	0.8508	0.8531	0.8554	0.8577	0.8599	0.8621
1.1	0.8643	0.8665	0.8686	0.8708	0.8729	0.8749	0.8770	0.8790	0.8810	0.8830
1.2	0.8849	0.8869	0.8888	0.8907	0.8925	0.8944	0.8962	0.8980	0.8997	0.9015
1.3	0.9032	0.9049	0.9066	0.9082	0.9099	0.9115	0.9131	0.9147	0.9162	0.9177
1.4	0.9192	0.9207	0.9222	0.9236	0.9251	0.9265	0.9279	0.9292	0.9306	0.9319
1.5	0.9332	0.9345	0.9357	0.9370	0.9382	0.9394	0.9406	0.9418	0.9429	0.9441
1.6	0.9452	0.9463	0.9474	0.9484	0.9495	0.9505	0.9515	0.9525	0.9535	0.9545
1.7	0.9554	0.9564	0.9573	0.9582	0.9591	0.9599	0.9608	0.9616	0.9625	0.9633
1.8	0.9641	0.9649	0.9656	0.9664	0.9671	0.9678	0.9686	0.9693	0.9699	0.9706
1.9	0.9713	0.9719	0.9726	0.9732	0.9738	0.9744	0.9750	0.9756	0.9761	0.9767
2.0	0.9772	0.9778	0.9783	0.9788	0.9793	0.9798	0.9803	0.9808	0.9812	0.9817
2.1	0.9821	0.9826	0.9830	0.9834	0.9838	0.9842	0.9846	0.9850	0.9854	0.9857
2.2	0.9861	0.9864	0.9868	0.9871	0.9875	0.9878	0.9881	0.9884	0.9887	0.9890
2.3	0.9893	0.9896	0.9898	0.9901	0.9904	0.9906	0.9909	0.9911	0.9913	0.9916
2.4	0.9918	0.9920	0.9922	0.9925	0.9927	0.9929	0.9931	0.9932	0.9934	0.9936
2.5	0.9938	0.9940	0.9941	0.9943	0.9945	0.9946	0.9948	0.9949	0.9951	0.9952
2.6	0.9953	0.9955	0.9956	0.9957	0.9959	0.9960	0.9961	0.9962	0.9963	0.9964
2.7	0.9965	0.9966	0.9967	0.9968	0.9969	0.9970	0.9971	0.9972	0.9973	0.9974
2.8	0.9974	0.9975	0.9976	0.9977	0.9977	0.9978	0.9979	0.9979	0.9980	0.9981
2.9	0.9981	0.9982	0.9982	0.9983	0.9984	0.9984	0.9985	0.9985	0.9986	0.9986
3.0	0.9987	0.9987	0.9987	0.9988	0.9988	0.9989	0.9989	0.9989	0.9990	0.9990
3.1	0.9990	0.9991	0.9991	0.9991	0.9992	0.9992	0.9992	0.9992	0.9993	0.9993
3.2	0.9993	0.9993	0.9994	0.9994	0.9994	0.9994	0.9994	0.9995	0.9995	0.9995
3.3	0.9995	0.9995	0.9995	0.9996	0.9996	0.9996	0.9996	0.9996	0.9996	0.9997
3.4	0.9997	0.9997	0.9997	0.9997	0.9997	0.9997	0.9997	0.9997	0.9997	0.9998

Note: Tabulated values are the probability that a standard normal random variable is less than or equal to the given value of z.

Example: $Pr\{z \leq 1.15\} = 0.8749$

TABLE B.2 SIGNIFICANCE LEVELS FOR THE t-DISTRIBUTION

Degrees of Freedom	t-values											
	0.2	0.4	0.6	0.8	1.0	1.2	1.4	1.6	1.8	2.0	3.0	4.
1	0.437	0.379	0.328	0.285	0.250	0.221	0.197	0.178	0.161	0.148	0.102	0.0
2	0.430	0.364	0.305	0.254	0.211	0.177	0.148	0.125	0.107	0.092	0.048	0.0
3	0.427	0.358	0.295	0.241	0.196	0.158	0.128	0.104	0.085	0.070	0.029	0.0
4	0.426	0.355	0.290	0.234	0.187	0.148	0.117	0.092	0.073	0.058	0.020	0.0
5	0.425	0.353	0.287	0.230	0.182	0.142	0.110	0.085	0.066	0.051	0.015	0.0
6	0.424	0.352	0.285	0.227	0.178	0.138	0.106	0.080	0.061	0.046	0.012	0.0
7	0.424	0.351	0.284	0.225	0.175	0.135	0.102	0.077	0.057	0.043	0.010	0.0
8	0.423	0.350	0.283	0.223	0.173	0.132	0.100	0.074	0.055	0.040	0.009	0.0
9	0.423	0.349	0.282	0.222	0.172	0.130	0.098	0.072	0.053	0.038	0.007	0.0
10	0.423	0.349	0.281	0.221	0.170	0.129	0.096	0.070	0.051	0.037	0.007	0.0
11	0.423	0.348	0.280	0.220	0.169	0.128	0.095	0.069	0.050	0.035	0.006	0.0
12	0.422	0.348	0.280	0.220	0.169	0.127	0.093	0.068	0.049	0.034	0.006	0.0
13	0.422	0.348	0.279	0.219	0.168	0.126	0.092	0.067	0.048	0.033	0.005	0.0
14	0.422	0.348	0.279	0.219	0.167	0.125	0.092	0.066	0.047	0.033	0.005	0.0
15	0.422	0.347	0.279	0.218	0.167	0.124	0.091	0.065	0.046	0.032	0.004	0.0
16	0.422	0.347	0.278	0.218	0.166	0.124	0.090	0.065	0.045	0.031	0.004	0.0
17	0.422	0.347	0.278	0.217	0.166	0.123	0.090	0.064	0.045	0.031	0.004	0.0
18	0.422	0.347	0.278	0.217	0.165	0.123	0.089	0.064	0.044	0.030	0.004	0.0
19	0.422	0.347	0.278	0.217	0.165	0.122	0.089	0.063	0.044	0.030	0.004	0.0
20	0.422	0.347	0.278	0.217	0.165	0.122	0.088	0.063	0.043	0.030	0.004	0.0
25	0.422	0.346	0.277	0.216	0.163	0.121	0.087	0.061	0.042	0.028	0.003	0.0
30	0.421	0.346	0.277	0.215	0.163	0.120	0.086	0.060	0.041	0.027	0.003	0.0
35	0.421	0.346	0.276	0.215	0.162	0.119	0.085	0.059	0.040	0.027	0.002	0.0
40	0.421	0.346	0.276	0.214	0.162	0.119	0.085	0.059	0.040	0.026	0.002	0.0
45	0.421	0.346	0.276	0.214	0.161	0.118	0.084	0.058	0.039	0.026	0.002	0.0
50	0.421	0.345	0.276	0.214	0.161	0.118	0.084	0.058	0.039	0.025	0.002	0.0
60	0.421	0.345	0.275	0.213	0.161	0.117	0.083	0.057	0.038	0.025	0.002	0.0
70	0.421	0.345	0.275	0.213	0.160	0.117	0.083	0.057	0.038	0.025	0.002	0.0
∞	0.421	0.345	0.274	0.212	0.159	0.115	0.081	0.055	0.036	0.023	0.001	0.0

Note: Table entries represent the probability of a t variable being greater than or equal to the given t-value t_ν with specific degrees of freedom ν, i.e. $Pr\{t \geq t_\nu\}$.

Example: With degrees of freedom ν (DF) = 15, $Pr\{t \geq 1.2\} = 0.124$

TABLE B.3 CRITICAL t-VALUES FOR DIFFERENT SIGNIFICANCE LEVELS

Degrees of Freedom	Probabilities								
	0.6	0.7	0.8	0.9	0.95	0.975	0.99	0.995	0.999
1	0.325	0.727	1.376	3.078	6.314	1.000	31.821	63.657	318.320
2	0.289	0.617	1.061	1.886	2.920	0.816	6.965	9.925	22.327
3	0.277	0.584	0.978	1.638	2.353	0.765	4.541	5.841	10.215
4	0.271	0.569	0.941	1.533	2.132	0.741	3.747	4.604	7.173
5	0.267	0.559	0.920	1.476	2.015	0.727	3.365	4.032	5.893
6	0.265	0.553	0.906	1.440	1.943	0.718	3.143	3.707	5.208
7	0.263	0.549	0.896	1.415	1.895	0.711	2.998	3.499	4.785
8	0.262	0.546	0.889	1.397	1.860	0.706	2.896	3.355	4.501
9	0.261	0.543	0.883	1.383	1.833	0.703	2.821	3.250	4.297
10	0.260	0.542	0.879	1.372	1.812	0.700	2.764	3.169	4.144
11	0.260	0.540	0.876	1.363	1.796	0.697	2.718	3.106	4.025
12	0.259	0.539	0.873	1.356	1.782	0.695	2.681	3.055	3.930
13	0.259	0.537	0.870	1.350	1.771	0.694	2.650	3.012	3.852
14	0.258	0.537	0.868	1.345	1.761	0.692	2.624	2.977	3.787
15	0.258	0.536	0.866	1.341	1.753	0.691	2.602	2.947	3.733
16	0.258	0.535	0.865	1.337	1.746	0.690	2.583	2.921	3.686
17	0.257	0.534	0.863	1.333	1.740	0.689	2.567	2.898	3.646
18	0.257	0.534	0.862	1.330	1.734	0.688	2.552	2.878	3.610
19	0.257	0.533	0.861	1.328	1.729	0.688	2.539	2.861	3.579
20	0.257	0.533	0.860	1.325	1.725	0.687	2.528	2.845	3.552
25	0.256	0.531	0.856	1.316	1.708	0.684	2.485	2.787	3.450
30	0.256	0.530	0.854	1.310	1.697	0.683	2.457	2.750	3.385
35	0.255	0.529	0.852	1.306	1.690	0.682	2.438	2.724	3.340
40	0.255	0.529	0.851	1.303	1.684	0.681	2.423	2.704	3.307
45	0.255	0.528	0.850	1.301	1.679	0.680	2.412	2.690	3.281
50	0.255	0.528	0.849	1.299	1.676	0.679	2.403	2.678	3.261
60	0.254	0.527	0.848	1.296	1.671	0.679	2.390	2.660	3.232
70	0.254	0.527	0.847	1.294	1.667	0.678	2.381	2.648	3.211
∞	0.253	0.524	0.842	1.282	1.645	0.674	2.326	2.576	3.090

Note: Table entries are critical t values t_ν such that the probability of a t variable being less than or equal to tabulated critical value is equal to the probability at the given degrees of freedom, i.e. $Pr\{t \le t_\nu\}$.

Example: With degrees of freedom ν (DF) = 5, $Pr\{t \le 0.920\} = 0.8$

ANSWERS TO SELECTED PROBLEMS

Chapter 4

P4-2. 37.4%.

P4-5. 15.75 days.

P4-6. $P_e = 720$ yd^3; $P_h = 128$ yd^3; $N_h = 6$ haulers.

P4-8. $P'_h = 75$ yd^3; $N'_h = 6$ trucks.

P4-10. (a) 25 minutes; (b) 5 minutes

P4-11. Total delay $= 56.25$ minutes; average delay $= 7.5$ minutes

P4-13. Maximum queue $= 42$; Total waiting time $= 239$ hours.

P4-14. Maximum queue $= 50$; Total waiting time $= 391$ hours.

Chapter 5

P5-1. Average total cost $= \$5.67$ million (in 1978 dollars).

P5-3. Total cost $= \$8$ million (in 1987 dollars).

P5-5. Total cost $= \$126,000$; Cost per daily output $= \$1,128$.

P5-7. Total cost $= \$23.27$ million.

P5-9. Total cost $= \$8.18$ million.

P5-11. Total cost $= \$15,381,788.50$.

P5-13. For normal mobilization, 2% at $t = 1$, 8% at $t = 2$, 18% at $t = 3$, 32% at $t = 4$, 50% at $t = 5$, 68% at $t = 6$, 82% at $t = 7$, 92% at $t = 8$, 98% at $t = 9$, and 100% at $t = 10$.

P5-15. Minimum cost $= 2,000 \, J \, L \sqrt{10 C_1 C_2 K R}$.

Chapter 6

P6-2. (a) \$39,774; (b) \$39,780; (c) \$39,780.

P6-4. (a) \$35,740; (b) \$36,757; (c) \$35,285.

P6-6. NPV $= \$15,613$.

P6-8. NPV $= \$12,992$.

P6-10. Minimum required annual revenue $= \$202,000$ for Design No. 1 and \$222,300 for Design No. 2.

P6-11. (a) \$23,635; (b) \$25,119; (c) \$23,112.

Chapter 7

P7-2. APV = $14,470 for 7-year bond; APV = $42,820 for overdraft.

P7-4. $456,590 for coupon bond refinancing.

P7-6. $22,640 uniform monthly payment for 36 months.

P7-8. $236,000 uniform annual mortgage payment.

P7-10. All values are in million dollars: (a) N_t = 1.250 for t = 0, −3.432 for t = 1, −5.681 for t = 2, −5.706 for t = 3, −4.075 for t = 4, and −2.014 for t = 5; (b) N_t = −1.250 for t = 0, −3.773 for t = 1, −6.524 for t = 2, −7.020 for t = 3, −5.736 for t = 4, and −3.842 for t = 5.

P7-11. (a) G = $900,000; (b) $\overline{G}$ = $749,100

P7-13. $\overline{G}$ = $95,769.

Chapter 8

P8-1. All values are in thousand dollars; (a) F = 720, P = 7,080; (b) F = 480, P = 7,080; (c) F = 960, P = 7,080.

P8-3. All values are in thousand dollars; (a) F = 450, P = 6,450; (b) F = 482.4, P = 6,542.4; (c) F = 426, P = 6,666; (d) F = 462.4, P = 7,058.4; (e) F = 474, P = 6,234; (f) F = 506.4, P = 6,626.4.

P8-5. Payments on unit price contract in thousand dollars: (a) 3345.0, (b) 3,478.8, (c) 3,512.3, (d) 3,646.1, (e) 3,411.9, and (f) 3,545.7.

P8-8. All values are in thousand dollars; (a) F = 500, P = 3,500; (b) F = 513.6, P = 3,633.6; (c) F = 485, P = 3,635; (d) F = 518.6, P = 3768.6; (e) F = 494, P = 3,554; (f) F = 519.6, P = 3,687.6.

Chapter 9

P9-6. For Part (a), 1. Clear B; 2 Place B on E; 3. Place A on B; 4. Place C on A; and 5. Place D on C.

P9-8. 1. Clear B; 2 Clear D; 3. Place B on A; 4. Place E on B; and 5. Place D on C.

P9-10. (i) 34 sec.; (ii) 44 sec.

Chapter 10

P10-5. Critical path: D–X–F–L–O where X is a dummy activity linking D and F; project duration = 41.

P10-7. Critical path: C–F–I–K; project duration = 41.

P10-9. Critical path: D–F–L–O; project duration = 35.

P10-11. Critical path: B–E–I; project duration = 18. Inclusive dates for activity start and finish in a trial solution for resource leveling: A, 1-3; B 1-5; C 1; D, 4; E 6-12; F, 9-14; G, 2-5; H, 12-14; I, 13-18; J, 15-18; and K, 16-18.

P10-14. Shift the following activities in the schedule for Problem P10-11 to new dates: D, 12; F, 12-17, H, 13-15; J, 18-20; and K 16-18. Projection duration = 21 days.

Chapter 11

P11-1. (a) mean = 41 and standard deviation = 23.2 for project duration; (b) probability = 0.329

P11-2. (a) mean = 23 and standard deviation = 3 for project duration; (b) probability = 0.027

P11-4. Project cost = $5,150 for all crash and $4,890 for project crash.

P11-6. Project cost = $3,265 for all crash and $3,065 for project crash.

P11-7. Project cost = $3,340 for normal duration and $3,515 for project crash.

P11-9. Project cost = $1,110 for normal duration and $1,230 for project crash.

P11-11. Critical path: $D-X-G-N-O$ where X is a dummy activity linking D and F; project duration = 43.

Chapter 12

P12-2. For Part (c), the expected percent expenditures are: (i) 107.5%; (ii) 112.5%; (iii) 90%

P12-3. (a) Forecast cost = $64,866, cost variance = $4,866; (b) Forecast cost = $55,347, cost variance = $5,347.

P12-5. (a) Estimated unit cost for all three resources = $2.38/yd^3 and experienced unit cost = $2.49; (b) Major problem is labor.

P12-7. (a) Average cumulative cost per unit: $40.00 for month 1, $37.69 for month 2, $37.73 for month 3, $31.58 for month 4, $29.90 for month 5, and $28.64 for month 6; (b) Forecast cost to complete based on proportion of work completed: $32,000 for month 1; $30,154 for month 2, $26,982 for month 3, $25,266 for month 4, $23,924 for month 5, and $22,909 for month 6.

P12-9. (a) Re-commenced project duration = 12 months; (b) NPV = $1,790; (c) Lump-sum payment = $92,379, and (d) NFV = $14,746.

Chapter 13

P13-2. (a) 0.74; (b) 0.93; (c) 1.

P13-3. (a) 0.74; (b) 0.92; (c) 0.97.

P13-6. (a) 0.92; (b) 0.55; (c) 0.19.

P13-8. (a) Use sample size 8 for normal inspection; (b) accept if no defective exists, and reject if one or more defectives exist.

P13-10. $U = 11.60$; $L = 9.66$.

Chapter 14

P14-3. (a) Possible data: job number, data, owner, etc., (b) a single relation could be used, with job number as key.

P14-5. Three possible relations: initial estimate information; activity network topology information; and monitoring information.

INDEX